"Let's talk sense to the American people. Let's tell them the truth. . . . Better we lose the election than mislead the people; and better we lose than misgovern the people."

— Adlai E. Stevenson accepting the nomination of the Democratic National Convention, 1952

Stevenson's oratory during the 1952 campaign was such that, as Richard N. Goodwin later wrote, "After he spoke, no leader of his party nor the dialogue of Democracy itself would ever sound the same again. . . . He told an entire generation that there was room for intelligence and idealism in public life, that politics was not just a way to live but a way to live greatly, that each of us might share in the passions of the age."

Stevenson's own words during that campaign — in letters, speeches, and press conferences — are presented in Volume IV of *The Papers of Adlai E. Stevenson: "Let's Talk Sense to the American People," 1952–1955*. It shows Stevenson vigorously criss-crossing the country after accepting his party's draft, eloquently speaking out on such issues as foreign policy and trade, civil rights, the atom bomb, Communism and Communist-hunters, the economy and fiscal responsibility, and Indochina. The volume also covers the years immediately succeeding his defeat, when resuming the same grueling schedule, he fought strongly and successfully to rebuild the Democratic party and elect a Democratic Congress in 1954, all the while devoting his best efforts

Walter Johnson, the editor of *The Papers of Adlai E. Stevenson,* is a professor of history who has taught at the University of Chicago, where he received his M.A. and Ph.D., and at Oxford, where he was Harmsworth Professor of American History. He presently teaches the University of Hawaii. He is the author and editor of nine previous books, including *1600 Pennsylvania Avenue: Presidents and the People 1929–1959, William Allen White's America, How We Drafted Adlai Stevenson,* and *Selected Letters of William Allen White.*

... er, originally worked in ... as a junior partner. In ... campaign for governor ... to Springfield as his per- ... him until July 1961.

Books by Walter Johnson

THE BATTLE AGAINST ISOLATION

WILLIAM ALLEN WHITE'S AMERICA

THE UNITED STATES: EXPERIMENT IN DEMOCRACY
(with Avery Craven)

HOW WE DRAFTED ADLAI STEVENSON

1600 PENNSYLVANIA AVENUE: PRESIDENTS AND THE PEOPLE, 1929–1959

THE FULBRIGHT PROGRAM: A HISTORY
(with Francis J. Colligan)

Edited by Walter Johnson

SELECTED LETTERS OF WILLIAM ALLEN WHITE

ROOSEVELT AND THE RUSSIANS: THE YALTA CONFERENCE
By Edward R. Stettinius, Jr.

TURBULENT ERA: A DIPLOMATIC RECORD OF FORTY YEARS, 1904–1945
By Joseph C. Grew

THE PAPERS OF ADLAI E. STEVENSON

Volume I: Beginnings of Education
Volume II: Washington to Springfield, 1941–1948
Volume III: Governor of Illinois, 1949–1953
Volume IV: "Let's Talk Sense to the American People," 1952–1955

The Papers of Adlai E. Stevenson

WALTER JOHNSON, *Editor*

CAROL EVANS, *Assistant Editor*

C. ERIC SEARS, *Editorial Assistant*

The Papers o

Advisory Committee

Adlai E. Stevenson

VOLUME IV

"Let's Talk Sense to the American People,"

1952–1955

LITTLE, BROWN *and* COMPANY • *Boston* • *Toronto*

FIRST EDITION

T 05/74

The editors gratefully acknowledge the permission of the following authors, publishers, individuals and institutions to reprint selected materials as noted:

Herbert Agar, Eugenie Anderson, Jacob M. Arvey, Harry Ashmore, Brooks Atkinson, William Benton, Carol Berendt, William McC. Blair, Jr., Julian P. Boyd, Don Brice, Stuart Gerry Brown, Mina R. Bryan, C. & T. Publications, Limited, the *Christian Century,* Columbia Broadcasting System, Inc., Alistair Cooke, Norman Cousins, Gardner Cowles, Bethia S. Currie, Jane Warner Dick, Harold W. Dodds, Doubleday & Company, Inc., Helen Gahagan Douglas, Cyrus Eaton, B. Ifor Evans, John Anson Ford, John Kenneth Galbraith, Lloyd K. Garrison, Judith Montagu Gendel, Richard Paul Graebel, Harper & Row, Publishers, *Harper's Magazine,* Gordon Havens, Mrs. Hubert H. Humphrey, Elizabeth L. Hutter, Johns Hopkins Press, Gerald Johnson, George F. Kennan, Alfred A. Knopf, Inc., Paul R. Leach, Walter Lippmann, Archibald MacLeish, John J. McCloy, Carl McGowan, The Macmillan Company, Dumas Malone, T. S. Matthews, Loring C. Merwin, Stephen A. Mitchell, The New American Library, Inc., *New Statesman,* the New York *Times,* Joseph L. Rauh, Jr., Franklin D. Roosevelt, Jr., Dore Schary, Eric Sevareid, Ellen Thorne Smith, John Sparkman, Modie J. Spiegel, Jr., Edith R. Stern, Laura B. Stevens, Syracuse University Press, Niccolo Tucci, Harriet Welling, Theodore H. White, and Stanley Woodward for all the items from their publications and writings as detailed in the footnotes.

Harcourt Brace Jovanovich, Inc., for lines from the poem "Names" by Carl Sandburg, reprinted from his volume *Complete Poems.*

Harper & Row, Publishers, for excerpts from *As We Knew Adlai: The Stevenson Story by Twenty-two Friends,* edited and with a preface by Edward P. Doyle. Copyright © 1966 by Harper & Row, Publishers, Inc.

Harper & Row, Publishers, for quotations from *What I Think* by Adlai E. Stevenson. Copyright 1954, © 1955, 1956 by R. Keith Kane.

J. B. Lippincott Company and John Murray, Publishers, Ltd., London, for eight lines from *Collected Poems in One Volume,* by Alfred Noyes. Copyright 1906; renewal 1934, by Alfred Noyes.

Random House, Inc., for excerpts from *Major Campaign Speeches of Adlai E. Stevenson, 1952.* Introduction by the author. Copyright 1953 by Random House, Inc.

Library of Congress Cataloging in Publication Data (Revised)

Stevenson, Adlai Ewing, 1900–1965.
    The papers of Adlai E. Stevenson.

    Includes bibliographical references.
    CONTENTS: v. 1. Beginnings of education, 1900–
1941.—v. 2. Washington to Springfield, 1941–1948.—
                    v. 4. Let's talk sense to the
American people, 1952–1955.
    1. Stevenson, Adlai Ewing, 1900–1965. I. Johnson,
Walter, 1915–   ed.
E748.S84A25 1972   973.921'092'4 [B]   73-175478
ISBN 0-316-46751-0 (v. 2)

*Published simultaneously in Canada
by Little, Brown & Company (Canada) Limited*

PRINTED IN THE UNITED STATES OF AMERICA

Foreword

Shortly after Adlai E. Stevenson died, Andrew Kopkind wrote: "He came at the right time. America in the Fifties needed a voice of reason and none could have equalled Mr. Stevenson." [1] And James Reston observed: "He tried to impose his own principles and conscience on American politics." [2]

After Governor Stevenson was drafted by the 1952 Democratic National Convention against his wishes, he conducted a campaign that, though he lost it, raised American political thinking to a high plane and bequeathed it certain enduring qualities. His campaign speeches — the speeches of the loser — became best-selling books at home and abroad. [3] "He lighted up the sky like a flaming arrow, lifting political discussion to a level of literacy and eloquence, candor and humor, that tapped unsuspected responses in the American electorate," George W. Ball wrote. [4]

Several months after his defeat, Stevenson wrote:

> For years I have listened to the nauseous nonsense, the pie-in-the-sky appeals to cupidity and greed, the cynical trifling with passion and prejudice and fear; the slander, fraudulent promises, and the all-things-to-all-men demagoguery that are too much a part of our political campaigns. Sometimes in the deafening clamor of political salesmanship, I've thought that the people might be better served if a party purchased a half hour of radio and TV silence during which the audience would be asked to think quietly for themselves.
>
> Politicians all applaud and support public education as democracy's

[1] "Adlai Stevenson: The Man Who Died Twice," *New Statesman*, July 23, 1965, p. 112.

[2] *Sketches in the Sand* (New York: Alfred A. Knopf, 1967), p. 84.

[3] The American hardcover edition of *Major Campaign Speeches of Adlai E. Stevenson, 1952* sold 34,268 copies. Letter, Bennet Cerf to Carol Evans, October 30, 1969.

[4] "With AES in War and Politics," in *As We Know Adlai: The Stevenson Story by Twenty-two Friends*, edited and with preface by Edward P. Doyle, foreword by Adlai E. Stevenson III (New York: Harper & Row, 1966), p. 148.

great monument and cornerstone, but does the politician, the agent and spokesman of democracy, have no responsibility for public education? Government by the consent of the governed is the most difficult system of all because it depends for its success and viability on the good judgments and wise decisions of so many of us. But judgment and decision depend on information and understanding. In matters of public policy, candidates then have the greatest responsibility of all to inform truthfully, so that the people will understand and will have the tools of good judgment and wise decision.[5]

Speaking specifically of the 1952 campaign, Stevenson said:

Believing utterly in democracy and the collective reason of properly informed people, I have always thought that political campaigns for offices of great responsibility are both an opportunity and an obligation to talk sensibly and truthfully about public questions and their full implications.

I felt that the danger, not only to the Democratic Party politically, but to the country, in this national campaign was that it would follow the pre-convention line and turn largely on Korea, corruption, communists in government, etc., which were really not controversial issues between the two candidates at all. No one was running on a pro-corruption ticket or in favor of treachery. Everyone wanted to arrest inflation, reduce the cost of living and end the stalemate in Korea as quickly as possible. These were all questions of men and methods for dealing with them, not of objectives or good intentions. But of basic and fundamental importance in the campaign was that we Americans who were destined to lead, whether we liked it or not, must face stern decisions at home and the brutal facts of a world half slave, half free, a world besieged from the east for the first time since the Turks were turned back at the gates of Vienna, a world in which two-thirds of the people were hungry and half could neither read nor write — a world, in short, in which tolerance, understanding and peace were not to be had easily, quickly or cheaply. Unless people faced these realities at home and abroad, unless they knew that sedatives are not solutions and peace and prosperity goals, not gifts, we would dissipate a great opportunity to "dyke and break-water," as William James put it, our sandbank of reason.

For these reasons, I said in accepting the nomination that I viewed the campaign not as a crusade to exterminate the opposition, "but as a great opportunity to educate and elevate a people whose destiny is leadership, not alone of a rich, prosperous, contented country, but of a world in ferment." And because you cannot banish the evils of society by banishing reason or waving wands, I also said in that speech: "Let's talk sense

[5] *Major Campaign Speeches of Adlai E. Stevenson, 1952*, with an introduction by the author (New York: Random House, 1953), pp. xxiv–xxv.

to the American people. Let's tell them the truth. . . . Better we lose the election than mislead the people." [6]

In March, 1953, Stevenson embarked on a tour of self-education to countries in East Asia, Southeast Asia, South Asia, the Middle East, and Europe. This trip was his first exposure to Asia and the Middle East. What he learned heavily influenced his attitudes thereafter. The trip is chronicled in Volume V of *The Papers of Adlai E. Stevenson* and is a study in depth to illustrate how Stevenson prepared himself — if called upon — to serve in the presidency.

Upon his return in August, 1953, as titular head of the Democratic party he continued to attract new people and furnish new ideas to the party. He played an important role in the successful campaign to elect a Democratic Congress in 1954, and he sounded the tocsin against drift and complacency. To use the phrase of Stuart Gerry Brown, Stevenson was the "conscience in politics." [7]

In this volume — as in the previous volumes of *The Papers of Adlai E. Stevenson* — Stevenson's own words are presented in letters, postcards, press conferences and speeches. These volumes are a documentary biography of Adlai E. Stevenson and, at the same time, a documentary history in his own words of the extraordinary, and often bewildering, changes that remolded the United States and the world during his lifetime, from 1900 to 1965.

In selecting the materials from Stevenson's papers to be published in these volumes, the editors decided to emphasize the documents that helped answer such questions as: How did he educate himself? How did he become the man he became? What were the key influences in his life? How did he understand his times? How did he articulate the problems of his times?

Because of the large volume of mail Stevenson received as governor of Illinois it was impossible for him to acknowledge it or properly respond to it without the help of his staff and, later on, his law partners. During his administration as governor he authorized his assistants to draft letters over his name, to be signed, usually by Mrs. Anne Risse at the State House or Carol Evans and Margaret Munn at the mansion, without going over his desk. Although he dictated and signed an impressive number of letters himself, he once told his secretary Carol Evans that he did not think his signature was important or added anything to a letter. Letters from personal friends were put on his desk, as

[6] Ibid., pp. xxv–xxvi.
[7] *Conscience in Politics: Adlai E. Stevenson in the 1950's* (Syracuse, New York: Syracuse University Press, 1961).

were those of special interest, and he either dictated replies or sent his own handwritten response. Usually letters of great importance went first either to Carl McGowan or to William McCormick Blair, Jr., depending on the nature of the matter, and were brought by them to the Governor's attention.

When letters were written over the Governor's name by an aide, the author's initials with those of his secretary were typed in the left-hand margin of the carbon copy to identify the writer and the person who typed the letter. For example, if on a carbon copy of a letter drafted for the Governor the initials "CMcG/FR" are found in the left-hand margin, this indicates that it was dictated by Carl McGowan and typed by his secretary, Frances Ruys. If Mr. McGowan deemed it unnecessary to clear the letter with Governor Stevenson before it went out, the letter was signed by one of the three secretaries authorized to do so. If the letter was considered important enough to be read by the Governor before mailing, it was usually presented to him first in draft form, then typed in final form and signed by one of the authorized persons or by the Governor himself.

When the Governor dictated letters, his initials with those of the secretary were placed on the left-hand margin of the carbon. Some of these letters were then returned to his desk for one reason or another (he sometimes added a postscript by hand, or he might redraft the letter) and were signed by him. The others were signed by one of the authorized subordinates.

Stevenson and his principal aides continued to follow these procedures during the 1952 presidential campaign. In addition, a large correspondence section was formed at the campaign headquarters in the Leland Hotel in Springfield to acknowledge the enormous amount of mail he received as a presidential candidate. Most of the letters sent from the campaign headquarters went out over the signature of Stevenson's campaign manager, Wilson W. Wyatt, or other campaign aides. We have used none of this material.

Generally speaking, the procedures used during Stevenson's governorship were followed later when, in 1955, he entered a law partnership with William McCormick Blair, Jr., W. Willard Wirtz and Newton N. Minow. All of his partners assisted him with his correspondence, and his personal secretary, Carol Evans, was authorized to sign his name.

Because the collection of Stevenson's papers consists mainly of carbon copies, it is impossible to know whether he or one of his authorized associates signed them. It is, of course, possible to determine whether he was actually their author. But whether he composed and signed them personally or not, the letters and memoranda are considered to be his because he authorized them to be done on his behalf.

When we have made deletions from letters, speeches or other papers we indicate this by ellipses. We have provided editorial comment on any item where it was necessary for clarity or continuity.

The editors had a large collection of papers available for Volume IV. This volume is, therefore, much more selective than Volumes I and II, and even more selective than Volume III on the governorship of Illinois. Stevenson provided in his will that material about his governorship be deposited in the Illinois State Historical Library and the remainder be deposited in the Princeton University Library. Stevenson's most important correspondence was at his home in Libertyville when he died. The editors selected some of the material for this volume from the material at Libertyville before the collection was divided between the two depositories. Some items are still in the possession of Adlai E. Stevenson III.

The editors searched widely for handwritten documents. Stevenson enjoyed writing by hand — he must have, since he wrote by hand so many letters and postcards. Some people, particularly before Stevenson became governor of Illinois, failed to save them. Many people were most cooperative, placing all their Stevenson items at our disposal. Some preferred to send us only selections from their collections. A few refused to send us any material at all.[8]

Some letters, which would cause unnecessary anguish to people still living, the editors have not included in these volumes, or they have made appropriate deletions within such letters. These deletions are indicated by ellipses.

Stevenson wrote many letters to Mrs. Edison Dick and her family over the years. Some were dictated and transcribed on the typewriter, and some were handwritten. Mrs. Dick submitted extracts to the editors from the handwritten letters she received from Stevenson. She has indicated with ellipses material that was deleted by her. The originals of all the handwritten letters are in her possession.

The location of handwritten letters, postcards or originals of typewritten letters is given in the footnote references. Otherwise, since the majority of the papers in Volume IV are in the Princeton University Library (some in the distribution, probably inadvertently, went to the Illinois State Historical Library in Springfield), the editors identify the

---

[8] Katie Louchheim wrote: "These were [some of] the women who owned a share in Adlai's destiny." *By the Political Sea* (Garden City, New York: Doubleday, 1970), p. 108.

location of only those papers that are *not* in the Princeton collection. (It should be noted that a few letters to Alicia Patterson are taken from copies at Princeton.) Those papers at the Illinois State Historical Library will be identified as "in A.E.S., I.S.H.L."

Most of Stevenson's letters were signed with his full name; some to close personal or political friends were signed "AD" or "ADLAI." Because we have had to work, in most cases, with carbon copies, it is impossible to know how these letters and memoranda were signed. Hence, signatures have been omitted from such items. Whenever we have located the original letter, and he signed it otherwise than with his full name, we have included the signature.

When he wrote by hand, Stevenson had several idiosyncrasies. He spelled "it's" without the apostrophe; he used "thru" for "through," etc. We have left such items as he wrote them and have not added a *sic*.

When references in a letter were not clear, the editors wrote to the recipient of the letter (or to his heirs) to seek clarification. The responses — many of them reflected in the footnotes — have been extremely valuable and have added a dimension to the editing that would not have been possible to achieve unless these volumes were edited shortly after Stevenson's death.

The editors generally did not include letters written to Stevenson. Publishing letters written by people still alive or recently alive requires obtaining formal permission — a time-consuming task. Instead, the editors have summarized the contents of an incoming letter where it was necessary to make Stevenson's reply understandable.

Adlai E. Stevenson, as those who knew him well realize, corrected copies of his speeches up to the minute or second of delivery. Moreover, many of these last-minute-corrected speeches the editors have been unable to locate in the depositories. Stevenson sometimes gave these to reporters and they apparently were not returned to him. The editors decided, therefore, to rely on the texts of Stevenson's speeches that he himself selected for publication in *Major Campaign Speeches of Adlai E. Stevenson, 1952* (New York: Random House, 1953). Without the copies of the finally corrected speeches, we felt the speeches as they appeared in this publication, the text of which Stevenson approved, were to be relied upon rather than a press release of the speech or a carbon copy. Whenever speeches are used that are not included in that publication, the editors indicate whether the text was taken from a press release, carbon copy, or some other source.

Under the legal agreement between Walter Johnson and Adlai Stevenson III, Borden Stevenson and John Fell Stevenson, Adlai III agreed to read each volume before publication. In the event of disagreement as to the inclusion of any item of his father's papers, the matter was to be referred to Judge Carl McGowan for final — and irrevocable — decision. Adlai III objected to nothing included in this volume.

Contents

	Foreword	*vii*
One.	*The Draft at the 1952 Democratic Convention*	*1*
Two.	*The 1952 Campaign*	*25*
Three.	*To the Man Who Said What He Meant*	*189*
Four.	*Appeals to Reason*	*263*
	Acknowledgments	*607*
	Index	*609*

Illustrations

(*between pages 238 and 239*)

Stevenson's comments when Richard Nixon's campaign fund was disclosed
Stevenson meets with campaign advisers in front of the executive mansion
Walter Johnson hanging Stevenson's picture
Springfield, Illinois, welcomes Stevenson home, July 18, 1952
"It's Still There" — political cartoon from the Chicago *Daily News*
Stevenson with Charles P. Farnsley and Alben Barkley, August 7, 1952
A barbecue for Stevenson at the home of Alben Barkley
Campaigning in Michigan in 1952

(*between pages 494 and 495*)

"Coming Out Swinging" — political cartoon from the Chicago *Daily News*
Conferring with Estes Kefauver during the campaign
Writing a speech at Wilson Wyatt's home, 1954
With Adlai III, Nancy Anderson, Borden, and John Fell at the Louisville airport, September 13, 1954
At the home of Mr. and Mrs. Ernest L. Ives, Southern Pines, North Carolina, 1955
With Mr. and Mrs. Ernest L. Ives and Borden in Southern Pines, 1955
On vacation in Jamaica, September, 1955
With Adlai E. Stevenson III and his bride Nancy Anderson on their wedding day, June 25, 1955

Part One

The Draft
at the 1952
Democratic Convention

*A*lthough Governor Stevenson in January and March, 1952, refused President Harry S. Truman's request that he consider the Democratic presidential nomination,[1] Stevenson wrote in 1953:

> All winter and spring people were coming to Springfield and telephoning from all over the country — newspapermen, columnists, commentators, political leaders, friends, leaders of organizations, etc., etc. The mail became a real burden. . . . To all, my explanation was the same: I was a candidate for Governor of Illinois; I was committed to run for that office and one could not run for two offices at the same time in good conscience, or treat the highest office within the gift of the people of Illinois as a consolation prize.[2]

On July 12 — the day the Republican Convention closed — William Flanagan, the Governor's press secretary, issued the following statement: "He is a candidate for re-election as Governor of Illinois, and as he has often said, wants no other office. He will ask the Illinois delegation to respect his wishes and he hopes all of the delegates will do likewise."

By this time many of the leaders of the Democratic party had given up hope of drafting Stevenson. A draft to them apparently required careful planning and assumed an agreement with the candidate to be drafted. No such agreement was forthcoming from Stevenson. Newsweek observed on July 7: "Democratic leaders are beginning to fear that, if Stevenson doesn't speak out soon, a draft may become impossible."

Some, however, refused to give up hope of a draft including a group of Illinois citizens who in February, 1952, organized a committee to prepare and distribute literature to acquaint the nationwide public with Steven-

---

[1] See Stevenson's letter to the President of March 31, 1952, in *The Papers of Adlai E. Stevenson*, Vol. III, p. 540.

[2] *Major Campaign Speeches of Adlai E. Stevenson, 1952*, with an introduction by the author (New York: Random House, 1953), pp. xxi–xxii.

son's outstanding record as governor.[3] On July 12 this committee — the
National Committee Stevenson for President — mailed a letter to every
delegate and alternate urging them to draft Governor Stevenson. Three
days later Stevenson wired the editor of this volume, who was cochairman
of the committee:

> Have just seen circular letter to delegates and am very much dis-
> turbed in view of my unwillingness to be candidate. Have consis-
> tently avoided trying to influence your committee's activities feeling
> that my position was manifest and that I could not properly ask you
> to cooperate as a friend if your group had other views in conflict with
> my wishes. . . . I do not want to embarrass you and I am grateful
> for your good will and confidence but my attitude is utterly sincere
> and I desperately want and intend to stay on this job, with your help
> I hope. Regards. ADLAI E. STEVENSON [4]

*The National Committee Stevenson for President was undaunted. Its
members believed the nation needed Stevenson for President. They were
convinced — although somewhat shakily at times — that in view of the
Governor's deep faith in public service he could not refuse a convention
draft. On July 16 the National Committee Stevenson for President opened
unofficial campaign headquarters at the convention hotel with two purposes in mind: to create newspaper, TV and radio news about Stevenson
and to provide a place where pro-Stevenson delegates could meet and
plan for the draft. The mere opening of the draft headquarters stimulated
increased newspaper, radio and TV comment about Stevenson, and about
three hundred delegates visited the headquarters during the first two
days it was functioning. On Sunday, July 20 — the day before the convention opened — the National Committee Stevenson for President called
the leaders of Pennsylvania, Indiana, New Jersey, and Kansas together to
plan the organization of the draft.*

*The next day Stevenson's speech of welcome to the delegates demon-
strated what a formidable, articulate leader he was.[5] The impact of this*

---

[3] Walter Johnson, *How We Drafted Adlai Stevenson* (New York: Alfred A. Knopf,
1955), describes the role of this committee in the draft at the convention. Jacob M.
Arvey, "The Reluctant Candidate — An Inside Story," *Reporter*, November 24, 1953,
and "A Gold Nugget in Your Backyard," in *As We Knew Adlai: The Stevenson Story
by Twenty-two Friends*, edited and with preface by Edward P. Doyle, foreword by
Adlai E. Stevenson III (New York: Harper & Row, 1966); and George W. Ball,
"With AES in War and Politics," in *As We Knew Adlai*, have useful information on
the draft.

[4] Quoted in Johnson, *How We Drafted Stevenson*, p. 54. A copy of this telegram
is in the possession of Walter Johnson.

[5] Arthur Krock wrote: "His two speeches at the Chicago convention . . . restored
the level of political oratory in this country to that which Woodrow Wilson occupied."
New York *Times*, September 15, 1952.

speech, the announcement the same day by the National Committee Stevenson for President that former Senator Francis J. Myers, of Pennsylvania, and Philadelphia City Council President James A. Finnegan would manage the draft movement, and the announcement the next day (Tuesday, July 22) that Governor Henry F. Schricker of Indiana would place Stevenson in nomination, all combined to create a fast-moving Stevenson bandwagon. On the evening of July 21, Vice President Alben Barkley withdrew as a candidate. President Truman, displeased with Stevenson's refusal to seek the nomination, had given his support to the Vice President. In a roundup story on the convention, the Alsops wrote in their syndicated column: "The plain fact is that Mr. Truman and the 'bosses' who are supposed to have maneuvered the Stevenson draft were themselves caught flat-footed when it became clear that the convention wanted Stevenson and nobody else.

"In effect, the professionals simply rushed to the head of the Stevenson parade which was already forming, and began frantically waving their banners." [6]

Many party leaders and many labor leaders had favored Stevenson in the spring of 1952. When he proved adamant (not "indecisive") in his refusal to be a candidate, they committed themselves to other candidates. Then, after the draft got under way at the convention, many of them returned to their support of Stevenson after honoring commitments to support others on the first or second ballots.

On Thursday, July 24, the day the names of various leaders were placed in nomination, President Truman's alternate in the Missouri delegation announced for the first time that he had been instructed by the President to cast a vote for Stevenson. The President arrived in Chicago on the day of the balloting. Following the second ballot, Averell Harriman wrote a statement urging his supporters to shift to Stevenson. After Harriman had already decided to do so, President Truman urged Harriman to withdraw in favor of Stevenson. [7]

The day before Stevenson was drafted on the third ballot, Walter Lippmann wrote:

---

[6] Chicago *Sun-Times*, August 3, 1952.

[7] Paul T. David, Malcolm Moos, Ralph M. Goldman, *Presidential Nominating Politics in 1952: The National Story* (Baltimore: Johns Hopkins Press, 1954), p. 154, adds, "But the President's influence was hardly necessary at this point." President Truman wrote that "my announced open support cinched his nomination." *Memoirs: Years of Trial and Hope, 1946–1952* (New York: Doubleday, 1956), p. 496. This simplistic interpretation has been accepted by a number of writers, including Alden Whitman, *Portrait: Adlai E. Stevenson, Politician, Diplomat, Friend* (New York: Harper & Row, 1965), and Alfred Steinberg, *Sam Johnson's Boy: A Close-up of the President from Texas* (New York: Macmillan, 1968).

There is no doubt, I think, that from the beginning Stevenson has seen the reality of the situation with extraordinary objectivity and penetration. He has not been coy. He has been wise in realizing what after 20 years in office it would mean to take over the leadership of the Democratic party.

It could be done only under conditions which, if not unique in politics, are very rare indeed. The new leadership had to draw its strength from the mass of the party, not from the outgoing president. There was no value in the kind of nomination for which Vice President Barkley was, so cynically and so briefly, considered.

The new leadership had to be drafted. It could not be appointed from the White House. A draft, as everyone knows, is almost never genuine. In the case of Stevenson, if he is nominated, there will have been a genuine draft. He will have been drafted because the party needs the man more than he desired the office. To have known this is the mark of wisdom. To have adhered to it is the mark of great public virtue.

If Stevenson is nominated under these conditions, he can, therefore, assume the leadership entirely in his own right, quite uncommitted to any faction.[8]

To Arthur M. Schlesinger, Jr.[9]

[June or July 1952]

Dear Arthur:

Thanks for your very interesting letter about the civil rights situation. I am sending it on to our National Committeeman, Col. [Jacob M.] Arvey.

If, as you say, it is Averell [Harriman] or me there will be no strain or conflict on my part and I will be doing my best for Averell! [10] I seem to be having a hard time convincing people that I donot want to be the candidate for President, and that I *do* want to be the Democratic candidate for Governor of Illinois, and nothing else!

Yours,
AES

[8] Chicago *Sun-Times*, July 24, 1952.
[9] Associate professor of history at Harvard University. This handwritten letter is in the Schlesinger papers, John F. Kennedy Library.
[10] Mr. Schlesinger worked for Harriman at the Democratic National Convention.

To John S. Miller [11]

June 14, 1952

Dear John:

Thanks for your note. It is getting dreadfully tough and I am apprehensive that if I don't get out — all the way out — before the Republican Convention I will never be able to get out regardless of whom they nominate.

I have lived from day to day with the confident hope and expectation that it would blow over and that a genuine draft was literally impossible, but now I begin to have my doubts — particularly as [Senator Robert A.] Taft's nomination seems to become more certain. I agree with all you say and I hope I can hold the line without too much ultimate embarrassment.

Yours,

To Alfred A. Knopf, Jr.[12]

June 17, 1952

My dear Mr. Knopf:

I have seen the galley proofs of Ben Thomas' "Lincoln." [13] It is a stirring story of a humble man who rose to greatness through his loyalty to his country's highest principles; a book from which adherents of democracy today may draw new inspiration.

Sincerely yours,

Mrs. Jacqueline Shaw, of Brookline, Massachusetts, wrote Stevenson that his decision was not in his own hands but God's. She added that Abraham Lincoln was one of the most uncertain of men.

To Mrs. Jacqueline Shaw

June 17, 1952

My dear Mrs. Shaw:

I was so glad to have your letter of June 3. It has been helpful, and your reference to Lincoln's indecisions and difficulties comforted me a lot,

[11] A Chicago lawyer and an old friend of Stevenson's.

[12] Secretary and director of the Trade Department of Alfred A. Knopf, Inc. A copy is in the Stevenson collection, Illinois State Historical Library (A.E.S., I.S.H.L.). In a carbon copy Stevenson wrote to Mr. Thomas: "Dear Ben: Your words are always better than mine. A.E.S."

[13] Benjamin P. Thomas, *Abraham Lincoln: A Biography* (New York: Alfred A. Knopf, 1952).

even if they have not solved mine! I think, as you say, that somehow "in His good time" I will find the answer. If it is merely what I want to do, I have it now, and that is to stay here.

With warm regards and my gratitude, I am

Sincerely yours,

Laura Magnuson, Stevenson's close friend for many years, wrote that she and her husband, Dr. Paul Magnuson, were leaving for Europe and wished to send their "love & best wishes for peace of mind (& soul) in all the tough decisions that lie ahead of you."

To Mrs. Paul Magnuson [14]

June 17, 1952

Dear Laura:

Your note comes just as I was working my way down the pile to a clipping of Paul's prompt and vigorous and estimable reaction to the A.M.A. speech.[15] I had meant to congratulate him long before this, but I hope *this* will suffice.

You were sweet to think of me before your departure. I wish I were going with you because my life hereabouts is acutely unpleasant and I am sorely tormented. I know well enough what *I* want, but all this pressure mingled with duty, obligations, causes, etc. is perplexing and confusing.

Have a wonderful summer, and my best to Paul.

Affectionately,

ADLAI

Stevenson entered Passavant Hospital in Chicago on June 21 for a minor operation to remove kidney stones.[16] While he was there, his old friend Fanny Butcher Bokum, literary editor of the Chicago Tribune *(under her professional name, Fanny Butcher), sent him a book.*

---

14 The original is in the possession of Mrs. Magnuson.

15 Dr. Magnuson, a well-known orthopedic surgeon and chairman of President Truman's Commission on the Health Needs of the Nation, spoke out on June 10 against the "public be damned attitude" of the American Medical Association, which was then meeting in Chicago. He warned that this attitude, which stemmed from the association's fear of socialized medicine, would only encourage federal regulation of the medical profession. See the New York *Times,* June 11, 1952.

16 See *The Papers of Adlai E. Stevenson,* Vol. III, pp. 572–576.

To Mrs. Richard Bokum [17]

Chicago, June 26, 1952

My dear Fanny:

You were sweet to send me the Winston Churchill book, and I even found time to read a bit of it while languishing at Passavant. It is charming and I am afraid will preoccupy entirely too much of my time.

As for Mr. Busch's book,[18] I hardly see how he contrived to write anything at all in view of the limited time he had and our very, very few conversations. I had hoped that the book would not be published but that was beyond my control, and after a hasty reading I think he did well with what he had to work with. It is getting harder and harder for me to recognize myself, however!

With warm thanks and affectionate regards to you both, I am

Sincerely yours,

To Paul R. Leach [19]

July 4, 1952

Dear Paul:

Count me in for December 13! [20] I hope I shall be delivering no speech, but that you will be entertaining the Governor and Governor-elect of Illinois.

I wish you would tell me what to do to make it clear that that is what I want and all I want!

Sincerely yours,

To Barry Bingham [21]

July 4, 1952

Dear Barry:

. . . I am more anxious every day to keep out of the presidential business and continue here. I think I have made a tragic mistake not

---

[17] A copy is in A.E.S., I.S.H.L.

[18] Noel F. Busch, *Adlai E. Stevenson of Illinois* (New York: Farrar, Straus & Young, 1952).

[19] Chief of the Washington bureau of the Knight newspapers. The original is in the possession of Mr. Leach.

[20] The annual dinner of the Gridiron Club of Washington, of which Mr. Leach was president.

[21] Publisher of the Louisville *Courier-Journal* and a close friend of Stevenson's. A copy is in A.E.S., I.S.H.L.

to indicate long before this that I could accept the nomination under no possible circumstances, but meanwhile I have drifted along trying to see my duty and do it, and confident that a draft was impossible and that I was safe. Now I am really worried.

I will see you in Chicago.

Sincerely yours,

The divorced wife of Admiral William A. Glassford, with whom Stevenson had worked while special assistant to Secretary of the Navy Frank Knox (1941–1944), wrote that Senator Taft was whistling in the dark if he thought he would be nominated. She expressed the hope that the Democratic Convention would be an improvement over the Republican Convention then taking place.

To Mrs. D. L. Glassford

July 11, 1952

My dear Mrs. Glassford:

Your letters always enchant me and the last one is no exception. "Daft Taft" was certainly "whistling in the dark" as you surmised. As for me, perhaps you are right, but I can hardly see it that way and I shall do my level best to stay right here in Illinois where I belong — which is my full measure. I am afraid "Ike," as you say, is in for some rude blundering and I hope he doesn't insult any more of our friends the way he did the French the other day.[22]

I had a feeling that the Republican convention was grossly deficient in a sense of humor. You would never make that mistake!

Sincerely yours,

Candidates and delegates began to arrive in Chicago on Monday, July 14. Governor Stevenson remained in Springfield secluded from the press. On Friday, July 18, he arrived in Chicago and was met at the airport by reporters, TV and newsreel cameras. He stated:

> I shall never be a candidate in the sense that I'll ask anybody to vote for me here. On the contrary, I'll do everything possible to discourage any delegate from putting me in nomination or nominating me.

[22] The Associated Press quoted Eisenhower as saying that the French had gone "astray" since they had become "50 per cent agnostic or atheistic." New York *Times,* July 11, 1952.

I cannot conceive that, with all the willing candidates available and with all the talent and ability at its disposal, the Democratic party would turn to an unwilling candidate who is running for another office.[23]

On Sunday, July 20, Governor Stevenson attended services at the Fourth Presbyterian Church, where the Reverend Harrison Ray Anderson preached on the text: "If any of you lack wisdom, let him ask of God, that giveth to all men liberally, and upbraideth not; and it shall be given him." The reporters present interpreted the sermon as being directed at Stevenson and that Reverend Anderson was admonishing him not to decline the nomination. When they asked Stevenson what he thought of the sermon, he replied: "Superb."

Later that afternoon Stevenson met with the Illinois delegation. Although reporters were barred from the caucus, by putting their ears to the space between the floor and the sliding partitions of the hotel room, they heard the give-and-take. Stevenson stated that he did not want to be nominated; he wanted to run for reelection as governor of Illinois. The reporters then quoted him as saying: "I do not dream myself fit for the job — temperamentally, mentally, or physically. And I ask therefore that you all abide by my wishes not to nominate me, nor to vote for me if I should be nominated."

The convention opened on Monday, July 21. As Stevenson stepped to the rostrum to welcome the convention to Illinois, his appearance set off wild applause. James Reston wrote in the New York Times: "The 'reluctant candidate,' who has been trying to talk himself out of the Democratic Presidential nomination for the last five months, talked himself right into the leading candidate's role this morning with a fifteen-minute address that impressed the convention from left to right."

WELCOMING ADDRESS TO THE
DEMOCRATIC NATIONAL CONVENTION [24]

As Governor of the host state to the 1952 Democratic Convention, I have the honor of welcoming you to Illinois. And, in the name of our nine millions of people, I extend to you the heartiest of greetings. Chicago and Illinois are proud that once again the party conventions by which we restate our principles and choose our candidates for the greatest temporal office on earth, are held here in Chicago — at the crossroads of the continent.

[23] Quoted in Johnson, *How We Drafted Stevenson*, p. 72.
[24] The text is from *Major Campaign Speeches AES 1952*, pp. 3–10.

Here, on the prairies of Illinois and the Middle West, we can see a long way in all directions. We look to east, to west, to north and south. Our commerce, our ideas, come and go in all directions. Here there are no barriers, no defenses, to ideas and aspirations. We want none; we want no shackles on the mind or the spirit, no rigid patterns of thought, no iron conformity. We want only the faith and conviction that triumph in free and fair contest.

As a Democrat perhaps you will permit me to remind you that until four years ago the people of Illinois had chosen but three Democratic governors in a hundred years. One was John Peter Altgeld, a German immigrant, whom the great Illinois poet, Vachel Lindsay, called the Eagle Forgotten; one was Edward F. Dunne, whose parents came here from Ireland; and the last was Henry Horner, but one generation removed from Germany. Altgeld was a Protestant, Dunne was a Catholic, and Horner was a Jew.

That, my friends, is the American story, written by the Democratic Party, here on the prairies of Illinois, in the heartland of the nation.

You are very welcome here. Indeed, we think you were very wise to come here for your deliberations in this fateful year of grace. For it was in Chicago that the modern Democratic story began. It was here, just twenty years ago, in the depths of shattering national misery at the end of a dizzy decade of Republican rule that you commenced the greatest era of economic and social progress in our history — with the nomination of Franklin Roosevelt; twenty years during which we fought total depression to victory and have never been more prosperous; twenty years during which we fought total war to victory, both East and West, and launched the United Nations, history's most ambitious experiment in international security; twenty years that close this very month in grim contest with the communist conspiracy on every continent.

But, our Republican friends say it was all a miserable failure. For almost a week pompous phrases marched over this landscape in search of an idea, and the only idea they found was that the two great decades of progress in peace, victory in war, and bold leadership in this anxious hour were the misbegotten spawn of socialism, bungling, corruption, mismanagement, waste and worse. They captured, tied and dragged that ragged idea in here and furiously beat it to death.

After listening to this everlasting procession of epithets about our misdeeds I was even surprised the next morning when the mail was delivered on time! I guess our Republican friends were out of patience, out of sorts and, need I add, out of office.

But we Democrats were not the only victims here. First they slaughtered each other, and then they went after us. And the same vocabulary was good for both exercises, which was a great convenience. Perhaps the proximity of the stockyards accounts for the carnage.

The constructive spirit of the great Democratic decades must not die here on its twentieth anniversary in destructive indignity and disorder. And I hope and pray, as you all do, that we can conduct our deliberations with a businesslike precision and a dignity befitting our responsibility, and the solemnity of the hour of history in which we meet.

For it is a very solemn hour indeed, freighted with the hopes and fears of millions of mankind who see in us, the Democratic Party, sober understanding of the breadth and depth of the revolutionary currents in the world. Here and abroad they see in us awareness that there is no turning back, that, as Justice Holmes said, "We must sail sometimes with the wind, sometimes against it; but we must sail and not drift or lie at anchor." They see in us, the Democratic Party that has steered this country through a storm of spears for twenty years, an understanding of a world in the torment of transition from an age that has died to an age struggling to be born. They see in us relentless determination to stand fast against the barbarian at the gate, to cultivate allies with a decent respect for the opinion of others, to patiently explore every misty path to peace and security which is the only certainty of lower taxes and a better life.

This is not the time for superficial solutions and endless elocution, for frantic boast and foolish word. For words are not deeds and there are no cheap and painless solutions to war, hunger, ignorance, fear and to the new imperialism of Soviet Russia. Intemperate criticism is not a policy for the nation; denunciation is not a program for our salvation. Words calculated to catch everyone may catch no one. And I hope we can profit from Republican mistakes not just for our partisan benefit, but for the benefit of all of us, Republicans and Democrats alike.

Where we have erred, let there be no denial; where we have wronged the public trust, let there be no excuses. Self-criticism is the secret weapon of democracy, and candor and confession are good for the political soul. But we will never appease, nor will we apologize for our leadership in the great events of this critical century from Woodrow Wilson to Harry Truman!

Rather will we glory in these imperishable pages of our country's chronicle. But a great record of past achievement is not enough. There can be no complacency, perhaps for years to come. We dare not just look back to great yesterdays. We must look forward to great tomorrows.

What counts now is not just what we are *against,* but what we are *for. Who* leads us is less important than *what* leads us — what convictions, what courage, what faith — win or lose. A man doesn't save a century, or a civilization, but a militant party wedded to a principle can.

So I hope our preoccupation here is not just with personalities but with objectives. And I hope the spirit of this Convention is confident reaffirmation that the United States is strong, resolved, resourceful and rich; that we know the duty and the destiny of this heaven-rescued land; that we can and we will pursue a strong, consistent and honorable policy abroad, and meanwhile preserve the free institutions of life and of commerce at home.

What America needs and the world wants is not bombast, abuse and double talk, but a sober message of firm faith and confidence. St. Francis said: "Where there is patience and humility there is neither anger nor worry." That might well be our text.

And let us remember that we are not meeting here alone. All the world is watching and listening to what we say, what we do and how we behave. So let us give them a demonstration of democracy in action at its best — our manners good, our proceedings orderly and dignified. And — above all — let us make our decisions openly, fairly, not by the processes of synthetic excitement or mass hysteria, but, as these solemn times demand, by earnest thought and prayerful deliberation.

Thus can the people's party reassure the people and vindicate and strengthen the forces of democracy throughout the world.

After delivering his speech, Governor Stevenson went into seclusion at the home of his aide Bill Blair.[25] Fashionable Astor Street was disrupted by the activities of reporters, photographers, television cameras and sound trucks. Linemen strung wires through the walled garden of the Blair house to the lawn area between the sidewalk and the street where six pay-station booths were set up for the reporters.

On July 24 — the day Stevenson's name was placed in nomination — the reporters gathered outside Blair's home sent Stevenson the following:

1.) Have you been in communication with President Truman or his representative either Wednesday or Thursday?

2.) Will you accept the nomination for President if the convention offers it to you after it becomes apparent no candidate can get a delegate majority?

And, here is our plea in verse:

> *Here we are anxious as a bride,*
> *While you sit so silently inside,*
> *Please answer our query*

[25] William McCormick Blair, Jr., was ordinarily known as Bill Blair, and he is referred to frequently by that name in the following pages.

> *Because we are getting weary*
> *While the world waits for you to decide.*

We wish to thank you for your hospitality — and patience with us.
Sincerely,
THE STEVENSON PRESS CORPS.
— *A Growing Party.*

Stevenson wrote in longhand at the bottom of the page of this request:

(1)   No. Who is his rep.? I don't know. No one has told me they were his representative.[26]

In response to another request by the reporters for a statement, Stevenson wrote:

> There was an old man named Adlay
> Who wanted to be Governor badly
> Said he with dismay
> Tho my heart's far away
> I'll give a prize for a last line — gladly.[27]

On the first ballot the next day, Governor Stevenson received 273 votes. On the second ballot the total jumped to 324½ votes. When the convention convened after dinner Averell Harriman's statement urging his supporters to vote for Stevenson was read to the delegates. State after state began to shift to Stevenson, and by the time the vote reached Pennsylvania, it was clear that he would receive the nomination on the third ballot.[28]

It was now past midnight. The delegates, while they waited to hear from the man they had drafted, listened to speeches by Senator Richard Russell and Senator Estes Kefauver. Finally, President Harry S. Truman spoke, and as he finished he introduced Stevenson.

Alistair Cooke, in analyzing the significance of Stevenson's nomination, wrote in the Manchester Guardian, *July 28, 1952:*

> So Stevenson emerged in triumph and in singularly happy independence. He owes nothing to the South, nothing to the Northern liberals. He is his own man. And in the last hour, after a jolly but

[26] There is no answer (2) in the original.
[27] The originals of both documents are in the possession of William I. Flanagan, the Governor's press secretary at the time.
[28] Stevenson needed 616 votes to carry the nomination. At 12:25 A.M. on the morning of July 26, he received 617½ votes on the third ballot. For the choice of Stevenson's running mate, see Kenneth S. Davis, *The Politics of Honor: A Biography of Adlai E. Stevenson* (New York: Putnam, 1967), p. 275.

perfunctorily received introduction by the President, he showed them what a formidable manner of man that is. His famous decorum hardened into magnanimity, his wit into principle, his integrity stayed the same. . . .

Out of this throbbing circus, its blowsy barkers and its super-subtle medicine men, emerged a humble and civilized man. It should not be forgotten that he was the choice of the gaping rustics and the family men who did not much fancy the glamour of the sideshows and the ringmasters and the miracle healers.

SPEECH OF ACCEPTANCE

July 26, 1952 [29]

I accept your nomination — and your program.

I should have preferred to hear those words uttered by a stronger, a wiser, a better man than myself. But, after listening to the President's speech, I feel better about myself!

None of you, my friends, can wholly appreciate what is in my heart. I can only hope that you may understand my words. They will be few.

I have not sought the honor you have done me. I *could* not seek it because I aspired to another office, which was the full measure of my ambition. One does not treat the highest office within the gift of the people of Illinois as an alternative or as a consolation prize.

I *would* not seek your nomination for the Presidency because the burdens of that office stagger the imagination. Its potential for good or evil now and in the years of our lives smothers exultation and converts vanity to prayer.

I have asked the Merciful Father — the Father of us all — to let this cup pass from me. But from such dread responsibility one does not shrink in fear, in self-interest, or in false humility.

So, "If this cup may not pass from me, except I drink it, Thy will be done."

That my heart has been troubled, that I have not sought this nomination, that I could not seek it in good conscience, that I would not seek it in honest self-appraisal, is not to say that I value it the less. Rather it is that I revere the office of the Presidency of the United States.

And now, my friends, that you have made your decision, I will fight to win that office with all my heart and soul. And, with your help, I have no doubt that we will win.

You have summoned me to the highest mission within the gift of any people. I could not be more proud. Better men than I were at hand for

---

[29] The text is from *Major Campaign Speeches AES 1952*, pp. 7–10.

this mighty task, and I owe to you and to them every resource of mind and of strength that I possess to make your deed today a good one for our country and for our party. I am confident too, that your selection of a candidate for Vice President will strengthen me and our party immeasurably in the hard, the implacable work that lies ahead for all of us.

I know you join me in gratitude and respect for the great Democrats and the leaders of our generation whose names you have considered here in this Convention, whose vigor, whose character, whose devotion to the Republic we love so well have won the respect of countless Americans and have enriched our party. I shall need them, we shall need them, because I have not changed in any respect since yesterday. Your nomination, awesome as I find it, has not enlarged my capacities. So I am profoundly grateful and emboldened by their comradeship and their fealty, and I have been deeply moved by their expressions of good will and support. And I cannot, my friends, resist the urge to take the one opportunity that has been afforded me to pay my humble respects to a very great and good American, whom I am proud to call my kinsman, Alben Barkley of Kentucky.

Let me say, too, that I have been heartened by the conduct of this Convention. You have argued and disagreed, because as Democrats you care and you care deeply. But you have disagreed and argued without calling each other liars and thieves, without despoiling our best traditions in any naked struggles for power.

And you have written a platform that neither equivocates, contradicts nor evades. You have restated our party's record, its principles and its purposes, in language that none can mistake, and with firm confidence in justice, freedom and peace on earth that will raise the hearts and the hopes of mankind for that distant day when no one rattles a saber and no one drags a chain.

For all these things I am grateful to you. But I feel no exultation, no sense of triumph. Our troubles are all ahead of us. Some will call us appeasers; others will say we are the war party. Some will say we are reactionary. Others will say that we stand for socialism. There will be the inevitable cries of "throw the rascals out"; "it's time for a change"; and so on and so on.

We'll hear all those things and many more besides. But we will hear nothing that we have not heard before. I am not too much concerned with partisan denunciation, with epithets and abuse, because the workingman, the farmer, the thoughtful businessmen, all know that they are better off than ever before and they all know that the greatest danger to free enterprise in this country died with the great depression under the hammer blows of the Democratic Party.

Nor am I afraid that the precious two-party system is in danger. Certainly the Republican Party looked brutally alive a couple of weeks ago, and I mean both Republican parties! Nor am I afraid that the Democratic Party is old and fat and indolent. After 150 years it has been old for a long time; and it will never be indolent as long as it looks forward and not back, as long as it commands the allegiance of the young and the hopeful who dream the dreams and see the visions of a better America and a better world.

You will hear many sincere and thoughtful people express concern about the continuation of one party in power for twenty years. I don't belittle this attitude. But change for the sake of change has no absolute merit in itself. If our greatest hazard is preservation of the values of Western civilization, in our self-interest alone, if you please, is it the part of wisdom to change for the sake of change to a party with a split personality; to a leader, whom we all respect, but who has been called upon to minister to a hopeless case of political schizophrenia?

If the fear is corruption in official position, do you believe with Charles Evans Hughes that guilt is personal and knows no party? Do you doubt the power of any political leader, if he has the will to do so, to set his own house in order without his neighbors having to burn it down?

What does concern me, in common with thinking partisans of both parties, is not just winning the election, but how it is won, how well we can take advantage of this great quadrennial opportunity to debate issues sensibly and soberly. I hope and pray that we Democrats, win or lose, can campaign not as a crusade to exterminate the opposing party, as our opponents seem to prefer, but as a great opportunity to educate and elevate a people whose destiny is leadership, not alone of a rich and prosperous, contented country as in the past, but of a world in ferment.

And, my friends, more important than winning the election is governing the nation. That is the test of a political party — the acid, final test. When the tumult and the shouting die, when the bands are gone and the lights are dimmed, there is the stark reality of responsibility in an hour of history haunted with those gaunt, grim specters of strife, dissension and materialism at home, and ruthless, inscrutable and hostile power abroad.

The ordeal of the twentieth century — the bloodiest, most turbulent era of the Christian age — is far from over. Sacrifice, patience, understanding and implacable purpose may be our lot for years to come. Let's face it. Let's talk sense to the American people. Let's tell them the truth, that there are no gains without pains, that we are now on the eve of great decisions, not easy decisions, like resistance when you're attacked, but a long, patient, costly struggle which alone can assure triumph over the great enemies of man — war, poverty and tyranny — and the assaults upon human dignity which are the most grievous consequences of each.

Let's tell them that the victory to be won in the twentieth century, this portal to the Golden Age, mocks the pretensions of individual acumen and ingenuity. For it is a citadel guarded by thick walls of ignorance and of mistrust which do not fall before the trumpets' blast or the politicians' imprecations or even a general's baton. They are, my friends, walls that must be directly stormed by the hosts of courage, of morality and of vision, standing shoulder to shoulder, unafraid of ugly truth, contemptuous of lies, half truths, circuses and demagoguery.

The people are wise — wiser than the Republicans think. And the Democratic Party is the people's party, not the labor party, not the farmers' party, not the employers' party — it is the party of no one because it is the party of everyone.

That I think, is our ancient mission. Where we have deserted it we have failed. With your help there will be no desertion now. Better we lose the election than mislead the people; and better we lose than misgovern the people. Help me to do the job in this autumn of conflict and of campaign; help me to do the job in these years of darkness, doubt and of crisis which stretch beyond the horizon of tonight's happy vision, and we will justify our glorious past and the loyalty of silent millions who look to us for compassion, for understanding and for honest purpose. Thus we will serve our great tradition greatly.

I ask of you all you have; I will give to you all I have, even as he who came here tonight and honored me, as he has honored you — the Democratic Party — by a lifetime of service and bravery that will find him an imperishable page in the history of the Republic and of the Democratic Party — President Harry S. Truman.

And, finally, my friends, in the staggering task you have assigned me, I shall always try "to do justly and to love mercy and to walk humbly with my God."

After the acceptance speech, Stevenson returned to Springfield to plan his campaign and to organize his staff. He received many letters of praise and support. President Truman wrote him by hand at 6:40 A.M. on Saturday, July 26, congratulating him on his performance at the nominating convention. It was, he said, one of the most remarkable nights he had ever spent in his life. He referred to Stevenson as a brave man with the necessary experience and education to become a fine president. He invited the Democratic nominee to meet with him in Washington in the near future to discuss campaign strategy.

To Harry S. Truman

July 27, 1952

Dear Mr. President:

I am deeply touched by your letter, written at 6:40 A.M., after that endless night. I am grateful beyond expression for your charity and good will. Last winter you paid me the greatest compliment within your gift, and now you have added something more that is very precious to me.

I am literally staggering under the new and unfamiliar burdens I have so abruptly assumed! But you know all about that. I would be delighted to take advantage of your suggestion that I come to Washington to discuss my miseries. Most any time would be convenient for me, I think, and if one of your staff called me we could work out a mutually satisfactory time, I am sure.

With my thanks, again, for your letter, and my everlasting gratitude for your confidence, I am

Faithfully yours,

Alicia Patterson and Adlai Stevenson had been friends since about 1926. In July, 1926, Stevenson went on a trip to Russia and Miss Patterson married and moved to London and later to New York. He did not see her again until he went to New York in 1946 as a delegate to the General Assembly of the United Nations, when they renewed their friendship. In 1948 (and until her death in 1963) Miss Patterson was publisher of Newsday *(Long Island), and, in private life, Mrs. Harry Guggenheim.*

To Alicia Patterson [30]

July 27, 1952

Alicia dear —

I finally got your note in the madness & mess at the house — but not until Sunday. Why didn't you come to the house — Blair House as we called it! — during the week? Everyone else did I think. I wanted so much a final glimpse and word and — but nothing's *final*. I refuse to believe that my life is over. Try to get in touch with me soon. I thought the piece you did in Newsday was excellent & I'm very proud. It's hard for me to think of myself as a candidate for Pres. & it gives me a wan & weary smile. I hope I can keep a straight face most of the time anyway. At the moment I'm so tired I don't feel as tho I had a face.

[30] This handwritten letter is in the possession of Adlai E. Stevenson III.

I'm on my way to Spfd by train with a full carload of reporters, police etc — triumphal stop in Bloomington & then parade, civic celebration and speech in Spfd. Oh God deliver me! I don't know how long I can last! . . .

The line to emphasize is that I am *not* Truman's candidate. He asked me and I turned it down. Then he turned to Harriman, then Barkley, but the convention turned to me after I had repeatedly said I was not a candidate and didnt want it.

Samuel Cardinal Stritch, Archbishop of Chicago, wrote Stevenson on July 26: "Your acceptance speech to the Convention was fine. In your own charming way you unwittingly gave to the country a master portrait of yourself. Through the trying hours I was deeply in sympathy with you because I knew your inner anguish. Your courage begotten of confidence in God will give you the strength of a man who forgets self for the common good."

To Samuel Cardinal Stritch

July 29, 1952

My dear Cardinal Stritch:

Nothing has touched me more in these anxious days than your letter. That you wrote me at all was enough. That you wrote me so understandingly heartens and encourages me beyond expression. Twice during the Convention I was on the eve of calling your house, thinking I might come over for an hour with you, but I concluded to spare you an exhibition of my anguish and confusion. Now that I have assumed the appalling task I shall do it as well as I possibly can, and I hope, with your prayers, with honor and dignity, which are more important to me than success.

Faithfully yours,

Playwright Robert E. Sherwood, who among other things had written Abe Lincoln in Illinois (*1939*), *wrote Stevenson:*

You know how I have felt for a long time about the supreme appropriateness of your nomination for the office of President of the United States, so I do not need to tell you how happy I am that it has come to pass. But I do want to thank you with all my heart for the nobility and courage and good humor with which you accepted this awful responsibility.

I saw and heard your acceptance speech on television, I read it in the morning papers and I saw and heard it again on a television repeat. It is a very great document, intellectually and artistically as well as politically. It had the true and rare savor of Sangamon County — and that is the highest praise that I could give to any speech.

To Robert E. Sherwood

July 29, 1952

My dear Bob:

Your letter touches me deeply. Without saying more for the moment, let me just request that, if at all possible, you stop off on your return trip East. There are trains from Chicago to Springfield (3 hours) and airplanes (1 hour) frequently. I should like very much to see you and get some of your precious counsel if I could.

I can, of course, send a car to pick you up in St. Louis (1 hour 45 min. by motor) if that is more convenient.

Yours,

Stevenson's old friend Archibald MacLeish, with whom he had worked so closely in Washington during World War II and during the formation of the United Nations,[31] wrote on July 26: "We know a little of what you have been going through. And we are very, very proud of you. . . . I don't need to tell you that I am at your service, typewriter, yellow pad and all. . . . God bless you my dear friend."

To Archibald MacLeish

July 30, 1952

Dear Archie:

Your letter refreshes me no end — if that is still possible! I am crushed with the burdens that have suddenly and unwillingly become mine. About all I can suggest for the moment is that you get out a typewriter, pad and pencil and go to work with fragments of any kind of things you think need to be said. I am sure we are not far apart on the latter score except that I cannot articulate them like you can. I hope and pray that I can keep my debate up on a level of honor, dignity and public enlightenment, and for that purpose there is only one MacLeish. I wish my mind was orderly enough to suggest precisely what, but my first engagement seems to be the American Legion Convention in New York on August 27 (still tentative), and I suddenly discover that henceforth I shall be able to do little of my own writing.

[31] See *The Papers of Adlai E. Stevenson*, Vol. II, pp. 230–235.

Enough for now, together with my thanks for your response to my silent prayer for help.

My love to Ada.[32]

Yours,

Mrs. Franklin D. Roosevelt wired Stevenson: "My warm good wishes and hopes that you will win and bring us the kind of administration which will help our country and the world to peace."

To Mrs. Franklin D. Roosevelt [33]

July 30, 1952

My dear Mrs. Roosevelt:

Nothing has pleased me more than your thoughtful and encouraging wire. I had hoped so much that I might see you while you were in Chicago, but I did have an opportunity to listen to your splendid speech.

I shall do the best I can with my limited experience and talents, and your good will will be a constant encouragement.[34]

Faithfully yours,

---

[32] Mrs. MacLeish.

[33] The original is in the Franklin D. Roosevelt Library, Hyde Park, New York.

[34] Mrs. Roosevelt was "exhilarated" by Stevenson's campaign speeches. See Joseph P. Lash, *Eleanor: The Years Alone* (New York: W. W. Norton, 1972), pp. 212–214.

Part Two

The 1952 Campaign

*S*tuart Gerry Brown wrote that Governor Stevenson faced the "nearly impossible task of asserting his unwilling leadership of a party loyal, for the most part, to a President from whom he felt a need to achieve independence, and to prove his independence to the nation. It was as complex a political situation as one could conjure. Yet it perfectly suited the complexity of Stevenson himself. He could and did reveal certain aspects of his intellect and character to best advantage under such circumstances."[1]

An important asset "little noted in the newspapers," Stevenson wrote, "which meant a great deal to me — I had literally no obligations to anyone." As a result, "I concluded to organize and run my part of the campaign my own way. As I was still Governor I established my headquarters in Springfield instead of New York, as in the past."[2] He appointed his old friend Wilson Wyatt, former mayor of Louisville, Kentucky, and former housing expediter and administrator of the National Housing Agency, as his personal campaign manager. The Governor replaced President Truman's chairman of the Democratic National Committee with his old friend Stephen A. Mitchell, a Chicago lawyer and an early promoter of Stevenson for public office in 1948. Stevenson called Senator J. W. Fulbright to Springfield to advise on political questions. And Stevenson asked his old friends, Hermon Dunlap Smith and Mrs. Edison Dick, to be cochairmen of the Volunteers for Stevenson. Another old friend, George Ball, was made executive director. William McCormick Blair, Jr., assistant to the Governor, continued in the same capacity during the campaign.

To fulfill the pledge in his speech of acceptance — "Let's talk sense to the American people. Let's tell them the truth. . . . Better we lose the elec-

---

[1] Stuart Gerry Brown, *Conscience in Politics: Adlai E. Stevenson in the 1950s* (Syracuse, New York: Syracuse University Press, 1961), pp. 11–12.
[2] *Major Campaign Speeches of Adlai E. Stevenson, 1952* (New York: Random House, 1953), pp. xxiii–xxiv.

tion than mislead the people" — *Governor Stevenson and his aide Carl McGowan prepared a list of major topics which the Governor wanted to discuss. These issues he discussed in major speeches in September, "thereby setting forth my whole program and identifying myself and my views as quickly as possible." October was reserved for "the exigencies and opportunities that were bound to develop as the campaign progressed, and for amplification and rebuttal in the debate that I thought would develop on some of the domestic issues at least. It did not develop and as the battle of words progressed, I felt more and more that people cared little about the issues and party records, or about precise definition of positions. They were weary of conflict, impatient and eager for repose. While discouraging, it was not surprising. Having said my piece with some precision on the problems of our country, I tried to stir deeper waters and talked more and more philosophically about faith and fear, and about the mighty and wondrous powers for good of free and independent-thinking Americans."* [3]

A research and writing staff headed by Harvard historian Arthur M. Schlesinger, Jr., was appointed to assist in implementing the substantive aims of the campaign. Among others in the group were David Bell, who had been an assistant to President Truman; Professor Willard Wirtz, of the Northwestern University Law School; John Fischer, editor of Harper's; *Professor John Kenneth Galbraith of Harvard University; Robert Tufts, who had been a member of the Policy Planning Staff of the Department of State; freelance writer John Bartlow Martin; William Reddig, former literary editor of the Kansas City* Star; *and freelance writer Sidney Hyman, who had helped Robert E. Sherwood write* Roosevelt and Hopkins: An Intimate Story *(New York: Harper & Brothers, 1948). Other writers who contributed ideas and drafts of speeches were David L. Cohn, Herbert Agar, Bernard DeVoto, Samuel I. Rosenman, Robert E. Sherwood, and Archibald MacLeish.* [4]

Governor Stevenson's pride in his own style was such that he rewrote and rewrote drafts of speeches submitted to him until the last minute before delivery.

"Did I talk over the people's heads?" Stevenson wrote. "No — and that's about the only aspect of the campaign I am sure of! As I have said above, I think candidates for important offices, let alone for the Presidency of the United States in this age and day, should not treat us as fourteen-year-olds but as adults, challenging us, in the ancient tradi-

---

[3] Ibid., p. xxvi.
[4] See John Fischer, "The Editor's Easy Chair — Footnotes on Adlai E. Stevenson," *Harper's*, November, 1965, which discusses the writing group. It was housed in the Elks Club in Springfield.

tion of all civilized people, with the assumption that we should and can and will respond to the appeal of reason and imagination." [5]

Richard N. Goodwin wrote: "After he spoke, no leader of his party nor the dialogue of Democracy itself would ever sound the same again. He was eloquent and was acclaimed for eloquence. But, finally, it was not how he spoke but what he said that mattered. Others would bring new accents and perhaps even greater powers to leadership. But it had all begun in Springfield, Illinois, in that hopeful dawn year of 1952." Goodwin added: *"He told an entire generation that there was room for intelligence and idealism in public life, that politics was not just a way to live but a way to live greatly, that each of us might share in the passions of the age."* By appealing to young and old alike to take an active part in the political process, Goodwin felt that Stevenson had *"changed the face of American politics, enriching the democracy, providing a base on which talent could aspire to power, opening a gateway to public life through which many who never heard his voice will some day enter."* [6]

Theodore H. White stated: "Adlai Stevenson was the John-the-Baptist of American politics. He changed the whole tone of American politics. . . . Young people across America responded to Stevenson in 1952 and this has affected them ever since." [7]

Washington Star *columnist Mary McGrory recalled listening to Stevenson's speech of acceptance on the radio with her brother in New Hampshire, when "suddenly at one in the morning the clipped tones of Stevenson rode out over the static and the majestic cadences of his acceptance speech fell on our unbelieving ears. Politically speaking, it was the Christmas morning of our lives. . . . In the campaign that followed, for the first time in my life I read political speeches for pleasure. Stevenson's speeches seemed beautiful to me. I did not realize until much later how bold they were."* [8]

To Lloyd K. Garrison [9]

August 2, 1952

Dear Lloyd:

My heartfelt thanks for your understanding letter. I am struggling to

[5] *Major Campaign Speeches AES 1952*, p. xxvii.

[6] *The Sower's Seed: A Tribute to Adlai Stevenson* (New York: New American Library, 1965), pp. 12–13.

[7] Interview with Walter Johnson, April 14, 1967.

[8] "The Perfectionist and the Press," in *As We Knew Adlai: The Stevenson Story by Twenty-two Friends,* edited and with preface by Edward P. Doyle, foreword by Adlai E. Stevenson III (New York: Harper & Row, 1966), p. 170.

[9] Member of the New York law firm of Weiss, Rifkind, Wharton & Garrison. He had met Stevenson in Washington during World War II, when Garrison was a mem-

perfect an organization here as I shall have no satisfaction from this campaign if I don't do it in character, and well.

I am sure there are many things you can do to help, and just what to suggest at the moment I hardly know, but feel free to write or wire or telephone me at any time.

And after November 4 I suspect you better get ready to move.

Love to Ellen.[10]

Yours,

ADLAI

To Carroll Binder [11]

August 2, 1952

Dear Carroll:

So many thanks for your fine letter and the enclosures, which I have read with much interest and gratification. You are always good to me and also understanding — which is so rare. I know that in the future you will not hesitate to send ideas or suggestions or bits and pieces of textual material which might be useful. Please do so. I value your judgment highly and your long friendship. I shall do my level best never to disappoint you. It is a fearful task that I have assumed.

Yours,

ADLAI

To Bernard DeVoto [12]

August 2, 1952

Dear Benny:

A thousand thanks for your good letter. I value enormously any bits and pieces of writing you can send me, and by all means give me that brief on the conservation of public lands planks in the Republican platform.[13] I never knew how much I didn't know!

Sincerely yours,

ADLAI

---

ber of the National War Labor Board. The original is in the possession of Mr. Garrison.

10 Mrs. Garrison.

11 Editorial editor of the Minneapolis *Tribune*. The original is in the possession of the Newberry Library, Chicago.

12 Editor of "The Easy Chair," *Harper's* magazine, and author of many books on the American West. The original is in the DeVoto collection, Stanford University Library.

13 The 1952 Republican National Convention adopted a plank reading in part: "We

To Marquis Childs [14]

August 2, 1952

My dear Mark:

I wish we had had the opportunity for at least a telephone call. If it had to be it came about the right way — no commitments, no agreements, not even "an understanding." I shall do it my own way as best I can with all the disadvantages of a late start, no staff, difficulties in Washington, unfamiliar surroundings, etc., etc.

I am so glad you think well of Oscar.[15] I intend to use him in most delicate work.

Now that it is over, may I add my thanks for your everlasting encouragement.

Yours,

ADLAI

To Samuel I. Rosenman [16]

August 2, 1952

Dear Sam:

I was delighted to have your understanding and comforting letter. Your confidence and encouragement hearten me. I hope you will not hesitate to give me any advice or suggestions as to what you should do or what you can do to help me. Nobody has ever challenged my amateur standing in the business of politics, and I am afraid it takes more than good will and vitality now.

With my warm thanks and great respect, I am

Cordially yours,

---

favor restoration of the traditional Republican public land policy, which provided opportunity for ownership by citizens to promote the highest land use. . . . In the management of public lands and forests we pledge the elimination of arbitrary bureaucratic practices. . . ." See the New York *Times,* July 11, 1952.

[14] Member of the Washington bureau of the St. Louis *Post-Dispatch.* The original is in the Childs collection, Wisconsin Historical Society.

[15] Oscar Chapman, Secretary of the Interior, 1949–1953.

[16] A New York lawyer, former justice of the New York Supreme Court and adviser to President Roosevelt, and author of *Working with Roosevelt* (New York: Harper, 1952).

To General George C. Marshall [17]

August 3, 1952

My dear General Marshall:

Nothing has pleased me more than your thoughtful and heartening letter. Knowing what confronts me, I am sure you can understand my disinclination to seek this appalling responsibility. I shall do my level best to keep your confidence and respect.

Please give my very warm regards to Mrs. Marshall.

Faithfully yours,

P.S. Southern Pines never looked better to me! [18]

To Allan Shivers [19]

August 3, 1952

My dear Allan:

I am so grateful to you for your kind letter. I should be delighted to see you most any time at your convenience. I am afraid I am woefully ignorant about the Tidelands business [20] and would welcome your views. I should think a little sober consideration of all the equities in an atmo-

---

[17] Chief of Staff of the Army during World War II and Secretary of State, 1947–1949. The original is in the George C. Marshall Research Foundation, Arlington, Virginia.

[18] The Marshalls had a home at Pinehurst, near the winter home of Stevenson's sister and brother-in-law, Mr. and Mrs. Ernest L. Ives, at Southern Pines, North Carolina.

[19] Governor of Texas, 1949–1957. A copy is in the Adlai E. Stevenson papers, Illinois State Historical Library (A.E.S., I.S.H.L.).

[20] In May, 1952, Congress passed an act granting to the states ownership of the offshore oil lands. President Truman vetoed the bill. The 1952 Republican platform pledged "restoration to the States of their rights to all lands and resources beneath navigable inland and offshore waters within their historic boundaries." Wilson Wyatt, who was present at a meeting with Governor Shivers at which this topic was discussed, later wrote: "Early in the same campaign I was present when a small delegation of powerful party leaders met with him at the Governor's Mansion in the Illinois capital. They were urging a position important to their region. He was not in accord. Finally in desperation, but with confidence that he had the unanswerable argument, the absolute trump of trumps, one of them said, 'But otherwise you can't win.' Coldly Stevenson responded, 'But I don't *have* to win.'" "What I Think Is Still What I Thought," in *As We Knew Adlai*, p. 107. Stevenson maintained his position that federal control of the offshore oil lands should be continued (see, e.g., his speech of October 10, 1952, at New Orleans, below), and Governor Shivers eventually bolted the Democratic party and supported Eisenhower. See Kenneth S. Davis, *A Prophet in His Own Country: The Triumphs and Defeats of Adlai E. Stevenson* (Garden City, New York: Doubleday, 1957), p. 422.

sphere of justice for all would remove some of the passion from this subject and yield sound ultimate results.

Please come whenever you wish and little advance notice is necessary.

Cordially yours,

To Eric Sevareid [21]

August 3, 1952

Dear Eric:

I am so grateful for your letter. Mr. Johnson [22] has been here. He is wholly delightful, eager to help, but, as you warned, very deaf and hardly fit for full time duty in this mare's nest. I think he can be very helpful in contributing ideas and drafts.

I shall pass along the suggestion of John Hayes [23] to Wilson Wyatt. He looks precisely like what we want although I assume he is attached to the National Committee rather than to me personally.

It was good to have a glimpse of you and I am at a loss for words to thank you for all you have done for me. I hope you are not misleading the people to your own destruction!

Cordially yours,

P.S. My regards to that wonderful Peter.[24]

To Vincent Sheean [25]

August 3, 1952

Dear Jimmy:

If I could only write like you my trepidation would subside. Things are slowly taking shape and I hope I can measure up to the demands of the long ordeal ahead of me.

By all means plan to come to Springfield with Mrs. Sheean. I cannot foretell just what degree of chaos there will be on the 12th or thereabouts. The Vice President, wife and stepdaughter arrive the 13th to speak with me at Governor's Day on the 14th. The town will be dreadfully crowded

---

[21] Commentator for the Columbia Broadcasting System.

[22] Gerald Johnson, columnist for the Baltimore *Sun* and author of many books on the history of the United States.

[23] Unable to identify.

[24] Mr. Sevareid and his son Peter had visited Stevenson in Springfield after the Democratic Convention.

[25] Author and foreign correspondent.

at that time but we can certainly squeeze you in somewhere or in a friend's house — doubtless to the delight of the friend!

Warmest regards and my everlasting thanks for your constant encouragement, confidence and understanding.

Yours,

To Gerald Johnson

August 4, 1952

Dear Mr. Johnson:

Our meeting was most profitable to me, and I hope you can work up a speech for the American Legion and also on the "time for a change" theme. I note that the New York Times puts particular emphasis on the latter as a justification for its position.[26] I wonder if we should counterattack, somehow, with the idea that Jenner,[27] Kem,[28] Watkins,[29] etc., would be a change for the worse if they captured the Republican party, the Senate and Eisenhower.

I should like to write you at length about the many thoughts that occur to me and promptly vanish in the chaos hereabouts.

Cordially yours,

MEMORANDUM TO: Mr. Wilson Wyatt
FROM: Governor Stevenson

My spy in the Eisenhower camp reports their strategy somewhat as follows:

(1) Foreign policy will be the No. 1 issue, with special attention to the Far East.

(2) Nixon will push hard on the [Alger] Hiss business.

(3) Every effort will be made to appease the [Senator Robert A.] Taft people; the liberal wing influence seems to be dying.

(4) A big play will be made to bring the farmers into line.

According to . . . one of Ike's advisers,[30] the plan is to let me develop as a shining knight until October and then hit me with horsemeat, cigarette tax scandals,[31] and whatever else they may have, feeling that they

[26] The New York *Times* supported Eisenhower.
[27] Senator William E. Jenner of Indiana, a leading figure in the senatorial investigation of Communist subversion.
[28] Senator James P. Kem of Missouri, who lost his seat in the 1952 election.
[29] Senator Arthur V. Watkins of Utah.
[30] Unable to identify.
[31] For a discussion of these, see *The Papers of Adlai E. Stevenson,* Vol. III, 489–490, 502, 509; Davis, *A Prophet in His Own Country,* pp. 362–365; and John Bartlow Martin, *Adlai Stevenson* (New York: Harper, 1952), pp. 126–138.

should save them until the end when the balloon is largest and most quickly deflated.

To Letitia Stevenson [32]

August 4, 1952

My dear Aunt Letitia:

It was a constant comfort to me to know that you were at the Convention with Buffy.[33] I think she needed you very much and it is a pity that Aunt Julia [34] couldn't have been with you. . . .

Spiritually, it is a support to me to feel my own standing by and supporting me with their love. These will be hard weeks and when the moment comes that you will be willing again to join with us, be assured we will call upon you. But never, in any way, let Buffy exhaust you. In her personal enthusiasm she may overlook the fact that you may not enjoy all the arduous things she attempts to do.

With heartfelt thanks.

Lovingly,

On July 31, 1952, Doris Fleeson wrote and enclosed a copy of her column from the Washington Star *of July 30 saying that Stevenson was being urged to organize his own campaign in his own manner and to proclaim his intention to clean house in Washington.*

To Doris Fleeson [35]

August 6, 1952

Dear Doris:

Thank you for your letter. I am quite sure you are correct about the necessity for changes. Even if it wasn't necessary to reassure the public, however, I would do it anyway, as you probably know. I think I have started already in establishing my headquarters here, selecting a personal campaign manager, and a personal staff of my own selection. There will be more changes to follow as time and the inordinate difficulties confronting a candidate who had no organization and no obligations permit.

You are most gracious to me and I am grateful.

Yours,

[32] Sister of Stevenson's father. A copy is in A.E.S., I.S.H.L.
[33] Stevenson's sister, Mrs. Ernest L. Ives.
[34] Mrs. Martin D. Hardin, Letitia Stevenson's sister.
[35] A copy is in A.E.S., I.S.H.L.

To Mrs. Albert D. Cash [36]

August 6, 1952

My dear Betty:

Word has just come to me that you were Betty Cassatt of Charlevoix. At least I always identify all of my childhood friends as "of Charlevoix"!

I want you to know how distressed I was to read about your husband's death. Fred Hoehler,[37] who has been my indispensable colleague here in Illinois has told me the unhappy story. You have my profoundest sympathy.

I hope some day that our paths will cross again. My memories of Charlevoix and our childhood are happy and forever green.

Sincerely yours,

To Harry S. Truman

August 6, 1952

Dear Mr. President:

I have just had a call from Mr. Connelly [38] inviting me to luncheon with you on next Tuesday. I have advised him that I shall most certainly be there, and I am grateful for your thought of me.

I have been in the anguished throes of the Convention sequel, but there is some blue sky on the horizon. My little headquarters organization here in Springfield is taking shape, and I have found an old friend, a Catholic, whom I think will be a suitable replacement for Mr. McKinney.[39] I hope to have him here for a meeting with Mr. McKinney on the latter's return from Colorado Springs the end of the week. Mike Monroney [40] has agreed to take John Sparkman's [41] place as Director of the Speakers' Bureau. I have not, however, found a suitable Treasurer for the National Committee. Several prospects have been unavailable, and any suggestions you could give me in this direction next week would be most helpful.

Faithfully yours,

Mrs. Edison Dick, cochairman of the Volunteers for Stevenson, wrote the Governor that some of his friends were concerned that Wilson Wyatt

[36] A copy is in A.E.S., I.S.H.L.
[37] Director of the Illinois Department of Public Welfare.
[38] Matthew Connelly, appointments secretary to President Truman.
[39] Stevenson replaced Frank McKinney with Stephen A. Mitchell as chairman of the Democratic National Committee.
[40] Senator from Oklahoma.
[41] Senator from Alabama and Stevenson's running mate.

and Arthur M. Schlesinger, Jr., two leaders of Americans for Democratic Action, were much too liberal in their views.

To Mrs. Edison Dick [42]

August 8, 1952

. . . Frankly your letter amazes me. This is the first time I've ever detected that the [Chicago] Tribune line — the extreme partisan line — could affect your judgment. Of course the opposition will smear and hurt me every way they can — be it Wilson Wyatt, Schlesinger, etc etc. But do you think they really have the views assigned them by the press? If so what evidence is there? Who was I to get for a manager to help me — an old line politician? an inexperienced novice knowing no one?

That . . .[43] et al could fall for the idea that I was a puppet in the hands of Wyatt & a young writer Schlesinger is exactly the equivalent of the idea the opposition will also spread that I'm a puppet of Truman. They don't seem to believe that, but they'll swallow the other eagerly. It makes me despair of "friends," just as you say. If they want to manage my campaign & staff my hqrs. and feel competent to do so, why don't they step forward. Maybe I'm getting a little tired & irritable after a long night with Dick Russell,[44] [Averell] Harriman & Moody! [45]

Forgive me — but just remind them and yourself that *I'm* the candidate and if they don't know me & what I stand for and I thought had demonstrated then perhaps Eisenhower is their best bet who doesn't know what he stands for and is surrounded with people that have neither depth of intellect or convictions that my friends have ever shown any affinity for.

Its hard — and I know *you'll* forgive this outburst of despair at doubts provoked by opposition newspapers which will get hotter & hotter as the campaign progresses.

I hope the Cttee [46] in Chi[cago] can help to reassure the faint of heart who believe their doubts & doubt their beliefs. . . .

Sir Gladwyn Jebb, British Ambassador to the United Nations — and a friend of Stevenson's from their association at the United Nations, 1945–1948 — wrote Stevenson on August 4 expressing his pleasure that an old friend, whom he admired and liked, should be a candidate for the Presi-

[42] This handwritten letter is in the possession of Mrs. Dick.
[43] This deletion was made by Mrs. Dick.
[44] Senator Richard Russell of Georgia.
[45] Senator Blair Moody of Michigan, who was filling the vacancy caused by the death of Arthur H. Vandenberg.
[46] Volunteers for Stevenson.

dency. He added: "I know how much the problem of power and of the effect of power on one's own character troubles you, as it must trouble all sincere and thinking people. But I also know that you are one of those rare persons whom power, if it should come to you, is more likely to exalt than to corrupt." He mentioned that during the presidential campaign of 1888, the British minister to the United States, Lionel Sackville-West (later Lord Sackville), had answered a letter, ostensibly from a naturalized Englishman asking for whom he should vote, by recommending President Cleveland. The letter was published, and amidst the furor over foreign interference in domestic affairs, the minister was handed his passport and he left the country, a fate which Sir Gladwyn hoped would not befall him as a result of his letter.

To Sir Gladwyn Jebb [47]

August 9, 1952

Dear Gladwyn:

So many thanks for your kind and thoughtful letter. Have no fear, I shall guard your correspondence from the press with the utmost caution, and you need not be haunted with the unhappy fate of Lord Sackville.

It is an appalling undertaking, which I did not seek and did not want. I shall do it as best I can.

With very warm regards to you and Cynthia,[48] I am

Sincerely yours,

To Richard Bentley [49]

August 11, 1952

My beloved Bentleys:

I have heard about your proffer of the house at Huron Mountain [Michigan] and I am so grateful for your thoughtfulness. I don't see how I can possibly use it, in view of the vast entourage which seems to accompany me henceforth.

But I can dream.

Yours,

ADLAI

[47] A copy is in A.E.S., I.S.H.L.
[48] Lady Jebb.
[49] A Chicago lawyer, who handled Stevenson's divorce case in 1949. The original is in the possession of Mr. Bentley.

On August 8, Archibald MacLeish wrote Stevenson outlining his ideas for a speech to the American Legion on the true nature of patriotism.

To Archibald MacLeish

August 11, 1952

Dear Archie:

The "stuff of patriotism" is just right, and is there not a sound and timely thread in the theme of combatting inflation by restraint in demands for spending and special consideration by all groups — including veterans? The idea of Americans first and veterans second?

Peace and national security are the obvious directions of this speech, and I think I could well add to the usual an obvious talk about strong defenses at home and abroad some stern, sensible, simple talk about what we, as citizens, owe to ourselves — strikes, profiteering, black markets, and all the ugly materialism of a people that have suffered little of the hard realities of sacrifice, discipline, self-control, want, etc., to keep their freedom. But I suppose all that is part of the anatomy of patriotism which you have in mind.

I get so sick of the everlasting appeals to the cupidity and prejudice of every group which characterize our political campaigns. There is something finer in people; they know that they *owe* something too. I should like to try, at least to appeal to their sense of obligation as well as their avarice.

My chaos here is incredible and I see less and less time for any adequate writing of my own. You comfort me beyond words.

Yours,

P.S. I enclose some pedestrian mouthings before American Legion Conventions here in Illinois. Also my veto of the Legion's anti-subversive bills in the Illinois Legislature.[50]

AES

P.P.S. I don't suppose I could use much more than 2000 or 2500 words.

AES

On August 9, Loring Merwin, publisher of the Bloomington Daily Pantagraph, *in which the Stevenson family owned a minority interest, wrote his cousin that he had been going through some of the "worst mental an-*

[50] For Stevenson's veto of the Broyles Bill, see *The Papers of Adlai E. Stevenson,* Vol. III, pp. 412–418.

guish of my lifetime" on the question of what the paper should do about his candidacy. He added that he felt the country needed a change in direction.

To Loring C. Merwin

August 11, 1952

Dear Bud:

Thanks for your note. Let me know when you get back and we will have a talk. Perhaps the attached editorial should put things in somewhat better perspective with regard to Wilson Wyatt. I have wondered who I might have found that was better balanced, more moderate, and who also had some practical experience in political management. I consider myself very fortunate that he is willing to sacrifice three months of his prosperous law practice.

. . . As to changes in direction we can talk. Some things must be clear — my headquarters in Springfield, Wyatt instead of an administration manager, and Steve Mitchell, who has been investigating the Department of Justice, as National Chairman. But it is hard for a hostile press to acknowledge the fact of change when the argument is so precious.

As to the editorial,[51] I should like to discuss it with you, as you will concede some of it is meaningless, such as "The people want a change from diplomatic empire building to a sane program of cultivating other free nations in a common desire for collective security." As to "the people want a change from extravagant welfare spending," you have noted in the paper that Eisenhower is all out for bigger, better, broader social security. I sometimes wonder if the press of the country is doing itself justice, let alone the people. There is so much bunk in the air and the people should have the truth from the press, if not from the politicians.

Yours,

T. S. Matthews, editor of Time *and a Princeton classmate of Stevenson's, wrote him on August 8 praising his speech of acceptance. But he made several criticisms of it, including his belief that some people were shocked at the Governor's quoting of the words of Christ in Gethsemane.*

[51] The *Pantagraph*, August 11, 1952, headed its editorial "Can Stevenson Effect Changes?" It argued that he had "one great handicap. He is the candidate of a party which has been in control of our national government for 20 years — a party which, under Harry Truman, has set all-time records for spending, scandal and inefficiency and has dragged respect for government to its lowest point in our history."

To T. S. Matthews

August 11, 1952

Dear Tom:

Thanks, and thanks again.

All of your criticism I need. I shall mark it well. The speech was rather hastily written in the confusion of the house on Astor Street [52] and turned out better than I expected. I am disturbed about sacrilege. I had always thought, perhaps too much like a Unitarian, that the words of Christ are our own words and where they express our feelings better than we can they are ours to use. I learn slowly, and my only defense is relentless effort to learn.

How I wish you *were* able to do some writing for me. For the first time I am suddenly confronted with the ugly reality that I cannot hope to do my writing *in toto* myself any longer, and I shudder at what it means, psychologically for me and publicly for the record. I am trying to build up a staff in the midst of this confusion but my acquaintance after years here is not good.

Please write me from time to time when you have suggestions. There will be no rewards except the thanks of the heart.

Yours,

On August 11, Senator Richard B. Russell of Georgia wrote Stevenson that he had enjoyed his visit to Springfield, and added: "Let me again assure you of my willingness to assist you in every way I can."

To Richard B. Russell

August 11, 1952

Dear Senator:

Warmest thanks for your note and the enclosure which I shall read promptly.

Your visit here heartened me. It is a comfort to feel that I have the understanding and support not alone of kinsmen but of profoundly respected and experienced leaders in our public life. I shall have to rely on your help very much, and I hope you will never hesitate to tell me if I am making mistakes.

[52] Bill Blair's Chicago townhouse, which Stevenson used as his headquarters during the Democratic National Convention. See Part One, above.

I think the National Chairman solution should prove advantageous from the viewpoint of public impressions, but Steve Mitchell will need patience and counsel in the intricacies of his new job.

Cordially yours,

To Harry S. Truman

August 13, 1952

Dear Mr. President:

Let me tell you again how much I enjoyed and profited from our meeting yesterday. I am mortified that we took so much of your precious time but for Senator Sparkman, the staff and myself it was heartening and invaluable — and delightful, as it always is with you.

I was sorely tempted to issue a sarcastic statement following Ike's outburst this morning but I thought of your advice and restrained myself.[53] I am glad to hear that he will be invited for a briefing too.[54]

My understanding is that we can count on you for speeches in October in the East and possibly Pittsburgh and St. Paul, winding up in St. Louis; and also for a trip to the Northwest if that seems necessary. I know how sincere you are about helping us and of your almost limitless energy, but we shall try not to impose on you unreasonably.

With renewed thanks for all your courtesies and encouragement, I am,

Faithfully yours,

To the Reverend Reinhold Niebuhr [55]

August 13, 1952

Dear Dr. Niebuhr:

And now I find myself in the very position which you wished and I fervently "diswished." My biggest disappointment is that I shall not have your brain and gifted hand at my command. But your spirit will help mightily and I hope you can say a prayer for me now and then and pass along any suggestions that may occur to you.

With earnest wishes for your rapid and full recovery,[56] I am

Sincerely yours,

[53] Eisenhower declared on August 12 that the American people wanted a change "in order to replace corruption with honesty, reckless spending with economy . . . mismanagement in foreign affairs with clear-cut policies and programs for positive peace." New York *Times,* August 13, 1952.

[54] President Truman arranged for briefings on international affairs for both candidates.

[55] Professor of applied Christianity at Union Theological Seminary. A copy is in A.E.S., I.S.H.L.

[56] Mr. Niebuhr had just suffered a stroke.

To Archibald MacLeish [57]

August 14, 1952

Archie — With hordes of people clamoring on the lawn (this is Gov's day at the State Fair) I'm returning this in accordance with your wire without time to even look at it. Also I'm enclosing some gratuitous suggestions from John Sullivan [58] — an old "Legion politician." Anything you say is so much better than I could say it — just write your way. Thanks from the troubled heart — AES

After reading the draft of a proposed speech, Stevenson sent the following handwritten memorandum, undated, to Arthur M. Schlesinger, Jr. [59]

Mr. Schlesinger —

I want to hit this idea of group influence in Govt. over and over — the Dem. party is the party of all the people not of any group etc. I said something about this in my acceptance speech —

AES

Stevenson made the following inserts on August 14 in a draft of a letter to the Country Gentleman, *a general interest monthly magazine for farm families.* [60] *In the October, 1952, issue, Representative Harold D. Cooley of North Carolina, chairman of the House Committee on Agriculture, published "The Case for Stevenson" in an attempt to woo the farm vote in the upcoming election.*

I believe this is essentially a state and local responsibility. By school and road improvements in Illinois we are making rapid progress toward equality and accessibility of school facilities. Likewise we have made rapid progress in hospital construction under the federal-state-local participation program.

[57] This handwritten letter is in the MacLeish papers, Library of Congress.

[58] John Lawrence Sullivan was President Truman's Secretary of the Navy. He was the first Navy Secretary under the National Security Act of 1947, which brought all the armed services under the Department of Defense. He had been commander of the New Hampshire Department of the American Legion in 1937.

[59] This handwritten memorandum is in the Schlesinger papers, John F. Kennedy Library. The editors have selected only samples of Stevenson's notes to Schlesinger during the campaign.

[60] The handwritten original is in the Schlesinger papers, John F. Kennedy Library.

I think our farm programs must be constantly reviewed and their value tested against their cost. After all the farmer is a taxpayer, too. The long range of course is stability and healthy growth for the whole economy, of which agriculture is a large part, but only a part. Just as we can't have healthy business without healthy agriculture, we can't have healthy agriculture without healthy business. I think there is sometimes a tendency to look at them separately rather than at the interdependence of farm and city, of agriculture and industry.

Mrs. Franklin D. Roosevelt wrote Stevenson on August 6, making several suggestions, including one that he consult Bernard Baruch. She added: "I have always found that while it took a little tact and some flattery to get on with the old gentleman I got enough information with valuable experience back of it to make it worthwhile." She closed by apologizing for adding one more headache to the many he probably already had.

To Mrs. Franklin D. Roosevelt

August 15, 1952

Dear Mrs. Roosevelt:

I am so grateful to you for the letter from a former State employee. Her confidence illustrates why I was so eager to continue with this work in Illinois where we have made such conspicuous progress and heartened so many faithful State employees.

. . . I was much interested in what you said about Mr. Baruch.[61] I have written him since the Convention and have planned to see him in New York when I am there. Although my acquaintance is meager, he has always been most friendly and cordial, and I know he is a mine of sound advice.

You have never added a "headache" and you never will. I hope you will give me any suggestions you can as the campaign progresses.

Faithfully yours,

Mrs. Hermon Dunlap Smith wrote Stevenson on August 12 about their long and close friendship and their happy times together at their summer home in Desbarats, Ontario, and at Lake Forest, Illinois. She expressed her gratitude that he had asked her husband to be cochairman of the Volunteers for Stevenson. She wrote: "Finally, I want you always to bear in mind that we will love you in the rain and blizzards of failure and ad-

---

[61] He supported Eisenhower.

verse criticism as well as in the fair weather of success." She added that Mr. and Mrs. McPherson Holt, formerly of Lake Forest, who had moved to California, and her niece Linda Spence were visiting her; and that Linda was writing on the back of her letters to California, "America Needs Stevenson."

To Mrs. Hermon D. Smith

August 16, 1952

Ellen dear:

Your sweet letter has brightened my day and lifted my heart — not to mention the balsam! The loyalty of you and Dutch through all these years, and so many trials, has been as precious a blessing as God has given me. I have moments when I feel, however, that I must have become a hideous burden to my oldest and dearest friends. That must never be and I must trust you not to let me impose on you too much. I have misgivings right now about Dutch and the sacrifice of his holiday.

As to "the rain and blizzards of failure and adverse criticism" — they will come and the comfort that you have been for so long will be there I know. And believe me, it is a comfort!

How I wish I was up there this very moment but they have forbidden me to leave the United States and it looks as though my two or three day holiday will be in Wisconsin, if at all.

Love to you and all the family, the Holts, and tell Linda to keep her barrage leveled at California.

Devotedly,

To Samuel I. Rosenman

August 21, 1952

Dear Judge:

I was delighted to have your letter, which I have only now had an opportunity to read. Your suggestions I have noted carefully, and, happily, they coincide largely with my own instincts, subject to the difficulty I find in taking myself very seriously. I have thus far exercised with some difficulty a good deal of restraint about my adversaries and what they have been saying. I hope I can continue to do so, and also avoid a dangerous tendency to casual wisecracks which are promptly distorted by the press.

I shall most certainly take prompt advantage of your suggestion about seeing Mrs. Roosevelt, whom I admire inordinately and know well; and I think you are quite right that I should have no reluctance about identifying myself with the Roosevelt regime. I have none, in fact, however.

As to my "conservatism," to which some of the papers have referred, I haven't detected any enthusiasm or particular praise on that score. The fact of the matter is, I must keep in character, and I *am* a moderate, I suppose.

Your proffer of help is heartening, and I have already asked some of my staff to get in touch with you and Bob Sherwood about doing a piece for me. I am in despair not alone of doing most of my writing but of doing any of it any more! And it is the most discouraging aspect of this whole business, but perhaps the writing will improve in the process!

We have been having some "skull practice" sessions hereabouts, and more will be needed. I hope we can work out some way for you to participate. There is so much I don't know!

Cordially and gratefully yours,

On August 16, President Truman wrote Stevenson emphasizing the importance of a bipartisan foreign policy. He was distressed to see this bipartisan approach becoming more partisan every day. The Republicans, he charged, were making foreign policy an issue because their stand on domestic issues attracted few votes. He closed by again offering his services to the campaign.

To Harry S. Truman

August 23, 1952

Dear Mr. President:

I am so grateful to you for your letter of August 16. I am a little alarmed by the evident anxiety of the Republicans to create the illusion of some positive foreign policy program of their own, and, thus, a partisan issue. I shall do my best to follow your advice and try to keep the bi-partisan policy concept uppermost in our thinking and speaking. It seems to me the very fact that foreign policy and domestic policy *are* so interdependent that it may occasion some difficulties, but if there is sabotage let it come from them.

I have had two and a half days of so-called rest, surrounded with newspaper men and photographers, in Wisconsin. Little by little I am learning the ropes — and I hope the knots! It has been difficult for me and I hope you will be patient with me and also point out my mistakes. There will be many I am afraid.

Faithfully yours,

J. E. Tufts, of Oneida, New York, whose son Robert was a member of the research staff of the Stevenson campaign organization, wrote on August 17, expressing his pleasure at his son's appointment.

To J. E. Tufts

August 23, 1952

My dear Mr. Tufts:

I was delighted to have your letter even as I am delighted to have Bob on my staff.

You are quite right that much of our trouble springs from the quality of people who are attracted to public service in this country. I have been preaching, or should I say howling, about this for years, and I hope I can make a whole speech of it some time during the campaign.

I have had some very practical experience with the difficulty of pushing good younger men along in the strictly partisan political route, but I think we are maturing as a nation in that regard.

Cordially yours,

Governor John S. Battle of Virginia wrote Stevenson on August 19 that there were rumors that he supported federal legislation for repeal of the poll tax, passage of an anti-lynching law, adoption of a compulsory Fair Employment Practices Commission, and federal aid to education. Battle added that it was believed that Stevenson and President Truman had reached an agreement on these issues.

To John S. Battle

August 23, 1952

Personal and Confidential

Dear John:

I was glad to have your letter, and I am not in the least surprised by the multitude of views that are expressed about my position on most everything. There seem to be countless people who know what I think and intend to do long before I do!

As to the civil rights business, I wish we had a chance to talk. I am convinced, and have been for years, that the sledge hammer approach has been all wrong, both in the Negroes' interest as well as others. I will say something about this in New York next week, speaking to the all-out civil rights people at the Democratic State Convention and at the

Liberal Party Convention. I think there is much we could do without any compulsory FEPC, which could not be passed anyway. Dick Russell [62] is confident that the South will support a poll tax constitutional amendment and that an anti-lynching law, although obsolete, could readily be enacted. If we could do something on the employment discrimination line in addition, I think we will have demonstrated both our purpose and direction as a party and have fully satisfied the expectations of the more moderate and understanding Negro leaders, many of whom have been here to see me. Their restraint has been somewhat surprising in view of the extremism that is so commonplace on the civil rights issue in the North.

As to Federal aid to education, I have not formulated my views conclusively. I think it is evident that there is not too much we can do in the present budgetary situation, but I am reliably informed by people working for Alfred Sloan,[63] in New York, that we may *have* to help medical schools, and very soon.

Incidentally, you will be interested to hear that not one of the suggestions enumerated in your letter was even mentioned when Senator Sparkman and I saw President Truman.

Please treat this with your own good discretion, as I am steering as best I can, albeit clumsily, between the countless pitfalls on this intricate and unfamiliar course.

You were good to write me with such candor and I am genuinely grateful. Please do it again; and I hope we can have a talk.

Cordially yours,

Paul Simon, editor of a weekly newspaper at Troy, Illinois, and strong supporter of Stevenson's work as governor, was now serving in the army in Germany.

To Private First Class Paul M. Simon [64]

August 25, 1952

Dear Paul:

I am touched more than I can say by your letter — and by your contribution. I can well imagine that the salary of a private first class is not such as to give him much room for leeway, and that a political contribu-

---

[62] Senator Richard Russell of Georgia.

[63] Chairman of the board of General Motors and president of the Alfred P. Sloan Foundation.

[64] The original is in the possession of Mr. Simon.

tion comes at the very bottom of the priority list. I can only say that I shall value this contribution much more than many larger ones I will receive.

You are also very generous in your indications of the other ways in which you hope to help. Now that this nomination has come, I expect to bring to bear on it everything I have. The vastness of it all is so great, however, that I realize I will need every bit of assistance I can get. Your own willingness to do all you can is heartening indeed.

I know that it has been hard to have your journalistic career interrupted by military service. I can only voice the hope that you are finding your stay in Germany interesting and full of material for future reflection. It is apparent from your letter that you know, better than most, what the real issues are in this campaign.

With warmest personal regards, and my every good wish, I am

Sincerely yours,

Stevenson addressed the American Legion Convention in Madison Square Garden, New York City, on August 27, 1952.

THE NATURE OF PATRIOTISM [65]

I have attended altogether too many conventions not to know how you are all beginning to feel here on the afternoon of your third day. You work hard at Legion business, and then devote the balance of your time to the museums, art galleries, concerts and other cultural monuments of New York. And, of course, you have to listen to speeches too! I console myself with the thought that this punishment, while cruel, is not unusual.

I have no claim, as many of you do, to the honored title of old soldier. Nor have I risen to high rank in the armed services. The fact that a great General and I are competing candidates for the Presidency will not diminish my warm respect for his military achievements. Nor will that respect keep me from using every honest effort to defeat him in November!

My own military career was brief. It was also lowly. An Apprentice Seaman in a naval training unit was not, as some of you may also recall, exactly a powerful command position in World War One. My experience

---

[65] The text is from *Major Campaign Speeches AES 1952*, pp. 17–22. Archibald MacLeish wrote on August 27: "It was a beautiful, beautiful job. Just what I had prayed for. Your own idiom — your own accent. Even the few phrases of mine that remained had undergone the sea change."

thus provided me with a very special view — what could be called a worm's-eye view — of the service. In 1918 I doubt if there was anything more wormlike than an Apprentice Seaman. I must add, though, that from a very topside job in the Navy Department during the frenzy of the last war I sometimes had nostalgic recollections of apprentice seamanship when someone else had to make all the decisions.

After the first war, many Americans lost sight of the fact that only the strong can be free. Many mistook an ominous lull for permanent peace. In those days the American Legion knew, however, that he who is not prepared today is less so tomorrow, and that only a society which could fight for survival would survive.

The Legion's fight to awaken America to the need for military preparedness is now largely won. We have made great advances in understanding the problem of national security in the modern world. We no longer think in terms of American resources alone. For the most part we now understand the need for a great international system of security, and we have taken the lead in building it.

We have joined our strength with that of others — and we have done so in self-protection. We seek no dominion over any other nation — and the whole free world knows it! If there are those behind the Iron Curtain who don't know it, it is because their masters don't want them to know it.

I am not sure that, historically, there has been another powerful nation that has been trusted as the United States is trusted today. It is something new under the sun when the proudest nations on earth have not only accepted American leadership in the common defense effort, but have also welcomed our troops and bases on their territory. Ports the world around are open to American warships by day or night. Our airmen are stationed in the most distant lands.

Yet all is not perfect. There are still vital interests which we and our allies are not militarily prepared to defend.

Some of us are reluctant to admit that security cannot be won cheaply by some clever diplomatic maneuver or by propaganda.

We have not yet really faced up to the problem of defending our cities against the rapidly growing threat of Soviet air power. There is, for example, a great shortage of volunteers for our civil defense ground observation corps.

And many only partly understand or are loath to acknowledge that the costs of waging the cold war are but a fraction of the costs of hot war.

So there remain important tasks for us. I believe in a strong national defense, and I believe that we must press forward to improve our position and not waver or hesitate in this interval when the scales are so precariously balanced. While I think it is true that today the fight for preparedness is going well, there are other and even more difficult tasks that we dare not neglect.

The United States has very large power in the world today. And the partner of power — the corollary — is responsibility. It is our high task to use our power with a sure hand and a steady touch — with the self-restraint that goes with confident strength. The purpose of our power must never be lost in the fact of our power — and the purpose, I take it, is the promotion of freedom, justice and peace in the world.

We talk a great deal about patriotism. What do we mean by patriotism in the context of our times? I venture to suggest that what we mean is a sense of national responsibility which will enable America to remain master of her power — to walk with it in serenity and wisdom, with self-respect and the respect of all mankind; a patriotism that puts country ahead of self; a patriotism which is not short, frenzied outbursts of emotion, but the tranquil and steady dedication of a lifetime. The dedication of a lifetime — these are words that are easy to utter, but this is a mighty assignment. For it is often easier to fight for principles than to live up to them.

Patriotism, I have said, means putting country before self. This is no abstract phrase, and unhappily, we find some things in American life today of which we cannot be proud.

Consider the groups who seek to identify their special interests with the general welfare. I find it sobering to think that their pressures might one day be focused on me. I have resisted them before and I hope the Almighty will give me the strength to do so again and again. And I should tell you — my fellow Legionnaires — as I would tell all other organized groups, that I intend to resist pressures from veterans, too, if I think their demands are excessive or in conflict with the public interest, which must always be the paramount interest.

Let me suggest, incidentally, that we are rapidly becoming a nation of veterans. If we were all to claim a special reward for our service, beyond that to which specific disability or sacrifice has created a just claim, who would be left to pay the bill? After all, we are Americans first and veterans second, and the best maxim for any administration is still Jefferson's: "Equal rights for all, special privileges for none."

True patriotism, it seems to me, is based on tolerance and a large measure of humility.

There are men among us who use "patriotism" as a club for attacking other Americans. What can we say for the self-styled patriot who thinks that a Negro, a Jew, a Catholic, or a Japanese-American is less an American than he? That betrays the deepest article of our faith, the belief in individual liberty and equality which has always been the heart and soul of the American idea.

What can we say for the man who proclaims himself a patriot — and then for political or personal reasons attacks the patriotism of faithful public servants? I give you, as a shocking example, the attacks which have been made on the loyalty and the motives of our great wartime Chief of Staff, General Marshall.[66] To me this is the type of "patriotism" which is, in Dr. Johnson's phrase, "the last refuge of scoundrels."

The anatomy of patriotism is complex. But surely intolerance and public irresponsibility cannot be cloaked in the shining armor of rectitude and righteousness. Nor can the denial of the right to hold ideas that are different — the freedom of man to think as he pleases. To strike freedom of the mind with the fist of patriotism is an old and ugly subtlety.

And the freedom of the mind, my friends, has served America well. The vigor of our political life, our capacity for change, our cultural, scientific and industrial achievements, all derive from free inquiry, from the free mind — from the imagination, resourcefulness and daring of men who are not afraid of new ideas. Most all of us favor free enterprise for business. Let us also favor free enterprise for the mind. For, in the last analysis, we would fight to the death to protect it. Why is it, then, that we are sometimes slow to detect, or are indifferent to, the dangers that beset it?

Many of the threats to our cherished freedoms in these anxious, troubled times arise, it seems to me, from a healthy apprehension about the communist menace within our country. Communism is abhorrent. It is strangulation of the individual; it is death for the soul. Americans who have surrendered to this misbegotten idol have surrendered their right to our trust. And there can be no secure place for them in our public life.

Yet, as I have said before, we must take care not to burn down the barn to kill the rats. All of us, and especially patriotic organizations of enormous influence like the American Legion, must be vigilant in protecting our birthright from its too zealous friends while protecting it from its evil enemies.

---

[66] George C. Marshall, who had served under President Truman as special ambassador to China (1945), Secretary of State (1947–1949), and Secretary of Defense (1950–1951), was a favorite target of Communism-in-government Republicans, who viewed as appeasement his policy of limited war. They held his views chiefly responsible for the "loss" of China to the Communists in 1949. Senator McCarthy charged that he was part of a conspiracy "so immense and an infamy so black as to dwarf any previous such venture in the history of man," and Senator Jenner referred to Marshall as a "living lie" and a "front man for traitors."

The tragedy of our day is the climate of fear in which we live, and fear breeds repression. Too often sinister threats to the Bill of Rights, to freedom of the mind, are concealed under the patriotic cloak of anti-communism.

I could add, from my own experience, that it is never necessary to call a man a communist to make political capital. Those of us who have undertaken to practice the ancient but imperfect art of government will always make enough mistakes to keep our critics well supplied with standard ammunition. There is no need for poison gas.

Another feature of our current scene that I think invites a similar restraint is the recurrent attacks in some communities upon our public schools.

There is no justification for indiscriminate attacks on our schools, and the sincere, devoted, and by no means overpaid teachers who labor in them. If there are any communist teachers, of course they should be excluded, but the task is not one for self-appointed thought police or ill-informed censors. As a practical matter, we do not stop communist activity in this way. What we do is give the communists material with which to defame us. And we also stifle the initiative of teachers and depreciate the prestige of the teaching profession which should be as honorable and esteemed as any among us.

Let me now, in my concluding words, inquire with you how we may affirm our patriotism in the troubled yet hopeful years that are ahead.

The central concern of the American Legion — the ideal which holds it together — the vitality which animates it — is patriotism. And those voices which we have heard most clearly and which are best remembered in our public life have always had the accent of patriotism.

It was always accounted a virtue in a man to love his country. With us it is now something more than a virtue. It is a necessity, a condition of survival. When an American says that he loves his country, he means not only that he loves the New England hills, the prairies glistening in the sun, the wide and rising plains, the great mountains, and the sea. He means that he loves an inner air, an inner light in which freedom lives and in which a man can draw the breath of self-respect.

Men who have offered their lives for their country know that patriotism is not the *fear* of something; it is the *love* of something. Patriotism with us is not the hatred of Russia; it is the love of this Republic and of the ideal of liberty of man and mind in which it was born, and to which this Republic is dedicated.

With this patriotism — patriotism in its large and wholesome meaning — America can master its power and turn it to the noble cause of peace.

We can maintain military power without militarism; political power without oppression; and moral power without compulsion or complacency.

The road we travel is long, but at the end lies the grail of peace. And in the valley of peace we see the faint outlines of a new world, fertile and strong. It is odd that one of the keys to abundance should have been handed to civilization on a platter of destruction. But the power of the atom to work evil gives only the merest hint of its power for good.

I believe that man stands on the eve of his greatest day. I know, too, that that day is not a gift but a prize; that we shall not reach it until we have won it.

Legionnaires are united by memories of war. Therefore, no group is more devoted to peace. I say to you now that there is work to be done, that the difficulties and dangers that beset our path at home and abroad are incalculable. There is sweat and sacrifice; there is much of patience and quiet persistence in our horoscope. Perhaps the goal is not even for us to see in our lifetime.

But we are embarked on a great adventure. Let us proclaim our faith in the future of man. Of good heart and good cheer, faithful to ourselves and our traditions, we can lift the cause of freedom, the cause of free men, so high no power on earth can tear it down. We can pluck this flower, safety, from this nettle, danger. Living, speaking, like men — like Americans — we can lead the way to our rendezvous in a happy, peaceful world.

Thank you — and forgive me for imposing on you for so long.

The next day Stevenson spoke to the New York State Democratic Convention in New York City.

EQUAL RIGHTS [67]

Lest you think I entertain any ill feeling, let me say at the outset that I have forgiven my friend Averell Harriman and the New York delegates to the National Convention for what they did to me there!

It is with great pride that I come among you this evening as the nominee of the Democratic Party. I must add that I also come here with some trepidation, because even in Chicago we have to admit that New York is important — at least on election day!

I am a Democrat by inheritance — but I am also a Democrat by conviction. I believe in the progressive policies of the Democratic Party.

[67] The text is from *Major Campaign Speeches AES 1952*, pp. 23–29.

I believe that they are the best policies for our country to follow, and I believe the people think so, too, and that the Democratic Party will win again in November. And I expect to win running like a singed cat. The singeing hasn't been very painful so far.

There is one face I miss here this evening — your great Senator and my honored friend, Herbert Lehman. But I don't begrudge him one minute of his well-earned holiday in Europe. And I doubt if he begrudges me one minute of my campaign in the United States! For many years Senator Lehman has been one of the best and purest influences in our public life. And today he exerts in the Senate a moral authority and leadership comparable to that provided twenty years ago by George Norris.[68]

We have a good time ahead of us this autumn. We have a good platform. A group of honest men got together in Chicago and made an honest attempt to grapple with the great problems of our day. They came out with good answers. I stand on that platform. And I don't feel the need — so understandably felt by my distinguished opponent — of having my campaign manager say that I will write my own platform.

We have a great Vice Presidential candidate. I hope you in New York will soon get to know him better. To me he is somehow the physical embodiment of the social and economic progress of the past two great decades of Democratic leadership.

John Sparkman was the son of a tenant farmer. He worked his way up from rural poverty to win an education, a law degree, and an outstanding position as a legislator. But John Sparkman has never forgotten his beginnings. It has been his ambition in life to make more freely available to other poor boys and girls the opportunities which only stubborn determination could win for himself.

He is a leading representative of the new liberalism which is changing the face and the folkways of the South. He has been the devoted champion of legislation promoting farm ownership, better housing, social security, the T.V.A., rural electrification, soil conservation, and crop insurance. None know the problems of the small businessman better than he, and his intimate knowledge of the revolutionary convulsions that torment our world has been accentuated by service on the United States Delegation to the United Nations Assembly. He has enlisted for life in the struggle to improve the economic lot and the security of all our people. I am very proud to have John Sparkman as my running mate. And I hope I can keep up with him.

We have, in addition, a Presidential candidate. Perhaps the less said

[68] Republican senator from Nebraska, 1913–1943.

about him the better. You know what we have done and tried to do in Illinois. I propose to outline in the next few weeks what I should like to do in the nation. Let me say now that I shall do my best to conserve our gains and to carry forward the great Democratic tradition of government in the service of all the people, the tradition of Franklin Roosevelt and Harry Truman.

The Republicans have been talking of late as if I was ashamed of the accomplishments in war and peace of the past twenty years which they, by some miraculous agility, both embrace and condemn at the same time. I have been tempted to say that I was proud to stand on that record, if only the General would move over and make room for me!

But it is not enough, it seems to me, just to stand on the successes of the past. The people know what *has* been done, and now they want to know what *will* be done. A party cannot live on laurel leaves. We remember what happened to Lot's wife. And the people whom we seek to govern, though prosperous and well, are sorely taxed and troubled by war and threats of war.

The transcendent problem before us and the great unfinished business of our generation is peace in the world. There is only one way to work for peace. It is not an easy way. There is no substitute for the long, complex and patient processes of building strength and unity in the free world — political strength, economic strength, military strength, and moral strength — the strength of a common faith that nations can be free and people can stand erect and unafraid.

I am disturbed by some of the Republican contributions to the foreign-policy debate. A Republican foreign-policy expert said the other day that the Democratic Party was interested only in Europe and regarded all other nations as "second-class expendables." This kind of statement is not simply absurd; it is also irresponsible and dangerous. And I hope that such excessive partisanship does not do irreparable damage to our country. Of course, we are interested in Europe. But if this country, and I mean Democrats and Republicans alike, stands for anything, it stands for freedom and against the expansion of communist dominion anywhere in the world. Does Mr. Dulles [69] think that President Truman by his prompt and courageous decision of June 27, 1950, treated Korea like "a second-class expendable"? If he does not think so, he would serve his party and his country and our friends in Asia better by more candor and less claptrap.

I hope that the Republican leaders will permit us to discuss our somber foreign problems on the plane where they belong — not on the

[69] John Foster Dulles was the chief Republican spokesman on foreign policy and became Eisenhower's Secretary of State.

plane of demagoguery, but on the plane of serious, factual discussion, and in terms of alternatives that are real, rather than epithets that are false.

And we could well apply the same rule to the problems here at home. One of these I want to mention here tonight is civil rights.

The phrase civil rights means a number of concrete things. It means the right to be treated equally before the law. It means the right to equal opportunity for education, employment and decent living conditions. It means that none of these rights shall be denied because of race or color or creed. The history of freedom in our country has been the history of knocking down the barriers to equal rights. One after another they have fallen, and great names in our history record their collapse: the Virginia Statute of Religious Freedom, the Bill of Rights, the Emancipation Proclamation, the Woman's Suffrage Amendment, down to the 1947 Report of the President's Commission on Civil Rights.

The record of our progress is a proud one, but it is far from over. Brave and important tasks remain. We cannot rest until we honor in fact as well as word the plain language of the Declaration of Independence.

This is our goal. It requires far more than action by government. Laws are never as effective as habits. The fight for equal rights must go on every day in our own souls and consciences, in our schools and our churches and our homes, in our factories and our offices — as well as in our city councils, our state legislatures and our national Congress. In this discussion, of all discussions, let us not be self-righteous. Let us work for results, not just empty political advantage. We are dealing here with fundamental human rights, not just votes.

This is a job for the East, the North and the West, as well as for the South. I know. I have been a Governor of a great Northern state. I have had to stop outrages committed against peaceful and law-abiding minorities. I have twice proposed to my legislature a law setting up in our state an enforceable fair employment practices commission. I am proud to say that the Democrats in our legislature voted almost solidly for the bill. But I must report in simple truth that the bill was lost in Springfield, Illinois, because of virtually solid opposition from the party which claims descent from Abraham Lincoln. All the same, gratifying progress has been made in Illinois toward the elimination of job discrimination by the initiative of business itself. And I would be less than fair if I didn't acknowledge it gratefully.

In saying this is not a sectional problem, I do not mean to say that there is no particular problem in the South. Of course there is a problem in the South. In many respects, the problem is more serious there than elsewhere. But, just as it is chastening to realize our own failures and shortcomings in the North, so it is both just and hopeful to recognize and admit the great progress in the South. Things are taking place in the South today that would have seemed impossible only a few years ago. In the last two years alone ten state universities have admitted Negro students for the first time to their graduate and professional schools. And that is only one of many examples that could be cited of the wonders that are working in the South.

We can agree that the problem is nationwide; we can agree that good progress has been made; but I think we can also agree that unremitting effort is the cause of most of that progress, and that unremitting effort is the way to assure more progress in the future. Part of that effort must be legislative. The Democratic platform of 1952 states the goals of Federal legislation.

I have often affirmed my belief in strong state and local administration. I believe — with your own great Governors, Al Smith and Franklin Roosevelt and Herbert Lehman — that affirmative state government can rise to meet many pressing social problems, and can thereby arrest the trend toward overcentralized Federal power. In Illinois I have worked to make the state government responsive to the needs of the people so that it would not be necessary for them to turn to Washington for help. I like to think that people are becoming more and more conscious of the role of the states in the Federal system; more and more conscious that we will save more money by doing the jobs at home than by screaming about waste and extravagance in Washington.

In the case of equal opportunity for employment, I believe that it is not alone the duty but the enlightened interest of each state to develop its own positive employment practices program — a program adapted to local conditions, emphasizing education and conciliation, and providing for judicial enforcement. That is the kind of law I proposed in Illinois.

I think the time has come to talk sensibly about how we can make more rapid progress in this field rather than how we can make more votes. I think — indeed, I know — that there are leaders in the South who are just as anxious as we are to move ahead. But we must frankly recognize their local difficulties. We must recognize, too, that further government interference with free men, free markets, free ideas, is distasteful to many people of good will who dislike racial discrimination as much as we do.

This is not the time to discuss all these familiar obstacles. Let me only say that in a spirit of give and take, of tolerance and understanding, we can clean up this fire hazard in our basement faster and more effectively.

But our platform also favors Federal legislation — particularly, I assume, when states fail to act and inequalities of treatment persist. The problem, of course, is what kind of legislation.

Personally, I have been much impressed by a bill recently reported favorably by the Senate Labor Committee. Only three members opposed it, one of whom was Senator Richard Nixon. Both your New York Senators [70] joined in sponsoring the bill.

It creates a Federal Commission and encourages it to stay out of any state with an effective commission; by the same token, however, it encourages the states to act because, if they do not, the national government has the power to do so. The bill requires the Federal Commission to undertake a nonpartisan and nationwide educational program, to proceed by persuasion as far as possible, and, in cases of complaints of violation, to proceed by very careful deliberation and full and fair hearings. Enforcement would be by order of a court, not an administrative body.

You know as well as I do that we have reached a sort of legislative stalemate in this field in the Congress. In so far as this is due to real, legitimate objections to the substance of the legislation, I think this Senate bill goes a very long way toward meeting such objections. It may be that it can be improved still further, especially in the direction of giving the states a reasonable time in which to act.

In so far as the present stalemate is due to misuse of the processes of deliberation and debate in Congress, the problem is somewhat different.

I believe firmly in the principle stated in our platform — the principle that majority rule shall prevail, after reasonable debate, in both houses of our Congress. And from my experience, with the practical workings of representative government, I would interpret "reasonable" very liberally, because majorities can be tyrannical too.

This principle of majority rule is important in a much broader area than that of civil rights — it is of vital importance, for example, in the field of foreign policy. One of the most famous of all filibusters occurred in 1917 in the debate over President Wilson's proposal to arm merchant ships for the protection of American lives and property against power-mad aggression. It is not inconceivable that a similar situation might occur today or tomorrow in the delicate state of our foreign relations. In these perilous times we cannot risk submerging our national purposes in a sea of interminable conversation.

The precise nature of the changes that should be made in the present rules of Congress is, of course, a problem for the Congress itself, for each House, under our Constitution, makes its own rules for doing business. As President I could not make the decision, but I could and would use whatever influence I may have to encourage the Congress to shake off its shackles.

I would urge in these fields and in many others that affect national

[70] Herbert H. Lehman (Democrat) and Irving M. Ives (Republican).

policy that all of us resolve to take a fresh look. There has been too much freezing of positions, too much emotion, too many dogmatic statements of irrevocable attitudes. We are dealing with human situations, with human emotions, with human intelligence; our purpose must be to reason together for the common betterment of us all; our interest must be, not in controversy, but in results.

This has been my attitude, and this will be my attitude. If there are those who disapprove, I will be sorry but not surprised. If there are those who approve, I bespeak their best efforts and pledge them mine, confident that in the long run results will be more eloquent than oratory.

I have been talking about methods. About goals there can, of course, be no disagreement. We believe in the equality of rights and the equality of opportunity for all Americans. In affirming this belief, the Democratic platform was but the mirror of our own conscience. We must continue this fight until it is won.

Also on August 28, Stevenson addressed the State Committee of the Liberal Party in New York City.

FAITH IN LIBERALISM [71]

I appreciate very much this opportunity to meet with you men and women of the Liberal Party, and I'm deeply grateful for your confidence and for the honor that you have done me. That your nomination of me (for President) was unanimous only increases my respect for your judgment and discrimination!

After listening to what Mr. Dubinsky [72] had to say a moment ago, I was tempted to think that when he concluded he was going to introduce not me but Benjamin Franklin. Evidently he couldn't get here.

Dr. Counts [73] said here a moment ago that the Liberal Party has tried to serve us as sort of a political conscience. Now I have, of course, read about you in the published writings of certain columnists and I am fully aware that you are very dangerous characters. I'm informed that attacks on you from the right are equaled in violence only by denunciations in the communist press.

Well, I know how that is. In my very brief political career I've some-

[71] The text is from *Major Campaign Speeches AES 1952*, pp. 30–34.

[72] David Dubinsky, president of the International Ladies Garment Workers Union; founder and vice chairman of the Liberal Party of New York; also a founder of Americans for Democratic Action.

[73] George S. Counts, professor of education at Teachers College, Columbia University, and later chairman of the New York Liberal Party, 1955–1959.

times wondered if I had any friends left. And then they suddenly nominated me for President, and I wondered if I hadn't too many friends. But if I have, by any chance, too many friends I am sure time will take care of that!

You know how it is in an election year — they pick a President and then for four years they pick on him.

I hope that the alert members of the press here present will note that I arrived at your convention under my own power. I was not escorted or dragged to this platform. And what's more I think I'm standing on my own feet. And, to the best of my knowledge, I've neither been drugged nor hypnotized. Now I offer this testimony in advance since, as you know, I'm alleged by the Republicans to be in a state of multiple captivity and you will, sooner or later, undoubtedly be included on the distinguished list of my jailers.

I've been much interested in the continued debate that's been raging in the newspapers as to whether I was headed right, center or left. I think it would have been rather more relevant had they asked: Is the man moving forward, backward, or is he grounded?

Now I sometimes think we're far more tolerant of a quarterback than we are of our candidates. An advance on the football field through left guard, or through right guard, or even straight through center, is generally counted as yardage gained. I think that is the sports writer's word for it. The only unforgivable thing is to be trapped by the Old Guard behind your line. Whatever may happen, I trust that it will at least be said of me that I know the difference between the goal line and the sideline.

Now there's no mystery about my program, whatever label may attach to it. I am running on the Democratic platform. I am for it; and I'll fight for it and I expect to win on it.

No platform, of course, can resolve all of our dilemmas. As vital, it seems to me, as the written word is the spirit and the resolution of those who embrace the written word. The real question is whether a platform represents the clicking of a ghost's typewriter, if I may put it that way, or the beating of a human heart.

Our opponents also have a platform. In modern times they've honored us Democrats by borrowing many phrases from past Democratic platforms. Now because of the timing of the conventions, this inevitably leaves them four years behind. But I suppose plagiarism must, nevertheless, be considered a form of progress.

And this is open season for that kind of progress. This is the time when even the most obsolete Republican becomes momentarily reconciled to the machine age. He listens — he's very apt to listen with a stiff upper lip — while his candidate calls for those greater social gains which a few minutes before they called wild-eyed socialism. In this season Republican candidates are even forgiven for whispering that there could be a better law than the Taft-Hartley Act.

The season when Republican hearts regularly throb with such thoughts is, of course, the autumn of Presidential years. This is indeed a truly remarkable interval, a sort of pause in the Republican occupation and I've often thought that it might well be called the liberal hour. But it should never be confused with any period when Congress is in session.

Now it's a misfortune — deserved, I fear — of the Republican leadership not just to be taken too seriously during these moments of imitation. Their forward look sometimes seems to me like a costume taken out of the closet every four years for the big masquerade ball. It often looks nice after a dry cleaning, but the stuffed shirt still shows.

I think it's ironic — but nonetheless revealing — that my distinguished opponent, my very distinguished opponent, feels compelled to prove that he was innocent of any association with Franklin Roosevelt and Harry Truman. After all, there were four occasions on which the people of the United States indicated their desire to continue such an association. Nevertheless, my opponent's trepidation is perhaps understandable. Joe McCarthy may get him if he doesn't watch out.

I certainly, for one, don't envy the General having to listen to all the conflicting advice about how to treat the slanderers of his dear friend and senior officer, General [George C.] Marshall. You can tell the size of a man by the size of the thing that makes him mad, and I hope that, regardless of my own political advantage, this matter is not finally resolved by the counsel of those who favor what has been described as the middle-of-the-gutter approach.

There is some low comedy in this minor Republican spectacle, but there is also, it seems to me, symbolic tragedy, too. For everything that our distinguished fellow citizen has accomplished in his great service to his country is imperiled by many men who propose to ride to Washington on his train.

They are not just the men who hunt communists in the Bureau of Wild Life and Fisheries while hesitating to aid the gallant men and women who are resisting the real thing in the front lines of Europe and Asia. They are also the men who would rather hold post-mortems over the loss of China than do something now to save India.

And they are, finally, the men who seemingly believe that we can confound the Kremlin by frightening ourselves to death. They would rather battle Democrats than communists any day. And, like the communists, their favorite sport is prophesying our imminent doom.

As I indicated at the start of this campaign, I don't intend to tell anyone that complicated things are simple and that all of the answers are in the back of a book which I will shortly produce. Only men who confuse themselves with God would dare to pretend in this anguished and bloody era that they know the exact road to the promised land.

You of the Liberal Party will perhaps understand me best when I vigorously disclaim infallibility. For it seems to me that an authentic humility, an awareness of the complexity of men's choices, a tolerance for diverse opinions, and a recognition for brave experimentation are the heart of any liberal faith.

But let no one make the mistake of believing that the liberal's tolerance for conflicting opinion makes him incapable of fighting hard for the things that he believes in.

For example, I yield to no man — if I may borrow that majestic parliamentary phrase — I yield to no man in my belief in the principle of free debate, inside or outside the halls of Congress. The sound of tireless voices is the price we pay for the right to hear the music of our own opinions. But there is also, it seems to me, a moment at which democracy must prove its capacity to act. Every man has a right to be heard; but no man has the right to strangle democracy with a single set of vocal cords.

There's another text that I should like to take from the Democratic platform. The near unanimity with which the civil rights plank was adopted at the Democratic Convention this year is in great part the result of things that have happened to us as a nation during the past decade. At the moment, as on so many occasions during World War Two, Negro Americans are fighting and working side by side with their white countrymen in many parts of the world. I venture to say that there are few men of either race who are not affected by that experience. And one could point to many other examples of the remarkable progress of the past decade, and I mean in the South as well as in the North.

The Federal Government has a direct responsibility to maintain this progress by helping to secure equal rights for all of our people.

I told the Democratic State Convention earlier this very evening that I have been impressed by the recent bill reported by Senator [Hubert H.] Humphrey on behalf of the Senate Labor Committee. Both your New York Senators joined in sponsoring the bill. We must continue to press forward along such lines as these — in our national Congress as well as in our states and our communities — until we have eradicated the curse of discrimination in this nation.

To meet the crisis of our day, we must have affirmative values and clear-cut objectives. The challenge to all of us is to prove that a free society can remain free, humane and creative, even when it is under heavy and ruthless fire; that it can combat poverty, injustice and intolerance in its own midst, even while resisting a monstrous foreign despotism; and that it can give man a glimpse of serenity and of hope, even while calling on them for sacrifice.

We shall be accused of idealism or some such crime for projecting so optimistic a vision. To which the only truthful answer is that we plead guilty. This is not to say that we guarantee a happy ending; it is only to say that we retain our confidence in man's ability to achieve the triumph of decency and of compassion in our lifetime.

After all, there was a man named Hitler, and it looked for a while as if he were invincible. Yet we despised and "decadent" peoples are still talking — and he hasn't made a speech in seven years. The "thousand-year Reich" already belongs to the history books while the idea of freedom has endured, even in the dreariest dungeons behind the Iron Curtain. So I say, let the demagogues beware.

I believe we are living in the twilight of the totalitarian gods; beyond the fury and the turmoil of our times lies an horizon of new hope for embattled humanity. With liberal faith, with cool heads, with warm hearts, we shall make that hope real for our nation and for our century.

Robert J. Lynch, assistant to Secretary of State Edward R. Stettinius, Jr., wrote Stevenson on August 22 that in case Stevenson's deposition about Alger Hiss [74] *assumed greater importance than was warranted he had some ideas that might be helpful.*

To R. J. Lynch

August 30, 1952

Dear Bob:

Many thanks for your good letter. I wish very much that you would send along anything you have that might be of interest in the Hiss matter. I think you know the circumstances. I gave a deposition early stating that what I had heard from others while I was in the State Department in 1945 and 1946, that he had a good reputation. There was nothing else I could have said honestly.

It was good to hear from you again and I hope all goes well with you.

Sincerely yours,

[74] For a discussion of this deposition and its text, see *The Papers of Adlai E. Stevenson*, Vol. III, pp. 100–104.

P.S. I rather doubt if the Republicans make much of the Hiss case but their more strident Press will doubtless do so. After all, Dulles hired him for the Carnegie job after I knew him.[75]

To John S. Battle

August 30, 1952

Dear Governor:

I have just returned from some "unfamiliar" campaigning in and about New York, and this is the first opportunity I have had to thank you for your kind and charitable remarks about me before the Virginia Central Committee. I hope that I shall not prove too much of a disappointment to you and my other friends there. This is an assignment, as you well know, which I did not want and I can only do my best as I see it which will probably satisfy no one.

With warm regards and my gratitude.

Cordially yours,

On Labor Day, September 1, Stevenson spoke at Cadillac Square, Detroit, at Hamtramck, Michigan, and delivered the following speech at Campau Square in Grand Rapids, Michigan.

BI-PARTISAN FOREIGN POLICY [76]

I am very glad to be able to be here in Grand Rapids on this Labor Day holiday. As a boy I spent my holidays up in Northern Michigan. But now I have made the unhappy discovery that in politics and public office there are no holidays — especially in campaign years.

I am privileged to count myself among the friends and admirers of one of your great citizens. I knew Arthur Vandenberg [77] well, and served with him at four or five of the great international conferences following the war. He paid me the courtesy of some flattering correspondence and proposed me as his successor on one of the major committees of the

[75] John Foster Dulles, as chairman of the board of the Carnegie Endowment for International Peace, had hired Alger Hiss to be president of the organization in December, 1946.

[76] The text is from *Major Campaign Speeches AES 1952*, pp. 42–45.

[77] Senator Arthur H. Vandenberg, Republican of Michigan, was a native of Grand Rapids and died there on April 18, 1951. He had worked closely with President Truman to maintain a bipartisan foreign policy and had been associated with Stevenson in the early stages of the United Nations. See *The Papers of Adlai E. Stevenson,* Vol. II.

United Nations in 1947. He was a great champion of our bi-partisan — or, as he preferred to call it, our un-partisan — foreign policy. Senator Vandenberg was never doctrinaire. He was a practical and realistic man whose primary concern was the protection and advancement of the welfare and safety of his country — a foreign policy that far-seeing men and women of both parties could support. And Arthur Vandenberg refused to play politics with foreign policy.

These are good rules to follow today. I, for one, intend to do my best to follow them because foreign policy is a deadly serious business these days. I think it should be discussed in this campaign soberly and with restraint. We could pay a sad price in misunderstanding or miscalculation abroad by what we say intemperately, unwisely and hypocritically to beguile the voters in this campaign. Our purpose should not be to exploit people's fears, not to make empty promises of magic solutions, but instead to discuss the real problems that confront our country in the world, and what we actually can and should do about them.

I want to say, clearly and unmistakably, that I believe the essential direction of our foreign policy is right — building the unity and collective strength of the free countries to prevent the expansion of Soviet dominion and control over one nation after another. I think we must join other nations in building military, economic and political strength which can gradually but surely lessen the relative power of the Soviet Union on world events. And I think we must continue to work steadily at the frustrating task of putting international affairs on a permanent basis of law and order.

These are the key purposes of our present policy as I understand it. They are the purposes that we are seeking to accomplish through the United Nations; through the Atlantic, Pacific and Western Hemisphere regional security treaties; through our programs of military and economic aid to other countries; through the Point Four program; and through our financial and commercial policies, including the reciprocal trade program. These things make sense. If we continue with steps like these, adjusting and changing and improving them as we can, war becomes an alternative of diminishing hope to the enemy, and communism an alternative of diminishing attraction among the vast uncommitted peoples of the world.

Now in all I have said here, I do not believe there is any fundamental issue between the Republican candidate for President and myself. As far as I know, he, like myself, approves the basic direction our foreign policy has been following.

Where there is an issue, however, is between the two Republican Parties that contested the nomination with such violence at Chicago, because the Republican Party is hopelessly divided over foreign policy. Senator Vandenberg, with all his great prestige and persuasiveness, was never able to win over the reactionary wing of his party to his own enlightened understanding of the twentieth century.

That wing of the party seems stronger if not wiser since we lost the benefit of Senator Vandenberg's leadership. And I say that with no partisan satisfaction, because the difficulties we confront as a nation in this revolutionary age transcend any considerations of political advantage. And I say to you in all sincerity that winning the peace is far dearer to me, as it is to you, Democrats and Republicans alike, than winning the election.

My distinguished opponent has already had occasion to disagree with conspicuous Republicans on foreign-policy issues. He has differed sharply with members of his party who have assailed the American action in Korea to stop and turn back communist aggression. He has gone further to set himself against the views of important members of his party who have called for enlarging the Korean War.

I think he has done us all a service by saying these things. He knows, as every realistic American knows, that if we had not chosen to fight in Korea, sooner or later we would have had to fight a bigger war somewhere else. The memory of Munich is still fresh. The quicker aggression is stopped the better. And, as it is, even with all the heartbreak and suffering and cost of Korea — even with the frustration of the long stalemate over the armistice — it is quite possible that our action in Korea may have headed off World War Three. We may never know the answer to that, but the tragic consequences of piecemeal aggression even in our lifetime are plain for all to see.

I don't envy the General's impossible dilemma as a result of the conflict within the party he now heads. Carrying out an effective, positive, forward-looking foreign policy in a democracy requires support not only in the executive, but also in the legislative branch of government. How is it possible when a large proportion of his party's members in the Senate, and more than half of them in the House, have consistently opposed what he approves? And if elected — he would probably carry back to Washington with him most of the same Republicans.

But the Republican leaders evidently have a solution for this dismal dilemma because their vice-presidential candidate the other day asserted his belief that Republicans in Congress who have opposed our bi-partisan foreign policy will change and reverse their attitude if their party is successful in this election. (Maybe this is what they mean by "it's time for a change"!) Now must we conclude from this that a lot of Republican leaders have been opposing our foreign policy just for political reasons?

Should matters of this extreme gravity be entrusted to men who trade their convictions so lightly? I may be naive but I don't think a man should be in public office whose attitude on our most important business depends on whether a Democrat or a Republican is in the White House. Surely a vote on foreign policy in the Congress is more important than voting in a popularity or a beauty contest.

Happily the Democratic Party is united on foreign policy. We have our differences. If we didn't we would hardly be Democrats, but our differences are not over foreign policy. Democratic support of this policy is no new, sudden, confused or pretended attitude. We have worked for the building of that program from the beginning with the advice and help of some far-sighted Republicans like Arthur Vandenberg. We know much about its weak points and its strong points, and the ugly and the happy realities of our period in history. We believe passionately in the rightness of our directions. Our deepest convictions and highest hopes are involved, for this is the means of preserving our most cherished institutions, our freedoms, our future as a Christian nation.

The price is high, dangerously high, and we look hopefully to the time when it can be reduced, but meanwhile we must forge the great tools for man's noblest work — achieving freedom, justice and dignity for nations and individuals. For a century, from Waterloo to the Marne, the British fleet protected us, but now it is our turn. It is up to this mighty nation with our allies to advance the hopes through which man may eventually fulfill his destiny as a child of God.

On August 9, Philip Noel-Baker, Member of Parliament and a friend of Stevenson's since they had worked together at the London meetings of the United Nations Preparatory Commission in the fall of 1945, wrote expressing his pleasure over the presidential nomination.

To Philip Noel-Baker [78]

September 2, 1952

Dear Philip:

I was delighted to have your letter and I am much heartened by your support and encouragement.

I should like very much to feel that whatever transpires in the election there can be no serious alteration of our directions in Europe. The Republican talk about "liberation" in Eastern Europe of late has disturbed

[78] A copy is in A.E.S., I.S.H.L.

me, as it doubtless has you. I hope that the British, however, can make some allowances for what we charitably call political expediency! [79]

With all good wishes and my thanks, I am

Sincerely yours,

President Truman wrote Stevenson on August 28 praising him for the speech on patriotism he delivered before the American Legion in New York City. He was sure the speech put the Republicans on the defensive. He closed his letter by again offering to help the candidate in any way he saw fit.

To Harry S. Truman

September 4, 1952

Dear Mr. President:

You were so good to write me, and I am, as always, profoundly grateful for your continuing encouragement.

The things you said about me in Milwaukee touch me deeply.[80] If I am as good as all that and as deserving of the people's confidence, I am beginning to feel that I should be running for Pope. However, I will quickly forgive and forget any of your generous excesses.

We are off tomorrow on a long journey to the West to remind the folks to keep their smokehouses locked if there are too many Republicans around.

Faithfully yours,

On September 5, Stevenson opened his Western campaign on a tour that took him to Colorado, Wyoming, Montana, Oregon, Washington,

[79] In Hamtramck, Michigan, a heavily Polish suburb of Detroit, on September 1, Stevenson said: "Last week the Republican candidate for President made a speech in New York [to the American Legion]. His speech aroused speculation here and abroad that if he were elected, some reckless action might ensue in an attempt to liberate the people of Eastern Europe from Soviet tyranny. . . . It should never be an issue among Americans, for we are all united in our desire for their liberation from the oppressor and in confidence that freedom will again be theirs. But I want to make one thing very plain: Even if votes could be won by it, I would not say one reckless word on this matter during this campaign. Some things are more precious than votes. The cruel grip of Soviet tyranny upon your friends and relatives cannot be loosened by loose talk or idle threats. It cannot be loosened by awakening false hopes which might stimulate intemperate action that would only lead your brothers to the execution squads."

[80] President Truman had said: "I don't believe the Democratic party has ever had a candidate better qualified to be President than we have this year in Adlai Stevenson." New York *Times*, September 2, 1952.

California, Arizona and New Mexico before returning to Springfield on September 13. He delivered the following speech at McCormack Junior High School in Cheyenne, Wyoming, on September 6.

THE NEW WEST [81]

I usually think of Wyoming, somehow, as a vacation state. I have had a very happy vacation today. It started at 5:30 this morning in Denver, and since then I have been to Minneapolis, to Rochester, to Kasson, to Rochester, to Minneapolis, to Cheyenne. I think I am the only man in history who ever decided to go from Denver to Cheyenne by way of Minnesota.

This restful day suggests to me that I am not running for President of the United States but flying to an insane asylum. But it has given me an opportunity that falls to the lot of few people, to see something of the enormousness, the might and the grandeur of the United States.

I have come in the past four years to know every corner, I think, every crossroad of my State of Illinois, and now I have the privilege that should be everyone's privilege, and, unhappily, is the privilege of all too few, to see — if not every crossroad — at least the principal centers of virtually all of the United States. I can think of nothing that is better calculated to increase one's sense of pride, one's respect for his fellow American and at the same time one's humility.

I have been in Wyoming before. I came here first in 1915, as a boy, and I spent a number of years here in the summer. I even earned my board and keep, working on cattle ranches. I used to tell the folks back home that I was a cowboy, but my recollection — and I think it is accurate — is that I spent the greater part of my time shocking barley, making hay and repairing irrigation ditches. The last time I came here to Wyoming was exactly two years ago, I believe, this week. I went fishing with my three sons up on top of the Continental Divide, at Bridger Lake and around the headwaters of the Yellowstone River. I must say that at that time it never occurred to me that I should be back here two years later fishing again, but this time fishing for votes. I have even concluded, out of the wealth of generosity that is within me, that if you treat me as well as the cutthroat trout did, I will buy a Wyoming fishing license — after November 4th.

I came out here once after college with a classmate of mine. We were on a secret mission; we had solemnly decided that we were going to make our careers in Wyoming, but we weren't telling our parents. The summer wore on and I didn't come home. Then my father ordered me home, and

[81] The text is from *Major Campaign Speeches AES 1952*, pp. 72–77.

the result was that Wyoming lost a great rancher and the American Bar Association gained a lawyer.[82] I am not sure who came off better, Wyoming or the Bar Association; I have been loath to ask either.

I had an experience on that last journey to Wyoming that perhaps many of you have had. Up on top of the Divide, there is a creek that separates and forms the Pacific Creek, flowing down the western watershed, and the Atlantic Creek, flowing down the eastern watershed. Sitting there on a bright summer afternoon on top of the world, I couldn't help but think of what had happened and the symbolic significance of this lovely spot, there on top of the Continental Divide where the winds blow from all directions. I thought of how the center of gravity in world affairs had moved in the past three thousand years from the valley of the Tigris and Euphrates, to the valley of the Nile, to Athens, to Rome, to Paris, to London, and in our time and in our generation had jumped the Atlantic and had come to the Western Hemisphere, had come to the United States of America.

Somehow, there on top of the Divide, with my feet in the creek — one in the Atlantic and one in the Pacific — I thought that this lovely wind-swept mountain side was perhaps the center of the center of gravity of the whole world — and just at that moment, in my reverie, I dropped my sandwich in the water. I don't know whether it went east or west but I went hungry for the rest of that afternoon.

I think one of the finest things you do out here is to keep alive the memories of the old West — they are such an important part of the American tradition — memories that are dear to all of us, whether we have ever been here or not. I wish I could have come here in time to see your Frontier Day. I am told that it captures most vividly the spirit of the old times. I used to try as a boy, there on the ranches of the Big Horn, to ride steers. I even tried to ride a bucking horse. Someone told me it took a strong back and a weak mind and I could qualify on at least one count. I hope nobody makes any comparisons with the way I ride the Democratic donkey.

In Minnesota today, the cattle rustlers and the acrobats on horseback of the motion-picture version of the old West had to take a back seat because my distinguished opponent made off with the farm plank of the Democratic platform — in broad daylight.

You know, what hurt most, however, was what he did to our platform. We don't object to his rewriting the Republican platform, but if he wants to stand on our platform, we think it only fair to ask him to take it as it is.

The Democratic platform is strong enough and it is broad enough in its present form to carry all of the progressive Republicans in the land. The

[82] See Davis, *A Prophet in His Own Country*, p. 139.

trouble is that some Republican candidates seem to be on the platform just for the ride from now until election day. They seem to be only interested in roping votes before the election, but they won't be doing any branding afterward.

But it wasn't my intention to talk to you about the old West, of course. I want to talk about the new West and only briefly. Of course, the two are closely related; both have evoked the pioneering spirit of the American people. The old West represented the challenge of new and unknown physical horizons. The new West has meant an exploration of less tangible frontiers — the frontiers of science, of technology and of resource development. Beyond these frontiers we can already see the outlines of a thrilling and exhilarating future. We know that increasingly the Western part of the United States is becoming a leading source of American food and fibers, of American power and American industrial might — and the West has always been a schooling ground of American venturesomeness and American ingenuity.

Speaking of the Republican platform, it reminds me of nothing so much as the Powder River. I don't say that the Republican platform is a mile wide. But you will be flattering it if you said it was an inch deep. And what is more, it tries to run uphill!

The new West is going to be more and more important to our national future. Every time I have come out here, everything seems to have doubled somehow in size. So far as I can see there are three main components in this staggering growth.

One is the energy and the resourcefulness of the people. Another is the wisdom of the people of the United States in determining that our natural resources be managed for the good of all of the people. A third factor is our free-enterprise system, which releases the creative energy and vigor of a people more effectively than any other economic system thus far devised by man.

People sometimes talk as if government and free enterprise were mortal enemies. In this part of the country you know that they are working together as partners. Land, water and minerals are the bone and the sinew of the West. It takes wise government policy to develop these resources in the interests of all of the people. The Democratic Party knows, as you know, that sound public-conservation policies provide the best foundation for healthy, private enterprise both here in Wyoming and throughout the West.

Now, what are some of the ways in which we have seen this established — proven?

You here in Wyoming have seen that Federal investment in sound irrigation projects will give individual ranchers a chance to own their own land and make a decent living. You have seen power from Federal projects form the basis for greater farm output and new and expanded private businesses.

You have seen sensible and forward-looking public-land leasing policies stimulate the exploration and the development of new oil reserves.

You have seen governmental research work demonstrate that coal and oil shale can be turned into liquid fuel by private enterprise.

These are not the actions of an arbitrary bureaucracy, my friends, seeking any socialization of our economy. They are the actions of a sensible government interested in creating the conditions under which free enterprise can thrive; under which private individuals can have greater opportunities to start farms and businesses, to get better jobs, to earn more money, to provide a more secure future for themselves and for their children. This is the kind of government I think you want to have in Washington. Certainly this is the only kind of government that I am interested in.

Now you might suspect I was slightly partisan, but I am frank to say I don't think the Republican Party can give you that kind of government. Divided, quarreling and disunited, none of the Republicans in either of the Republican Parties has yet offered a single new idea for meeting any of the major issues ahead of this country. They complain, they denounce, they criticize and they fairly burst with self-righteousness. But when are they going to get down to cases?

Here we are, a great industrial nation, seeking to achieve a constructive relationship between employers and workers in the interest of ever-growing production and ever-higher standards of living for us all.

Last week in Detroit I made some specific suggestions for moving ahead in this field. My very distinguished opponent so far has suggested only that we might be able to turn the problem over to a university for study. I suggest that the all-important goal of good labor-management relations is entitled to a higher priority on our action list.

We are likewise a great agricultural nation, seeking to develop farm policies that will give us abundant production with fair prices to consumers and fair living standards for farmers. Earlier today in Minnesota I offered a specific program for moving ahead toward this goal. It is a program which has been written into the Democratic platform and which has been supported by Democrats in and out of Congress. And I can tell you now it will not be realized if we turn the country over to a party more than half of whose members in the House of Representatives voted only two months ago to deny the farmers of this nation firm price supports.

We face real problems — hard problems — in this country. Labor relations and farm policy are only two of many that will not be solved by platitudes or pious good will or extravagant bids for votes. They will only be solved by concrete, specific, practical action. That is what I have been talking about and what I intend to go on talking about. So far, I am sorry to say, we have been getting very little of that kind of talk from our Republican friends.

Even in the field of foreign policy I have been disappointed. There has been much trumpeting by the Republicans to the effect that they were about to unveil a new, a positive and dynamic, streamlined foreign policy. Well, it was unveiled Thursday night by my most distinguished opponent. And what did it turn out to be? Three of the ten planks were "throw the rascals out." And the others turned out to be exactly the foreign policy this nation has been following. It is a good foreign policy. I am glad that the Republican candidate is for it. But does he not realize that this foreign policy has been bitterly fought and obstructed and sabotaged by prominent Republican leaders in the Senate and in the House? Many of the men who have been most indifferent to our allies, who have fought hardest against the Marshall plan, against the Voice of America, and the Point Four Program and the other major pillars of our foreign policy are now running on the same Republican ticket with the candidate who endorses all of these measures.

What with the endorsement of all the social gains of the last twenty years, the adoption of our agricultural platform, and going us one better on this, I am beginning to wonder what sort of a shell game this is — what kind of razzle-dazzle is it? But I guess, after all, there is room for such a distinguished hitchhiker on the Democratic platform. I don't mind it. I welcome it; and so do you. It is just those one-eyed guys with knives in their teeth who are scrambling aboard with him that make me a little uncomfortable.

The Republican candidate on Thursday night repudiated the records of at least half of the Republicans who are running for the Congress, but he does not appear disposed to repudiate the candidates. I think the American people are too smart not to realize that a positive, constructive foreign policy cannot be carried out by a negative, destructive Republican majority in Congress. I think the people of this country are grown up and I think they can tell oratory from common sense. I think people want serious issues discussed seriously. I think the people of this country know that the problems of war, of inflation, poverty, greed cannot be washed away by saying every day that we are for peace and prosperity. To solve such problems means hard, sweaty, back-breaking labor, pain and anguish and unhappiness. We believe that they can be solved, for we are ready to pitch in with heart and mind and soul to tackle the natural and human difficulties that confront us and stand in our way.

If we do that — if we buckle down to work with the fortitude and energy that our pioneering forefathers showed when they subdued this continent, then we can win through this stormy night to the dawn of a peaceful world.

But, my friends, I don't think I am going to wait that long before I come back to Wyoming to go fishing!

Stevenson spoke at the Portland Journal *luncheon for Oregon newspapermen in Portland, Oregon, on September 8, 1952.*

THE ONE-PARTY PRESS [83]

It is very pleasant to consider today that I have a group of editors and publishers temporarily at my mercy. I know it won't last long. But, since the press — some of it — keeps describing me as a captive candidate, I particularly enjoy speaking to a captive audience.

In addition, I have had a strange feeling these past weeks that people are following me. They all seem to be friendly, inquisitive and rumpled; they wear hats and keep writing things down on pieces of paper. I cannot drink a milk-shake or put on a pair of shoes without their friendly but implacable surveillance. Given this relentless observation, I find it an agreeable change to stand here and look straight back at such a distinguished group of what I believe are called "opinion molders."

If ignorance, apathy and excessive partisanship are still the greatest enemies of democracy — as I believe Bryce said some forty or fifty years ago — then of course it is up to a free press to help us on all three counts and all the time. Otherwise neither democratic government nor a free press can be sure of permanency.

In short, government — our brand of representative government — depends on you, and, something which I think your profession sometimes overlooks, you depend on government, for the ultimate protection of a free press is in the Constitution.

That is why the rock-bottom foundation of a free press is the integrity of the people who run it. Our press may make a million mistakes of judgment without doing itself permanent harm so long as its proprietors are steadfast in their adherence to truth. I have no doubt whatever that the bulk of owners and publishers and editors are doing an honest job with the news.

I ought to know, because I am straining the impartiality of the press to the limit these days. Yet, as a candidate in a hard-fought campaign, I have

[83] The text is from *Major Campaign Speeches AES 1952*, pp. 78–82.

been well impressed by the fair treatment accorded me by most newspapers, including most of those aligned editorially with the opposition. I am convinced that nearly all publishers are doing their honest best, according to their lights — even if I must confess that sometimes their lights seem to me a little dim.

I am glad to pay this tribute to the press. It is true, and I think it should be said. I am grateful for the impartiality and fullness of your news columns. Yet I am not recommending complacency. And, from my vantage point, certain defects are apparent. If I were still an editorial writer I suppose I would say that there are some ominous tendencies, or even that these tendencies could weaken the fabric of the Republic.

In my new role in life, I can't help noticing from time to time — I want to put it as delicately as I can — that the overwhelming majority of the newspapers of the country are supporting the opposition candidate. This is something, I find, that even my best friends *will* tell me! And I certainly don't take it personally. In fact, I would have been somewhat startled and unhappy if I received much press support after the reception given my Democratic predecessors, Mr. Truman and Mr. Roosevelt. Some people might even have considered such support an ill omen.

It would seem that the overwhelming majority of the press is just against Democrats. And it is against Democrats, so far as I can see, not after a sober and considered review of the alternatives, but automatically, as dogs are against cats. As soon as a newspaper — I speak of the great majority, not of the enlightened ten per cent — sees a Democratic candidate it is filled with an unconquerable yen to chase him up an alley.

I still haven't got over the way some of our nation's great papers rushed to commit themselves to a candidate last spring, long before they knew what that candidate stood for, or what his party platform would be, or who his opponent was, or what would be the issues of the campaign. I know where a young publisher's fancy turns in that season of the year, and I don't blame them for a moment. But I feel that some of them may yet regret the impetuosity of their wooing now that autumn is here.

I am touched when I read in these papers solicitous editorials about the survival of the two-party system. Now I really can't bring myself to believe that the Republican Party is about to fade away, even if it loses in 1952. If so, it is staging one of the longest and loudest deathbed scenes in history. How can the Republican Party disappear when about 90 per cent of the press for ten or fifteen years has been telling the American people day in and day out that the Republican Party alone can save the Republic? Surely Republican publishers and editors don't honestly believe that they have so little influence!

I am in favor of a two-party system in politics. And I think we have a pretty healthy two-party system at this moment. But I am in favor of a two-party system in our press too. And I am, frankly, considerably concerned when I see the extent to which we are developing a one-party press in a two-party country.

I earnestly wish that the newspapers so highly agitated over the two-party system in politics would contemplate the very real dangers of the one-party system in the press. I don't say this because of any concern over the coming election. My party has done all right in recent elections in spite of the country's editorial pages, and I have a hunch we will do all right this year too.

But, as an ex-newspaperman and as a citizen, I am gravely concerned about the implications of this one-party system for our American press and our free society.

A free society means a society based on free competition and there is no more important competition than competition in ideas, competition in opinion. This form of competition is essential to the preservation of a free press. Indeed, I think the press should set an example to the nation in increasing opposition to uniformity.

What I think I detect is a growing uniformity of outlook among publishers — a tendency toward the trade-association mentality of uniformity of attitude toward the public, the customer, if not toward one another as producers of consumer goods. I doubt if this shoe fits the peculiar function of the newspaper.

I think you will agree that we cannot risk complacency. We need to be rededicated every day to the unfinished task of keeping our free press truly free. We need to work even harder for the time when all editors will honor their profession, when all publishers will have a sense of responsibility equal to their power and thus regain their power, if I may put it that way.

It's not honest convictions honestly stated that concern me. Rather it is the tendency of many papers, and I include columnists, commentators, analysts, feature writers, and so on, to argue editorially from the personal objective, rather than from the whole truth. As the old jury lawyer said: "And these, gentlemen, are the conclusions on which I base my facts."

In short, it seems to me that facts, truth, should be just as sacred in the editorial column as the news column. And, as I have said, happily most papers, but by no means all, do struggle with sincerity for accuracy in the news. Coming from Chicago, of course, I am not unfamiliar with the phenomenon of an editorial in every news column!

What I am saying is that the press cannot condemn demagoguery, claptrap, distortion and falsehood in politicians and public life on the one hand and practice the same abuses on the public themselves, on the other. I know the people are smarter than many politicians think and sometimes I suspect that even editors underestimate them.

The free press is the mother of all our liberties and of our progress under liberty. That's easy to say, but while saying it, it is well to remember what it means.

Having delivered myself of this, let me say a few words about the campaign. It is going to be a tough campaign, and I am not kidding myself about the difficulties. My opponent is a great General, who has served the Army and the nation well. He has behind him a vigorous and active party — a good deal of whose vigor and activity is devoted to the continual scrimmage between the rival Republican teams. Indeed, I wait breathlessly for each morning's newspaper to see which Republican Party is on top that day. Nonetheless, I would be the last to underestimate the effectiveness or the determination of the professional Republican organization.

But I think we have certain advantages too. One of them is that we are a relatively united party — not just in organization, but, and this may be more important, on our major problems. I do not think the people will install a party which may seem less capable of governing as time goes on. I doubt if this fretful, distracted and divided Republican Party has that capacity. If it cannot govern itself, why should we suppose that it could govern the country?

Another way of saying the same thing is that the Democratic Party has policies. It has a foreign policy, and it has a domestic policy. Some Republican leaders like our policies; most Republican leaders hate our policies; but none of them seems to have any very distinctive policies of their own to offer.

We have policies, I think, because we have ideas. I know, of course, that the Democrats aren't supposed to have any ideas. We are supposed to be stale and weary and intellectually and morally bankrupt — except on the occasions when we are supposed to be so vital and energetic and overflowing with new ideas as to constitute a danger to the Republic — or, at least, to the Republicans. As for myself, I continue to regard the Democratic Party as the party of constructive change in this country. It is always time for constructive change, and that is what I hope we can continue to offer the American people.

In short, I know it will be a hard fight. I hope it will be a clean one. We have had a lot of ground to make up. We have made up some. I figure that we still have a little distance to go. But I think too that we are gaining steadily. As for more detailed predictions, I think I will leave that to you gentlemen!

Of course, the campaign itself bulks large in our eyes today. I would like to conclude with the warning that we must not let it obscure the outlines of the world crisis in which we are involved. This generation has been summoned to a great battle — the battle to determine whether we are equal to the task of world leadership. I am deeply persuaded that the press can be our shield and our spear in this battle. I believe Jefferson said, "If a nation expects to be ignorant and free in a state of civilization it expects what never was and never will be."

We must look largely to the press for the enlightenment that will arm us for this conflict. We should be able to look to the press for much of the sober certainty that will carry us to victory and peace. Our government and our arms and our wealth will avail us little if the editors do not accept this invitation to greatness. The agents of confusion and fear must not usurp the seats of the custodians of truth and patriotism.

In saying this, I want to emphasize my belief that the leadership for this development of a free press must come entirely from the profession itself. Government has its co-operative part to play. It must do everything possible to oppose censorship and to free the channels of communication. Beyond that point, it cannot safely go. The basic job can be done only within and by the free press itself, by you gentlemen. I know you can do it superbly. We have solemn reason to pray it will be done that way.

Stevenson spoke in the Veterans Memorial Auditorium in San Francisco on September 9, 1952. Four days later, David E. Lilienthal, former chairman of the Tennessee Valley Authority and later chairman of the Atomic Energy Commission from 1946 to 1950, noted in his diary: "Stevenson is putting on one of the greatest performances in public life in my recollection. His speeches are simply gems of wisdom and wit and sense." [84]

WORLD POLICY [85]

I want to share with you, if I may, a letter from a California lady who knew my parents when they lived here fifty years ago. She writes that after Grover Cleveland was nominated for the Presidency in 1892 and my grandfather was nominated for Vice President, she named her two kittens Grover Cleveland and Adlai Stevenson. Grover, she writes me, couldn't stand the excitement of the campaign and died before the election. But Adlai lived to be a very old cat.

[84] *The Journals of David E. Lilienthal,* Vol. III: *Venturesome Years* (New York: Harper & Row, 1966), p. 337.
[85] The text is from *Major Campaign Speeches AES 1952,* pp. 91–99.

And this, my friends, is obviously for me the most comforting incident of the campaign so far.

As your chairman said, because of my prior service here [at the United Nations Conference in 1945] and because San Francisco is our window to the Far East, I want to talk soberly tonight about foreign policy.

We think and we talk a lot these days about our dangers. We should think and talk more about our opportunities as well.

Victory or defeat for a nation, as for a man, springs, first of all, from its attitudes toward the world. The men who built the West had victory in their hearts and songs on their lips. They were doers, not worriers. They really believed that the Lord helps those who help themselves.

There is something badly wrong, it seems to me, with the perspective of men who call the last ten years the "dismal decade."

And there is something odd, too, in a point of view which at once endorses the nation's foreign policies and promises to save you at the same time from such enlightened bungling.

It was some such curious mixture which was served up in Philadelphia on last Thursday. Now I am reluctant to believe that my honored opponent has been persuaded that bad history is good politics — perhaps he hopes that the Republican Old Guard will swallow his bitter pill of approval of our policies if it is sugar-coated with condemnation of Democrats.

At any rate, however we interpret it, his speech in Philadelphia does not dispose of foreign policy as an issue in this campaign. The General's ten-point foreign program, of which three points were "throw the rascals out," and seven were a recital of the same foreign-policy goals which the "Democratic rascals" have been following for years, does not, it seems to me, contribute much to our foreign-policy discussion.

But foreign policy consists of much more than the setting of goals. Even the extremist wing of the Republican Party will not really argue that peace and prosperity are bad or that the nation does not want allies.

The rub comes in doing anything to make progress toward these goals which we are glad the Republican candidates agree upon. A President can suggest but he cannot pass laws. That's the job of Congress.

And the most powerful and numerous wing of the Republican Party — the wing that would control all of the important Congressional committees — would not support the program which the Republican presidential candidate endorsed last Thursday.

How do I know? Well, because the Old Guard has been fighting that same identical program for years.

Let me illustrate.

My opponent spoke approvingly of foreign trade. Now, among other things, it is not exactly a new idea to Democrats that a thriving foreign trade means better markets for American agriculture and industry and a better balance in world economy.

I don't think even the Republicans will try to take credit for the Reciprocal Trade Agreements program. Certainly the Old Guard won't. It has been trying to wreck that program every time it comes up for renewal — as it does again next year.

I don't think that a Republican President could even get a bill to renew it out of a committee — not, at any rate, without crippling amendments. Or are we to assume that the Republican leaders in Congress have been opposing it in the past not from conviction but just because it was a Democratic program?

I could go on — talking of their attacks on our assistance program, even on the defense budgets, and similar knife work — for the Republican record in Congress is as long as it is wrong.

How, then, can a disunited party unite the country for the hard tasks that lie ahead? I don't think it can. No matter how great their commander, divided and embittered men do not win battles.

America is threatened as never before. The question history asks and which we must answer is whether the idea of individualism — the idea of personal freedom for you and me — is equal to the idea of collectivism — the idea of personal subordination to the state; whether the idea of maximum personal liberty is equal to the idea of maximum personal discipline.

This ancient contest between freedom and despotism, which is renewed in every generation, is acute in ours. And the most important single event, it seems to me, in our history is that it is our turn to be freedom's shield and sanctuary.

I don't think that war is an inevitable part of this contest. Even the most ambitious and ruthless men do not deliberately invite destruction of the basis of their power. They can throw the iron dice, but they know they cannot foretell the fortunes of war.

We who are free must have great strength in order that weakness will not tempt the ambitious. And the measure of the strength we must have is not what we would like to afford but what the adversary compels us to afford.

With 85 per cent of our budget allocated to defense, it is the Soviet Union which now fixes the level of our defense expenditures and thus of our tax rates. The only way to emancipate ourselves from this foreign control, and to cut taxes substantially, is first to develop our strength and then to find the means of ending the armaments race.

And here let me say something to those abroad who may mistake our present wrangling for weakness. We have always had differences of opinion which have produced all sorts of noises and confusion — especially in campaign years! But it is the kind of noise that, to the inner ear, is the sweet music of free institutions. It is the kind of noise that has produced the harmony of firm purpose whenever our people have been put to the test. The costliest blunders have been made by dictators who did not quite understand the workings of real democracy and who mistook diversity for disunity.

No one can predict, and it would be foolish to try to predict, how and when the peaceful purpose of our power will succeed in creating a just and durable peace. But are our efforts conditional upon assurance of prompt success? To answer "yes" would be to accept the certainty of eventual defeat.

Co-existence is not a form of passive acceptance of things as they are. It is waging the contest between freedom and tyranny by peaceful means. It will involve negotiation and adjustment — compromise but not appeasement — and I will never shrink from these if they would advance the world toward a secure peace.

Though progress may be slow, it can be steady and sure. A wise man does not try to hurry history. Many wars have been avoided by patience and many have been precipitated by reckless haste.

In Europe, our efforts to build patiently for peace are meeting with success. The Marshall Plan has brought, as we all know, a striking improvement in political and economic conditions. The North Atlantic Treaty Organization is building a strong system of military defense. Europe is not yet wholly secure against subversion from within or attack from without, but this goal of security is, at least, in sight.

I wish I could say the same for Asia, but there would be no greater disservice to the American people than to underestimate the gravity of the dangers that America faces in this area, perhaps for many years to come.

Now, it's about America's relations with Asia that I should like to talk with you tonight, soberly and realistically.

Across the continent of Asia more than a billion of the world's peoples are churning in one of history's greatest upheavals. All the struggles of man over the centuries — economic, political, spiritual — have come together in Asia and now seem to be reaching a climax.

The causes behind that upheaval are many and varied. But there is nothing complicated about what the people want. They want a decent living — and they want freedom.

The word used most frequently by Asians to describe their aspirations is nationalism.

Nationalism to Asians means a chance to stand on their own feet, a chance to govern themselves, a chance to develop their resources for their own welfare, and a chance to prove that the color of their skins has nothing to do with their right to walk with self-respect among their fellow men in the world. Nationalism to them means the end of a legalized inferiority. It means pride, spirit, faith.

This type of nationalism is not inconsistent with closer co-operation among nations nor with the need for an enforceable peace. The Asians actually regard freedom and national independence as the doorway to international order — just as we do.

Russia's interest in Asia is nothing new.

The expansionist aims of Russia did not change with the passing of the Czars. But today the steel glove of a revolutionary ideology covers the heavy hand of imperialist expansion.

The strategy of communism in Asia is to pose as the champion — the only champion — of the Asian peoples. Communism has not created the cause or the forces behind Asia's vast upheaval. It is attempting to give direction to those forces. It seeks to impose its own label on the multiple revolutions going on in Asia today by identifying itself with the deeply felt needs and hopes of the Asian peoples.

There's an important difference, it seems to me, between communism as we view it and communism as some of the Asian peoples view it. When we think of communism we think of what we are going to lose. When many of the Asiatics think of communism they think of what they are going to gain — especially if they believe that they have nothing to lose.

It's important that we know these things and think about them, for we shall never be able to cope with communism unless we understand the emotional basis of its appeal.

The communists have failed to incite the workers to revolution in Western Europe. They have failed to turn the Western Allies one against the other.

But the communists may well believe that in the aspirations and the grievances of the East they now have the key to world power. They hope, and perhaps even expect, that the West cannot rise to the challenge in the East.

Furthermore, they may not feel the same need for quick and tidy solutions that is felt in certain quarters in our own country. They may believe that they can afford to have a patience equal to the stakes involved.

And the stakes are nothing less than an overwhelming preponderance of power — for with Asia under control, they could turn with new energy and vast new resources in an effort to win a bloodless victory in a weakened, frightened Europe.

These communist expectations define the dimensions of the threat we face in Asia and of the tasks which lie ahead for us — tasks which can be met only by disciplined, resourceful, imaginative, and reasoned effort. It is an effort which has two parts: defense and development.

There is active fighting, as we all know, in Malaya and Indo-China. Have we given fitting recognition to the hard, bitter and prolonged efforts of the British, the French, the native Malayan and Indo-Chinese forces? These efforts have involved heavy loss of life and great material costs.

What will the defensive task require of us in these areas, and in the Philippines, Formosa, Japan, and Korea? What contributions, what commitments to security in this area should we make and can we make to the emerging system of Pacific defense?

These are some of the questions, the hard, the ugly questions we must face before disaster, not afterward. This is no time, it seems to me, to kid ourselves with press agents' platitudes.

In Korea we took a long step toward building a security system in Asia. As an American I am proud that we had the courage to resist that ruthless, cynical aggression; and I am equally proud that we have had the fortitude to refuse to risk extension of that war despite extreme communist provocations and reckless Republican criticisms.

Whatever unscrupulous politicians may say to exploit grief, tragedy and discontent for votes, history will never record that Korea was a "useless" war, unless today's heroism is watered with tomorrow's cowardice.

On other occasions I have spoken and written much about the solid accomplishments which the Korean war has made possible. Tonight let me say only this:

I believe we may in time look back at Korea as a major turning point in history — a turning point which led not to another terrible war, but to the first historic demonstration that an effective system of collective security *is* possible.

Having failed to defeat us on the field of battle, the enemy there now seeks to defeat us by prolonging the negotiations and by exhausting our patience.

But some men in this country seem to think that if definitive victory cannot be won, we should either take reckless military action or give the whole thing up. Such advice plays into the enemy's hands. The contest with tyranny is not a hundred-yard dash — it is a test of endurance.

This defensive effort in Korea and elsewhere in Asia is building a shield behind which we have the opportunity to assist in the other great task — the task of development.

Listening to the debate over China this past year, I had the distinct impression at times that the very Congressmen whose vocal cords were most active in the cause of isolation and against foreign entanglements were the same ones who were now talking as if they had wanted us to take part in a civil war in China.

The time to stop a revolution is at the beginning, not the end. But I don't recall any pleas from these critics for help for Sun Yat-sen and Chinese democracy back in the twenties. Nor did I hear them demanding intervention by the United States in the mid-thirties when civil war with the communists broke out. Indeed it was not until quite recently, when the Chinese wars were about over, that there was even an audible whisper that we help fight a hindsight war, that we should have given more help to China than we did.

It would seem to me, my friends, that the Republican critics could better demonstrate the good faith of their concern for Asia by doing something about India and Pakistan today rather than talking about China yesterday. I don't think that tearful and interminable post-mortems about China will save any souls for democracy in the rest of Asia, the Near East and in Africa.

India is not caught up in civil strife. It can be helped in a way that is natural to us and best for it; help in the ways of peace and of social progress. India has to grow more food. It has to restore its land. It needs new resources of power. In short, it needs a democratic helping hand in the development programs it has already charted for itself.

The same is true of many other countries.

It is help of this kind that we can provide by sending agricultural experts, engineers and other trained people to these countries, and through programs of assistance to economic development.

By working with each country to expand the production of goods which are needed by other countries in the region, a self-generating and self-financing cycle of trade and development can be initiated, which will reduce and can eventually eliminate the need for American aid. At the same time, we can enlarge our export markets and develop new sources of the products we need to import.

Land reform is, of course, fundamental to the problem of Asia. But in these ways and by this kind of friendly advice and counsel we can help to guide this economic development in ways which will give powerful support to democratic political institutions.

These programs are in accordance, it seems to me, with our best traditions. And I want to assure our friends in Asia that America will never seek to dominate their political and their economic development. We will not try to make their societies over in the image of our own. On the contrary, we respect the integrity of their institutions and the rich values of their cultures. We expect to learn as well as to teach.

These programs are primarily concerned with the material needs and wants of individual men and women. Yet we do not make the mistake of believing that the answer to communist materialism is a different brand of materialism.

The answer to communism is, in the old-fashioned phrase, good works — good works inspired by love and dedicated to the whole man. The answer to the inhumanity of communism is humane respect for the individual. And the men and the women of Asia desire not only to rise from wretchedness of the body but from abasement of the spirit as well.

In other words, we must strive for a harmony of means and of ends in our relations with Asia — and indeed with the rest of the world. The means of our co-operation are primarily material.

If we believe the communist threat to Asia is dangerous to us, then it is in our own self-interest to help them defend and develop, adjusting our policies to the constantly changing circumstances in a world of accelerating change. But we must not, in our necessary concern for the urgent tasks of defense and development, permit the means to obscure the end. That end is the widening and the deepening of freedom and of respect for the dignity and the worth of man.

Some may say to you that this is visionary stuff. To this I reply that history has shown again and again that the self-styled realists are the real visionaries — for their eyes are fixed on a past that cannot be recaptured. It was Woodrow Wilson, with his dream of the League of Nations, who was the truly practical man — not the Old Guard who fought him to the death. And in the fateful summer of 1940 it was the vision of a Churchill that saw beyond Dunkerque to victory.

I say that America has been called to greatness. The summons of the twentieth century is a summons to our vision, to our humanity, to our practicality. If these provide the common purpose of America and Asia, of our joint enterprise, of our progress together, we need have no fear for the future. Because it will belong to free men.

Alicia Patterson sent Stevenson her article "The Case Against Wechsler," which appeared in the Bulletin of the American Society of Newspaper Editors, *September 1, 1952. She criticized the sponsor of a radio discussion program for dropping James Wechsler, editor of the New York* Post, *from the program because he had been a member of the Young Communist League while in college in the 1930's.*

To Alicia Patterson

September 14, 1952

Dear Alicia:

Bravo! Your statement in the Bulletin on the Wechsler case was superb, courageous and wholly right. Thank God you stood up to that one. And knowing nothing about the situation I am a little surprised that Spike Canham [86] would even continue as moderator of the program. I wish I had your pen at work on my speeches, which are driving me insane, what with the want of time and the incessant pressure.

I come East this week and will probably be in New York Friday night, September 19, and perhaps Sunday the 21st and Monday, the 22nd. I doubt if the party you have in mind would be possible, although I think we could arrange for a little get-together in my quarters in the Biltmore [Hotel] on the afternoon of September 22, if possible for you and the others. Why not send me a wire if you think it worth while to try to do something about it and I will let you know as promptly as I can when the plans are formulated.

The trip was a great success politically, but very tiring for an amateur who is evidently trying to do things a little better than in the past. . . .

Yours,

To Paul C. Smith [87]

September 14, 1952

Dear Paul:

Chaos and fatigue followed me back to the hotel and I had no opportunity to call you after the meeting. I had hoped for a little more of your counsel, and I will hope that you will send along any ideas, addressed to me personally and marked confidential, at the Executive Mansion. I shall not embarrass you.

Even a glimpse of you was good, and I was enchanted to see the lovely Nan again. [88] And now I march East on my dreary pilgrimage.

Yours,

Paul H. Buck, provost of Harvard University, wrote to advise Stevenson that the university had granted Professor Arthur M. Schlesinger, Jr., a leave of absence so that he could work on Stevenson's campaign. Mr. Buck expressed his pleasure that Professor Schlesinger would have "this opportunity both to serve and to learn."

[86] Erwin D. Canham, editor of the *Christian Science Monitor*.

[87] Editor of the San Francisco *Chronicle*. A copy is in A.E.S., I.S.H.L.

[88] Mrs. Dennis McEvoy, the former Nan Tucker, whose grandfather founded the *Chronicle*. In 1952, her uncle, George Cameron, was publisher of the paper. Before her marriage, Mrs. McEvoy had worked for the paper for about five years.

To Paul H. Buck

September 15, 1952

My dear Mr. Buck:

I am grateful to you for your letter of September 12, and to the Harvard Corporation for its willingness to grant a leave of absence to Mr. Arthur M. Schlesinger, Jr. I cannot tell you how much I value this generous evidence of good will.

I do not know what other participants may get out of this campaign, but I can assure you that my own education is proceeding apace.

With renewed thanks, and my every good wish, I am

Sincerely yours,

To Mrs. John Kenneth Galbraith

September 15, 1952

Dear Mrs. Galbraith:

I address you as the real victim of Ken's participation in this campaign enterprise.[89] I know with what disappointment you must have watched him vanish — just at vacationtime — into the wastes of the Illinois prairies, and I want you to know how much I value your willingness to view the loss with good temper.

It does not help you much to know how effective and useful I have found Ken's presence here to be, but it is a point I wish to make for whatever worth it may be to you.

Thanks again, and I hope I shall one day have the opportunity to speak my gratitude in person.

Sincerely,

To Mrs. John Paul Welling [90]

September 16, 1952

My dear Harriet:

Many thanks for your letter. I am shocked by the news about Charlie.[91] I had not heard a word. He was a really old friend whom I saw all too little and I can imagine what misery this must be for you.

---

[89] Professor Galbraith, of the Harvard University Department of Economics, was a speech drafter in Stevenson's campaign.

[90] A copy is in A.E.S., I.S.H.L.

[91] Mrs. Welling's brother, Charles Morehead Walker, Jr., who had died recently.

I think your surmise about Ellen is correct and I shall dismiss that idea.[92]

I am so glad you think well of what I have been saying. It has been a hideous strain with such ghastly pressures, but I believe we learned some brutal lessons in the West which will not be repeated.

Affectionately,

To Franklin P. Adams [93]

September 16, 1952

Dear Frank:

Your notes have been a most welcome interlude in the sea of paper which has descended upon me. I hope you will keep them up, although I shall probably do a completely inadequate job by way of reply.

In any event, I am both grateful for your good wishes and encouraged by them; and I send my warmest personal regards.

Sincerely,

To Richard B. Russell

September 16, 1952

Dear Senator:

I tried to reach you by phone on my return yesterday from the West, but I find that you have already left for Venezuela.

I am disturbed that you feel that I am "reaching to the left," and I hope that on your return we can have another candid talk. Thus far, I do not feel that I have yielded any positions which are inconsistent with my own views, nor do I intend to. But because I value so highly your own judgment I should like to be informed about my mistakes when your convenience permits. Also I feel that your active support, particularly in the South, can be of inestimable value in some areas which are better known to you than to me.[94]

I hope you have a happy journey. Our trip to the West was most reassuring, indeed, far more so than I had anticipated.

Sincerely yours,

---

[92] Since many of Stevenson's handwritten letters to Mrs. Welling were not made available to the editors, it has not been possible to explain this reference to Ellen Stevenson.

[93] A copy is in A.E.S., I.S.H.L.

[94] Senator Russell did not issue a public statement in support of Stevenson until the closing weeks of the campaign.

On September 12, to enlist the positive support of Senator Robert A. Taft, General Eisenhower conferred with him at Columbia University for the first time since the Convention. Taft submitted a list of issues to ascertain the Republican candidate's position. After the meeting, Taft announced that he would heartily cooperate in the campaign. Taft told a press conference that Eisenhower agreed that the main issue was "liberty against creeping socialization." The senator explained that while he did not agree with all of Eisenhower's views on foreign policy, "I think it is fair to say that our differences are differences of degree." [95]

Stevenson observed in a speech at Albuquerque, "The elephants put their two heads together in New York today for a peace conference. . . . It looks as if Taft lost the nomination but won the nominee." [96]

To Archibald MacLeish [97]

SEPTEMBER 16, 1952

PLEASE SEND STATEMENT ON TAFT EISENHOWER AGREEMENT AIR MAIL HELP HELP. I AM DESPERATE FOR WRITING ASSISTANCE. WILL BE IN HARTFORD THURSDAY NIGHT AND SPRINGFIELD, MASSACHU-SETTS FRIDAY NOON AND NEW YORK FRIDAY NIGHT SEND ANYTHING AND ALL THE TIME.

ADLAI

President Truman wrote Stevenson praising his recent speeches in the West. He advised the candidate not to change his method of attack. He did admit, however, that he was worried about the pace of the campaign, which he feared would peak too early before the election. He closed by praising Stephen A. Mitchell, who he thought was well qualified to handle his job as chairman of the Democratic National Committee.

When President Truman published Years of Trial and Hope: 1946–1952,[98] *he criticized Stevenson for firing Chairman Frank McKinney and for establishing campaign headquarters in Springfield to disassociate himself from the administration. Truman charged that there was little coordination between Springfield and the National Committee in Washington, and as a result there were really two campaigns. He also wrote that Stevenson asked him to get into the campaign too late.[99]*

Stephen A. Mitchell wrote a memorandum on February 22, 1955, about

95 New York *Times*, September 13, 1952.
96 Ibid.
97 This telegram is in the MacLeish papers, Library of Congress.
98 New York: Doubleday, 1955.
99 *Years of Trial and Hope*, pp. 498–499.

the Truman charges. Mitchell denied there had been faulty coordination between him and Wilson Wyatt. He stated that it was essential to fire McKinney in order to establish a "clean look" in national headquarters. Mitchell agreed there were two campaigns in 1952, "one by Stevenson and the other by Truman. This seemed to me to make the best of a bad situation because each man had his appeal but the appeals were different and they were effective with quite different groups of people. . . . I think the two separate campaigns were a reflection of the differences between the two men and proved the validity of their independence of each other."

As to the charge that Stevenson asked Truman to come into the campaign too late, Mitchell noted that Stevenson asked him, at their first meeting in the White House on August 12, to make six speeches. But, Mitchell added, Truman's first trip to Milwaukee on Labor Day blossomed into a full-scale whistle-stop campaign: "The first trip then to Milwaukee naturally whetted the appetite of the political fire horse Truman and put his entourage in the White House fully into the campaign and from then on there was a full-scale effort to build Truman's part in the campaign."

Mitchell remarked: "My personal opinion is that Truman's campaigning did a lot of good in the places where he appeared and with the audiences who heard him. But I do think the Republican press gave more space to his tart or acidulous comments than they did to Stevenson's campaign speeches and then these papers would claim they were giving the Democrats just as much attention as the Republicans." [100]

To Harry S. Truman

September 17, 1952

My dear Mr. President:

I was so glad to find your letter of September 10 on my return from our trip through the West. I share somewhat your anxiety about the campaign moving a little too rapidly, but I hardly know what to do about it except plow ahead and run like a singed cat until I drop — which I hope will not be before November 5th!

The articles you enclosed with your letter were so reassuring. I find it so difficult to keep up with the press while I am writing and talking and trying to handle my work here at the same time.

The westward journey was most reassuring. I cannot say the situation is bad in any of the 10 states we passed through, although I gathered

[100] This memorandum is in the Mitchell papers, Harry S. Truman Library, Independence, Missouri.

that Senator McFarland may have some real ground for apprehension in Arizona.[101] The Party, I was told everywhere, was never more unified and aggressive, and I am disposed to believe it. The crowds exceeded any expectation of mine and there also seems to be some new and very healthy working leadership emerging in several of the states we passed through.

The situation in California was particularly gratifying. While the Kefauver people have pretty much taken over, I gather that they are making a sincere effort to keep the other elements actively participating and several of the latter confirmed this. I gather that Jackson's prospects against Cain are excellent, which will be pleasing to you as it is to me.[102]

With my thanks and every best wish, I am

Faithfully yours,

To Dore Schary [103]

September 17, 1952

Dear Mr. Schary:

Reviewing our pilgrimage through the West, I want to thank you and Mrs. Schary again for that extraordinary extravaganza on your lovely lawn in Brentwood. I feel as though I owe you more than thanks — at least half a dozen gardeners for a week!

It was a delightful but all too brief interlude for me and I am profoundly grateful to you for your courtesy and your disarming hospitality. My son [104] is still babbling about "the movie stars" he saw, while his father just babbles!

With my very kind regards to Mrs. Schary and those enchanting daughters, I am

Cordially yours,

To Norman Cousins [105]

September 17, 1952

Dear Norman:

I told Jane Dick today by telephone that I would welcome any speeches you can find time to write. Your material is by far the best

---

[101] Barry Goldwater defeated Senator Ernest McFarland in the November election.
[102] Henry Jackson defeated Senator Harry Cain of Washington in the November election.
[103] Hollywood producer and director and a strong supporter of Stevenson. The original is in the possession of Mr. Schary.
[104] Borden.
[105] Editor of the *Saturday Review*.

that I receive, and if I take liberties with it I am sure you will understand.

Specifically, I think that some time I would like to talk about Youth. A group of University of Illinois — Students for Stevenson — called on me today, and reminded me that I had not talked on their future — military service, jobs, etc.

Also, I have felt that there was a theme that could be developed in the idea of government by consent, not by command. I apologize for imposing on you incessantly and presenting my ideas in such loose and limited form. It seems to be all I can do to keep pace with the day's difficulties, with no time to think about tomorrow.

Cordially yours,

Stevenson spoke at Bushnell Memorial Auditorium in Hartford, Connecticut, on September 18, 1952.

THE ATOMIC FUTURE [106]

I am glad to be here in Connecticut. I first came here to school not far from Hartford about thirty-five years ago as a small boy.[107] I have always gratefully recalled the warmth with which your citizens took me in, and also the patience with which my teachers tried to educate me. Some of them are here tonight and I am deeply touched by their continued interest in this Democratic heretic from the prairies of the West. Or should I attribute it to the fact that the last twenty years have won most of the more enlightened to the Democratic standard!

In recent weeks my distinguished opponent has adopted the singular theory that a candidate for President should support all state and local candidates on his party ticket — good, bad, indifferent — and regardless of their views and records.[108]

I believe this is a new theory, even in the Republican Party. It was not too long ago when Governor Dewey, as party leader, honorably refused to support a Republican Congressman who had distinguished him-

[106] The text is from *Major Campaign Speeches AES 1952*, pp. 134–139.

[107] See *The Papers of Adlai E. Stevenson*, Vol. I, Part Two, for Stevenson's education at the Choate School in Wallingford, Connecticut.

[108] At a press conference on August 22, Eisenhower praised General George C. Marshall, whose patriotism had been bitterly attacked by Senator Joseph McCarthy and Senator William Jenner. When a reporter asked whether Eisenhower would support McCarthy for reelection, he replied: "I will support him as a member of the Republican organization." He added that a Republican President needed a Republican Congress: "For that reason, I have to accept the decisions of the voters of a state, as much as I can." New York *Times*, August 23, 1952.

self by incessant and noisy opposition to vital national policies. But the General's theory is not only novel, it is dangerous. If the voters of this nation ever stop looking at the record and the character of candidates, and look only at their party label, it will be a sorry day for healthy democracy.

Win or lose, I will not accept the proposition that party regularity is more important than political ethics. Victory can be bought too dearly.

But this exhibition of Republican expediency is not what I wanted to talk to you about. I wanted to talk here tonight about something which transcends politics — atomic energy, which is the new dimension in all our thinking — and also about the relation of power to peace.

I was moved to select this topic because atomic energy is a major component of our power and because our decisions and actions in atomic energy matters, as they relate to preparedness for both war and peace, will long bear the imprint of our wise and lamented friend, Brien McMahon of Connecticut.[109]

Brien McMahon was among the first to see the great potentiality for good and evil which was opened up by this advance of the frontiers of knowledge. He sought to reconcile the needs for security with the needs for information — both to encourage further scientific advances and an intelligent public opinion. He saw the need for civilian control. He fought to keep the sights of the development program high.

We have already, for example, opened up new fields of medical research. Brien McMahon died of cancer. With luck and the help of atomic research, our children may be safe from this grim disease.

We have already produced, with an atomic reactor, the steam to generate electric power. We are building now — and in a Connecticut shipyard — an atomic-powered submarine. We can begin to dream of electric stations, ships, airplanes and machinery to be powered by the atom. Men are at work today with atomic tools trying to find out how plants convert energy from the sun into food. It is not too fantastic to think that we may, in time, unlock new doors to boundless energy for our homes and industries.

This is a field in which government and industry can work in ever more fruitful partnership. The people of this country have invested more than six billion dollars in atomic development. This work must be for everyone's good, and not just for the profits of some. But more can be done to work out new relationships in this field between government and business — relationships which will safeguard the public interest and yet allow full room for private initiative.

[109] Senator Brien McMahon, who had led the struggle to achieve civilian control of atomic energy, had died on July 29, 1952.

This is the excitement of the future which awaits us. The age of atomic abundance is still far off. And we will never be able to release the power of the atom to build unless we are able to restrain its power to destroy. This is the merciless question of the present — the question of what we should do with atomic power in a divided world.

Here again we face a bitter decision. We shrink from the use of such weapons — weapons which destroy the guilty and innocent alike, like a terrible sword from heaven. The memory of Hiroshima is fresh within us — described in enduring prose by one of the most accomplished of contemporary writers — John Hersey [110] — who, I am proud to say, is head of the Volunteers for Stevenson in Connecticut. But we can't renounce the power which science has given us when renunciation might expose our people to destruction.

In the decision to move ahead Brien McMahon again played a leading role. He demanded that we constantly step up our reserves of atomic weapons. He worked always to keep the sights of the atomic energy program high and its policies bold — and the United States has made a notable contribution to the security of the free world by its rapid development of atomic power.

Yet there has always seemed to me a danger in making the atomic bomb the center of defense strategy. The bomb is but one part of a general system of defense. It cannot be a substitute for such a general system. It cannot be our only answer to aggression. But the bomb remains an essential part of our defense system. Until it is subjected to safe international control, we have no choice but to insure our atomic superiority.

But there can be no solution in an arms race. At the end of this road lies bankruptcy or world catastrophe. Already the earth is haunted by premonitions in this shadowed atomic age. Mankind must deserve some better destiny than this.

Because our Government knew the futility of the arms race, it made its great decision to seek an international system for the control of atomic power. We went to the United Nations and Bernard Baruch, a beloved and wise elder statesman, offered on behalf of the United States to share with other nations the good in atomic energy. In return, we asked that other nations join with us to curb its power for evil.

I think this decision was right — profoundly right. Few things we have done since 1945 have so clearly demonstrated our national determination to achieve peace and to strengthen international order. By this offer, all nations were asked to diminish their own sovereignty in the interests

110 John Hersey, *Hiroshima* (New York: Alfred A. Knopf, 1946), originally published in *The New Yorker*, August 31, 1946.

of world security — just as each of us gives up some degree of personal independence when communities establish laws and set up police forces to see that they are carried out.

Unfortunately, as we all know, the Soviet Union has thus far refused to join in a workable system. The reason is obvious. To be effective, such a system would require effective United Nations inspection; and the Kremlin fears to open up the windows and doors of its giant prison. It fears to have the rest of the world learn the truth about the Soviet Union. It fears even more to have the Russian peoples learn the truth about the rest of the world.

And so the negotiations have long been deadlocked. And, in irritation and disgust, some of us have rebelled against the whole idea of negotiation itself. Some of us have even felt that our possession of the bomb makes negotiation unnecessary and, if our allies are alarmed by our uncompromising attitude, so much the worse for them. When we have the bomb as our ally, some of us may say, we need no other.

Such ideas are folly. If we started throwing our atomic weight around the world, no stockpile of bombs could remotely make up for all the friends we would lose. And the irony is that it is our allies who make our atomic strength effective. We built the bomb with the help and co-operation of foreign scientists. Our atomic-production program today depends on foreign supplies of uranium. Our air power would be gravely crippled without foreign bases. Even in terms of the bomb itself, going-it-alone would simply be a shortcut to national disaster.

A year ago some Republican leaders contended that the best way to stop the war in Korea would be to extend it to the mainland of China. In the same vein, Republican leaders today seem to be arguing that the best way to deal with Soviet power in Europe is to instigate civil war in the satellite countries. These are dangerous, reckless, foolish counsels and likely to lead to the sacrifice of the lives of the very people whom we hope to liberate.

And likewise the Democratic Party opposes that weird Republican policy which proposes to reduce our contributions to free-world strength, on the one hand, while it steps up its verbal threats against the enemy, on the other hand. Theodore Roosevelt used to say: "Speak softly and carry a big stick." But these modern Republicans seem to prefer to throw away the stick and scream imprecations.

The Democratic Party will never desist in the search for peace. We must never close our minds or freeze our positions. We must strive constantly to break the deadlock in our atomic discussions. But we can never yield on the objective of securing a foolproof system of international inspection and control. And we will never confuse negotiation with appeasement.

In the long run, the strength of the free nations resides as much in this willingness to reduce their military power and subject it to international control as in the size of their military establishments. This desire and willingness of the free nations to give up their preponderant power and to abandon force as an instrument of national policy in the interests of peace is not only unprecedented — it provides the moral justification for the amassing of great power. And we must never delude ourselves into thinking that physical power is a substitute for moral power which is the true sign of national greatness.

I hold out no foolish hopes. We all know the character of the men in the Kremlin — their fanaticism, their ruthlessness, their limitless ambitions — but we know too that their realism has restrained them thus far from provoking a general war which they would surely lose, and they know that they can have peace and freedom from fear whenever they want it and are prepared to honor their wartime pledges and the obligations assumed when they signed the United Nations Charter. We may hope that the steady strengthening of the free world will increase their sense of the futility of aggression; that the intensification of peaceful pressures against the Soviet Empire will sharpen the internal contradictions within that empire; that, in time, free peoples may lift their heads again in Eastern Europe, and new policies and leadership emerge within the Soviet Union itself.

No one can be certain about the meaning of peace. But we all can be certain about the meaning of war. The future is still open — open for disaster, if we seek peace cheaply or meanly, but open for real peace, if we seek it bravely and nobly.

In any case, let us not cower with fear before this new instrument of power. Nature is neutral. Man has wrested from nature the power to make the world a desert or to make the deserts bloom. There is no evil in the atom; only in men's souls. We have dealt with evil men before, and so have our fathers before us, from the beginning of time. The way to deal with evil men has never varied; stand up for the right, and, if needs must be, fight for the right.

To my Republican listeners I would say: the atomic adventure transcends partisan issues. Win or lose, we Democrats will work with you to follow this adventure to the end of peace and plenty for mankind.

To my fellow Democrats I would close by repeating what Brien McMahon said in his last public appearance. He said: "The way to worry about November is to worry about what is right. If we do not stand for the right, ten thousand campaign speeches will never help us. If we do stand for the right, we will again be asked to lead our country."

Stevenson spoke at City Hall in Springfield, Massachusetts, on September 19, 1952.

THE NEW ENGLAND TRADITION [111]

I don't know why it is that an American, no matter where he was born or where he lives, has a feeling in New England of coming home. Perhaps it is because this country of yours looks so homelike; perhaps it is because the people and their welcome are always so friendly; perhaps it is because so much of what we are as Americans came out of these valleys and these hills — our habit, for example, of making up our own minds in our own way, and saying what we think — our habit of respect for each other, and for ourselves — our habit, if you please, of freedom.

At all events, I have felt very much at home today in Massachusetts, and yesterday traveling through Connecticut. I hope I feel equally at home up here after November 4th. Maybe I feel particularly at home in Springfield because I, too, live in Springfield, albeit some two hundred years younger than your Springfield, but equally famous.

Now, my friends, I have thought that the proper way to conduct a campaign was to discuss the issues, and by that I mean the choices that people have to make between alternative courses of conduct. It has been a little hard for me to get a discussion of the issues in this campaign. Our Republican friends, to be sure, are in favor of throwing the rascals out, but they are also in favor of throwing the rascals in. While approving everything that has been done for the past twenty years by the Democrats, they say the country is headed for perdition and they call us all dreadful names.

Indeed, to keep this campaign on the highest possible level worthy of its significance, I have been tempted to make a proposal to our Republican friends: that if they would stop telling lies about us, we would stop telling the truth about them. Which reminds me that about the only place where they have really taken issue with us seems to be on the subject of humor. The Republicans are against it. And those of us who have found a certain friendly amusement in the antics of the two-headed elephant have been rebuked — an elephant, we are given to understand, is no laughing matter. Well, for myself, I can't think it a hideous offense to believe that

[111] The text is from *Major Campaign Speeches AES 1952*, pp. 140–145.

the American people have a sense of humor. We used to call Al Smith "the Happy Warrior."

In fact, he was given this name by another happy warrior, Franklin Roosevelt, who got his title "the Great Humanitarian," by the way, in this city of Springfield, Massachusetts. In the midst of the terrible years of the Civil War, Abraham Lincoln — and the Republican Party still claims him — at least at election time — said of humor:

"If it were not for this occasional vent, I should die."

It is a far cry from Lincoln to these solemn individuals who want to banish it from American public life. I have about concluded that what G.O.P. really means is "grouchy old pessimists."

Maybe this feeling about a little humor to enliven our lives goes far to explain the General's remark last week about Oliver Cromwell. I found myself somewhat puzzled when he announced that Cromwell was going to be the model of the Great Crusade.[112]. Why should he have chosen Oliver Cromwell? Obviously it could not be because Cromwell sent his Roundheads on a bloody crusade against the people of Ireland with religious persecution, starvation and the sword as his weapons. It could not be because Cromwell led his army into the House of Commons to seize control by force of the Parliament of England. But now I think I know why the General admired Oliver Cromwell. Whatever else you may say about Cromwell, you can never accuse him of having cracked a joke.

I suppose we must not be too critical. To be surrounded by the Republican Old Guard night and day would be a melancholy fate for anyone and I can understand why it is no laughing matter for the General. In fact, Senator Taft seems to be getting most of the amusement. When he walked out of the General's house in New York with the surrender in writing I have never seen such a contented smile since the cat swallowed the canary.

I have been wondering sometimes what that brutal battle in Chicago last July was all about.

I am glad to note that not all of the crusaders who marched into battle against Senator Taft so gallantly are prepared to follow their leader in his inglorious retreat.

Let me say to the good Republicans of New England: there is always

---

[112] Eisenhower, speaking to state representatives of the Citizens for Eisenhower and Nixon in New York City, had praised the volunteers' spirit, comparing it to that which Oliver Cromwell had inspired during the English Revolution: "Cromwell proved that you can have the most iron discipline that any army ever knew and at the same time the greatest elan. His secret was this: He bound his people together by their devotion — not to Cromwell (he was a rather ornery-looking old fellow who wasn't very personable) but he bound them to a cause and the cause he used was religion." New York *Times*, September 14, 1952.

a light in the Democratic window and a warm welcome awaiting you in the Democratic Party. We know how to make people feel at home, and that's why we win elections.

Let me further say that if I should be elected President in November, I will be President, and I will not be honorary head of a regency.

Now, my friends, you all know how this country has been transformed in the last twenty years. The Democratic Party took over when the nation was almost in a state of receivership in 1933. Fortunately, we had a great and revered leader — Franklin Roosevelt. Under his leadership the Democratic Party dedicated itself to improving opportunity and security for all of our citizens. In the last twenty years we have restored and reconstructed the nation. Where there was once poverty, there is now prosperity. Where there was once anxiety, there is now security. Where there was once discrimination, we now have opportunity. Democratic administrations have produced the great social reforms of our era. We will defend these reforms against all of those humorless people who haven't been happy since the days of William McKinley. And, we will defend these reforms and this free society of ours — we will defend them against those on the extreme left, the admirers of Lenin and Stalin, who would bind all of us to the service of an omnipotent and all-powerful state.

It is the Democratic administration in Washington, assisted by many good Republicans, who followed in the train of Arthur Vandenberg, which has rallied the free world against communism in the last seven years. Indeed, if it had not been for the wisdom and the courage of our national leadership, Europe might have by now fallen to the communists. If it had not been for the wisdom and the courage of our national leadership, communist aggressors would by now have swallowed Korea and swarmed over all of Asia.

The fight for freedom and for security takes place on many fronts. You of New England, by the way, have been waging your own battle in recent years — a battle to maintain the economic health and the vitality of this region.

A few days ago in a report to the President by the Council of Economic Advisers, I found this comment about New England — I think many of you are familiar with it. It said: "Its people are noted for their independence and self-reliance. They seem to look less to the Federal Government for help than do the people of any other region."

Now, if I were a New Englander, I would be mighty proud of this compliment.

I want to say to you here in New England what I have said elsewhere. I believe the Federal Government must not hesitate to do those things that are necessary for the country's welfare, which the people of the states and the localities cannot do for themselves. Decisions on Federal expenditures must not be made simply in response to local or regional pressures, or the demands of particular pressure groups. Such decisions would reward those who bring the most pressure, and at the expense of those who bring the least. We must see that modesty is never penalized.

I am also conscious of the things that disturb New England — the textile mills and the shoe factories that have been closing or moving south; the unemployment in some mill towns when jobs elsewhere have been plentiful; and the fact that any drop in business hits New England with special severity. The relatively slight recession, even of 1949, was keenly felt in many New England communities.

Now the Federal Government must never seek to impede the growth of one part of the country to help another. Nor have I ever heard any New Englander suggest that the salvation of New England lies in blocking the advance of the South or of the Midwest. But government can work toward fair standards of competition between regions. We know that Massachusetts pioneered not alone in manufacturing, but in a decent and dignified life for the men and women who work in industry. Your standards of unemployment compensation, of accident compensation, protection for women and children, have always been high. Unions in New England are strong and alert to the interests of their members.

Competition which derives its advantage from lower wage standards, less protection for workers, or lower living standards, is not always healthy competition.

We must have, it seems to me, reasonably uniform wage and hour standards. We must have reasonably uniform standards of social security throughout our country. That has been the policy of the Democratic Party, as I understand it, during these past twenty years. New England's greatest resource is in its people, its unparalleled supply of skilled labor, its experienced and thrifty management, its knowledge of how to produce to the highest standards of workmanship. Any region with such a resource is assured of a great future. In the next twenty years we shall have in the United States an increase in population of over thirty million persons. New England is certain to be called upon to supply many of the needs — from fine textiles to grinding wheels — of this expanding population. Of that there can be no doubt.

The success of New England in meeting this challenge of a growing population with a rising standard of living will depend in the future, as it has in the past, on New England brains, initiative and leadership. You haven't been waiting here in this section of the country for Washington to tell you how — and there is no danger that you will.

There are some ways, however, in which the Federal Government can help. Some of them are immediate. Your new industries — and many of your old ones — produce things that are vital to our national security. The small New England manufacturer and the firm that is new in its business must get a fair break on Government orders. Orders must be guided to communities where men and plants are idle. It is poor economy indeed to pay unemployment compensation and provide public assistance in one place while defense orders go where labor is scarce.

There is also here the problem of power. I am told that the power rates in New England are nearly twice as high as for the country as a whole. This means higher production costs in factories, higher costs and smaller use in homes and on the farms.

You still have an important resource in water power that awaits development. The decision both on our power development and on flood control on your streams is a decision that belongs to the people of New England. And the Federal Government, my friends, should stand ready here, as in other parts of the country, to help local people develop resources which they cannot develop themselves.

In many parts of the country, New England has resources that are better known than its factories. The farms of the Connecticut valley looked good even to a man from Illinois, and that is saying something. Also you take care of our insurance out in this part of the country. You educate a lot of our children and you seem to do them much good. I can testify to that because I was educated here myself and so have all of my boys learned something about the rigors of New England climate, and also its classrooms! You are the custodians of some of the greatest monuments to our past and of some of the finest scenery in our land. The day will surely come when every American, at least once in his lifetime, will come up the Connecticut valley, will go over to visit Lexington and Concord, will go on to Boston, and then go on for a vacation somewhere in the Green Mountains or the White Mountains or the coast of Maine. I wish I was up there myself!

I am sure that New England has a brilliant future — a future to match its brilliant past. Men and women who trace their ancestry to Ireland, to Italy, to France, to Poland, and a dozen other lands have joined their traditions and energies with those who first landed here in New England to build the New England way of life.

I have said many times during this campaign that we have hard, heartbreaking tasks ahead of us. I don't minimize them, but I say to you that we will win through, and we will win through, my friends, with the Democratic Party — I hope!

On September 18, while Stevenson was campaigning in Connecticut and Massachusetts, the New York Post *headlined:* SECRET NIXON FUND. *The paper charged that a "millionaire's club" in California had collected a "slush fund" for the "financial comfort" of the Republican vice-presidential candidate. In the uproar that ensued, the Republican New York* Herald Tribune *declared that Nixon should offer to withdraw from the campaign, and the New York* Times, *which was supporting the Republican ticket, editorialized that Nixon had shown poor judgment in accepting the gift.*[113]

Stevenson wrote the following statement on Biltmore Hotel stationery.[114]

I have been repeatedly pressed for comment on the matter of Senator Nixon.

From what I have heard about it, the questions seem to be: who gave the money, was it given to influence the Senator's position on public questions, and have any laws been violated?

I am sure the great Republican party will ascertain these facts, will make them public, and act in accordance with our best traditions and with due respect for the second most important position in the land.

Condemnation without all the evidence, a practice all too familiar to us, would be wrong.

On September 20, Adlai E. Stevenson III received his commission as a second lieutenant in the United States Marine Corps. His father spoke at the commissioning ceremonies at the United States Marine Base at Quantico, Virginia.

TO THE YOUNG MARINES [115]

You know something about the life of a candidate for high office in this country. You know what happens to him, what is expected of him. He is supposed to have something to say about every sort of issue to

[113] Nixon discussed the fund and his struggle to stay on the Republican ticket in his *Six Crises* (New York: Doubleday, 1966). Garry Wills, "Nixon's Dog: How the 37th President of the United States Brilliantly Outwitted the 34th President of the United States, *Esquire*, August, 1969, pp. 91ff, is a revealing analysis.

[114] This undated, handwritten statement is in the possession of William I. Flanagan. The phrase in paragraph two "and have any laws been violated" is in Mr. Flanagan's handwriting.

[115] The text is from *Major Campaign Speeches AES 1952*, pp. 146–148.

every kind of audience. He does his best to put his beliefs, his convictions, into words so that the people who listen to him can think about them and judge for themselves. His whole concern is to find the right words, the true, faithful, explicit words which will make the issues plain and his position on those issues clear.

Well, there are times when the words are very hard to find and this is one of them.

Let me just say that I am proud that my son and each one of you has achieved the special distinction of a commission in the Marine Corps. I am proud that my country has a military unit with the spirit of the United States Marines.

You are being trained to fight, and if you are called on, you will fight as Marines have always fought. Yours is a great tradition. You are part of the shield of our Republic in a time of peril. Do not underestimate the effect that you, and others like you in all our armed forces, are having in the hard and painful work of creating peace.

In one way or another each generation has to fight for its freedom in the conditions of its time. Our times are hard — as hard as any in our history. We, your fathers, have asked you to make ready to fight so that you and your children may walk upright and unafraid.

Your country does not accept the inevitability of world war. But the way to peace is essentially a work of construction, by far the largest we have ever undertaken. It is nothing less than the rebuilding of a ruined world and the establishment of conditions in which free government can take root and grow elsewhere, as it has long since taken root and grown here in America.

Marines have always manned the places of great peril, and also of great honor. Your job, wherever you are sent, will be the first line of defense or assault to halt aggression before it gains ground and momentum. More than that, you will be ambassadors to men in other lands whose hopes for freedom are dimmer than ours. Understand them and their hopes. You may have many a chance to compose the differences and to ease the conditions that provoke wars.

You carry with you not alone the hope, the prayer and the love of the people who gave you birth. You carry the same hope, the same prayer, and the same love of people around the world who do not know your names, but who do know you by your cause and your great tradition. Not alone America, but all free men winced when the flag was lowered on Wake Island. Not alone America, but humanity was vindicated when the flag was raised again on Iwo Jima. Our fate rides with you.

I know something of the massive threats you face. But I know, too, something of the mighty heart of your Corps. I've seen it, face to face, in the steaming jungles.[116] And I shall never forget it.

But with all that, I know full well that I have not yet answered the question in the hearts of many of you. It is a question which your presence here asks of us all.

Why must you defend your country when your country seems to lie in peace around you? Is it because of some mistake made in the past by those older than yourselves — some failure of foresight or decision? Is it for that you must offer the sacrifice of the young years of your lives?

Certainly there have been failures and mistakes. The course of human history is a record, a tragic part, of things done which should not have been done, things not done which should have been done. Our own history is like the rest. But of one thing I, for myself, am certain and I think you also can be certain.

It is not to make good the errors of the past that you are here but to make good the promise of the future. The fighting in which we are now engaged in Korea is fighting undertaken in the name of the common collective security of the great majority of the nations of the world against the brutal aggressiveness of one or more of them. It is fighting which might, conceivably, have been avoided on that particular battlefield had we acted otherwise than we did — though, as to that, no man can surely say. But it is fighting which must inevitably have been faced, somewhere in the world, so long as the Soviet Union pressed its purpose to subjugate the free peoples of the earth, and so long as the United States and the free peoples of the earth retained their purpose to resist.

We and our friends found the courage to resist two years ago. It is to press that courage home, to affirm and to establish the faith that a peaceful world can in truth be built, that you and the thousands upon thousands of young men like you have been asked to serve your country with the hope and promise of your lives.

I guess it is just that simple. But the verities are simple. I hope you understand. I hope every man in your commands will understand.

I wish you God speed and all good fortune.

Later that day Governor Stevenson spoke at a rally at Mosque Auditorium in Richmond, Virginia.

[116] See *The Papers of Adlai E. Stevenson,* Vol. II, pp. 66–106, for Stevenson's tour of the Pacific Theater in 1943.

THE NEW SOUTH [117]

I was reminded that my grandfather, then a candidate for Vice President, spoke here in Richmond exactly sixty years ago this week in the old Academy of Music. According to the newspaper account, the audience responded "enthusiastically" to his "exposure of the iniquities of the Republican tariff system," and he took his seat amid "deafening applause."

For the deafening applause his grandson is prepared to await the conclusion of his remarks, and meanwhile any reference to Republican iniquities will be wholly unintentional!

Here in Richmond tonight, in Virginia, rich both in history and in the knowledge of its history, I am moved to talk for a few minutes of the past.

This is not an idle task. We can chart our future clearly and wisely only when we know the path which has led to the present. A great American philosopher has said that those who can't remember the past are condemned to live it again.

The South is a good place to take our bearings, because in no part of the country does the past — a past of great nobility and great tragedy — more sharply etch the present than in the South. It is a good place to think of the grim problems of war and peace which weigh so heavily on all of us today. For here we can best learn the lessons suggested by the peace of 1865, made when the great voice of moderation had been stilled. (I have been privileged to live for four years in Springfield, Illinois, the home of Abraham Lincoln.) The victor's settlement permitted the South to keep its charm, its mockingbirds, and its beaten biscuits. For himself the victor retained only the money and the power.

It took the South decades to recover. During these bleak years, from 1865 to 1912, the Republican Party was constantly in power except for the two discontinuous terms of Grover Cleveland. In one of them my grandfather was privileged to serve as Vice President. And, again, between Woodrow Wilson and Franklin Roosevelt, the Republican Party had another long term of rule. The Democratic Party, therefore, had the dubious distinction of wandering in the desert for a longer time than the Children of Israel after their flight from Egypt.

For the South this period was a desert without an oasis. But, however hard it was to bear at the time, we in the more fortunate present can view it with a semblance of charity. For the Republican leadership did not neglect the South and other Democrats simply because you were Democrats. In its frozen impartiality it also neglected Republican

[117] The text is from *Major Campaign Speeches AES 1952*, pp. 149–156.

farmers, small businessmen and working people. Men earned the neglect of the Republican leaders not by their political affiliation, but by being small and poor. And this is why so many people have shifted to the Democratic Party.

The Republican leadership did not merely treat the South with arrogant and massive neglect. It did more. It shackled the South, and millions outside the South, through its control of Congress; its control of money and banking; its favoritism to powerful interests; its espousal of high tariffs, high interest rates and unfair freight rates.

In the larger sense you became colonials of an empire which, if it was not alien, was at least absentee. Yours was primarily an agricultural economy, depending for cash income largely on cotton and tobacco. Of these you produced far more than could be consumed at home.

You paid exorbitant rates of interest for mortgage and crop loans. Nobody consulted you about freight rates. You just paid them. Crops sold for what they would bring because farmers could not hold them for higher prices. Bitterly they witnessed prices rise only after their crops had gone out of their hands.

It is interesting to recall that more than half a century ago Southern and Western farmers pleaded for government warehouses where they could hold their crops for better prices in exchange for certificates at 80 per cent of the market value. The plan was denounced by Republican leaders as socialistic, a phrase they evidently never get tired of. But now, since the Democrats have enacted essentially the same plan, the Republicans approve enthusiastically. Indeed, bidding for the farm vote up in Minnesota the other day, the Republican candidate for President pulled the Democratic platform right out from under me!

But to return to the past. When you marketed your crops abroad, you sold in free markets for the going price. But when you bought manufactured goods at home, Republican tariffs compelled you to pay through the nose. You have been protesting this injustice since at least the year 1828.

Of course the Republican tariff wasn't all bad. It generously permitted Americans to worship at duty-free altars; eat from duty-free tin cans; import duty-free yachts; be hanged with duty-free rope; and admire duty-free paintings in museums.

The Republicans were still at their old game only a little while ago, and I wish we could be sure they would not return to it if they have a chance. Over the protest of over a thousand American economists, they enacted the Smoot-Hawley tariff that raised rates to an all-time high.[118]

118 The Smoot-Hawley Tariff Act raised duties on many items, in some cases setting duties on raw materials at fifty to one hundred per cent above 1922 levels. It

I need not tell Virginians, or your tobacco-growing and tobacco-processing neighbors, what that did to tobacco exports. Nor need I remind Southern cotton growers and cotton manufacturers how they were harmed; or say that this tariff was a turning point in precipitating the worldwide depression of the 1930's.

But I am not going to talk about the depression when the average yearly income of the families of one Southern state was $500. I have said — and I repeat — that I am not running against President Hoover. Indeed, I think all of us have reason to be grateful to him for the work of the Hoover Commission. And the fact of the matter is, I don't know who I am running against, but I strongly suspect it is Senator Taft after all.

But I most certainly am running against the unchanging and apparently unchangeable attitudes of the Republican leadership. Presidents come and go. But attitudes remain. For a political party, as a man, is the sum total of its inheritance, environment, experience and attitudes.

Thus, for example, when the depression was coming on, the Secretary of the Treasury was Andrew Mellon. What was his formula for dealing with the depression? How did he propose to act when the magnificent promise of American life seemed at a shabby and ignominious end? Mr. Hoover, in his recently published memoirs, tells us. It was: "Liquidate labor, liquidate stocks, liquidate the farmers, liquidate real estate." [119]

That is certainly one way to deal with a depression — the graveyard way. But somehow the American people were less than enthusiastic about it, and they turned to the Democratic Party which held out the prospect of life and hope.

The Democratic Party of today was born, then, of the sufferings of the people. It is neither all-wise nor all-knowing, for these are not man's gifts, but God's. But it is now — as it always has been — compassionate, merciful, humane; no stranger to human needs and wants and fears.

The task of striking off the shackles of the South, begun by Woodrow Wilson, has brought you to your rightful place in the Union, not as a matter of charity, not as a sectional matter, but because a happy, purposeful people in a strong, prosperous country is the democratic goal. The Southern states, too, it seems to me, have played a large part in liberating men's creative energies and reaching these goals.

Everywhere this liberation of man's powers during the Democratic decades has brilliantly succeeded, but nowhere has its success been more

---

was signed by President Hoover on June 17, 1930, despite objections by over a thousand economists, and by the end of the following year over twenty countries had initiated retaliatory measures.

[119] *The Great Depression, 1929–1941* (New York: Macmillan, 1952), p. 30.

marked than in the South. Here has come the richest flowering of a great region our nation has witnessed. A new vitality and creative energy is apparent in every aspect of Southern culture, material, intellectual and spiritual. Your colleges are crowded. There is a keen interest in the arts.

Some years ago a famous American critic said that the South was the wasteland of the mind. Yet at that very moment, I am told, so many of your housewives had novels simmering with the soup — among them *Gone with the Wind* — that many husbands had to wait for supper. And men — in an effort perhaps to keep up with their women, among them your own Ellen Glasgow — were writing books and plays, too. So it was that the Nobel Prize for Literature came to the Mississippian, William Faulkner, a prize that he accepted in an exalted address, extolling the unconquerable spirit of man.

If this means much to the nation, it also, I am sure, means much to you. Your way has often been hard. Yet you have always held that civilization is something more than the bending of the resources of nature to the uses of man. Man cannot live without bread, but his spirit cannot live by bread alone.

In the course of this resurgence, I hope that it may be possible for us to keep all that was good of the Old South, while embracing all that is good of the New South. Technicians can make a country, but they alone cannot create a civilization. There are riches in your inheritance which are sometimes overlooked — riches which the rest of the nation could borrow with great profit. I believe it was Gladstone who said that no greater misfortune could befall a people than to break utterly with its past.

Among the most valuable heritages of the Old South is its political genius, which in many respects was far ahead of its time. Even today some of the finest products of Southern governmental thought are only beginning to win the general acceptance which they have so long deserved.

A classic example, it seems to me, is the Constitution of the Confederacy. Scholars of constitutional law have long recognized it as a sound and most thoughtful document. It contained some brilliant innovations, including the so-called item veto — authorizing the President to disapprove individual items in an appropriation bill, without having to veto the entire measure.

This inspiration of the Confederate statesmen has since been incorporated into the constitutions of about three-fourths of our states, including my own state of Illinois.

Is it too much to hope that our Federal Government may soon adopt this priceless invention of Southern statesmanship? I hope not, because it is a most useful tool. It has enabled me to veto more appropriations, involving more money, than any Governor in Illinois history. And, by the way, forty-six other states had higher state tax burdens than Illinois in relation to the income of their citizens last year.

In other fields, I am glad to note, the Southern talent for government has won the recognition which is its due. Many of your states are among the best governed in the land. Southern diplomats have earned whole-hearted respect in Asia and Europe. In Congress Southern leaders once again give wise and distinguished service to the nation, especially in the all-important area of foreign affairs. I am proud to have one of them, Senator John Sparkman of Alabama, as my running mate. And I am also proud that other such leaders — each himself a candidate for the Presidency — have given me their support — Senator [Estes] Kefauver of Tennessee, and my distant kinsman, Senator Richard Russell of Georgia.

Just as the governmental contributions of the South sometimes were not fully appreciated in the past, so too, I suspect, some of the problems of the South have not been fully understood elsewhere. One of these is the problem of minorities — a problem which I have had occasion to think about a good deal, since my own state also has minority groups.

One thing that I have learned is that minority tensions are always strongest under conditions of hardship. During the long years of Republican neglect and exploitation, many Southerners — white and Negro — have suffered even hunger, the most degrading of man's adversities. All the South, in one degree or another, was afflicted with a pathetic lack of medical services, poor housing, poor schooling, and a hundred other ills flowing from the same source of poverty.

The once low economic status of the South was productive of another — and even more melancholy — phenomenon. Many of the lamentable differences between Southern whites and Negroes, ascribed by insensitive observers to race prejudice, have arisen for other reasons. Here economically depressed whites and economically depressed Negroes often had to fight over already gnawed bones. Then there ensued that most pathetic of struggles: the struggle of the poor against the poor. It is a struggle that can easily become embittered, for hunger has no heart. But, happily, as the economic status of the South has risen, as the farms flourish and in the towns there are jobs for all at good wages, racial tensions have diminished.

In the broad field of minority rights, the Democratic Party has stated its position in its platform, a position to which I adhere.[120] I should justly

[120] *"Civil Rights.* The Democratic Party is committed to support and advance the individual rights and liberties of all Americans.

"Our country is founded on the proposition that all men are created equal. This

earn your contempt if I talked one way in the South and another way elsewhere. Certainly no intellectually dishonest Presidential candidate could, by an alchemy of election, be converted into an honest President. I shall not go anywhere with beguiling serpent words. To paraphrase the words of Senator John Sharp Williams of Mississippi, better to be a dog and bay the moon.

I should like to say a word about the broader aspects of minority rights.

First, I utterly reject the argument that we ought to grant all men their rights just because if we do not we shall give Soviet Russia a propaganda weapon. This concept is itself tainted with communist wiliness. It insultingly implies that were it not for the communists we would not do what is right. The answer to this argument is that we must do right for right's sake alone. I, for one, do not propose to adjust my ethics to the values of a bloodstained despotism, scornful of all that we hold dear.

Second, I reject as equally contemptible the reckless assertions that the South is a prison in which half the people are prisoners and the other half are wardens. I view with scorn those who hurl charges that the South — or any group of Americans — is wedded to wrong and incapable of right. For this itself is an expression of prejudice compounded with hatred, a poisonous doctrine for which, I hope, there will never be room in our country.

---

means that all citizens are equal before the law and should enjoy equal political rights. They should have equal opportunities for education, for economic advancement, and for decent living conditions.

"We will continue our efforts to eradicate discrimination based on race, religion or national origin.

"We know this task requires action, not just in one section of the Nation, but in all sections. It requires the cooperative efforts of individual citizens and action by State and local governments. It also requires Federal action. The Federal Government must live up to the ideals of the Declaration of Independence and must exercise the powers vested in it by the Constitution.

"We are proud of the progress that has been made in securing equality of treatment and opportunity in the Nation's armed forces and the civil service and all areas under Federal jurisdiction. The Department of Justice has taken an important part in successfully arguing in the courts for the elimination of many illegal discriminations, including those involving rights to own and use real property, to engage in gainful occupations and to enroll in publicly supported higher educational institutions. We are determined that the Federal Government shall continue such policies.

"At the same time, we favor Federal legislation effectively to secure these rights to everyone: (1) the right to equal opportunity for employment; (2) the right to security of persons; (3) the right to full and equal participation in the Nation's political life, free from arbitrary restraints. We also favor legislation to perfect existing Federal civil rights statutes and to strengthen the administrative machinery for the protection of civil rights."

Official Report of the Proceedings of the Democratic National Convention, July 21–26, 1952 (Washington: Democratic National Committee, 1952), pp. 274–275.

So long as man remains a little lower than the angels, I suppose that human character will never free itself entirely from the blemish of prejudice, religious or racial. These are prejudices, unhappily, that tend to rise wherever the minority in question is large, running here against one group and there against another. Some forget this, and, in talking of the South, forget that in the South the minority is high. Some forget, too, or don't know about strides the South has made in the past decade toward equal treatment.

But I do not attempt to justify the unjustifiable, whether it is anti-Negroism in one place, anti-Semitism in another — or for that matter, anti-Southernism in many places. And neither can I justify self-righteousness anywhere. Let none of us be smug on this score, for nowhere in the nation have we come to that state of harmonious amity between racial and religious groups to which we aspire.

The political abuse of the problem of discrimination in employment, the exploitation of racial aspirations on the one hand and racial prejudice on the other — all for votes — is both a dangerous thing and a revolting spectacle in our political life. It will always be better to reason together than to hurl recriminations at one another.

Our best lesson on reason and charity was read to us by Robert E. Lee. It was not the least of his great contributions to the spirit of America that, when he laid down his sword, he became president of a small college in Lexington — now the splendid Washington and Lee University. There he remained the rest of his life; unifying, not dividing; loving, not hating.

As the autumn of 1865 was coming on, General Lee, in one of the noblest of American utterances, said: "The war being at an end, the Southern states having laid down their arms, and the questions at issue between them and the Northern states having been decided, I believe it to be the duty of everyone to unite in the restoration of the country and the re-establishment of peace and harmony . . ." Later he said: "I know of no surer way of eliciting truth than by burying contention with the war."

We have great need of Lee's spirit in this hour of peril to our country, when voices of hatred and unreason arise again in our land. As free men we shall always, I hope, differ upon many things. But I also hope that we shall never be divided upon those concepts that are enshrined in our religious faith and the charters of our country's greatness.

No one could stand here in Richmond without reverence for those great Virginians — Washington, whose sturdy common sense was the mortar of our foundations, and Jefferson, that universal genius who, proclaiming the Rights of Man when few men had any rights anywhere, shook the earth and made this feeble country the hope of the oppressed everywhere. And so it is today after nearly two centuries.

Fortunately for us all, the Southern political genius still lives. It flamed not long ago in Woodrow Wilson. It burns steadily today among Southern members of Congress, and among many of the leaders of your states.

Good politics make good government. In this campaign I shall not try to minimize the tasks which we confront. That we shall pass through these troubled times I am sure, not by grace alone, but by faith, intelligence and implacable determination.

In my travels about the country of late in quest of your confidence I have felt that determination, that indomitable spirit. But nowhere more than here where I suspect it is as strong today as it was in the spring of 1865, when the Army of Northern Virginia returned to their homes. They found a wasteland of burned houses and barns, fences fallen and ditches caved in, weeds, and sorrow brooding over the fields.

That was in April. But by June a crop was growing. The next year the crop was larger, and the next year it was still larger, and so, painfully and slowly, with no help except their hands and the benison of God, the South started on its long march from desolation to fruitfulness.

This is part of your great heritage. And if I could speak for all Americans as I now do for myself, I would say that it also is part of the great heritage of America.

On Governor Stevenson's return to Springfield from his campaign trip, a letter from President Harold W. Dodds of Princeton University was awaiting him. Dodds wrote: "The University bathes in your reflected glory and is proud of its son who represents such high ideals of political responsibility and leadership qualities." He added that he had just returned from the peace and quiet of Nova Scotia.

To Harold W. Dodds

September 24, 1952

Dear Harold:

I was delighted to find your letter on my return from my weary journey. You should not have mentioned that remote spot in Nova Scotia. I shall dream about it all night.

I am so grateful for your flattering and heartening comments. If I can perform in the Princeton tradition it will be my reward — win or lose.

Cordially yours,

Mrs. Eugenie Anderson, ambassador to Denmark, wrote Stevenson on September 15: "You may have heard already from others abroad, but I can assure you that you are making an extremely favorable and reassuring impression on our friends here in Europe. If they could vote in our elections — as they sometimes wish they could — I am sure you would receive a West-European landslide!"

To Eugenie Anderson

September 24, 1952

My dear Mrs. Anderson:

I am so grateful for your very thoughtful and encouraging letter. It is a pity we can't use some of those good Democratic precincts in Western Europe!

With all good wishes, I am

Sincerely yours,

To Arthur M. Schlesinger, Jr.[121]

September 25, 1952

Mr. Schlesinger —

For Pete's sake pls. [please] tell the writers to cut down on the *attack* stuff.

On September 26, Stevenson campaigned in Indiana and praised his friend Governor Henry F. Schricker, who was campaigning for the United States Senate. On September 27, he spoke at Memorial Auditorium in Louisville, Kentucky.

KOREA [122]

While I feel very much the uncomfortable politician trying to beguile your votes here tonight, I do not feel at all like a stranger in Kentucky.

My great-great-grandfather and great-great-grandmother were married here in Kentucky. In fact some historians say that their marriage is the first recorded marriage in Kentucky. They built a home near Danville more than 150 years ago which is still standing.

My Grandfather Stevenson was born here before his parents moved to

121 This handwritten memorandum is in the Schlesinger papers, John F. Kennedy Library.
122 The text is from *Major Campaign Speeches AES 1952*, pp. 181–188.

Illinois 100 years ago this year. He was a student at Centre College where he fell in love with the President's daughter — always a sound policy for a struggling student — and thus I acquired a Kentucky grandmother also.

So you will forgive me, I hope, if I claim a very close kinship to Kentucky. But if that's not enough, I'll also claim kinship with Alben Barkley — the greatest Kentuckian of them all.

And I also have Kentucky to thank not only for my ancestors but also for Wilson Wyatt — once the Mayor of this great city and now my campaign manager.

So, my fellow Kentuckians, I want to talk to you tonight about the war in Korea.

When I entered this campaign, I expressed my hope that Democrats and Republicans alike would regard this election year as a great opportunity to educate and elevate a people whose destiny is leadership. I hoped that both parties would talk sense to the American people.

But I have been increasingly disturbed about the tone and spirit of the campaign.

Last Monday the General spoke in Cincinnati about Korea.[123] He said that this was a "solemn subject" and that he was going to state the truth as he knew it, "the truth — plain and unvarnished." If only his speech had measured up to this introduction! And since he has tried, not once but several times, to make a vote-getting issue out of our ordeal in Korea, I shall speak on this subject and address myself to the record.

We are fighting in Korea, the General declares, because the American Government grossly underestimated the Soviet threat; because the Government allowed America to become weak; because American weakness compelled us to withdraw our forces from Korea; because we abandoned China to the communists; and, finally, because we announced to all the world that we had written off most of the Far East.

That's what he says — now let's look at the record.

First, the General accuses the Government of having underestimated the Soviet threat. But what about the General himself? At the end of the war he was a professional soldier of great influence and prestige, to whom the American people listened with respect. What did he have to say about the Soviet threat? In the years after the war, the General himself saw "no reason" — as he later wrote — why the Russian system of government and Western democracy "could not live side by side in the world." In November, 1945, he even told the House Military Affairs Committee: "Nothing guides Russian policy so much as a desire for friendship with the United States."

[123] For the text of Eisenhower's speech, see the New York *Times*, September 23, 1952.

I have no wish to blow any trumpets here. But in March, 1946, I said: "We must forsake any hope that the Soviet Union is going to lie still and lick her awful wounds. She's not. Peace treaties that reflect her legitimate demands, friendly governments on her frontiers and an effective United Nations Organization should be sufficient security. But evidently they are not and she intends to advance her aims, many of them objectives of the Czars, to the utmost."

My opponent's next point is the question of demobilization. We know how self-righteous the Republican office seekers are on this question today. But what were they saying at the time? In the 1944 campaign, the Republican candidate of that year accused President Roosevelt of deliberately delaying demobilization and promised that the Republicans would do it quicker. "I believe," he said, "that our members of the armed forces should be transported home and released at the earliest practical moment after victory." Although the General warned against too rapid demobilization, he later said — in September, 1946 — that: "Frankly, I don't think demobilization was too fast."

Demobilization did go too far and too fast. But it would have gone farther and faster if the Republicans had been in power — and it is nonsense to pretend otherwise.

Next, take the question of the withdrawal of American forces from Korea. The General acts as if this were the result of some secret White House decision. I would call his attention to the fact that while he was Chief of Staff of the United States Army, the Chiefs of Staff advised that South Korea was of little strategic interest to the United States, and recommended withdrawal of the United States forces from the country.

Next, my distinguished opponent has recently begun to parrot the charge of some of his recently acquired political tutors that the administration abandoned China to the communists.[124] He did not talk this way once; but then he has changed in a good many respects of late. Maybe he's competing for the title of Mr. Republican as well as Mr. President. But he still must know in his heart, even if he does not choose to admit it, that in the past six years nothing except the sending of an American expeditionary force to China could have prevented ultimate communist victory. Did he propose that; did any of the Sunday-morning quarterbacks on the Republican team propose that?

Distinguished American military men — including at least one Republican — have testified that the Chinese Nationalists did not lose for want of supplies or American support. Their armies were larger and better

---

[124] For a discussion of this attack, which had been growing during the past three years, see Walter Johnson, *1600 Pennsylvania Avenue: Presidents and the People Since 1929* (Boston: Little, Brown, 1960), chapters 28 and 29.

equipped than the communist armies. They had every physical advantage.

Has my opponent forgotten the wise words of the most responsible Republican of them all, Senator [Arthur] Vandenberg? Here is what Senator Vandenberg said in December, 1948, on this subject of China.

"The vital importance of saving China cannot be exaggerated. But there are limits to our resources and boundaries to our miracles . . . I am forced to say that the Nationalist Government has failed to reform itself in a fashion calculated to deserve continued popular confidence over there or over here . . . If we made ourselves responsible for the army of the Nationalist Government, we would be in the China war for keeps and the responsibility would be ours instead of hers. I am very sure that this would jeopardize our own national security beyond any possibility of justification."

So spoke Senator Vandenberg and his view was shared by intelligent and responsible men in both parties. Now who talked sense about China: Senator Vandenberg or the General?

Then there is the question of "writing off" Korea. The General condemns the Secretary of State's excluding Korea from our defense perimeter in 1950.[125] But the General fails to point out that this defense perimeter was a line developed by the military authorities themselves. Surely it is a gross and discreditable distortion to say that the Secretary of State took the lead in this matter. Twice in 1949 General MacArthur, then our top commander in the Pacific, defined our defense perimeter in the terms later used by the Secretary of State. It was on the recommendation of our military authorities that Korea and Formosa and mainland areas were not included in a direct military commitment.

And I am, frankly, astonished that my great opponent stooped at Cincinnati last week to the practice of lifting remarks out of context. Why did he quote only a part of what the Secretary of State said — why did he skip the Secretary's pledge that, if there should be an attack on these countries, "the initial reliance must be on the people attacked to resist, and then upon the commitments of the entire civilized world under the Charter of the United Nations"? [126] The United States Government thus clearly announced its determination to seek United Nations action against aggression. And that's exactly what we did.

The true significance of the Secretary's remark, therefore, is that the military situation made it necessary for him to do what he could diplomatically to give some assurance of our interest in the security of the

[125] On January 12, 1950, Secretary of State Dean Acheson had spoken of the "defense perimeter" of the United States in the Pacific and described it as running from the Aleutian Islands to Japan to Okinawa to the Philippines. New York *Times,* January 13, 1950.

[126] Ibid.

Republic of Korea. Why does the General not only skip this but distort the whole meaning of these developments? And how does he honestly square this campaign-time charge of writing off Korea with his own statement in July, 1950, that "when our Government guaranteed the Government of South Korea, there was no recourse but to do what President Truman said and did."

I deeply regret the necessity for this recital. I was prepared to ignore the political license and false charges of extremists and reactionaries. But I cannot ignore them now when they are uttered by the Republican nominee himself, a man personally identified with and presumed to be intimately informed about the recent course of our foreign affairs.

Nor do I list these mistakes in judgment and errors of prediction in order to lay any personal blame on the General. I would never have brought these things up had he not pointed the accusing finger. Many Americans of both parties made the same mistakes. Better we refrain from competing in denouncing each other in a scramble for votes, admit our common mistakes — and get on with our business.

Let's talk sense. Let's admit that mistakes were made. America did demobilize too rapidly and too severely. America did allow the Russians to develop an undue superiority in conventional arms and in ground forces. Perhaps this country should have given a direct military guarantee to the Republic of Korea. And it might well have been wiser if American forces had not crossed the 38th parallel in the fall of 1950.

There is another curious example of my opponent's uncertainty that is worth noting.

At Abilene, Kansas, on June 5th, shortly after his return to this country, he said that: "There has been built up behind the Yalu River a very definite air strength that would make very dangerous any attempt to extend the war at this moment, until we have a bigger build-up of our own."

Three months later the General says this: "I have always stood behind General MacArthur in bombing those bases on the Yalu from which fighter planes are coming . . ."

What kind of straddle is this? On one occasion he is against bombing across the river. And a little later he is for it. I confess I am bewildered.

This seems to me to be too serious a matter for such wandering opinions.

But enough about the past, and even about the past inconsistencies of my opponent. I have always agreed with Winston Churchill that if the present tries to sit in judgment on the past, it will lose the future. The important thing is to draw the right lessons from the past and to get on with the job.

One lesson which I had hoped that most of us had learned from the past is an understanding of what the present threat to our freedom really is. I thought that my distinguished opponent, of all Americans, would agree that this threat is the threat of world communism.

But it develops that he has now adopted the theory of Senator Taft, who unsmilingly states that the greatest threat to liberty today is the cost of our own Federal Government!

It is surely fundamental to the making of wise policies to decide whether the threat to the United States is internal or external. Either the threat to our security is world communism or it is not.

This is surely more than the "differences of degree" which, according to Senator Taft's statement following the peace conference on Morningside Heights, are all that separate him from the General on foreign policy matters. It is not a question of degree whether we measure our defense by an arbitrary budget or measure our budget by the needs of survival.

If we should follow out this theory that the threat is internal, we would undertake the deliberate and systematic weakening of ourselves and our allies. And such a policy of national weakness and international weakness can lead to a single result: that is, to invite the expansion of Soviet power.

By adopting this theory, the Republican candidate has reversed the advice of Theodore Roosevelt to speak softly and carry a big stick. The new advice is to talk tough and carry a twig.

You saw this policy proposed a year ago for Asia when some Republicans wanted at one and the same time to cut the defense budget and expand the war. Now you see it proposed again for Europe by those isolationists who would reduce our aid to our allies and our own defense appropriations and simultaneously speak with "cold finality" to the Soviet Union. This is the policy of tougher words backed up with smaller armies.

I wonder if the General realizes the full implications of the agreed statement issued by Senator Taft. Senator Taft has evidently reassured him by saying that their differences in foreign policy are just differences in degree.

Differences of degree, indeed!

Is it a difference of degree to be for or against the North Atlantic Treaty?

Is it a difference of degree to blame the Korean War on Stalin or on our own President?

Is it a difference of degree to be for or against the strengthening of our allies?

Such differences of degree may well turn out to be the difference between success and disaster — between peace and war.

Tough talk about communism will not deter the Soviet Union from new adventures. The thing which will save the world from war is American strength, and real strength need not be loud or belligerent. Nor is it just a matter of our national strength alone. It is equally the strength of the free world — the strength of the nations which stand between us and the Soviet Union.

Strength is the road to peace. Weakness is the road to war. This is the simple truth of peace and war in our times. The Democratic Party has been consistently the party of strength — and thus the party of peace. With equal consistency, the opposition has been the party of weakness — the party which persists in the dreary obsession that we must fear above all, not the Kremlin, but our own Government. And as the party of weakness, it gives evidence of pursuing, once in power, a policy of weakness which would demoralize the free world, embolden the Soviet Union to new military adventures, and, in the end, pull down the world into the rubble and chaos of a third world war.

Let's talk sense to the American people. Peace is far more important than who wins this election. Whichever party wins, the American people must be sure to win. Let us not place victory in a political campaign ahead of national interest.

And let's talk sense about what we have gained by our determination, our expenditures, and our valor in Korea.

We have not merely said, we have proven, that communism can go no further unless it is willing to risk world war.

We have proven to all the peoples of the Far East that communism is not the wave of the future, that it can be stopped.

We have helped to save the peoples of Indo-China from communist conquest.

We have smashed the threat to Japan through Korea and so have strengthened this friend and ally.

We have discouraged the Chinese communists from striking at Formosa.

We have mightily strengthened our defenses and all our defensive positions around the world.

We have trained and equipped a large army of South Koreans, who can assume a growing share of the defense of their country.

We have blocked the road to communist domination of the Far East and frustrated the creation of a position of power which would have threatened the whole world.

We have asserted, and we shall maintain it, that whenever communist soldiers choose freedom after falling into our hands, they are free.

We have kept faith with our solemn obligations.

These are the values won by the fidelity and prowess and the sacrifices of young men and women who serve their country. We have lost many of our beloved sons. All Americans share in the bereavement of so many mothers, and fathers, of wives and sweethearts. The burden lies heavily on us all. We pray God that the sacrifices and the sorrows will soon end.

I would say one thing more about the great debate over our foreign policy. My opponents say the threat to our liberty comes from within.

I say that the threat comes from without — and I offer the fate of the enslaved peoples of the world as my evidence.

My opponents say America cannot afford to be strong.

I say that America cannot afford to be weak.

I promise no easy solutions, no relief from burdens and anxieties, for to do this would be not only dishonest; it would be to attack the foundations of our greatness.

I can offer something infinitely better: an opportunity to work and sacrifice that freedom may flourish. For, as William James truly said, "When we touch our own upper limit and live in our own highest center of energy, we may call ourselves saved."

I call upon America to reject the new isolationism and to surpass her own glorious achievements. Then we may, with God's help, deserve to call ourselves the sons of our fathers.

On September 23, the day that Senator Richard M. Nixon went on television and radio to explain the "Nixon Fund," Kent Chandler, former mayor of Lake Forest, Illinois, and vice chairman of the A. B. Dick Company, sent a telegram to Stevenson asking how the fund he had as governor differed from the Nixon fund. Chandler also demanded that the names of donors and recipients be made public.[127] The names of the donors, the amount of each gift, and the names of the recipients were released to the press on September 27.[128] The next day the New York Times *printed the information in full. Stevenson also released to the press copies of his income tax returns going back as far as 1942.*

On September 29, Stevenson spoke about the fund over radio and television from Chicago.

[127] The editors discussed the fund in *The Papers of Adlai E. Stevenson*, Vol. III, pp. 9–10; see also pp. 303–304. The fund was not secret. The money went largely to supplement the low state salaries of a number of able people whom Stevenson persuaded to take official positions to help him improve the government of Illinois.

[128] See memorandum by Robert W. Notti, "The Stevenson Fund," December 2, 1966. A copy is in the possession of the editors. See also Arthur Edward Rowse, *Slanted News: A Case Study of the Nixon and Stevenson Fund Stories* (Boston: Beacon Press, 1957).

FIRST FIRESIDE SPEECH [129]

I am grateful to the Volunteers for Stevenson for affording me this opportunity to visit you in your homes as nearly as may be — perhaps I should say returning your visit, because so many of you were good enough to come out to see me during my recent travels around the country.

First let me say that I suppose some of you have been curious about the presents that I have given some of my associates as Governor of Illinois. I am frank to say, immodestly perhaps, that I am very proud of what we have accomplished in the state government of Illinois in these past four years. Most of the daily newspapers of this state — preponderantly Republican, of course — who have followed our work in Springfield, have expressed their approval. I cannot, much as I should like to, detail everything that has been done in Illinois during these past four years, but I should have no reluctance in matching our reforms and our progress in all of our state services in the same interval with any other state in the Union. While running for President I shall not deprecate my opponent's great services to his country as some Republican governors are now attempting to deprecate what we have accomplished in the State of Illinois. I am content with the record, and I am beholden for it to men of both parties whom I induced to work for the State of Illinois when I came into office.

In my inaugural speech in January, 1949, I said: "It is obvious to all that many of the senior positions in the state's service do not pay enough to support, let alone attract, the quality of management and leadership these positions demand and the people deserve, except upon a basis of unselfish sacrifice. And too often, as many have noted, the reward for sacrifice in public service is not gratitude in lieu of dollars but abuse, criticism and ingratitude.

"Government cannot, will not and should not attempt to match the salary scales of private business, but government can and must, if it is to be good government, pay salaries which are not an invitation to carelessness, indolence, or even worse, corruption."

Some of the men I brought into the state government did so at great financial sacrifice. Pending better salaries, I made gifts of money to a few of these men on my immediate staff from political contributions. At least four of these men, while serving me in Springfield, have had offers in private employment of double or more their state salaries. Some have had financial worries known to me. None ever asked me for help, and

129 The text is from *Major Campaign Speeches AES 1952*, pp. 189–198.

none could have been improperly influenced by these gifts, because I gave them and I appointed them to their jobs and I could have discharged them at any time. Two of them have left the state service long since — one to become vice-president of the Federal Reserve Bank of Chicago, and the other is now a justice of the Illinois State Supreme Court.[130]

I do not consider this public curiosity either a smear or a Republican plot. It was never a secret. Indeed, I discussed the difficulty of getting competent people into state service frequently and publicly. Actually I think the public interest in the compensation of government servants is very healthy. It is a problem that perplexes everyone who holds major public responsibility in either elective or appointive positions. I am glad that I have been of some help to a few of the people who have been of tireless help to me in a job of great difficulty to which I have given everything that is in me for the past four years. To attract and employ better people in state government is never easy. It has been my greatest satisfaction in Illinois. You will only get good government from good people. But I have no brief for the means I used except that I had no other. If it is wrong to give money to people in appointive jobs which could not influence them, then it must be wrong to give money to people running for elective office which *could* influence them. Yet, we give political contributions to candidates every day in the week.

It is no simple question. But I hope I have not discouraged anyone from contributing to the Democratic Party! However distasteful, public service makes you public property, and I have long felt that candidates for high office should make a full disclosure of their personal finances so that there can be no misgivings about their connections and independence. But it should be possible to do this through some confidential means without invading a man's legitimate privacy. No such machinery being available to me, I have made my income tax returns for the past ten years public, and Senator Sparkman, my running mate, will provide similar information. Actually, as few people seem to realize, President Truman proposed more than a year ago in a message to the Congress that high officials in all branches of government should place on record each year full information concerning their income from all sources as a step toward insuring the integrity of public service and protecting government officials against false charges.

But I don't want, and must not spend all evening talking about the intricate and all-important problem of getting better men into govern-

---

[130] George Mitchell served under Stevenson as director of finance. He became vice president of the Federal Reserve Bank of Chicago in 1951. Walter V. Schaefer, who was Stevenson's administrative assistant in 1949, was elected to the Illinois Supreme Court in 1951.

ment service. To get back to the campaign and to your choice for President and Vice President in this fateful year. I have traveled now through some twenty states from coast to coast. I have expressed my views as clearly as I could on a great variety of public questions, not that I am confident that my views are always right, or that I am particularly wise, but because I think you are entitled to know what my views are. I could not expect everyone to agree with everything — and there are many who say that too much candor is a dangerous way to campaign — that it is better to talk in generalities, capitalize [on] discontents and leave solutions cloudy or uncertain. But I said when I accepted the Democratic nomination in Chicago that it would be better to lose the election than to mislead the people. So, I have talked about the cost of living, labor problems, farm policy, conservation — about civil rights, corruption, and economy in government, and about the overshadowing issues of war and peace.

I have expressed my views as best I could. I have done the best I could to keep my promise to talk sense to the American people. I had hoped that my opponent would also state his position on the issues so that we could debate them out in the American way. But he has chosen instead to insist that he and his running mate are the only candidates of sufficient integrity to assure the nation clean government during the next four years. I think that the object of opening the mind, as of opening the mouth, is to shut it again on something solid. But what the General now believes on most of the big questions that trouble us, I do not know. There is one exception, however — agriculture — where the General has jumped off of his platform onto ours. But he knows that the Republicans in Congress won't follow him.

While talking a lot during this past month, I have also done some listening, and some reading from the thousands of letters that come to me. Among things that evidently trouble people most seem to be these four questions: Korea; how serious is the communist danger in this country; is our prosperity in danger; and how can we get the highest integrity and efficiency in government. Now let us work backward up this list.

A number of people have written in to ask, in effect: "You and your Republican opponent both say that you will give us an honest administration. How do we know?" It is a fair question. One kind of answer comes from a lawyer in Kansas who fills five pages of single-space typewriting indicting the graft, the thievery and the corruption under state and national Republican administrations during his lifetime. Everything he says is true, but this is not answer enough. No approach to the problem of corruption in government is good enough if it ignores the deeper problem of corruption in men — of men. We do not say that a bank is corrupt because the cashier embezzles. The problem of corruption — of graft, in its simplest form — is a problem of individual morals, public and private.

Behind every crooked tax collector is a crooked taxpayer. Although I have done so before, and on many occasions, I think this topic is evidently important enough to talk about it again at length, and I propose to do so. In that speech I will outline some ideas for a program of action. Tonight I would only remind you that the Democratic Party is the party of Senator [Estes] Kefauver, Senator [Paul H.] Douglas, Senator [J. W.] Fulbright, Congressman [Frank] Chelf of Kentucky, Congressman [Cecil] King of California — men who have distinguished themselves in the fight against evil in and out of government. With the help of men like these, and many more like them, I have no doubt that we can keep the Federal service clean.

Now I want to turn to the question of whether this country is heading for runaway inflation, or for depression, or whether we can look forward to a continuation of the prosperity we have been enjoying for some years.

Driving through Connecticut the other day, an older man came close to the car and said to me this: "Why don't you just tell people how good they have it and how bad it used to be?" And a little later, as we passed a mill town a man waved one of those home-made signs you see so often, reading, "If you can't stand prosperity, vote Republican."

There has been a real temptation to base this campaign on the plain and pleasant fact that the Democratic party has been in control of this nation and has led it out of an awful depression into the greatest prosperity it has ever known, and through a world-shattering war and a great wave of social reform. It is a great temptation to point out that the Republican leadership has opposed us almost every step of the way. And now, while adopting everything and proposing to repeal nothing, at least publicly, their orators still sneer at everything we now have and shout about socialism. They call our lives of pride and dignity, "cradle-to-the-grave rides through the welfare state."

Moreover, the Republican candidate has agreed to agree on all domestic matters with the Republican Old Guard. I don't know whether the Old Guard would take it away if they could, but I do know, on the basis of the record of the past twenty years, that if they had been in the saddle they would never have had it to take away.

I think we can keep production and employment high in this country, and I think we can and must arrest inflation — the rising prices which make it so difficult for many.

In Baltimore last week I outlined a program to stop inflation — a pay-as-you-go tax policy for the Government; the strictest possible control of all government expenditures; restraints upon excessive private borrowing;

and closing the loopholes in the present wage-and-price controls if these other measures don't work. I think if we have the guts to do it, this program will do the job. But it will be carried out only if you send to Congress men and women who have the courage to force through these measures over stubborn opposition. We will stop rising prices and wages which just eat each other up if you will do your part. We have laid out the lines of defense and you must support them if you really mean business about these rising costs of living.

Now, about the questions regarding communism, especially communists in government, I think I will devote a whole speech to this, perhaps next week, but I will give you a brief answer right now. These mortal enemies cannot be permitted to get close to the bloodstreams of America, particularly its Government. I don't believe oaths and affidavits are much good, for a real communist never hesitates to lie, nor is catching and punishing communists after their treachery enough to end the hazard.

I think generally that close screening of government employes and the quiet professional work of the F.B.I. is the best way to turn over every stone in this country to see what lies beneath it. This is a job for professionals, and I think it can be done without slandering innocent people. I distrust those who have made political capital out of broadside charges discrediting hundreds of loyal government employes. I do not believe that we can jettison our processes of justice without endangering freedom for every American.

Beyond this I say to you that the battle against communism in America is an infinitely tougher and harder battle than most of the Republican leaders have ever admitted or evidently even understood. Why is it that these politicians that scream loudest about communism in America have fought hardest against every Democratic program to fight communism itself? They criticize our efforts to block the communist invasion of Korea. They have opposed our efforts to make the people of Europe and of Asia secure enough to reject the false gospels. They have opposed making the people of America secure enough so that they will never turn again, as some did in the thirties, to the false prophets.

The F.B.I. figures show that we have in this country now only a fraction of the communists we had twenty years ago. The point is that we have got to fight communism, not just communists. We have got to see to it that the soil is so healthy that communism just can't grow and survive in it, and that means the creative and constructive work of assuring good jobs, decent homes, good education and free political institutions.

These are some of the things I should like to talk about further. Finally, now, peace and war. You know the kind of letters I receive;

so many of you have written me about Korea and about your soldier sons. Every one of us knows in his heart why we have to stand up and fight in Korea. We all know that when the communists attacked across the 38th parallel that was the testing point for freedom throughout the world. The men in the Kremlin thought that they would be unopposed, and if they were, the whole question of the future could be settled in one blow. If they had been allowed to conquer free people in Korea, they could have picked away at the free world and engulfed more millions, piece by piece, one by one. Sooner or later we would have had to fight, and the later we made our stand, the bigger and the harder the war would have been. Stopping the enemy in Korea before Japan was threatened and before East Asia with all of its resources of manpower, rubber, tin, oil, etc., fell to the communists was received with enthusiastic shouts of approval by the majority of the American people and even by the Republican leadership.

Now, however, they attempt to make you believe that it was almost an act of treason, but what do you think they would be saying now if we had not stopped the enemy in Korea, if Japan was threatened and if East Asia was falling bit by bit to the enemy? Would they not be saying now that Harry Truman and Joseph Stalin were boyhood friends in Outer Mongolia?

And another thing the Republican leadership is now telling us is that the danger to this nation is from within, not from without; the danger lies not with Moscow but in Washington; your enemy is not Joseph Stalin but Harry Truman — or even possibly Adlai Stevenson.

A campaign addressed not to men's minds and to their best instincts, but to their passions, emotions and prejudices, is unworthy at best. Now, with the fate of the nation at stake, it is unbearable; with the darkest evil, the mightiest force ever gathered on earth arrayed against us and our friends, this is no time for such talk. It is not for me to stand in judgment upon the men who pilfer truth and say such things, but for your sake and for mine — for the sake of my sons and your children, and the future of millions of our friends overseas, and the future of our nation, and for those who languish imprisoned behind the Iron Curtain — we must know the truth and come to grips with the facts of life, look them in the face and stare them down, and in so doing, triumph over them.

We are not, I take it, a race of whimpering adolescents who can't face the truth, but a race of men and women, proud, courageous and unafraid. I shall state the facts as they appear to me from some years of experience, not only in domestic affairs but in foreign affairs. The Republican leadership blows thin drafts of crafty words down your neck, but it fails to tell you the following things.

Eighty-five per cent of the Federal budget goes for past wars and for preserving our present and our future liberty. The world has been at war almost continuously now for forty years. The intervals between the wars grow shorter; the wars increase in dimension and in destructiveness. The last war was man's first true world war. The revolutions of our times are manifold revolutions; their flames burn from one end of the globe to the other. The intercontinental airplane makes counties of continents; it makes lakes of oceans. In the words of the song, "There is no hiding place down there." Much of mankind is changing its entire outlook upon the world; whatever was, is cast out; whatever is, is questioned. Mankind and its hundreds of millions is on the march, toward what goal and with what destruction on the way no man can foretell. Whole nations have sunk out of sight behind iron curtains; whole peoples have disappeared from view.

Today there is less communication between great groups of men than there was in the roadless world of a thousand years ago. We can no more communicate with half of mankind than we can raise the dead. The while the anti-Christ stalks our world. Organized communism seeks even to dethrone God from his central place in the Universe. It attempts to up-root everywhere it goes the gentle and restraining influences of the religion of love and peace. One by one the lamps of civilization go out and nameless horrors are perpetrated in darkness. All this is done by an enemy of a kind that we have never faced before. He is primitive but he is also advanced. He goes with a piece of black bread in his hand, but in his mind he carries the awful knowledge of atomic energy. He is careful, cool, calculating, and he counts time, not impatiently as we do, not by the clock, but by decades, in terms of centuries. Much of what he is trying to do today his ancestors were attempting to do four hundred years ago.

The problems of a tortured, convulsive humanity stagger the nation. Unprecedented times demand of us unprecedented behavior. The task that confronts us will try our souls. It will exact a high price in discipline of mind and in austerity of spirit. It will determine whether we are worthy of our high place in the world, whether we are worthy of our forefathers who converted a wilderness into a country, fair and free, and left to us all the riches, material and spiritual, that they wrought in pain.

Long ago we asserted a great principle on this continent: that men are, and of right ought to be, free. Now we are called upon to defend that right against the mightiest forces of evil ever assembled under the sun.

This is a time to think, a time to feel, a time to pray. We shall need all of the resources of the stubborn mind, the stout heart, the soul refreshed, in the task that confronts us.

It is the most awesome task that any people has ever faced. For we are become the leader and mainstay of one great wing of humanity in conflict with another wing of humanity. As such, we must play the principal part in saving ourselves, our friends, and our civilization.

Whose task is this? It is inescapably your task. You and you alone will decide the fate of your family and your country for decades to come. You will decide whether you are to be slaves or free — to live gloriously or perish miserably. You may seek comfort at the feet of false leaders who, like medicine doctors, beat drums to ward off evil spirits. You may listen to false leaders who tell you that there is an easy way; that all you have to do is elect them and thereafter relax in a tax-free paradise — the political equivalent of sending ten cents to cover the cost of postage. You may, fearing to face the facts squarely, be distracted by phony issues that have no bearing upon the life-and-death controversy of our times. But, so deluded, you run the risk of being beguiled to destruction, for there is no easy way.

What is the lesson of history and of all human experience? What is the primary law of life? You struggle and you survive — you fail to struggle and you perish. The ways of the world are marked with the bones of peoples who hesitated.

Your salvation is in your own hands; in the stubbornness of your minds, the tenacity of your hearts, and such blessings as God, sorely tried by His children, shall give us. Nature is indifferent to the survival of the human species, including Americans. She does not weep over those who fall by the way.

I repeat, then, that the task is yours. Yours is a democracy. Its Government cannot be stronger or more tough-minded than its people. It cannot be more inflexibly committed to the task than they. It cannot be wiser than the people. As citizens of this democracy you are the rulers and the ruled — the law-givers and the law-abiders — the beginning and the end. Democracy is a high privilege. But it is also a heavy responsibility whose shadow stalks you although you may never walk in the sun.

I say these things to you not only because I believe them to be true, but also because, as you love your country, I love my country and I would see it endure and grow in light and become a living testament to all mankind of goodness and of mercy and of wisdom.

If telling you the truth about the world as I see it should cause you to cast me down, and revile me, and with me the Democratic Party, I should still tell you the truth as I see it. For no office within your gift — including the Presidency itself — is worth the price of deception.

I say we must know the truth, for the truth alone will make us free. What American is content to chew the cud of comfort in fancied security?

What American — I ask you — blessed as no other man in history, would blind himself to the ancient wisdom; the wisdom which tells us that much shall be asked of him to whom much is given? [131]

How long can we keep up the fight against the monster tyranny? How long can we keep on fighting in Korea; paying high taxes; helping others to help ourselves? There is only one answer. We can keep it up as long as we have to — and we will.

That is why we cannot lose, and will pass from darkness to the dawn of a brighter day than even this thrice-blessed land of ours has ever known.

To Hermon D. Smith [132]

September 30, 1952

Dear Dutch:

What with all your work and all your loyalty and encouragement these many years, I now find you have also contributed most generously. I am beginning to feel like a dreadful nuisance to my friends, and most of all to you. I wish I thought there was some way to repay such friendship.

Yours,

ADLAI

To John S. Battle

September 30, 1952

Dear Governor:

I am mortified that I have not had an opportunity prior to this to thank you and Mrs. Battle for your extraordinary hospitality in Richmond. It was a memorable day for me and the best of it was a chance to see you both again in your charming home. Somehow I felt that I was in the presence of two great Virginia aristocrats — the kind of people I like to think my Virginia ancestors were.[133]

With warm thanks to you both.

Sincerely yours,

---

[131] This paragraph and the preceding one were omitted from the radio speech due to lack of time.

[132] The original is in the possession of Mr. Smith.

[133] Among these was Joshua Fry (1700–1754). See *The Papers of Adlai E. Stevenson*, Vol. II, p. 111, and for Stevenson's accidental discovery of Fry's house, Vol. I, pp. 358–359.

To Alicia Patterson

September 30, 1952

Dear Alicia:

I have been worrying about your "operation." [134] I hope all goes well and that you will report in full on conditions, personal and otherwise, in due course.

Yours,

To Richard Bentley [135]

September 30, 1952

Dear Dick:

I get simultaneous advice that you have contributed very handsomely to the Volunteers for Stevenson and are afflicted with an ulcer. I hope there is no association. I feel as though I had become an awful burden to my friends, but your everlasting loyalty touches me deeply. I wish I could lay on hands and cure your misery. But I don't seem to have achieved those gifts!

Love to Phoebe.[136]

Yours,
ADLAI

To Arthur M. Schlesinger, Jr.[137]

October 2, 1952

Mr. Schlesinger — Pls [please] have all drafts indicate who wrote them so I know whom to address questions to — Initials will do.

AES

To Arthur M. Schlesinger, Jr.[138]

[no date]

Mr. Schlesinger — We should weave the McCarthy episode into the Time for a change speech somehow — maybe its time for a change from his ilk etc —

AES

[134] The editors have been unable to discover what operation Stevenson refers to.
[135] The original is in the possession of Mr. Bentley.
[136] Mrs. Bentley.
[137] This handwritten memorandum is in the Schlesinger papers, John F. Kennedy Library.
[138] This handwritten memorandum is in the Schlesinger papers, John F. Kennedy Library.

To Hermon Dunlap Smith [139]

October 2, 1952

Dear Dutch:

I am glad to know that so many businessmen have expressed their desire to work with Volunteers-for-Stevenson. The Democratic party, in my judgment, is the natural home for American businessmen — for all those who want to keep our economy expanding and our enterprise system vigorous and competitive. I don't need to tell you how deeply I believe in our free system. As I put it in a speech in 1949: "I don't like any interference with free markets, free men and free enterprise."

Our nation owes much of its greatness to the creative genius of our industrial leadership. I hope that we shall never stop producing these men whose perseverance and ingenuity and inspiration blaze new trails into greater productivity and thus raise living standards for all our people.

The kind of America I want is one that will continue to nourish such leaders — to assure them a fair chance, to reward their initiative, and to secure for them an honored place in our society.

In the future, as in the past, America must remain the land of opportunity. I shall do my best to keep it that way.

Yours ever,

Mrs. William McAdoo, of Santa Barbara, California, daughter of President Woodrow Wilson, wrote Stevenson volunteering her assistance and praising him for his Wilsonian qualities.

To Eleanor Wilson McAdoo

October 2, 1952

My dear Mrs. McAdoo:

I was delighted to have your letter. To be identified in your mind in any way with your father is the ultimate compliment. He has been my life-long hero. I met him at the age of twelve at Seagirt, I believe it was, when my father took me to call during his campaign that year. Later I went to Princeton and finished my Wilsonian saturation.

I am so grateful for your suggestion of help and I shall quickly inform the staff about your proffer. I should think there might well be something you can do, and I hope they will get at it at once.

With my gratitude and warmest regards, I am,

Sincerely yours,

[139] The original is in the possession of Mr. Smith.

There were widespread rumors that the New York Times *might with-draw its support of Eisenhower and shift to Stevenson. New York phi-lanthropist and author James P. Warburg sent Stevenson a copy of his letter to the* Times *urging them to switch.*

To James P. Warburg

October 5, 1952

Dear Jim:

Thanks for your letter and the piece to the Times. I hope it has some effect, although I doubt if they can bring themselves to a complete switch. I am told the Washington Post is particularly vulnerable.

Hastily yours,

P.S. I certainly hope the Times prints the letter and that you send me a few copies if it does.

Eric Sevareid, covering the campaign for the Columbia Broadcasting System, wrote to Carl McGowan on October 2:

What, after all, is the Eisenhower appeal to people? It is not only his great fame and popularity. In psychological terms, he is a father-image. He is not only appealing to people's prejudices and animosities and ignorance — more than that, he is appealing to their sense of weary perplexity. Millions of people seem to be tired of trying to think out the answers to problems like Russia, Korea and inflation, that seem to have no clear answers. Eisenhower gives them no answers, to be sure, but what he does give them is an illusion of Authority, of Competence. He is saying, just trust me and my friends and somehow, somewhere we shall find the answers. He is careful not to ask them to think; he never suggests that the answers really lie with the people themselves, that it is their responsibility. He merely asserts and asserts, and millions seem ready to close their eyes and their minds and blindly, hopefully, put the whole painful, perplexing business on to Father's broad shoulders. They want to vote for a man who *acts* as though he knew the answers and they are in no mood to really examine his credentials.

Adlai takes the opposite approach. In his almost painful honesty, he makes it clear that he does not know all the answers, that nobody really can or does; he clearly demonstrates the enormous size of the problems and he demands that the people think and more than that, think about their own responsibilities. He has been analyzing, not asserting; he has been projecting, not an image of the big, competent father or brother, but of the moral and intellectual proctor, the gad-fly called conscience. In so doing he has revealed an integrity rare in American politics, a luminosity of intelligence unmatched on the political scene today; he has caught the imagination of intellectuals, of all those who are really informed; he has excited the passions of the *mind;* he has not excited the emotions of the great bulk of half-informed voters, nor, among these, has he created a feeling of Trust, of Authority of Certainty that he knows where he is going and what must be done. Eisenhower does create that feeling, or that illusion, because, God knows, he is empty of ideas or certitude himself. But this the people by and large fail to see. It is my impression that great numbers of people don't want their problems analyzed, however brilliantly and truthfully; that is just too painful an effort, to follow it; they simply want somebody to take the problems over.[140]

Stevenson spoke in the Masonic Temple in Detroit on October 7, 1952.

SAFEGUARDS AGAINST COMMUNISM [141]

I've been trying in this campaign to talk about all the public questions that affect your welfare as Americans, sanely, sensibly, and forthrightly. I hear it said, now and then, that I am talking over the heads of the people.

Well, if it is a mistake to appeal to intelligence and reason, instead of emotion and prejudice, then I plead guilty to the charge.

Besides that, I would rather be charged with talking over your heads than behind your backs.

People are smarter than some may think — "There's still a God's plenty left in people of the little red schoolhouse and the tall white steeple."

So you'll just have to forgive me if I go on trusting your intelligence.

I want to talk to you tonight about a disease. It is a disease which may have killed more people in this world in the last several years than cancer, than tuberculosis, than heart disease — more than all of these combined.

It has certainly killed more minds, more souls, more decent human hopes and ambitions, than any corruption — including the darkest days of Hitler.

I want to discuss with you the ways that communism has attacked this nation — and the ways in which this attack has been met.

This subject is swathed in fog and confusion. Most of this has been created by the communists themselves, seeking under confusion's cover to advance their evil purposes. But some of it has been created by political demagogues, who are hunting for votes much more than for communists.

140 This letter is in A.E.S., I.S.H.L.
141 The text is from *Major Campaign Speeches AES 1952*, pp. 213–219.

I propose tonight to do what I can to penetrate this fog and dispel this confusion. I propose to make precisely clear the record and the position of the two political parties on this problem. Unhappily facts sometimes get smothered in falsehoods.

These are the facts:

Twenty years ago the most serious threat of communism this country ever faced — a threat arising from poverty and despair, following, as it happens, twelve years of Republican administrations — was stopped by a Democratic administration.

For twenty years my party has helped the people of America to build that economic strength and that faith in freedom which make communism impossible — and every step we have taken has been opposed, ridiculed and sabotaged by the Republican Old Guard.

For years your Government in Washington has been desperately rallying and strengthening the free peoples of the world against communism, and leading the way in building the collective strength which is the only bulwark against communist expansion — and this, too, over the bitter protest and unrelenting opposition of the Republican Old Guard.

Again, Democratic leadership has built an elaborate internal security system to protect this nation against communist subversion — a system which has put the leaders of the Communist Party in this country where they belong — behind bars.

Let's look at the record a moment.

Agents of Soviet communism first began making headway in this country in the 1920's. The administration, you will recall, was Republican at that time. A month ago the junior Senator from Wisconsin quoted what he said was a Department of Justice document to prove the existence of communists in the State Department. It is true that he found the quotation in a Department of Justice document. But he neglected to say that it described the situation in 1928, and that what it proved was the existence of a communist plot under the Presidency of — Calvin Coolidge.

But, as I have said, the great communist conspiracy had its first real chance when the Republicans fumbled and bungled this nation into the Great Depression. ("Fumbled and bungled" is not mine but one of their favorite oratorical epithets for everything the Democrats have done for twenty years.) You remember the bitter winters of 1930 and 1931. Farmers in Arkansas — conservative, law-abiding farmers — organized to march on towns and loot the stores. Children left home to spare their parents another mouth to feed; so many of them left that the railroads put on special open boxcars to keep the kids from breaking into the closed ones. Millions of American men and women waited in the breadlines. An army of ragged veterans actually marched on our national capital.

It is little wonder that across the land men and women — and especially the young — began to drift toward the terrible conclusion that free government had reached the end of its rope. Reaching out for a solution — any solution — the communist agents found ready converts among the unemployed, the farmers, the workers. It was then that some persons like Alger Hiss and Elizabeth Bentley,[142] witnessing the devastation of capitalism and the menacing rise of Hitler, became entangled in the communist conspiracy.

In the election of 1932, almost one million Americans voted against the capitalist system. If the paralysis had continued in Washington, the one million votes cast against capitalism in 1932 might have swelled to ten million in 1936.

But in 1933 the Democratic Party brought to this nation a great leader — Franklin Roosevelt.

From that day onward, the swelling menace of discontent and communism in this country began to wane. President Roosevelt brought to us a new spirit, a new hope. The Government acted swiftly and decisively to give the farmer a market, to give the worker a job, to give the unemployed a means of saving their self-respect, to give youth opportunity and hope. America's faith in itself was restored. Under his leadership the American people unlocked from within themselves the strength to drive out communism.

This country was saved from depression and despair. Communism in the United States was turned back and as long as we hold fast to the progressive spirit of human welfare that inspired that leadership we need never fear a communist revolution in this country — and every honest man knows that is true.

And where were the Republican leaders during this fight? They cannot conceal the record. They tried to block, to trim, to obstruct, to prevent, the collective-bargaining laws that mean security to the worker, the price-support laws that mean security to the farmer, the social-insurance laws that mean security to the aged and the infirm.

The plain truth is that the Democratic administrations saved this country from depression and from communism or fascism over the opposition of the Republican leadership, because these near-sighted gentlemen never have understood that the way to make this country secure is to work for the security of all of the people in it. These men still control the Republican Party. That is why thoughtful people of this country are apprehensive that a Republican victory this November would be an Old Guard victory

---

[142] Elizabeth Bentley was a courier for a Soviet spy ring operating within the United States. Testifying before the House Un-American Activities Committee in 1948, she implicated a number of government officials, among them President Roosevelt's wartime adviser Lauchlin Currie and his Secretary of the Treasury's assistant, Harry Dexter White. See the New York *Times,* July 31, 1948.

and the forerunner of another great depression. We must prevent another economic disaster, for that would open up the greatest opportunity the Kremlin could hope for to take over the free world, not by arms but by invitation.

We licked the communist hope for a revolution in the thirties. But the years of misery, Republican years, had left a heritage of fanatics and agents in our midst. Communism was finished as a political threat; it survived as an instrument of subversion and espionage. Soviet secret agents and their dupes burrowed like moles in the ground, trying to undermine the foundations of this and every other government in the world.

They penetrated the Nazi Government in Germany.

They penetrated the Government of Imperial Japan — so successfully that they learned in advance about the Japanese plot against Pearl Harbor.

They penetrated the anti-communist Government of Chiang Kai-shek in China — despite the long experience of his secret police in dealing with them.

They penetrated the Governments of a dozen European countries — no matter how anti-communist their policies or pretensions.

No government in the world has been immune from their penetration. Nor has ours. Nor will any government be safe from espionage and the secret communist attack so long as the Soviet Union pursues its goal of world dominion.

We must never forget the dedication, tenacity and fanaticism of this inscrutable, ruthless, restless conspiracy. As General Bedell Smith, the director of the Central Intelligence Agency, warned us last week, we cannot let our guard drop even for a moment. The only safe assumption is that no place is safe.

We must, to protect our Government from infiltration, combine vigilance with vigor. This is a long and continuous struggle — no single action can win the campaign.

And the Democratic administration has been conducting this fight for a long time. In 1939 the Roosevelt Administration made it unlawful for communists to work for the Federal Government.

In 1940 there was passed the Smith Act, under which the Department of Justice in President Truman's administration subsequently convicted the thirty-one leaders of the American Communist Party.

During the war, the Civil Service Commission and the F.B.I. conducted a continuous screening of Federal employes. Nearly 1500 men and women were denied Federal employment because of doubtful loyalty.

In 1947 President Truman set up a new and tighter Federal loyalty-control program. Many people have thought it was too tight, fearing an invasion of our ancient principle that a man is innocent until proved guilty. In the same year the Attorney General established a list of subversive organizations. In 1948 and 1949 the Department of Justice indicted and convicted the communist leaders.

The list of subversives uncovered in these years has been long. By hard, patient, silent work these men were exposed, be it noted, in the years before 1950 — before the junior Senator from Wisconsin suddenly appeared on the scene and began his wild and reckless campaign against the integrity of our Government itself.[143] Some people have been impressed by his loud talk. But the record is clear on this, too. For all his bragging and fear-mongering the junior Senator from Wisconsin has yet to produce evidence leading to the conviction of one single communist agent, either in or out of government.

The reason for this is clear. Catching real communist agents, like killing poisonous snakes or tigers, is not a job for amateurs or children, especially noisy ones. It is a job for professionals who know their business and their adversaries.

The professionals of the Federal Bureau of Investigation make up a magnificent instrument for the protection of our Government. For years, the F.B.I. has been quietly and remorselessly uncovering the communist plot against America. It has exposed one conspirator after another. It provided the evidence that sent the thirty-one leaders to prison.

I have often wondered what the Republicans think they would do to improve the situation if they were elected. The General has joined loudly in the clamor about the Communist menace in Washington. First he said the communists in government were the result of incompetent, loose security policies. More recently, I'm sorry to say, he implies that the Federal Government is deliberately concealing communists. But he has offered only thundering silence about a cure. What would he do? Would he fire J. Edgar Hoover? Would he fire General Bedell Smith, head of the Central Intelligence Agency and his own former Chief of Staff? Would he discharge General Smith's deputy, Allen Dulles, the brother

143 On February 9, 1950, Senator McCarthy spoke in West Virginia. He explained all the difficulties in one sentence: "The reason we find ourselves in a position of impotency is not because our only powerful potential enemy has sent men to invade our shores, but rather because of the traitorous actions of those who have been treated so well by this nation." And he charged: "In my opinion the State Department . . . is thoroughly infested with Communists." Reporters present insisted that McCarthy said he had a list of two hundred and five Communists in the State Department. On February 10, 1950, the senator charged there were "Fifty-seven card-carrying members of the Communist party" in the State Department.

of his own chief adviser on foreign affairs? Would he discharge the experienced men who now protect our nation's security?

I think we are entitled to ask, is the Republican candidate seriously interested in trying to root communists out of the Government, or is he only interested in scaring the American people to get the Old Guard into the Government?

For my own part, I will tell you straight out, I believe the F.B.I. has been doing a superb job. I think J. Edgar Hoover and General Bedell Smith are excellent, experienced, devoted and trustworthy men in these posts of great responsibility. I would back them to the hilt.

And let me say one more thing, so there will be no shadow of a doubt. If I find in Washington any disloyal government servant, I will throw him out ruthlessly, regardless of place, position or party. I expect to review thoroughly the present loyalty system and if it can be strengthened or improved in any way, it will be done.

As far as I'm concerned this fight will be continued until the communist conspiracy in our land is smashed beyond repair. And I think my record is the best evidence that this fight will be conducted with full respect for our system of justice, and for the Bill of Rights of the United States.

Let us never forget that tension breeds fear, fear, repression, and repression, injustice and tyranny. Our police work is aimed at a conspiracy, and not at ideas or opinion. Our country was built on unpopular ideas, on unorthodox opinions. My definition of a free society is a society where it is safe to be unpopular.

I want to keep our America that way.

I agree with the Roman Catholic Bishops in their pronouncement last November. "Dishonesty, slander, detraction and defamation of character," the Catholic Bishops said, "are as truly transgressions of God's Commandments when resorted to by men in political life as they are for all other men."

We of the Democratic Party have fought communism in America for twenty years — in the Government, in the union halls, in the farm grange halls, in the schools and in our homes. We have met and destroyed this disease as it has not been met or destroyed in any other country in the world. And we have done it without false accusation, without the assassination of honest characters, without destroying the principles of freedom upon which this society is based. Carelessness about our security is dangerous; carelessness about our freedom is also dangerous.

And let me say another thing that needs saying. I have not said and I do not think for a moment that a single responsible Republican leader in those days of boom and bust in the twenties and early thirties when communism sank its roots in this country was deliberately plotting the downfall of capitalism or covertly encouraging communism. And we will make a lot more progress in solving this problem when we stop capitalizing [on] communism for political advantage and think more of the welfare of the Republic than of how we can spread fear and smear and mistrust.

But if the Republican leaders insist on talking incessantly about softness toward communism, I must point out the record shows that even today the Republican Party opposes those cost-of-living controls which the Democratic Party supports in order to prevent another boom and bust — another period when the beckoning finger of communism's false light would grow stronger in America.

The record shows the Republican Party has steadily tried to block and hobble our worldwide fight against communism time and time again; the Republican majority in Congress has voted to slash economic and military aid to our allies.

But there is no cheap answer to communism, to world peace, to anything worth having.

The Democratic Party rejects this policy of loud words and soft deeds. We stand for a foreign policy of strength, for that is the only policy that can lead to peace.

We will protect ourselves from communism, and, at the same time, we will protect our liberties, too — those liberties which, above all, distinguish the United States from the police state.

Stevenson spoke at the University of Wisconsin in Madison on October 8, 1952.

THE AREA OF FREEDOM [144]

After what Wisconsin did to Illinois last Saturday [145] I suppose you are here not out of curiosity about a candidate for President, but as a mark of charity to the grieving Governor of Illinois. I think your manners are very good, and therefore I will be charitable and not detain you long enough to tell you the whole Democratic story!

I rarely miss the opportunity of visiting a university. Perhaps I discovered, at long last, the reason for this mysterious attraction a few days ago when I overheard some of my staff talking about "egg-heads." They

[144] The text is from *Major Campaign Speeches AES 1952*, pp. 220–227.
[145] The Wisconsin football team defeated the University of Illinois, 20-6.

were quoting some newspaper columnist who said that only "egg-heads" could understand my speeches.

For a few minutes I took this egg-head talk personally in injured silence. But I couldn't stand it and summoned up the courage to ask them what an egg-head was. The answer, I discovered, is that an egg-head is anyone who has gone to college! So at least today I have a lot of company.

It makes me shudder a little to think that I graduated from college thirty years ago last June and how doddering and venerable the thirtieth reunion class looked to me then. If I look to you the way they looked to me, I wouldn't vote for me! Having uttered that sentence, I quickly comfort myself by reminding you that you haven't any younger alternatives!

Nothing so dates a man as to decry the younger generation. Yet this has been a favorite attitude of old fogies throughout recorded time. They were at it 4,000 years ago in Memphis and Philadelphia, Egypt, just as some of their contemporaries are at it today in Memphis, Tennessee, and Philadelphia, Pennsylvania.

Perhaps the solution to this aberration is to be found in the flashing epigram of La Rochefoucauld that "The old begin to complain of the conduct of the young when they themselves can no longer set a bad example."

Sometimes, however, such being the infirmities of these my sere and ivy years, I find myself repeating this maxim to myself so that I may conduct myself with seeming parental grace in the presence of my own young sons. Occasionally the tendency to decry the younger generation — a form of mental arthritis for which there is as yet no cure — takes on large proportions. Before we entered the last war a number of misguided writers busied themselves with telling the country that if we should go to war, all would be lost. The reason, they said, was that the young men of this generation were weak and soft, debilitated by ice-cream cones and Cadillacs for the rigors of armed conflict.

This, of course, was nonsense; a confection of which we are presently having an overproduction. The men of our armed forces in the last war were as courageous and enduring as they ever were in the history of this nation, and indeed they prevailed against conditions more terrible than those known to Andrew Jackson's men. They fought without hate, they griped with fervor, and they laughed at themselves with characteristic and saving American humor. And serving with them, in uniform and out of uniform, were millions of American women.

I have never believed that whiskers and wisdom are necessarily synonymous; sometimes indeed whiskers merely adorn blank spaces on blank faces. Going upon this assumption I have been able to persuade many young men to throw in their fortunes with me in a common fight for good government, and if I should be given a lease on the White House I shall hope to induce many young men to join me in a high adventure as I have done in Illinois.

Most of you students were born, I suppose, in the early thirties and do not remember the state of the world at that time. Looking back, it must be hard for most of you to realize that such a world ever existed. Your world has troubles of its own — perhaps greater troubles than those of twenty years ago. But one worry you are spared is the worry of finding a job. When you finish college and military service, you will enter a world which wants and needs you.

This seems a natural thing — when you have it. It is a terrible thing when you don't. As we look around our booming country, it is almost incredible to think that mass unemployment was ever a problem. Yet a short twenty years ago millions of people were engaged in a desperate search for work.

If you are incredulous, let me say that my generation went into the depression with much the same incredulity. I finished college in 1922. That was the era of flappers, bathtub gin, Freud — the threshold of the gay and carefree period of the twenties — the era of wonderful nonsense, about which a fellow Princetonian of mine, F. Scott Fitzgerald, wrote some enduring prose.

This decade marked a curious pause in American life and growth — a last interlude of national self-indulgence between the testing of the First World War and the testing of depression. It was our last time of daydreams before crisis made us face the dark ordeal of the twentieth century.

The men who ran our country in that decade assured us that they had found the secret of permanent prosperity. Most of us believed them, and bought stocks. Then, in 1929, came the crash — and, as prosperity crumbled away before our eyes, we discovered that its copyright owners had no program against depression — nothing but wails and exhortation and whistling in the night. Our masters in Washington and Wall Street threw up their hands. Some jumped out of windows. In the face of economic disaster we were leaderless.

Of course modesty forbids me to tell you which party was in control of the country and had been for many years at that time!

It was a sullen and hostile world — a world which had little for youth of opportunity, of hope, of a future. The system was running down, like a broken clock. The wonder is, not that so many young men and women turned to socialism or to communism, but that there were so few.

The election of 1932 was, in a way, a last chance for a free America.

Nearly a million votes were cast against capitalism that year. That million might well have swelled to ten million by 1936 if the economic paralysis had continued.

But, as you all know, the election of 1932 brought Franklin Roosevelt and the Democratic Party, and also the vitality and guts to tackle our economic problems within the framework of the democratic system. The growth of extreme radicalism was arrested by bringing an end to human distress and economic chaos. In 1936, not ten million but a bare 250,000 people voted for socialism and communism. I firmly believe, therefore, that the man who was more responsible than any other for checking the spread of communism in America was Franklin D. Roosevelt.

We came very near a revolution in 1932 — and no place was more revolutionary in those days than our old, sober, sedate farm belt. Hunger and want were turning law-abiding American farmers into rebels. When a season's produce could no longer earn the cost of production or meet the interest on mortgages, it seemed time for action. In Wisconsin, in Iowa, in Nebraska, in Kansas, farmers banded together to resist foreclosures, to prevent the sale of farms for taxes, to keep surplus milk off the market by dumping it on the roads — violence and irresponsibility which we do not condone, but which were symptomatic of a dying faith in our system.

I remember those bitter days well, because my first government job was with the Agricultural Adjustment Administration — the old triple-A.[146] Although a city lawyer in Chicago at the time, I came from the corn belt of Illinois and like many other young lawyers and businessmen and college professors, I jumped at the chance to work for a government which was doing something for the farmer who had not even flourished in the roaring twenties.

In those years, too, we began the process of the reform and reconstruction of our economic system — the process which has made our economy so much more foolproof today than the vehicle in which we careened to disaster in the twenties and which was manned by Republican chauffeurs and mechanics.

I go into this because it is something more than ancient history. I would have hoped that all Americans could accept the gains we have made in the last generation, and that on this basis we could move forward together. But I fear the struggle is not over. The minority which fought this effort at every step along the way is still fighting. Senator Bricker [147] spoke for them when he cried at the Republican convention this year that the "last vestige of the New Deal" must be "destroyed."

I hope this was just partisan elocution, but the record is not reassuring

[146] See *The Papers of Adlai E. Stevenson*, Vol. I, pp. 246–253.
[147] Senator John W. Bricker of Ohio.

that the constructive work which has been done is secure. And it is well for you who can't remember where we have been to know where we are. This freedom and this security are part of the landscape of your world. But they have only been part of that landscape for a short time.

The remaking of our country in this last generation has made America a beacon of progress on an otherwise stormy and darkening earth. I cannot say that you young men and women will go out today into a safer world than that of 1932. But I do say that you will go out into a stronger America — an America which welcomes you, which has a place for you, and in which you may live and work and serve with dignity and faith.

It seemed to me appropriate to discuss these great changes here at the University of Wisconsin, because the democratic impulse of the thirties owed a great deal to the Wisconsin tradition in our national politics.

There were a number of elements in that Wisconsin tradition. The basic element, of course, was a deep and abiding faith in the American people and the American soil. No matter how much our nation becomes overgrown with the tall towers of great cities, we can never forget that our democracy had its roots in the land. It was a Wisconsin historian — Frederick Jackson Turner — who first made the nation understand that the American democracy came out of the wilderness.[148] In our century, few have symbolized better the ancient Jeffersonian faith than the great leader of Wisconsin progressivism, Robert La Follette.[149]

But the Wisconsin tradition meant more than a simple belief in the people. It also meant a faith in the application of intelligence and reason to the problems of society. It meant a deep conviction that the role of government was not to stumble along like a drunkard in the dark, but to light its way by the best torches of knowledge and understanding it could find. The La Follettes were never ashamed to call on the experts.

Above all, the Wisconsin tradition meant a belief in the value of the free intellectual community — the belief which has found such splendid embodiment here in this city. If we value the pursuit of knowledge, we must be free to follow wherever that search may lead us. The free mind is no barking dog, to be tethered on a ten-foot chain. It must be unrestricted in the play of its inquiry. If we insist on conclusions before the search is over, we are committed to playing the game of the mind with marked cards.

The Wisconsin idea — the faith in the free mind and in the application of reason to government — was one of the hopeful ideas of our cen-

---

[148] Turner proposed this famous thesis in *The Frontier in American History* (New York: Holt, 1920), and it brought him considerable fame and a Harvard professorship in the years that followed.
[149] Governor of Wisconsin, 1900–1906; U.S. senator from Wisconsin, 1906–1925.

tury. Today we find that idea everywhere under attack. Throughout the world, the whole conception of the free intellectual community is menaced by those who fear freedom more than they love it. As darkness falls upon this earth, the area of freedom shrinks. New philosophies arise — new theories of the state — which recoil from freedom, detest it, exterminate it, and seek to found new societies upon its extermination.

In the Soviet Union we see the totalitarian state in its gloomy reality. The first casualty of the communist regime is the free mind; and, once the free mind disappears, all else must follow. Thus in Soviet Russia today the last trace of freedom has been extinguished. Not only history and economics and politics, but science and art and music are enslaved by the regime. The unorthodox experiment, the unacceptable melody, the extreme painting, become evidences of disloyalty. Unorthodoxy is treason to the state.

This process reaches its grim climax, of course, in the Soviet courts. Here injustice, wearing the gowns of justice, stages the last act of the cruel joke. Men are accused at random of infamous and fantastic charges; they are transformed into enemy agents, spies, traitors; documents are misrepresented and falsified; past associations are uncovered and distorted, past remarks torn from context; guilt comes in the end, not just by association, but by accusation. And triumphant above all rises the figure of the great accuser whose word can brand men's lives, make falsehood true, create evidence where none existed before, and spread through all society the reign of suspicion and terror.

Because we believe in the free mind, we are opposing communism with all our will. We are opposing it abroad, where its relentless pressure seeks further to narrow the area of freedom. We are opposing it at home, where its agents and its dupes seek to undermine our society and strangle our freedom in its own paradoxes.

As President, I would use all the power of the Federal Government to expose and identify communist activity, to remove communists and their tools from places of position and prestige in our society, and to protect our free institutions from communist espionage, sabotage and subversion.

But, because we believe in the free mind, we are also fighting those who, in the name of anti-communism, would assail the community of freedom itself. The liberties of expression and conscience are the basic liberties of American society. They are sustained by our whole structure of law and justice. That structure has sufficed for us in the great crises of our past. I see nothing in the future which requires us to throw it overboard now.

I would call to your mind the words of a great Republican patriot,

Theodore Roosevelt. "No greater harm can be done to the body politic," he said, "than by those men who, through reckless and indiscriminate accusation of good men and bad men, honest men and dishonest men alike, finally so hopelessly puzzle the public that they do not believe that any man in public life is entirely straight; while, on the other hand, they lose all indignation against the man who really is crooked."

And in case you have not been reading all the philosophers, I remind you that Aristotle said: "History shows that almost all tyrants have been demagogues who gained favor with the people by their accusation of the notables." Way back there!

Disturbing things have taken place in our own land. The pillorying of the innocent has caused the wise to stammer and the timid to retreat. I would shudder for this country if I thought that we too must surrender to the sinister figure of the Inquisition, of the great accuser. I hope that the time will never come in America when charges are taken as the equivalent of facts, when suspicions are confused with certainties, and when the voice of the accuser stills every other voice in the land.

So long as America is populated by Americans, this can never be the case. We shall defend the free mind and the free spirit, as we always have in the past. We love and cherish the light of freedom. We will not be stampeded into the dark night of tyranny. With faith in our great heritage of individual freedom, we can — and will — keep America the land of the free.

This challenge to freedom has its compensations. It has forced us to re-define our own values. It has made us restate the ideal of freedom for the complex industrial society of the twentieth century. And the process of redefinition and restatement — for most of us, anyway — has only strengthened our faith in the durability of free society.

We are hearing a lot today about American division, weakness, hesita-tion, fear. Some, perhaps, find it politically profitable to cultivate the vine-yards of anxiety. I would warn them lest they reap the grapes of wrath.

I have said elsewhere in the campaign that this election is a struggle between accusation and fear, and confidence and faith. I say to you today that we need not dwell in fear. We have shown in these twenty years the mighty things we are capable of — if we but maintain faith in ourselves, in our heritage of liberty and in the invincibility of free men.

Fear begets fear, as faith begets faith. My party knows where it has been and where it is going. The opposition doesn't like the road we have traversed and is sharply divided about the road ahead. The future stretches ahead, untrodden and uncharted — but ours to take and to master. That future is mostly yours; the roads yours to choose.

On October 11, Stevenson returned to Springfield for a three-day respite from campaigning to work on speeches, confer with aides, and answer some of his correspondence.

To Barnet Hodes [150]

October 12, 1952

Dear Barney:

Word has just come to me that you have made a very large and welcome contribution to the Volunteers for Stevenson. I seem to be thanking you repeatedly for your charity to me, and this is a very exceptional deed indeed!

My thanks and best wishes.

Sincerely

To Marshall Field III [151]

October 12, 1952

Dear Marshall:

I have been hoping for an opportunity to see you personally and to thank you for the letter you sent to the Sun-Times.[152] It has been difficult for me for many reasons, and your own loyalty and support are as gratifying as anything that has happened during this campaign which I had hoped to avoid, as you well know.

With love to Ruth [153] and my everlasting gratitude, I am

Sincerely yours,

The widow of the highly regarded columnist Raymond Clapper wrote Stevenson on September 30: "I count myself fortunate to be alive today to see and hear the greatest Presidential candidate of my time and per-

---

[150] Fifth Ward Democratic committeeman in Chicago. The original is in the possession of Mr. Hodes.

[151] A copy is in A.E.S., I.S.H.L.

[152] Mr. Field, the founder of the Chicago *Sun* and an ardent supporter of Stevenson, had turned control of the *Sun-Times* over to his son, who supported Eisenhower.

[153] Mrs. Field.

haps the greatest the United States has ever had the good fortune to have."

To Mrs. Raymond Clapper [154]

October 12, 1952

Dear Mrs. Clapper:

I have read your letter and feel a little giddy. I remember your husband so well from my days in Washington and the occasional visits he made to Colonel Knox' office, and, of course, I read him regularly. I wish he were here now and I have little doubt I would have another voice in the rather drafty halls of journalism.

You were more than good to write me and I am heartened.

Sincerely yours,

Stevenson issued the following statement on October 12, 1952.

I have received a letter written on the stationery of THE NEW YORK TIMES reading as follows:

October 3, 1952

Governor Adlai E. Stevenson
The Governor's Mansion
Springfield, Illinois

Dear Governor Stevenson:

"Policy sits above conscience," but here is a small contribution from eight minor keepers of the conscience of a great institution, who are devoted to that institution and to the cause for which you are fighting.

(Unsigned)

The letter contained $100.00 contribution in cash.

I cannot accept this money because anonymous contributions are prohibited by the Federal election laws. Nevertheless, I deeply appreciate the sentiment behind this letter. I have given some thought as to what should be done with the money and have sent it to The New York Times as a contribution to the annual fund raised at Christmas time by the New York Times for the "100 Neediest Cases."

---

[154] A copy is in A.E.S., I.S.H.L.

To Alicia Patterson [155]

October 12, 1952

Alicia dear —

I'm back in Spfd. after the last of the exhausting journeys for 48 hrs & then off again on this endless pilgrimmage.

A letter from Josephine [156] brings me the shocking news about your operations, that you can't talk by phone etc. . . .

I'm bewildered by it all — you've always seemed so strong, and I pray that all goes well with you. Even from my very brief experience in the hospital with my kidney this summer, I know a little of all the bodily miseries in recuperation and the aggravations of enforced idleness with people peering at you all the time. In short, I'm suffering with you a bit, and I wish I could see you to report on my late adventures (I'm trying to write while a photog[rapher]. from the P.D. [St. Louis *Post-Dispatch*] is working — such is the value of each moment in this dreadful pitiless business).

When will you be out of the hosp.? Where will you be? I get to N.Y. toward the end of the ordeal and hope I can catch a glimpse of the convalescent — and also hear about her operations!

My prayers are with you — and I can use any you have to spare — not just for victory but for survival. I hope this reaches *you* —

Love
ADLAI

To Mrs. Herbert Agar [157]

October 13, 1952

DISTRESSED TO HEAR OF YOUR ILLNESS.[158] HERBERT REPORTS GOOD PROGRESS. WE WILL KEEP HIM TOO BUSY TO WORRY.[159] WARM REGARDS.

To Arthur M. Schlesinger, Jr. [160]

October 13, 1952

Mr. Schlesinger —

I want to *change* the prosperity and peace formula — and talk more

[155] This handwritten letter is in the possession of Adlai E. Stevenson III.
[156] Mrs. Ivan Albright, Miss Patterson's sister.
[157] A copy of this telegram is in A.E.S., I.S.H.L.
[158] Mrs. Agar was in Huntington Hospital, Huntington, Long Island.
[159] Mr. Agar was writing speech drafts for Stevenson.
[160] This handwritten letter is in the Schlesinger papers, John F. Kennedy Library.

soberly about the difficulties of both: the necessity of moving *forward* — *progressivism,* rather than to risk standing still or retreating — the idea that "what man does not alter for the better, time, the great innovator will alter for the worse."

There may be some ideas in the attached — I've not read it over. A little more sobriety about the difficulties — a little more "sense" — than the continued flat assertion that we Dems. can & will continue prosperity and win the peace — a little more challenge to the people to understand the difficulties and help us solve them for their benefit etc —

AES

To Mrs. Franklin D. Roosevelt [161]

October 14, 1952

TO THE RESPECT OF A NATION WHICH IS GRATEFUL FOR YOUR LIFE- TIME OF SERVICE AND ACCOMPLISHMENT, MAY I ADD MY OWN WARM WISHES FOR MANY MORE YEARS OF HAPPINESS AS WELL AS OF CONTINUED SERVICE.[162]

The editors have selected two speeches from a campaign trip that in- cluded visits to Louisiana, Utah, California, and Texas. The following speech was delivered in New Orleans on October 10.

TIDELANDS OIL — FOREIGN TRADE [163]

When I was a little boy I spent several winters here in New Orleans out near Audubon Park and I used to ride up and down Canal Street on the streetcars. No one ever paid any attention to me, and now I come back forty years later and thousands come out to greet me on Canal Street. Something has happened and you've touched my heart. But the fact of the matter is that I love New Orleans — either way!

For here in New Orleans you have made an admirable civilization. It is a jambalaya containing all that makes for the body's pleasure, the mind's delight, the spirit's repose. Here each man seasons the dish to his own taste, for in this amiable society each man is master of his own seasoning.

I wish I could linger over this delectable dish. But such a luxury is not permitted the campaigner. If, then, you will forgive me my bad manners, I shall talk at once about things of mutual concern.

[161] This telegram is in the Franklin D. Roosevelt Library, Hyde Park, New York.
[162] Mrs. Roosevelt was born October 11, 1884.
[163] The text is from *Major Campaign Speeches AES 1952,* pp. 235–244.

As you know, I stand on the Democratic Party platform with respect to minority rights. I have only one observation to make on this subject, one that must sadden you as it saddens me. It is that, after two thousand years of Christianity, we need discuss it at all.

Let me speak for a moment on a subject of special interest to Louisiana. That is the question of the tidelands or, more accurately, the submerged lands which lie between the low-water mark and Louisiana's historical boundary three miles to seaward.

These are the lands in controversy — and no other. The Federal Government lays no claim to the true tidelands (those between the low- and high-water marks) nor to lands underlying inland waters; and, indeed, it could not because the United States Supreme Court has long since expressly recognized that ownership of all these lands clearly resides in the states. I have no designs upon the oysters of Maryland or the clams of Massachusetts!

Now I have been Governor of a state and I know, better than most, something of the problems of the states. I know that Louisiana, like other states, has important functions to perform for its people. It takes money to do those things and each state needs every resource it can muster for this purpose.

I am not surprised, therefore, that Louisiana has been greatly disappointed in the decision of the Supreme Court holding that the right to the oil beneath the coastal submerged lands is vested in all the people of the United States and not just those of Louisiana. The people and the Governor of Illinois would be equally disappointed had they lost a similar lawsuit.

But I am not runnng for Governor. And if I am elected on November 4th, I will be representing all of the people and not just some. What will be the position I will then find myself in with respect to this controversy? And how, therefore, should I state my view on it now, if I am to be a responsible President and fair with everyone?

Well, I have stated my position on this — and only *one* position — and I want to make clear that I lack the versatility of my opponent, who has had at least three separate positions on the tidelands question. I tried to make my views as clear as I could at the time Governor [Allan] Shivers of Texas paid his widely advertised visit to me in Illinois.[164] But what I said then has apparently not been circulated widely or set forth fully in this part of the country, and so I am going to say it again now.

The man who becomes the next President of the United States must, in my judgment, take up the submerged-lands controversy at the point

[164] See note 20, above.

where the Supreme Court left off. He cannot and should not begin to go behind Supreme Court decisions, saying that this one is right and that one is wrong and acting accordingly. I think he takes them as they come, whether they involve submerged lands or the seizure of the steel industry.

There was one great Louisianian who, I am sure, would have agreed with me on this. He was a distinguished Confederate officer who fought long and honorably for this state in the Great War. And as a lawyer on earlier trips to New Orleans I have stopped to look at the statue of Edward Douglas White, Chief Justice of the United States Supreme Court.

If the submerged lands, by virtue of the ruling of the United States Supreme Court, are a national, and not a state, asset, the question presented is one of wise policy in the disposition of that asset. I do not think it is wise policy for the Congress to institute a practice of giving away such national assets to individual states. I believe this in the case of the submerged lands as much as I would believe it in the case of the national forests, the national parks, the national grazing lands, and all of the other public lands which, though located within the boundaries of individual states, belong to the people of all of the states. I believe it is the duty of the President to conserve the national assets, the national domain, be it dollars in the treasury or forests in Oregon.

But to say this is not to solve the problem of the submerged lands. That problem is how to use the submerged lands for the benefit of the people of the country, including the people of Louisiana. The solution lies ultimately with the Congress which makes our laws. At the moment we are on dead center.

I don't believe in keeping matters in an unsettled state so that they may be exploited for political purposes. I believe that what is most needed in the case of the submerged lands is to get rid of the politics, to face the problem with sense and reason and good temper, and to get on with the business so that development can proceed.

I said to Governor Shivers, and I say to you of Louisiana, that my hope and desire is to see the early enactment of legislation which will provide for a fair and equitable arrangement for the administration of these lands and the division of their proceeds. We did this in the case of other public lands years ago — allocating in some cases 37½ per cent of the royalties to the state where the land is located.

I do not know whether the same formula should be followed in the case of the submerged lands. And I do not think that matters of this importance can be settled wisely in the frenzy of a national campaign or as a means of getting votes. I am equally sure that a settlement fair to all, including the people of Louisiana, can be worked out in a realistic, rational spirit. A President who was careless with the people's assets could hardly be a careful steward of your trust.

But there is something else I want to talk about here tonight. The windows of the port of New Orleans open upon seas and continents. They open also upon the incomparable empire of the Mississippi Valley. The great river, the sea, and your energies, have made you — in the romantic old phrase — a company of merchant adventurers.

You are deeply concerned both with foreign trade and domestic trade. But the two are now one. Our economic power in the world is so great that a slight downtrend here produces earthquake shocks elsewhere. These shocks immediately register upon the sensitive indicators of your commerce. So, too, Republican barriers to trade, such as quotas and high tariffs, are quickly reflected upon your docks, in your stores and in your homes as men lose their jobs.

This is a powerful industrial city. Last year, more than $200,000,000 worth of industry moved into the area. So far this year, more than $100,000,000 of new industries have arrived.

In 1952, this port may handle close to $2,000,000,000 worth of cargo. This is twice the volume of only five years ago.

In brief, a new giant has arisen on the shores of the Mississippi. But giants need more elbow room and more of everything than smaller figures.

Yours has been a long, steady, slow growth. During the past twenty years, however, the progress here has been spectacular. When depressions came in the old days, you could comfort yourselves that you would be less harmfully affected than cities whose growth had been faster than yours. But this is no longer true.

You are geared to a bigger and faster moving wheel than ever before. Louisiana must, therefore, seek the right answer to this question:

Is the Democratic Party or the Republican Party the more likely to promote foreign and domestic prosperity?

Perhaps a few questions may throw light on this subject.

Has not the Republican Party always been the party of quotas and high tariffs?

Did not the last Republican administration raise tariffs to the highest point in history? Didn't that cripple your foreign trade, injure your home market and set in motion events that exploded in the world's most destructive depression?

When these tariffs were rivets on your necks, did not the Republican leadership treat your complaints with contemptuous silence?

What of unfair and discriminatory freight rates that long ran against the South? Did the Republican leadership help right this wrong? Or was it content to see the South pay through the nose?

The Democratic Party has always been for world trade and liberalized tariffs. These are things for which the South has always stood. It is, therefore, no accident that President Roosevelt chose Cordell Hull as his Secretary of State almost twenty years ago. Chief among his great achievements was his program for Reciprocal Trade Agreements to encourage and increase our foreign trade, and incidentally the prosperity of New Orleans.

And what of the Republican record on Reciprocal Trade Agreements? Its leadership has always opposed them. If this leadership prevails, what will happen then to your great port and the thousands of people who earn their living through it? If you have any doubts on this subject, remember the Republican record. Then read the Republican platform and please tell me what it means, if you can.

How do you reconcile the Republican position with your International House or your International Trade Mart; your Dock Board and Foreign Trade Zone? New Orleans has done a magnificent job building cordial personal and business relations with Latin America. How long do you think these relations will last if our Latin-American friends have trouble earning a living by trading with the United States? What will it do to our Good Neighbor Policy — and I say to you that the further strengthening of our Good Neighbor Policy will be a major objective of my administration.

It is not possible for this nation to be at once politically internationalist and economically isolationist. This is just as insane as asking one Siamese twin to high dive while the other plays the piano. And that is exactly what the Republican leadership has long been doing. And that, I believe, is what it would do if it should again come into power.

Even if the Old Guard thinks of foreign trade as a one-way street, that trade is, and must be, a two-way street. We cannot sell without buying and we cannot go on exporting dollars forever.

On October 7th, Senator [Robert] Taft told an audience at Elgin, Illinois, that he had voted time after time against Reciprocal Trade Agreements.

I cannot exaggerate the deadly importance of this statement. It foreshadows more than the blight that would descend upon New Orleans if his views should prevail. And it foreshadows even more sinister results at the hands of Soviet Russia.

I am not a man given to exaggeration. Nor do I want to frighten you into voting for me. I shall continue to try to appeal to your minds rather than to your solar plexus. Yet I now beg you to listen carefully.

The Soviet Party Congress recently convened in Moscow. Its meeting was described by *Pravda,* the chief Soviet Government newspaper, as "the greatest event in the ideological life of the Communist Party and the Soviet people."

Stalin wrote a book for the occasion. The book is an instrument of Soviet foreign policy. It lays down the line that the Soviets may be expected to follow for perhaps the next decade.

This, briefly, is what he tells communists everywhere: That the world struggle will revolve around Western Germany and Japan; that basic Soviet policy is to emphasize that it will be difficult for Western Germany and Japan to earn a living within the non-communist world. Therefore Soviet Russia will play up the economic opportunities that will be offered these countries to trade with the communist world. And Stalin concludes that conflicts between the free world and Western Germany and Japan will grow as these countries get on their feet and compete more sharply with the free world; that is, with such great trading nations as the United States, Britain and France.

In short what Stalin is saying is this: that he is not so foolish as to engage us in a great shooting war; that he will simply wait it out because we are so blind and so stupid that he will not permit Western Germany and Japan to trade with the free world. They must, then, eventually trade with the Soviet world. So doing they will fall within Soviet domination.

Here I bid you pause and think before it is too late. The mentality of the Republican party in foreign trade has been well assessed by Stalin. He has seized upon one of the keys that may open the door to our downfall, if we permit him to use it. I say to you with the utmost conviction, that if we follow the suicidal foreign-trade fanaticism of the Republican Party, we may condemn this nation to isolation and destruction.

Stalin, then, proposes to conquer us, not by arms, but by taking advantage of what he believes to be our stupidity. This is not a battle that can be won by cannon or bombs. And it cannot be won by a few minutes' briefing of Army officers on the immensely complicated area of foreign trade and foreign finance — particularly by Republican politicians to whom reciprocal trade is distasteful.

But, to come back to the South after this brief excursion abroad. Friendliness for the South is nothing new in my family. Let me tell you what I mean.

In the 1870's, New Orleans men fought carpetbaggers on Canal Street. Standing with them, there was, I am proud to say, my grandfather Adlai

Stevenson. A Congressman from Illinois, he fought a Republican project to compel the use of troops at Southern elections. This project was known as the Force Bill. He expressed his distaste for a measure that would have compelled the South to go Republican at bayonet point.

Time passed. In the 1890's the Republican leadership was still unable to convert Democrats to Republicanism through reason. But it was still determined to do it through force. By then, my grandfather was Democratic Vice-Presidential candidate on a ticket headed by Grover Cleveland, a ticket that was elected. In 1892, just sixty years ago, he again opposed the Force Bill. He said that its passage might mean the election of Congressmen by bayonets, and that the South was faced with the counterpart of the horrors of the Reconstruction Period.

I hope, therefore, that with no violation of grace, I may claim spiritual kinship with you in your struggle for freedom and equity. Today it is the struggle of the ordinary man to get his rightful share of the goods produced by him and his community against those who would grab the greater share for themselves. The struggle never takes quite the same form, but its objective is always the same. Only the weapons change. Yesterday they were bayonets. Today they are a Republican campaign of fear and intimidation.

For decades these forces were pitilessly arrayed against you. The strong exacted of you what they could, and you granted what you must. The sufferings of those times are painful recollections of thousands of Louisiana families. Your physical hardships were great. But — more important — your self-respect was wounded. The wounds of the body are superficial. But the wounds of the spirit are grievous.

These mournful recollections, however, have been fading in the sunshine of happier times. Woodrow Wilson's New Freedom, forty years ago, began your liberation. Twenty years ago, Franklin Roosevelt, leading a strong Democratic Party in the name of a long-suffering people, began to bring you what had so long been denied you. Ever since that time, you have been moving toward a better life.

If I now, for a moment, speak of the past, it is not because of an urgent interest in history. It is because the past and present illustrate two different views of the Republican and Democratic Parties toward man and his place in society.

Let us then look homeward here in Louisiana. It was — and still is — one of our potentially richest states. Petroleum, gas, sulphur, salt exist here in prodigal abundance. Your fisheries are rich. You have a great sugar bowl and a valuable fur catch. Your forest resources are enormous. Your cotton and rice fields are wide.

You long had everything that makes for prosperity. But, for decades, the great majority of the people of Louisiana ate the dry crusts of poverty. Many of them dragged out their lives in the shadowy world of under-nourishment. They were too weak to live fully and too strong to die.

Malaria, pellagra and other diseases sapped the strength of thousands. Your health services were pitifully inadequate. How many people died because they couldn't get medical treatment, no one knows except God and their families. Your roads were poor, especially your farm-to-market roads. There were too few schools and teachers for your children. In rural areas, school terms were often too short for genuine education. There was not enough money for longer terms and many men couldn't live at all unless their children worked and added something to wretch-edly low family incomes.

Farmers sold their produce for what they could get. Working people sold the sweat of their faces and the toil of their hands for a pittance. And so there rested upon this lovely state, this potentially rich state, the bone-chilling breath of poverty.

By 1933 the people of the United States had lived for almost forty years — except for one eight-year interval — under Republican rule. Most of you had little to show for it except perhaps a corner of the earth where you vainly sought shelter against the arrows of misfortune. By 1933 your condition was little better than that of the natives of India. Your average yearly income per person was then $222.00, or 65 cents a day.

The thin pretense was maintained that you were sovereign citizens of sovereign States. Actually, Louisiana and the South had long been converted through Republican leadership, with its control of money and banking, into an American India. That leadership had succeeded in making the whole South colonies of the rich industrial Northeast. They were your absentee landlords. They used every method possible to keep yours a primitive, agricultural economy through their control of the money and banking systems of the nation. It is only during the past twenty years that you were liberated from colonialism and began to come into your rightful estate as free citizens of a free country, fully participat-ing in all of its privileges.

This process of liberation has been described by the Republican leaders — with their usual skill in calling things by their opposites — as "social-ism." I don't need to tell you that our Democratic program is the strongest bulwark against socialism that a free society could have. I have repeatedly said that I do not favor socialization — socialization of medicine, sociali-zation of law, socialization of industry or anything else. Those who say that we cannot meet the people's needs without destroying free enter-prise are the worst enemies of free society.

But enough of old, unhappy, far-off things. For some years you have been living in a world bright and fresh. Prosperity walks upon your farms and in the streets of your towns. More people of this state now own — or are on their way to owning — more houses and farms than ever before. Their savings are greater than ever before. Your children can now find opportunities at home instead of having to go elsewhere for them. And we no longer have eroded people living on eroded lands.

In determining our course for the future, I think that there is a simple method. We know what we have. We know how far we have gone. We must now decide how to get from what we have in the present to what we want in the future.

The relationship of the Democratic Party and the people during the twenty years past has been a relationship of good will. The Democratic Party has been responsive to the needs of the people and the people have responded by keeping it in power. I have no doubt at all that this harmonious relationship will be continued at the ballot box next month.

I want to conclude by saying a few words about something that means a good deal to Louisiana — and to me. Some hard words have been said this year by the General — in unmalicious haste, so I hope and suppose — about that great nation which has been the actual motherland for so many of you and a spiritual motherland of us all.

Je voudrais maintenant dire quelques mots à la population de langue française. Je vous adresse mon salut car je suis un grand admirateur de la France et de la civilisation française.

Quiconque dit que la France est en train de dépérir ou de dégénerer oublie les belles qualités françaises qui furent apportées ici, en Louisiane, par les ancêtres de la population de langue française, qualités qui fleurissent toujours dans la patrie d'origine de cette population.

Vous êtes de bons citoyens Americains mais vous avez conservé beaucoup de ces belles qualités du peuple français que vos ancêtres ont apportées dans ce pays, et je vous en félicite.

On October 14, Stevenson spoke in the Mormon Tabernacle in Salt Lake City, Utah.

ON LIBERTY OF CONSCIENCE [165]

I cannot speak tonight in this tabernacle without an awareness of the links between its history and that of the State from which I come.

Many of us who reside in Illinois have tasted the wholesome tonic of

[165] The text is from *Major Campaign Speeches AES 1952*, pp. 245–250.

humility in contemplation of the mistakes to which our history bears witness at Nauvoo — the Beautiful Place — in Illinois where your forefathers stopped on their long journey and built another temple.

It was 106 years ago now that there were those "burnings," the persecution, the mob violence and the murders which finally drove the men and women of the Mormon faith on westward.

When the caravans of those who today seek public office in this nation stop here with you, to meet with you in this, your tabernacle, they stop their clamor and haranguing. They seek the response of your hearts and your minds rather than of your hands or your voices.

I wish that all of our political campaigning could be conducted in the spirit which this meeting place inspires. It is a spirit of faith, a faith that triumphs over any obstacle.

And tonight I want to talk in this Temple to the great confident majority of Americans — the generous and unfrightened, those who are proud of our strength and sure of our goodness and who want to work with each other in trust, to advance the honor of our country.

Needless to say this includes many millions of Republicans. If all virtue were in one party the nation would be in a sad way. But this confident majority, I am sorry to say, does not include the Republican speechmakers of this campaign. How do they picture our magnificent America?

Sometimes they whine about our troubles — describing us as half-defeated, half-bankrupt and wholly self-pitying.

Sometimes they boast about our self-sufficiency — describing us as choosing to live alone, friendless, on a remote island, indifferent to the fate of man, a huge hermit-crab without a soul.

Sometimes they call large sections of us dupes and fellow-travelers — a people without a purpose and without a mind.

But at all times they picture us unworthily — scared, stupid and heartless. They thus betray the conquering, hopeful, practical yet deeply moral America which you and I know.

We all know it is nonsense, and that in fact the reverse is true. To the dismay of the enemies of America, we proved after 1945 that we have learned in the last twenty years not only to produce mightily, but to distribute among all our people an increasingly fair share of that production. We have evolved a stronger and a better form of economy, which makes nonsense of the Russian textbooks.

The friends of freedom everywhere have rejoiced. They have noted our rising and widespread wealth and well being. They have noted that we had no depression and no unemployment at the end of the war — in spite of headlong demobilization and disarmament. And remember that all this happened before the Marshall Plan, before the revival of our armed might, before Korea. Every liberty-loving European gave thanks that we had showed ourselves not only strong but stable.

Must this inspiring record now be ridiculed for campaign purposes? Must our credit for using our capitalist system wisely and humanely be undermined in Europe — and by General Eisenhower of all men? Must our proud all-American achievement be pictured as a Democratic Party plot?

During the war, you remember, when we all knew America was in danger, we only wanted the best, the most unselfish. We had no time for building political mantraps or for inventing derogatory tales. It was a heartlifting moment.

But a cold war leads the timid and the discontented into frustration. And out of frustration comes pettiness — the niggling, pitiful picture of a confused, divided country which these office-seekers are now painting. And this, of course, was the very purpose for which the Russians invented cold war and imposed it upon us.

They hoped we would feel frustrated, shackled by circumstance. They hoped we would fall to quarreling among ourselves and thus betray our mission.

But the American giant will not be shackled!

We shall not be tempted by the cold war to be half-regretful, half-ashamed of our strength — or frightened of it, which is worse. Regretful (God help us!) in the face of the stirring truth that Lincoln's vision has come true, that now we are indeed the "last, best hope of earth" — so recognized by all the free world, which implores us to be great, to lead with magnanimity and, above all, with patience. The very powerful, if they are good, must always be patient.

And still some of us regret it! Some of us say: "Why can't life leave us alone? We don't want to lead. We want to be undisturbed."

What would our Fathers have said to such talk? From the dawn of our Revolution they saw America as the saviour — not merely in terms of power, but in terms of goodness.

They knew that Providence had given us this empty, unexploited Continent for a purpose. And they knew that it must be a purpose which includes all men — for the same God made us all.

In 1787 George Washington said: "The preservation of the sacred fire of liberty, and the destiny of the republican form of government, are justly considered as deeply, perhaps as finally staked, on the experiment entrusted to the hands of the American people."

At that time we had less than four million inhabitants. But there was no doubt, no fear, in Washington's mind regarding our destiny.

In 1858 Abraham Lincoln said: "Our reliance is in the love of liberty which God has planted in us. Our defense is in the spirit which prized liberty as the heritage of all men, in all lands everywhere."

At that time there were about thirty million Americans. And we were threatened with civil war. But there was no doubt, no fear, in Lincoln's mind. He saw the war and the dissolution of the Union as a threat to the new, revolutionary idea of the free man and to democratic aspirations everywhere.

In 1915 Woodrow Wilson said. "The interesting and inspiring thought about America is that she asks nothing for herself except what she has a right to ask for humanity itself."

By that time we were a world power, about to enter into a world war. But there was no doubt, no fear, in Woodrow Wilson's mind. He knew, as in truth we have always known, that we were destined to be an example and to assume the burden of greatness.

So we are marked men, we Americans at the mid-century point. We have been tapped by fate — for which we should forever give thanks, not laments. What a day to live in! What a flowering of the work and the faith of our fathers! Who in heaven's name would want America less strong, less responsible for the future?

And precisely because we are tapped by fate, we must be wise and patient as well as strong. This means that we must live, intensely live, the faith which has made us free and thereby invincible. "Despotism may govern without faith, but liberty cannot."

American power is not just coal and iron and oil; cotton and wheat and corn. It is not just our forests and our mountain-ranges, and the huge meandering rivers of our central plains, and the high dry cattle country, and this lucky land of yours between the mountains and the sea. It is not even all these things plus a hundred and sixty million people. It is these things, plus the people, plus the idea!

So a second temptation of the cold frustrating war — which we also proudly reject — is to become so distracted by our troubles that we take this faith too much for granted, that we salute it (as some of us salute our religion), and then go our own way unchanged. If we do not make it part of us — keep it forever before us, intense and demanding and clear — the faith might die and we should then die with it.

What is this "American idea" which we so justly venerate? I suggest that the heart of it is the simple but challenging statement that no government may interfere with our conscience, may tell us what to think. All our freedoms, all our dynamic unleased energies, stem from this.

We Americans just naturally talk like this: "No government can tell me what to think. No government can tell me what to do, unless it can prove that the common good is served by such interference." This is the American way of living.

Yet the same Republicans (the dinosaur-wing of that party) who object to service from our Government — who call everything "creeping socialism," who talk darkly of "dictatorship" — these same men begin to hint that we are "subversive," or at best the tools of our country's enemies, when we boast of the great strides toward social justice and security we have already made, and of the still greater strides we plan. They laugh at us, superciliously, when we say we are the political party with a heart.

To honor and uphold our faith, therefore, we must never let them confuse us about the difference between what government should do if possible and what it must never do if America is to survive.

It should strengthen us in our freedom by fostering widespread ownership and as much economic independence as possible. In the towns and counties, in the state capitals and in Washington, that great work goes forward today.

But never must government step across the line which separates the promotion of justice and prosperity from the interference with thought, with conscience, with the sacred private life of the mind.

If you like, this is the distinction between the things that are God's and the things that are Caesar's. The mind is the expression of the soul, which belongs to God and must be let alone by government. But farm prices, minimum wages, old-age pensions, the regulation of monopoly, the physical safety of society — these things are Caesar's province, wherein the Government should do all that is humanly possible.

But those among us who would bar us from attempting our economic and social duty are quick with accusations, with defamatory hints and whispering campaigns, when they see a chance to scare or silence those with whom they disagree. Rudely, carelessly they invade the field of conscience, of thought — the field which belongs to God and not to Senators — and not to protect the Republic, but to discredit the individual.

Let us remember also that the first of the Seven Deadly Sins is spiritual pride: the sin which assures me that I know and you don't, so that I give myself permission to use any dubious or dishonest means to discredit your opinion.

Because we have always thought of government as friendly, not as brutal, character assassins and slanderers in the Congress of the United States have a free hand in the methods they use. We never foresaw that the cult of thought-control and of the Big Lie would come to America. So if their conscience permits, they can say almost anything. And if my opponent's conscience permits, he can try to help all of them get re-elected. But will he have strengthened or weakened the American idea?

This is no small thing, this remorseless attack upon freedom of conscience, freedom of thought. A few peddlers of hate and fear would be of little consequence if they had not been welcomed as satellites by Senator Taft and included in the leadership of this strange crusade. And none of them would be significant if the General — who was implored to come home by Republican leaders so that they might be quit of Senator Taft — had not yielded to the demands of his beaten foe. But because of that surrender, because of those strange allies in his queer crusade, our role in world-history, our faithfulness to the men who made the United States, is challenged in this election.

Finally, then, let us recall that our basic faith in liberty of conscience has an ancient ancestry. We can trace it back through Christian Europe, and through pagan Rome, back to the Old Testament prophets. It is by no means exclusive with us. It is in fact our bond of unity with all free men. But we are its ordained guardians today.

Let us lift up our hearts, therefore — glad of our strength, proud of the task it imposes. So far from being half-defeated, half-divided, half-bankrupt — while we are true to ourselves, we can never be defeated; while we accept the honorable burden of leadership, we can never be divided. And in the name of that burden we shall find the means and the determination to spend in money and in labor and in hard thought whatever is needed to save ourselves and our world.

John W. Davis, the 1924 Democratic presidential candidate, wrote Stevenson on October 14 that it was his duty to support Eisenhower: "I do this, believe me, without any reflection upon yourself. . . . May I take this occasion to compliment you on the form and quality of your speeches as well as on your ability to withstand the rigors of the campaign."

To John W. Davis

October 20, 1952

Dear Mr. Davis:

Thank you for your letter. I am confident that you arrived at your conclusion honestly and thoughtfully, and I can ask nothing more than that from anyone.

I suspect few have any conception of what you properly call the "rigors of the campaign," especially in view of the limited press and funds that we have. But it has been an experience for which I shall ever be thankful.

Cordially yours,

Stevenson delivered the following speech at the Cleveland Arena in Cleveland, Ohio, on October 23.

THE HISS CASE [166]

The hour is growing late in this autumn of our political decision. But I find it necessary to talk here tonight of things which are more fundamental than the immediate political questions before us.

For three months now I have done my best to talk sensibly.

I believed with many of you that General Eisenhower's hard-won victory in the Chicago Convention was a victory of the constructive and progressive men in the Republican Party over its bitter and reactionary elements.

I believed that an educational and elevating national discussion would result. But, instead, in the past two months the General has, one by one, embraced the men who were so savagely against him at Chicago. He has lost the support of men like Senator Wayne Morse of Oregon and has won the support of men like Colonel McCormick of the Chicago *Tribune*.

Meanwhile, his Vice Presidential candidate and other principal speakers on his behalf have given the Republican campaign its distinct shape and pattern.

It is not a campaign by debate. It has become a systematic program of innuendo and accusation aimed at sowing the seeds of doubt and mistrust.

The Republican candidate for Vice President has himself set the pace. This week and next — in these last days before the election — the Republican high command is counting heavily on this kind of campaign.

Next Monday, I'm informed, the junior Senator from Wisconsin is going to make a highly advertised speech — the man who said last week that, if he were put aboard my campaign train with a club, he might be able to make a good American out of me.[167]

Now plainly I have no concern about what the junior Senator from Wisconsin has to say about me. As an isolated voice he would be unimportant. But he has become more than the voice of a single individual who thinks the way to teach his brand of Americanism is with a club. This man will appear on nationwide radio and television as the planned

---

[166] The text is from *Major Campaign Speeches AES 1952*, pp. 269–275.

[167] At one point in October, 1952, Senator McCarthy said, "If somebody would only smuggle me aboard the Democratic campaign special with a baseball bat in my hand, I'd teach patriotism to little Ad-lie." See Fred J. Cook, *The Nightmare Decade: The Life and Times of Senator Joe McCarthy* (New York: Random House, 1971), p. 6; see also p. 581 for an explanation of the source of this and other similar quotations.

climax of the Republican campaign — as the voice of the wing of the Republican Party that lost the nomination but won the nominee. You will hear from the Senator from Wisconsin, with the permission and the approval of General Eisenhower.

Only last week, stung by charges that he had surrendered to the Old Guard, the General said that the decisions in this campaign "have been and will be mine alone." He added: "This crusade which I have taken to the American people represents what I, myself, believe." Crusade indeed!

In 1950 a group of Republican Senators, headed by Senator Smith of Maine, issued a Declaration of Conscience denouncing the tactics of smear and slander.[168] The General might have endorsed that Declaration of Conscience. He might have made it the testament of a real Crusade. Instead, by ignorance or choice, he has turned not to the Republican signers of that declaration, but to the Republican Senator who called Senator Smith a thief and defender of the communists.

I had not expected that the General would ever countenance such a campaign by his "crusaders." But this was before the General gave his hand to Senator [William E.] Jenner of Indiana who had called General George C. Marshall a "living lie" and "a front man for traitors" — Marshall, the architect of victory and General Eisenhower's greatest benefactor. It was before General Eisenhower struck from the speech that he was to give in Wisconsin words of praise for General Marshall at the request of the junior Senator from Wisconsin who had termed Marshall "so steeped in falsehood" that he "has recourse to the lie whenever it suits his convenience." [169] And it was before General Eisenhower last week quietly reinserted the words of praise for General Marshall in New Jersey once he was safely out of McCarthy and Jenner territory.

If the General would publicly embrace those who slandered George Marshall, there is certainly no reason to expect that he would restrain those who would slander me.

The Republican Vice Presidential candidate — who asks you to place him a heartbeat from the Presidency — has attacked me for saying in a

---

[168] On June 1, 1950, Senator Margaret Chase Smith delivered a Declaration of Conscience to the Senate. She criticized confusion arising from the lack of leadership from the White House, but she stated: "Certain elements of the Republican party have materially added to this confusion in the hopes of riding the Republican party to victory through selfish political exploitation of fear, bigotry, ignorance, and intolerance." Republican senators Charles W. Tobey, George D. Aiken, Wayne C. Morse, Irving M. Ives, Edward J. Thye, and Robert C. Hendrickson joined her in the declaration.

[169] On June 14, 1951, Senator McCarthy, on the floor of the Senate, accused General George C. Marshall of being part of "a conspiracy so immense, an infamy so black, as to dwarf any previous such venture in the history of man." See Walter Johnson, *1600 Pennsylvania Avenue*, Chapter 28: "Politics of Revenge."

court deposition that the reputation of Alger Hiss was good.[170] And let us always be clear where the responsibility lies. As the Republican Vice Presidential candidate put it last Monday, General Eisenhower "is the captain of the team." Senator Nixon added significantly: "With due regard for his team members and their abilities, he is calling the plays."

Now what are the facts? In the words of Al Smith, "Let's look at the record." I had known Hiss briefly in 1933 when I worked about five months for the Agricultural Adjustment Administration in Washington, where he was also employed. I did not encounter him again until twelve years later, in March of 1945 in the State Department. I saw him intermittently from March of 1945 to March of 1946 in the course of our official duties. Half that time I was in London for the Government. He never entered my house and I never entered his. I saw him twice in the Fall of 1947 at the U. N. General Assembly in New York. I have not seen him since.

In the spring of 1949 I was requested by the lawyers for Alger Hiss to appear at his first trial and testify as to his reputation. I refused to do so because of the burden of my official duties as Governor of Illinois. I was then requested to answer questions submitted under order of the court with regard to his reputation, as I had learned about it from others.

I said his reputation was "good" — and it was. I didn't say it was "very good"; I didn't say he was a "great patriot"; I didn't say any of the things the Wisconsin Senator, whose best weapon is carelessness with facts, says I said. I said his reputation was "good" so far as I had heard from others, and that was the simple, exact, whole truth, and all I could say on the basis of what I knew.

This was his reputation as the General, himself, has good reason to know.

These same spokesmen have challenged my sworn statement that I didn't believe that I had seen Hiss between March, 1946, and the fall of 1947. They say I introduced him at a speech in Chicago on November 12, 1946. All of the records make clear that my recollection was accurate. For on November 12, 1946, I was in official attendance as a U.S. delegate to the United Nations in New York, and was not in Chicago.

I am a lawyer. I think that one of the fundamental responsibilities not only of every citizen but particularly of lawyers is to give testimony in a court of law and to give it honestly and willingly. It will be a sorry day for American justice when a man, particularly one in public life, is too timid to state what he knows or what he has heard about a defendant in a criminal trial, for fear that the defendant might be later convicted.

[170] For the text of the deposition see *The Papers of Adlai E. Stevenson*, Vol. III, pp. 101–104.

And I might add that here in your own state of Ohio a Republican Congressman was recently convicted for unlawful acts.[171] Before his conviction, your own Senator Taft appeared and testified that this man's reputation was "excellent without question." Senator Bricker [172] and Congressman Joseph W. Martin, Jr., Republican minority leader, gave the same testimony.

My testimony in the Hiss case no more shows softness toward communism than the testimony of these Republican leaders shows softness toward corruption.

At no time did I testify on the issue of the guilt or innocence of Alger Hiss as a perjurer or a traitor. As I have repeatedly said, I have never doubted the verdict of the jury which convicted him.

I testified only as to his reputation at the time I knew him. His reputation was good. If I had said it was bad, I would have been a liar. If I had refused to testify at all, I would have been a coward.

But while the brash and patronizing young man who aspires to the Vice Presidency does not charge me with being a communist, he does say that I exercised bad judgment in stating honestly what I heard from others about Hiss' reputation. "Thou shalt not bear false witness," is one of the Ten Commandments, in case Senator Nixon has not read them lately. And if *he* would not tell and tell honestly what he knew of a defendant's reputation, he would be a coward and unfit for any office.

The responsibility of lawyers to co-operate with courts is greatest of all because they are officers of the court. And Senator Nixon is a lawyer.

He has criticized my judgment. I hope and pray that his standards of "judgment" never prevail in our courts, or our public life at any level, let alone in exalted positions of respect and responsibility.[173]

These are the plain and simple facts. I would suggest to the Republican "crusaders" that if they were to apply the same methods to their own candidate, General Eisenhower, and to his foreign affairs adviser, Mr. Dulles, they would find that both these men were of the same opinion about Alger Hiss, and more so. And more important, I would suggest that these methods are dangerous, not just to the Republican candidate, but to the very processes of our democracy.

In December, 1946, Hiss was chosen to be president of the Carnegie

---

[171] Walter E. Brehm, Republican congressman from Ohio since 1943, was convicted on April 30, 1951, and fined five thousand dollars for receiving illegal campaign contributions from his office employees. He was not a candidate for reelection in 1952.

[172] Republican Senator John W. Bricker of Ohio.

[173] The handwritten draft of this and the two preceding paragraphs — from which the typed copy of the speech was made — is in the Schlesinger papers, John F. Kennedy Library.

Endowment by the Board of Trustees, of which John Foster Dulles was Chairman and several leading Republican businessmen were members. After Hiss was elected, but before he took office, a Detroit lawyer offered to provide Mr. Dulles with evidence that Hiss had a provable communist record. No such report or warning ever came to me. Under date of December 26, Mr. Dulles responded. Listen to what he said:

"I have heard the report which you refer to, but I have confidence that there is no reason to doubt Mr. Hiss' complete loyalty to our American institutions. I have been thrown into intimate contact with him at San Francisco, London and Washington . . . Under these circumstances I feel a little skeptical about information which seems inconsistent with all that I personally know and what is the judgment of reliable friends and associates in Washington."

That, my friends, is what John Foster Dulles, the General's adviser on foreign policy, thought.

In May, 1948, General Eisenhower was elected to the Board of Trustees of the Carnegie Endowment at the same meeting at which Hiss was re-elected president and Dulles Chairman of the Board. This was months after I had seen Hiss for the last time. I am sure the General would never have joined the Board of Trustees if he had any doubt about Hiss' loyalty.

After he had been indicted by the grand jury, Hiss tendered his resignation as president and trustee of the Carnegie Endowment. The Board of Trustees, of which General Eisenhower was a member, declined to accept his resignation and granted him three months' leave of absence with full pay so that he might defend himself. The General was not present at the meeting, but I do not find that he ever voiced disapproval of this concrete expression of trust and confidence. In May of 1949, the month in which I gave my deposition, and again in December, 1949, after the first trial of Alger Hiss, the Board of Trustees, of which General Eisenhower was still a member, again voted to reject Hiss' resignation.

Alger Hiss, General Eisenhower and Dulles continued as fellow members of the Board of Trustees until after the conviction of Hiss.

I bring these facts to the American people not to suggest that either General Eisenhower or John Foster Dulles is soft toward communists or even guilty of the bad judgment with which the General's running mate charges me. I bring them out only to make the point that the mistrust, the innuendoes, the accusations which this "crusade" is employing, threatens not merely themselves, but the integrity of our institutions and our respect for fair play.

I would remind General Eisenhower of the wisdom of yet another General. One day, after inspecting his troops, the Duke of Wellington said: "They may not frighten the enemy, but gad sir, they frighten me."

I might observe to the General that although his troops do not frighten us they ought to frighten him.

I do not suppose that the Hiss case exhausts the arsenal of accusation with which the General's high command hopes to obtain victory. But these things I can tell you about myself and they are on the record. In 1943, during the war, after leading an economic mission to Italy, I warned against the spread of Soviet influence in the Mediterranean. In 1945 and 1946, just after the war, I engaged in constant and heated debate with Soviet representatives in the United Nations in support of the interests of the United States. I repeatedly pointed out that appeasement doesn't work. In March, 1946, I said to an audience in Chicago that: "Russia and communism are on the march . . . We must forsake any hope that she is going to lie still and lick her awful wounds."

This was not long after General Eisenhower had told a House Committee: "Nothing guides Russian policy so much as a desire for friendship with the United States." As late as June of this year he said, "There is no more reason to fear the 190 million backward people living on the Eurasian continent than there is to fear pollywogs swimming down a muddy creek."

I would never have believed that a Presidential contest with General Eisenhower would have made this speech necessary.

It may well be that the General has been misled by his lack of experience in civil life. This is not a war; it is a political contest in a free democracy; and the rules are different. We who believe in our system have always considered it to be the responsibility of candidates to promote wider understanding of the true issues — and not to stir up fear and to spread suspicion.

I resent — and I resent bitterly — the sly and ugly campaign that is being waged in behalf of the General, and I am deeply shocked that he would lead a so-called "crusade" which accepts calumny and the big doubt as its instruments.

Because I believe in freedom I am opposed to communism. And I think I know more about it and more about the Soviet Union than most of these self-appointed Republican custodians of patriotism. I even went to Russia more than twenty-five years ago to see for myself, before, I dare say, some of these crusaders even knew what was going on in the world,[174] and I have negotiated face to face with the Russians and their satellites in San Francisco, London and New York.

We are opposing communism abroad, where its relentless pressure seeks further to narrow the area of freedom. We are opposing it at home

---

[174] For Stevenson's visit to Russia in 1926, see *The Papers of Adlai E. Stevenson,* Vol. I, pp. 167–169; Davis, *A Prophet in His Own Country,* pp. 153–159.

where its agents and converts seek to undermine our society and corrupt our government. As I have repeatedly said, the Federal Government must use all its resources to expose and identify communistic activity, to keep communists out of places of responsibility in our society, and to protect our institutions from communist espionage, sabotage and subversion.

But I know and you know that we do not strengthen freedom by diminishing it. We do not weaken communism abroad or at home by false or misleading charges carefully timed by unscrupulous men for election purposes. For I believe with all my heart that those who would beguile the voters by lies or half-truths, or corrupt them by fear and falsehood, are committing spiritual treason against our institutions. They are doing the work of our enemies.

In the end such tactics serve directly the interests of the communists and of all other foes of freedom.

Even worse, they undermine our basic spiritual values.

For in the final accounting, "What shall it profit a man if he shall gain the whole world, and lose his own soul?"

Before starting off on his final campaign tour of New York and New England, Stevenson, from his rich experience in the founding of — and participating in the early days of — the United Nations, delivered the following radio speech marking United Nations Day on October 24, 1952.

THE UNITED NATIONS:
OUR HOPE AND OUR COMMITMENT [175]

We do more today than to observe the anniversary of an institution. What we do today is to hold communion with an idea.

I speak of the idea of peace on earth.

The pursuit of this idea is at once old and new. It is as old as man's discovery that he could conquer and enslave other men. In the same sense it is as old as the will to resist, as old as the power of a righteous cause. But it is also a young idea, this pursuit of peace, for it is only in our century that human wisdom and energy have sought to bring all the nations of the earth under a rule of law through world organization.

If the pursuit of peace is both old and new, it is also both complicated and simple. It is complicated, for it has to do with people, and nothing in this universe baffles man as much as man himself. Much of nature's mystery has come under man's mastery. Heat, cold, wind and rain have lost their terrors, but the environment man has created for himself has yet to

[175] The text is from *Major Campaign Speeches AES 1952*, pp. 276–277.

be brought under control. Nature's jungle has been conquered, but man still lives in the larger jungle of his fears.

Yes, it is complicated, this pursuit of peace, but there is also an inspiring simplicity to it. We can win the war against war because we must. Progress is what happens when impossibility yields to necessity. And it is an article of the democratic faith that progress is a basic law of life.

If I thought that the human race was no longer capable of human progress, I would not be trespassing now upon the time and attention of the American people. Instead, I might be off on a remote hilltop silently contemplating the closing scene of the final act of the human comedy.

But I do not believe it is man's destiny to compress this once boundless earth into a small neighborhood, the better to destroy it. Nor do I believe it is in the nature of man to strike eternally at the image of himself, and therefore of God. I profoundly believe that there is on this horizon, as yet only dimly perceived, a new dawn of conscience. In that purer light, people will come to see themselves in each other, which is to say they will make themselves known to one another by their similarities rather than by their differences. Man's knowledge of things will begin to be matched by man's knowledge of self. The significance of a smaller world will be measured not in terms of military advantage, but in terms of advantage for the human community. It will be the triumph of the heartbeat over the drumbeat.

These are my beliefs and I hold them deeply, but they would be without any inner meaning for me unless I felt that they were also the deep beliefs of human beings everywhere. And the proof of this, to my mind, is the very existence of the United Nations. However great the assaults on the peace may have been since the United Nations was founded, the easiest way to demonstrate the idea behind it is by the fact that no nation in the world today would dare to remove itself from membership and separate his country from the human hopes that are woven into the very texture of the organization.

The early years of the United Nations have been difficult ones, but what did we expect? That peace would drift down from the skies like soft snow? That there would be no ordeal, no anguish, no testing, in this greatest of all human undertakings?

Any great institution or idea must suffer its pains of birth and growth. We will not lose faith in the United Nations. We see it as a living thing and we will work and pray for its full growth and development. We want it to become what it was intended to be — a world society of nations under law, not merely law backed by force, but law backed by justice and popular consent. We believe the answer to world war can only be world law. This is our hope and our commitment, and that is why I join all Americans on this anniversary in saying: "More power to the United Nations."

Stevenson delivered the following speech at the Nelson House in Poughkeepsie, New York, on October 25.

FRANKLIN DELANO ROOSEVELT [176]

I am sorry I kept you waiting. I have just been up at Hyde Park and the Roosevelt Library and then I went over to Val Kill cottage for breakfast with Mrs. Roosevelt and Franklin Roosevelt, Jr. It was hard to tear myself away from a scene so thronged with memories for any Presidential candidate or, indeed, for any Democrat — or for any American.[177]

As I came across upstate New York yesterday, I reflected a little on the meaning of Franklin Roosevelt for our time and for our nation.

As a man, he remains a vivid and unforgettable figure in all our minds. His courage, his gallantry, his world vision and his passion for democracy will stay always alive in the national memory. Of course, I know he had — and has — his enemies too. Like all great historical figures, he aroused contention and controversy. But, when I look at those enemies, I can only remember the statement made about another great New York Democrat: [178] We honor him for the enemies he has made.

He made enemies because he led the party of progress — and those who benefit by the vested privileges or injustices of an existing order always resent and resist change.

Franklin Roosevelt became President at one of the turning points in our history. The old order had reached the end of its tether. Our nation either had to revolutionize itself from within — or risk revolution from without. It had to recognize the existence of the twentieth century.

At home, the disorder and collapse of the security markets and then the economy, the misery and despair of the people, threatened revolt and violent social change.

Abroad, the old order had built one wall after another, insulating America from the world, until it had succeeded totally in neutralizing our

176 The text is from *Major Campaign Speeches AES 1952*, pp. 278–281.

177 Franklin D. Roosevelt, Jr., wrote Stevenson on October 27: "It was a great privilege for Mother and me to have you for breakfast at her cottage, and I heard nothing but praise for your speech at Poughkeepsie."

178 Grover Cleveland, governor of New York, 1882–1884, and President of the United States, 1885–1889 and 1893–1897.

power and withdrawing us from the world balance of forces. War threatened.

Fortunately we had in President Roosevelt a man with the historical insight to understand the problems and with the will and leadership to do something about them.

At home, he knew that the economy of a great nation could not be weak, anarchic, undermined by speculation and influenced by selfish and unscrupulous concentrations of wealth and power. He stood for a strong economy — and he knew that the people's government had an essential role to play in releasing the energies of the people.

Under his leadership, the American people drew up programs by which they could gain the assurance of economic and social security. His New Deal put solid foundations under our free economic system — foundations designed to maintain the buying power of the people and thus to prevent another collapse into the dark pit of depression and despair. Sense and sanity and responsibility were restored to our economic life.

The result was that our nation, so weak and battered and despairing in 1932 in the greatest economic misfortune of our history, was able ten years later to serve as the arsenal of democracy in the greatest war of our history — and today is riding the crest of the greatest prosperity of our history.

As Mr. Roosevelt believed in strength at home, so he believed in strength abroad — because he knew that, without strength, America would be without influence, and without influence America could not make her proper contribution to the maintenance of peace. From the beginning of his administration, he led the way in building up American military and naval power.

Some of you will remember that his early requests for naval appropriations horrified certain of his liberal friends. They tried to explain it away by saying that it was a kind of hobby for him, like sailing his favorite sailboat! Well, if it was a hobby, it was a fortunate one for the American people. Those aircraft carriers and destroyers built with PWA money turned out to be mighty useful just a few years later.

But Roosevelt did not believe in strength for the sake of strength. He believed in strength for the sake of co-operation with other free nations in the service of peace. Unfortunately, by the time he could persuade the rest of us of the vital importance of an affirmative foreign policy, the Second World War was upon us. Once war had begun he understood that we could best defend America by helping our friends in the world defend themselves. And in the fire and fury of war, he never lost sight of the ultimate objective — the building of a structure of world security which would reduce the chances of another such global holocaust.

The concept of the United Nations was his final legacy to the American people. It is one of the proudest incidents in my own life that I was able to play a role in its birth and its formative years. The United Nations and its specialized agencies are today the world's best hope for peace.

At home and abroad, President Roosevelt understood the moral and historical imperatives of our age. Under his leadership America came to terms with the needs of our own industrial society and with the needs of the emerging world community. We shall continue his struggle for sanity and responsibility at home and for the collective strength of freedom abroad. We shall never go back to the pre-Roosevelt period — to the reign of the Republican Old Guard — no matter how much the old enemies of Roosevelt inveigh against us, nor how successful these men are in recapturing the Republican Party.

Some of them have spoken loudly and defiantly of their determination to destroy the last vestiges of the works he wrought. But I don't think they will do any better this time than they have in any election since 1932 — even with a General to lead their legions.

I have said that this nation would never retreat from affirmative, forward-looking policies at home and abroad. Nor shall we stand still. We shall move ahead — and I hope we may do so with some of the same creativeness and enterprise and the same faith in free Americans which Franklin Roosevelt has written large across our history.

New conditions create new problems. We will not be bound by the past, any more than Roosevelt felt himself bound by Woodrow Wilson's era. Nor would he have it so, for his deepest belief was that the obligation of government was to keep pace with the changes wrought by science and experience in our society — and by ideas in the minds of men.

We cannot rely on past solutions in 1952, any more than he could in 1932. But, as we move ahead, we shall always be faithful to the spirit of Franklin Roosevelt. We shall always be fired and inspired by his courageous example. We shall attempt to achieve at last that America — free and friendly and strong and responsible — of which he always dreamed.

At the Madison Square Garden rally for Stevenson on October 28, many endorsements of him were read to the audience, including a telegram from Albert Einstein: "I am happy to support your candidacy for the Presidency because I trust your integrity, judgment and independence." Among those who spoke about Stevenson was his old friend Carl Sandburg, poet, folk interpreter of America, and biographer of Abraham Lincoln:

"I have known Adlai Stevenson for twenty-five years and I am not

cutting any corners nor shading any phrase when I say that he is a great and a consecrated man, one more embodiment of the finest human flame out of the American past, a farmer, business man, lawyer, able governmental executive, a father of three sons, one of them a marine officer who will see service in Korea.

"Long before this time of ours America saw the faces of her men and women torn and shaken in turmoil, chaos and storm. In each major crisis you could have seen despair on the faces of some of the foremost strugglers. But their ideas won. Their visions came through. They live in the sense that today their dream is on the faces of living men and women. They ought not to be forgotten — the dead who hold in their clenched hands that which became the heritage of us, the living.

"This is the reminder, the high memory, the gospel of faith, the lighted torch that Adlai Stevenson has carried this summer from coast to coast, from the Great Lakes to the Gulf. Adlai Stevenson sees America not in the setting sun of a black night of despair ahead of us. He sees America in the crimson light of a rising sun fresh from the burning creative hand of God, with splinters of the golden flame saying there can be hope of great days to come, great days possible to men and women of will and vision." [179]

Stevenson delivered the following speech at Madison Square Garden.

THE NEW FORCE IN AMERICA [180]

We are reaching the final hours of the long campaign voyage. A week from today you and millions of your countrymen will retire to the solitude of the voting booth for a moment of communion with your conscience. The blare of the loud-speakers will be silenced; the Republican air raid will be over; the all-clear will have sounded; the candidates, the politicians, the experts, the pollsters will all have slipped into the shadows, and the people will take the stage.

As I speak here I am aware that the world will quickly forget what I say tonight, but it will long — (*voices say "no."*) — oh, yes, it will, but it will long remember what you do on next Tuesday. And I will long remember your welcome to me, a son of Illinois, here in New York tonight.

To stand here in Madison Square Garden on this traditional occasion is to be enveloped with the memories of two great men of this State and of the Democratic Party — Alfred Smith and Franklin Roosevelt. It was

[179] The original draft is in the possession of Miss Margaret Sandburg, Flatrock, North Carolina.

[180] The text is from *Major Campaign Speeches AES 1952*, pp. 286–291.

these men who led the Democratic Party to its great revival. Picking up after a long period of Republican rule and ruin, they gave to New York State and then to this nation a whole, complete program of liberal social reform. They took up once more the spirit of the idea of an immortal American — that government must be of the people, for the people, and by the people. It is the principle immortalized at Gettysburg which animates and guides our party today — the principle of government with a heart — government not content with merely governing, but dedicated to reflecting and expressing the interests of people — their needs, their dreams, their highest hopes and aspirations.

To travel this country as I have these past two months is to realize that there is a new force alive in America. People are looking for something more in the conduct of their public affairs. I sense at this mid-point of this great century of revolution a kind of driving desire in people to find a more exalted meaning in democracy. They are willing to do for their party more than they have done before, and they are demanding of those who would be their leaders, some new, not wholly defined, imperfectly perceived element of uplift in the execution of democracy's purpose. The record of this election will be the record of the response of our two great parties to this new challenge of the people.

The Republican Party rose last spring from a generation of lethargy and caught for a moment the spark of this new desire and exaltation. They cradled the fire in the slogan of change. And then, as the nation cheered, the Republican Party cast out its old and weary rigid leadership and turned instead to a man whose name has become a national symbol of high purpose.

However, that the spark which had been kindled in the higher desires of thousands of our Republican friends was then snuffed out is a sordid triumph of expediency over principle. These hopes and aspirations were shaken to their roots when the Republican crusader said "I do" to the lifelong cheer-leader for a dear, departed, quiet past that is also dead. These hopes were wholly destroyed in the chain reaction of compromise which followed the first surrender of principle to expediency. Today there is the dreary dullness of disillusion; the stark realization that the venerable Republican Party has within it forces of reaction once more unconquerable. It is in all ways proper that Democrats extend a warm, affectionate welcome to these thousands of courageous souls — these refugees from all walks of life who were thrilled by the General's victory at Chicago, and are now disheartened by this negotiated peace with the enemy. It has been part of the price of that surrender that much of the purpose of this campaign and of this election has been lost — for us as well as them.

America faces today great questions of its destiny. This should have been a time, in this campaign, for the two great parties to lay before America their precise programs for America's future. I have tried to do this — for you, for the Democratic Party, for the independents who wear no label — to the fullest of my ability. I have enjoyed it. There have been great satisfactions in honoring as best I could my commitment to talk sense to the American people. But there has been no opportunity for actual debate, for evidently part of the price of the embrace on Morning-side Heights has been to lay no affirmative program before this nation for its approval.

The general headquarters of the great crusade are agreed upon what they are against, which is, in a word, Democrats. But, they are not agreed on what they are for. And the record is clear that most of what they are for is what most of the people of America are against — and have been for twenty years. So, speech after speech has come forth from Republican rostrums, always in the same pattern. Volumes of sound about all that the Democrats have done wrong, followed by an angels' choir — the angels in costume, of course.

The biggest single fact before the American people in this election is that there is no Republican program for the future. It is not enough that they tell us that they are against high prices. It is not enough that they cry out in alarm about false prosperity. They offer no facts to support their prophecies of doom and no evidence that they have departed from their 1930 patented formula of "let boom and let bust."

It is not enough to be told that every decent Republican hates communism. So does every loyal American. What we wanted to know was how the Republican leadership would meet this problem. And, of that we know nothing, except that the General gives us his assurance that we can do it justly and fairly and in full observance of the American system of justice. We do not know even whether the Republican program would include fighting communism by helping our allies, as the General professed before he was a candidate; or, whether he changed his mind when he took up Senator Taft's demand for tax reductions that could only be accomplished by halting virtually all aid to Europe.

There is no point in going on. The pattern is clear on issue after issue. To recognize the problem, to engage in self-righteous denunciation, and then to present two offerings: one, unspoken but plain from the record, is the persistent answers of a group of Old Guardians who are once again in the places of decision. We have said in five straight elections that we don't like those answers — and will say it again. The other answer which has come so often these past two months is the assurance that a great General will somehow continue to deal with these problems fairly and justly. It is in no disrespect that we say this is not only too little — it is dangerously too much. A democracy cannot afford to make its elective process simply a determination to rely on the unrevealed wisdom of one man. History offers too many warnings against that course.

On July 12th, in Chicago, speaking to a group of old-line Republican leaders, the man who was then seeking the Republican nomination sought to reassure his listeners against their doubts about his political qualifications. Would he do, they were asking in effect, what they considered necessary to win the election? He gave them full and sufficient assurance, and these were his words: "In the military, when strategical principles conflict with the tactical, the tactical always goes. Which means that long-term programs are not nearly so important as winning the next battle."

Now, it isn't perhaps for me to argue before the bar of the American people whether a background of military or civilian experience is a better qualification for the Presidency. Anything I might say would be misinterpreted as a denial of my unqualified respect for those who have served our country with courage and with devotion. Yet the Republican candidate, drawing upon his own military experience to explain his campaign tactics, gives those tactics he has subsequently employed a fuller meaning which the voters of America are entitled to have made clear.

High prices, labor relations, farm programs, social security, communism — are these in the General's view matters right now only of campaign tactics? Are America's long-term programs for meeting these problems of lesser importance than winning this election? Is this only a battle that we have before us? Do the tactics of winning it justify false fears and false promises? Is it all right to count the American people too ignorant to understand? Are no long-term answers necessary? Is it just bread and circuses, and if there has to be an answer, is it to offer fairness, justice and the services of a man whose familiarity invites respect?

In this record is the complete rejection by the Republican Party of what I have called earlier the new force alive in America today, the desire of people to find a new, a more exalted kind of meaning in the public life of this democracy.

Are we ready, we of the Democratic Party, to meet this challenge? I say that we are. An awareness of it has been the guiding star of this campaign. I have spent — and my colleagues with me — two long, yes, hard months, spelling out a complete program of policy for the people to consider and to vote on next Tuesday. In any campaign there may be some words uttered that one wishes later had remained unspoken. I am not above reproach. I have not been able in the exigencies of time and circumstances to spell out every problem, every question in minute detail. But my conscience — that thing that usually feels so bad when everything else feels so good — my conscience does not trouble me.

I have spoken my piece with candor, and often. I have been subjected to the solemn charge that I am being too funny, and at other times I have been accused of being too intellectual and somber. I shall have to let you judge whether I am too prone to invite people to laugh or weep. Both, in my judgment, are good for the spirit, and I hope the Republicans don't contemplate any legal prohibitions against them!

I can approach this day of the people's judgment with the confidence that I have never attempted to be different things to different men. There is only one candidate for the Presidency on the Democratic ticket. It will never, I hope, be said that the Governor of Illinois has ever whispered anything to the Governor of South Carolina that he would not say aloud to the Governor of New York. I have said the same thing about the great cause of equal rights for all men in Virginia and in Harlem. I have not been an isolationist in Chicago and an internationalist in New York. I have not praised my friend in one breath and then moved on quickly to grasp hands with those who slander him.

We have talked to — not down or up — we have talked *to* the American people. This is the beginning of our answer to men and women who are saying, "We want no smallness of vision in those who seek our trust — no compromising with what some mistakenly think are our weaknesses."

It was a great poet who said, "Not failure, but low aim, is a crime." Those who aspire to the leadership of America, if they offer Americans something unworthy of their own beliefs and interests, will fail.

I do not say to you that I, or any member of our party, has a vision of America large enough that its people will not outstrip that vision in a score of years. I say to you only that it is our purpose, our intent to work up toward the level of high purpose for America which you hold unspoken in your hearts. We offer you what we think is an awareness of your aspirations for our country as it turns into the second half of this troubled century. You want your public affairs to be in the hands of a government which is clean so that it may be strong. You want the tremendous affairs of America administered so that you can live in a world of plenty and of peace. You accept the obligations of leadership of the world of free nations, asking only that these obligations entail no more of sacrifice than is wholly essential and required.

We have learned that to act with enthusiasm and faith is the condition of acting greatly.

We have learned that to plan boldly is to make dreams come true.

We offer for America, for leadership, no fear, no counsels of little cautiousness — nothing small and petty. Facing America, we offer an awareness of its call for something better, and nothing less than the finest which is in us.

And finally, my friends, you have been very patient, and I have some good news for you. On Sunday last, the Chicago *Tribune* came out for the General, and Colonel McCormick is in the forefront of the great crusade, without any loss of rank. But the Milwaukee *Journal* came out for Stevenson — and guess who lives in Wisconsin?

To Alicia Patterson [181]

October 28, 1952

. . . I'm back in Hoboken on the train after a hideous day beating my way thru the crowds in N.Y. and N.J. and speaking speaking speaking ad nauseum — for them as well as well as [sic] me I fear.

When Oh when will this ghastly ordeal end!

I had hoped for a moment alone to call you but the throng never opened and now you're asleep and so am I, or should be. The note at the Hotel when I arrived late last night from Conn. via Harlem was a warm blessing & relief although Virginia Pasley [182] had already brought the word that you were "sprung" from the hospital. But I pine for details of your journey thru the valley of the shadow — how could it all have overtaken you so rapidly, so unexpectedly etc etc. And are you really mending — your letter sounds so tired — and so am I — deathly tired and baffled & wondering, why oh why. Please, please take care — no impetuous decisions to get up and have at it again.

The campaign is going well — I guess — at least measured by crowds and hysteria which seem to be the politicians yard stick. Indeed it looks almost too good, with virtually every state at least a battle ground and many "safe" — as the wise guys say. And woe to him who wins. Why oh why did I do it? I had to, didn't I?

I must to bed — or die — and sometimes I wish it was both.

. . . ADLAI

P.S. I did a poor "rally" speech at the [Madison Square] Garden tonight — but it was intended to be diffe[re]nt than the usual rally, pour it on, conventional type thing. But alway[s], always too little time to prepare!

---

[181] This handwritten letter, postmarked October 29 and mailed from Scranton, Pennsylvania, is in the possession of Adlai E. Stevenson III.

[182] A feature writer for *Newsday* who covered Stevenson's campaign for that paper.

Governor Stevenson concluded his campaign on Saturday evening, November 1, with a speech at the Chicago Stadium.

THE CAMPAIGN IS OVER! [183]

Tonight we have come to the end of the campaign, and a long, long journey — and I have come home to old friends and to familiar surroundings. There's no place like home.

There have been times when I have wondered whether you, my friends here in Illinois, couldn't have found some easier way of getting rid of me. In fact, before the Convention I wrote a song about it, only the Democratic Party took the song and changed the words. My song was called "Don't Let Them Take Me Away."

It has been a great campaign. I have enjoyed every minute of it. It has been the most exhilarating and most heartwarming and most uplifting experience a man could have.

The story of this campaign is written in the record of the changing meaning of the Republican talk about change. It was, in its July form, the one thing they had to offer the nation. And what a different meaning it has in November can, it seems to me, be illustrated by one fact. Never once in this whole campaign, so far as I have been able to determine, has the General ever mentioned the name of Wendell Willkie, who was really the founder of the modern tradition of progressive Republicanism. I can understand that it is difficult to mention him, for Wendell Willkie placed the principles of the new Republicanism above compromises and expediency. And there are evidently a lot of Republicans who haven't forgiven him yet.

This stadium reminds me most vividly of Wendell Willkie, for it was here, in March of 1941, and at my invitation — which I personally went to Rushville, Indiana, to extend to him — that he spoke eloquently to a great mass meeting on the life-and-death issue of aid to our friends abroad who were then sorely pressed by the Nazi tyranny.

It was this kind of selflessness following so closely on the disappointment of political defeat that has kept, and will always keep, Wendell Willkie's memory alive for all Americans, and especially for those of his party who wanted to perpetuate his tradition.

My friends of Chicago, it has not only been a great campaign for me — it's also a winner. There has been an electric feeling of victory in the air all the way home.

Well, that's the way it always goes with Democratic campaigns. In July the Republicans pull each other's hair and kick each other's shins,

[183] The text is from *Major Campaign Speeches AES 1952*, pp. 306–312.

and practice up for the rest of their campaign by calling each other the names they are going to call the Democrats later on. This is known as creating unity in the Republican Party.

Then, in August, the newspapers compete with each other in predicting Republican landslides. They tell us we might just as well save the expense of campaigning because we don't have a chance. The polls show that the Republicans will carry every State except Rhode Island and Georgia, and they're doubtful. This is the month, my friends, when the Republicans place their big orders for confetti and balloons.

In September the newspapers tell us that the Democrats are gaining a bit, and that no one needs to worry, for reason has prevailed and the Republicans are really truly united. In September the polls begin to worry them a little, so they accuse us of talking over people's heads. They even accuse us of having a sense of humor.

Then, by the first of October, the newspapers sense that something is wrong and they begin to get nervous. They accuse their own candidate of running like a dry creek.

By mid-October the pollsters begin to concede that the election will be fairly close. This is the time of year when the Republicans start to complain that the campaign is going on too long — it is too hard on the candidates, and, besides, the Democrats are socialists, communists, crooks, or a little of each.

By the first of November the newspapers say that it's impossible to predict the outcome of the election; and now they say that the Republic is in danger and that they have documentary proof that all Democrats are dreadful and depraved, and that to find out how dreadful we are everyone should tune in on Monday night to hear the real low-down — although, of course, they disapprove heartily of such techniques.

And then, of course, on Election Day, the Democrats win. And so it goes, my friends, election after election.

I think you know and I know that they have never really been ahead at any time. They just throw so much confetti at each other, read so many of each other's editorials, and cheer each other's speeches so loudly, that they begin to think that everyone agrees with them. Well, they don't. And I think you can rely on the American people every time to tell who is really talking sense and who isn't.

And it's even more than a question of sense. It is, above all, a question of which party has faith in the future of America — which party has a program — which party has earned the people's trust. The answer to this question is now, as it has been for these many years, the Democratic Party.

Then this time, perhaps because the Republicans wanted discipline in their ranks, they chose a General to lead them. He and they have taken a bewildering variety of positions. And in the Republican choir the General has shown an admirable capacity to sing bass and baritone and tenor all at once. When he was here in the Middle West he identified himself with the most reactionary and isolationist wing of the Republican Party. But he recognized that the songs he sang in what he mistakenly considered isolationist territory would not be music to the ears of Eastern Republicans. So, when he went East he summoned a new ghost from the Republican haunted house and asked for a new script.

Which General do you read? And which do you believe? Is it the one who is in agreement on all basic issues with Senator Taft in Taftland? The one who signs up Senators Jenner and McCarthy on his team? Or, is it the General who proclaims in New York and California his devotion to all the social gains achieved by the Democratic administrations in the past twenty years?

We have been offered a strange picture of an anguished, reluctant, respected figure reciting distasteful words, shaking hands that make him shudder, walking in strange, dark alleys, caught in a clamor of conflicting voices. And that picture, I fear, appeals not just to soft hearts, but to soft heads.

I do not ask you to withhold your compassion for my opponent in the ordeal he has endured. But I say, does he, therefore, deserve your confidence and trust?

It occurred to me last night, on Hallowe'en, that the General who started out with a new broom has ended up on an old broomstick, and he is surrounded by a vintage collection of ghosts, of spooks and bogeymen.

Some still cling to the fact that he doesn't really mean it; that immediately after the election he will wave a wand and there will be a flash of fire and he will be transformed into what they call the "Old Eisenhower." And that will be the neatest Hallowe'en trick of them all.

They say that then he will turn in righteous wrath upon those who have held his hands throughout this melancholy autumn.

Well, I don't believe it, and neither do they. This suggestion that he will double-cross his new-found friends as soon as he gets into office does credit neither to the General's integrity nor to Senator Taft's vigilance.

Can independents really believe that victory would strengthen progressive Republicans? Will Senator Taft, having laid down the General's program, be humbled and routed by the General's success? Will the big gun — not-so-secret weapon of these last weeks of the Republican campaign — the Junior Senator from Wisconsin — will he be enlightened and chastened by the heady wine of triumph? — the Wisconsin Senator who told the country the truth for once the other day when he said that his power in Washington depends upon the General's election? Let's not deceive ourselves, because it is quite clear who will run the country in the event of a Republican triumph.

Many progressive Republicans, like Senator Wayne Morse, for that reason are fighting on our side because they know what the fate of the progressive Republicans would be under an administration like that. Hence, I have noticed as I have traveled in this autumn weather that the Ike buttons are falling faster than the leaves.

This, my friends, is the transformation that has been wrought in three months. And, as a result, instead of the hopeful, resurgent Republican Party, the contrast between the two today is exactly what it has been for twenty years. The Democratic Party remains the party which has fought for a strong America — a nation strong at home, strong abroad, dedicated to strengthening the purpose and the meaning of life for all of our citizens.

The Republican Party, despite the honorable efforts of many individuals, remains the party not of a strong America, but of a little America. Its leadership stands for a rudderless and drifting economy, at the mercy of every gust and squall, careening recklessly between the extremes of boom and bust.

That's a change, my friends, we need just as much as we need a good attack of appendicitis.

And, abroad, the Republican Party stands similarly for a little America — fearful to take its place in building the strength and the unity of free peoples.

We entered this campaign with a bipartisan foreign policy, virtually united except for a few stubborn men — united as the leader and the hope of the free. The campaign closes with an alarming chasm reopening between us. Here is change indeed — frightening change — that reflects a guiding purpose no higher than political ambition.

It was irresponsible politics first to hold out hopes of early liberation to those among us with families and close friends behind the Iron Curtain.

It was dangerous politics to promise tax cuts of tens of billions at the risk of endangering our own defenses and those of our allies in Europe and Asia.

It was sorry politics to urge the re-election of the few figures in public life who still preach unreconstructed isolationism.

And it was cheap politics to suggest that one candidate is more deeply concerned than the other about getting our sons home from Korea.[184] And, on this let me add just one thing. Yesterday the New

[184] Stevenson wrote in his Introduction to *Major Campaign Speeches of Adlai E. Stevenson, 1952*, p. xxvii: "While foreign affairs was bound to enter the campaign

York *Times* published a poll taken among some of our troops in Korea — and the Democratic candidate got twice the votes of the Republican candidate.

I grieve, and so should you, that the Republicans have made an issue of war and peace when there was none four months ago, because this far transcends politics or the political fortunes of any man. The stakes are life and death; the stakes are civilization itself, and not votes in an election campaign.

It's time for a change. It's always time for a change. And we Democrats have accomplished tremendous changes despite stubborn obstruction and resistance, consecutively for twenty years. But, we are far from where we seek to go. So let's talk in these closing moments of this campaign about the future, and not about the past — about our hopes, and not about our fears.

The things we seek for ourselves we seek for all Americans: good education for our sons and daughters; the dignity of security in advancing age; the equality of opportunity for all, not just some of God's children.

The only guiding stars are those which reflect the needs and the aspirations of people — of living men, women and children.

Let us build our program for change not on fear, but on faith — faith which we know is rooted in the vast resources of this land and the unmeasured capacities of its people.

I wish you could all have made this two-month journey with me. No American could travel the long road I have traveled and not find his faith renewed, his faith in his country and its future.

I have traversed the New England hills, ablaze with autumn color, and felt the touch of the soft air of the Southland.

I have flown over the mighty mountains to the Golden Gate and the blue Pacific.

I have flown over the fir-clad slopes and the rolling wheatlands of the great Northwest, and over the lonely cattle lands of the old Southwest.

I have traveled the route my forebears followed westward to Illinois.

---

significantly and properly, I had assumed that it and our unhappy situation in Korea particularly would not be a politically fruitful tree to shake in view of my adversary's past utterances. In early August I decided, if elected, to make a quick journey to Japan, Korea and India 'to see for myself,' meet the people with whom I would have to deal, and to give the best possible evidence of our profound concern for the Orient. We kept the plan secret, fearful that it might be construed as a political gesture. This may have been a mistake, and while I cannot approve the General's speech about going to Korea and the implication of early settlement or the misleading use that was made of it, I think he did the right thing to go out there and that we will all benefit from his first-hand information."

I have seen the old stone houses in the Pennsylvania hills, and I have come home to the sweep and the swell of the free soil of our beloved Illinois.

I have seen an America where all of the signs read "Men at Work."

But, we have much to do in this century in this country of ours before its greatness may be fully realized and shared by all Americans.

As we plan for change let us be sure that our vision is high enough and broad enough so that it encompasses every single hope and dream of both the greatest and the humblest among us.

I see an America where no man fears to think as he pleases, or say what he thinks.

I see an America where slums and tenements have vanished and children are raised in decency and self-respect.

I see an America where men and women have leisure from toil — leisure to cultivate the resources of the spirit.

I see an America where no man is another's master — where no man's mind is dark with fear.

I see an America at peace with the world.

I see an America as the horizon of human hopes.

This is our design for the American cathedral, and we shall build it brick by brick and stone by stone, patiently, bravely and prayerfully. And, to those who say that the design defies our abilities to complete it, I answer: "To act with enthusiasm and faith is the condition of acting greatly."

On the day before the election, Carl McGowan, Governor Stevenson's closest aid, wrote to him:

11/3/52

To AES:

I don't know who is going to win *tomorrow*, but it is clear to me that *today* all of the honest and sensitive and intelligent people in this country know who should.

Who can say, then, that victory has not already come?

CMcG

On election evening Stevenson, after writing his telegram to General Eisenhower conceding defeat, drove to the Leland Hotel where the Springfield campaign staff, leading journalists including James Reston and Raymond P. Brandt, such national figures as Senator J. W. Fulbright and John L. Lewis, and many friends from across the country were listening to the returns. In the automobile ride between the mansion and the Leland, Stevenson recalled a story told by Abraham Lincoln, and Benjamin P. Thomas, the noted Lincoln scholar, who was riding with him, told the Governor that he had quoted Lincoln's words exactly. At the Leland, the Governor stood before his friends — many of whom wept, many of whom said, "No, no" — and spoke:

THE VERDICT — WE PRAY AS ONE [185]

I have a statement that I should like to make. If I may, I shall read it to you.

My fellow citizens have made their choice and have selected General Eisenhower and the Republican Party as the instruments of their will for the next four years.

The people have rendered their verdict and I gladly accept it.

General Eisenhower has been a great leader in war. He has been a vigorous and valiant opponent in the campaign. These qualities will now be dedicated to leading us all through the next four years.

It is traditionally American to fight hard before an election. It is equally traditional to close ranks as soon as the people have spoken.

From the depths of my heart I thank all of my party and all of those independents and Republicans who supported Senator Sparkman and me.

That which unites us as American citizens is far greater than that which divides us as political parties.

I urge you all to give General Eisenhower the support he will need to carry out the great tasks that lie before him.

I pledge him mine.

We vote as many, but we pray as one. With a united people, with faith in democracy, with common concern for others less fortunate around the globe, we shall move forward with God's guidance toward the time when His children shall grow in freedom and dignity in a world at peace.

I have sent the following telegram to General Eisenhower at the Commodore Hotel in New York:

THE PEOPLE HAVE MADE THEIR CHOICE AND I CONGRATULATE YOU. THAT YOU MAY BE THE SERVANT AND GUARDIAN OF PEACE AND MAKE THE VALE OF TROUBLE A DOOR OF HOPE IS MY EARNEST PRAYER. BEST WISHES,

ADLAI E. STEVENSON. [186]

[185] The text is from *Major Campaign Speeches AES 1952*, pp. 319–320.
[186] The handwritten original of this telegram is in the possession of Mrs. Margaret Munn, Springfield, Illinois.

Someone asked me, as I came in, down on the street, how I felt, and I was reminded of a story that a fellow-townsman of ours used to tell — Abraham Lincoln. They asked him how he felt once after an unsuccessful election. He said he felt like a little boy who had stubbed his toe in the dark. He said that he was too old to cry, but it hurt too much to laugh.

A small group of old friends joined the Governor at the mansion after his statement at the Leland Hotel. George Ball wrote:

> Finally, he announced that since he had lost the election the least he could do was to make the toast. And so, with Adlai, we all raised our glasses while he offered a tribute to "Wilson Wyatt, the best campaign manager any unsuccessful politician ever had."
>
> He described himself wrongly, of course, as we all knew. He was no "unsuccessful politician," but a brave leader who had given a whole generation of Americans a cause for which many could, for the first time, feel deeply proud — a man of prophetic quality who, in Arthur Schlesinger's phrase, "set the tone for a new era in Democratic politics."
>
> Only one person present that evening would have dared to call Adlai Stevenson "unsuccessful" — and we loved him for it. For we had each of us, at different times and in different ways, discovered that sense of decency and proportion, humility and infallible good manners which led him so often to understatement — particularly when he spoke of himself. And we would not have had him otherwise.[187]

[187] "With AES in War and Politics," in *As We Knew Adlai,* pp. 152–153.

Part Three

To the Man
Who Said What He Meant

*L*etters and telegrams poured into Springfield the day after the election
and for days and weeks thereafter. They came from the known and
unknown — and from people in many lands.

Some came from those who voted for Eisenhower but praised
Stevenson for the quality of his campaign. One woman wrote that both
she and her husband thought the Governor was far more able than
Eisenhower but they felt the country needed a Republican as President.
A Scottish clergyman wrote: "Many in Britain regret as I do that you
are not President-elect." A barman in a Swiss hotel wrote: "All the
sympathy of my customers was for you." Ambassador Stanley Woodward
wrote: "I write you simply to tell you that I am terribly sorry you were
not elected, and how much I admired your conduct of the campaign."
John Steinbeck wrote: "I hope you will have rest without sadness. The
sadness is for us who have lost our chance for greatness when greatness
is needed." Julian Boyd and his aides on The Papers of Thomas Jefferson
wrote: "We wish again to express our thanks to you for your efforts in
furthering, during your campaign, the ideals of American democracy
which are vital to our survival." Norman Thomas, who voted for the
Socialist candidate, wrote: "It has been my lot, as a campaigner myself
for a minor party, to have read the speeches of presidential candidates
rather closely, ever since 1928. You set a new standard in campaign
oratory." An enlisted man in Korea wrote: "This letter has just one
purpose: to express my pride in your exemplary record during this past
campaign." Seventeen members of the Air Force wrote: "It was and is
sad to realize that our country's leadership has been temporarily deprived
of your unique qualities." An Italian wrote: "I did not believe it possible
to be able to moderate the exigency of a battle with chivalry and good
taste." A British Member of Parliament wrote: "I hope it will not be considered an impertinence if a stranger does give expression to his admiration for the elevated manner in which you conducted your campaign." A

nineteen-year-old Japanese wrote: "In Japan, we supported you as a President of the U.S." A thirteen-year-old schoolboy from New Rochelle, New York, wrote: "I guess that it is needless to say how I listened and learned from your magnificent campaign talks." One envelope read: "To the Man 'Who said what he ment — and — ment what he said' Springfield, Ill." Carl Sandburg wrote: "You are cherished and remembered in multitudes of deep prayers." Winston S. Churchill wrote on December 30 thanking Stevenson for a bound copy of the speech of welcome and the speech of acceptance: "Thank you so much for your kindness in sending me this gift, which I value as a tangible and most interesting reminder of your distinguished campaign." [1]

The Governor answered as many letters as he could, but the majority had to be answered by a form letter. "The mail and messages have literally crushed us to death since the election," Stevenson wrote on November 11. "All very gratifying but what a headache." [2] *By November 14, Stevenson staff members estimated that over fifty thousand letters and telegrams had been received in Springfield.* [3] *Their final estimate reached a hundred thousand.*

Stevenson worked to make sure that the affairs of the State of Illinois were in order for transfer to the new Republican Governor. He spoke on November 9 at Alton, Illinois, at the dedication of the historical marker to the martyred Elijah Lovejoy; he spoke at the Philip Murray Memorial Dinner at Atlantic City on December 3; he spoke at the Gridiron Club dinner on December 13. On January 8, 1953, he made a Farewell Report to the Citizens of Illinois. He visited Washington, D.C., and New York en route to a vacation at Barbados at the home of Mr. and Mrs. Ronald Tree. While there he selected the speeches for Major Campaign Speeches of Adlai E. Stevenson, 1952 *(New York: Random House, 1953) and wrote an introduction for the volume.*

On the way to board ship at San Francisco for a trip of self-education through many countries of Asia, the Middle East, and Europe, he spoke at Los Angeles on February 26, 1953.

Stevenson's old friend Mrs. John Paul Welling wrote him on November 2: "The poetic close of your gorgeous speech at last night's rally [at the Chicago Stadium] so expressed and suggested my own passion and hope for America, that I realize even more clearly how and why the people who had scarcely heard of you in July now think they feel as

[1] These letters and telegrams are in the Adlai E. Stevenson collection, Princeton University Library.

[2] This handwritten letter is in the possession of Mrs. Edison Dick.

[3] Letter, William McCormick Blair, Jr., to Leland Stowe, November 14, 1952.

close to you as do all of us who have loved you from way back for your-self alone." She wrote later in the letter: "You have endured greatly, my dear — I know. And you have triumphed gloriously." [4]

To Mrs. John Paul Welling [5]

November 6, 1952

Dear Harriet:

I have read and re-read your lovely letter. I am sure that the ordeals of the past may be a bit of philosophy that I have unwittingly accumulated and made this one that much easier.

I have no regrets — except that I have seen and talked to you all too little of late. Perhaps I can now do something about that, too.

Love,

To Alicia Patterson [6]

November 6, 1952

Alicia dear —

Thanks for your wonderful wire and the letter. I'm glad, so glad, you're mending rapidly.

I've no regrets; did the best I could, didn't trim, equivocate or clasp dirty hands. But the 20 yrs. the moribund Dem[ocratic]. organization, Korea (a disposable & dangerous thing to have put into the campaign!) etc etc were too much. I really don't know, but many newsmen etc. dropping in to say goodbye seem to feel that HST's campaigning hurt far more than it helped by raising the target again and diluting my coverage.

Sometime we will talk again — maybe by the black river.[7]

ADLAI

To Sidney Hyman

November 6, 1952

Dear Sidney:

I am sorry I did not have an opportunity to express to you adequately before you left my deep personal gratitude for the help which you gave

[4] This letter is in the Adlai E. Stevenson collection, Illinois State Historical Library (A.E.S., I.S.H.L.).

[5] A copy is in A.E.S., I.S.H.L.

[6] This handwritten letter is in the possession of Adlai E. Stevenson III.

[7] Miss Patterson had an estate near Kingsland, Georgia, on the St. Mary's River. The river, the dividing line between Georgia and Florida, is called the Black River locally because of the dark color of the water, caused by mangrove roots.

during the campaign. I thought that the performance of the Elks Club group [8] was magnificent from beginning to end, and I know that you played a vital role in it.

I believe that we can all take the satisfaction that comes from having dealt with the issues sharply, uncompromisingly and literately, and that is a continuing value of great importance.

I hope I shall have the opportunity of seeing you again in the future. Meanwhile, be assured of my warmest thanks and my every good wish.

Sincerely,

To Arthur M. Schlesinger, Jr.

November 7, 1952

Dear Arthur:

Despite the lingering reverberations of the voice of the people in my ears, I can still hear the voice of the Elks Club speaking clearly, forcefully and intelligently. It may not have been heard by enough people, or perhaps its message was garbled in transmission, but it had a lot to say and it said it well.

I am deeply grateful to you for your own contribution to that effort. When I think of the trouble and inconvenience to which you were put, and especially how it took you away from your family, I am overcome with contrition. In any event, you and your wife have my warmest thanks — and my every good wish.

Sincerely,

To Maude Myers [9]

November 7, 1952

Dear Miss Myers:

Disappointment over the outcome of the elections, together with the fact that there will be a change in the State administration in January, may tend towards a letdown on the part of key officials and State employees generally. I appreciate the fact that some of this reaction would stem from loyalty to me, for which I am most grateful.

However, an even more basic loyalty is that which we owe to the peo-

[8] The research and drafting of speeches was done in offices in the Springfield Elks Club. See Kenneth S. Davis, *A Prophet in His Own Country: The Triumphs and Defeats of Adlai E. Stevenson* (Garden City, New York: Doubleday, 1957), pp. 410–411.

[9] President of the Illinois Civil Service Commission. The original is in the possession of Miss Myers.

ple of Illinois; and it can be discharged only by rigorous adherence to the highest standards of public service during the remainder of our terms.

It is my earnest desire that we turn the State government over to the new administration in first-rate condition. I hope that you will communicate my determination that there be no letdown to the appropriate personnel under your direction.

We started this administration with a new concept of public responsibility, and we must end it that way.

Sincerely yours,

To Gerald W. Johnson

November 10, 1952

My dear Mr. Johnson:

The tumult and the shouting having died, it is now possible for me to send you this word of thanks for the help you were kind enough to provide during the campaign. It appears that we were swimming against a very heavy tide, but I am reasonably satisfied that we put our best foot forward in terms of the intellectual fare we provided the people. Your own contribution to that end was substantial, and I shall be eternally grateful to you for it.

I hope that the future will provide me with opportunities to renew our acquaintance. I have found it a most pleasant and stimulating one.

With thanks and my every good wish, I am

Sincerely yours,

Senator Hubert Humphrey of Minnesota praised Stevenson's candidacy and campaign as "two of the finest things that have ever happened to American politics." He urged the Governor to continue to be the leader of the Democratic party.

To Hubert Humphrey

November 10, 1952

Dear Hubert:

So many thanks for your telegram. I am afraid I have been a dreadful disappointment to many people, and none gave me more support and encouragement than you; but somehow, I have no regrets or any trouble with my conscience. We shall meet soon I hope.

Sincerely yours,

Senator Estes Kefauver of Tennessee wired: "You fought a good and courageous fight without compromise and based entirely upon the issues."

To Estes Kefauver [10]

November 10, 1952

Dear Estes:

So many thanks for your fine and thoughtful telegram. I have no regrets, but I am afraid I have been a miserable disappointment to many loyal friends like yourself who gave so much to the campaign. Perhaps it is all for the best. Much will depend upon the quality and purpose of our opposition. About that I hope we can talk sometime.

Meanwhile, my enduring thanks for all you have done and my warmest good wishes.

Sincerely yours,
ADLAI

To William E. Stevenson [11]

November 10, 1952

Dear Bill:

One of the most effective members of our research staff here in Springfield during the campaign was an alumnus of Oberlin. His name is Robert Tufts, and I believe he was originally a member of the class of 1936 at Oberlin, although his actual graduation was delayed until 1940. Before he came to Springfield to participate in the campaign he had been a member of the Policy Planning Staff at the State Department, a very responsible post which he resigned in order to help me out. He had been most highly recommended to me by people in the Department as not only one of the most thoughtful persons there but also as having a real gift for the articulation of policy. His work in the campaign certainly bore out all of the high recommendations I had received about him.

He has now returned to his job in Washington, but his disposition is strongly toward teaching, and I think that his own college is the place where he would like to do it most. I believe his field of study was economics, but I am sure he would be effective not only in that department but in such related areas as government and political science, and of course his recent experience in foreign affairs at the Planning Staff level is formidable.

I would hope at least that it might be possible for you or someone at

[10] The original is in the Kefauver papers, University of Tennessee Library.
[11] President of Oberlin College and a Princeton classmate of the Governor.

Oberlin to talk with him, and this letter is written primarily for that purpose. His home address is 3607 R Street, N.W., Washington 7, D.C.

I cannot state too strongly the high regard I have for Bob both as an individual and for what I conceive to be his exceptional ability. I think he would be an excellent man for you, and I hope it will be possible for you to canvass the possibilities with him.

Yours,

To Ralph McGill [12]

November 10, 1952

Dear Mr. McGill:

Your telegram heartens me enormously — and so did Georgia! [13] I have no regrets about the campaign and my conscience is comfortable, but I am afraid I have been a miserable disappointment to some valiant supporters, yourself among the foremost. And I shall never be able to express my gratitude properly.

I was disappointed that we had no opportunity to talk while you were traveling with us. I hope that time may come and soon. There is much work to be done in this country, as you know, and I hope we can share a little of it along the way.

Sincerely yours,

Walter Lippmann wired on November 5: "You have won everything that a good man could want except only the election. That was impossible for a Democrat to do this year. You should think of your campaign as the big beginning. Affectionate regards."

To Walter Lippmann [14]

November 10, 1952

Dear Walter:

I was touched and delighted by your thoughtful telegram. I have no regrets except for the disappointment of so many of my friends and supporters.

I shall hope to see you both again before too long.

Cordially yours,

ADLAI

[12] Editor of the Atlanta *Constitution*.
[13] Stevenson had received 456,823 votes in Georgia, as against Eisenhower's 198,979.
[14] The original is in the Lippmann papers, Yale University Library.

To Robert Tufts

November 11, 1952

Dear Bob:

I enclose herewith for your information a copy of a letter which I have sent to President Stevenson of Oberlin College. I believe that he has gone on a trip abroad and there may be no immediate reply to this, but I am hopeful that sooner or later you and he can get together.

I have tried to reflect in the enclosed letter the high regard I place on your performance here in Springfield during the campaign, but I would like to reiterate these feelings directly. In retrospect it appears that we were laboring under many handicaps, but one of them was certainly not the caliber of the material we placed before the people. I marvel at the job done by the research staff, and I know in particular of your great contributions to that effort. I think none of us should be so disappointed by the result that we overlook the great satisfactions we are entitled to take from this positive aspect of the campaign.

I am deeply indebted to you for the inconvenience to which you exposed yourself and your family in my interest, and for the intelligence and industry which you brought to bear on my behalf.

With warm thanks, and my every good wish, I am

Sincerely yours,

To Mrs. Franklin D. Roosevelt [15]

November 11, 1952

My dear Mrs. Roosevelt:

You were, as always, more than good to write me so promptly. I have no regrets about the campaign except the disappointment of many friends. On the contrary, I feel a profound sense of gratitude for the experience and to countless friends who gave me help and encouragement. You are at the front of the list, and I shall never be able to thank you properly.

With my utmost respect and affection, I am

Faithfully yours,

President Truman wired Stevenson on November 7 that he hoped, as head of the Democratic party, he would soon revitalize the Democratic National Committee in order to ensure victory in the 1954 elections. He promised to help Stevenson any way he could to organize such an effort.

15 The original is in the Franklin D. Roosevelt Library, Hyde Park, New York.

To Harry S. Truman [16]

November 11, 1952

MANY THANKS FOR YOUR TELEGRAM. HAVE DISCUSSED STEPS TO RE-
ORGANIZE NATIONAL COMMITTEE. CAN COME TO WASHINGTON NO-
VEMBER 29 OR 30 TO SEE YOU IF CONVENIENT. WILL TELEPHONE
CONNALLY [17] LATER FOR INSTRUCTIONS. WARM REGARDS.

To Mr. and Mrs. Archibald MacLeish [18]

November 11, 1952

My beloved MacLeishes:

Your wire lifted my heart. As a matter of fact, my heart seems to be much higher than my friends' hearts! I have no regrets except their disappointment.

I shall not be able to thank you for the literature you contributed to my public offerings, but I think you know how I feel. We shall all live to fight another day.

Affectionately,
ADLAI

Bernard DeVoto wrote Stevenson on November 5: "I want to say to you now only that in all American history no one else has made so fine, so honorable, so truthful and distinguished campaign as yours." Mrs. De-Voto added a postscript: "I am so very proud that Benny was privileged to work for you. You have our undying admiration and devotion."

To Bernard DeVoto

November 11, 1952

Dear Benny:

I have just read your letter of November 5, and my heart is very full. I hesitate to question your judgment or your perspective as a historian and shall let your flattery rest in my grateful bosom undisputed.

But the simple facts are that I am the beneficiary of the hearts and minds of many people who made this campaign which you call mine. I am the debtor and they are the creditors, and you are one of the foremost.

---

[16] A telegram.
[17] Matthew Connelly, President Truman's appointments secretary.
[18] The original is in the MacLeish papers, Library of Congress.

For me it was an adventure for which I shall be eternally grateful to my party and to the good and the wise who rallied to our standard.

There is much work ahead in which I hope to find some means to play some part. In that I shall want and need you, and count this but the beginning of our association.

Among the blessings is the opportunity, at last, to read a little De Voto and his last book [19] which is traveling to Arizona with me tomorrow.

My thanks to your wife for her endearing postscript, and my respect and affection to you.

Yours,

Eve Curie, the French scientist and daughter of the discoverers of radium, wrote Stevenson from France on October 26: "I wish I could express with what deep satisfaction I read your speeches. . . . By calmly stating true facts and speaking your faith, by refusing to exploit popular prejudices, you have affirmed your fundamental respect for the people of the United States."

To Eve Curie

November 11, 1952

My dear Mademoiselle Curie:

I have been very much flattered by your kind letter of October 26. It was good of you to write me and I shall long cherish the generous comments of such a civilized Frenchwoman whom we respect so much in the United States. Perhaps I shall have the good fortune to meet you on another journey to this country.

Sincerely yours,

To Albert Einstein

November 18, 1952

Dear Dr. Einstein:

I think nothing has pleased me more than your support of my candidacy. I am both deeply grateful and immensely flattered by your confidence.

With the utmost respect and my thanks, I am

Cordially yours,

19 *The Course of Empire* (Boston: Houghton Mifflin, 1952).

On November 5, Bernard M. Baruch, who had supported General Eisenhower, wrote that Stevenson had made a "valiant fight." In the future, he hoped Stevenson would not have to "carry so many old men of the sea on your back."

To Bernard M. Baruch

November 18, 1952

Dear Mr. Baruch:

So many thanks for your very thoughtful and flattering note. I have no regrets — except for the disappointment of many friends whose hopes were high.

I shall certainly take the liberty of calling on you when I can get to New York from time to time. I value your advice and extraordinary wisdom immensely, and I think the Democratic party must make a calm and penetrating appraisal of its role and position in our future national life.

Sincerely yours,

Stevenson's old friend Trygve Lie, Secretary-General of the United Nations, wrote him on November 11, praising the way he conducted the campaign and the "extraordinarily high quality of your speeches." He added: "Having established yourself as a world figure to whom millions look for leadership, I crave for you and for the peoples who need your leadership, a full realization of their hopes." He explained that he was resigning his office in hopes his successor might be able to cope with the split between East and West.

To Trygve Lie [20]

November 18, 1952

Dear Trygve:

I thank you deeply for your thoughtful and charitable letter of November 11. I read the announcement of your resignation in the papers with no surprise, in view of our prior conversations. I have been in Arizona and have no personal information, but my guess is that you will have to continue for another year. All the same, I think the proposal of resignation was probably wise and may serve a useful purpose.

[20] A copy is in A.E.S., I.S.H.L.

We most certainly must talk, and I shall hope to see you when the dust settles a bit — if I may use that unhappy expression!

Faithfully and gratefully yours,

To Estes Kefauver [21]

November 18, 1952

Dear Estes:

What with telegrams and letters I feel that I have repaid your courtesies shabbily, but the mail is appalling and it is hard to segregate the important ones.

Let me say how grateful I am for your very major contribution to our ill-fated campaign. Personally I have few regrets except for the disappointment of countless friends and supporters who seem to take it harder than I do. And I am glad to note a philosophical acceptance of our destiny from your letter of November 6. I hope we can keep in touch, because, obviously, there is much work to be done to restore our party to public confidence. In that I should like to help to some extent if I possibly can.

With my thanks and warm regards, I am

Sincerely yours,

ADLAI

To Hubert H. Humphrey

November 18, 1952

Dear Hubert:

I am deeply grateful for your charitable and comforting letter of November 8.

Some time we must talk about this "leadership" business. I am a little perplexed. I should like to do what I can, consistent with earning a living, to be of future help to the party, and I am sure we both agree that it can and must recapture public esteem and confidence. Much will depend, of course, upon our coherence and purposefulness in Congress. And in no small measure that means yourself. We must find an opportunity to talk about these things.

Meanwhile, I agree that restaffing the National Committee for its new mission is the first order of business — besides cleaning up the national deficit.

[21] The original is in the Kefauver papers, University of Tennessee Library.

With my warm regards and my everlasting thanks for your tireless help in my late adventure, I am

Sincerely yours,

Winston Churchill's niece, Lady Judith Montagu, wrote Stevenson on November 8, urging him to visit England in order that his "rooters" could get a glimpse of him. She concluded by saying that "it's impossible to tell you what passions of hero worship have been stirred up."

To Lady Judith Montagu [22]

November 19, 1952

My dear Judy:

I was delighted with your letter but "passions of hero worship" frighten me a little. I had wanted to travel and come to England for a bit next year, but now I dare not. Such passions must not be obliterated by reality!

You were good to write me and I hope and fully expect that things will turn out not too badly.

Cordially yours,

General George C. Marshall wrote Stevenson on November 6: "I send you my sympathy over the results of the campaign. You fought a great fight. Your political speeches reached a new high in statesmanship. You deserved far better of the electorate, but you will be recognized increasingly as a truly great American."

To General George C. Marshall

November 20, 1952

My dear General Marshall:

Nothing has touched me so profoundly as your thoughtful and flattering note. I have no regrets, except the disappointment of my friends and supporters, and your letter alone would be sufficient reward for what I did and hoped to do better.

With my kindest regards to you and Mrs. Marshall, I am

Faithfully yours,

[22] A copy is in A.E.S., I.S.H.L.

To Edward D. McDougal, Jr.[23]

November 20, 1952

Dear Ed:

I am crushed with work, and have been obliged to decline Mr. Quigg's request.[24]

Likewise I see no hope of speaking before the Commonwealth Club.[25] My situation is frightening, and besides I shall have to be very guarded in my talking hereafter because the "excitement of perpetual speech-making is fatal to the exercise of the highest powers."

Yours,

ADLAI

Professor Stuart Gerry Brown of the Maxwell Graduate School of Syracuse University, in a letter to Stevenson on November 17, in analyz-ing defections from the Democratic party to Eisenhower, emphasized that Stevenson carried the independent vote: "It is clear that they voted for you precisely because you did not promise things no one could carry out, and because you were not a father symbol. This means that they voted for you as an expression of the growing political maturity and responsibility in America." For the future, Brown recommended a reorganization of the Democratic party and maintaining and building the volunteer organizations which expressed the will of independents.

To Stuart G. Brown [26]

November 28, 1952

Dear Mr. Brown:

Your letter fascinates me. Some of the conclusions I had come to my-self from the evidence. I had not, however, pieced together the im-portant conclusions that we *did* win the independents. I agree em-phatically on our opposition role. It was never more important nor the opportunity never greater. Can we break past traditions, harness our re-

[23] A former law partner of Stevenson in the firm of Cutting, Moore, and Sidley and in its successor, Sidney, McPherson, Austin and Burgess, and in 1952 general counsel and an officer of International Minerals and Chemicals Corporation in Chi-cago. The original is in the possession of Mr. McDougal.

[24] Philip W. Quigg, editor of the *Princeton Alumni Weekly*, had asked Stevenson to write an article for the magazine.

[25] Stevenson had previously addressed this Chicago businessmen's group, of which he was a member. See *The Papers of Adlai E. Stevenson*, Vol. II, pp. 16, 237 ff, 280.

[26] The original is in the Brown papers, Syracuse University Library.

sources of manpower, persuade politicians that it is better to win long battles than little scrimmages? I don't know, but I am willing to try a little, in spite of the handicaps of defeat, some of our Southern friends and ever present ambitions — not mine!

I shall read your books [27] and I earnestly hope you will pass along any and every idea that occurs to you.

My regards to Paul Appleby.[28]

Sincerely yours,

To Joseph Bohrer [29]

November 20, 1952

Dear Joe:

Chal Taylor [30] tells me that you are "off your feed," as the old folks used to say. I hope this is not post-election depression, because I never felt better and have no regrets, except for the disappointment of my friends. Among the latter you are at the top of the list, and all I expect now is that you pull yourself together and we'll live to fight another day.

When you feel like it, gather up Margaret [31] and come down for a night with me — and I'll give you a blow-by-blow account of my late adventures in the great jungle.

Yours,

Eric Sevareid, the Columbia Broadcasting System television commentator, wrote Stevenson on November 6: "No one has conducted a campaign so intelligent, so courageous and with such unswerving devotion to the simple cause of truth as you have done. . . . Yours remains the only powerful, believable voice for tolerance, sanity and social progress in the country. . . . You can reorganize and revitalize the Democratic party in the name of the young and the hopeful; they will look to you for that. There is no other effective national champion of civil liberties, of free speech, of the true American liberal movement and philosophy except yourself."

[27] *The Social Philosophy of Josiah Royce* (Syracuse, New York: Syracuse University Press, 1950) and *The Religious Philosophy of Josiah Royce* (Syracuse, New York: Syracuse University Press, 1952), both edited by Mr. Brown.

[28] Dean of the Maxwell Graduate School, Syracuse University.

[29] A Bloomington friend of Stevenson's since their childhood. See "Boys in Bloomington," in *As We Knew Adlai: The Stevenson Story by Twenty-two Friends*, edited with preface by Edward P. Doyle, foreword by Adlai E. Stevenson III (New York: Harper & Row, 1966), pp. 1–14.

[30] Chalmer C. Taylor, of Bloomington.

[31] Mrs. Bohrer.

To Eric Sevareid

November 22, 1952

Dear Eric:

I have pondered your letter, and that I am grateful for it and for your support, early and late, I hardly need say. As for the campaign, I have no regrets and my conscience is comfortable. My only misery is the State of Illinois and the apparent disinterest of masses of good people in preserving what we so painfully accomplished here.

I am comforted by your thought that I have some further public utility. As to what to do and how to do it, and earn a living, I am a little perplexed. But we will see. In the meantime, I hope there will be an opportunity to talk with you somewhere along the way. The problem of "party leadership" has infinite difficulties and hazards, as you well know, particularly if one has no further political ambitions and a great desire to come to rest in some work both useful, permanent, stable and profitable!

My affectionate regards.

Yours,

On November 21, President Truman invited Stevenson to have dinner and spend a night in the White House to discuss political matters. He said he was glad to be out of active politics, although he would be more than happy to advise Stevenson if he desired such advice. He hoped that Stevenson would take charge of the party and provide it with the leadership it would need in the future.

To Harry S. Truman

November 26, 1952

Dear Mr. President:

Thank you for your letter. I look forward to the dinner eagerly and I so am grateful to you for thinking of me and also of my sister, who has just telephoned me from Southern Pines that she has been invited too.

I have to speak at the CIO at Atlantic City at the memorial meeting for Philip Murray on Wednesday afternoon, and I find that the only plane I can get from Atlantic City to Washington does not arrive at the Washington airport until 5:28 — Eastern Airlines. I shall plan to be on that plane and come at once to the White House unless that is inconveniently late for you, in which event I can come the following day, Thursday, any time you appoint.

If you would prefer me to come Wednesday evening at that time, I shall come direct to the White House, and I will be delighted to stay the night if that is entirely convenient. I am distressed about the communications from Atlantic City, but this seems to be the best I can do. It may be possible, when I arrive there, to charter a plane to enable me to arrive in Washington somewhat earlier, but it has been impossible to make any arrangements from here.

Faithfully yours,

To Chester Kerr [32]

November 26, 1952

Dear Chester:

I want to collect some wisecracks about the campaign which I might use at the Gridiron dinner. You told one at the [Edison] Dicks the other night which I promptly forgot — after my fashion. If you can possibly pass it along to me, together with any other comments — in lighter vein — in regard to the campaign, they will be most welcome and very precious to your harrassed hero!

Yours,

Stevenson's running mate wrote him on November 25: "I just want to say that I deemed it a great honor to be on the ticket with you. I think you made a magnificent fight. . . . As a loyal Democrat I look to you for leadership. I know that many millions of Americans do likewise. I feel confident that you will speak out and will give to us that leadership."

To John Sparkman

November 28, 1952

Dear John:

You were so good to write me and I feel that I was by no means adequate to our appalling task. But there was never a moment of misgiving about your adequacy. And there is a comfort in one's close associates that is easier to feel than to express.

[32] Secretary and later director of the Yale University Press. A copy is in A.E.S., I.S.H.L.

I know this is but the beginning of a long and I hope fruitful collaboration.

With my affection and respect and hope for an early visit, I am

Cordially yours,

Nicolo Tucci, of The New Yorker, wrote Stevenson a lengthy letter on November 5. Among other things he said: "The climate is McCarthy, so it could not be Stevenson. But this is one more reason to keep our Stevenson and keep him vocal. What we needed before he appeared on the political stage was some enthusiasm, some real fire to counteract the 'enthusiasm' of the so-called defenders of whatever it is, on which McCarthy and Eisenhower and so many other fools can agree. We have it. Stevenson is the first great American optimist after Jefferson, the first real 'grand seigneur' of our age, so why should we complain?" Later in the letter he wrote: "Stevenson's voice was a new thought: Jefferson had come back, we had not lost our friend, here he was, in his unchanged antiquity. . . . His presences made the television screen seem wise and noble, his very first words broke the sinister link between stupidity and the political tradition in this country (they had seemed so inseparable for much too long), if he won, a new era in America would win: even magazine editors and publishers would stop catering to the twelve-year-old idiot; people would once more be challenged, in the ancient tradition of all civilized countries, with the assumption that they could understand what was being said to them." Near the close of the letter he wrote: "Stay with us, speak for us, keep us together and we will all keep you busy airing, repairing and sharpening the dusty weapons of the great wise men in history."

To Nicolo Tucci [33]

November 29, 1952

Dear Mr. Tucci:

I apologize for neglecting your remarkable letter. I have read it and reread it. Please don't feel that I feel either defeat or despair. I don't. And I count myself well rewarded that some like yourself perceive the design and intent of the campaign. That it succeeded as well as it did, given the handicaps, actually gratifies me.

But as to your eloquent and compelling call to carry on, I think you both misjudge my talents and my temperament. I shall do a little I trust but I am not a fearless, tireless knight and find the bright lights distaste-

[33] A copy is in A.E.S., I.S.H.L.

ful and the trumpets a little chilling. Perhaps one gets this way after some 12 years of almost ceaseless and sleepless public work.

At all events, I am deeply grateful and I shall try to fulfill your hopes in some minute measure. I wish you would sit down and write a speech for me saying whatever you think needs saying. Some day I shall use it, by bits and pieces, because I am dry and hopelessly distracted with pressures from all directions.

My thanks for this acquaintance.

Cordially yours,

On December 3, Stevenson spoke at the Philip Murray Memorial Dinner, Atlantic City, New Jersey. Mr. Murray, the president of the Congress of Industrial Organizations, had died on November 9, 1952.

THE LEGACY OF PHILIP MURRAY [34]

It is hard on occasions such as this to distinguish between the lasting darkness of loss and the passing darkness of its shadow.

Our lives take their meaning from their interlacing with other lives, and when one life is ended those into which it was woven are also carried into darkness. Neither you nor I, but only the hand of time, slow-moving, yet sure and steady, can lift that blanket of blackness.

I am, of course, deeply conscious of the honor that I share in taking part in this tribute to the memory of Philip Murray. But even more keenly, I feel that it is appropriate for someone outside the labor movement, like myself, to participate in this memorial. I say that because Mr. Murray was more than the President of the C.I.O., more than a leader and spokesman for organized labor.

Those of you who worked with him knew him first and foremost as a trade-unionist, a man of sagacity at the bargaining table, a militant leader in your times of stress, and a shrewd negotiator. Those of you, among the thousands who called him "friend," knew him as a beloved companion, a thoughtful advisor, a generous man with a boundless sense of humor and kindness. As time softens the first sadness of his death, I think we can better see Phil Murray in perspective, and describe him properly in terms that would have embarrassed this unassuming man in his lifetime.

In the truest sense of the words that we often abuse, his life was a success story. The world is better off because he lived in it. Without that fact as a basic ingredient, you cannot give validity to a success story. Too

---

[34] The text is from Adlai E. Stevenson, *What I Think* (New York: Harper, 1955), pp. 43–46.

often, in judging what man is a success, we think in terms of the market place, and measure him a success because he moved into the big house on top of the hill. But the test is rather "how and why." And Phil Murray's success in life cannot be measured in a probate court.

The inspiration in Mr. Murray's life, the lesson for the world, lies in the fact that a boy humbly born in another country could come to America, his knuckles blackened with the coal dust of the Scottish pits, hew out an illustrious career for himself in service to his fellow man, and die a man of simple tastes and modest means, but leave a legacy of material goods in the homes of millions of workers in these United States — not only material goods measured in wages, in pension benefits, and other gains for the workers he led, but the goods of the spirit. Millions of workers have a personal dignity their fathers never knew because Phil Murray and others like him helped these workers to stand on their own feet.

My acquaintance with him was not intimate and my contacts were few. Perhaps that qualifies me all the better to comment on what to me was his most conspicuous quality. Humbly born, after a stormy life of democratic leadership and great achievement he humbly died. Yet it has been too often true that the very humbleness, even the disadvantages, of a man's beginnings have led him to abuse authority subsequently attained. Rank and power expose humility to the rust of pride. We know those who, in the very telling of how they "came up the hard way," acknowledge in the telling that they have lost the lesson of their experience.

Phil Murray's humility was deeper rooted. It did not change with the seasons of experience or the years of growth. He knew that in our system of things the conferring of authority on particular individuals is largely accidental, that its compliment is slight, and that the man who exercises it is no different from his fellow men or from what he was himself before he assumed the role of leadership.

It was often remarked, and to some it seemed strange, that the President of the C.I.O. was moved easily to laughter and not infrequently to tears. Perhaps his greatness found its sustenance there, or at least its reflection — for it is emotions that link us closest with each other. So much of democratic leadership is just the understanding of the people's needs and hopes, and looking to them rather than to one's own ideas for guidance and for strength, the maintaining of a oneness between leadership and following.

No democratic organization can afford the risk of leadership which lacks humility. It is that element which gives men — which gave Philip Murray — the ability to lead a people who distrust the power to command.

His was not an easy career. The path of the man who chose a career in organized labor in Murray's youth was not strewn with N.L.R.B. [National Labor Relations Board] orders directing an employer to bargain. Too often the life of the labor organizer was more akin to the career of an underground leader, in terms of frustration, even terror.

What motivated and sustained him in the long struggle? What was the guiding purpose that drove him on with a disregard for self that resulted finally in death? I suspect the mature, the compelling purpose, was to bring dignity and meaning into lives which had lost these qualities. It was plainer to those in the coal mines of Pennsylvania in 1902 in his boyhood than it was to a good many other people in America what a price we had paid, in human values, for the fruits of the industrial revolution. The coal dust and the sweat and smoke of factories had settled not only on men's faces and in women's kitchens but on their lives. Work had become, for millions, something much less — much meaner — than it had been when men were carving homes and farms out of forests and wilderness and working as craftsmen in small shops. In too many minds the men and women beside the assembly lines became indistinguishable from the machines.

This, then, is our heritage from Philip Murray. It is no lesser for not being written in the words of great books or in the masonry of proud structures — for it is written rather in the lives of men and women and built into the meaning of democracy. It is the example of what leadership means in a system that finds its strength in its insistence that leaders be only servants. To realize this heritage is to deny all but the personal elements of loss, of ending, in what has happened. There are those who are ready to accept, to carry on — and even to build upon — the example which has been left, the tradition which has been established.

Behind the grief of great loss there is the stimulus to assume the increased responsibility to go on. The whole lesson of history is its essential continuity. It is the fullest recognition and memorializing of those who have departed that those who remain feel no despair — for otherwise the task was not fully done. I cannot presume to say that I know what Mr. Murray's view of the future was. But I do know that his life and work spanned a dramatic evolution in the status of labor and in our thinking about labor in this country. From the unspeakable conditions of fifty or sixty years ago he lived to see organized labor grow to its present vast power and influence in our economy and our society. And I suppose that this transition is as important a single fact as any in the past half-century.

While there are inequities and injustices in our laws that still demand remedy, labor's long battle for status and recognition has been largely won. Violence and ruthlessness by employers and unions alike are now obsolete. The doctrine that the end justifies the means should be a thing of the past in labor relations.

Labor has been afflicted with Communist infiltration. It has been afflicted with hoodlums and racketeers. These battles for clean unions have been fought and will be fought as long as necessary. But the bigger job of the future is the proper exercise of organized labor's vast responsibility, not just to the workingman but to the country. Some of the attitudes, habits of thought, and methods of the past are no longer relevant. How soon will the modern idea that Big Labor is here to stay, that its constituency is no longer just the union member but the nation, pervade the ranks of labor leadership? The largest task now, as I see it, is the conduct of relations with industry, always in the larger framework of the national interest on which labor and business and all the rest of us are dependent.

I'll say nothing poetic about the twilight of the era of your great gains. Rather it is for us to make this interval of labor's transition from "far-off things, and battles long ago," the dawn of a better era for all of us — for America.

I like to think that Phil Murray was familiar with these words: "A fool who stands fast is a catastrophe; a wise man who stands fast is a statesman."

It is, then, in a spirit of gratitude for what he did with his life and of gratitude for the opportunity that is the handmaiden of the power he helped bestow upon you, that we say to Philip Murray: "Hail and Farewell," and that we say to Death, "Be not proud."

The following letter was written from the White House on Thursday evening, December 4.

To Mrs. Edison Dick [35]

December 4, 1952

. . . After this I shall inscribe a message to Eisenhower as follows:

> Dear General —
> I got here first, pal!
> Yours,
> AES

[35] This handwritten letter is in the possession of Mrs. Dick.

But what an ordeal! Last night I finished with the Pres. about 11 & betook meself to bed — the Lincoln room & the vast bed. First I read a bit and then the trouble commenced when I tried to go to sleep — the ghosts and shadows that fill that room, bits and pieces of imperishable words that were conceived, perhaps written here on this table where I am sitting at this moment — the very table on which he signed the Emancipation Proclamation after all those months of torment. As if these reveries were not enough — the whole room filled with ghosts — strange faces some of them, bearded, some ugly, some good — all manner of clothes. They seemed to fairly jostle each other for my attention to the imperatives of their speechless mouths. And then it all receded and the portraits came marching up the stairs and down the halls and into my room, or did I leave my room and walk thru the halls and down the stairs and pass them all one by one? I don't know. But behind each in some strange dimension stretched out all the miseries, the burdens, the doubts and anguish that afflicted him here in this house.

At 3 am I gave up and took a sleeping pill and then another for good measure. And this morning they had to wake me up and there were Pres. & Mrs. T. patiently waiting outside for for breakfast with their irresponsible guest.

I hope to do better tonight & tomorrow morning too, or I'll have to come to Lake Forest for a nights sleep on Woodland Rd.[36]

To Louis A. Kohn

December 3, 1952

Dear Lou:

I have written the people on the list you gave to Miss [Carol] Evans except for Sidney Salamon [37] and I did not have his address. But most of all I think I should write you and say what I have said so many times — what is Stevenson without Kohn.[38] Some day I hope we can have a good post-mortem instead of those frenzied automobile rides when I am always so preoccupied and nursing my worries.

Yours,

---

[36] The Dicks' home.

[37] A St. Louis insurance executive, who was active in the Democratic National Committee, serving as treasurer in 1950–1951.

[38] Mr. Kohn had been urging Stevenson to run for public office as early as 1946 and was active in the Stevenson for Governor Committee in 1948. See *The Papers of Adlai E. Stevenson*, Vol. II, pp. 453–456.

To Frank E. Karelsen, Jr.[39]

December 3, 1952

Dear Mr. Karelsen:

Before another day passes I want you to know how grateful I am for all your help during the campaign. I remember well your earnest interest in me from early last winter and I have also heard about your devoted service during the campaign.

I am deeply touched and grateful.

Sincerely yours,

To Walter T. Fisher [40]

December 7, 1952

Dear Walter:

Only on this last trip to the East did I have an opportunity to read your eloquent article in the Christian Century.[41] I can see why it took some time to write it, and I could not have been more flattered or pleased. I am mortified that I have not thanked you before, but my home work has been grossly neglected for weeks and months, as I am sure you know.

With a heart full of gratitude for this, and much much more besides!

Yours,

To Edwin A. Lahey [42]

December 7, 1952

Dear Ed:

Many many thanks for your excellent contribution to my little speech at the CIO meeting. If you have seen it you will recognize some of that imperishable prose — and I only hope that no one else does!

Yours,

ADLAI

---

[39] A New York City lawyer active in liberal Democratic politics. The original is in the possession of Mr. Karelsen.

[40] Chairman of the Illinois Commerce Commission. A copy is in A.E.S., I.S.H.L.

[41] "Why I Shall Vote for Stevenson," *Christian Century*, October 8, 1952.

[42] Columnist for the Knight newspapers based in Washington, D.C. The original is in the possession of Mr. Lahey.

Fanny Butcher, literary editor of the Chicago Tribune, *invited Stevenson to attend a birthday celebration for Carl Sandburg.*

To Mrs. Richard Bokum [43]

December 7, 1952

Dear Fanny:

I hardly know what to say — except yes! But the hell of it is — and it is real hell! — that the 6th will be in the midst of my hideous travail from New Years until I am evicted on the 12th. Indeed, that is the day the legislature convenes, but perhaps I am wrong. At all events, I have a major concluding speech to make by radio to the people about that time [44] and one to the new legislature, together with the inaugural preparation problems, the turnover of the state government, and the frightening physical problems of moving myself out of this house and to Chicago so that it will be ready for its new occupants, all at the same time.

The foregoing by way of saying that while I will make every effort — indeed "bust a gut" (something Chaucerian maybe) — to get there, I just must be excused from any speech other than such extemporaneous and brief words as I can marshal at the moment. I hope you will understand. It's a pity Carl had to be born the 5th of January 75 years ago. I think it very thoughtless of him.

Yours,
ADLAI

Stevenson, while in New York City and Washington, D.C., met with Dwight Palmer and Stephen A. Mitchell, treasurer and chairman, respectively, of the Democratic National Committee. They discussed ways of paying the deficit from his campaign and also discussed plans to revitalize the party.

To D. R. G. Palmer [45]

December 7, 1952

Dear Dwight:

Somehow a talk with you now and then seems to ease my mind and simplify my thinking about a lot of things. Our talks in New York and

---

[43] The original is in the possession of Mrs. Bokum.

[44] The speech was delivered on January 7, 1953. See *The Papers of Adlai E. Stevenson,* Vol. III, pp. 589–595.

[45] A copy is in A.E.S., I.S.H.L.

Washington were immensely comforting. For reasons that probably find their roots in my Scotch and Quaker ancestry, I have felt uneasy about the deficit and I want to do anything I can to help with it. Last night while he was here, Bennett Cerf [46] suggested that I make a broadcast asking for contributions from as many people, in any amount, as possible. I have not thought the thing through, but if it has merit in the judgment of better heads, I will do it, although perhaps the New York dinner will serve the same purpose.

Your survey idea of state organizations seemed to me excellent and I have discussed it with several people. Perhaps not in identically the form you suggest, but in some manner it should be done, and I think we could enlist the *ad hoc* services of some of our better political leaders to do some traveling in the winter to that end. I am going to talk further about it to Mitchell et al.

But the purpose of this letter was to thank you for your note of December 1 and the beautifully framed and touching little note with the twenty-dollar gold piece. It will be among my most precious reminders of the late adventure and it is obvious that I now owe you $20.00 along with all my gratitude. I am writing to the people, of course.

Sincerely, yours,

To Thomas M. Storke [47]

December 8, 1952

Dear Mr. Storke:

The News-Press is a member of a very select group, it seems, for it was one of some 200 daily newspapers which supported my candidacy during the recent election. I am deeply grateful to you, and to the members of your staff, for that support. I hope that I did nothing to discredit it, and I hope that I may always merit your confidence. Certainly you have earned my enduring thanks.

Cordially, yours,

To Stephen A. Mitchell

December 8, 1952

Dear Steve:

I know that the flood of proposals and recommendations and plans of

---

[46] President of Random House. Mr. Cerf was trying to persuade Stevenson to publish a volume of his campaign speeches, which appeared the following year as *Major Campaign Speeches of Adlai E. Stevenson, 1952*.
[47] Publisher of the Santa Barbara, California, *News-Press*.

all kinds and from all quarters has you as bewildered as it does me. Therefore, let me add another!

We have various Democratic leaders around the country like Finnegan,[48] O'Mahoney,[49] DiSalle,[50] Chapman,[51] Doyle,[52] Butler,[53] Rawlings,[54] etc., etc. I wonder if there would be some merit in considering requesting some of these gentlemen to give a few weeks time to the National Committee on an ad hoc basis for the purpose of a careful survey and analysis of the exact political and party situation in various states assigned to them on some sort of a regional basis.

Without elaborating the idea, it seemed to me that you could well ask them to give you a hand to do some traveling at the Committee's expense to review the situation and estimate the prospects for new blood, new leadership for issues, program, etc. I cannot see how you could possibly do all this yourself and some quiet, intensive survey work by discreet, sophisticated, experienced men might yield a much more accurate inventory of our situation than we are likely to get otherwise.

Yours,

On November 16, Miss Lynn Pierson (nine years old), of Appleton, Wisconsin, wrote Stevenson that she was sorry he lost the election. She mentioned that her father was a minister and knew Dr. Richard Paul Graebel, minister of the First Presbyterian Church of Springfield, Illinois. She enclosed a photograph of herself and her three-year-old sister Juli.

To Lynn Pierson

December 8, 1952

Dear Lynn:

You were very sweet to write to me and the picture of you and Juli is very pretty. I wish you weren't quite so far away!

Yes, I do go to the Presbyterian Church here and Dr. Graebel is a brilliant and inspiring preacher. Perhaps you know that my great grandfather [Lewis Warner] Green was a Presbyterian preacher, too.

---

[48] James A. Finnegan, president of the Philadelphia City Council.
[49] Senator Joseph O'Mahoney of Wyoming.
[50] Michael DiSalle, director of the Office of Economic Stabilization.
[51] Oscar Chapman, Secretary of the Interior.
[52] James E. Doyle, state chairman of the Democratic Organizing Committee of Wisconsin.
[53] Paul Butler, national committeeman from Indiana.
[54] Calvin Rawlings, national committeeman from Utah.

I hope you have a Very Merry Christmas and I wish to congratulate you on your very good handwriting.

Every good wish to you and Juli.

Sincerely,

Random House, Harper and Brothers, and Doubleday and Company each proposed to Stevenson that a volume of his campaign speeches be published. Random House published Major Campaign Speeches of Adlai E. Stevenson, 1952, *while Stevenson was in Asia in 1953.*

To Lloyd K. Garrison [55]

December 9, 1952

Dear Lloyd —

I'm hastily sending you this to read before I call you by telephone to discuss my publishing problems. Random House has some prior claim to a book of campaign speeches, Harpers, thanks to [John] Fis[c]her & [Cass] Canfield, has a prior claim on my affections, yet the Doubleday proposition looks awfully good. Would Harper match it? And if so can I pass Random House & use the speech book as one of the three?

I think I need a lawyer, also a clear head, also a friend with some knowledge of the publishing business. Consider yourself all of those things and me your client. I'll call you for advice by phone in a day or so.

Yrs hastily —

ADLAI

Stevenson sent the following telegram to be read at a meeting of the Democratic Organizing Committee of Wisconsin.

To James E. Doyle

December 9, 1952

I REGRET MY INABILITY TO BE WITH YOU IN PERSON TO EXPRESS MY GRATITUDE FOR YOUR UNTIRING EFFORTS ON BEHALF OF THE DEMOCRATIC TICKET IN THE CAMPAIGN. I HAVE ESPECIALLY FOND MEMORIES OF MY VISIT TO WISCONSIN IN OCTOBER. I WAS TOUCHED BY THE WARMTH OF YOUR WELCOME AND IMPRESSED WITH THE CALIBER OF YOUR CANDIDATES AND LEADERSHIP.

SINCE THE ELECTION MANY THOUSANDS OF PEOPLE HAVE TAKEN

[55] This handwritten letter is in the possession of Mr. Garrison.

THE TROUBLE TO SEND ME MESSAGES OF COMFORT AND ENCOURAGEMENT. THE OVERWHELMING MAJORITY OF THESE PEOPLE — MANY OF WHOM IDENTIFIED THEMSELVES AS REPUBLICANS OR INDEPENDENTS — WISHED MOST OF ALL TO COMMEND THE CHARACTER OF THE DEMOCRATIC CAMPAIGN. THEY WANTED IT KNOWN THAT THEY ENDORSED THE POLICY OF "TALKING SENSE" TO THE PEOPLE, OF REFUSING TO COMPROMISE PRINCIPLES, OF APPEALING TO THE INTELLIGENCE OF THE VOTERS. IT SEEMS CLEAR THAT OUR PARTY HAS EMERGED FROM THIS ELECTION WITH THE RESPECT OF A VAST NUMBER OF VOTERS, INCLUDING MANY WHO DID NOT CAST THEIR BALLOTS FOR THE DEMOCRATIC TICKET THIS TIME.

ONE OF THE ENDURING SATISFACTIONS OF THE CAMPAIGN FOR ME HAS BEEN THE PARTICIPATION AND SUPPORT OF SO MANY INDEPENDENTS. SUCH ACTIVITY IS NOT ONLY GRATIFYING TO ME, BUT IS INDISPENSABLE TO A HEALTHY DEMOCRATIC SOCIETY. I HOPE THIS POLITICAL INTEREST AND POSITIVE PARTICIPATION WILL CONTINUE, AND, NATURALLY, I HOPE IT WILL EXPRESS ITSELF THROUGH THE DEMOCRATIC PARTY!

I WOULD LIKE TO SAY A WORD ABOUT THE FUTURE. I THINK THE PARTY MUST IN THE YEARS IMMEDIATELY AHEAD ASSUME A ROLE OF POSITIVE AND INTELLIGENT OPPOSITION. THAT OPPOSITION MUST BE THOUGHTFUL AND DISCRIMINATING; WE SHOULD NOT, AND I HOPE WE WILL NOT, AUTOMATICALLY OPPOSE THE ADMINISTRATION MERELY ON GROUNDS OF PARTISANSHIP. WE SHOULD SUPPORT THOSE POLICIES WHICH WE RECOGNIZE TO BE GOOD FOR THE NATION, OPPOSING ONLY THOSE WE BELIEVE TO BE INJURIOUS. TO THE EXTENT THAT I CAN CONTRIBUTE TO THESE ENDS I HOPE TO DO SO. THE DEMOCRATIC PARTY WILL RISE AGAIN. IT HAS SERVED THE NATION WELL IN AN ERA OF TESTING WITHOUT COUNTERPART IN OUR HISTORY. IT MUST NOW PROVE THAT IT CAN MEET THE TEST OF DEFEAT AS COURAGEOUSLY AS IT HAS THE CHALLENGE OF VICTORY. I AM CONFIDENT THAT THE PARTY HAS THE CHARACTER AND THE INTELLIGENCE TO DO THIS. IN THE YEARS BEFORE US, I BELIEVE THE PARTY WILL CONTINUE TO FUNCTION AS A DYNAMIC, CONSTRUCTIVE FORCE IN AMERICAN LIFE AS IT HAS FOR THE PAST 150 YEARS.

To Mrs. Franklin D. Roosevelt [56]

December 10, 1952

My dear Mrs. Roosevelt:

I have your letter of December 6 this morning, and I am passing it

[56] The original is in the Franklin D. Roosevelt Library, Hyde Park, New York.

along promptly to Mr. Mitchell at the Democratic National Committee in Washington.

I hope they can contrive to keep Miss Blackburn.[57] You know the situation: the necessity for a close husbanding of our resources, the liquidation of the deficit, and the reorganization of the staff to fulfill its new mission of research and publicity and political reorganization around the country. I hope we can make the Committee something really useful during this interval in which we will have no access to the resources of the Executive Departments and no patronage. After twenty years it will be quite a new concept and enterprise.

If I were to write you a dozen letters I could not hope to succeed in thanking you for your help, morally and actually, during my late ordeal. But some time soon I hope to have a chance to try in person!

Faithfully yours,

Robert Kintner, president of the American Broadcasting Company, suggested to Stevenson that he appear regularly on radio and television as a representative of the Democratic National Committee and comparable time be offered the Republicans.

To Robert E. Kintner

December 10, 1952

Dear Bob:

I am mortified that I have not long since acknowledged your telegram of November 20. I think very well of the idea of allotting time for both parties and would be glad to discuss it with you after the dust has settled a little bit following the expiration of my term here in Springfield.

I cannot foresee the future with any clarity just yet, but it might well be that all of the proposals with regard to television and radio which have come in would yield attractive ideas for future exploitation. This, too, I should like to discuss with you.

For the meanwhile, I shall be saying little if anything. As to the latter, the future will probably reflect no change from the past!

My affectionate sentiments to Jean [58] and you.

Sincerely yours,

[57] Miss Catherine "Casey" Blackburn, who worked for the Democratic National Committee doing political research on newspaper files from the early 1940's until the mid-1950's.
[58] Mrs. Kintner.

At Stevenson's request, Norman Cousins, editor of the Saturday Review, *wrote a lengthy memorandum on November 12 entitled "Whither A.E.S.?" He noted: (1) "The biggest job by all odds is to articulate America to the rest of the world. . . . Let's put this down then as a primary obligation of A.E.S." (2) Stevenson was a "Custodian of the Public Conscience." "That Custodian gave Americans of both parties a sense of largeness about public life and on public issues that had been too long denied them. . . . Millions of Americans made a profound emotional investment in you. They expect and indeed demand the right to rally around you. You could not default on this obligation if you wanted to. . . ." (3) The Democratic party needed to be rebuilt with "new people, new methods, new ideas." In contributing to this rebuilding, Cousins insisted that Stevenson had to be clear that recommendations one and two came before three in order to retain his position as "citizen-at-large." Cousins suggested the formation of a new "High Council" for the Democratic party to analyze and state the issues and to search for new candidates. He warned against the danger of the Democrats becoming a Labor party, and he recommended a magazine outlet for Stevenson's writings.*

To Norman Cousins

December 10, 1952

Dear Norman:

Last night I read again your letter and the memorandum of November 12. You try me sorely! I want to do all the things that you suggest, but in the present confusion and the difficulty of resolving so many questions at one time, I am making little progress, I fear.

On two counts I emphatically agree. My own best hope for influencing opinion and exercising "leadership" is as a "citizen at large" rather than as head of the Party without authority and with divided following. In short, I agree that my "power" within the Party is likely to flow from leadership outside the Party.

Also, I emphatically agree that we must avoid any attempt on the part of the labor movement to take over the Democratic Party. I hear that there are conflicting counsels in the labor movement about this but there is no conflict in my mind.

I am loath to speak on a regular spot because I should have to talk whether I had anything to say of importance and I feel it would be desirable to maintain some scarcity value for the product.

As to the magazine idea, I wish we had a proper outlet, but I would hesitate to be editor and therefore stuck, in a way, with whatever was printed.

As the dust settles, we can talk again, I hope about all these things. A little progress is being made in Washington toward the reorganization of the Party with a view to your point 3.

Hastily yours,

Brooks Atkinson of the New York Times *wrote Stevenson on November 6: "I never expected in a political campaign to hear America discussed in terms of the dreams of Jefferson, Lincoln, Emerson and Walt Whitman had for it when the concept was new, and Stephen Vincent Benét had when it was already mature. . . . Expressed in terms of your own character and experience, to say nothing of your extraordinary articulate literary style, this attitude toward America has been the most uplifting element in any campaign in my time." Atkinson then expressed his concern over the wide schism between liberal intellectuals and the rest of the country.*

To Brooks Atkinson

December 10, 1952

Dear Mr. Atkinson:

I have only now found your letter of November 6 which was hopelessly smothered in the post election avalanche. I have read and reread it, and if you were moved by my part in the campaign I am shattered by your part in the congratulatory aftermath!

I shall count your letter one of my richest rewards for all the effort.

While I cannot view the future or interpret the election with the same misgivings that you do, I do feel that there is truth in what you say about the position of the liberal intellectuals. The diagnosis of any complicated disease is difficult, but we are, I think, in an interval of mistrust and for the moment at least the liberal and the intellectual is "mistrustworthy."

I am not in the least discouraged. The pendulum swings wide in our country, and statistically the popular vote figures were by no means bad, indeed good. This was the more remarkable in view of the General's household popularity and my obscurity, the accumulation of twenty years of irritations, Korea, etc. etc.

I hope we can find a chance to talk of these things some time. My sister and brother-in-law were pleased by your remembrance.

With my warm regards to Mrs. Atkinson and the utmost gratitude to you, I am

Cordially yours,

To Alicia Patterson [59]

December 12, 1952
Friday midnight & very sleepy & weary

Alicia dear —

Only 10,000 letters left to ans[wer]!!

I see little chance of Georgia within 2 weeks after Dec. 27. I don't get evicted from Spfd. until Jan 12 & then I must have a few days in Chi-[cago]. looking for a place to live temporarily,[60] getting settled on some interim basis etc etc. I thought then I would try to get a little holiday — out of reach — in the West Indies & work on a little book to make some money. Then perhaps around Mar 1 I was thinking of going around the world for self education & to escape while Congress is in session, before I put my foot in it with some of my beloved Democratic brethern. All this in confidence — as if it was important!

I don't know about the eggheads or what they're up to — all I want is to be left alone! — but I hope it doesn't become subversive in the land of Jefferson to like intelligent, educated, sensitive people or to be proud that they voted for you. But it looks as tho that was the wave of the future. Tonight the Gridiron dinner in D.C. & a witty speech by the loser.

A

Paul R. Leach, of the Washington bureau of the Chicago Daily News, *made the following introduction of Stevenson to the Gridiron Club dinner at the Statler Hotel in Washington on December 13: "Gentlemen: It is the American way to put everything we have into a political campaign, especially for the presidency. It is an office worth having. Therefore it is worth fighting for. But when the votes are counted, and the victor and vanquished exchange regards, we present a solid front to the rest of the world, and let no man say otherwise. The Gridiron Club is happy to present a man who was staunch in his campaigning, truly American in defeat. Gentlemen: The Leader of the Loyal Opposition; the Governor of the Prairie State of Illinois — the Honorable Adlai E. Stevenson."*

[59] This handwritten letter is in the possession of Adlai E. Stevenson III.
[60] Stevenson's house in Libertyville was rented to Marshall Field IV.

AN ADDRESS BY GOVERNOR ADLAI E. STEVENSON
BEFORE THE GRIDIRON CLUB DINNER [61]

A funny thing happened to me on the way to the White House! — Let me tell you something about it all.

While I did not carry many states, I seem to have run way ahead in the Fourth Estate, excluding, of course, you publishers. I can think of no state I would rather have carried, and perhaps I should begin by apologizing to those of you who work for a living and who thought I was out in front, somewhere beside Mississippi, Britain and France. The fact was, of course, that the General was so far ahead we never saw him. I was happy to hear that I had even placed second.

It is apparent that I was not the first choice of a great many. But no one will say, I trust, that I snatched defeat from the jaws of victory. Which reminds me that four years ago, occupying the seat I occupy to-night, was another great Governor — excuse me, the Governor of another great State — some say the second greatest State in the Union.[62] What has just happened to me had just happened to him. In fact, it had just happened to him for the second time. But did he despair? He did not. He said to himself — if I may take a newspaperman's license and tell you what a man says to himself — he said: "If I cannot be President myself, I can at least make somebody else President." Which, blast his merry heart, he proceeded to do. And look at him now. He's as contented as the cat that swallowed the canary, or should I say the cabinet.

At that Gridiron dinner just four years ago the newly elected Governor of Illinois sat down there with you common people — which reminds me that I rather enjoy talking over your heads — at last! I was happy and carefree and had nothing to worry about; nothing except the organization of a new administration to clean up the State of Illinois after the long years of the usual Republican misrule. (And now I don't even have that to worry about!)

I, a Democrat, had just been elected Governor by the largest majority ever received in Republican Illinois. And here I am, four years later, and just defeated by the largest majority ever received in Democratic America.

Wasn't it Jim Watson [63] who said that he entered the Senate with almost *no* opposition from the people of Indiana, and that he left the Senate, with *none?*

[61] The text is based on a printed copy prepared by friends of Stevenson for private distribution.

[62] Thomas E. Dewey of New York.

[63] James Eli Watson, Republican representative from Indiana, 1895–1897 and 1899–1909, and U.S. senator, 1916–1933.

I feel a little the same way. But I wonder if I'm not entitled to some kind of a record. Did anyone starting from scratch ever *enter* our public life with such widespread approval, and then *leave,* with such widespread approval — all in the space of four years? Frankly, I think the chroniclers of our times have overlooked the meteoric beauty and brevity of my political career.

Well, I had not planned it that way. I had wished to continue as Governor of Illinois, there to erect and fortify a shining temple of administrative purity and political probity. But the gods decreed otherwise — after meeting in the Chicago stockyards. Mindful of the Chinese maiden's philosophical acceptance of unwanted and aggressive attentions, I concluded to accept my fate gallantly and joyfully, with consequences that were reported by most of your publishers — also joyfully!

Now I content myself that it is all for the best. After all, didn't Socrates say that the duty of a man of real principle is to stay out of politics? So you see I'm delighted that the sovereign people have put an even higher value on my principles than I did.

Yes, I have much to be thankful for and it would be out of character if I didn't frankly confess my happy state of mind, even here, surrounded by my late executioners.

As you all know, I just love to make speeches. Especially light-hearted speeches. For laughter most of all distinguishes us from the lower — or untaxed — animals, and I am much relieved that the Republicans evidently decided not to prohibit humor in politics by Federal law. Maybe they are going to leave it to the states to deal with this newest threat to the Republic.

I am happy that almost 27 million voted for me. I was a little baffled by the emergence of that word "egghead," to describe some of my supporters — a word which I am glad to bequeath to the nation's vocabulary. It seems to have been first used to describe the more intelligensiac members of that lunatic fringe who thought I was going to win. I am happy to note that you have refrained from saying of the eggheads that the yolk was on them!

That figure, 27 million, still staggers me. But I need a much stronger verb to describe what the still larger number of those who liked Ike does to me!

I have not compared notes with the President-elect on how he enjoyed the campaign. Indeed, now that the affair is over, I hope some time to know him, which recalls many editorials and articles you gentlemen wrote last spring about how I wanted to run against Senator Taft but not the General who was my old friend. It has seemed to me odd that the simple truth that I did not want to run against anyone had so little news value.

I would tell him that for my part I enjoyed the campaign — in spots. There were times, I confess, when I was afraid I wouldn't die, times when I felt I wouldn't do it to a dog. Let me add, by the way, that, like every red-blooded American patriot, I own a dog. It was not a campaign contribution. And I think the General would say to me that there are times when he wishes he was in my shoes — you see I had them fixed.[64]

A lot of wonderful things happened to me during the campaign. People shook hands (have you ever shaken 4,000 hands, one after the other, with a happy smile and a bright word for the owner of each hand?) They even shouted, "Good old Ad-lai!" If any of you gentlemen run for public office and have a slightly unusual name, let me advise you either to change it before you start, or be prepared to take other people's word for it.

I travelled. In San Francisco a woman in the crowd shook hands with me through the car door and shortly announced that she had lost a diamond ring. I travelled tens of thousands of miles, up and down this vast country, on such a sightseeing tour as few men are privileged to make. And all free! Free, that is, if blood and sweat, money and deficits don't count.

I got several hours sleep a night; they fed me pretty regularly; I got a little tired of cheese on rye sandwiches and coffee in cardboard containers. And I frequently thought, unhappily, of Froude's line in his life of Bunyan: "The excitement of perpetual speechmaking is fatal to the exercise of the highest powers." I became very familiar with the sound of my own voice. I hope the Recording Angel will note that I did not say the "sound of my own *words*" — although, if you want to raise this ghostly subject, I should be quite willing to open my speech-writing books, if the Luce publications and Readers Digest will open theirs.[65]

And speaking of books, although I clearly won the bosom-baring and public-stripping contest of last fall, I am now prepared to go a step further and disclose my pre-nomination expenditures in full:

Before the Convention:

(1) 3-Cent postage stamps to explain, mostly *to* the press,
    why I was not a candidate for the nomination $150.00

After the Convention commenced in Chicago, a large number of persons took up their residence on the street and lawns around my house —

---

[64] William F. Gallagher, of the Flint, Michigan, *Journal,* took a widely circulated photograph of Stevenson, which prominently showed a hole in his shoe, and for which Mr. Gallagher was awarded a Pulitzer Prize in 1953. The photograph is included in the illustrations to this volume.

[65] The Luce publications and the *Reader's Digest* were vitriolic opponents of Stevenson during the campaign, and *Life* in its October 6 and 13, 1952, issues did not carry even one picture of him.

and you know who they were — and the following expenditures were incurred before I could escape:

(2)	68 cases of beer — *for* the press	$272.00
(3)	16 cases of non-alcoholic beverages *for* the press	34.00
(4)	8 cases of other beverages — *for* the press	480.00
(5)	Hire of truck from house to Convention Hall — *for* the press	30.00
(6)	Hire of bus from house to Convention Hall — *for* the press	50.00
(7)	Special police assigned to protect house — *from* the press	500.00
	TOTAL	$1,366.00

There is a further item, not yet available, for restoring lawns destroyed, if not permanently scorched, *by* the press.

The eggheads present, if any, will identify and understand, then, why I think of those words: "How sharper than a serpent's tooth it is to have a thankless — press."

Of course, I make this further and positively final revelation with no expectation of political reciprocity, but merely to suggest, with characteristic delicacy, that the ANPA [American Newspaper Publishers Association] can send its check to me.

And now that the tumult and the shouting have died, and Walter Lippman[n] and Joe Alsop have gone back to writing the next chapter of the Doomsday Book, how does the vanquished hero feel, and what of the future?

Well, gentlemen, there are certain pleasurable aspects of defeat. Although there seemed little perceptible editorial enthusiasm for me during the campaign, except in some of the better papers, I have been stirred by the virtues which so many assayists [essayists] discovered in me the moment it became clear that the outs were in. Much of this comment seemed to suggest that it couldn't have happened to a nicer guy. And, lest you get ahead of me, I say that I couldn't have lost to a nicer guy. And I'll still think so, even if the boys are not out of the trenches by Christmas!

Then there were the letters. We gave up counting before long and began to weigh them. So many of them were from people who voted for the General, and evidently felt that they owed me an explanation; curious why people will go to all that trouble to write a long letter when a little X in the right place would have been so much easier. But I am grateful to them all, and I wish there was some refined way befitting my station to explain to each of them that we spent a lot of money we didn't have, etc. But I suppose if I did they might write again, in less friendly vein, and say: "Just like a Democrat."

As to my future: Well, there are those like the man who changed the sign on his car after the election from "Switched to Stevenson" to "Switched, Bothered and Bewildered," who feel that I should devote my classic talents to the welfare of mankind by frequent talking; then there is another smaller group who insist that God, and/or the election, has appointed me the scourge of the Republican party; and finally there is the much smaller group that feel that it is not wholly unworthy or improper to earn a living. My sons are numbered in the latter group.

But despite anything you may have read or written, there are some future plans of action that I definitely have rejected. I have declined an invitation to become President of the National Association of Gag-writers. And I will not go into vaudeville. It is equally definite that I will not become manager of the Washington Senators — I mean Clark Griffith's, not Mr. Taft's.

To those of us who constitute what I trust will be known as the responsible opposition, these are times of unusual complexity. Mention of Mr. Taft suggests, for example, that for the moment, at least, we Democrats are intruders in a family quarrel. Indeed it is difficult to be certain, for the present, whether we Democrats will be disagreeing with the new President, or acting as his bodyguard.

But whatever happens to the Republicans, the Republic will survive. I have great faith in the people. As to their wisdom, well, Coca Cola still outsells champagne. They may make mistakes. They do sometimes. But given time they correct their mistakes — at two or four year intervals. I have faith in the people, and in their chosen leaders: men of high purpose, good will and humble hearts, men quite prepared to stand aside when the time comes and allow even more humble men to take over.

As to you, the press, a last word. It is the habit of journalists, as of politicians, to see the world in terms of crisis rather than continuity; the big story is turmoil and disaster, not the quiet spectacle of men working. I trust that there will be none among my party who will hope for just a small, dandy little catastrophe to vindicate us. I am aware of the thesis that bad news sells papers. But neither politicians nor publishers have the right in this age to hope for the worst. Every newspaperman has talked at one time or another of how to handle the story of the end of the world; but who will be around to buy the extra?

Every lesson of history is that democracy flourishes best when speech is freest. No issue is more important — and more troublesome — in this time of conflict with massive repression than the preservation of our right, even to bore each other. (I was flattered, by the way, by an unsigned letter last week that said: "Please start talking again, Governor, or we'll be bored to death before we're starved to death.") Never was the responsibility of the majority press greater to make clear that it is concerned about the freedom of all Americans, and not merely about its own liberty to agree with itself. Your typewriter is a public trust. Its sound may be the most beautiful noise you know, but it has meaning and justification only if it is part of the glorious discordant symphony of a free society.

I am grateful to the Gridiron Club for inviting me and to all of you for your courtesy and patience with me.

To the minority among you, I say "chins up," and "There, there, little mink coat, don't you cry, For you'll be a teapot by and by."

The daughter of James P. Warburg, then three weeks old, "dictated" a letter to Stevenson on December 12 saying that her father told her that Governor Stevenson was going to "lie in the weeds" for a while. She advised: "Take a pillow when you go to the weeds because if you don't they will tickle your ear."

To Jennifer Joan Warburg [66]

December 15, 1952

Dear Jennifer:

Thank you so much for your superb letter. I have never had a better letter from one so young. Indeed I have never had one from one so young.

And thanks for reminding me about the pillow when I lie in the weeds. But if you were a weed I would very much like you to tickle my ear; and I should like to have you tickle my ear anyway.

Your very old friend,

To the Reverend Reinhold Niebuhr [67]

December 15, 1952

Dear Reinhold:

I have only now found your letter of November 11 in the avalanche that engulfed me. I could not be more grateful.

Just the other day I was talking about you with one of your myriad admirers in Washington. I wonder if you know how many people pray for

[66] A copy is in A.E.S., I.S.H.L.
[67] The original is in the Niebuhr papers, Library of Congress.

you, and I am honored to be included as an irreverent member of that chorus.

I think you are quite right about the failure of the administration to explain the Korean war during the past years. But at the same time they had little help from a press from which the public deserve better.

You have paid me a great compliment and I am your debtor.

With warmest best wishes, I am

Cordially yours,

A Chicagoan wrote Stevenson that a friend from India had been extremely impressed by the Governor's campaign.

To Dahyabhai Patel [68]

December 15, 1952

My dear Mr. Patel:

Mr. Chapin [69] advises me that you thought well of me and of my campaign for the Presidency. I am very much flattered and I am also grateful indeed for your support and good will.

I earnestly hope that you will take back to your country a vivid impression of our policies and a wholesome respect for our democratic system. We believe in the people. Not that they are always right but that they ultimately correct their errors, — and please don't feel that I think their decision this time was an error! Think of the anguish and misery it saved me.

With my thanks and warm good wishes, I am

Sincerely yours,

Claude G. Bowers, ambassador to Chile and former newspaperman and author of many books, including Jefferson and Hamilton (*Boston: Houghton Mifflin, 1925*) *and* Jefferson in Power (*Boston: Houghton Mifflin, 1936*), *wrote Stevenson that his speeches were "superbly courageous and were addressed to the intelligence of the people." Bowers expressed bewilderment over the loss of New York to Eisenhower and explained he was writing James A. Farley for his analysis. Bowers pointed out that in many Southern states the Democratic party was in the hands of oligarchies which had to be ousted.*

[68] A copy is in A.E.S., I.S.H.L.
[69] Unable to identify.

To Claude G. Bowers

December 15, 1952

My dear Mr. Ambassador:

Only now has your extraordinary letter of November 10 emerged from the avalanche that engulfed me after the election. You have educated me — as you always do — and you have also flattered me far beyond my deserts. But I like it! And I shall file your letter away with a carefully selected few thus to haunt you when calmer judgment emerges.

I was much interested in what you had to say about the South. We have a problem there which I think you have analyzed perfectly. The ancient Democratic coalition has little reason for further existence and we shall have to build anew relying on different leadership in many places. It may take a long time.

As for New York, I think as Jim probably told you that the organization was woefully weak — this in confidence! — and that there was tremendous disaffection among the Irish Catholics because of "communists in government." Also the expenditure of appalling sums of money by the Republicans for every kind of publicity device both there and elsewhere had its effect. I suppose that the most important contribution to the Republican victory was the impression that General Eisenhower created that he could settle the Korean war promptly. Our reports from many places indicate that women turned out in astonishing numbers and even among the labor group deserted their husbands to vote for Ike.

Well, I am rewarded by a few letters like yours and have no regrets. Thank you so much.

Cordially yours,

Former congresswoman Mrs. Helen Gahagan Douglas of California wrote Stevenson: "There were many tears shed election night, but tears will not dissipate the fear that is abroad today. You have the intelligence and the spiritual strength to generate the hope and faith that is needed, but it must be backed up by a Democratic National Committee Program that is vital and alive in every county."

To Helen Gahagan Douglas [70]

December 16, 1952

Dear Helen:

I am so grateful for your letter of November 12 which has only now emerged from the heap.

I think we *must* take advantage of past experience, and I am passing your letter along to Steve Mitchell. I think he has some regional surveys in contemplation. There is much party organization work to be done, if my observations are correct.

Cordially yours,

ADLAI

Mrs. Ronald Tree wrote Stevenson on December 15, thanking him for his hospitality on the recent visit she and Mr. Tree made to Springfield. She urged the Governor to vacation at their home in Barbados.

To Mrs. Ronald Tree [71]

December 16, 1952

Dear Marietta:

This is but a hasty note to acknowledge your sweet letter this morning. Perhaps Arthur [Schlesinger, Jr.] and the others hereabouts are right and I should try to vanish for a bit of repose shortly after my term here in mid-January. I can imagine nothing more perfect than the Barbados — but I had hoped that you would be there, too, and February 1st looks very distant! As the dust settles, I may call you by phone and take advantage of your generosity.

My best to Ronnie.

Affectionately,

Helen Keller wrote Stevenson on December 3: "Your noble philosophy, applied to statesmanship, inspires me with an unwavering faith that the principles and practices of democracy will yet be reaffirmed and renewed."

[70] The original is in the possession of Mrs. Douglas.
[71] A copy is in A.E.S., I.S.H.L.

To Helen Keller

December 16, 1952

Dear Miss Keller:

Thank you so much for your beautiful letter. I only wish I merited it. I have never been more flattered.

Cordially yours,

To Richard Bentley [72]

December 17, 1952

Dear Dick:

Henry Tenney [73] brought me the news of your operation. I seem to have been out of communication with the outside world for some time! Reports are that the progress is good and I am delighted to hear it. I have yearned to see you all again in more tranquil circumstances than have been mine and healthier circumstances than have been yours.

My love to Phoebe.[74]

Yours,
ADLAI

To Donald J. Walsh [75]

December 19, 1952

Dear Don:

Thanks for your note. I have decided to try to do the book of speeches with a little introduction for Random House right after I get through here. The possibility of a travel book — and the possibility of travel! — is in the offing with Harper's in the lead. I have noted carefully your admonition to withhold serial and all other rights. I shall act accordingly.

Now hurry and get off your duff — but not too soon.

Yours,
ADLAI

---

[72] The original is in the possession of Mr. Bentley.
[73] A Chicago lawyer active in the Volunteers for Stevenson.
[74] Mrs. Bentley.
[75] Former director of Public Safety during Stevenson's governorship, afterwards with the Chicago *American*. The original is in the possession of Mr. Walsh.

To Henry Steele Commager [76]

December 19, 1952

My dear Professor Commager:

I hope you will forgive me for being so late in thanking you for your assistance in connection with the education speech. Norman [Cousins] has told me that you put everything aside in order to prepare this material for me at a time when you were about to leave for London. I am most grateful, and mortified that you were put to this trouble because I concluded not to speak on the subject.

Most of the fun in running for President is the chance it gives you to have some contact, however remote, with so many sympathetic and helpful people. I am suggesting it to all my friends!

May I also take this opportunity to thank you for your courageous and inspiring writings.

With all good wishes, I am

Cordially yours,

Trygve Lie, Secretary-General of the United Nations, wired Stevenson on December 23: "The impact you have made through your magnificent campaign will not be lost. I wish you continued success in carrying on the education of your fellow citizens in the responsibilities of world leadership."

To Trygve Lie [77]

December 23, 1952

Dear Trygve:

I was delighted to find your thoughtful and gracious telegram. My thoughts have been very much with you in these recent months and I pray for the best for you, whom I shall always count a dear and honored friend, and for the United Nations which is freighted with the hopes and fears of so many in these fateful days.

Please give my warm regards to Mrs. Lie, and may the New Year bring you peace of mind.

Yours,

[76] Professor of history, Columbia University.
[77] A copy is in A.E.S., I.S.H.L.

To Hiram Haydn [78]

December 23, 1952

Dear Mr. Haydn:

I have seldom been more flattered than by your letter of December 11, inviting me to serve a term on the Editorial Board of The American Scholar. Indeed, this is my closest approach to authentic scholarship!

However, in view of my very uncertain plans and the probability that I may be away for a considerable period, I think I had best decline for the reason that I should be of no possible value and without a free moment for at least a year to come.

I am deeply grateful to you and to the Phi Beta Kappa Senate, and I hope you will express to them my gratitude and regret.

Cordially yours,

Stevenson's former law firm held an annual Christmas luncheon. The Governor sent the following telegram to one of the partners of the firm.

To Kenneth F. Burgess

December 24, 1952

SORRY I CANNOT GET THERE FOR LUNCH TO WISH YOU ALL A MERRY CHRISTMAS ESPECIALLY THE DEMOCRATS IF ANY. AS FOR A PROSPEROUS NEW YEAR I AM SURE THE LAW CLERKS ARE PRAYING THAT THE FUTURE OF SIDLEY, AUSTIN, BURGESS AND SMITH WILL BE AS GOOD AS ITS PAST. AFFECTIONATE REGARDS TO MR. SIDLEY AND ALL OF YOU.

To Sir Louis and Lady Spears [79]

December 26, 1952

Dear Louis and Mary:

You were so sweet to send me that thoughtful cablegram on Christmas. I am mortified that in the appalling chaos hereabouts I not only sent you nothing but even forgot to wire you. Please forgive me and know that my thoughts and heart are very much with you.

I have hopes now of commencing the long journey through the Orient, the Middle East, etc. beginning around March 1, with the probability

[78] Editor of the *American Scholar*, published by Phi Beta Kappa.
[79] Lady Spears, the former Mary Borden, was Ellen Stevenson's aunt.

that I may be in England in late May or early June. I would like to avoid the Coronation confusion,[80] and somehow meet Borden [Stevenson] after college for a little travel or "retreat" with him before I return to this country and he proceeds on his first exploration of Europe. Sir Maurice Bowra, the Vice Chancellor at Oxford, has asked me to make the Romanes Lecture there some time before the 13th of June. I am tempted — and horrified at the prospect!

With affectionate good wishes, I am

Yours,

To Hermon D. Smith [81]

December 26, 1952

Dear Dutch:

Thanks for the report. I confess I have not had an opportunity to read it yet what with this incessant clamor, complicated by Christmas, but I am sure it will be useful for future reference.

Please tell Ellen [82] that the Smiths could have thought of no better Christmas present than the deficit check. But why any present! You and Ellen and Adele [83] are my presents! And tell Adele that I am going to hire her to read the morning paper at breakfast to me — for one dollar.

Yours,

ADLAI

Gerald Johnson wrote Stevenson on December 23 and urged him to speak out: "We don't need a campaign argument — not yet. But we do need a manifesto that will polarize liberal opinion, not against any individual, but against heresy, regardless of who preaches it."

To Gerald Johnson

December 28, 1952

Dear Gerald:

I have your interesting letter, and I think you are right about taking advantage of the interval in which my views might command some respect as nonpolitical. However, there are many difficulties: the President, the Democratic members of Congress, the ambitions, etc.

80 The coronation of Queen Elizabeth II was to be held in June, 1953.
81 The original is in the possession of Mr. Smith.
82 Mrs. Smith.
83 The Smiths' daughter.

However, the expression of some philosophical base to "polarize liberal opinion," as you put it, does seem to me desirable. My present situation is hopeless, and when I leave here in a few weeks I am committed to some work and then some travel.

The conclusion is obvious: Gerald Johnson must draft the manifesto of the liberals at the mid-century point!, and then send it to me at 11 South La Salle Street in Chicago! I am not sure how good a ghost such a distinguished writer can be, but if there is any Johnson ghosting I want it myself. There now; get to work — and let this be a lesson to you when you feel like nudging me again.

Cordially yours,

P.S. And the sooner the better. I might be able to use it in a piece I must do very soon as a foreword to a little book of speeches.

A.E.S.

John Milder, of Brooklyn, New York, wrote Stevenson on December 20 that a group of students at Columbia University, who had worked for his campaign, planned to publish a liberal magazine: "It is the kind of thing that your campaign inspired."

To John B. Milder, Jr.[84]

December 29, 1952

My dear Mr. Milder:

I have read with interest your recent letter in which is described the plan of you and your associates to publish a magazine generally devoted to questions of current concern in our social and political life. Although I understand — and certainly hope — that this enterprise is in no way related to my own future political fortunes, I am gratified that it is apparently an outgrowth of associations formed and common interests discovered in the course of activities on my behalf during the recent campaign.

A losing election campaign seems at first blush like the emptiest thing in the world in terms of permanent and positive effects. This is especially true of the feelings of those who have labored actively in it; and I must confess that there have been moments since Election Day when this reaction has assailed me with almost overwhelming force. However, these are transient emotions — not unnatural under the circumstances — and they grow less frequent as the days go by. My dominant impression is that our campaign, disappointing as was its outcome, had values of its

[84] A copy is in A.E.S., I.S.H.L.

own which justify all the time and trouble and heartbreak that went into it.

This feeling on my part is only strengthened and confirmed by the news that one group of young people who worked in it acquired thereby an understanding of the vital issues pressing upon our country, and a purpose to discuss them calmly and sanely with others through the medium of a magazine.

I wish your project well. I hope that it will always, if I may use once more a phrase that still rings true to my ear, talk sense to its readers. This requires a willingness to face the facts as they are even though they may clash with the preconceptions of either a liberal or a conservative point of view. It means a refusal to substitute generalities and clichés for the painful processes of thought. It demands a readiness to speak out for the truth as it is given to one to see it, no matter how unpleasant or unpopular.

If your publication is unwavering in its adherence to these exacting standards, then it will have helped mightily in the eternal effort to push [back] both the forces which make for irrational, prejudiced, or fuzzily wishful thinking — and this whether its life be one issue or a thousand. I hope it will be the latter.

Sincerely yours,

P.S. I have no objection to your using this letter in your first issue if, as indicated in your letter, you desire to do so.

A.E.S.

To Lloyd K. Garrison

December 29, 1952

Dear Lloyd:

I think I gave you some papers about recordings. Here is another to add to them for future discussion. Also, find enclosed letters from Knopf and Farrar Strauss for your "book" file.

I sometimes think it will take me the rest of my life to work through this labyrinth!

I am now planning definitely to fly to Barbados on Tuesday, January 20, and will plan to be in New York on the 18th and 19th. Perhaps we could reach some decision at that time about the travel articles and/or book. I could come a day earlier if need be.

I should like to get off on my journey March 2 by boat from San Francisco to Hawaii and thence by air. There will be much preparatory work to be done, so that my time gets more precious. Meanwhile, the

The **BILTMORE**

FRANK W. REGAN, PRESIDENT
DAVID J. MARTIN, MANAGER

MADISON AVENUE AT 43RD STREET
New York City
TELEPHONE - MURRAY HILL 7-7000

ADJOINING GRAND CENTRAL

I have been repeatedly pressed for comment on ~~Senator~~ the matter of Senator Nixon.

From what ~~little~~ I have heard about it, the questions seem to be: who gave the money, ~~and~~ was it given to influence the Senator's position on public questions, I and have any laws been violated?

I am sure the great Republican party will ascertain these facts, will make them public, and act in accordance with our best traditions and with due respect for the second most important position in the land.

Condemnation without all the evidence, a practice all too familiar to us, would be wrong,

*Stevenson's comments when Richard Nixon's
campaign fund was disclosed*

Stevenson meets with campaign advisers
in front of the executive mansion

Walter Johnson hangs a picture of the non-candidate in the "Draft Stevenson" headquarters in the Hilton Hotel, Washington, D.C.

Springfield, Illinois, welcomes Stevenson home, July 18, 1952

*Mayor Charles P. Farnsley of Louisville, Kentucky, presents
the Democratic nominee with the key to the city, August 7, 1952.
Looking on is Vice President Alben Barkley*

*Vice President Alben Barkley holds a barbecue for Stevenson
at his home near Paducah, Kentucky, September 28, 1952. In the
background are campaign manager Wilson W. Wyatt and former
Kentucky Governor Lawrence Wetherby*

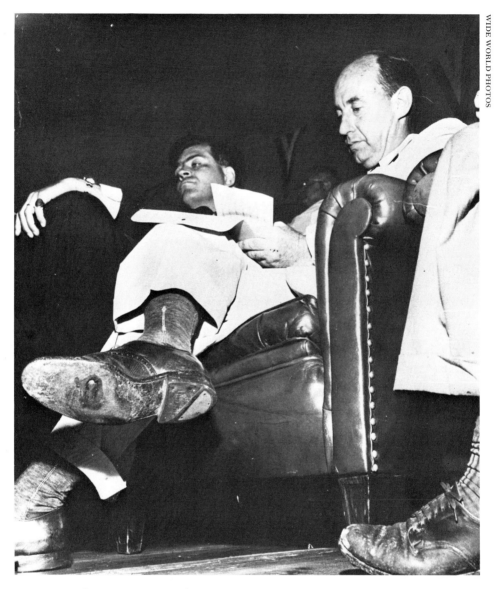

Campaigning in Michigan in 1952. Governor G. Mennen Williams is with Stevenson

Random House book stares in my frightened face! I must do it all in Barbados between January 21 and my return to New York the 10th or 12th of February.

Yours,

P.S. For the travel magazine pieces, I have thought of the idea of setting them up in the form of letters to my sons, light treatment, geography, what I saw, who I talked to, what I heard, etc., reserving the more ponderous thought about world problems for the second portion of a book to follow the letters. What do you think?

A.E.S.

David L. Cohn, who had been a member of the "Elks Club group" of speechwriters during the campaign, wrote Stevenson on December 21, urging him to accept an invitation from Professor James Silver to speak at the University of Mississippi: "The more so since Mississippi not only remains — as when I was a boy there — poor, proud, and prolific — but also Democratic." He added that he was back at his farm in Hopewell, New Jersey, "an overweight Simon Legree grinding down the wretched peasantry who toil for me."

To David L. Cohn [85]

December 30, 1952

My dear David:

Your engaging letter lifted a dreary morning. I do not recall hearing from Professor Silver, but I did have a letter from Governor [Hugh] White and was obliged to tell him that circumstances too involved to recite would make it impossible for me to come to the University of Mississippi at the appointed time.

I am noting that Hopewell telephone number and may have to inspect Simon Legree's operation. You know how suspicious I've been of those cruel landlords.

My plans are confused — as always! If I can ever get disentangled here and relocate in Chicago, I propose to escape for a bit and then come March perhaps take a long, long journey. I hope it neither odd nor unwise that I feel like vanishing to new scenes for a bit — a big bit!

May all your days be joyous!

Sincerely,

[85] A copy is in A.E.S., I.S.H.L.

Max Ascoli, founder of the Reporter, *wrote Stevenson urging him to write for the magazine and asking for a list of the Volunteers for Stevenson.*

To Max Ascoli

December 30, 1952

Dear Max:

I have your letter of the 19th and am delighted to hear of the growth and your plans for the future of The Reporter. I thought your previous letter sounded a little discouraged, and this one is very heartening.

I shall take steps at once to see what, if anything, can be done about getting some sort of list of the Volunteers into your hands, and also of the major contributors. I think Roger Stevens [86] in New York, who was the Treasurer, would know best about the latter. Whether the National Headquarters, which is gradually folding up in Chicago, has any comprehensive list I do not know.

I should most certainly like to do a piece for The Reporter sometime, but I have been so mercilessly besieged here in Springfield that I am constantly behind in my day-to-day chores. When my term expires, there lies ahead of me the "Speech Book" and then a long journey, followed by a book, I suppose.

But let us talk of these things. I shall hope to have a day or so in New York around the 18th or 19th of January, and will let you know against the chance that we could talk then or when I come back once more in February.

Sincerely,

P.S. Among my bushels of Christmas cards, one is very conspicuous — from "1/1,000,000th" of my supporters — and, I am happy to say, a much larger percentage of your employees! Is there some way you can thank, bless and kiss them all (I mean the females) for me? No, reserve the caresses for me! But do thank them, and tell them that my heart is full.

A.E.S.

Historian Allan Nevins, of Columbia University, wrote Stevenson: "Your speeches and bearing lifted party activity in this country to the highest plane it has ever touched. From beginning to end it was superb. There was a combination of elevation and solid sense in everything you said that carried us straight back to Lincoln."

[86] A Broadway theatrical producer and real estate broker.

To Allan Nevins

January 3, 1953

Dear Allan:

I have your letter of December 26 and the effect is dangerously infla-
tionary! If I contributed anything to a higher level of campaigning for
the highest office, I am content; that you think so makes me doubly content.

I wish I were going to see you at the Carl Sandburg dinner. Unhappily, I find that the Democratic members of the Legislature are holding a caucus dinner that night and the following morning I have to speak
at the joint session. I must remain at my post of duty to the end, so I
shall miss this memorable affair to my enduring regret. But I comfort
myself with the thought that we shall meet in the future in Chicago,
perhaps even in New York, if not in this lovely old house.

Sincerely yours,

STATEMENT BY ADLAI E. STEVENSON
ON THE OCCASION OF THE 75TH BIRTHDAY CELEBRATION
OF CARL SANDBURG, JANUARY 6, 1953 [87]

Carl Sandburg is the one living man whose work and whose life epitomize the American dream. He has the earthiness of the prairies, the
majesty of mountains, the anger of deep inland seas. In him is the restlessness of the seeker, the questioner, the explorer of far horizons, the
hunger that is never satisfied. In him also is the tough strength that has
never been fully measured, never unleashed, the resiliency of youthfulness which wells from within, and which no ageing can destroy.

To Archibald MacLeish

January 6, 1953

Dear Archie:

I wish you had not written me that lovely letter.[88] I was contented,
indeed elated, by the prospect of a visit with the [Ronald] Trees in
Barbados. Even the work which I must do there preparing an introduction for a book of speeches which Random House is publishing did not
depress me.

But then comes your letter — and now I want to go to Antigua, like

[87] The text is based on a carbon copy.
[88] Mr. MacLeish had invited Stevenson to vacation at their home on Antigua.

[*241*]

a fickle woman, but I cannot. I must not now — but it is not to say I will not. We shall see and if I can find any time in my brief days there, I'll land on you.

Love to Ada [89] and a thousand thanks.

Yours,

P.S. That I must write an introduction for the speeches and haven't the remotest idea what to say reminds me of you! Have you any idea what I should say? If so, you'll know how to say it — and you will say it as lengthily or briefly as you please and send it to me post haste care Ronald Tree in Barbados or care Mrs. Ralph Hines,[90] 237 East 61st Street in New York if you say it before I depart on January 20.

A.E.S.

Herbert Agar wrote Stevenson on January 6, 1953: "I doubt if you could possibly know what an impression you have made upon the people of England and France. . . . I also doubt if you can possibly know how low is the stock of our country in England and France today. . . . My profound belief is that you can do more than can the Government of the United States" to alter the situation. He urged Stevenson to visit England and lecture.

To Herbert Agar [91]

January 6, 1953

Dear Herbert:

I have read and reread your letter and aside from a dangerous inflation I feel a little bewildered and futile. How can all this be? And what can I really do to help in a situation which I know is bad, acutely bad. I should like to, of course, but my old trouble of hopeless inadequacy afflicts me again.

But to business: my plans are becoming clearer now. I am off the 20th to Barbados with the Trees for some sun and to try desperately to meet the Random House deadline on the speech book; then back to New York to speak at the big Democratic clambake in middle February; then to Washington for "consultations" and then the West Coast for one more speech and off March 2 for my journey through the Orient. The schedule is by no means clear but it looks now as though I could not be in England before mid or late June which, I am afraid, will be too

---

[89] Mrs. MacLeish.
[90] The former Betty Borden, Ellen Stevenson's sister.
[91] A copy is in A.E.S., I.S.H.L.

late for lecturing, even if you were to prepare my "lectures." This all rather suggests that maybe I better defer any public speaking in England until another journey a year hence if it could be then contrived.

At all events, I yearn for the Sussex countryside and the beloved Agars. But for the present, I am afraid you better restrain the eager, which will probably sustain the illusion about me a little longer.

My love to Barbie [92] and there will be more communications to you.

Yours,

P.S. Barry Bingham is going with me, at least through the Far East and I hope all the way.

P.P.S. I'm afraid I have written you to some fanciful and incorrect address which must have been manufactured in my fevered head.

Gordon Havens, of the New York Times, *wrote Stevenson: "Before you leave Springfield, I just want to tell you that the newspapers seem to be pretty dull these days without your speeches in them — and that things won't seem really right until you're making them again."*

To Gordon Havens

January 9, 1953

Dear Mr. Havens:

Your note of January 4 was most kind and I am grateful for it. Your observations with reference to my speeches are much too generous, but I do hope to be expressing myself from time to time on public questions when the need and an appropriate occasion coincide.

Thank you again for your expression of good will, which I value highly.

Sincerely yours,

Before Governor Stevenson left Springfield he delivered a message to both houses of the legislature and made a radio report to the people of Illinois.[93] His old law firm, Sidley, Burgess, Austin & Smith, 11 South La Salle Street in Chicago, generously loaned him space enough for his numerous files, an office for himself and his secretary, Carol Evans, and his aide, William McCormick Blair, Jr., and Blair's secretary, Phyllis

[92] Mrs. Agar.
[93] See *The Papers of Adlai E. Stevenson,* Vol. III, pp. 589–595.

Gustafson. After establishing himself in his office, he visited New York City to make arrangements with Look *magazine for a series of articles about his forthcoming trip of self-education through countries stretching from Japan to the United Kingdom. He then flew to Barbados for a vacation and to make the final selection of his campaign speeches to be published in* Major Campaign Speeches of Adlai E. Stevenson, 1952 *and to write an introduction for the volume.*

To Harry S. Truman

January 16, 1953

Dear Mr. President:

My heart is very much with you and Mrs. Truman on the eve of your departure from that House and that post where you have found so much of anxiety, of misery, of misunderstanding, and also of joy and triumph. Having just left my residence in Springfield, I have tasted something of what you are feeling, but I pray that your spirit is serene, that you are content, confident that as these troubled, crowded years recede there will emerge a recognition and gratitude for the wisdom and the courage of the great decisions that were yours.

I am leaving now for a visit with friends in the West Indies, and, unhappily, some work! About the first of March I plan to take a long journey through the Orient and back by the Middle East and Europe in early July. I have traveled much in Western Europe, and the Mediterranean, but Asia is *terra incognita* for me and this seems a logical time to have a look for myself.

I shall hope for a good visit with you on my return. Meanwhile, my warmest wishes to you and Mrs. Truman and Margaret.

Respectfully yours,

Stevenson left on January 21, 1953, for a three-week vacation in Barbados. The following note was written sometime during his stay there.

To Carol Evans [94]

[no date]

Carol — Have to mail this in great haste — no time for a proper note. Just back from 3 days in Dominica, little changed since the 18th

[94] This handwritten letter is in the possession of Miss Evans.

century. Struggling desperately to make progress with this darn book and *pray* that corrections are being made as I send the sheets back.

Hope all is well —

Hastily

AES

On February 14, 1953, Stevenson spoke at the Jefferson-Jackson Day Dinner in New York City. Before his speech he was interviewed by Edward P. Morgan for the Columbia Broadcasting System.[95]

MORGAN: Governor Stevenson, you appear to be one of the most healthy-looking defeated candidates that I've seen. You're sunburned and alive and everything — what's happened to you?

STEVENSON: Well, I've just had a vacation. I've just come back from Barbados in the British West Indies where I had almost three weeks, the first real vacation I've had in thirteen years.

MORGAN: Well, it has obviously agreed with you, but I see that you're planning another trip. Where are you going to go, Governor?

STEVENSON: Well, I'm going to — I've never traveled to the Orient. I've been in Europe a great deal and this seemed to me a very logical opportunity between jobs to do some travel for my self-education, and I plan to go from the United States to Japan by way of Honolulu early in March and thence, if possible to Korea, then to Formosa, Hong Kong, Indochina, the Philippines, Indonesia, and back to Singapore, I suppose, and then to Burma, Thailand, India, Pakistan and on into the Middle East and back through Europe.

MORGAN: It sounds as if you're deliberately hitting the areas of actual or imminent contention with communism. That's a tough job — why are you doing that? Have you picked them deliberately?

STEVENSON: Well, it's partially deliberate and partially because the imminent impact is everywhere. And I think it's universal in the Orient and it's probably the most formidable problem we will confront for a generation or for a long time at least, and I should like to know something about it first hand.

MORGAN: Do you expect that this will be an official trip in any way? Are you going to report to Washington when you come back?

[95] The text is based on a tape recording of the interview in the Morgan papers, Wisconsin State Historical Society.

STEVENSON: Oh, I hadn't intended that. I am just going to travel as a private citizen and I hope that it will be anything but an official visit.

MORGAN: But so far as the use that you make of the education en route, that may be official insofar as your leadership in the Democratic party is concerned — there's no rules that will bar you from using it in experience as the head of the loyal opposition, so to speak.

STEVENSON: Well, I don't know, Ed, whether I'm head of the loyal opposition or not. I've always found this problem of leadership a little ambiguous, and I really have no ulterior motive here and no objective other than self-information. It seems to me that it's terribly important for anyone who is speaking or writing about contemporary affairs to understand something of this struggle for this revolution that's going on in the colonial areas of the world, and in Asia particularly.

MORGAN: You are going to do a little writing and a little speaking after you get back to share your experiences and education with the people at large?

STEVENSON: Well, I've agreed to do some writing while I traveled for *Look* magazine in the United States, and when I come back I may or may not attempt a book — I don't know. I shall probably have some occasion to talk, to speak, and I certainly feel that the information that I will obtain from firsthand observation will be useful to me, and I hope to my listeners.

MORGAN: Governor, some other people have been traveling — Mr. [John Foster] Dulles, the Secretary of State, just got back from Europe. You've indicated, I think, that the administration by its policies and declaration might be reviving what has been known as dollar diplomacy. Is it likely that you're going to expand critical remarks of that kind in your speech in New York tonight?

STEVENSON: Well, yes, I shall make some reference, I think, in this speech — I haven't quite finished it — merely expressing my hope that there is not in contemplation revival of an old and discredited practice, dollar diplomacy. I hope very much that I have misread the signs, the indications, in the news that there might be some threat or coercion of that kind in what's been implicit in what's transpired. I hope very much that that's not the case. I'm actually reasonably confident that it isn't but it's a source of apprehension, of course.

MORGAN: Still on the subject of trips, Governor Stevenson, have you gotten any idea of which way you might be traveling in, say, 1956?

STEVENSON: Well, that's a long time off, before I see anything, I'm afraid.

MORGAN: You mentioned a minute ago about the titular leadership of the party, whether you were or whether you weren't. Mark Childs, the Washington columnist, has just written that the big question now is whether you are a politician ready to accept responsibility for the leadership of the Democratic party. Do you want to say anything about that at all?

STEVENSON: I don't know what I could say about it. I undertook the — I accepted the nomination that I had not asked for, and did not want, I ran for President as my party's nominee as best I could, I gave it the best I had. I, in other words, discharged the responsibility that was assigned me with the best spirit and purpose that I could summon. Now, just beyond that what my obligations are and what my role is is not entirely clear to me. Certainly I want to do all I can to further the basic concepts of our party and to contribute intelligently and constructively, if I can, to my generation.

MORGAN: You've been generous with your time, Governor Stevenson. Bon voyage, and thank you very much.

STEVENSON: Thank you, sir.

Stevenson spoke in New York City on Jefferson-Jackson Day, February 14, 1953.[96]

It is now some 3 months, 9 days, 19 hours and 47 minutes since we conceded the election of General Eisenhower. Watching the conduct of our party during that time, I can only say that I am prouder than ever to be a Democrat. And that is my best valentine!

In that interval General Eisenhower has had the honors of victory and also the misery, while I have had the miseries of defeat and also a vacation. But, as the newspapers say, to the victor belongs the toil.

It seems to me very appropriate that the party with a heart should be having this great dinner here in New York on St. Valentine's day. I am sure we Democrats are in a mood to love everybody. And, of course, we would be delighted if a few million more people would love us.

I have questioned my qualifications to be speaking here this evening. My most recent distinction, after all, is the dubious one of being the first Democrat defeated since Al Smith 24 years ago. But I derive some personal satisfaction out of being associated with Al Smith — even in misfortune! and, while I make no prediction, I would remind you that the Democratic party made a very rapid recovery after the disastrous election of 1928.

[96] The text is from the St. Louis *Post-Dispatch*, February 15, 1953.

There was even talk then of dissolving the Democratic party. What a difference today! There have been few, if any, recriminations; little crying over spilt milk; nearly all the inevitable post-mortems have been intelligent and constructive. I think of no instance where a party has so quickly and so spontaneously recovered its spirit. It is astonishing, exhilarating and also contagious.

I freely admit that the sportsmanship, courtesy and charity shown me by so many of you leaders of our party following the election have comforted and fortified me immensely. I am very grateful also for the deluge of messages that has engulfed me from people in and out of our party all over the country. I must confess that I began by nibbling at this mass of correspondence, but it made me feel so good that I gradually increased the dosage. Even if it is not as good as a few million votes, it certainly eased the pain.

The new Administration has been in power for 25 days. This is not a very long time as we Democrats count time in office, and therefore I do not believe what I hear murmured around the country — that it is time for a change! This seems to me hasty and quite unjust for the team, as they call it, has hardly begun to play. Indeed, it had a little trouble getting started. The star Defense man looked ideal.[97] He weighed four or five million. I mean he was good and heavy. But he got into an argument right away with the referee and was penalized for holding!

There is a real temptation for us Democrats to relax in our unaccustomed position on the sidelines — to sit back and enjoy it, as Monday morning quarterbacks, while the Republicans have the novel experience of scrimmaging with reality. For 20 years they developed blocking to a fine art. Now they must do something themselves about the awful problems of our revolutionary age.

But we cannot succumb to this temptation. I hope we have learned from the Republican example how not to be an opposition party! This is an unfamiliar role for us, and one we have not filled with invariable distinction in the past. As the opposition party, we must be very careful how we interpret our title.

We shall fight them to the end when we think they are wrong. But our central purpose, our guiding light, must be something different: It must be to keep on working positively and constructively for the good of the country. Of course, it is easier to express these lofty sentiments than to practice them. Undoubtedly we will have our partisan moments. But let us never be content merely to oppose: let us always propose something better.

Thanks to President Truman and his Cabinet, gravely conscious of the perils of our times, the Government has been transferred smoothly and

97 Charles E. Wilson, president of General Motors.

with the heartiest good will. This is as it should be. We differ upon many things. But we wear in common the seamless garment of love of country. The Government is our Government as well as theirs.

May I say, then, that we wish President Eisenhower, his official family, and the Congress, godspeed in the awful trials they face. Our prayers go with them in dark, evil-haunted night they must traverse, confronted with an enemy whose massive power is matched only by its malevolent purpose. The outcome of their efforts will profoundly affect all men everywhere for good or evil. As they see or fail to see, understand, act or fail to act, so may the warm sun continue to shine upon living men or the cold moon rise upon an empty earth.

We, the opposition, in these fateful days must contribute much more than epithets, smears and witch hunts to the solution of our problems. And I have been delighted to see that the Democrats in the Congress, led by such fine Americans as Sam Rayburn in the House and Lyndon Johnson in the Senate, have been following exactly this kind of positive, intelligent opposition.

But the Congress will not be the only place where the Democrats write their record. Democrats hold many offices in states and cities — and we are going to hold many more I will add, a couple of years from now. But there is only one sure way to do so — that is by offering better candidates, better programs, better organization than our opponents. In the townships, the cities, the counties, the congressional districts, the states, as well as the nation, our job is to make the Democratic party stand for sound and progressive policies, so that it will attract honest, forward-looking and independent-thinking citizens.

Last fall there was a formidable upsurge of interest by the people of our country in politics. Men and women took part in the campaign who had never before participated in political activities — ringing doorbells, addressing envelopes, doing the pick-and-shovel jobs on which success depends. Many did this in the regular parties; many were in the independent citizens' groups. These people are the new blood of our political life. We need them, and to keep them we must have programs and candidates which will command their active allegiance.

The Republican party is attempting what has not been tried for a long time — government by business men. America has always been a nation ripe for experiment; we Democrats have experimented boldly and accomplished miracles. Because the Republican experiment is new and different in these times, doesn't mean that it is bad. On the contrary it 'deserves a thorough and fair test. And it faces this test under far more favorable conditions than we Democrats had when we inherited a broken and despairing nation 20 years ago.

Today the misery and despair are forgotten. Three weeks ago we were able to pass on to the Republicans a thriving, healthy concern. Never has our land been more prosperous, never have more men and women been working, never have more goods flowed from our farms and factories to our people. And this is true — even though during the campaign it sometimes sounded as if we were tottering on the brink of economic and moral disaster. Fortunate indeed is the Administration which has been happy enough to inherit such a rich and abundant estate!

I, for one, am prepared to give this business administration my heartiest support — so long as it works faithfully for the public interest. But history warns us, I think, that government by a single group, no matter how high-minded and patriotic it may be, exposes government to genuine dangers. There is always the tendency to mistake the particular interest for the general interest — to suppose, in the immortal thought recently uttered before a committee of Congress, that what is good for General Motors is good for the country.[98] There is always the possibility that the successor of the New Deal will turn out — after the fine words have faded away — to be the Big Deal, while the New Dealers have all left Washington to make way for the car dealers — I hasten to say that I do not believe the story that the general welfare has become a subsidiary of General Motors.

Yet this most recent experiment in the management of our public affairs demands our support and sympathy, if only because of the crises we all face together in the world. And let us not deceive ourselves about the size of the Communist conspiracy. The sullen, somber men, the morbid misanthropes, of the Kremlin, hardened and disciplined by their monstrous philosophy, dispose of staggering resources in population, in land, in raw materials, and in the zeal which is the product of fanatical faith as well as of ugly fear and ruthless ambition.

At the present time, according to the best estimates, their production is growing at a rate approximately twice our own — and this in a period of remarkable expansion in our own economy. And they are in the struggle to stay. We delude ourselves if we think that a few words uttered on the short-wave radio will cause this iron regime to shatter

---

[98] Charles E. Wilson was asked by a senator at the Senate hearings on his appointment as Secretary of Defense: "I am interested to know whether if a situation did arise where you had to make a decision which was extremely adverse to the interests of your stock and General Motors Corporation, or any of these other companies, or extremely adverse to the country, in the interests of the United States Government, could you make that decision?"
Mr. Wilson replied: "Yes, sir; I could. I cannot conceive of one because for years I thought what was good for our country was good for General Motors, and vice versa." New York *Times,* January 24, 1953.

and disintegrate — that a few blasts on the trumpets of psychological warfare, and the walls will come tumbling down.

The last thing we want, I would suppose, is to stand alone against this threat — to get into a situation where our young men must bear by themselves the full brunt of the Communist assault. That is why our policy has been one of collective strength and mutual security. Our allies share with us, not only bases and raw materials and manpower, but — more important — the common faith in the worth of free men which is our most potent weapon.

We need them as they need us. The fact that we have been in a position to contribute most to the collective defense in the way of arms and money does not entitle us to preach or threaten. And I hope I have misunderstood some news of late that sounds to me better calculated to provoke distaste for us than respect. We want not sullen obedience, but friendly cooperation from our allies.[99] We want understanding from them of our problems and heavy tax burdens, even as we patiently try to understand their difficulties. We want no satellites; we want companions in arms, the companionship of embattled free men in common cause.

For we of the NATO countries and the other free nations are banded together, once and for all, in sickness and in health, till — or rather — lest atomic death us do part. I hope I have misread the signs of the revival of the discredited "dollar diplomacy." I hope we are forging no silver chains. We have heard much about the new "psychological" offensive; but we will frighten no Russians by threatening financial sanctions against our allies. On the contrary, the Kremlin is encouraged by all signs of division in our ranks.

We Democrats have always favored greater European unity as the only permanent way to make Europe economically solvent and militarily independent. Since 1947 it has been a prime object of our policy. The very core of the Marshall plan lay in its treatment of Europe as an entity. Using private persuasion, rather than public ultimatums, we have helped create the organization for European Economic Co-operation; the European payments union, and now the Schuman plan for pooling coal and steel. A European constitution is being fashioned, and a European Defense Community is a near reality.

[99] Secretary of State Dulles had said: "If it appears there were no chance of getting effective unity (in Europe), and if in particular France, Germany and England should go their separate ways, then certainly it would be necessary to give a little rethinking to America's own foreign policy in relation to Western Europe." See James Reston, "Foreign Diplomats Puzzled by Dulles' Off-Cuff Speech. Lack of Precision in His Remarks Causes Uncertainty about New U.S. Policies," New York *Times,* January 29, 1953.

These achievements are not accidental; they are the result of a purposeful policy and of friendly persuasion.

A genuine partnership operates through consultation and persuasion. There is no room in it for the big stick or the ultimatum, be it a small or medium ultimatum, or the large economy size. Ours must be the role of the good neighbor, the good partner, the good friend — never the big bully.

And we cannot enlist the support of ordinary people abroad if we do not trust them at home. The Democratic and Republican parties today are separated by the same old principles which divided Jefferson and Hamilton when parties first began in the United States. Hamilton felt that only the men of wealth and business affairs were qualified to understand and conduct government. Jefferson had faith in all the people — and, in their faith, our party has fought for the poor and humble and weak when they were oppressed by the wealthy and strong. This has been the central concept of our party — given fiery expression by Andrew Jackson, and renewed by the great Democratic leaders of our own century, by Woodrow Wilson, by Franklin D. Roosevelt, and by that man of Independence, our nation's leading private citizen, Harry Truman.

And it is interesting to note, by the way, that after all the clatter and criticism and denunciation of the campaign, the two laws which President Eisenhower wants to amend, the Taft-Hartley Law and the McCarran Act, were both vetoed by President Truman.

There has never been a time in history when it is more necessary to reaffirm our democratic faith, in all its vigor and all its majesty. Some in America today would limit our freedom of expression and conscience. In the name of unity, they would impose a narrow uniformity of idea and opinion. Let no one mistake where the Democratic party stands on this. We glory in the multiplicity of strains and cultures and ideas that are woven into the tapestry we call America. We share Jefferson's "eternal hostility to any form of tyranny over the mind of man."

Our farms and factories may give us our living. But the Bill of Rights gives us our life. Whoever lays rough hands upon it lays rough hands on you and me. Whoever profanes its spirit diminishes our inheritance and beclouds our title to greatness as a people. If we win men's hearts throughout the world, it will not be because we are a big country but because we are a great country. Bigness is imposing. But greatness is enduring.

Only a government which fights for civil liberties and equal rights for its own people can stand for freedom in the rest of the world.

Only a people who can achieve the moral mastery of themselves can hope to win the moral leadership of others.

Opposition confers opportunity; adversity tests the soul and strengthens the will. "Yield not thy neck to fortune's yoke, but let the dauntless mind still ride in triumph over all mischance."

The Democratic party understands the nature of the contemporary challenge. The party of all the people, it speaks to all people everywhere. The party of the poor and humble, it can understand the strivings of the poor and humble everywhere. The party of freedom and opportunity, it can hold high the torch of democracy and light the way to liberty for men and women everywhere. And because the Democratic party understands the challenge of history, history will reward it once again with responsibility.

After listening to Stevenson's February 14 speech on the radio, Harry S. Truman sent a wire to David D. Lloyd in Washington asking him to tell Stevenson that it was a good speech and that he and Mrs. Truman were very satisfied that he was taking over as head of the Democratic party. They both pledged their support.

To Harry S. Truman

February 18, 1953

My dear Mr. President:

Dave Lloyd was good enough to deliver your telegram to me in New York. I was delighted and more gratified than I can tell you. The New York dinner was a huge success — and Margaret [Truman] the most successful part of it!

I was in Washington for a couple of days and saw something of the Democrats. I found them, to my delight, in better spirits and more eager for the job ahead than I had thought possible. The manner in which you turned over the government has also stood us in good stead with much of the more discriminating press, and I am sure will pay important dividends in the long run.

I am off on my travels the first of March and returning about the middle of July. I think things are shaping up in comforting fashion in the National Committee, and the financial situation looks brighter than I had anticipated at this stage. I think Dwight Palmer has done an admirable job and Steve Mitchell seems to be winning more confidence and respect as he goes along.

With warmest thanks for your thoughtful wire and my very best wishes to you and Mrs. Truman, I am

Cordially yours,

To Mr. and Mrs. Ronald Tree [100]

February 18, 1953

My beloved Trees!

Everything was all right as far as San Juan. Indeed, we were grossly neglected in Antigua. But at San Juan the past caught up with me with a vengeance. Instead of reaching New York at 5:30, I reached there at 12, after festivities with Munos Marin [101] and assorted Democrats of the Island. In New York it was a horror — news reels, TV, reporters and crowds at midnight. There followed three days that reminded me of the campaign and bleached my lovely tan. Then to Washington by special train surrounded by the faithful, and three more days of wild commotion culminating in luncheon (uninformative) with President Eisenhower.

And now I am back in Chicago, bedeviled with a multitude of things and but a week before I set sail again for California and points west by west by west.

The serenity and the blue sea of Barbados haunts me, and, given the choice, I should rather be sitting beneath the MacNeil's [102] (that poisonous clan!) sipping rum punch a la Tree, than anything I can think of. And I guarantee it is better than sipping anything around the White House.

It was my great hour, and I find all my conversation drifting off into engaging stories of 17th Century life amid the peerage of Barbados. My audiences generally drift off too. But, all the same, my heart and head are somewhere between Farley Hill at twilight and the Hotel Tree by moonlight. I shan't attempt to thank you. It was simple salvation. Even the work turned out all right, at least the publishers are ecstatic and LIFE grabbed the Introduction at a substantial price in twenty minutes.[103] As for me, I think it is lousy.

Much love; and my course is set for London and a reunion with you in June or July. Could you contrive a flying fish pie!

Affectionately, and so much gratitude,

P.S. I found the Democrats in New York and Washington full of spirit and gaiety. I could hardly believe it.

From February 15 to 17 Stevenson was in Washington visiting with Democratic senators and congressmen and workers at the Democratic

[100] A copy is in A.E.S., I.S.H.L.
[101] Luis Munoz-Marin, governor of Puerto Rico, 1949–1965.
[102] Unable to identify.
[103] "Candidate Tells Candid Story," *Life,* March 2, 1953, pp. 94–96.

National Committee. After a few days in Chicago, Stevenson flew to Los Angeles to speak at a Jefferson-Jackson Day Dinner for Democrats from the Western states on February 26.

CAMPAIGN MYTHOLOGY AND THE PUBLIC WEAL [104]

While we may be a defeated party, we are not a beaten party. We are not a beaten party for many reasons, and the most important is that we have been honest with the people. We made no effort to sugar-coat bitter problems so that they would be easier to swallow. We told the truth; we spoke our minds. And we emerged from the campaign with more good will in the bank than any other defeated party in recent history. I am confident that if we continue to be forthright with the American people, our bank account of respect will continue to grow.

We must, therefore, be honest with the people by supporting the new administration when we believe it to be serving the national interest.

We have all been heartened by the occasions on which our new President, under the sobering responsibility of authority, has shown that he respects the public weal more than ebullient campaign oratory. He has quite properly rebuked Republicans in Congress for unseemly haste in cutting taxes before making the hard decisions on where, when, and if expenses can be cut. Democratic Congressmen, I am proud to say, supported the President with responsible realism.

And in the resolution he has just proposed, the President has repudiated the Republican campaign mythology about dark and sinister agreements at Yalta, Teheran, and Potsdam.[105] The proposed resolution relates to the breach of those agreements by the Soviet government, shameless violations which have long been denounced by everybody, Democrats and Republicans alike. Let us, I say, no longer make cynical political capital by pretending that our country ever conspired in the tragedy that has befallen once great and independent peoples.

Tempting as it is, I shall not dwell on the unworthy and misleading words that have been uttered of late about the Seventh Fleet, words im-

---

[104] The text is from *What I Think*, pp. 59–63.

[105] The 1952 Republican platform promised: "The Government of the United States under Republican leadership will repudiate all commitments contained in secret understandings such as those of Yalta which aid Communist enslavements." Eisenhower sent Congress a resolution that declared that the United States had never acquiesced in the subjugation of free peoples. He refused to do what the extremists wanted, however: to repudiate, in their entirety, the agreements reached at the Yalta Conference. See Dwight D. Eisenhower, *Mandate for Change, 1953–1956* (New York: Doubleday, 1963), p. 211.

plying that President Truman's purpose was to protect Red China rather than Formosa.[106]

But while supporting the Republicans when they act in the national interest, we have an equal responsibility to oppose them when they do violence to the public interest.

In the coming months many questions await resolution by the Congress and the people. One of the first is tidelands oil. On this issue I have long since expressed my views.[107] But, however the Congress may decide the question, let us make sure that it does not set in motion the piecemeal dismemberment of our great public domain which is held for the benefit of all the people of the United States.

There are powerful interests who have interpreted the election as heralding an open season for the retail and wholesale transfer to the states of our great national assets — the forests, the grazing lands, the water, and the minerals.

In this connection, if you will indulge me for a moment, you may be amused, as I was, by a telegram to Senator Earl Clements [108] from a man in Kentucky which I saw the other day:

> Chattanooga Daily Times . . . quotes Senator Walker in Lincoln Day speech as favoring sale of Post Office Department to private interests. Please advise when bids are to be opened. I represent eight plumbers and one Republican who wish to acquire this property.[109] Also interested in United States Mint and Fort Knox if they are for sale.

I hope we don't forget that the public domain belongs to Democrats and Republicans alike, and, as Theodore Roosevelt warned us long ago, the descendants of both will pay the price if we do not preserve their heritage. And I confidently expect that the Democrats in Congress will be the Public's guardians of our forests and our parks; our grazing lands and our minerals; guardians, too, of our great reclamation programs and our family-sized farms; and of low-cost power for all the people.

Likewise, we must vigilantly protect the great programs of social

[106] In his first State of the Union Message, Eisenhower stated that the Seventh Fleet would "no longer be employed to shield Communist China" from attack from Taiwan.

[107] See note 20 to Part Two, p. 32, and Stevenson's New Orleans speech of October 10, 1952, also in Part Two, pp. 150–158.

[108] Earle C. Clements, senator from Kentucky, 1950–1957.

[109] President Eisenhower's Cabinet appointments (ten in all, not nine) were drawn from leaders in business and industry with the exception of Martin Durkin, Secretary of Labor. Mr. Durkin was president of the Plumbers Union and a Stevenson supporter. The makeup of the Cabinet was humorously referred to as "nine millionaires and a plumber."

progress which we have initiated in the past twenty years and which may be in for something less than sympathetic treatment.

Incidentally, I had been under the very distinct impression, a few months back, that the Republicans had made off with the Democratic farm plank. I guess I was wrong. They just borrowed it temporarily, and returned it immediately after the election.

But it was not so much of these things that I wanted to talk tonight. One of the most exhilarating aspects of the 1952 campaign for me was the activity of so many independent-minded citizens, many of whom had never before participated in a political campaign. They found it exciting and satisfying to join in making the nation's greatest decisions; what our government is to do about war and peace; about depression and prosperity; about human rights and human liberties. But politics, good politics, is not merely a quadrennial or biennial burst of enthusiasm; nor is it a function reserved to the so-called professionals. In its highest and truest sense, politics is leadership; and leadership is a time-consuming, brain-consuming, and energy-consuming job — a job that is open to all citizens.

This means that we must organize in our communities; we must get and give the truth. In the places where our organization has been deficient we must set ourselves to the tough task of putting our house in order.

Forty years ago the Democratic party was just assuming power, after a long period out of office. In that moment of triumph Woodrow Wilson said this in his First Inaugural Address: "The success of a party means little except when the nation is using that party for a large and definite purpose." Now that is a chastening statement of principle which our Republican friends would do well to bear in mind. And each of us as citizens, owing as we do our first allegiance to the purposes of our country rather than to those of our party, should be careful never to obstruct the one in order to advance the other.

Wilson's sober appraisal of the significance of party victory can be validly applied to our own present situation. A political party which cannot in defeat make itself an effective instrument of larger national purposes is without significance in the future political life of the country; and sooner rather than later, it will be so marked by the people to whom it must look for the return of trust and confidence and victory.

One of the most challenging aspects of this job is that it seems never to have been done well in the past. Latterly, in twenty years of opposition, the Republican party never distinguished itself except by the shrill vehemence of its criticism of the imperative adjustments to the facts of life, both at home and abroad, which were made under the imaginative and determined leadership of Franklin Roosevelt and Harry Truman. Our

Republican friends evidently thought the definition of minority was the converse of maturity; that responsible conduct was not required until they attained majority status. Growing up is always a painful process. The necessity for doing so swiftly makes it worse.

There is, then, a unique opportunity for our party to achieve a new distinction. If we make the most of it, we not only best assure our own eventual triumph, but we may create a pattern of political conduct for others to see and follow, to the lasting benefit of the nation. For the party out of power, principle — and not patronage — must inevitably be the only solvent. Let us not fail to make a virtue of our necessity.

Yes, we Democrats have a special duty — we who chafed under the yoke of responsibility during the postwar years while Europe was saved and Communism stopped — we who suffered all the while the taunts of irresponsible opposition. We must continue, I say, to tell the people the truth; that there are no magic, cheap, short solutions to global conflicts long in the making.

We must not yield to the temptation to goad the Republicans to produce quick miracles and dazzling successes. Let us never sow division when it is so important to harvest unity.

The tensions and difficulties may get worse before they get better in Europe, in the Middle East, in Asia — all around this world, divided and in revolution. Millions of people are as sorely puzzled as many of us here at home. The nature of the struggle is by no means clear to them and, unlike this heaven-favored land, there is lacking to many the same incentives to make the struggle. We must labor to increase these incentives, to prove to misery-laden millions that democracy can provide the right to think, to believe, and to eat, as well as vote.

That others have reservations about our unerring wisdom, that some cannot or will not fall in step at our pace must not exasperate and defeat us. And, in the dark majesty of the issue of life or death, none of us will advance our overriding interest in peace by outbursts of temper against each other or by ill-considered muscle-flexing against the common foe. We shall have to take care not to amuse our foes and frighten our friends.

Patience — firm, intelligent, understanding — seems to be in short supply. Yet it is the indispensable quality of leadership of the diverse elements of the free world and of the uncommitted millions groping their way into the sunlight of a better world. It is also the essential quality of a political party which, after the exhilaration of executive responsibility, finds itself in the less dramatic role of proving again its qualifications for public confidence.

What we as a party must cultivate is what the nation must have. In defeat we can make ourselves servants of the national purpose for peace. There is no greater or better political destiny.

President Truman wrote Stevenson on February 19, again praising the February 14 speech, and requested an autographed copy of it. The former President added that his daughter, Margaret, told him that it was about the best speech she had ever heard. Truman, referring to the source of the comment, concluded that it was quite a compliment. Stevenson wrote the following letter from California.

To Harry S. Truman

February 28, 1953

Dear Mr. President:

I am profoundly flattered by your letter of February 19, including Margaret's charitable appraisal of my "effort" at the dinner in New York. I enclose a copy; and when President Truman asks Stevenson for an autographed copy of a speech, the latter is tempted to think that the former's oratorical judgment may be slipping!

I hope you are making the adjustment to private life with ease. I am sure it is with grace. I pray that there will be some time for tranquillity and the peace of mind we all covet and seldom find, which you so richly deserve.

With very warm regards to Mrs. Truman, I am

Faithfully yours,

Arthur Krock, of the Washington bureau of the New York Times, *wrote Stevenson on February 19 that their friendship seemed to have diminished since he criticized the Governor's position on labor during the campaign. Krock suggested that Stevenson should wait for evidence before criticizing the Administration's attitude toward France as he had done in his February 14 speech. Krock concluded: "My plea is that you take every care to preserve your great reputation for constructive comment and criticism, and hence your leadership that extends beyond party lines. For you may well be the American who will save our basic system from its greatest threat in history."*

To Arthur Krock [110]

February 28, 1953

Dear Arthur:

Thanks so much for your good letter. I am a little bewildered by your feeling that our friendship had diminished. It certainly has not on my part, although I hope you don't, like some journalists and some politicians, dislike my complaints about misinterpretation. I can hardly believe I have the formidable destiny you assign me, and I must say that the future is a little bewildering to me. But "sufficient unto the day is the evil thereof," and I am not tempted to cross any bridges for the present, until I finish my appalling journey and have an opportunity to re-appraise — that useful bureaucratic word — the situation.

As to the criticism of the "get tough" policy in my New York speech, it may well be that the Department [of State] had requests from the Germans and the French, as Scotty's [111] piece indicates. While I hardly expect to measure my criticism by past Republican standards in checking for information and adhering to facts, I think the responsible French were as much surprised by the new tone as I was, and that that could be verified. I did.

I hope I can be "constructive," but I also propose to be critical when I disagree. Indeed, I have been rather flattering myself about my temperance to date.

But enough of all this; and I am really grateful for your letter.
Love to Martha.[112]

Yours,
ADLAI

To Mr. and Mrs. Ronald Tree [113]

March 1, 1953

My dear Trees:

I am dictating this on the West Coast on the eve of my departure on this appalling adventure, because you and Barbados are still very much with me. I had a couple of days at Palm Springs after the festivities in Los Angeles and found myself lecturing the Californians on the virtues and advantages of Barbados. What a politician!

The Los Angeles dinner was a "sell out" and will serve to further reduce

[110] The original is in the possession of Mr. Krock.
[111] New York *Times* columnist James Reston.
[112] Mrs. Krock.
[113] A copy is in A.E.S., I.S.H.L.

the party mortgage by about $50,000. The spirit is good beyond one's dreams everywhere, but here, as always, organization and leadership is woefully weak.

The reaction to my speeches has been for the most part good, friendly, but at least one of the hired hands, David Lawrence,[114] is still screaming imprecations.

I shall probably reach England the end of June or early July and will hope for a reunion — with Barbados rum! It seems likely, now, that at least one or two of my sons may go abroad after school to join me for a bit before I return, and will probably be in England with Mary Spears before I get there.

I yearn for the sands of St. James and all the delights of l'Hotel Tree — including the Trees.

Affectionately and gratefully,

Just before leaving Springfield, Stevenson talked to State Representative Paul Powell and agreed not to oppose Powell as Democratic minority leader in the House provided Powell and his allies would support putting Stevenson's former aide Lawrence Irvin in the State Central Committee headquarters to develop an active program for downstate Illinois. Stevenson's letter to Richard J. Daley, county clerk of Cook County, failed to achieve this purpose, and the Democratic party downstate hibernated.

To Richard J. Daley [115]

March 1, 1953

Personal and Confidential

Dear Dick:

I had hoped to talk to you again before I left Chicago. I was disturbed to hear from Jim Ronan [116] that he was having difficulty with the project we had in mind about putting Lawrence Irvin in the State Central Committee headquarters to carry on an active program of party development in the downstate counties. Evidently there is opposition from some members of the legislature who, I presume, are more opposed to me than to Lawrence.

My feeling about this is that we should be doing in Illinois, and promptly, what is being done in so many other states, in proximity notably

---

[114] Syndicated newspaper columnist and editor of *U.S. News & World Report.*
[115] A copy is in the possession of Lawrence Irvin.
[116] Illinois Democratic state chairman.

Michigan and Wisconsin, to rehabilitate the party, improve local leadership, get better candidates and integrate the independent resources, which developed so extensively during the last campaign. It is not that I feel that Lawrence, as an individual, is the indispensable man; it is rather that he knows the situation downstate better than anyone, has the personal attributes which we need, and will go in the right direction or not at all.

As you know, virtually all of the money that the State Committee has had since I became Governor has come from me, directly or indirectly. After I was nominated for President, Don Forsyth,[117] who had started the fund solicitation downstate, carried on for Sherwood Dixon,[118] who feels exactly as I do. The money, plus whatever I personally have contributed to the strength and esteem of the party in Illinois, makes me feel that my view should be entitled to some weight. I have asked for little in the past and this does not seem an excessive request in the circumstances.

Jim Ronan must move carefully, of course, to avoid any further disruption, and tells me that if the matter were submitted to an open meeting of the State Central Committee his suggestion about putting Irvin in the headquarters as executive director, or something, would be voted down. I should think if the Committeemen from Chicago were asked to hold fast and support such a proposal, together with whatever support he would have downstate, it would be sufficient.

I am taking the liberty of sending copies of this letter to Joe Gill,[119] whom I was disappointed not to see while in Chicago, and to Jim Ronan. I do not think Lawrence can be asked to wait around much longer.

The dinner in Los Angeles was a huge success and served to cut the party deficit by another $50,000 or more. The spirit everywhere seems to be animated and wholesome and I am much heartened by what I have seen in New York, Washington and out here.

With all best wishes to you and the Daleys, large and small.

Yours,

[117] Springfield businessman and a supporter of Stevenson.
[118] Stevenson's former lieutenant governor and unsuccessful Democratic candidate for governor of Illinois in 1952.
[119] Cook County Democratic party chairman.

Part Four

Appeals to Reason

On March 2, 1953, Stevenson sailed from San Francisco to begin his world trip. This trip is chronicled in Volume V of The Papers of Adlai E. Stevenson. A separate volume is devoted to this trip to provide a study in depth of how Stevenson educated himself — how he prepared himself to serve more intelligently as the "conscience" of American politics.

Stevenson arrived back in Chicago on August 20, 1953. A citizens' committee, headed by Laird Bell, sponsored a meeting at the Chicago Opera House on September 15 so that he could make a report to the nation on his trip.

Stevenson explained that after the trip he planned to help rejuvenate the Democratic party. "New leadership is emerging," he stated on September 5, 1954. "More young people are taking an active interest in party affairs."

He also remarked that he planned to make many fund-raising speeches to pay off the deficit from the 1952 campaign. By the fall of 1954 this objective was attained. "For weeks past, his life had been one of rushing from hotels to planes and back to hotels . . . handshaking . . . endless meetings with state and national Democratic party leaders," Don Whitehead wrote on September 5, 1954.[1] When asked whether he had found anything on his travels around the United States that disturbed him above all others, Stevenson replied that he was deeply disturbed over a trend toward conformity — "a growth of anti-intellectualism which manifests itself in a sneering attitude toward education, science and the arts."

He added: "I've been appalled at the use of the technique of exploiting fear of communism for political gain, and saddened by the fact the administration has at times encouraged this technique and has not fought it."

Stevenson then observed: "There is a great hunger among the people for moral leadership that remains unsatisfied. We have placed too much em-

[1] Chicago Sun-Times, September 5, 1954.

[265]

phasis on materialism. Most political appeals have been appeals to the belly rather than to the spiritual, the intellectual, the moral and educational." [2]

Stevenson did not spare himself in the autumn of 1954 in campaigning in many states to help elect Democratic candidates for the Senate, House and governorships. The Democrats captured control of both houses of Congress and won a majority of governorships. With the removal of Senator McCarthy and others from key committee chairmanships, President Eisenhower was now freed from the restraints of the extremists in his own party. The Democratic Congress under Senate Majority Leader Lyndon B. Johnson and Speaker of the House Sam Rayburn generally gave support to many Eisenhower proposals.

Meanwhile, during 1955, Stevenson returned to the practice of law and adopted a reduced writing and speaking schedule until he announced on November 15, 1955, that he would be a candidate for the Democratic nomination.

Upon Stevenson's return to the United States, the Secretary of State wired him and expressed a desire to see him and get the "benefit of your impressions."

To John Foster Dulles

August 23, 1953

Dear Foster:

Thank you so much for your thoughtful telegram. You may be sure I shall look forward to a little visit with you when I have an opportunity to come to Washington.

Meanwhile, let me say again how very grateful I am for the many courtesies extended by the Department officials along my endless road. They were more than a little helpful and I suspect I would be wallowing somewhere between Asia and Europe in impotent frustration if it had not been for their everlasting helpfulness.

With warm good wishes from one who has at least a slight appreciation of your problems.

Cordially yours,

[2] Ibid.

To Carroll Binder [3]

September 5, 1953

Dear Carroll:

. . . I am much concerned about many things, but it is difficult to express myself with utter candor without being charged with partisanship and losing all resonance. Our prestige and esteem abroad is low and getting lower, as you well know. Also, a little travel persuades one that the Orient is the big area of contest in the future and our ignorance at home is only matched by their ignorance of us.

I hope we shall meet, and if I come that way of course I will hope to see you. My best to Tommy.[4]

Yours,

ADLAI

P.S. Your editorial was excellent. Keep it up.

Thomas K. Finletter, Arthur M. Schlesinger, Jr., David Bell, Robert Tufts, Willard Wirtz, John Kenneth Galbraith, and others comprised an informal group that wrote position papers and drafts of speeches for Stevenson. During the next several years they met occasionally with him to discuss issues.

To Arthur M. Schlesinger, Jr.

September 5, 1953

Dear Arthur:

So many thanks for your letter of the 31st and the fat enclosures. Lord knows when I will have time to read them, but read them I will. I feel already as though I should like to start around the world again!

I have already read Bob Tufts' excellent piece, which amused and enlightened me no end, but I suspect his conclusion about the indifference to foreign affairs is right. I shall also write Miss Wickenden.[5]

I hope you will thank Dave Bell, and may this also serve as a thanks for the speech draft. I find concentration terribly difficult, what with distractions, weariness and chronic intellectual confusion.

Yours,

---

[3] The original is in the possession of the Newberry Library, Chicago, Illinois.
[4] Mrs. Binder.
[5] Elizabeth Wickenden prepared material on Social Security.

To Thomas K. Finletter

September 5, 1953

Dear Tom:

Thanks for your note. I hope we can get together soon. I shall be coming East probably around the end of the month. I will be in New York then and could we have an evening, perhaps with some others, for some skull practice? Just let me know your general plans until mid-October. I am going to speak very little, indeed hardly at all and only for fund-raising affairs for the National Committee for a few months. Perhaps this is wrong, but I am woefully tired and disorganized and I have to plan a bit for the future.

Love to Gay.[6]

Yours,

Paul M. Butler, Democratic national committeeman from Indiana, wrote Stevenson on September 2 praising the work of Stephen A. Mitchell, but added: "What we need of course, is your own vigorous and active leadership of the party."

To Paul M. Butler [7]

September 8, 1953

Dear Paul:

I was deeply touched by your letter. Perhaps if you stay over the 15th we could have a leisurely talk some time on the 16th in Chicago. I shall hope so. If not, we can arrange something later on when the dust settles — if it ever does!

I share your regard for Steve, as you know, and I think the accomplishments in reorganizing and reorienting the Committee are superb.

Cordially yours,

To Mrs. Franklin D. Roosevelt [8]

September 8, 1953

My dear Mrs. Roosevelt:

So many thanks for the clipping from Britain. I had a busy time, as you

[6] Mrs. Finletter.
[7] A copy is in the Adlai E. Stevenson papers, Illinois State Historical Library (A.E.S., I.S.H.L.).
[8] The original is in the Franklin D. Roosevelt Library, Hyde Park, New York.

will understand. Now I find myself relaxing so utterly that I can't summon the wits or energy to do much of anything. Sometime you must tell me how to avoid total collapse after total effort — for years and years!

Faithfully,

The Democratic National Committee met in Chicago on September 13 and 14. On September 14, Stevenson delivered one of the speeches at a fund-raising dinner. David E. Lilienthal, former chairman of the Tennessee Valley Authority and of the Atomic Energy Commission, wrote: "The most reassuring thing about the sessions was to see how Adlai Stevenson stands head and shoulders over any of the second-raters who would like to be considered Presidential timber. His wit is a genuine thing, he is an extraordinarily good speaker; a modern orator one might say." [9]

On September 15, Stevenson delivered his report to the nation at the Civic Opera House. [10] *Former President Harry S. Truman, who was present, wired to congratulate him the next day.*

To Harry S. Truman

September 17, 1953

Dear Mr. President:

I am so grateful for your thoughtful wire. I am afraid the speech hardly deserved it, and it sounded a little mild in spite of the non-aggression pact proposal which the press hereabouts has utterly overlooked. But you know all too well how hard it is to strike a balance between temperance, responsibility and what an avid public wants, which is often what they shouldn't have, especially in foreign affairs.

The meeting seems to have been an unqualified success — thanks to you.

With my profound thanks for coming and everlasting gratitude for your confidence and encouragement and for that precious evening with you.

Cordially yours,

Former Ambassador Stanley Woodward wrote on September 3 expressing his regret that Stevenson had not been able to visit with him and Mrs. Woodward in Salzburg, Austria. He urged Stevenson to advocate a reduction in American tariffs in order to help the European economy. He

[9] *The Journals of David E. Lilienthal,* Vol. III: *Venturesome Years* (New York: Harper & Row, 1966), p. 425.
[10] For the text of this speech, see *The Papers of Adlai E. Stevenson,* Vol. V.

expressed concern over the impact of Senator McCarthy's attacks on the Department of State and the decline in morale of Foreign Service officers.

To Stanley Woodward [11]

September 17, 1953

Dear Stanley:

I have finally found your letter; and I agree emphatically with everything you say. You will detect some thread of it in the attached copy of a speech I gave here in Chicago the other night. I have no doubt that the trade policy will be as difficult a problem for the next Congress as any that we have faced in years, and I am reasonably hopeful that the Democrats will show much more unity in the direction of liberalization than the Republicans. I had thought to take a much more positive tone about McCarthyism, but it is hard to get so much into one short speech, as you well know. And besides there seems to be a lot of feeling here that McCarthy and his works are on the decline and he should not be provided with a welcome lifeline to rehabilitate himself attacking Democrats. As it is, as our politicians say, he is the Republicans' headache.

I am a little confused about the whole thing, I confess, but I have a feeling it is not as important here at home as I thought it was abroad.

I shall tell Ike most emphatically the reaction I had about demoralization in the State Department. I have been a little loathe, nor have I had the opportunity, to say too much about this in public for fear it would lose its effect and be attributed to the usual political criticism, but I found it very serious.

I hope we see something of each other after you return; and I shall always regret that I missed my chance to come to Salzburg.

Cordially yours,

ADLAI

James P. Warburg praised Stevenson for advocating the exploration of all avenues of negotiation with the Soviet Union in his speech of September 15. Mr. Warburg in his letter of September 16 suggested Stevenson place some constructive alternatives before the American people "in place of the present inflexible insistence upon unconditional surrender in Asia and Europe."

---

[11] The original is in the possession of Mr. Woodward.

To James P. Warburg

September 21, 1953

Dear Jim:

Thanks for your letter, and greetings to my girl friend Jennifer.[12]

I tried to make it clear that I was firmly against the all too aptly called "inflexible insistence upon unconditional surrender in Asia and in Europe." As to Germany, I would eagerly welcome your materials, as always, but I came back more convinced than ever that there are possibilities, if remote, in greater European integration which would have little prospect of success without the participation of the largest and strongest European state. I wish I could place some "constructive alternatives" before the people, as you imply. So send along your ideas, which will be constructive I am sure.

Yours,

To Richard Neuberger

September 21, 1953

Dear Dick:

Chicago was saturated with good Democratic gossip here the other day — and so was I! An important item was the news that Dick Neuberger might be a candidate for the Senate, with brither [brighter] prospects than the Democrats have had for a long time.[13]

I returned from my journey horribly weary and full of wisdom, which I shall be glad to impart to you if you will let me know when you come this way.

My best to Maurine.[14]

Yours,

Tallulah Bankhead wired Stevenson on September 8:

DEAR MR STEVENSON AM DEEPLY IMPRESSED BY YOUR ARTICLES.[15] THEY SHOULD BE READ BY ALL THINKING PEOPLE. THE MOST HUMILI- ATING DAY OF MY LIFE WAS WHEN I WAS MISQUOTED BY TIME MAG-

---

[12] Mr. Warburg's baby daughter.
[13] Mr. Neuberger was elected to the Senate from Oregon in 1954.
[14] Mrs. Neuberger.
[15] Articles on Stevenson's trip appeared in *Look* magazine. See *The Papers of Adlai E. Stevenson*, Vol. V.

AZINE BY SAYING I WOULD MARRY YOU. THE ONLY PERSON I WOULD
EVER MARRY IS KUKLA OF KUKLA FRAN AND OLLIE OR MY FATHER
THEREBY ADDING INCEST TO INJURY. DONT FORGET ST MATTHEW
WHEN HE SAID HE TOOK THE CUP AND GAVE THANKS DONT FORSAKE
US WE NEED YOU NOW MORE THAN EVER KINDEST REGARDS.

To Tallulah Bankhead [16]

September 22, 1953

Dear Miss Bankhead:

I was delighted with your engaging telegram. I shall not forget St.
Matthew nor, unhappily, that you say you were misquoted!

Cordially yours,

*Mrs. Lucille Taylor, of Lancaster, Pennsylvania, wrote Stevenson on
September 17 urging him not to retire to law practice, for "we need you."
She added that a disc jockey in discussing the weakness of the Philadel-
phia Phillies said: "We need more power. Why, if all the guys we left on
base this year had of voted for Adlai Stevenson, that fellow would be
President now."*

To Lucille Taylor [17]

September 22, 1953

Dear Mrs. Taylor:

I was delighted with your charming letter and Jack Pyle's remark, but,
heavens!, I had no idea the Phillies were that weak at bat! You are very
heartening and maybe I should get a job as a disc jockey. Unhappily I
can't carry a tune.

Cordially yours,

*Brooks Atkinson of the New York Times was one of the many journal-
ists on the paper who supported Stevenson. He wrote on September 5
urging him to speak at Antioch College. He also mentioned that Walter
Locke, editor of the Dayton News, was one of Stevenson's most eloquent
advocates.*

[16] A copy is in A.E.S., I.S.H.L.
[17] A copy is in A.E.S., I.S.H.L.

To Brooks Atkinson

September 5, 1953

Dear Mr. Atkinson:

I was enchanted to hear from a "loyal insurgent" again. I share your regard for Antioch, on the basis of what I have heard about it, and I should like to go there in April. My future, however, is so uncertain that I dare not make commitments that far ahead. At the moment I am in the process of declining some four hundred fifty speaking engagements to try to find a little repose, rest and sanity. I am sure you will understand, and I hope we can meet again.

My warm regards to Mrs. Atkinson.

Cordially yours,

P.S. I have read Walter Locke's column often and that is someone else I want to meet, more than he wants to meet me. I wish I had a pipeline into his mind and reservoir.

To Alicia Patterson [18]

September 19, 1953

Dear Alicia —

The damnable "schedule" has just been worked out. I leave here for Wash[ington] to see Ike Sept 29th. Go to N.Y. the 30th or 1st, spend the week end in the country seeing some characters and return to Chicago Mon or Tues Oct 5 or 6. I pray I won't miss you both places. Probably going to Bloomington for a few days this coming week after the boys leave for school returning to Chicago Sunday the 27th. . . .

As for me, well its damn hard to be "responsible" and "helpful" and all those sweet things. And when you are the Reps. [Republicans] beat you up. But maybe I don't care enough — and certainly not enough for my more aggressive Democratic brethren.

Love
ADLAI

[18] This handwritten letter is in the possession of Adlai E. Stevenson III.

To Mrs. Ernest L. Ives [19]

September 28, 1953

Dear Buff —

It was a wonderful visit [20] & I sometimes wonder why I don't just collapse into that quiet comfort for a bit. (At the moment the telephones in the office are all clattering!)

The cost of the car for Borden and John Fell was $1491.42 and your half is $745.70 — if you really want to give Bordie such a generous birthday present!

Love
ADLAI

Stevenson visited Washington to see President Eisenhower and Secretary of State John Foster Dulles. He spent several days in New York City and then visited with Mr. and Mrs. Chester Bowles at Essex, Connecticut.

To Mr. and Mrs. Chester Bowles

October 6, 1953

Dear Bowles:

It was as agreeable a feast of reason as I can recall. I wish there could be more, and often — but what a cruelty that would be to your menage!

So, many many thanks for a delightful visit, good food, exquisite view and charming company.

Cordially yours,

Harry A. Legge, of Urbana, Ohio, asked Stevenson on September 14 if he were quoted correctly that "the Democrats would have won the last election if it had been held anywhere between England and Korea." Mr. Legge enclosed a column from an Ohio weekly labor paper which read: "To take Adlai at his word then, nobody likes the Eisenhower administration except Americans, who voted for Eisenhower. . . . We might humbly suggest that if Adlai thinks he can be elected to something in Europe, he move from Illinois to London and stand for Parliament."

[19] This handwritten letter is in the Elizabeth Stevenson Ives collection, Illinois State Historical Library.
[20] Stevenson had just stayed with his sister at the family home in Bloomington.

To Harry A. Legge

October 6, 1953

Dear Mr. Legge:

I have your letter. I probably must plead guilty, although I have no distinct recollection. It is well known that the Democratic party was in strong favor in most of Europe and Asia and the quote that you refer to evidently may have come from any number of foreign newspapers, although I can't see that it has much to do with anything nor can I concur in Mr. Reinig's [21] conclusions. I also once made a remark that I seemed to have carried most of the states that I didn't visit during the late campaign. Perhaps there is nothing funny in that either.

Sincerely yours,

To Mrs. India Edwards [22]

October 9, 1953

Dear India:

I have just heard about your departure from the National Committee and your approaching move to California. I feel a little as though this was the end of an era, and somehow you have a very large place in my political career as well as my heart. I have thought often of your everlasting encouragement and smiling reassurances in my trials. And somehow I don't think you are going to be out of my sight for keeps, at least I hope not.

I was glad to hear that you are continuing as Vice Chairman. I, for one, and there are thousands more, will never forget what you have done for the party and what you have brought to it in the way of a vigorous advocacy and concern for the women.

Blessings, and affectionate good wishes.

Yours,

Miss Mary Anne Tornincasa, of Troy, New York, who was seventeen, wrote Stevenson on August 27, thanking him for "arousing in me an interest in politics through your wonderful campaign speeches." She added: "I'd rather listen to that recording of your speeches than Eddie Fisher!"

---

[21] C. W. Reinig, editor of the *Weekly Labor Forecast and Review.*
[22] Vice chairman of the Democratic National Committee. A copy is in A.E.S., I.S.H.L.

To Mary Anne Tornincasa

October 9, 1953

Dear Mary Anne:

This is the first opportunity I have had to thank you for your very kind and thoughtful letter which was sent to Springfield and for some reason just reached my office here in Chicago a few days ago.

I am glad that you liked my book of campaign speeches and I note with delight that you would rather listen to a recording of my speeches than Eddie Fisher. Coming from anyone, that's a compliment!

With every good wish and my thanks for your thought of me, I am

Sincerely yours,

On September 30, Loring C. Merwin, president of the Daily Pantagraph, *sent his cousin a column by David Lawrence and asked for his comments. Mr. Merwin said that his brother, Davis Merwin, "has two extremely strong convictions vis-à-vis Russia which I have at least partially shared: (1) Russia is a gangster nation and hence any negotiations with her is futile because her word means nothing and (2) we have gone as far as we can in 'persuading' our allies and we must now set a positive course which they must follow because they dare not do otherwise. Obviously you don't agree but I'm not at all sure that I understand the reasons why not."*

To Loring C. Merwin

October 13, 1953

Dear Bud:

. . . I hardly know what you expect me to answer to reply to David Lawrence's wild talk and distortions. And why doesn't he call Churchill, Laniel,[23] Adenauer,[24] yes, and Ike and Dulles, "appeasers" too? All of them know, if Lawrence doesn't, that the best, probably the only present hope of reunification of Germany *and* EDC [European Defense Community] is assurance to Russia against German aggression. Also, our foolish assumption that the Soviet "peace" propaganda falls on deaf ears is mistaken and dangerous. They must not be left with that initiative.

The flavor of your letter and his article — of "go it alone" and our allies will follow because they have to — is dangerous. If you have been following the press and magazines you must have seen the reports of a

[23] Joseph Laniel, prime minister of France.
[24] Konrad Adenauer, chancellor of the Federal Republic of Germany.

growing spirit of independence of the United States, and I believe that holding the alliance together is the most important and difficult task we have. Intemperate refusal to even *try* to reduce the tensions will only confirm the prevalent suspicion that we are inflexible; indeed, that our objective may be a war of extermination.

It does no good to repeat that Russia is a gangster nation and untrustworthy. We have known that for many years. We also know that they will liquidate an unsuccessful enterprise, viz. Greece, Berlin blockade, Korea, etc. And how are we going "to be sure of our own security," as Lawrence says, baffles me. I think there has been agreement for a long time that absolute security is impossible. As for his insistence on building strength, isn't that what we have been doing for years in order to restore the power balance with a view, I thought, to something better and less expensive and perilous. There is probably little hope now, as I said, but pray heaven it will never be said that we didn't try or that we create the impression abroad that we did not *want* to try. And if Lawrence thinks that an absolute embargo on East-West trade is possible he is duller than I thought, and sounds more like a demagogue than a commentator, unless, of course, he is ready to propose not a discontinuance of economic aid but *more* aid, which we can't afford and they don't want. Usually he is clamoring at the same time about waste, extravagance, balancing the budget, reducing taxes, etc.

Ho hum; you must excuse me from a long dissertation. You will find my views briefly stated in the speech of September 15, which many papers printed in full, but not the Pantagraph, and, of course, I would be glad to talk with you about it all. The attached clipping, by the way, lay next to your letters in the pile. I have read only the last paragraph but the phrase "know nothing approach" of Ferguson caught my eye.

Yours,
Aᴅ

P.S. I just heard that Dave [Merwin] was here the other day and I am sorry I missed him.

To Frank Lausche [25]

October 13, 1953

Dear Frank:

I noticed with interest and satisfaction the report of your appointment of Mayor Burke [26] to the Senate vacancy, in the paper this morning.

---

[25] Governor of Ohio. A copy is in A.E.S., I.S.H.L.
[26] Thomas A. Burke, mayor of Cleveland, Ohio.

Somehow it reminded me that I had been meaning to suggest to you for a long while that I hoped you would find an opportunity to talk a little with William E. Stevenson, the President of Oberlin College. I am sure you know him. He is an old friend and classmate of mine and was very helpful to me in the last campaign as head of the Volunteers for Stevenson in Ohio, although he is a registered Republican. I think he is getting more and more interested in politics and on our side of things. I am sure he could be useful and that it would flatter and encourage him if he felt that you were interested.

With warm good wishes to you and Mrs. Lausche, I am

Cordially yours,

To John Foster Dulles

October 13, 1953

Dear Foster:

I was sorry my appointments in New York prevented an evening with you in Washington, and you were good to invite me.

I said something to the President about the uncomfortable state of mind among our government employees — particularly the foreign service — which I sensed or encountered abroad. He asked me to tell you about it orally or by memorandum. But I am sure you are quite familiar with the situation and the reasons for it. As things settle down, I suspect this uneasiness will improve and probably already has.

With my thanks for your thoughtful invitation and warm regards to you and Mrs. Dulles, I am

Sincerely yours,

Professor John Kenneth Galbraith wrote Stevenson that the problem was how to keep the Democratic party "intellectually alert and positive." He suggested a study committee to formulate policies for the party.

To John Kenneth Galbraith

October 16, 1953

Dear Ken:

Strangely, your letter of September 23 was carted off in a file for more careful examination and has only now come to my attention. It is a perfect statement of our problem, which I have thought about for a long time. Indeed, it has clarified my own thinking immensely. Your phrase about the future of the Democratic party, "lies not in its being the party of the right or the left but the party of both the knowledgeable and responsible and truly public action" I hope I don't forget!

I talked about something of this kind to Averell Harriman when I came back from Europe in August. Since then I have had some talks with others, including Charles Murphy [27] and Tom Finletter. The latter indicated he would take an interest in exploring the possibilities a little further. I think he has done so and has probably talked with you or will presently.

Murphy felt that it should be established as a project in the National Committee. Without very coherent reasons I have an instinctive feeling it had best start in a less formalized way, until we see what we can evolve.

While in Britain I talked to some old friends in the Labor Party, and was impressed with the fact that they are totally becalmed and have exhausted their program and have no present basic objectives except to stop Bevanism. [28] We may be in the same position, and I emphatically agree that now is the time to start to review what has been done and consider what should be done.

Of course, I want to help any way I can, but I am eager to avoid any impression that this is a Stevenson brain trust operation. I think you will understand my sensitivities.

Do talk to Tom [Finletter]. I think he might be useful, what with time, intelligence and some background, but he will need somebody like yourself to help him not only to assume responsibility for specific projects but to counsel him with names, ideas, etc.

I had thought to come to Boston for the Harvard-Princeton game with my boys and for an evening with you, Arthur [Schlesinger], Dave [Bell] and such others as you cared to assemble. It now looks as though I will not be able to come, due to the fact that my work here is far behind schedule.

I am delighted that I find myself in total agreement with you, and those "ancient and flea-bitten cliches in the absence of anything involving thought" still haunt me, with what I suspect is a decisive political escapism.

Bless you.

Yours,

The provost of University College, London, wrote Stevenson on September 23: "I have felt that the future of the free countries depend very much upon the development of ideas such as those that you hold and

[27] Former special counsel to President Truman.
[28] The left-wing faction of the Labour party was led by Aneurin Bevan.

indeed on your own powerful expression of them." He raised the question whether people in England could make a positive contribution to Stevenson's efforts.

To B. Ifor Evans [29]

October 22, 1953

My dear Dr. Evans:

I was deeply touched and pleased by your letter. I wish I knew what to suggest because I should not be in the least embarrassed if we could develop something of a dialogue between thoughtful people in our countries. It seems to me it is both essential and it would also be most pleasant! However, I have no views other than to suggest that if you have any ideas for me from time to time they would be more than a little welcome.

With cordial regards and my utmost thanks for your gracious letter, I am

Cordially yours,

To Wilson W. Wyatt

October 29, 1953

Dear Wilson:

I thought the attached might interest you. I think we are in total agreement as to the desirability of approaching the study program informally and with a minimum of commotion, at least for the present. After talking with you I talked to some others, notably Tom Finletter, who has taken hold with his usual perception and energy. I am taking the liberty of passing your letter along to him so that he will have both your views and the name of Philip Coombs [30] as a possibility should he need help as the project progresses.

I was much impressed with John Sharon's [31] letter and the memorandum on reciprocal trade which has been very informative to me. I should like to embrace their suggestion at once but I am a little loathe to put so many friends to so much work until it becomes more evident as to just how and when I can use it. With no staff here even for writing, let alone research, I am in a difficult spot and shall have to contrive some way out of it if I am going to do much sensible talking in the future. In the mean-

---

[29] A copy is in A.E.S., I.S.H.L.

[30] Secretary of the Fund for the Advancement of Education of the Ford Foundation.

[31] Washington lawyer and law partner of George Ball.

time I seem to be bogged down with routine burdens and work in hand in a discouraging way.

Perhaps what I should do is to ask John Sharon to proceed, as he suggests, and then at least I would have at hand the research background for my own use, or someone else's use, if I can get some writing help when the occasion for a speech arises. My hesitancy springs, as I say, from reluctance to impose such a burden on them without more certainty as to the use of the material. Do you think I should tell them to go ahead?

Yours,

P.S. On further thought I have asked Miss [Carol] Evans to send a copy of this letter to John Sharon. I propose, as you know, to speak very seldom for some time. Indeed, I have no choice what with the work in hand and my state of mind.

Miss Brenda Nagel, a junior high school student in Vidor, Texas, wrote Stevenson that she had worked for him in the campaign and asked how she could become a better Democrat.

To Brenda Nagel

October 30, 1953

Dear Brenda:

It sounds to me from your letter as though you already know how to be a good Democrat. When you tell me that you are getting all the information you can and that you worked hard during the election I know that you're doing the best kind of job.

Let me just add this suggestion. Try to figure out what you think people want and have to have — not just the people you know, but all the people in this country and in the world. Then ask yourself what is needed to give them a chance to get these things if they are willing to work hard for them. And ask yourself what we have to do to be as sure as we can be that there will be peace in the world instead of war. If you work out the best answers you can to these questions you will be one of the best citizens anyone can be — and a better Democrat too.

Sincerely yours,

Susan Roach, of Old Lyme, Connecticut, thirteen-year-old supporter of both Stevenson and the Democratic party, wrote that she was preparing a class report on why young people should join the Democratic party and asked for Stevenson's views on the subject.

[281]

To Susan Roach

October 30, 1953

Dear Susan:

I have your letter of September 29 and I think that perhaps the best way of answering your question as to why young people should support the Democratic party is to repeat what I said at the Democratic Convention in 1952.

At that time I said that:

> People here and abroad see in us, the Democratic party, that has steered this country through a storm of spears for twenty years, an understanding of a world in the torment of transition from an age that has died to an age struggling to be born. They saw in us relentless determination to stand fast against the barbarian at the gate, to cultivate allies with a decent respect for the opinion of others, patiently to explore every misty path to peace and security which is the only certainty of lower taxes and a better life.

I hope that this letter will be of some help to you.
With every good wish, I am

Sincerely yours,

Mrs. Raymond Lewis, of Buffalo, New York, wrote that she and her husband were very much impressed with Stevenson's views on a variety of issues. She asked: "What can average young people like my husband and me do to help get a better group of people — especially you! — into responsible positions in our Federal Government?"

To Mrs. Raymond S. Lewis

November 5, 1953

Dear Mrs. Lewis:

In my desire to reply to your letter of September 16th as soon as possible, I failed to answer an important question that you raised: What can you do to help qualified citizens win responsible positions in government?

It seems to me the key word in your question is "do." Progress requires responsible action — political progress especially so! Within the framework of our two-party system, we can be most effective by channeling our efforts through a party. Of course, I believe the Democratic Party best represents the ideals you are striving for. But it can only continue to do so — and do an even better job in the future — through the support and activity of interested and intelligent persons such as you and your husband. A party is only as good as its participants.

If you are in doubt as to how to go about working in your own community, may I suggest that you write to the Democratic National Committee at 1001 Connecticut Avenue, Washington, D.C. I am certain they will be delighted to help you.

With my every best wish.

Cordially yours,

Mrs. Doris Valentine, of San Diego, California, who grew up in Bloomington, wrote on October 27 asking for information about Stevenson for a speech she was to deliver.

To Doris Dooley Valentine [32]

November 7, 1953

Dear Mrs. Valentine:

I have read your good letter with all of the reminders about our home town of Bloomington. I wish there was something I could send you that would be helpful, but I am afraid my story, such as it is, has been written and rewritten, notably in biographies entitled "Adlai Stevenson of Illinois," by Noel Busch and published by Farrar, Strauss, and one by John B. Martin entitled "Adlai Stevenson," published by Harper & Brothers.

I must confess I have read neither of them myself,[33] and have found myself exceedingly tiresome and uninteresting to myself! I wish I could be more helpful, and I must also amend your letter to add that I have never said I would run for President again. That is a decision which will have to be deferred, as you will understand.

Sincerely yours,

P.S. I am returning the clipping herewith.

Loring Merwin wrote concerning Stevenson's return to the board of directors of the Bloomington Daily Pantagraph — *a post he resigned*

---

[32] A copy is in A.E.S., I.S.H.L.

[33] Stevenson, for some reason, denied that he read books about himself, yet he did. Cf. his letter to Mrs. Richard Bokum of June 26, 1952, in Part One, p. 9.

when he became governor. Merwin asked whether he preferred a three-man or a five-man board.[34]

To Loring Merwin

November 7, 1953

Dear Bud:

Thanks for your letter of November 4. I am sure you appreciate that I get a hundred or more a day and it is difficult for me to keep up to date and do anything else.

I can see little advantage in a five-man Board and would be quite content to resume the old arrangement of yourself, Bunting[35] or Gunn,[36] and me. That would provide you with a quorum on hand when necessary and afford me an opportunity to keep in touch with things, either through more regular attendance at Directors' meetings or from minutes. I think it might be a good idea to circulate them in the future as you did this time.

As for being an officer, I don't care about becoming a Vice President again, and it might be more comfortable for you if I was not, due to politics, etc.

I was surprised to read about the expenses as well as the salary for Dave [Merwin] for editorial advice, "particularly on matters of national defense." I don't want to appear captious, but it would seem to me like a lot of money in addition to his regular editorial payroll. As you said, I have no doubt that Dave needs money. But so do I. I now have a payroll which I must personally carry of two or three girls and an assistant, and my situation will become extremely awkward before long. But I certainly don't intend to ask the Pantagraph for any help, and it can have recourse to my counsel whenever it wants it, as you know. Perhaps, however, I don't understand the whole situation, but I am sure you will appreciate this came to me as something of a surprise in view of the closed and intimate character of this corporation.

Yours,

p.s. I like the new form of monthly accounting.

---

[34] For the Stevenson family's involvement with the *Daily Pantagraph,* see *The Papers of Adlai E. Stevenson,* Vol. I, pp. 153–154.

[35] Joseph M. Bunting, treasurer of the Pantagraph Corporation and general manager of the newspaper.

[36] Emmet V. Gunn, secretary of the Pantagraph Corporation and business manager of the newspaper.

To General George C. Marshall

November 7, 1953

Dear General:

May I say that no one, or at least very few, were made happier by the Award of the Nobel Prize than I was.[37]

Cordially yours,

The Reverend Richard Paul Graebel of the First Presbyterian Church of Springfield wrote Stevenson on November 4: "You are Destiny's Child. Whether you ever or never hold office again, you will be a force of destiny in the American Republic from here on out. . . . And if you find life on a Pedestal lonely, let me come and help sustain you anytime." From a selfish point of view, Graebel wrote, he was happy Stevenson was not President.

To the Reverend Richard Paul Graebel

November 7, 1953

Dear Dick:

Bless you for that letter. It *is* lonely and I am afraid I don't understand the job very well! But on one thing we can agree — I am glad I *ain't* it!

Yours,

Look, November 3, 1953, published an article by Lauren Bacall (Mrs. Humphrey Bogart) entitled "I Hate Young Men." Miss Bacall listed the qualities of six older men whom she found attractive: a sense of humor, humility and dignity — and named as her first choice Adlai Stevenson, "because he possesses all of the qualities. He combines humility and sophistication, a practically non-existent combination. None of it is studied. He is a man who never tries to impress anyone — just does. With great charm and honest simplicity, he has the rare faculty of being able to put anyone at ease. Conversation with him is never strained; he is interested in what you say, and listens. Listening is what most people have forgotten how to do, and what a gift it is! Stevenson is the politest man I have ever met, a characteristic which surely must have gone with the 'good old days' I've heard so much about. At least I have seen little of it from the

---

[37] General Marshall had been awarded the Nobel Peace Prize for the Marshall Plan.

younger men. Above all, he is a man of complete integrity, of wisdom and humor. He seems to have it all — the ability to make you laugh at the most difficult moments, innate good sense and uncompromising convictions."

To Mrs. Humphrey Bogart [38]

November 12, 1953

Dear Betty:

It was a delightful article and you have at least six gentlemen blushing, I am sure. But I am *not* sure, for one, how becoming the state of lowered lids and self-conscious confusion is for a man both humble and sophisticated, charming and simple, wise and humorous. I think I detect an awkward lout immensely pleased with himself, stammering something that sounds very much like "Aw, fellers" — and those virtues I have now acquired from such an authoritative source! What am I to do? My clay feet are showing. What a task you have given me, and what a task you have given yourself, for now you will be consigned, like sufferers before you, to write and write.

Thanks for your charity; and the respectful regards of another pencil sharpener.

Yours,

Mrs. Carol Berendt, of Syracuse, New York, wrote Stevenson on November 13 that she had been planning to write him ever since the day he swam alone from a villa on the Cap d'Antibes to Eden Roc and back. She urged him next time to have a rowboat alongside because he was "valuable public property."

To Carol Berendt [39]

November 17, 1953

Dear Miss Berendt:

I was charmed with your letter and also your concern for Stevenson afloat! In such delicious water I felt both safe and, as you say, alone at last! But I shall be discreet, not to "protect valuable public property" but probably because I am just that way.

You were sweet to think of me.

Cordially yours,

[38] A copy is in A.E.S., I.S.H.L.
[39] A copy is in A.E.S., I.S.H.L.

James Boyd, of New York, wrote to express his concern about what he believed to be the "lethargic attitude" of the Democratic party and its lack of direction.

To James Boyd [40]

November 20, 1953

Dear Mr. Boyd:

I have read with much interest your thoughtful letter of October 28. I agree with you that the Democrats should not sit idly by without protest in the present climate of affairs in our country. To some of the things you mention, particularly foreign affairs, I spoke in Chicago in September. To others I am referring in Georgia this week. Moreover, I suspect as a new session opens and the Republican program, if any, unfolds, you will hear more and more Democratic opposition from our Congressmen and Senators.

A party like ours, national in scope and containing every element, can hardly "formulate a plan of action," as you suggest, with any persuasion or discipline. This has, of course, been one of the problems and one of the contrasts between the American political system and the British, for example, for many years. The problem is always one of finding the maximum area of agreement on policy within the framework of diversity, but I think it safe to say that our common grounds, North and South, East and West, are enlarging as the party becomes more harmonious and integrated.

I am so grateful for your most interesting letter and I hope you will keep plugging for what you believe in, which sounds very much like what I believe in!

Cordially yours,

Mrs. Roosevelt wrote Stevenson on November 18 urging him to attend the Columbia University Bicentennial Conference.

To Mrs. Franklin D. Roosevelt [41]

November 20, 1953

Dear Mrs. Roosevelt:

So many thanks for your letter. I have accepted the Columbia invitation, and I am beginning to quake with anxiety already. I wish I had

[40] A copy is in A.E.S., I.S.H.L.
[41] The original is in the Franklin D. Roosevelt Library, Hyde Park, New York.

mastered the speech preparation problem like you have — and a lot of other things besides!

Sincerely yours,
ADLAI

Stevenson spoke in Atlanta, Georgia, on November 24. He wrote the following letter by hand while en route. After Atlanta he visited in Alabama and Washington, D.C.

To Carol Evans [42]

November 23, 1953

Dear Miss E—

I neglected to tell you that I absent mindedly left the green wrapped package of pillow cases (?) you gave me on the 5:35 commutation train Friday night. It was in the rack above the last seat on the right hand side of a car about midway in the train & probably was removed by the conductor at the end of the run and turned in at the "lost and found" place in the N W [Northwestern] station in Chicago.

Please call there and ask if they have such a package. So far as I know it had no identification — name — on it but I didn't examine it carefully nor do I remember what store it was from — probably M.F. [Marshall Field & Company].

Forgive my everlasting confusion. The Southland approaches!

AES

P.s. If you have Mrs. Dennis McEvoy's [43] Wash[ington]. address & telephone number send it to me at Tydings' [44] Maryland address — if you have that. I left everything!

Stevenson addressed the Georgia legislature on November 24, 1953.[45]

I have been the Governor of a great state so I do not feel altogether alien here today before the Legislature of Georgia. Indeed, Illinoisian though I be, I feel more comfortable here in Atlanta among so many good

---

[42] This handwritten letter is in the possession of Miss Evans.
[43] Nan Tucker McEvoy, whose family owned the San Francisco *Chronicle.*
[44] Senator Millard Tydings of Maryland.
[45] The text is based on a mimeograph copy of a press release. The editors have silently corrected a few obvious typing errors and have made capitalization consistent.

Democrats than I used to sometimes feel in Springfield where the Legislature was so solidly infiltrated with gentlemen of another political persuasion.

I am profoundly grateful for your invitation to address the General Assembly, to you Governor [Herman] Talmadge for your hospitality, and to all of you (even the Republicans, if any) who have set aside some of your busy day for me. Indeed, I wanted to come to Georgia last year when we were engaged in one of these quadrennial great debates which are always great and seldom debates — and, I might add, seldom "Crusades" either.

But perhaps it is just as well I didn't, because I seem to have fared better in the states I didn't visit than in those I did. At all events, my heart is full of gratitude to the Georgians who gave your neighbor, Senator [John] Sparkman, and myself our largest majority.[46] I am very proud of your confidence last year and the honor you do me today. And I hope none of you are regretful that Georgia has never voted Republican. But if such there be, I commend to you the letter I had the other day from another Southern state which said, "We voted in haste and are repenting at leisure."

I thought coming down here of other things besides votes for which I was thankful to Georgia: of the great names of Georgia's past and present; of Senator Walter George, whose wisdom and prudence have earned the Nation's respect; of the great influence in our councils of Senator Richard Russell, with whom I am honored to claim a common ancestor who struck a memorable blow for freedom 175 years ago; [47] of Carl Vinson whom I was privileged to know during the war when my boss was Frank Knox, the Secretary of the Navy, and a Republican who did not mistake his party for his country.

But mostly I thought of the amazing progress of our Southland. As a former Governor of a sister state where Democratic Administrations are very good but not very frequent, I am not unmindful of the achievements of Georgia under the administration of Governor Talmadge.

The increases in late years in the level of income in Georgia, in bank deposits, employment, new industries, are a mirror of the South, indeed of the nation, fortunately, for the nation cannot be healthy if segments are unhealthy, as you in the South once had good reason to know.

There have been mistakes, injustices and failures during these decades of national growth. But the record of remarkable progress is clear, and

---

[46] Stevenson received 456,823 votes in Georgia in the 1952 election, compared with Eisenhower's 198,979.

[47] John Brevard, a French Huguenot who settled in the area about 1740 and became a justice of the peace and member of the North Carolina Assembly.

much of it has been made by the Democratic Party. Conscious of our deficiencies, let us not overlook our achievements.

Consider labor. For decades it was treated as a pariah in many areas. But for the past twenty years millions of working men and women have found their rightful place in the sun through organized collective bargaining.

Consider public health. Federal, state and private efforts have banished many diseases. The South is now vital in large part because we have eliminated yellow fever, malaria, pellagra, hookworm. Our national life expectancy constantly increases.

Consider agriculture. Formerly farmers did not share in the nation's general prosperity. But for the past twenty years most of our farmers have enjoyed a fairer share of our national income. I say "most" because we have on our consciences more than a million people in agriculture whose income averages less than one thousand dollars a year. And now with exports and farm prices falling all the farmers are apprehensive — even in Georgia.

You know, after the brave speeches in last year's campaign I thought the Republicans surely had a better farm policy. But they didn't. They didn't have anything but speeches. Now they have a study commission and we have promises of a new and better program. I hope it is, and if it is they can count on Democratic support. For we know that the present program is far from perfect, but we also know that an imperfect farm program is better than a bad farm depression.

What of minorities? Negroes were long our most depressed minority. Happily, their position has enormously improved. I unhesitatingly applaud the progress in the South which, by contrast with the past, is even more conspicuous than in the North. I believe, and I think in common with the great majority of thoughtful white people of the South that this improvement must and will continue, particularly in enlarged opportunities for Negro employment and advancement in the South's expanding industries.

For familiar reasons, American Negroes might have seemed fair prey for Communism. But, trusting in the performance and promises of American life, our Negro citizens are overwhelmingly anti-communist. This is a solemn vote of confidence in the democratic way. It is also of tremendous importance for our democratic cause in the eyes of the great nonwhite populations of the world where the malicious and the ignorant fan the anti-white, anti-Western fires.

I could go on and on listing the areas of our remarkable progress, for, undismayed by the doubts and shouts of the faint-hearted and reactionary, the nation has surged forward in the past twenty years under Democratic influence and the South has moved with it. With hope in your hearts and tools in your hands, your burst of long repressed creative energy marked an astounding renaissance.

Once tens of thousands of the South's ablest young people had to go elsewhere in search of opportunity. You brought them up. You set them on their way. Then they had to leave home. The hands and minds that were sprung of the South and might have contributed deeply to its advancement, contributed instead to other communities. Now this leakage from the heart of the South has been stopped and there is abundant opportunity for youth and enterprise, boldness and imagination, in the new South.

Fortunately, the making of a nation or a region is never completed. We Americans are inspired by the challenge to bridge the gulf between what is and what may be. But much remains to be done in the South and elsewhere, and tomorrow as yesterday the Democratic Party must help the people to do it.

Until lately the dopesters were freely predicting that the North-South cleavage would pull the Democratic Party apart at the seams. Our ill wishers egged us on. They reminded me of the boy who said: "Let's you and him fight."

But instead of disintegrating, the Democratic Party looks more united than it has for a long time. We lost an election in 1952, but we did not lose our vitality or sense of mission. And the sheep that strayed are daily coming back into the fold. For my part, they are welcome; including those that somewhat sheepishly return.

Now there are doubtless extremists in both the North and the South, and the East and the West, who are more interested in having their way than in having an effective Democratic Party or having a Democratic Party at all. But it isn't in the nature of a party structure that covers a nation to have total discipline and total conformity of view. There are bound to be disagreements, and it is well there are, because self-criticism, conflict and controversy are not only the ingredients of democracy, they are also the ingredients of progress. But we can and we do agree on a great many more things than we disagree on, and we need one another in order to advance the great body of ideas we agree upon. There is, I believe, a growing desire in both North and South to go forward together, without bitterness, in good will, mutual respect and with a decent concern for the opinions of one another.

Because Democrats are finding broader common ground and rebuilding their shattered citadels, we are on the way not only to healing the rifts that have plagued us so long but to a better, wiser, stronger instrument of the public will, which, after all, is the only reason for the existence of a political party.

And it is well we are because the real, the serious chasm is in the Republican Party. The days of Democratic minority, the days for reflection and rebirth, may be short as people come to realize more and more that a nation cannot be governed nor a world guided by promises, postponement, paralysis and slander.

A year ago many newspapers, and I don't include your justly famous papers in Atlanta,[48] were saying that the Republicans must be elected to save the Grand Old Party from destroying itself by even more irresponsible opposition; that given office they would measure up to the responsibility, somehow heal their divisions, reduce taxes, balance the budget, cut waste, cut military expenditures, strengthen the free world, liberate the enslaved, restore peace and light, milk and manna to the world.

Well, that would have been about as easy as for one Siamese twin to jump off Brooklyn Bridge while the other kept the skillet hot for the fish fry. And today the gulf between their promises and their performance is as wide as Texas. Nor, as the people are realizing, can you reconcile the irreconcilable, and many Republicans in Congress act as though they were still in the opposition. On two-thirds of the key issues in the last session, Democrats saved the Republican Administration from the Republican Congress. The attitude of many Republican leaders seems to be "I like Ike, but I don't like what Ike likes."

They have opened a campaign to elect a Republican Congress in 1954, which, as somebody said, is certainly an anti-Eisenhower move if there ever was one. And now the sorry counsels of partisan desperation seem to have prevailed, and our country has been humiliated before the world.

I remind you citizens of Georgia that it was by this identical tactic of smearing the Democratic Party as the party of disloyalty that the Republican Party kept itself in power for a generation after the Civil War. Then they called it "waving the Bloody Shirt," and they clung to political power even when their policies were corrupt, reactionary and bankrupt. And now, divided, becalmed and frightened, they are waving not the Bloody Shirt, but the Red Shirt — at a former President of the United States who has done more than any living man to check the forward thrust of Communism and preserve the blessings of freedom for mankind.[49] In a series of bold decisions President Truman revitalized the

[48] The Atlanta *Constitution*, under the editorship of Ralph McGill, and the Atlanta *Journal*, its evening counterpart, were both liberal in editorial policy.

[49] On November 6, 1953, Attorney General Herbert Brownell contrasted the Administration's new security program with Truman's, and charged: "Harry Dexter White was known to be a spy by the very people who appointed him to the most sensitive and important position he ever held in Government service." Since Truman had appointed White, there was a furious outcry. At a stormy press conference on November 11, when asked if he thought Truman knowingly appointed a Communist spy to high office, Eisenhower eased some of the rancor when he replied: "No, it is inconceivable."

free world, restored its will power, fortified its nerve, united its strength, concerted its purposes — against stubborn Republican opposition most of the way — and led the free peoples in their fight against imperialist Communism.

Yet, before a luncheon club, reckless words implying disloyalty have now been spoken about this man by the same politician who engineered the ruthless, reckless attack on the ethics of Senator Taft and his followers in the last Republican Convention. Government by postponement is bad enough, but it is far better than government by desperation.

General Eisenhower promised the people a new morality. But his lieutenants have chosen their weapons without regard for their effect on America's position in the world, or on the level of political debate in our own halls, or on the level of political responsibility in our own hearts and consciences. They have taken McCarthyism away from McCarthy. What an end to the Great Crusade!

Root out, I say, the agents of this satanic worldwide conspiracy; disclose the mistakes and failures of the past; assess the responsibility, let the chips fall where they may. But for the love of heaven let us do it with dignity, objectivity and justice, and with some better motive than partisan strife that can only seriously weaken the United States in its mortal struggle with the total evil that besieges the world.

No one wins this way. Suspicion of past Democratic mistakes is balanced by suspicion of present Republican motives. The people are confused, confidence in both parties undermined, the nation injured. The issue isn't which party detests Communism most, but how to deal with the serious problem of espionage in our government. And it won't be resolved to the nation's advantage by shouting matches and degrading circuses for political profit. Surely the people are entitled to have the facts in the Harry Dexter White and similar cases developed, evaluated and disclosed soberly, honestly, impartially in a manner consistent with the national interest, security and dignity.

I am proud, as I say, of the Democratic record in the last Congress and nobody should be more thankful than the President. Democrats supported the Administration when they thought it was right, which has sometimes been confused with supporting the President for his sake rather than Democratic principles for their sake. It will be harder now after this degrading assault on President Truman.

It will be harder now after the Administration's eagerness to accept Democratic assistance and then repudiate Democrats. It will be harder now with the major issues of farm policy, labor legislation, taxes, foreign trade, etc., postponed to an election year. And it will be harder now in a constant drumbeat of indictment by suspicion, of conviction by accusation which seem to be the Republican program. I note, by the way, that President Eisenhower says he hopes Communist espionage will not be an issue in next year's elections, but Mr. [Leonard] Hall, the Republican Chairman, says it will be the main issue. And they laughed when I stood up last year to talk about a two-headed elephant! But we are getting used to these contradictions.

In spite of the difficulties I respectfully urge that we persist in the constructive pattern the Democrats have established and resist the temptation to oppose for the sake of opposition. The business of the minority, of a loyal opposition, is still the government of the nation, not its injury to win empty political victories. Our party exists to serve the country, not the office seekers.

I have recently returned from a trip around the world. Over much of it beat the wings of the Satan of Darkness. And I say to you that we shall not die because of our quarrels over domestic affairs, but we may die if we do not move wisely and boldly in our foreign relations.

Fortunately, Southern vision has never failed the nation in the life or death affairs that have concerned it since 1914. Insight, memory and a strong sense of history have combined to enrich the South's wisdom. For Southerners alone among Americans know what it is to suffer the horror and humiliation of invasion.

On the shores of Galilee I understood better than before the meaning of those words: "Where there is no vision the people perish." What is vision? Is it not the ability to look beyond the crowded landscape to the high hills where truth resides and new ages are coming to birth? Is it not the ability to hear the quiet voice of reason above the shouting of the haters?

Happily, this vision is still among us — Democrats and Republicans alike — and whatever the provocations, pray heaven that we Democrats will struggle shoulder to shoulder, North and South, East and West, to insure its triumph.

Nothing we do with arms or aid will avail us long if America's moral image is one of confusion and cowardice, hysteria and fear.

But we are not frightened, frustrated brutes trembling before our pitiless destiny. We are not smothered in the cold filth of suspicion and the hot lava of hate. We are not delinquents scrawling dirty words on alley fences. We are calm, confident Americans, united by the vast majesty of freedom in its most solemn crisis of the Christian era.

And that image of gallantry and greatness the Democratic Party must reflect. For that is America!

To Ralph McGill [50]

December 1, 1953

Dear Ralph:

I had a fine Thanksgiving with my sons in Maryland, but even Millard Tydings could produce no ducks.

I enjoyed my visit to Atlanta and I hope it did more good than harm. Certainly if there was any of the latter, between you and the politicians it was well disguised.

I have wanted to tell you that one of the few satisfactions I have found in my exposed life of late is your confidence and good will, so often and so eloquently expressed. I wish to heaven I had you for a "ghost" and perhaps I could speak more often, and certainly better.

With so many thanks to you for all your sensitive thoughtfulness and agile management.

Cordially yours,

To Mr. and Mrs. Millard E. Tydings [51]

December 1, 1953

My dear friends:

I escaped the Washington frenzy quickly and I am now back amid the snows and horrible accumulations of Chicago, but, happily, with joyous memories of my visit with you in that lovely place. Somehow your hospitality and thoughtfulness have made this Thanksgiving memorable for myself and my children — with or without ducks!

I am fearful that descending on you in such an inconsiderate way may have been a nuisance, but if it was you left us happily oblivious.

I am so glad to have had an opportunity to meet Joe,[52] and can see for him the honors and contributions of his father who commands such widespread respect and affection.

Please forgive me for invading your security, and my heartfelt thanks for your infinite courtesy. You even restored my health, if not my figure!

Cordially yours,

Chester Bowles wrote Stevenson on November 25 that he was preparing a paper on economic problems at the suggestion of Thomas Finletter.

---

[50] The original is in the possession of Mrs. Ralph McGill.
[51] A copy is in A.E.S., I.S.H.L.
[52] Their son.

Bowles thought that the word "full" should be added to the Employment Act of 1946.

To Chester Bowles

December 1, 1953

Dear Chet:

Thanks for your letter. I heard you did a superb job at the CIO Convention, and I think your full employment suggestion has much merit. I hope to see Ken Galbraith myself soon and will talk about it some more.

Yours,

P.S. The portions of your book [53] that I have been able to read are really excellent and I think you have written something of importance and usefulness which will have a wide audience. As for mine, I have about abandoned it in view of the impossibility of finding adequate time.[54]

To Carroll Binder [55]

December 1, 1953

Dear Carroll:

I am just back this moment from a trip East and find your letter. My week-end is so confused that I suggest you telephone me at Libertyville 2-2233 as soon as you arrive in Highland Park and we will try to work out something mutually satisfactory. Saturday night may be all right but the schedule seems to indicate that I have a couple of people arriving from the East who may stay for dinner and the night.

Hastily,

ADLAI

P.S. Zafrullah Kahn [Khan], Foreign Minister of Pakistan, will be there for lunch on Saturday if you should arrive by that time and care to join us. I think we could successfully pretend that you are not a newspaper man, or even more successfully that you are a reliable one!

To John Sparkman

December 7, 1953

Dear John:

I am sorry I could not join you for lunch in Washington, but I had a

---

[53] *Ambassador's Report* (New York: Harper, 1953).

[54] Stevenson had planned to write a full-length book on his 1953 trip to Asia, the Middle East, and Europe, but by May of 1954 he had decided to abandon the project. See *The Papers of Adlai E. Stevenson*, Vol. V.

[55] The original is in the possession of the Newberry Library, Chicago, Illinois.

long standing engagement with Bob Meyner, the new Governor of New Jersey, and a fearfully crowded day — as usual!

My evening with the Secretary [56] did not bring forth any specific requests for cooperation. He did indicate that he looks heavily to you and also that he is evidently under heavy pressure to decrease Democrats in the Department, let alone add more. What with the witch hunters and the patronage hunters and the general climate, I doubt if much happens in that direction.

I was delighted with your foreign trade speech, a perfect primer for an ignorant beginner!

Cordially yours,

Miss Edith Gifford, who lived in Brooklyn, New York, and worked for a newspaper clipping bureau in New York City, began a scrapbook on Stevenson in 1952 and continued the project for years.[57]

To Edith Gifford

December 7, 1953

My dear Miss Gifford:

And now I have had an opportunity to examine Volume 2. I marvel at your industry and loyalty. I shall be eternally grateful, because scrapbooking is one of the areas in which I have been grossly negligent and there may come a time when I shall find more leisure to enjoy them and relive my departed glories.

I emphatically agree with you about the decay of the American editorial. Indeed, there is much that could be said about that whole field, but a politician, millionaire or poor man, hardly dares say anything about anything. Isn't it dreadful what has happened to our language? Even negotiation seems to be a synonym for appeasement. I hope peace, decency and dignity are not totally obsolete or epithets in our lifetime.

You have been very good to me and I appreciate it greatly.

Sincerely yours,

Ellen Stevenson's aunt wrote on November 29 praising Stevenson's speech in Atlanta. She mentioned that Senator McCarthy's attacks on the Department of State were having a serious impact in England.

[56] Secretary of State John Foster Dulles.
[57] The scrapbooks are in the Adlai E. Stevenson collection, Princeton University Library.

To Lady Mary Spears

December 7, 1953

Dear Mary:

Your good letter has come and it was sweet of you to write me.

I have not been speaking much of late, although I must do another one in Philadelphia this week. The situation here, as you surmise, is not good, but I believe the Republicans have gone too far and that the reaction may be setting in. The situation becomes so bitterly partisan that it inhibits my utility, for obvious reasons, but other devices are afoot to halt the sickening trend. I suppose you have seen the public letter of the Presbyterians.[58]

I have had a quiet fall in the country, busy as always and disgracefully unproductive. I will have to get down to the horrid business of earning a living again.

My best to you and Louis.

Affectionately,

David Cohn wrote Stevenson on November 27 that after the Atlanta speech he had visited with newspapermen, politicians, and voters and found widespread praise for the speech. "So, suh, my congratulations upon your appearance in the Confederacy," he added, and urged him to get to know, or at least write and thank, Milton Cummings, of Huntsville, Alabama, a liberal who had raised twenty-five thousand dollars for Stevenson's 1952 campaign.

To David L. Cohn [59]

December 9, 1953

Dear Dave:

Many thanks for your note. I wish I had had some opportunity to talk with Milton Cummings. I had heard much about him but I had no opportunity to do more than shake hands during the "southern invasion." I shall certainly write him a note, and promptly. I am glad you thought so

---

[58] Dr. John A. Mackay, moderator of the Presbyterian Church, U.S.A., mailed a letter on November 2 to eight thousand Presbyterian churches which stated: "Some Congressional inquiries have revealed a distinct tendency to become inquisitions . . . [which] begin to constitute a threat to freedom of thought in this country. Treason and dissent are being confused. The shrine of conscience and private judgment . . . is being invaded." New York *Times*, November 3, 1953.

[59] A copy is in A.E.S., I.S.H.L.

well of the visit and its results. Personally I enjoyed it and had no em-
barrassments whatever, but I suppose some of our Northern liberal
friends are upset.

Hastily yours,

*Mrs. Roosevelt wrote Stevenson on December 1 and quoted an un-
identified Yale graduate student as saying: "With the daily paper full of
mud-slinging and smear, complete with all the trappings of a three-ring
circus, the only refreshing thing that happens these days seems to be
when Adlai Stevenson speaks out." He added that "no one since the death
of Franklin D. Roosevelt has so captured the imagination of the American
people" as Stevenson had done.*

To Mrs. Franklin D. Roosevelt

December 10, 1953

My dear Mrs. Roosevelt:
  I wish I could thank that Yale boy for "them kind words" in person.
Perhaps you will do it for me.

Faithfully yours,

*Claude Bowers, ambassador to Chile from 1939 to 1953, wrote Steven-
son on November 25, praising the Atlanta speech and calling his attention
to Edward Livingston's and Thomas Jefferson's struggle to prevent the
Bill of Rights from being destroyed in the 1790's.*

To Claude Bowers [60]

December 15, 1953

My dear Mr. Ambassador:
  I was delighted to have your letters and that remarkably pertinent
quotation from Livingston. Indeed, I had Jefferson and Hamilton [61] on
the desk to look it up when I found your second letter had arrived.
  The other day I lunched with an old Chilean friend, Hernan Santa
Cruz, who gave me a faint impression of the dismay in Santiago when
you left.[62] The reward for your long service there is evidently deep in
the hearts of many Chileans.

[60] A copy is in A.E.S., I.S.H.L.
[61] Claude G. Bowers, *Jefferson and Hamilton* (Boston: Houghton Mifflin, 1925).
[62] Mr. Bowers had resigned as ambassador to Chile when the Eisenhower Administration took office.

Now that you are back here I hope so much you will send me bits and pieces of material from time to time which you think I could properly use. I find it so difficult to write freshly and so often these damnable speeches, with little assistance. I should so much like to have a copy of your lectures when published,[63] and I am glad to hear you are going to carry a message to the heart of Indiana.

Cordially yours,

To Milton Cummings [64]

December 15, 1953

Dear Mr. Cummings:

I suffered but one disappointment in my Southern journey. I had hoped for an opportunity to talk with you a bit, but what with the "entertaining" there seemed to be no chance to do so. I know how generous you have been to the party and I want you to know how grateful I am.

David Cohn has written me that he saw something of you while he was down there — and I am a little jealous.

With best Christmas wishes and my hope for better luck another time, I am

Cordially yours,

To Arthur Perry [65]

December 15, 1953

My dear Arthur:

I was much flattered by your invitation to give the commencement address this spring. Unhappily, I have already made commitments at Columbia, Princeton and Vassar — two of them commencement addresses. In the circumstances, I am afraid I must decline, not to spare John Fell's embarrassment but my own and your commencement guests! [66]

You were good to think of me and I hope you will forgive me, but I am sure you fully appreciate the horrors of preparation in the tumult of my unhappy life.

I am reasonably confident that John Fell will spurt, like his brothers did, and begin to mature rapidly, if late, once he is in college, so I am praying that he will be admitted this spring, and I hope he can demon-

---

63 Possibly a reference to *My Mission to Spain: Watching the Rehearsal for World War II*, published the next year.

64 A copy is in A.E.S., I.S.H.L.

65 Headmaster of Milton Academy. The original is in the possession of Milton Academy.

66 John Fell Stevenson was a senior at Milton Academy.

strate that he deserves it on his merits. There will be some parental talk at Christmas, although I am never sure it has any effect. Yet, somehow, I feel it has more effect with him than it had with the others.

Adlai proceeded the same way, as you recall, but had no trouble in college and is now making a record in the Marines that would warm the heart of an even more critical parent. Moreover, he shows a degree of enthusiasm about Law School which exceeds anything I can recall in my own case.

With warmest Christmas wishes to you and Emilie [67] I am

Cordially yours,
ADLAI

To Marshall Field III

December 15, 1953

Dear Marshall:

I am enclosing a letter from Richard Neuberger. He writes extensively and exceedingly well for the magazines, mostly about Alaska, public power and government. You may know him, and it is on that off chance that I am bringing this to your attention.

I don't ask you to add another charity to the many, but this is certainly one of the young men who encourages me about the future of the Democratic party. He has long been in the Oregon legislature, and so has his wife, and has resisted pressures for many years to run for higher office. This time he seems to want to do it. [68] Will you please return this letter at your convenience so that I can write him? I suspect the senatorial committee will have some money but I doubt if they can divert much to any individual candidate. And *please* don't feel that you must do anything for him on my account.

Affectionate Christmas wishes to you and Ruth. [69]

Yours,

To Richard L. Neuberger

December 15, 1953

Dear Dick:

I am mortified that I have neglected your letter of November 16, thanks to trips in the South and the East. I shall try to look into the possibilities forthwith.

---

[67] Mrs. Perry.
[68] Mr. Neuberger was preparing for his successful campaign for the U.S. Senate.
[69] Mrs. Field.

As you know, I have been devoting this autumn and winter trying to raise money for the Democratic National Committee to restore their solvency. The progress is good, but there is still a long way to go to have anything like generous funds above operating expenses for the next Congressional campaign. There doesn't seem to be anything the matter with our party anywhere that money would not cure, but I certainly agree that you should have something substantial in sight in Oregon. I had rather hoped that with the reanimation of the party out there that some large local support might be uncovered, yet I know how desperately difficult it always is, indeed I know only too well! I shall write you again if I can discover anything of interest.

Cordially yours,

On December 8, Stevenson spoke to the Council on Foreign Relations in New York City. Two days afterward he spoke in Philadelphia, and on December 13 he received an honorary degree from Yeshiva University.

To Chester Bowles

December 17, 1953

Dear Chet:

I wish to heaven I had had a little chance to see you in Philadelphia. As for the surprise question at the Foreign Affairs meeting, I should have had presence of mind enough to say that if Chester Bowles asks a question about Asia our foremost authority should answer it: Chester Bowles.

Christmas wishes to you both, and with them my hope for an early encounter.

Yours,

To Thomas K. Finletter

December 17, 1953

Dear Tom:

I enjoyed myself enormously the other night, and I hope you and the enchanting Gay [70] will forgive me for springing on you that way.

It occurs to me that we should also have some thoughtful work done on wire-tapping legislation and the Bricker amendment,[71] against the hope

[70] Mrs. Finletter.
[71] Senator John Bricker's proposed amendment would have restricted the scope of treaties and executive agreements. The proposed amendment read:
   Section 1. A provision of a treaty which conflicts with this Constitution shall not be of any force or effect.
   Section 2. A treaty shall become effective as internal law in the United

that we can develop some Democratic solidarity in the next session. As to the latter I think Dean Rusk [72] has some ideas that might be helpful. Postponement for more careful consideration might be the most expedient approach.

Hastily yours,

Stevenson received a letter from W. H. Flanagan, of Rock Island, Illinois, who asserted that neither Stevenson nor President Truman had ever made any effort to remove even one Communist from government. He added that he wished that he lived where he could vote for Senator Joseph McCarthy, Senator Pat McCarran, and Senator William Jenner — all of whom were leaders in the congressional campaign against subversive activities.

To W. H. Flanagan

December 19, 1953

Dear Mr. Flanagan:

I wish I knew how to reply to your bitter and ill-considered letter. Are you charging me with the defense of treason? If so, will you please indicate where and when?

As to what the last administration did to combat communism throughout the world, I am sure you must be informed as to what it did in this country. I am neither defending or accusing, but I take the liberty of pointing out that appropriations for the FBI were increased from some three million to over ninety million dollars between 1932 and 1952; that the previous administration instituted the loyalty review system in Federal employment; that all of the anti-subversive legislation was enacted in either the Wilson, Roosevelt or Truman administrations; that the last administration prosecuted and convicted all of the first and second rank Communist leaders in the nation and in many of the states. Some of these cases are still pending.

Sincerely yours,

States only through legislation which would be valid in the absence of treaty.

Section 3. Congress shall have power to regulate all Executive and other agreements with any foreign power or international organization. All such agreements shall be subject to the limitations imposed on treaties by this article.

Section 4. The Congress shall have power to enforce this article by appropriate legislation. . . .

In amended form it was rejected by the Senate on February 25, 1954.

[72] President of the Rockefeller Foundation and former Assistant Secretary of State.

To Alverta Duff [73]

December 24, 1953

My dear Alverta:

Am I mad at you! You would have made our family reunion complete if you had come up for the holidays. I am suspicious of what you are doing down there in Bloomington and why you are so reluctant to expose yourself to life on the prairie.

I have abandoned the book.[74] There just isn't time to do a proper job, but I have to do some lectures at Harvard that must be published,[75] and when am I going to do those? I shall thank my unknown friend from Texas for the nuts, but that is the last thing I need!

Affectionate regards and all best wishes,

Yours,

Vera Micheles Dean, editor of the Foreign Policy Bulletin *of the Foreign Policy Association, sent Stevenson an advance copy of an article from the December 1 issue of the* Bulletin.

To Vera Micheles Dean

December 24, 1953

My dear Miss Dean:

Somehow I have grossly neglected your letter of November 20 and the proof from the Foreign Policy Bulletin. I am so glad you thought of it, and I only wish it had wider currency. I hope some time that I can take advantage of this to some useful end, and here perhaps I should shamelessly confess that I have taken advantage of much of your writing in the past!

And the last book — "Foreign Policy Without Fear" [76] — is the best contribution of late to our perspective.

In the present climate of opinion and press I am afraid I am a poor spokesman for history and truth. There seem to be more than a few who will discount or distort anything a politician says, and of the latter breed I seem now to be one.

Sincerely yours,

---

[73] Housekeeper in Stevenson's Bloomington home during his youth. See *The Papers of Adlai E. Stevenson,* Vol. I. A copy is in A.E.S., I.S.H.L.

[74] See note 54, p. 296.

[75] The Godkin Lectures, published as *Call to Greatness* (New York: Harper, 1954).

[76] New York: McGraw-Hill, 1953.

To the Reverend Reinhold Niebuhr [77]

December 28, 1953

Dear Dr. Niebuhr:

So many thanks for your charitable letter about my speech in Phila-delphia. Need I add that a word of encouragement from you is as heartening as anything that comes my way. And you were more than generous with them, too!

Cordially yours,

P.S. I have been delighted to hear the encouraging reports from many quarters about your progress and I pray that you are not overexerting yourself again.

A.E.S.

Stevenson addressed the Association of American Law Schools in Chicago on December 28, 1953.

THE REPUTATION OF THE GOVERNMENT [78]

For me to undertake a discussion of the subject of "Government and Private Reputation" seems, to me at least, peculiarly appropriate. My interest in government, involving as it has a double exposure to the popu-lar franchise, has evaporated whatever pretensions I might once have had to the possession of private reputation.

I could, I suppose, provide an object lesson by showing my scars, for, as Professor Priest has said, in words that never occurred to Horace, *"Dura est ovicipitum via"* [79] — or, the way of the egghead is hard.

So I can only wistfully suppose that there *are* people who still have reputations to protect and that, perhaps, I could help them most by say-ing merely: "Keep your necks well in and never run for office."

While I am patently beyond rehabilitation, I like to think that the law and the press continue to provide ports of refuge for the normal in-dividual, and recognize the opportunities that daily fall in their paths to formulate sound and sensible principles for the protection of at least private reputations.

---

[77] The original is in the Niebuhr papers, Library of Congress.

[78] The text is from Adlai E. Stevenson, *What I Think* (New York: Harper, 1955), pp. 164–169. See also *Harper's*, April, 1954, pp. 25–28.

[79] Professor Madison Priest of Princeton University coined this phrase during the 1952 campaign.

I will not attempt to define the dimensions of the problem in terms of the irreparable injury done to reputations by reckless or malicious assaults. I should like, instead, to suggest that there is some value in the exploration of this problem in terms of the reputation of the government, as distinct from that of the individual. The condition of the government's reputation at any particular point in time may have, it seems to me, a great deal to do with the bringing of the evil into being and, once the evil begins to manifest itself, there is too little appreciation of the wounds which government itself receives when the private reputations of its citizens are insecure against official attack. This latter aspect especially has too much substance to be overlooked in any multi-sided discussion of the problem.

Government exists for all of us as a very real and ever-present force, and one with which we are in continuous, albeit sometimes shadowy, contact. We know that we owe it certain duties and marks of respect, and yet we also have a sharp, if inarticulate, sense that our obligations to render them are affected by countervailing responsibilities owed to us by government. Certainly the alacrity, enthusiasm, and effectiveness with which we discharge our part of the bargain is heavily conditioned by the degree to which we think our government is living up to its.

Let me give you an example of what I mean. During the election of 1952 corruption in government was one (and, I hasten to add, only one!) of the issues which appeared to contribute to the idea that it was time for a change. Now I think it fair to say that the particular instances disclosed were not, certainly as we have known governmental corruption in the past, markedly sensational. They did not reach to as high places as before, nor were they an improbable sequel to depression, war, boom, social dislocation — and the vast expansions of government and public spending.

The electorate did not, so far as I was able to observe, see the issue in the unsophisticated terms of one candidate's being for corruption in government and the other against, nor did I see much evidence of the naive error of distinguishing between Republicans and Democrats on the basis of moral virtues inherently peculiar to either. Why, then, did the issue have any significance? In large part I find the answer in what seems at first blush to be a wholly disparate and unrelated issue, namely, the Korean War.

To me the Korean War is, and I suspect always shall be, the supreme example in my lifetime of the essential need for mutual trust and confidence between the ordinary citizen and his government. Coming as it did upon the heels of the prolonged and exhausting struggle of World War II; involving as it did a far-off unfamiliar country and people and no immediate and visible interest of our own; becoming as it did a costly stalemate with victory, in the guise it has always come to us before, nowhere to be seen or felt — surely no government was ever obliged to ask its citizens to put forth greater efforts in reliance for the most part on bare official assurance that the long-range national interest required it.

Our people, with that sixth sense which is at once the inner grace and outward shield of democracy, seemed to know, however imperfectly, that they were being summoned to the highest kind of duty; and they met the challenge in the face of confusions, provocations, falsehoods, and frustrations beyond description because of their respect for the right of government to ask the ultimate in sacrifice for aims judged by government to be necessary.

Under such extraordinary circumstances what were they entitled to expect of government? Not that while its leaders were asking for sacrifice, some of its hangers-on should be fixing tax cases or selling influence. When it was suggested that such things might be going on simultaneously, the resentment was, I suspect, wholly out of proportion to what might have been generated in more normal times. Warren Harding's government, you will recall, never had to ask the people to do anything except relax and watch taxes go down. And, as the 1924 election indicated, such a government is not held to account by the most exacting standards.

It seems not unlikely, however, that the job of being President of the United States will never again be as pleasant as Calvin Coolidge presumably found it; and that future administrations will all find a return to normalcy, whatever that may be, an inadequate and impossible objective. The preservation of the free world, the staving off of atomic disaster, the accommodation and adjustment of new forces in ferment in our own society and about the globe — all will combine to subject government to the most rigorous tests of strength and statesmanship. And the demands upon it will, of necessity, magnify its demands upon us. The concern of government thus must be to create such a relationship between itself and its citizens that the response of the latter in time of crisis is prompt, trustful, and generous.

Leadership to be greatly served must be cloaked in greatness. Idealism at the center must not be frayed around the edges.

But the reputation of government is, of course, damaged by other kinds of disloyalty than the familiar problem of corruption. The disloyalty of the occasional Communist, or subversives of any stripe, who creep into government service, is destructive, too, and I suspect our people feel an almost personal affront about some of these disloyalties in government. While the sophisticated analysis of this problem, in terms of the disease being so much less dangerous than the cure, is probably true, it does not make me at all certain that the analysts know what the real danger was, or is. That danger never was that a small group of people could exercise any major influence over American foreign policy or deliver the government into the hands of either Communism or bankruptcy. The plan for reducing Germany to a pastoral state which has been ascribed to Harry Dexter White, for example, was not only rejected by the Truman administration which helped to rebuild Germany industrially, but so far as I can discover, it was also rejected by Stalin, who wanted German goods to rehabilitate the wrecked Russian economy. A danger greater than disloyal influence or espionage was that they hurt the reputation of government in the eyes of the people, and thereby loosen dangerously the magic bonds which tie a democracy together.

So as we seek for ways to protect private reputations against governmental attack, let us realize that the only time we have a problem at all is when the most vital reputation in the world — that of our government — itself is impaired.

It is the part of realistic wisdom to recognize that the vast majority of people in this country are not going to be too concerned about the private reputations of anybody if they sense a threat to the essential reputation of their government. This admittedly has its ugly side, but there is something also of the mysterious essence of democracy in the surviving desire of a people to rise up and strike out against a threat which is more damaging to the ideal of government they cherished than to the policies of the treasury of that government.

There is always, however, the other side of the coin of democracy. If we expect government to observe high standards of loyalty and honesty, we expect it no less to maintain the highest standards of freedom and liberty. One disloyal or dishonest person in government weakens democracy dangerously; no less, and perhaps even more, does one tyrant, arrayed in the panoply of authority and heedless of those who fall in his way.

The tyrants, and the political opportunists who use them, do the same kind of damage as the dishonest and the disloyal. They chip away at the pride which American citizens have in their government — a pride which is a corollary of devotion to the principles of decent, effective, fair government.

For greatness in a government is not to be found in money honesty alone, in wisdom and vision in the formulation of primary policy, or even in unfailing expertness in spy-catching. There must be, beyond all these, quality of what, if you please, I can only call justness — the meeting of the popular expectation that government is a protector of the basic equities, with a compassionate eye and a strong arm to see that each individual, no matter how weak or unappealing, is dealt with fairly and justly.

With this capstone virtue, government can command ". . . that loyalty on the part of the citizen which never fails to arise from the confidence that justice will always be done." Without it, to quote again, ". . . government writes its own epitaph. . . ." And in these trying times, no government — and certainly not one that bears the fateful responsibilities of the government of the United States — can afford to jeopardize that loyalty. For the price tags on peace and freedom which the government must collect from its citizens are forbearance and sacrifice and effort — and these are not eagerly given by the disillusioned.

Americans have, I am confident, a strongly developed sense of fair play. It is a rock against which many tides of racial and religious intolerance have beaten in the past, dangerously but vainly. At the moment there are mounting currents of repression and conformity, set in motion by our deep distaste for Communism and our frustration about the stubborn world, and swelled by impure springs of political expediency. But these, too, will recede in time, if the rock is not riven by other forces.

This natural instinct for justice focuses upon government. In large measure it is either realized or disappointed by governmental attitude or act. We had a notable instance of this in the case of the young lieutenant in Michigan who, although of proven loyalty himself, was about to be expelled from the Air Force as a security risk because he was related by blood to persons of allegedly doubtful loyalty.[80] Well, "the government" did do the right thing, and our faith that "the government" would never let itself be guilty of such an outrage bore fruit.

The Air Force that day armed itself with a kind of weapon which, in the long run, is more damaging to our enemies than all of the atomic bombs now stored at the ready.

For the morality of government is, like the law, a seamless garment, and it cannot be rent in one small place without endangering the whole fabric. It is always a lamentable thing when the good name of an individual citizen is unfairly taken from him by anyone, but when the filching is done by government or with its connivance, government does immeasurable harm to itself and the effects on the world we live in

[80] On November 7, 1953, the allegations were made public against Lieutenant Thomas Shepard. He won loyalty clearance on December 23, 1953. New York Times, November 8, December 24, 1953. For a discussion of the Eisenhower security program and the political use of the dismissal of alleged subversives, see Walter Johnson, 1600 Pennsylvania Avenue: Presidents and the People Since 1929 (Boston: Little, Brown, 1963), pp. 284–285, 287–295.

are calamitous. The cause of freedom, of human decency, does not advance in measured tread. There are times of retreat and times of enduring advances. It may be given to our time to recognize that the reputation of our government, of surpassing importance in the affairs of men, reflects in no small measure the extent of its concern for justice, honesty, and restraint in dealing with all its citizens at all times and under all circumstances.

And let me say also that government, to the man in the street, is frequently as all-inclusive as it is ill-defined. He is not much given to speculation about the separation of powers; and the executive, the legislative, and the judicial often manage to get hopelessly intermingled in his mind. He does not distinguish too sharply between a cabinet member, a district judge, or a Congressional committee chairman. He simplifies and personifies, and government takes its coloration for him from the acts of all. All have, therefore, a responsibility for the picture that emerges. Anyone can deface it.

The short of the matter is that the survival of our freedom, individual and collective, is closely linked to the good name, the private reputation, if you please, of our government. Its preservation is necessary to evoke the loyalties, both at home and abroad, upon which government must make heavy drafts.

L. F. Bishop, of Clifton Spa, New York, wrote on December 18 that when Stevenson spoke on radio and television thousands of his listeners were not Democrats. He added: "With your persuasive eloquence you have them sailing gayly along with you over a sparkling sea, until suddenly your tone seems strident as you say 'We Democrats.' Whoosh — You have heaved them all overboard with one word."

To L. F. Bishop [81]

December 29, 1953

Dear Mr. Bishop:

Thank you for your letter. You are quite right and I know precisely what you mean. The trouble is that most of these speeches that are nationally broadcast originate from Democratic Party meetings. It is awfully difficult to talk both to the partisan audience in front of you and to the invisible non-partisan audience. I shall try to do better.

Sincerely yours,

[81] A copy is in A.E.S., I.S.H.L.

To Alben W. Barkley [82]

January 4, 1954

Dear Alben:

Steve Mitchell reports that you couldn't reach me at Libertyville because my phone was unlisted and that I "would have to remedy that in order to hear from us common people." The sad fact is that I am so damned common that I have to rent my house and the phone is listed in the tenant's name! [83] I was distressed that I had missed you as I had promised my sister and brother-in-law, who arrived for the holidays, that you would most likely be here and that we would have a "Barkley Day" in Libertyville.

My love to Jane [84] and all the best.

Yours,

Mrs. Margaret Munn, who had been one of Stevenson's secretaries at the executive mansion in Springfield, sent him as a Christmas present a bottle top in the form of a donkey.

To Margaret Munn [85]

January 4, 1954

My dear Margaret:

So many thanks for that most useful donkey. He is already ornamenting the top of a half-filled bottle and he will move on and on, even as the bottles.

We missed you this Christmas, and I had some moments of yearning for what I choose to call "the good old days."

With affectionate good wishes, I am

Yours,
AES

---

[82] A copy is in A.E.S., I.S.H.L.
[83] Marshall Field IV.
[84] Mrs. Barkley.
[85] The original is in the possession of Mrs. Munn.

To Kitty Clark [86]

January 5, 1954

Dear Miss Clark —

Many nice things have come to me at Christmas time in the past and again this year. By "things" I mean things, thoughts, people, spirit. I think you know the common collective of "things."

But your "Christmas Wish" from a stranger, almost I think, is by itself. Are you a poetess, a writer, a philosopher, a theologian? Are you all of them? Where do you find such words, such perception, such sensitivity? You must live in two worlds — *yours* and *ours.*

I shall guard those two little sheets of precious paper — illuminated by a gentle, understanding, inspired artist. And what's more I shall pilfer words, phrases shamelessly.

And some day I shall meet and thank her for enveloping such an erring, earthbound mortal in such gracious mercy.

Thank you. Bless you, and a peaceful New Year to you — Kitty Clark.

To Frank E. Karelsen, Jr.

January 5, 1954

Dear Mr. Karelsen:

Thanks for your letter and for the Christmas card.[87] I could not be more flattered, and I think this is one card from 1953 which I shall preserve to impress my grandchildren.

I am sorry about the unfortunate remarks of Mr. Mitchell regarding the A.D.A.[88] His attitude, in so far as I know it, has been a growing feeling that these good friends of the Democratic party should be working in the party and not independently. I hope the misunderstanding is not serious, and I am sure he must share the same regard for so many of the members as I do, and, for that matter, all liberal Democrats.

With very best wishes, I am

Cordially yours,

86 This handwritten letter is in the possession of Mrs. Kitty Clark Gibbons.

87 Mr. Karelsen quoted Stevenson on his Christmas card: "Fear begets fear, as faith begets faith. . . . We shall defend the free mind and the free spirit. . . . We will not be stampeded into the dark night of tyranny. . . . With faith in our great heritage of individual freedom, we can — and will — keep America the land of the free."

88 On a television panel in Chicago, Stephen A. Mitchell had said that the Democratic party "could get along without" any endorsements from the ADA. The organization, he said, "has been developed very much in the press and by Republican speakers — out of proportion to what little I know of the organization's size and

Colonel Arvey wrote just before Christmas: "You have contributed greatly to the intellectual awakening of the American electorate. . . . In the small part I played in bringing you into public life, I shall always be proud." He added that had Stevenson been elected President, he "would have retired from all public life" in order to "emphasize the lack of ambition for myself and the fact that your service in a responsible role was all that I sought."

To Jacob M. Arvey

January 5, 1954

Dear Jack:

I have read and reread your letter. It touches me deeply, and I know from long experience the depth of its sincerity. I only wish I had proved a more genuine hero, but my failings are not the measure of my appreciation for your loyalty, support and counsel since you first talked to me about running for public office in the winter of 1947.

But perhaps there is some compensation in my failure at the polls last year: at least you have *not* retired from politics!

With renewed thanks for your magnificent Christmas present, and warmest regards to you and Mrs. Arvey, I am

Cordially yours,

Senator Kefauver sent Stevenson a copy of a letter he had written to Senate Minority Leader Lyndon B. Johnson. Kefauver urged the Democrats to refrain from partisan utterances on foreign policy even though the Eisenhower Administration failed to consult them. Moreover, the Democrats should protect Eisenhower "from the partisans within his own party." Kefauver explained that he was aghast at the excesses of certain congressional committees in the field of "so-called subversive investigations." He recommended a joint congressional committee with exclusive jurisdiction in such matters.

To Estes Kefauver

January 5, 1954

Dear Estes:

Many thanks for your letter, which, I am sorry to say, was lost in the Christmas shuffle, or perhaps "chaos" would be better.

importance." See Clifton Brock, *Americans for Democratic Action: Its Role in National Politics* (Washington, D.C.: Public Affairs Press, 1962), p. 148.

I think you have made a good point and also some sound proposals. Particularly I agree that if we followed recent Republican precedent we would frustrate and embarrass our foreign policy and injure the country. In spite of precedent and provocation that we must not do. Besides, I think a temperate, cooperative attitude in this field will disclose a degree of Democratic solidarity, maturity and good sense which should pay dividends politically as contrasts with the Republicans, past and present, emerge. At the same time there will be, I suspect, ample opportunity to ridicule the Republican divisions and the sharp moderation of attitudes that have accompanied Republican responsibility, viz. China of late. And what has happened to all the shouting about "liberation," renunciation of "secret treaties," etc., withdrawing the 7th Fleet's protection "from the Communists?" It was all cynical and dangerous political nonsense to catch votes at the price of confusion.

I, too, have thought well of the joint committee idea for loyalty investigative matters and I suspect some of our Republican brethren would gladly unload some of the cats on their backs. But I'm not informed on the Congressional situation in our party in this regard.

As to a Democratic "program," I hope the session will reveal a high degree of Democratic solidarity on some of the major issues which will only highlight the Republican division congressionally, and its incapacity to govern effectively.

With best wishes to you and Mrs. Kefauver, I am

Cordially yours,

To Paul Simon

January 8, 1954

Dear Paul:

I have your circular letter and I am much interested to hear of your candidacy for the legislature. As you know, I am an enthusiast for younger people with ideas and convictions getting into politics, especially Democratic politics!

Warm good wishes.

Cordially yours,

On January 10, John Pontrelli, the lad who delivered newspapers to Stevenson's 11 South La Salle Street office in Chicago, wrote that he was giving up his job and would not be seeing him any more.

To John Pontrelli

January 14, 1954

Dear John:

Just a note to wish you the best of luck and to thank you for looking after us during the past year.

I enjoyed catching a glimpse of you every so often and hope that our paths will cross soon again.

Sincerely,

Mr. Finletter sent Stevenson a number of policy papers prepared by members of the informal "Finletter group."

To Thomas K. Finletter

January 15, 1954

Dear Tom:

Yesterday I spent some time which should have been devoted to something more pressing, reading the enclosures with your letters of January 6 and 11. I was profoundly impressed and I think you are really getting some important results from the research work. I am glad to hear that Chester [Bowles]'s memo is going to be further developed in more specific detail.

I have to speak at a fund-raising dinner in Miami in late February. This time I shall insist that it be broadcast only locally. If you have, as a result of your evidently profound and extensive thought, any positive notions as to what I should talk about at that time they would be most welcome. Do you think, for example, that I ought to assail the Bricker Amendment? That's the way I feel.

Hastily,

To T. S. Matthews

January 19, 1954

Dear Tom:

What's this I hear about you and Martha Gellhorn? [89] But if I hear correctly I am delighted. Being a longtime admirer of hers and having, from time to time, charitable feelings for you, I view the whole thing

[89] Correspondent and author. She and Mr. Matthews were to be married within a few weeks.

[315]

with more satisfaction than I expected to find in your next matrimonial adventure.

I am not sure what I am dictating on this confused and busy morning, but whatever it is I mean to say "hurray" — with special love and kisses for that remarkable gal.

Yours,

P.S. I thought by this time you would have loaded me with all sorts of speech material. How about concentrating on a commencement address for Columbia or Vassar — both in June? I shall be at my wits' end for a time, and of course without ideas as usual.

P.P.S. And what are your plans anyway?

P.P.P.S. And why must I hear about your intimate plans from others or read about them in hostile journals?

H. M. Baggarly, publisher of the Tulia Herald, *Tulia, Texas, wrote that a brick was thrown through his window for displaying Stevenson's picture. He asked for an autographed picture to hang in his office over the brick.*

To H. M. Baggarly

January 26, 1954

Dear Mr. Baggarly:

I am sending you the photograph you request, but I am not laughing because of the brick-throwing Republicans, but because this is the only photograph I have.

I am sorry indeed that I caused you such annoyance, not to mention expense, and I am still more unhappy that bricks are a Republican weapon anywhere in America, let alone in Democratic Texas.

With best wishes to you and my gratitude for your loyalty and support, I am

Cordially yours,

To Clayton Fritchey [90]

January 28, 1954

Dear Clayton:

Thanks for the stuff on the Bricker Amendment. I enclose a copy of

---

[90] Editor of the *Democratic Digest*.

what I issued to the press this morning, a portion of which I suppose will be picked up by TV and radio.

I am much interested in your memo on foreign affairs and defense, but it might be better to wait until you get it shaken down. Two basic questions occur to me:

(1) If we are basing defense primarily on retaliation are we not returning to the pre–April 1950 situation when we were thinking in terms of a large, strategic Air Force? If so, is this a "new" concept, as advertised by Dulles and Ike? And is it a wise policy in view of our experience? [91]

(2) In public talk about the budget, the emphasis is on the Air Force to provide the means of retaliation. But is not the explanation for the budget increase largely payment for the obligational authorizations previously incurred in Democratic administrations? If that is the case, then, in effect, we have not abandoned the balanced force concept. What is the truth, and are we being sold a bill of goods to reassure the people that the administration can accomplish both sets of promises, i.e., reduced spending and tax reduction, plus better defense?

But enough of this.

Yours,

STATEMENT ON THE BRICKER AMENDMENT
by Adlai E. Stevenson [92]

In response to many requests for my views, I welcome this opportunity to express my opinion on the proposed Bricker Amendment to our Federal Constitution which the Senate is now debating.

I think this is a dangerous, a radical and unnecessary proposal. Moreover, it seems to me very unwise to propose a constitutional amendment which so few Americans understand or know anything about. I think we should be very cautious and conservative about tampering with our Constitution which has served us so well for 165 years.

It should be amended, as it has been in the past, only in cases of demonstrated need and in response to wide-spread public understanding and agreement. But admittedly few people understand the vast implica-

---

[91] In a speech before the Council on Foreign Relations on January 12, Dulles explained that the "new look" in military policy placed its emphasis on air-atomic power, on the "deterrent of massive retaliatory power" to supplement "local defensive power." The United States now would "depend primarily upon a great capacity to retaliate, instantly, by means and at places of our own choosing." New York Times, January 13, 1954.

[92] The text is from the Chicago Sun-Times, January 29, 1954.

tions of this proposal. Nor in my opinion, has the need for it been demonstrated.

Now — in a few words — why is it radical, dangerous and unnecessary?

It would shift the treaty-making power and, in effect, the conduct of our foreign relations, from the President to the Congress, and even to the 48 states. This is a radical alteration of powers between the President, the Congress and the courts.

It is dangerous because it would cripple the President and his secretary of state in the day-to-day direction of our myriad transactions with foreign governments, and at a time when they need the utmost prestige, initiative and flexibility; at a time when we have to deal with dictators whose word is law and who consult neither their people nor a Congress; at a time when the very survival of the free world depends on prompt, effective action in our foreign affairs.

It is unnecessary because a treaty cannot violate the Constitution and because Congress can always repeal as internal law the provisions of any treaty.

And it is a reactionary proposal, too, because when we deal with other nations we must speak and act as one; otherwise we are impotent, as the founding fathers well knew from their unhappy experience before the states were united. Yet this reactionary amendment would restore to the states the very power to nullify treaties which they relinquished when they adopted the Constitution.

If the reason for Sen. Bricker's amendment is fear of some possible abuse of the treaty-making power, then it reflects a lack of confidence in the Senate itself which must approve treaties by a two-thirds vote.

If the reason is fear of some possible infringement of the Constitution, then I point out that in 165 years not a single treaty has been ruled unconstitutional while scores of Acts of Congress have been.

If it is fear of the many agreements the President makes which are not submitted to Congress as treaties, then I say all power may be used unwisely, even the power to amend the Constitution.

But let us not paralyze the President's initiative in the conduct of foreign affairs in order to guard against some hypothetical danger. Let us not scuttle our opportunity and our efforts of many years to strengthen and defend freedom from communism's assaults. Let's not "secede from the world," as Dean [Joseph] O'Meara of Notre Dame law school says.

The issue, I believe, is one of confidence in the wisdom of the founding fathers who gave us our remarkable Constitution; confidence in the Supreme Court which interprets and protects it; confidence in our President, whoever he may be; confidence in the Senate of the United

States; and finally, confidence in the American people themselves who elect the President and the Congress, and from whom, in a democratic society, all power springs.

I hope President Eisenhower will stand firm against this ill-considered attack on the Constitution which few of our people yet understand. I hope he will stand firmly for the preservation of the integrity of his office and its indispensable powers.

On January 26, George F. Kennan, who had retired from the Foreign Service in 1953 and rejoined the Institute for Advanced Study in Princeton, wrote Stevenson: "I have never approved a policy in which our military strength is founded on the weapons of mass destruction and is unsubstantial without them. I feel that our position should be: we will hold such weapons, reluctantly and regretfully, only as an addendum to our normal military establishment, only for purposes of retaliation in case they are used against us or our allies, and only in such quantities as will suffice for deterrent purposes; we will be happy to dispense with them the moment satisfactory international arrangements can be made."

To George F. Kennan [93]

January 30, 1954

Dear George:

Your letter and the enclosures are very helpful and I am most grateful. I shall probably plagiarize shamefully!

If it is really true that we have embarked on a new policy, and I am by no means sure from the budget figures, I think it demands more and more public scrutiny. At least we should know what it really is, economy or defense. Meanwhile, I suppose our allies are guessing, and very nervously.

If you write any more on the "new look" I hope I can see it.

Sincerely yours,
ADLAI

To Cyrus Eaton [94]

January 30, 1954

My dear Mr. Eaton:

Thanks so much for your note and the clipping reporting the C. & O.

---

[93] The original is in the possession of Mr. Kennan.
[94] Cleveland industrialist and philanthropist.

transaction.[95] I am profoundly impressed — again! — by your extraordinary enterprise at a time of life when most men think of tranquillity.

That you even thought of me as a possible Director is flattering and I am grateful indeed. I should like to do some things of this kind and get back a little into the business community where I lived and worked so long.

I enjoyed our lunch and you stimulated me; something that doesn't happen every day hereabouts. I hope there will be more opportunities, including further discussion of the big business, banking, SEC [Securities and Exchange Commission] impact on smaller financing. Do let me know when you come this way again.

Cordially yours,

To Robert Tufts

January 30, 1954

Dear Bob:

Your letter is helpful and provokes my languid spirit. I must be in Florida about March first. If you have time to draft a portion of a speech, asking temperately and responsibly (that awful word!) some of the right questions to unmask the "new look" in defense for what it really is, I would be sorely tempted to dive into this subject a little. If you are too busy, don't bother.

Yours,

P.S. I am in touch with Paul Nitze [96] on this subject who may send me some material too.

Averell Harriman wrote Stevenson on February 1, expressing concern over the "new look" speech by Secretary of State Dulles at the Council on Foreign Relations on January 12. Harriman also felt the Democrats should demand real bipartisan consultation on foreign policy.

To Averell Harriman

February 2, 1954

Dear Averell:

Thanks for your letter. I agree that the "new look" is disturbing, and

---

[95] Mr. Eaton replaced Robert R. Young as chairman of the board of directors of the Chesapeake and Ohio Railway. See the New York *Times*, January 20, 1954.

[96] President of the Foreign Service Educational Foundation, Washington, D.C., and former director of the Policy Planning Staff, Department of State.

to me it is also confusing. On the basis of the new obligational authority requested in the budget it doesn't look as though there was any conspicuous emphasis on the Air Force, even if they do propose to rely on retaliation, which looks to me like a retreat to the pre-1950 situation.

It is all very bewildering, and I wish I knew just what the effect was abroad.

I have been loathe to say much, but I thought in Miami early in March I might advert to the new foreign policy with some questions at least. I hope we can have a talk before too long, and I wish you would let me know where you will be in the second half of March and early April.

Hastily,

P.S. If they seek bi-partisan support for the new policy — and if it *is* a new policy — I should think we should be very loathe to volunteer much help. I am afraid bi-partisanship to this administration means support for what they previously decide. I could tell you something about what the President said to me in our meeting in late September about his hope for bi-partisanship from the "inception" of policy. But I see no evidence that this has come to pass.

Farwell Smith, son of Mr. and Mrs. Hermon D. Smith, married Nora Stone, daughter of Melville E. Stone and Mrs. Mott B. Schmidt. Mrs. Schmidt was a friend of Stevenson's from his early Chicago days.

To Farwell Smith [97]

February 2, 1954

Dear Farwell:

Your family gave me a preview of your most recent adventure and I had meant to write you long before this.

Not only do I approve most heartily, as I do of all your adventures, but such a long one as this deserves special notice. As an extreme admirer for many years of your companion's mother, I think I perceive at least some of the reasons for your selection. I am delighted, and I only hope she doesn't end up in a remote jungle at midnight in a broken down jalopy on your honeymoon.

Affectionate wishes to you both.

Yours,

[97] A copy is in A.E.S., I.S.H.L.

On February 1, Mr. and Mrs. John Currie wrote Stevenson that trying to stay politically alert in Detroit was difficult because of a blackout of news about him. They added that even Arthur Krock in the New York Times *gave only one sentence to him the previous week.*

To Arthur Krock [98]

February 5, 1954

Dear Arthur:

Hooray for Krock and the N.Y.T. which can pierce even the sound barrier of Detroit!

And this isn't the first letter of this kind. Please return for my most precious file — entitled "entertainment."

Yours,
ADLAI

To Alicia Patterson [99]

[no date; probably February 8, 1954]

Alicia dear —

So many thanks for your birthday note. We had the usual riotous party this year at Ed McDougal's with many verses, speeches — and square dancing!

I've been living like a hermit in Libertyville this winter — a couple of days a week in town & occasional public appearances; trying desperately to keep up with the appalling load of mail, visitors etc. And now I'm in the interrupted throes of trying to put together some lectures I must give at Harvard in mid March.[100] With nothing to say its an awful chore, and bedevilled with languor and indifference its worse.

I must go to Miami for a Democratic fund raising clambake on March 6 & to Harvard March 17. Depending on the progress of the damnable lectures I may stay in the South & East between the two dates. . . . I had hoped to see you out here long before this & pine for news of your world — and you. . . .

AES

Apologies for this note — written on the Northwestern [Railroad]!

[98] The original is in the possession of Mr. Krock.
[99] This handwritten letter is in the possession of Adlai E. Stevenson III.
[100] The Godkin Lectures.

Tom Lehrer, who had taught mathematics at Harvard, also composed satirical music and wrote poetry. He sent Stevenson a copy of one of his humorous records.

To Tom Lehrer [101]

February 10, 1954

Dear Mr. Lehrer —

Thanks for the record. It came just after I gave away mine to an insistent visitor, who thereby acquired it as I had acquired mine! I shall now resume my diet of Lehrer for all and sundry visitors to my corner of the prairie.

But, please, please send me "Adlai, We Need You Badlai"! You know how we old soldiers love to reflect on battles long ago. I mean of course if it is on a record and you have a copy.

My current Harvard son, Borden, a Junior, tells me fabulous tales of your talents — mathematical, musical, literary. He needn't. But I hope some day to see and hear for myself. Thanks again — and I am sending along the book with a clumsy, hasty inscription. But please don't read it; you have other more mirthful things to do. And, the Republicans to the contrary notwithstanding, that is important too.

Cordially

In December, 1953, Thomas E. Dewey denounced President Truman and the Democrats for "bungling our country" into the Korean War and for the "loss" of China. He stated: "Remember that the words Truman and Democrat mean diplomatic failure, military failure, death and tragedy." And on a speaking tour to commemorate Lincoln's birthday in February, 1954, Senator Joseph McCarthy assailed the Democrats for "twenty years of treason." He added: "The hard fact is that those who wear the label — Democrat — wear it with the stain of an historic betrayal."

On February 12, Edward R. Murrow interviewed Stevenson at his Libertyville home. Stevenson used the following handwritten notes for part of the discussion. We reproduce them as he jotted them down.[102]

What to you is Lincoln's greatest lesson or meaning to us today?
Lincoln had a broad conception of the Civil War. Not only union

---

[101] A handwritten draft of this letter is in the possession of Carol Evans.
[102] This handwritten draft is in the possession of the editors.

imperilled, but the fate of democracy everywhere. America was democracy's proving ground. The masses of other lands looked to us with hope. If our experiment succeeded they too might win self government.

So he resolved that govt. of the people, by the people, for the people must not fail — "shall not perish from the earth." The civil war was deciding more than the fate of these United States. Americans were dying for the new, revolutionary idea of govt. by consent of free men. They were dying to save the union, and also the hope of all people everywhere.

And so it is today when the idea of the free man and freedom for all to choose their way of life is assailed by the global communist conspiracy and is hanging in the balance everywhere.

Also in his most thoughtful and considered speech — the Cooper Union speech [1860] — he begged the South to listen and stop denouncing the Reps. as reptiles and outlaws. And he implored the Rep. leaders not to think evilly of the South. But humility, forbearance and moral elevation were not the order of the day. The results were very sad. And perhaps thats a lesson for today when his birthday seems to be a signal to strike a new low in language and abuse.

Alistair Cooke, correspondent for the Manchester Guardian, *wrote Stevenson on February 8 and mentioned that in 1948 he had written of Thomas E. Dewey: "He has gone after the presidency with the humorless calculation of a certified public accountant in pursuit of the Holy Grail." Cooke recommended that Stevenson not criticize the Republicans for the economic recession that had set in: "It seems to me that a doctor who assures a man in public that he is going to get cancer will be thought a malign son-of-a-bitch if he's wrong and not much better if he's right."*

To Alistair Cooke [103]

February 16, 1954

Dear Alistair:

Thanks so much for your delightful letter and that line about Dewey which I had not heard before. It will interrupt my Libertyville nightmares — I hope! As you have observed, I have kept out of the recession business as you recommend. I made a speech in Philadelphia in mid-December which I thought struck an optimistic note, in the direction of discounting the fears of depression. However, the press and the cartoonists seem to persistently identify me with the business and there is nothing I can do

[103] A copy is in A.E.S., I.S.H.L.

about it. I have a feeling sometimes that the Republican idea is to hear, speak and see no recession — at least by Democrats.

Warm wishes and many thanks.

Cordially yours,

P.S. Keep the advice coming and also those delicious lines. Life is dreary hereabouts.

Don Brice, of the WKBN Broadcasting Corporation of Youngstown, Ohio, wrote Stevenson about the broadcast with Edward R. Murrow: "The brief comment you made on the present political muckraking and its effect on the international situation was apt, timely and direct to the point. . . . You are the only really strong voice to speak out for the millions of people, in this country and in many others, who believe in morality and ethics in government and politics." Brice urged him to continue to speak out against bigotry.

To Don Brice

February 16, 1954

Dear Mr. Brice:

Thanks so much for your flattering report on my performance with Ed Murrow. I was not altogether too pleased with it, and felt that we spent too much time on trivia and not enough on Lincoln, let alone my great grandfather Fell!

I too am apprehensive about the public climate, but I have difficulties finding time and strength for speech writing along with a multitude of other things which have fallen on me, with limited staff to help, etc.

I shall do the best I can and I know you likewise will try to incessantly combat this spreading evil.

Sincerely yours,

Under President Truman there were separate loyalty and security programs. One covered all employees, and dismissal occurred when there was a reasonable doubt of loyalty. The other applied to eleven "sensitive" agencies, including the Departments of Defense and State, and provided for dismissal of employees if their habits — including loose talk, drunkenness and homosexuality — or subversive 'activities made them risks to the national security. The Eisenhower Administration eliminated the separation between the two programs.

On October 23, 1953, the White House announced that 1,456 government employees had been dismissed or had resigned under Eisenhower's security program. During 1954 the Administration raised the figure to 2,200, to 6,926, to 8,008, and finally stopped the statistics at 9,600. While some Republican orators clutched the figures with sheer delight, newspapermen asked how many were actually dismissed as Communists, former Communists, or fellow travelers. The Alsops denounced the program as "Security-Firing Fakery" in their syndicated column January 22, 1954. In 1955, the Civil Service Commission admitted that more than 90 per cent of the 9,600 employees described as security risks had left the government by regular civil service procedures without hearings to test any security charges. Up to September 30, 1955, only 1,016 employees actually had been charged under the security program. And, of these, only 342 were dismissed under security procedures. The commission also revealed that more than 50 per cent of the 9,600 had been hired during the Eisenhower Administration.[104]

On February 10, Frank Altschul, chairman of the board of General American Investors Company, sent Stevenson some material about the "new look" and stated that a dangerous pattern was being formed by the government's claim that it had fired so many subversives hired by the Truman Administration.

To Frank Altschul

February 16, 1954

Dear Frank:

So many thanks for your letter of February 10 and the enclosure which seems to me excellent. I have been thinking about this problem, what to say and when to say it. Your document is helpful and I think I may take occasion to ask some questions, responsibly I hope, in a speech in Miami in early March.

I have little hope that the President is going to take any positive steps either with his "family" or the party and that the present line of attack will persist as long as the Republican leaders think it is paying dividends politically.

I am sure we should press insistently to disclose the fraud in the 2200 subversives, etc. The problem is out [how] to keep on the attack and not to appear on the defensive. The adversary may be helping us with his excesses in that regard.

Sincerely yours,

[104] Report of the Committee on Post Office and Civil Service (U.S. Senate, 84th Congress, 2nd Session, Senate Report 2750).

To M. A. Floyd

February 19, 1954

Dear Mr. Floyd:

I am most grateful to you for your very thoughtful and interesting letter regarding the outrageous attacks which have been made of late on members of the Democratic party.

I shall do what I can, as I have in the past, and I am delighted that more and more people are taking a solemn view of all these developments. I hope to have something more to say on this matter in a speech at Miami on March 6.

Sincerely yours,

To Paul H. Nitze

February 26, 1954

Dear Paul:

Ever so many thanks for your splendid memo on the defense policy. I wish I could, and I probably will, lift portions of it for a forthcoming oratorical effort.

Which reminds me that I am in the throes of trying to write some damnable lectures for Harvard and, again, I wish I could plagiarize your excellent speech at Dartmouth.

Many many thanks and best wishes.

Yours,

On March 5, Stevenson left for Miami, Florida, to attend a meeting of the Democratic National Committee. On March 7, he spoke at a fund-raising dinner.

CRUSADES, COMMUNISM, AND CORRUPTION [105]

I do not propose to respond in kind to the calculated campaign of deceit to which we have been exposed, nor to the insensate attacks on all Democrats as traitors, Communists, and murderers of our sons.

Those of us — and they are most of us — who are more Americans than Democrats or Republicans count some things more important than the winning or losing of elections.

There is a peace still to be won, an economy which needs some atten-

[105] The text is from *What I Think,* pp. 64–71.

tion, some freedoms to be secured, an atom to be controlled — all through the delicate, sensitive, and indispensable processes of democracy — processes which demand, at the least, that people's vision be clear, that they be told the truth, and that they respect one another.

It is wicked and it is subversive for public officials to try deliberately to replace reason with passion; to substitute hatred for honest difference; to fulfill campaign promises by practicing deception; and to hide discord among Republicans by sowing the dragon's teeth of dissension among Americans.

The loyalty and patriotism of a whole political party, of one-half of the nation, has been indicted. Twenty years of bipartisan effort, highly intelligent and highly successful, have been called "Twenty Years of Treason" — under the auspices of the Republican National Committee.

When one party says that the other is the party of traitors who have deliberately conspired to betray America, to fill our government services with Communists and spies, to send our young men to unnecessary death in Korea, they violate not only the limits of partisanship, they offend not only the credulity of the people, but they stain the vision of America and of democracy for us and for the world we seek to lead.

That such things are said under the official sponsorship of the Republican party in celebration of the birthday of Abraham Lincoln adds desecration to defamation. This is the first time that politicians, Republicans at that, have sought to split the Union — in Lincoln's honor.

This system of ours is wholly dependent upon a mutual confidence in the loyalty, the patriotism, the integrity of purpose of both parties. Extremism produces extremism, lies beget lies. The infection of bitterness and hatred spreads all too quickly in these anxious days from one area of our life to another. And those who live by the sword of slander also may perish by it, for now it is also being used against distinguished Republicans. We have just seen a sorry example of this in the baseless charges hurled against our honored Chief Justice.[106] And the highest officials of the Pentagon have been charged with "coddling Communists" and "shielding treason." General Zwicker, one of our great Army's finest officers, is denounced by Senator McCarthy as "stupid, arrogant, witless," and "unfit to be an officer," and a "disgrace to the uniform." [107] For what?

106 Earl Warren. Stevenson may refer to remarks made in the Senate hearings leading to Mr. Warren's confirmation as chief justice on March 1, 1953, which included a ten-point summary of "charges," e.g., that he was at one time connected with a liquor lobbyist, that he lacked judicial experience and so forth.
107 Senator McCarthy, who had assailed the Information Program of the Department of State during 1953, turned next to the Army. He charged that there were "earmarks of dangerous espionage" in the Signal Corps at Fort Monmouth. On February 18, McCarthy, at a hearing, shouted at General Ralph Zwicker: "You are a disgrace to the uniform. You're shielding Communist conspirators. . . . You're not

For obeying orders. This to a man who has been decorated thirteen times for gallantry and brilliance; a hero of the Battle of the Bulge.

When demagoguery and deceit become a national political movement, we Americans are in trouble; not just Democrats, but all of us.

Our State Department has been abused and demoralized.

The American voice abroad has been enfeebled. Our educational system has been attacked; our press threatened; our servants of God impugned; a former President maligned; the executive departments invaded; our foreign policy confused; the President himself patronized; and the integrity, loyalty, and morale of the United States Army assailed.

The logic of all this is — not only the intimidation and silencing of all independent institutions and opinion in our society, but the capture of one of our great instruments of political action — the Republican party. The end result, in short, is a malign and fatal totalitarianism.

And why, you ask, do the demagogues triumph so often?

The answer is inescapable: because a group of political plungers has persuaded the President that McCarthyism is the best Republican formula for political success.

Had the Eisenhower administration chosen to act in defense of itself and of the nation which it must govern, it would have had the grateful and dedicated support of all but a tiny and deluded minority of our people.

Yet, clear as the issue is, and unmistakable as the support, the administration appears to be helpless. Why? The Stevens incident [108] illustrates what preceding events have made memorably plain: A political party divided against itself, half McCarthy and half Eisenhower, cannot produce national unity — cannot govern with confidence and purpose. And it demonstrates that, so long as it attempts to share power *with* its enemies, it will inexorably lose power *to* its enemies.

Perhaps you will say that I am making not a Democratic but a Republican speech; that I am counseling unity and courage in the Republican party and administration. You bet I am! — for as Democrats we don't believe in political extermination of Republicans, nor do we believe in political fratricide; in the extermination of one another. We believe in

---

fit to be an officer. You're ignorant." On March 11, the Army charged that McCarthy, his aide Roy Cohn, and his subcommittee staff director, Francis Carr, had tried by improper means to force the Army to grant preferential treatment to G. David Schine, who had been drafted the previous fall. McCarthy fired back with forty-six charges against the Army. For thirty-six days the Army-McCarthy hearings were held in Washington and televised to the nation.

[108] Robert Stevens, Secretary of the Army before Senator McCarthy's attack on General Zwicker, had tried to appease McCarthy by suspending those at Fort Monmouth accused by the senator.

the republic we exist to serve, and we believe in the two-party system that serves it — that can only serve it, at home and abroad, by the best and the noblest of democracy's processes.

And there is nothing, by the way, except abuse of democracy's processes in this deception about the employees allegedly removed from government jobs as "security risks."

We were told in October, 1954, by the White House that 1,456 government employees had been removed as security risks. The President later raised the figure to 2,200. And we were told — by Governor Dewey of New York, the Postmaster General, the Counsel to the President, and countless other Republican leaders — that most of these were "subversives," "spies and traitors" who had been "kicked out of government." Some of these orators even suggested they had been planted in the government.

You remember all the campaign talk about Communism and corruption, and what the Republicans were going to do if they won to clean up "the mess in Washington," as they called it. Well, as you may have heard, they won, and when they didn't find the government "crawling with spies and traitors," they started this numbers game to show how well they were doing.

The figure has now been raised to 2,427; but the only thing we know for sure is the government's reluctant admission that out of more than two million federal employees only one alleged active Communist has been found.

It looks as though the Great Crusade had practiced a Great Deception. They may consider this good politics. But it is vicious government. We will await the final results with interest, and also the administration's apologies to the many innocent, loyal people who have been injured by this unscrupulous, un-American numbers racket.

Everyone hopes the administration will find and remove all the real subversives and keep them out of our government. For a single disloyal or dangerous employee is one too many, and I do not hold that the past should be closed. On the contrary, experience will remain a powerful, ever-present reminder of the price of anything less than eternal vigilance. But I do hold that past errors do not excuse new ones; that democracy's ideals and vitality must not be despoiled by those who purport to defend them.

The President has said he disapproves all these goings-on — this slander and deceit, this bitterness and ugliness, these attempts to subordinate a nation's common purposes to a divided party's political ambitions. He has said so repeatedly in statements to the press — but the nation's ideals continue to be soiled by the mud of political expediency.

This internal crisis makes it all the more urgent that the Democratic party remain strong, responsible, and attentive to the nation's business. I note that no Democrat has charged that the whole Republican party is corrupt merely because three Republican Congressmen in a row have been convicted of defrauding the government.[109] We know that Republicans and Democrats alike want better government — government that measures up to the ideals of proud people, to the dignity which befits the leader among nations, to the standard we think of as the reward citizens receive from a democracy for which they pay and work and pray and fight, and see their sons die to preserve.

Now, more than ever, America must be a citadel of sanity and reason. We live in a troubled, dangerous world where the great issues are peace or war and the stakes are life and death.

Perhaps these melancholy diversions explain, for example, why there has been so little public curiosity about such a genuine concern as the "new look" in national defense and foreign policy. I had hoped that there might be a resumption of the bipartisanship of President Truman's administration when Secretary Dulles and many prominent Republicans, including the President himself, served in important roles.

At all events, without the benefit of bipartisanship, the administration has unveiled this "new look." It has been presented to us as a program of more for our money, national security in the large economy-size package, "a bigger bang for a buck."

While I don't presume to understand its full implications, they are sobering enough to require searching, responsible discussion. The background of any evaluation of this new program must be stern realization that the peril of the free world is not diminishing.

We are told, and I am quoting the words of Secretary Dulles, that we have rejected the "traditional" policy of "meeting aggression by direct and local opposition." We have taken the decision, he says, "to depend primarily upon a great capacity to retaliate instantly, by means and at places of our choosing." But some "setbacks to the cause of freedom," some "Communist successes," Mr. Dulles says, should be regarded as "normal."

All this means, if it means anything, is that if the Communists try another Korea we will retaliate by dropping atom bombs on Moscow or Peiping or wherever we choose — or else we will concede the loss of another Korea — and presumably other countries after that — as "normal" in the course of events.

Is this a "new look" or is it a return to the pre-1950 atomic deterrent

---

[109] Those convicted were J. Parnell Thomas, of New Jersey, for payroll padding and salary kickbacks; Walter E. Brehm, of Ohio, for receiving illegal campaign contributions; and Ernest K. Bramblett, of California, for payroll kickbacks.

strategy which made some sense as long as we had a monopoly of atomic weapons together with a strategic air force. Yet even then it didn't deter attack, and brought us to the brink of disaster in Korea where atom bombs were useless, and we were only saved by heroic exertion to re-create conventional ground forces.

But, you say, we did not use the bomb against Russian and Chinese targets for fear of enlarging the war. Exactly; and if we should now use them in retaliation that way it would certainly mean World War III and atomic counter-retaliation. For the Russians have massive power of retaliation with atomic weapons just as we do, and our cities are also susceptible to destruction.

Another question: what if we are confronted with something less than a clear case of overt aggression? What if we had relied exclusively on a policy of "massive retaliation" since the close of World War II? Would we have resorted to global atomic war in order to meet the Communist threat in Greece and Turkey? To counter the Berlin blockade? To resist aggression in Korea?

If the answer is no, then the so-called "new look" in foreign policy is no "new look" at all, but merely a continuation of the policy of adapting our methods of resistance to the method of attack — a policy that has brought the free world through many crises without precipitating a Martian catastrophe.

Instead of greater freedom of choice, does this decision to rely primarily on atomic weapons really narrow our choice as to the means and the places of retaliation? Are we leaving ourselves the grim choice of inaction or a thermonuclear holocaust? Are we, indeed, inviting Moscow and Peiping to nibble us to death?

This is the real danger. This is the real problem. Will we turn brush fires and local hostilities into major conflicts? Will our allies go along?

Using weapons short of war, and relying upon our reluctance to embark on global war, the Communist imperialism will attempt to absorb country after country, to close the ring around us, and to decide the issue between tyranny and freedom long before a final outburst of atomic fury.

It seems to me that the new weapons — even if we had a complete monopoly — are no answer to all the complicated aspects of this worldwide struggle, for armed aggression is only one of the many shapes of the Communist menace. And the only thing new about the "new look" appears to be the weakening of our Navy and ground forces and reducing the non-atomic programs and policies that we need to win the cold war.

Was the administration caught between two conflicting sets of promises — to reduce the budget and simultaneously strengthen our defenses? Did it choose the former because the one thing that could not be cut, the *sine qua non* of our security, was the new weapons and air power?

I don't know, but if true bipartisanship in the formulation of policy in matters of such grave import is impossible, at least we are entitled to the facts and the truth unadorned. If our military policy is beyond the further financial endurance of the country; if this reliance on retaliation is the only reasonable policy for the long haul, then frankly tell us so and why. But don't confuse us and frighten our allies by misbranding disengagement as advance and retrenchment as initiative. Don't tell us we have something new and better for less, when we haven't.

It may be that they don't mean what they say or that I have misinterpreted what they say. But issues of life and death should be clarified and not clouded, for security in our age cannot be brought by slogans and gimmicks.

It is only in the strength of freedom, in the fortitude and sacrifice of free peoples; it is only in the humility of all men under God that we can create a future not scratched from the wreck and rubble of war or from the chaos of domestic disorder but rising from the love and faith and devotion of unconquerable humanity.

I hope that we can begin to talk with one another about our affairs more seriously, moderately, and honestly, whether it be our foreign policies or the patriotism of our people and public servants. There has been enough — too much — of slander, dissension, and deception. We cannot afford such wastage of our resources of mind and spirit, for there is important work to do which will be done together or not at all. It is for us, all of us, to recapture the great unifying spirit which still surges so strongly through the hearts and minds of America. Let us, as Democrats, resist the ugly provocations of this hour and try to cut the pattern of America's future, not from the scraps of dissension and bitterness but rather from the full, rich fabric of America's ideals and aspirations.

"Let us," in Thomas Jefferson's words, "restore to social intercourse that harmony and affection without which liberty and even life itself are dreary things," and without which, I could add, tomorrow's misfortune will mock today's expectations.

"Few speeches in these years have had such instantaneous effect on the opinions and behavior of political leaders," Stuart Gerry Brown wrote. "It was too powerful and too forthright to be ignored. Many Democratic leaders were, to say the least, uncomfortable. Some feared that it would backfire on the Democratic party in the coming congressional election." [110] *The New York Times wrote in an editorial on March 8: "Mr. Stevenson, as we have learned to expect, spoke as something more than a partisan.*

[110] *Conscience in Politics: Adlai E. Stevenson in the 1950's* (Syracuse, New York: Syracuse University Press, 1961), p. 66.

He spoke as a conscientious American citizen. . . . This speech will have to be answered by some Republican whom the people know and respect. It compels an early and definite decision on the McCarthy issue — which will be awaited with interest."

On March 9, the Republican National Committee, after consultation with President Eisenhower, announced that Vice President Nixon, not Senator McCarthy, would reply to Stevenson. On March 10, President Eisenhower, at his press conference, denied that the Republican party was half Eisenhower and half McCarthy. He did, however, commend Senator Ralph E. Flanders for accusing McCarthy of "doing his best to shatter" the Republican party.

On March 13, Vice President Nixon, speaking for the Republican party and the Eisenhower Administration, officially repudiated McCarthy: "Men who in the past have done effective work exposing Communists in this country have, by reckless talk and questionable method, made themselves the issue rather than the cause they believe in so deeply." [111]

To Arthur M. Schlesinger, Jr. [112]

March 7, 1954

Just back from the hall — weary but reasonably content with what I uttered — after 4 weary hours of banquet and speeches in a ghastly hall. But if you want to disclaim the baby I'll understand. Anyway, thanks!!!

A.E.S.

To Dore Schary [113]

March 15, 1954

Dear Dore:

Your wonderful letter finally caught up with me here in Hobe Sound [Florida] where I have been trying desperately to do some deadline work on some lectures I must give at Harvard in a few days. And, to borrow a word from Schary, it's a helluva place to work!

You were more than good to write me and I am delighted you thought well of the speech. I get little partisan satisfaction out of the Republicans' embarrassment in this predicament, and I hope and pray that sanity, sense and dignity is coming in one door as McCarthy goes out the other. But I have my fingers crossed.

Sincerely yours,

ADLAI

---

111 New York *Times,* March 14, 1954.
112 This postcard is in the Schlesinger papers, John F. Kennedy Library.
113 The original is in the possession of Mr. Schary.

Harry S. Truman wrote Stevenson on March 15 that he thought his Miami speech was entirely in accordance with his own thinking.

To Harry S. Truman

March 21, 1954

My dear Mr. President:

I have finally found a moment here in New York to catch up with my mail, including your gracious and heartening note about the speech in Miami. I was particularly disturbed by the "new look" and I think we have smoked the administration out on that one a little, which should reassure our allies and disclose another "hoax."

I have little misgiving about the ultimate destiny of McCarthy and his tactics, and I pray that your estimate of the durability of this wave of unreason is correct.

Faithfully yours,

P.S. I am ever so grateful for your approving remarks about the Miami "effort" in New York.[114] Evidently some of our Senatorial brethren did not think so well of it, but I am told their misgivings are not serious and some have felt better about it since the explanations of the "new look" and McCarthy's counter-attacks.

A.E.S.

On March 17, 18, 19, Stevenson delivered the Godkin Lectures at Harvard University. They were published under the title Call to Greatness *(New York: Harper & Brothers, 1954). They are included in Volume V of* The Papers of Adlai E. Stevenson.

John J. McCloy, chairman of the Chase National Bank of New York and former U.S. High Commissioner for Germany, wrote Stevenson on March 8: "I read your Miami speech and appreciated what you were trying to do to help my Party to unity." McCloy asked for copies of the Godkin Lectures.

To John J. McCloy [115]

March 21, 1954

Dear Jack:

I have your letter and I am most grateful for your heartening approval of what I was attempting to do in Miami. I am afraid, as usual, the per-

[114] In a letter dated March 15, 1954, Mr. Truman said that he had issued a statement endorsing Stevenson's Miami speech in its entirety.

[115] A copy is in A.E.S., I.S.H.L.

ception was not too acute, and after listening to Nixon's speech I am afraid that goes for the administration as well.

I have been much relieved by the further explanations of the "new look," as I am sure you are.

I am asking the office in Chicago to pass along some copies of the lectures at Harvard. But I would emphatically urge you not to read them. You have more useful things to do, and they are the fruit more of exhaustion and impatience than wisdom.

Yours,

P.S. I shall get home early in April and have an opportunity to read what you said at Andover. I wish I had it this minute and I would probably plagiarize shamelessly for some talking I must do in Princeton tomorrow.

To John Kenneth Galbraith [116]

March 21, 1954

Dear Ken:

Before the Cambridge chaos recedes too far, I must thank you and your bewitching lady for your infinite kindness to me. It was an exhilarating adventure for me, if not for my victims. And I was reminded again of my indebtedness to you and others thereabouts for provoking my torpid mind over and over again.

The luncheon at your house and my brief exposure to some people who know what they are talking about aggravated some lingering discontent with my lot. But perhaps it is better to be in and out of such groups than to be in until I am thrown out!

So many thanks to you and Mrs. Galbraith.

Yours,

To Mrs. Averell Harriman [117]

March 21, 1954

My dear Marie:

I don't suppose that Averell has yet returned to that sunny nest [118] from his western wanderings, so this goes to you, and with it my everlasting gratitude for a memorable interlude.

The lectures at Harvard turned out better than they deserved, and the

[116] The original is in the possession of Mrs. John Kenneth Galbraith.
[117] A copy is in A.E.S., I.S.H.L.
[118] Stevenson had stayed with the Harrimans at Hobe Sound while he was in Florida.

multitudes of students and faculty were large and enthusiastic, although I believe after three nights of my mouthings there was little new light in Cambridge. At all events, I felt that those endless hours in Mariner with the sea beating on the beach were not wholly in vain.

You and Averell were so, so good to us, and I shall never contrive again such a happy combination of working conditions, playing conditions and spirited conversational divertissements! I wish the whole thing were in front of me instead of behind me — in spite of the damnable work.

With fond hopes for an early reunion and the warmest thanks to you and Averell from Bill [Blair], Miss [Carol] Evans and me.

Affectionately,

P.S. I am dictating this on the wing in New York en route to Princeton and more chaos — which is by way of explanation for its inadequacy.

To Estes Kefauver [119]

March 21, 1954

Dear Estes:

Thanks so much for your letter; and I am deeply grateful to you for inserting the Miami "effort" in the Congressional Record. I have been reassured of late that it has really served some purpose in provoking further explanation from the administration of the "new look."

Warmest good wishes.

Cordially yours,
ADLAI

On March 22, Stevenson spoke at the senior class banquet at Princeton University.

THE EDUCATED CITIZEN [120]

I am informed that this senior class banquet is being held at the expense of your accumulated reserves. I suggest that inviting me here is a very perilous thing to do because certainly within a few hours the Republicans will ask for equivalent time.

I was delighted to witness a moment ago your emphatic approval of my program for Princeton some thirty-two years ago — unlimited cuts, non-compulsory Chapel, and student firing of the Dean. I always con-

[119] The original is in the Kefauver papers, University of Tennessee Library.
[120] The text is from *What I Think*, pp. 172–181.

sidered that it was wise in politics to have — shall we say — a popular program. The trouble is that when I went into politics it appears that I changed my views.

I feel as though I were opening the hunting season on college seniors. From now until mid-June, college seniors are fair game for all of us uplifters, viewers with alarm, Chautauqua-style orators, even for occasional unemployed politicians. From now until mid-June college seniors are to be repeatedly reminded how fortunate they are and what they should do with their hard-won educational disciplines; they are to be warned repeatedly that the old order is changing, that the sky is overcast, visibility low; and they are to be urged and goaded and implored to accept the challenge to remake the future.

Thirty-two years ago — and I might say quite a number of pounds and a good many inches around the waist ago — when I graduated I believe I listened to these same challenges flung down by orators whose names I have completely forgotten. Now it is my turn to be forgotten. In doing my homework this morning on this evening's oration, I not only let my mind run back to the state of the world thirty-two years ago when I graduated from Princeton but I also glanced at the *Nassau Herald* of 1922 in the hope that I could find something about myself that would impress you. I discovered that when my senior class voted to bestow the sobriquet of "biggest politician" upon one of its members I received only eight votes — but when it voted on *"thinks* he is biggest politician" I won second place, and that was due to a conspiracy among my roommates.

Thirty-two years ago my classmates and I graduated into a world that was quite different from the one you enter in 1954. Before settling down to the business of trying to earn a living, I did some more traveling. It was a happier, more helpful world than the one I saw on a recent journey around the globe. A terrible war to make the world safe for democracy had just ended victoriously. A noble concept, the League of Nations, had emerged from the chaotic aftermath of that elemental struggle. It was the twilight of kings, the dawn of world-wide democracy. Optimism was boundless and people proclaimed that we were on the threshold of the new era of universal and perpetual peace and prosperity.

It didn't turn out that way. It wasn't a threshold after all. Ernest Hemingway soon wrote: "I was always embarrassed by the words sacred, glorious, and sacrifice and the expression in vain. We had heard them, sometimes standing in the rain almost out of earshot, so that only the shouted words came through, and had read them, on proclamations that were slapped up by billposters over other proclamations, now for a long time, and I had seen nothing sacred, and the sacrifices were like the stockyards at Chicago if nothing was done with the meat except to bury it."

But I don't need to tell you, a generation that was born and nurtured in the depths of depression and came to consciousness in war and to maturity in the confusion of world revolution — I don't need to tell you that your elders have made something of a mess of things. Things didn't turn out as we had thought they would in 1922, and somehow the hope and easy confidence we felt dissolved as more and more the articulate and vocal among us doubted their beliefs and believed their doubts.

Nor do I need to enumerate for you in sepulchral tone the problems that you face. You know them only too well. Perhaps you can solve them. I would not presume to tell you how to do it. This university has given you the tools with which to try. Moreover, even if I would guide you, I could not. What a man knows at fifty that he did not know at twenty is, for the most part, incommunicable. The laws, the aphorisms, the generalizations, the universal truths, the parables and the old saws — all of the observations about life which can be communicated handily in ready, verbal packages — are as well known to a man at twenty who has been attentive as to a man at fifty. He has been told them all, he has read them all, and he has probably repeated them all before he graduates from college; but he has not lived them all.

What he knows at fifty that he did not know at twenty boils down to something like this: The knowledge he has acquired with age is not the knowledge of formulas, or forms of words, but of people, places, actions — a knowledge not gained by words but by touch, sight, sound, victories, failures, sleeplessness, devotion, love — the human experiences and emotions of this earth and of oneself and other men; and perhaps, too, a little faith, and a little reverence for things you cannot see.

Nonetheless, I would speak to you not of the past, when my generation held its hopes so high, but rather of the future, and if I cannot advise you on how to solve the momentous problems of your future, perhaps I can venture to suggest some duties and, if you please, some rules of conduct that, it seems to me, devolve upon the educated man. I would speak, then, about the educated man and his government, and about the educated man and his university.

The political organization that goes by the name of the United States of America consists of no fewer than 155,000 governing units, school boards, conservation districts, municipalities, states, the nation, etc. It is operated by some one million elected officials, ranging from mosquito district trustee to President, and by some six million full-time employees. Our government is so large and so complicated that few understand it well and others barely understand it at all. Yet we must try to understand it and to make it function better.

For the power, for good or evil, of this American political organization is virtually beyond measurement. The decisions which it makes, the uses to which it devotes its immense resources, the leadership which it provides on moral as well as material questions, all appear likely to determine the fate of the modern world.

All this is to say that your power is virtually beyond measurement. For it is to you, to your enlightened attention, that American government must look for the sources of its power. You dare not, if I may say so, withhold your attention. For if you do, if those young Americans who have the advantage of education, perspective, and self-discipline do not participate to the fullest extent of their ability, America will stumble, and if America stumbles the world falls.

You know that our record as citizens in recent years has been something less than perfect. Too often our citizens have ignored their duty to their government. Too often they have not even bothered to vote. But this is not all. Participating in government in a democracy does not mean merely casting a ballot on election day. It means much more than that. It means an attitude, a moral view, and a willingness to assume a day-to-day responsibility. How many good citizens do you know who constantly deplore waste, inefficiency, and corruption in government, and who also go out and ring doorbells for candidates they believe in? Not very many. Far more say, "Politics is dirty" — and that is about their only protest about the quality of government, and far more use the word "politician" as a term of opprobrium, disrespect, and dishonor — and this in the land of Washington, Jefferson, and Lincoln. How many respectable citizens do you know who protest loudly about the lawlessness and venality but don't hesitate to fix a traffic ticket? And then there are the unscrupulous for whom anything goes if it is within the letter of the law, or at least not too far outside; the numerous kind for whom legality and morality are synonyms. "The Fix" has become endemic in our political life.

I would remind you of an axiom of political science! People get the kind of government they deserve. Your public servants serve you right. Our American government may be defined, perhaps, as the government that really cares about the people. Just so, our government demands, it depends upon, the care and the devotion of the people.

Now it is sadly true that there are corrupt officials that don't get caught, if not as many perhaps as the cynical suspect. It is also true that there are at every level of our government able, patient, patriotic, devoted public servants, but all too often their reward is ingratitude, contumely, and lately even investigation. In years gone by we required only of our career servants, upon whom the successful operation of this huge mechanism of government depends, that they serve at a financial sacrifice and that they serve with little glory or public recognition. Increasingly, it appears, we also require them to run the risk of being branded as "subversive," "undesirable," as "security risks." It becomes increasingly hard to attract good men to government, and no wonder. Thoughtful men do not enjoy living in an atmosphere of constant guerrilla warfare and suspicion.

You who have spent four years on this campus know better than most people that your greatest satisfactions, your greatest rewards, resulted from the free interplay of ideas. You know that your most penetrating insights resulted from the exchange and the interchange and clash of ideas. And I would remind you that just as a great university cannot operate in any but an atmosphere of intellectual freedom, neither can a great government. It is the function of the democratic form of government to nurture freedom. No less does the democratic form of government require freedom as the condition in which it can function at all.

I would suggest, then, that it is the duty of an educated man in America today to work actively to put good men into public office — and to defend them there against abuse and the ugly inclination we as human beings have to believe the worst. I would suggest that it is not enough merely to vote but that we, all of us, have the further obligation to think, and to maintain steadfastly the rights of all men to think freely. It is always true that when the citizens of a democracy become apathetic, a power vacuum is created, and corrupt men, or incompetents or worse rush in to fill it. But today our situation is even more dangerous than that. In ordinary times the corrupt or the incompetent can be suffered for a while and then ejected. But these are no ordinary times. The world's fate now hangs upon how well or how ill we in America conduct our affairs. And if a bad man is elected trustee of a sanitary district, or if an able man in Washington is left to shift for himself in the face of unjustified attack, then our government is diminished by that much — and even more because others will lose heart from his example. So you as educated, privileged people have a broad responsibility to protect and improve what you have inherited and what you would die to preserve — the concept of government by consent of the governed as the only tolerable way of life.

We in our country have, indeed, placed all of our faith, we have placed all of our hopes, upon the education, the intelligence, and the understanding of our people. We have said that ours is a government conducted by its citizens, and from this it follows that the government will be better conducted if its citizens are educated. It's as simple as that. We believe

[341]

that the people will find their way to the right solutions, given sufficient information. We believe with Lincoln, "Why should there not be a patient confidence in the ultimate justice of the people?" (although I must confess to having entertained certain private fleeting doubts upon occasion). We have bet all our chips, if you please, on the intellectual improvement of our people. This is a magnificent gamble — but it is a gamble, for it raises the question whether we have reached the awesome pinnacle of world power we now occupy too soon, before we have sufficiently elevated our national mind to lead the world wisely. Only the educated man entertains doubts, and doubt is the beginning of wisdom; but doubt is not wisdom's fulfillment, and in a time of crisis the man who doubts may fall prey to the strong dumb brute — to the man on horseback.

There is in the moiling masses of Asia a tremendous power, potentially the greatest power on earth, and today our enemies conspire to gain the mastery of this power. They have at their disposal, as we all know, a powerful weapon, for Communism is a perversion of the dream of justice. And while we see its leading attribute as the perversion, the illiterate, the toiling masses still have their eyes fixed on the dream.

We, too, have a powerful weapon, truth, and we gain our strength from our thoughtful citizenry, which seeks and holds the truth with both its heart and its mind. The question is, however, whether we have come to decisive responsibility too early, before we were ready, before we had matured sufficiently. No man can say with certainty. Personally I am optimistic and confident, but this question will not be answered tomorrow; it will be answered in your lifetime, and it will be answered in large part by you, the privileged American.

If I have made your tasks and your responsibilities sound formidable, which indeed they are, may I also remind you that this is what makes the prospects of your careers so exciting. There is a wonderful passage in Emerson — and happily I couldn't lay my hands on it — I'll spare you from it. I hope sometime you will read that essay. It says the time to live is not when everything is serene, but when all is tumult — when the old admits being compared with the new. This is the time of early morning, when it is fresh and exciting. I think this is your generation, I cannot be sure. Change is the order of life and difficulties its meat. You live in a time of historic change and of infinite difficulty. But do not let the difficulties distract you. Face the problems of your time you must, deal with them you must. But do not allow the alarms and excursions and partisanship of our political scene to distract you, do not let even the awful problems of the Atomic Age claim all your attention. Dare, rather, to live your lives fully, boldly; dare to study and to learn to cultivate the mind and the spirit, even though it isn't fashionable in your community. For though our people become prosperous as never before and though our foreign policy triumphs, these things are but instruments of the proper purpose, the higher purpose, of Western man — the cultivation of the mind and of the spirit.

It would be presumptuous, and out of character, for me to lecture you about your spirit. That I must leave to wiser, and to better men. But perhaps you'll forgive me if I draw on what experiences I have had — I have not always been an unemployed politician, you know — to say a word about intelligence and experience as attributes of the good judgment you will need — the good sense, if you please.

Don't be afraid to learn; to read, to study, to work, to try to know, because at the very best you can know very little. And don't above all things be afraid to think for yourself. Nothing has been, in my judgment, more disheartening about the contemporary scene the last several years in America than the growth of the popularity of unreason — of anti-intellectualism. One thinks of those chanting, screaming crowds that walked over precipices in Germany — and not so long ago. The conformists abominate thought. Thinking implies disagreement and disagreement implies non-conformity and non-conformity implies heresy and heresy implies disloyalty. So obviously thinking must be stopped. This is the routine. But I say to you that bawling is not a substitute for thinking and that reason is not the subversion but the salvation of freedom. And don't be afraid of unpopular positions, of driving upstream. All progress has resulted from people who took unpopular positions. All change is the result of a change in the contemporary state of mind. Don't be afraid of being out of tune with your environment, and above all pray God that you are not afraid to live, to live hard and fast. To my way of thinking it is not the years in your life but the life in your years that count in the long run. You'll have more fun, you'll do more and you'll get more, you'll give more satisfaction the more you know, the more you have worked, and the more you have lived. For yours is a great adventure at a stirring time in the annals of men.

"University" is a proud, a noble and ancient word. Around it cluster all of the values and the traditions which civilized people have for centuries prized more highly. The idea which underlies this university — any university — is greater than any of its physical manifestations; its classrooms, its laboratories, its clubs, its athletic plant, even the particular groups of faculty and students who make up its human element as of any given time. What is this idea? It is that the highest condition of man in this mysterious universe is the freedom of the spirit. And it is only truth that can set the spirit free.

The function of a university is, then, the search for truth and its communication to succeeding generations. Only as that function is performed steadfastly, conscientiously, and without interference, does the university realize its underlying purpose. Only so does the university keep faith with the great humanist tradition of which it is a part. Only so does it merit the honorable name that it bears.

When you depart, think occasionally upon your university's inherent ideas and purposes, as its outward trappings recede. Don't forget that Princeton is a university, as well as *your* university; and that it has obligations to the whole of mankind not just to you — obligations which it can neither ignore nor shirk, and which cannot, consistently with its honorable name and its place in the community of scholarship, be sacrificed to passing passions and prejudices.

The right to the serene pursuit of truth did not descend like manna from heaven; it was won by hard fighting, and the fight goes on and on to the end of time — even as the struggle between good and evil. In this continuing battle for freedom, Princeton and her sister universities are at the farthest front, and so should you be who are Princeton's children. As the archive of the Western mind, as the keeper of Western culture, the university has an obligation to transmit from one generation to the next the heritage of freedom — for freedom is the foundation of Western culture. As graduates of this university, as individuals who have made in it an investment of the golden, irretrievable years of your lives, you have an obligation to oppose the efforts of anyone, for whatever reason or in the service of whatever interest, to divert Princeton or any sister institution from her classic objective. If you are to be true to your democratic traditions and realize your own best selves you cannot, I suggest, do less.

And I hope you will carry away with you some of the wise serenity of the timeless courage, the unhurried objectivity which is the atmosphere of Princeton and which represents the collective imprint of its founders, students, and teachers who have gone before you.

I came here last night in darkness, after an absence of four or five years. I came with an old friend, an old classmate. We drove a little through the campus, after dusk. It was soft, the air fresh with the beginning of spring. I thought of some words that I read here long ago, written by the English poet, Alfred Noyes, who stayed for a time on the Princeton campus. They went something like this if I am not mistaken:

> Now lamp-lit gardens in the blue dusk shine
> Through dogwood red and white,
> And round the gray quadrangles, line by line,

The windows fill with light,
  Where Princeton calls to Magdalen, tower to tower,
  Twin lanthorns of the law,
And those cream-white magnolia boughs embower
  The halls of old Nassau.[121]

Sentimental? Yes. Nostalgic? Perhaps. Yet beautiful, true. Your days are short here; this is the last of your springs. And now in the serenity and quiet of this lovely place, touch the depths of truth, feel the hem of Heaven. You will go away with old, good friends. And don't forget when you leave why you came.

After his speech at Princeton University, Stevenson delivered a speech at Charlotte, North Carolina, and spent a few days vacationing with Mr. and Mrs. Ernest L. Ives at Southern Pines, North Carolina. The following letter was written from there.

To Carol Evans [122]

[no date]

Miss E —

Be sure to send copies of the Godkin lectures & the Princeton speech — if you have it — to Adlai.

Also please deposit this check & the voucher in the 1954 income tax file.

It's raining and overcast & I despair of seeing the sun in the sunny south.

AES

Bill [Blair]'s bearing up in spite of the dullness — but John Fell was certainly smart to head to Florida and abandon his old man.

Stevenson had suffered from kidney stones, for which he underwent an operation in June, 1952.[123] A second attack occurred on March 28, 1954, during his stay with Mr. and Mrs. Ives. He spent three days at Duke University Hospital in Durham, North Carolina, for tests and was released.

[121] From *Collected Poems*, Vol. III, by Alfred Noyes. Copyright, 1906, Renewal, 1934, by Alfred Noyes. Reprinted by courtesy of J. B. Lippincott Company.
[122] This handwritten letter is in the possession of Miss Evans.
[123] See *The Papers of Adlai E. Stevenson*, Vol. III, pp. 572–576.

To Alicia Patterson [124]

April 5, 1954

. . . I landed in Chicago an hour ago — just a month from the day I left and what a month — Florida, Mass. R.I., N.Y., N.J. & N. Carolina — and not a days peace except in a hospital with doctors peering at me. Its a damn good thing I didnt try to fly back to the Black River [125] & get caught there with my wretched kidney stone. . . .

After the Miami clambake I spent a week with the [Averell] Harrimans at Hobe Sound working day & night on my lectures for Harvard — and working in a vacation spot is a moral exercise of which I've had enough! I came down from Cambridge to N.Y. with John Fell on a Saturday afternoon, took him to the theatre and went on to Princeton Sunday afternoon after a jolly day "conferring" with the N.Y. pols [politicians]. There was nothing I could do so I didn't assail you by telephone. . . .

Are you coming this way and when. I need a little of that cold impersonal wisdom of yours. . . .

AES

Joseph Rauh, a Washington lawyer and vice chairman of Americans for Democratic Action, wrote Stevenson on April 3, praising the speech in Miami and adding: "Most of what is favorable in the McCarthy picture today can be traced directly to that speech. Unfortunately much of what is unfavorable in that picture is equally traceable to the unbelievable timidity and silence of otherwise responsible Democratic senators."

To Joseph L. Rauh

April 6, 1954

Dear Joe:

Thank you so much for your heartening letter about my late utterances. I hope the brethren on the Hill are not feeling too badly about them. I saw Hubert Humphrey here last night and he said that his own view had changed about the wisdom of what I had done in Miami, and he heartily approved. He could give me no assurance, however, that his attitude was uniform on the Hill.

With kind wishes and my thanks, I am

Sincerely yours,

[124] This handwritten letter is in the possession of Adlai E. Stevenson III.
[125] Miss Patterson's estate in Georgia. See note 7 to Part Three, p. 193.

To Lady Mary Spears [126]

April 6, 1954

Dear Mary:

I was so glad to have your letter and to hear that there is some prospect of a glimpse of you this autumn. I don't know why you persist in coming only during campaign intervals, but I suspect it is the best opportunity to see America in its nakedness.

I was delighted to hear that you had finished another book. How you do it is beyond me. It takes me hours, days and infinite anguish even to write a simple speech, let alone a lecture. I have just finished three lectures at Harvard and they are my last!

While there I had a glimpse, all too brief, of Barbara Ward, [127] who is your ecstatic admirer, as you know.

My love to you both.

Affectionately,

ADLAI

P.S. I have not seen Betty [128] since the autumn but I talked with her on the phone in New York the other day and she reports encouraging progress.

The spectacle of President Eisenhower's legislative program being bogged down in Congress prompted Democratic charges of Republican "inaction," while the Republicans replied that the President was at a disadvantage in the Senate, where Democrats outnumbered Republicans. Senator Harley M. Kilgore, Democrat of West Virginia, delivered a speech in Indiana on March 27 charging the Republicans with an obsessive concern with their investigating committees "while constructive legislative work slows to a standstill." [129]

To Harley M. Kilgore [130]

April 6, 1954

Dear Senator:

I have just seen your splendid speech of March 27 and I find to my

---

[126] The original is in the possession of General Sir Louis Spears.

[127] The English author and writer for the *Economist*, who was on a three-month tour of the United States at the time. See her article "Report to Europe on America," *New York Times Magazine*, June 20, 1954, p. 7.

[128] Mrs. Ralph Hines, Lady Spears's niece and sister of Ellen Stevenson.

[129] See the New York *Times*, March 28, 1954.

[130] A copy is in A.E.S., I.S.H.L.

great satisfaction that we are in accord. That you saw fit to quote from a speech of mine flatters me immensely. I think what we are seeing is precisely what we foresaw, that the Republican party is incapable of governing in its present condition, and we hope the price the country pays for its re-education is not too heavy.

Cordially yours,

Leon B. Poullada, a member of the U.S. Foreign Service stationed at Lahore, Pakistan, had accompanied Stevenson on part of his trip through Pakistan the year before. He wrote Stevenson on February 26, 1954, enclosing pictures of the Khyber Pass area, which they had visited together, and a summary of the Indian press, prepared by the United States embassy in Delhi, regarding the impression Stevenson had made during his stay in India.

To Leon B. Poullada [131]

April 6, 1954

Dear Leon:

I was delighted to have your letter and the enclosures, which reminded me so vividly of our days together which, for me, were exciting and fascinating. I am just back today after an absence in the East and South of more than a month, and I shall take the first opportunity to read your article.[132]

I hope you don't despair of penetrating the Asian veil. I had a feeling that you had already proceeded further in that direction than most of the Americans I had met. I laugh at myself when I think of the temerity of myself, as well as my predecessors, in undertaking to write about that area, but we must try to understand and sometimes ever [even?] superficial reactions are not too erroneous, especially when there are opportunities to check them with people like yourself.

I was much interested in what you said about the undertone of unconscious anxiety to see more rather than less American influence. Perhaps you have something there that I had not wholly felt.

With warm regards, in which Bill Blair joins me, I am

Cordially yours,

P.S. As far as Bill is concerned he would just as soon never see Nathiagali or mutton curry again.[133] But I am still game!

[131] A copy is in A.E.S., I.S.H.L.
[132] "Economy . . . True . . . and False," *Foreign Service Journal*, May, 1954.
[133] See *The Papers of Adlai E. Stevenson*, Vol. V.

On April 1, Lloyd Garrison wrote expressing concern at the news that Stevenson had had to be taken to a hospital while in North Carolina. As Stevenson's lawyer, Mr. Garrison also said that Cass Canfield, of Harper & Brothers, was eager for a book on his world trip. Stevenson in May definitely abandoned the plan to do a lengthy book. Later in 1954, Harper published his Harvard lectures under the title Call to Greatness.

To Lloyd K. Garrison

April 6, 1954

Dear Lloyd:

"Privately," and evidently not much more privately than the front page of the newspapers, I have a stone below the kidney on the left side which bit me savagely the other day in North Carolina and I was carried off half unconscious to a distant hospital. Whether to have the thing operated on, which would mean a month of incapacity at least, or to live with it against the hope that it will pass away or be more accessible as it works down, is the question. I am suffering no pain at the moment, never felt better, but the ugly monster can strike again without warning and it is sort of a nuisance when you are traveling and trying to maintain difficult schedules, etc.

I was glad to have the news about the book. Actually, I dread the job of getting to work again what with all the everlasting distractions hereabouts, but I think I will have a try at it if I can have a little uninterrupted time. In any event, I must go ahead with the lectures and I am trying to persuade Cass [Canfield] to get them ready promptly so that they can come out promptly if the book is abandoned.

You are quite right that the great chance for important leadership is in the foreign field, but I am at a loss for positive proposals beyond what I attempted to do at Harvard, i.e., settle down for a long, steady, sober pull, which will lift no hearts and splash no water.

Some time I hope to get together with some of the bright boys on foreign affairs and talk it out. It is all so difficult to find time for half the things one would like to do. The sort of people I should like to meet with are [Dean] Acheson, [Dean] Rusk, [Paul] Nitze, [George] Kennan and perhaps one or two others like Chet Bowles.

Yours,

Shortly after he returned to Chicago from the South, Stevenson suffered another attack of kidney stones. He entered Passavant Hospital, where he was operated on successfully on April 12, and he was released on April 20.

To Mrs. Franklin D. Roosevelt [134]

April 9, 1954

Dear Mrs. Roosevelt:

I regret that I shall not have an opportunity to greet you in Chicago at the convention of Americans for Democratic Action.[135] A long time ago I made some engagements in Indiana for this weekend, but instead of going to Indiana I have gone to the hospital. And instead of talking with Indiana Democrats, I'm talking with Chicago doctors, which should provide even better opportunity for missionary work. The trouble is they are doing most of the talking!

At all events I am out of commission and so I must content myself with this inadequate greeting to you and to the ADA, which was formed to keep alive our progressive movement and to combat the influence of Communism in the liberal community. Those seem to me very worthy objectives. Yet I have noticed that your organization is often attacked and denounced by some people and newspapers, but without specifying the reason. I hope it does not mean that there are those among us who don't believe that you can be *for* greater freedom, justice and opportunity for all Americans and *against* Communism at the same time.

With respectful and affectionate regards to you and best wishes to my friends in ADA, I am

Cordially yours,

To Mr. and Mrs. James F. Oates [136]

April 18, 1954

My dear Oates' —

Thanks for your letters and thanks for *not* sending any more flowers. At one of my lowest moments I heard one interne mumble to another while they were all peering down at me attentively that my room looked and smelled like a wake. And one night I had a dream that I was Dion O'Bannion [137] dying gallantly for sin among my flowers.

[134] The original is in the Franklin D. Roosevelt Library, Hyde Park, New York.

[135] Mrs. Roosevelt was honorary chairman of the organization.

[136] A Chicago lawyer who had been a partner in the firm of which Stevenson was a member until 1941. See *The Papers of Adlai E. Stevenson*, Vol. I, p. 209. This handwritten letter is in the possession of Mr. Oates.

[137] A Chicago gang leader during the early years of Prohibition, who maintained a flower shop as a front and did a flourishing business supplying floral arrangements for the numerous and lavish funerals of Chicago's underworld. Rival gangsters shot him to death at noon on November 10, 1924, in his own shop.

But the carnation I've worn proudly on my dressing gown lapel during my recuperative walks in the corridor — fairly makes a fellow feel that he's walking, not hobbling! And now for home at last and I hope a glimpse sometime of my beloved Oates —

Love
ADLAI

To Alicia Patterson [138]

April 19, 1954

Dear Alicia —

I've had a major operation for a damn kidney stone and been really sick in the hospital for two weeks. Old stuff to you but new to me. But soon I'll be released to go to Libertyville to recuperate, thank heavens. But I'll have to cancel my trip to Louisville for the [Kentucky] Derby and most everything else for a couple of months I guess. So I'll miss a glimpse of you and the ponies.* Let me know when you can come to Libertyville for a visit & thanks for your note.

Love
ADLAI

* Hope you win again. Make a bet for me if you have a good chance. $10-10-10.

Stevenson had spent a short vacation on Dick Jenkins's ranch after the 1952 campaign. Mr. Jenkins was in St. Mary's Hospital in Tucson, Arizona, recuperating from a heart attack when the following telegram was sent.

To Dick Jenkins

April 20, 1954

AM JUST OUT OF THE HOSPITAL AND GOING HOME TO RECUPERATE. EXPECTING YOU TO FOLLOW MY LEAD PROMPTLY. CHIN UP AND BEST WISHES FROM AN OLD KIDNEY STONE.

A.E.S.

To Richard J. Daley [139]

April 20, 1954

With that splendid ticket headed by Paul Douglas the Democratic

[138] This handwritten letter is in the possession of Adlai E. Stevenson III.
[139] Chairman of the Cook County Democratic party organization. The original handwritten draft is in the possession of Carol Evans.

party is offering the people of Illinois as much as it ever has in history. I think the people will take advantage of it in Nov. I will leave no stone unturned to help. In fact I have already started and I am only sorry I cannot be there tonight.[140] Regards to your distinguished guest and my esteemed friend Senator [John F.] Kennedy.

AES

To David L. Cohn [141]

April 22, 1954

Dear David:

Thanks to a kind fairy I have whiled away a happy interval during my painful convalescence reading "Politics In A God-Fearin' Key." [142] It is utterly delightful and it also reminds me that I am committed to speak at a Hillbilly festival at Meridian, Mississippi on May 26. I may have long since mentioned to you that I submitted to this importunity from Governor [Hugh L.] White months and months ago. The doctor tells me there is a better than even chance I will be fit enough by then to undertake the journey.

It would be wonderful if Dave Cohn was with me, and it is almost indispensable that some of his southern wisdom be with me! If you have any bright ideas for a politician for a speech for a Hillbilly Festival and an enormous crowd send them along, Godless or God-Fearin'.

Yours,
ADLAI

To William Benton [143]

April 22, 1954

Dear Bill:

I have just seen your letter from Rome. It is all very exciting, and, of course, I am delighted and flattered that the Bentons would really like to have John Fell come along. I have passed the letter along to him with instructions to take it up with his mother. It is all a little difficult, for reasons that you can understand, and may take some time, and I am

---

[140] The Democratic party in Illinois was holding a fund-raising dinner after the primary in which Senator Paul H. Douglas was nominated.

[141] The original is in the Mississippi collection, University of Mississippi Library.

[142] *Saturday Review*, April 3, 1954.

[143] The original is in the possession of the estate of William Benton. Mr. Benton died on March 18, 1973. At the time this volume went to press, his papers were to be distributed to his widow and four children, all of whom had indicated that they wished to deposit the papers at the University of Chicago.

self-conscious about keeping you waiting with such an exciting proposition to offer someone else. I shall try to let you hear from us as promptly as I can.

I have done with the wretched operation and after a couple of ugly weeks in the hospital I am back on the Libertyville farm now recuperating. The doctor has ordered everything cancelled until the end of May, by which time I ought to be restored to a reasonable degree of health and strength. It has been a sharp warning to me and I propose to behave myself henceforth in spite of the demoralizing influence of Senator Benton, Robert Hutchins, et al.

Hastily,
ADLAI

David Lloyd, executive director of the Harry S. Truman Library, Incorporated,[144] *wrote Stevenson on April 13: "I think you have been making some excellent speeches of late and that their effect on the opposition has been even more remarkable. Never in my recollection . . . has a defeated candidate for the Presidency had so much influence or been regarded with so much awe, if not respect, by the opposition."*

To David D. Lloyd

April 22, 1954

Dear Dave:

Thanks for your letter! It rather inflated me, when I was altogether too inflated anyway. However, I am returning to normal size in all directions and I hope maybe somewhat less size in some directions.

Warm regards.

Cordially yours,

To Rabbi Jacob J. Weinstein [145]

April 22, 1954

Dear Rabbi:

Ever so many thanks for your note and for that wonderful prayer. The Lord, with an assist from Dr. Riba [146] and doubtless the Chaplain of the

[144] The Harry S. Truman Library, Incorporated, was the private organization which raised the money for the construction of the library building. The Harry S. Truman Library did not come into existence until 1957.

[145] Rabbi of the K.A.M. Temple, Chicago. The original is in the possession of Rabbi Weinstein.

[146] Dr. Leander W. Riba, the Chicago surgeon who performed Stevenson's kidney stone operation.

Plumbers Union Local 130, "doest wondrously indeed." I am mending rapidly at last.

Cordially yours,
ADLAI

To Paul H. Douglas

April 22, 1954

Dear Paul:

So many thanks for your note to the hospital. It was an ugly ordeal but, in the vernacular, I should be telling you about hospitals! [147] I hear the party the other night was a great success and that things look good around the Democratic front, in Cook County at least. We have repair work to do downstate, I have no doubt, and it will not be easy what with the intramural struggles. I think you must take care that we don't have any changes for the worse in the State Committee headquarters. For some time it will be difficult for me to do much, I am afraid, but I hear alarming rumors that have probably come to your attention too.

I am mending slowly and will probably be myself again, sometime, although at the moment it hardly seems to me likely.

Cordially yours,

To Mr. and Mrs. Wilson W. Wyatt

April 22, 1954

Dear Ann and Wilson:

So many thanks for those exquisite flowers that all but cracked a table top. We finally had to divide the Wyatts in two or three parts and I am not sure but what some of the Wyatts ended up in the psychiatric ward!

It was bad enough to have this horrid misfortune but what's worse, I am now forbidden to come to Louisville or to do much of anything for another six weeks. After a winter of no fun whatever, this was to be my big adventure. I am so very sorry; and I wish you would both come up and stay a week-end with me to talk things over and hear about my operation. If you wait very long I may forget some of the details.

Affectionately,

Joseph Bohrer, Stevenson's lifelong friend from their boyhood days in Bloomington, Illinois, sent him a copy of the remarks of outgoing Governor Joseph W. Fifer, Mr. Bohrer's grandfather, to the Illinois legislature at

[147] Senator Douglas had been severely wounded in World War II.

the inauguration of Governor John Peter Altgeld in 1893. Fifer, who had just been defeated by Altgeld, said: "We do not steal away from place and power in disgrace and shame; but, with the just pride of duties performed and pledges redeemed, we proudly place in the hands of our victorious opponents a high trust and a grave responsibility." Mr. Bohrer wrote of the speech: "Probably as good as anything between 1893 and when you came upon the scene."

To Joseph F. Bohrer [148]

April 22, 1954

Dear Joe:

I was glad to have your letter at the hospital and that morsel of Governor Fifer's exquisite eloquence. Somehow it seems to me that our political dialogue has grown coarser and coarser, and this reminder of the gallantry of partisanship in those rugged days all but convinces me. I shall not "throw it away." I shall keep it, perhaps memorize it, and certainly plagiarize it!

I am back from the hospital after an ugly ordeal, sans stone, sans strength, joie d'vivre and most everything else! But they assured me I will be myself again some time somehow.

Love to you both,

ADLAI

On April 23, Arthur M. Schlesinger, Jr., wrote Stevenson that Alfred W. Stern, a Lincoln collector, was unable to find the Lincoln story that Stevenson had used in his speech conceding defeat in 1952. Schlesinger added: "This is a plea to you to come clean. As one historian skeptically remarked at the Stern luncheon, 'It all sounds to me more like Stevenson than like Lincoln.'"

To Benjamin P. Thomas [149]

[no date]

Dear Ben —

And now I really am in trouble! I can't for the life of me remember where or when I first heard this "Lincoln story" but I know it has been in the back of my head for decades and somehow I have always asso-

---

[148] The original is in the possession of Mr. Bohrer.
[149] This handwritten letter is in the possession of Mrs. Benjamin P. Thomas.

ciated it with Lincoln. I don't believe I could possibly have dreamed it up. Help, help! — and if you can't no one can!

Yrs

ADLAI

To Mrs. Humphrey Bogart [150]

April 29, 1954

Dear Betty:

It was sweet of you to write me and I was enchanted with your thoughtful and heartening letter. I have been discharged after a brutal carving and I am now back on my little farm, *sans* stone and also *sans ma force et ma gaiete.* But I am assured that I shall be better than ever — some time.

I hope you had a gay journey abroad and shall look forward to hearing about it, either here or there, although the prospects of "there" are remote indeed.

Warmest good wishes.

Cordially yours,

Mrs. Roosevelt wrote Stevenson that Mr. Lewi Tonks wanted to work for his election and to serve in his administration.

To Mrs. Franklin D. Roosevelt

April 29, 1954

Dear Mrs. Roosevelt:

So many thanks for your letter of April 12 and the enclosure from Mr. Lewi Tonks. I have written to him. Many thanks. I shall keep him in mind, although the prospects of that "Stevenson Administration" seem to me both distant and distasteful at the moment! I am recovering from my hideous ordeal but it has been an unpleasant shock and I shall have to take it easy for a while.

With affectionate best wishes to you, I am

Sincerely yours,

Clayton Fritchey sent Stevenson an advance copy of the June Demo-cratic Digest. He also enclosed the text of a statement by Sam Bright-man of the Democratic National Committee.

[150] A copy is in A.E.S., I.S.H.L.

To Clayton Fritchey

May 3, 1954

Dear Clayton:

Maybe it was just as well you didn't use it. After all, with all those solemn Republicans around somebody might not understand what Sam meant by "the rock"!

I hope the June Digest proves good for my kidney; I know it is no good for my incision where every laugh causes pain!

Yours,

To John Paulding Brown [151]

May 3, 1954

Dear John:

So many thanks for your letter. I have had a grisly time of it but I will not be able to come to Washington. However, I am mending rapidly.

I quite agree that the ghastly vaudeville would be worth it if McCarthy disappeared in the ashes, but it looks as though the Secretary of the Army was hardly demolishing him yet.[152] Many thanks my brave lad.

Yours,
ADLAI

To Paul H. Douglas

May 3, 1954

Dear Paul:

I have had a bad time of it in the hospital but I am coming to life gradually.

Please find enclosed my check for $500 as a contribution to your campaign. I wish it could be more and will try to improve on this later on when I have paid the hospitals, doctors, nurses and sundry other creditors!

All good wishes.

Cordially yours,

[151] A Washington lawyer whom Stevenson had known since 1933–1934. The original was in the possession of the late Mr. Brown.
[152] The Army-McCarthy hearings were being broadcast by television.

In response to Stevenson's undated letter of late April, 1954, Mr. Thomas supplied the source of the Lincoln quotation that Stevenson had used in his speech conceding defeat in 1952.

To Benjamin P. Thomas [153]

May 4, 1954

Dear Ben —

You have saved me from the horrid fate of academic ridicule. Proudly, defiantly, I've scattered copies of your letter — with your advice to Harvard skeptics underlined in red crayon!!

I have, as Pepys puts it, been "cut of the stone" and am mending rapidly. Pray heaven I can come to Springfield soon — as long as none of you will come to see me!

Ys

ADLAI

P.S. Rousseau was similarly afflicted and Dave Cohen [Cohn] tells me sometime went walking in the woods at Fontainbleau always attended by a clutch of beautiful young duchesses. Occasionally, suffering from the stone, he would turn aside for painful relief in the bushes. But when he emerged, fortunate man, there were the glorious duchesses waiting to mop his brow with scented linen and give him their lovely, youthful shoulders to lean upon.

Me? Well the contrasts between Libertyville and Fontainbleau are sharp — but I did have a Swedish nurse and I wonder how good the Duchesses were at massage!

Blessings, thanks and love to Sally [154] —

AES

To Richard Patterson

May 5, 1954

Dear Mr. Patterson:

I am sending along my check for $70.00 to the Truman Library Fund and with it my profound regret that I cannot join you at the dinner celebrating President Truman's 70th birthday. Tell him, if you will please, that I am recovering from a geological expedition into my interior. The explorers came out with some minerals that are of no value

---

[153] This handwritten letter is in the possession of Mrs. Benjamin P. Thomas.
[154] Mrs. Thomas.

to man or beast, but they assure me the operation was a great success, and it *is* true that I am still alive.

I venture to say that President Truman will find in the temperance of time a unique place in our annals. History assigned him some of our most grave national decisions and he made them decisively and wisely, I think. He enriched the world's vision of a resolute and magnanimous America that would spend and struggle and fight, if need be, for freedom, peace and justice. Certainly he left none in doubt where he stood on the great issues of his troubled time in office.

And like few of his predecessors he has suffered the ugly barbarities that we Americans who honor so volubly the republican form of government seem to reserve for our highest officer.

His papers are the record of his stirring times and a national historical treasure. I share the hope of all of you that they will be suitably housed in reach of all scholars. Hence the enclosed token, and I am disappointed not to be there to do honor on a birthday of traditional significance to a great American whom I am proud to call my friend.

Cordially yours,

James Reston wrote in the New York Times, *May 4, 1954:*

Secretary of State John Foster Dulles will face the most serious criticism of his career tomorrow when he returns from the Geneva conference.

He is scheduled to report to Congressional leaders of both parties Wednesday morning and to the Senate Foreign Relations Committee Wednesday afternoon.

The criticisms being leveled against him here are these:

He proposed in public a policy of "united action" to block the Communist aggression in Indo-China before finding out in advance whether he had the support of the Congress, the French and the British, whose backing of the "united action" policy was known by him to be essential.

He went to London and Paris to press for adoption of this policy on the eve of the Geneva conference with the Communists on Indo-China and was met (a) with a public refusal by the British, and (b) with a French request for immediate United States air intervention in the war. The intervention was refused by Washington.

The result of these things was a public demonstration, not of "united action" by the Western Powers, but of "disunited inaction," which greatly weakened the Western position at Geneva and exposed American leadership to its worst diplomatic defeat since the fall of Continental China.

The criticism of the Secretary of State is being heard not only on Capitol Hill but in the embassies of friendly countries, in the Defense Department, and even in the State Department.

To James Reston [155]

May 6, 1954

Dear Scotty —

A bulletin from a convalescent: Your piece of May 4 — Bravo! That weird performance was a *major* blunder. And now after years of deprecating Korea, Truman's war, etc., followed by "massive retaliation" and defense cuts how are they going to sell Americans on Indo China quickly? Or are the advertising boys moving back in?

Kidney stones are no good — but *you're* good for them!

Cordially —

The New York Times, *March 28, 1954, published a letter from Lewis Mumford appealing to the American government to stop the continued development of weapons of total destruction. He pointed out that the U.S.S.R. had "equal scientific powers" and there was the possibility someone might be overcome by paranoia and trigger a holocaust. He concluded that submission to Communism was better than the final destruction of civilization.*

To Lewis Mumford [156]

May 10, 1954

Dear Mr. Mumford:

I have read your letter and the clipping from the *Times* with interest and sympathy.

I should have responded long ago, but I have been diverted by many things — mostly internal!

I share your sense of urgency concerning the problems raised by these dreadful weapons. I must confess, however, that I do not see that any form of unilateral action or renunciation by the United States or by the free nations will have much effect except to worsen our predicament. Your estimate, I take it, would be that such action on our part would in

[155] This handwritten letter is in the possession of Mr. Reston.
[156] A typewritten draft, with handwritten interlineations, is in the possession of Carol Evans.

some way pierce "the strong political armor of our present enemies," presumably leading to political reactions within the Soviet Empire which would prevent the Soviet leaders from exploiting our military weakness. I would be less than frank if I did not say that such an estimate seems to me recklessly optimistic, and that here, as elsewhere, weakness would surely tempt aggression and strengthen the most fanatical among our enemies. It rather seems to me that the course you propose, if I understand it, would invite perpetual dread of what the inscrutable Russians might be up to, and, in a state of growing intimidation, compound our anxieties rather than relieve them. In the end this course might be far more "catastrophic" than present policies (though that is saying a good deal I quickly confess!)

Until we can establish some form of effective international control, in short, I do not see how we can concede the atomic race to the USSR and cease atomic experimentation while the Soviet Union prosecutes it. We could not escape thereby, it seems to me, our responsibility for the hideous possible consequences of unilateral atomic disarmament.

Surely we are involved in an ironic moral dilemma — that our possession of these ghastly weapons, which promise to destroy the world in another war, may yet be the best hope of preventing that war. It is a slim hope perhaps; yet I cannot but feel that the existence of our thermonuclear stockpile is a better deterrent to Soviet expansion than the unilateral destruction of that stockpile would be.

These somber reflections do not much help the crisis of total extermination which, as you eloquently and rightly point out, hangs over us more every day. I certainly am without conviction that I see all the points clearly or that I have thought these problems through. Our nation, depressed by the sheer immensity and fatefulness of these questions, for the present at least I don't see how we can sensibly entertain any doubts that Soviet totalitarianism is bent on extending its power as far as the weakness outside will permit; I believe that our atomic strength has been to some degree a shield against such expansion; I doubt if it is much longer now that we are coming into balance, but I would not like to take the responsibility for the terror and the tyranny which might well result from the removal of the shield.

I have, as you may know, made several earnest statements during the past six months about disarmament or limitation. In that direction I think we must never rest or despair.

You were good to write me and I am flattered. We have not talked about the cobalt bomb which must bring us *without its development* very close to the end of this madness.

Sincerely yours,

To Mrs. Walter Baumgarten, Jr. [157]

May 11, 1954

Dear Judy:

I am sure your prayers did it! My recovery is speedy, but never as speedy as one would wish, and I am glad that sympathetic doctor spouse of yours understands what it is like.

I had enchanting letters from the dear Aunts [158] and also flowers, just at the right time, after my first glories had faded.

We shall hope to see our beloved St. Louis kinfolk at Tim's [159] wedding.

Love to all,

To Anna Melissa Graves [160]

May 11, 1954

Dear Miss Graves:

Thank you for your letter. I remember so well our meeting long ago in Russia [161] and I was delighted to hear from you again.

Evidently you do not keep in close touch with contemporary American journals because there have been countless articles about seeing ourselves as others see us. Indeed, I have spoken and written on that subject not infrequently myself. I am quite familiar with all you have reported about attitudes, especially in France where I spent a month last year and spoke with everyone, from Auriol [162] to the butcher. For your information I enclose a copy of a speech I made last September on my return from a long journey around the world and also one in Florida more recently. There have been others on the foreign and domestic aspects of McCarthyism.

I had hoped we would have done with McCarthy long before this but, of course, the administration has profited from him politically and it has not been until he began to attack them directly that they have fought back. I should think that people living abroad, such as yourself, could do a great deal to preserve the proper perspective of America by keeping these excesses in proper proportion in the minds of foreigners. I was

---

157 A copy is in A.E.S., I.S.H.L.
158 Julia Hardin and Letitia Stevenson.
159 Timothy Ives, Stevenson's nephew.
160 A copy is in A.E.S., I.S.H.L.
161 For Stevenson's trip to Russia in 1926, see *The Papers of Adlai E. Stevenson*, Vol. I, pp. 167–169; Davis, *A Prophet in His Own Country*, pp. 153–159.
162 Vincent Auriol, first president of the French Fourth Republic (1947–1954).

personally astonished how many Americans resident abroad seemed rattled and out of focus about their country.

I am sorry you saw fit to suggest that I write through rose-colored glasses. I don't know what you have read, but I write as I see things and as responsibly as I can, and I certainly did not see "what I wanted to see" on this last journey any more than you evidently do in your country. As to seeing the "boughts," I saw and talked with every, I repeat *every* chief of state, foreign minister, etc., from Tokyo to London. If they were *all* "bought" they didn't talk that way to me, and I suppose I have shared more intimately the confidence of more of them than anyone alive.

Sincerely yours,

P.S. Let me put it this way on rereading this hasty dictation: America is *not* "taken in" by McCarthy; *some* Americans are and the Republican party has used him until recently as a paid speaker. As to my being "calmed" about the U.S.S.R. by somebody, I'm afraid that is quite impossible and that after years of association with those people during and since the war, after extensive observation of their methods here and everywhere, anyone who could be tolerant of their methods or ignorant of their objectives must like what I detest or detest what I like.

A.E.S.

Ralph McGill, editor of the Atlanta Constitution, *wrote that his wife suffered from kidney stones and he therefore had some understanding of what Stevenson had gone through. Mr. McGill praised an article by Gerald Johnson in the* New Republic, *April 12, 1954, entitled "The Superficial Aspect." In this bitingly satirical article, Mr. Johnson wrote among other things that whether Stevenson could defeat President Eisenhower in an election was irrelevant, but that his ability "to eradicate some of the idiocies" in politics was certain. He concluded with his wholehearted endorsement of Stevenson.*

To Ralph McGill [163]

May 11, 1954

Dear Ralph:

I was delighted to have your letter, and the story of your wife's appalling misery with this ugly affliction has squeezed the last ounce of self pity out of me! And that is something else I have to be grateful to you

---

[163] The original is in the possession of Mrs. Ralph McGill.

for. I hope and pray that with her next kidney operation she is through with this horrid business.

I *did* read Gerald Johnson's article, but I wish I felt a little more enthusiastic for the goal he so graciously fixes for me.

With warmest wishes and salutations to Mrs. McGill and that fine boy, I am

Cordially yours,

To Harry S. Truman

May 12, 1954

Dear Mr. President:

I have read your speech to the Birthday Dinner in defense of the Executive.[164] I think it an utterance of enduring consequence regardless of the timeliness in the context of these lamentable times. Moreover, I am tempted to believe that it may do the Executive some positive good which will benefit us all.

We all, as citizens, have you now to thank for something more. I am sure I shall feel the same way when I have an opportunity to read your address to the National Press Club.

I am mending rapidly from my unhappy adventure in the hospital, but I was bitterly disappointed to miss the dinner in Washington and your birthday celebration in New York.

With warmest respect and regards to you and Mrs. Truman, I am

Respectfully,

On May 6, Senator Lyndon B. Johnson criticized President Eisenhower's handling of American policy toward Indochina and he ridiculed Vice President Nixon, ascribing one of Nixon's statements to the Nixons' dog, Checkers, and claiming that President Roosevelt's dog, Fala, would never have made such a statement.[165]

To Lyndon B. Johnson

May 12, 1954

Dear Lyndon:

I have at last had an opportunity to read what the others heard in Washington. It was a grand speech and stirred my blood and funnybone. I only hope it doesn't stimulate the kidneys. I can't stand much more!

Yours,

[164] See the New York *Times*, May 9, 1954.
[165] See the New York *Times*, May 7, 1954.

To Loring Merwin

May 17, 1954

Dear Bud:

Now that I am restored to the land of the living, I must report another gripe. I am informed from several quarters that Martin Agronsky [166] has been dropped by WJBC.[167] I wonder if this is true and, if so, for what reason. Some time I would like to talk to you about the dangers which concern many thoughtful people of this spreading and coercive conformity.

Yours,

To Mrs. Franklin D. Roosevelt [168]

May 17, 1954

Dear Mrs. Roosevelt:

Thank you so much for your sweet letter. When I read in the newspaper of your travels, energy and productivity I am the more mortified that I fell by the wayside. I have recovered rapidly and soundly but I shall never catch up with you.

Affectionately and devotedly,

Yours,

ADLAI

Mr. Truman wrote on May 17, expressing his appreciation for Stevenson's letter of May 12. He ended his letter by writing that he hoped Stevenson would recover soon and would advise the Democrats what to do to win the upcoming congressional and presidential election. Truman added that he would always regard Stevenson as the leader of the party.

To Harry S. Truman

May 19, 1954

Dear Mr. President:

I have just read your letter — and have a collector's item for my descendants! Thank you from the bottom of a full heart.

[166] Washington correspondent for the American Broadcasting Company, 1943–1964, and recipient of the Peabody award for distinguished reporting, 1952; later with the Columbia Broadcasting System.

[167] The Bloomington radio station owned by the *Pantagraph*.

[168] The original is in the Franklin D. Roosevelt Library, Hyde Park, New York.

As to telling *you* what to do to win the Congressional elections; well, I have tried a lot of foolish things in my life, but I shan't try that! I think you have done much on this trip East to set the tone and the direction for the campaign. I hope I can hew to that line. The bipartisanship problem seems to me infinitely complicated by both the Republicans' political indifference to bipartisanship in the past and their present apparent reluctance to use Democrats in policy forming positions. I really don't know how we are going to get very far until we can erase some vivid history and also slake the patronage thirst of the Republican National Committee. Both are Herculean tasks and every day they contrive to make them worse.

I hope we can talk of these and many things before long. I am almost fit again and doing my best to catch up with you.

Faithfully yours,

To Arthur M. Schlesinger, Jr.[169]

May 19, 1954

Dear Arthur —

So many thanks for your letter and the helpful enclosure. As to my speeches, I seem to be drifting for the present in agreeable aimlessness. Somehow I'll have to snap out of it — and how I look forward to the day when they will be few and far between.

I'm delighted that you can draft something for Harrisburg.[170] I had thought of a round denunciation of the McCarthy spectacle; a little moralizing about why chickens come home to roost; the failure to accomplish much of anything beyond verbal triumphs (do you remember Wilson's remark "Nothing was ever done so systematically as nothing is being done") and finally some foreign policy lamentations; ending up with strong plea for Democratic statesmanship, patriots not partisans, adm[inistration]. must succeed because America must succeed. And best guarantee of that is more Democrats in public office. Something about Pa. campaign at start and may be end would be appropriate — but I know nothing about it. Do you think its time to use some of your quotes from T.R.? Or would the autumn be better — after Congress etc? I rather think the latter.

I'm recovering rapidly — and getting very lazy and indifferent. Try it sometime, but not when I need you!

Yours
ADLAI

169 The handwritten draft of this letter is in the possession of the editors.
170 Stevenson was to speak in Harrisburg, Pennsylvania, on June 6, 1954.

P.S. I doubt if you can find time to do anything on this speech until after Columbia.[171] Between June 6 and 9th I'll have to do my editing job on what you can provide me. I have a strong feeling that the tone should be temperate, more of sorrowful patient hope and good humor than righteous injured indignation.

P.S.S. I enclose some wonderful stuff in Marshall's [172] letter which I've told him I'm going to use somewhere soon as a quotation from a letter from a friend or something.

AES

To Bernard DeVoto [173]

May 28, 1954

Dear Benny:

I was so glad to get your letter and the copy of your forthcoming article.[174] I wish you had also sent me a suitable commencement speech for Vassar!

I *am* planning, presently at least, to go up to the Northwest, and possibly on up to Alaska, in July. I want to take it easy and do very little speaking or political "work" and would like to think it largely as a holiday with one of my boys, if I possibly can. I believe the National Committee plans for me to make one so-called major speech, and that for my old friend Dick Neuberger, et al.

I am more and more persuaded that conservation as well as public power is going to become a major issue and that you are dead right in your estimates of its value, politically as well as to the country.

I have been in the national forests and had a fascinating time with that fine old man — was it Kittredge? [175] — in Yosemite about ten years ago. I have also visited one of the Oregon forests with Neuberger and the head forest man up there who is now retired. I cannot recall if it was Lyle Watts.[176] The suggestion of a little field trip in the arid country is excellent and I am going to see if we can't contrive it on this trip. I think Missoula might be the best chance and perhaps on the way back. I will talk to [Bill] Blair about this.

I wish somehow some time I could pull together all the threads properly

[171] Stevenson was to speak at the Columbia University Bicentennial Conference in New York City on June 5, 1954.

[172] C. B. Marshall, formerly of the Policy Planning Staff, Department of State.

[173] The original is in the DeVoto papers, Stanford University Library.

[174] Stevenson probably refers to "Conservation: Down and on the Way Out," *Harper's*, August, 1954.

[175] Unable to identify.

[176] Unable to identify.

on soil conservation, forests, grazing lands, parks, as well as public power, for a speech addressed to the layman, who understands thrift and husbandry in personal terms at least.

Hastily yours,
ADLAI

P.S. How Samuel Pepys got "cut of the stone" — and without an anaesthetic — I will never understand.

To Gerald Johnson

May 28, 1954

Dear Gerald:

I was distressed to miss your visit to Chicago. I have been in Mississippi for a couple of days visiting Governor [Hugh L.] White and speaking, or attempting to speak, at a hillbilly music festival in a stadium at night in the rain. Sometimes I wonder how many horrors there still are in store for me.

Sincerely yours,

To Chester Bowles

May 28, 1954

Dear Chet:

Thanks so much for your letter, together with the splendid memorandum to the Senators.[177] I rather hope, however, that they don't issue a draft statement just now, although if they do I think yours would do little harm and might do some good. I feel that we should miss no opportunity to point out the incessant political attacks of the Republicans on the foreign policy of Roosevelt and Truman, in spite of what you call the "successful bipartisanship" during those administrations. Actually, it seems to me that "bipartisanship" is never binding when a policy works out badly and yet can never be really successful unless it eliminates foreign affairs from the arena of irrational partisan controversy. That has certainly not been the case in the past decade or two.

It seems to me our situation now is as menacing as anything we have confronted since the war — that not only is Asia in peril, but our alliances in Europe with the consequent growth of neutralism and further American isolation. The erratic performance of the Republicans in the past few months has about persuaded me that they have no more self-discipline

[177] Mr. Bowles had enclosed a copy of a memorandum on Indochina that he had prepared for several Democratic senators.

and conviction in this field than in the others. I don't want to let them off easily for political reasons, and even more so for the value to adult education in our country about the dangers of irresponsible partisanship in this field.

I hope so much that I can see you when I am in New York. When I find out how the schedule develops I shall let you know and if there is any way to fit into yours I shall do so. . . .

Yours,

Stevenson delivered the following address at the Columbia University Bicentennial Conference in New York City on June 5, 1954.[178]

I am a great believer in national humility, modesty, self-examination, and self-criticism, and I have preached these virtues vigorously, although, of course, I haven't practiced them very diligently. Of late I have been disturbed, as I am sure many of you have, by what seems to me to be the course at home and abroad of irrational criticism, abuse, and mistrust of America, its conduct, its motives, and its people. I don't mean just the voices that have been raised, we thank God, in protest against our current deficiencies, against the attacks on academic freedom, the pressure for conformity, our failures abroad, or the present wretched manifestations in Washington of our national neurosis. Nor do I mean the wholesome and continuous debate and self-examination that should and must go on among us and among allies; the candid controversy that makes for good neighbors and for good friends. Rather I am talking of the malice, distemper, and the new fashion of being cynical, sarcastic, skeptical, deprecating about America or fellow Americans.

There are rising voices here and abroad that forget that although America occasionally gags on a gnat, it also has some talent for swallowing tigers whole; voices that tell us that our national energy is spent, that our old values have decayed, that it is futile to try to restore them; voices that say that at best we are as Rome: that once our bridges, our skyscrapers, our factories, and our weapons fall before the iron law of decay, no trace will be left — no great issues, no great cause to mark our past in universal history.

And there are voices that seem to say that we are as Carthage, that our vital principle is commerce, just commerce; our ethics, our politics, our imaginative faculties, they say, are all bent and twisted to serve our sovereign — commerce. Other voices cry havoc, fear that America is not equal to the task; that Communism is the way to the future — is irresist-

178 The text is from *What I Think*, pp. 47–55.

ible, just as Fascism was for them not so long ago. Even novelists and poets seem to have been infected. The very excitement in a time of change and testing is cynically suspect.

Some of this talk, of course, may reflect a wholesome attitude abroad and a wholesome attitude here of self-criticism, if in a slightly fevered form. Some of it may even mark the reaction to the easy and the groundless optimism of the nineteenth century. I don't know, but I do know that if we doubt ourselves we will persuade no one. If we doubt our mission in the world, we will do nothing to advance it. And if we are craven before the slanders that fill our ears we will secede from each other.

But to view our present and our future with such sickly anxiety is to ignore the lessons and the achievements of our past. For the plain truth is that we here in America have written the greatest success story in human history. The plain truth is that on the record of performance, we here in America have in a few years made Socialism obsolete, shown that Communism is nothing but a noisome stagnant pool of reaction.

And it wasn't merely in 1776 that America left its footprints on eternity. For in our lifetime, we, the seventh generation of free and independent Americans, have given a tidal force to the forward roll of what was set in motion by the first generation. If we but lift our heads for a moment above this storm of criticism, of abuse, doubt, and "un-American activities," and survey the past fifty years, I think you will say with me: "Hooray for America!"

The first and most obvious thing we have to cheer about is our material progress. The miracle of American mass production is commonplace. And under our capitalist system we have increased our wealth to an extent almost unimaginable fifty years ago, at the turn of the century.

Now this increase in our wealth has, of course, greatly changed our country. The change for the sake of change — as I've tried with a notable lack of success to point out to my countrymen — isn't worthy of applause. What matters is not that we have changed but how we have changed.

Our national income is distributed far more equitably than it was at the turn of the century. As late as 1935–36 there were only about a million American families and unattached individuals, as they commonly say, with incomes of $5,000 or more, and 17,000,000 with incomes of less than $1,000. Fifteen years later, in 1950, these proportions were just about reversed, and even after allowing for inflation, the change is still dramatic.

It is not in terms of money and products that we can see most clearly the change that America has undergone. Rather it is in the attitude of the people and in the role of the government. For we have succeeded not only in making our society prosperous but in keeping it fluid.

And, while this was easy enough in the days of the frontier, it seemed all but an idle dream by 1900. The frontier was closed; the homestead land was gone; women and children labored in dingy sweatshops, and robber barons plundered at will. Miners in company towns and immigrants compressed in filthy tenements were fast becoming a miserable proletariat.

How could the roads of opportunity be kept open? How, short of revolution, could we adjust modern capitalism to democratic ends? To many it seemed hopeless. Yet see what happened: the gap between rich and poor has been greatly narrowed without revolution, without Socialism, and without robbing A to give to B — although there may be some dissent to that down in Wall Street!

Our wealth has been mightily increased and better distributed. The rising tide has lifted all the boats.

How has this transformation been accomplished? By increasing productivity and by putting government to the service of the people. Woodrow Wilson, Theodore Roosevelt, Robert La Follette, and so on, led a revolt of the American conscience, followed by the reforms under Franklin Roosevelt. They've altered the face of America.

The child labor laws, wage and hour laws, the antitrust acts, banking legislation, rural electrification, soil conservation, social security, unemployment compensation, the graduated income tax, inheritance taxes — it may be too much to say that all this and more amounts to a bloodless revolution, but it certainly amounts to a transformation of our economic and social life.

Now why was all this done? Why did America adopt the concept of man's responsibility for his fellow man? Our decision that the well-being of the least of us is the responsibility of all of us was, of course, not merely an economic and a political decision; it was, at bottom, a moral decision. And it was not, as some are now saying in the nation's capital, all a sinister conspiracy of the great philanthropic foundations.

It rested upon the conviction that it is the duty of the government to keep open to all the people the avenues of opportunity that stretched so broad and so far before us in the days of our frontier. It rested upon the conviction that the government must safeguard the people against catastrophe not of their making.

But this great decision has brought us face to face with vexing problems which have engaged your attention, as I understand it, during this past week — the problems of the conflict between freedom and security, between the individual and his social safeguards.

It seems to me there is something gallant about man's fight to become the master rather than the slave of nature; but there is something rather tragic about his struggle to keep himself free from the impositions of his own social creations.

Now it would be fatuous to claim that we are anywhere near solving this conflict, in my judgment, as it would be fatuous to say that because our material well-being increases year by year all must be well with America. It isn't.

Too many of our people still dwell in wretched slums or on worn-out land. Once again our topsoil, our national skin, is blowing away out on the plains. Our schools and hospitals are overcrowded; so are our mental institutions and our prisons. Too many of our cities are wasting away from neglect. And how can we boast of our high estate when more than one of every ten citizens still do not enjoy fully equal opportunities?

Nonetheless our progress has been astonishing — more Americans are living better than ever before. The middle class, whose disappearance Marx so confidently predicted, has expanded as never before in the history of any other nation. And while the Communist conspirators fulminate about the cruel capitalists, the lackeys of Wall Street, and the downtrodden masses, we have created a free society that promotes the general welfare of all far better, far more successfully than it has ever been promoted by any other system or social organization.

Briefly, I think America's record is "terrific" — if I may borrow a word from my sons. And it is my view that its performance abroad is even more spectacular.

Since the turn of the century we have successively and emphatically renounced, first imperialism, then isolation, and finally our historical neutrality. We have transformed our foreign policy as completely as our domestic policy. Twice America has decisively tipped the scales for freedom in a mighty global exertion.

Instead of isolation, our policy is total involvement; instead of non-co-operation we have been the prime mover in the United Nations; instead of neutrality we have organized the greatest coalition in history. And in Korea we fought and bled almost alone for the United Nations and for collective security.

But this isn't all. In the process America has fathered three unprecedented ideas: Lend-lease for Hitler's intended victims in war, the Marshall Plan for Stalin's intended victims in peace, and Point 4 to help undeveloped areas. And to pay for it all Americans have borne a tax load, I mean a *collected* tax load, that is without counterpart save in Britain, and that few beyond our borders appreciate.

And what have we asked in return? Why have we done all of this? Some will say self-interest, and there is truth in that because Communism follows the geography of human misery. Some will say magnanimity, and there is truth in that, too. For it would have been easy to go home as we did after the first war, or go it alone as some of our people have proposed.

Call it what you will; the point is to help others help themselves, to help make independence and democracy work, to share the burdens of the less fortunate, to raise the tide a little all around the world, lifting all of the boats with it, just as we have done here at home. It was bold and imaginative. It was wise and responsible; it was good for them and it was good for us. As Edmund Burke said: "Magnanimity is not seldom the truest wisdom."

Now, while I emphatically approve and loudly cheer America's purposes abroad, past and present, I don't mean to imply for a moment that I approve of all our foreign policies and conduct, past or present — especially present!

My purpose has been just to suggest the main outlines of a success story in which we can all take pride. As we look back to 1900 and look around us today the infinite evidence of our creative impulses and of our vast achievements ought to be heralded, not mocked.

We have heard the "least of these." We have enlarged our vision, opened our heart, and we have disciplined our strength. We have turned it into a servant of justice — justice not alone for ourselves, but justice for the world-wide commonwealth of free men and of free institutions.

Here, indeed, is a case where mankind has a right to knowledge and to the use thereof — the knowledge of what America has done, how America has spread out the decision-making process, within its many parts.

It is the knowledge of how we have committed 160,000,000 people to vast social projects, not by coercion, but by persuasion and consent, and by a balancing of the rights of the one with the needs of the many.

I say it is a grand and glorious story. On the basis of the record we have out performed any rival proposals of Communism or of Fascism; and America has nobly accepted her responsibility and proudly met her time for greatness in a troubled age.

Why then all this abuse and criticism? Why then have we of late grown afraid of ourselves? Why have we of late acted as though the whole of this nation is a security risk? Why do you suppose we have given in to the bleatings of those who insist that it is dangerous for a man to have an idea? Why do we talk of saving ourselves by committing suicide — in the land of Jefferson?

So, having said: "Three cheers for America — you've done a great job of work," we have to add: "But look out, America, your work has just begun; though you've nobly grasped the present you could meanly lose the future."

What's the matter with us anyhow? The usual diagnosis is ignorance and fear. Ignorance leads many to confuse ends with means, to act as though material progress were an end in itself rather than a means to great and noble ends. This, I suggest, is the peril of our hardheaded, pragmatic attitude that has helped us so much to achieve our vast social and economic transformation, for if we ever succumb to materialism the meaning will go out of America.

And ignorance begets fear — the most subversive force of all. If America ever loses confidence in herself, she will retain the confidence of no one, and she will lose her chance to be free, because the fearful are never free.

But I wonder if all of these alarming concerns are not America's surface symptoms of something even deeper; of a moral and human crisis in the Western world which might even be compared to the fourth-, fifth-, and sixth-century crisis when the Roman Empire was transformed into feudalism and primitive Christianity, early Christianity, into the structure of the Catholic Church, or the crisis a thousand years later when the feudal world exploded and the individual emerged with new relationships to God, nature, to society.

And now in our time in spite of our devotion to the ideas of religious and secular humanism, I wonder if we are in danger of falling into a spirit of materialism in which the aim of life is a never-ending increase of material comfort, and the result a moral and religious vacuum. Is this leading, as lack of faith always must, to a deep sense of insecurity and a deterioration of reason? And I wonder, too, if today mass manipulation is not a greater danger than economic exploitation; if we are not in greater danger of becoming robots than slaves.

Since man cannot live by bread alone, is not the underlying crisis whether he is going to be inspired and motivated again by the ideas of the humanistic tradition of Western culture, or whether he falls for the new pagan religions, the worship of the state and a leader, as millions of believers in the Fascist and Soviet systems have already done?

That we are not invulnerable, that there is a moral and a human vacuum within us, is, I think, demonstrated by many symptoms, of which McCarthyism — which has succeeded in frightening so many — is only one.

But it is even more certain that there are millions who see or at least who dimly sense the danger, and who want to make life in its truly human meaning the main business of living; who want to express the humanistic tradition of reason and of human solidarity — who want to understand the truth and not be drawn into the mass manipulative influence of sentimentality and rationalization.

I venture to say that there are in the world many with a deep, intense longing for a vision of a better life not in a material, but in a spiritual sense; for love for human solidarity. There is a hunger to hear a word of truth, a longing for an ideal, a readiness for sacrifice. Churchill's famous speech at the beginning of the war is an illustration and so is the totalitarians' appeal to emotional forces rather than to material interests.

But the conventional appeal seems to be so often to the better life in *material* terms, I wonder if people are not eager to hear about the better life in *human* terms.

And I think that deep down the ideas of independence, of individuality, of free initiative, represent the strongest appeals to Americans who want to think for themselves, who don't want to be creatures of mass suggestion, who don't want to be automatons.

The question is, I suppose, whether the human and rational emotions can be aroused instead of the animal and irrational to which the totalitarians appeal. But fill the moral vacuum, the rational vacuum, we must; reconvert a population soaked in the spirit of materialism to the spirit of humanism we must, or bit by bit we too will take on the visage of our enemy, the neo-heathens.

As I have said, in my judgment America has accomplished miracles at home and abroad. But, despite all of this wisdom, this exertion, this goodness, the horror of our time in history is that things are worse than ever before. There is no real peace; we are besieged, we are rattled. Perhaps we are even passing through one of the great crises of history when man must make another mighty choice.

Beset by all of these doubts and difficulties, in which direction then do we look?

We look to ourselves — and we are not ashamed. We are proud of what freedom has wrought — the freedom to experiment, to inquire, to change, to invent. And we shall have to look exactly in the same directions to solve our problems now — to individual Americans, to their institutions, to their churches, to their governments, to their multifarious associations — and to all the free participants in the free life of a free people.

And we look, finally, to the free university whose function is the search for truth and its communication to succeeding generations. Men may be born free; they cannot be born wise; and it is the duty of the university to make the free wise. Only as that function is performed steadfastly, conscientiously, and without interference does a university keep faith with the great humanist tradition of which it is a part.

More than a hundred years ago William Ellery Channing defined the free mind this way:

> I call that mind free which jealously guards its intellectual rights
> and powers, which calls no man master, which does not content itself

with a passive or hereditary faith, which opens itself to light whence-
soever it may come, and which receives new truth as an angel from
heaven.

I wonder how many of us fulfill Channing's definition. And I wonder if
our failure to do so could be part of our trouble today.

To Mrs. Edison Dick [179]

June 13, 1954

. . . At 1 AM the speech was ready for Vassar and I was ready for bed!
I'm not sure about it. In the interests of more reasonable length I've cut
it a lot, and then of course I've had to add a lot of stuff that had best been
left unthought of — including a line about the Oppenheimer case [180] — a
science of security which would deny us the security of science — which
I think could be the only *news* value in the speech. Also — well — I've
spoiled largely your heroic work I fear and may have lost me my best
ghost!!!! [181]

Its been a wild & wooly week. Things went fine at Columbia — the excited welcome speech etc. & a fascinating if not important fight in the
Univ. over an honorary degree for me. Barbara Ward was exquisite — I
mean her speech — and she frail and weary I thought, but charming, dignified and a brilliant conversationalist of course. The week in the country
destroyed me — I tried tennis & long walks and was practically prostrate
for 2 days; indeed felt lousy all week but filled the schedule, appalling as
usual, and now am ready for Vassar — bless you! . . .

P.S. Horrors — Ive regained 5 of my lost 10 pounds! I'm damn tired and
want to come home again — and how long must it be before strength is
normal?

*On his visit to the East Coast, Stevenson also spoke at Harrisburg,
Pennsylvania, on June 9; delivered the Commencement Address at Vassar
College on June 14; received an honorary degree from Princeton Univer-
sity; and returned to Libertyville on June 17.*

---

[179] This handwritten letter is in the possession of Mrs. Dick.

[180] For an analysis of the revocation of J. Robert Oppenheimer's security clearance,
see Philip M. Stern, *Security on Trial*, collaboration by Harold P. Green, with a
special commentary by Lloyd K. Garrison (New York: Harper & Row, 1969).

[181] Mrs. Dick, in a short memo to the editors, wrote: "No one will be surprised
to learn that of the 'heroic work' Adlai finally used a few scattered excerpts — a fate
which, I suspect, befell more 'ghosted' scripts than the ghosts themselves are prone
to admit."

Professor Dumas Malone, biographer of Thomas Jefferson, wrote Stevenson on June 8: "The memory of the Presidential campaign is one that will always remain with me, along with the conviction that you emerged from it as the most appealing American public figure of my time."

To Dumas Malone

June 18, 1954

Dear Mr. Malone:

You have written me a letter that I shall long cherish and probably frequently reread. I remember so well your visit to Springfield, including your superb paper! I wish there were to be more visits. I trust you will let me know some time when you are passing this way.

Sincerely yours,

While in New York City, Stevenson stayed both at the apartment of William Benton and at the home of Mr. and Mrs. Ronald Tree.

To Mr. and Mrs. Ronald Tree [182]

June 18, 1954

The wanderers [183] have returned — full of honors, degrees, exhaustion and happy memories of the beloved Trees — if little else about the late mission of the East!

You were angels — as always — and I would gladly have subsided there for ever and without a struggle — or even another long walk!

With love & everlasting gratitude to dear, dear friends —

ADLAI

Former President Truman had just had his appendix and gall bladder removed in an emergency operation at Research Hospital in Kansas City, Missouri, when the following two telegrams were sent.

To Harry S. Truman

June 21, 1954

ENJOY THE SENSE OF DELICIOUS TOTAL DETACHMENT THAT COMES WITH SURGERY WHILE YOU CAN BECAUSE YOU WILL BE UP AND AT IT AGAIN SOON ENOUGH. BEST WISHES FROM A VETERAN.

[182] This handwritten letter is in the possession of Mrs. Tree.
[183] Stevenson and Bill Blair.

To Margaret Truman

June 21, 1954

AM WIRING ALL THE TRUMANS TODAY TO WISH YOUR FATHER A
SPEEDY RECOVERY AND YOU A SUCCESSFUL OPENING.[184] I CONFESS I
WOULD RATHER SEE YOU ON THE STAGE THAN HIM IN THE HOSPITAL.
I'VE SEEN ENOUGH OF THE LATTER BUT TOO LITTLE OF THE FORMER.
BEST WISHES.

Cyrus Eaton, chairman of the board of the Chesapeake and Ohio Railway Company, wrote Stevenson: "If the Democrats want to win in November and in '56, they ought to advocate an end to the present combination of a few men in one spot manipulating for their own personal ends the nation's insurance companies, banks, railroads, public utilities and industrial corporations, as well as the press and radio."

To Cyrus Eaton

June 22, 1954

Dear Mr. Eaton:

I have been traveling around in the South and East for some weeks, which is a bad way of recuperating from an operation!

This is the first opportunity I have had to acknowledge your letter of May 27. I am off now for Indiana, thence to the Northwest Coast and Alaska. I return to Chicago in mid-August in time for a little speaking in the Congressional campaign.

I think you have a point of importance and political significance, and some day I would welcome an opportunity to talk with you about the influence of a few in the affairs of many.

Sincerely yours,

To T. S. Matthews

June 25, 1954

Dear Tom:

I have been beating about the East, enlightening the academics and politicians and sundry other gentry for the past several weeks and on my return I find your letter, just as I am leaving for the Northwest and Alaska. Hence I will be delighted to read your piece, although I must say for

[184] Miss Truman was appearing in a play at the Pocono Summer Theatre, Mountain Home, Pennsylvania.

Matthews to submit anything in writing to Stevenson for comment is either the subtlest flattery I have enjoyed or you are getting rattled.

While in Princeton, where the Trustees honored me with a degree to my astonishment, I called on that beautiful mistress of the Cuyler household.[185] There I saw Sandy,[186] who was well mannered, good-looking, enthusiastic, healthy, and did me the honor of knowing me. I could not have been more delighted. He also seemed excited and genuine about going to school in England. My boys would have bawled, or at least I think so. I shall hope very much to see you and Martha [187] when you travel to St. Louis and have already alerted her devoted friend Winston Elting.[188]

Yours,

Novelist James T. Farrell wrote from Paris describing his impressions of anti-American feelings in France and praising Stevenson's speech at Columbia University.

To James T. Farrell [189]

June 25, 1954

Dear Mr. Farrell:

I was delighted with your most interesting letter of June 7 about France. How you can write! I am sending along copies of the speech, although they seem to be bogged down in New York and have not yet arrived in Chicago. I am so glad you thought well of it. I think I would rather not send copies direct to the gentleman in Holland. If you wish to do so you are at liberty to do so, of course.

Sincerely yours,

To Mrs. Humphrey Bogart [190]

June 30, 1954

Dear Betty:

You were sweet to write me and I wish we were coming to California on this journey, but the directions lie to the North. Should you be fishing in Alaska later in July we might cut some bait and cast some flies and do likewise to some Republicans.

[185] Mrs. Lewis B. (Margery) Cuyler.
[186] Mr. Matthews's son, William Alexander Procter Matthews.
[187] Mrs. Matthews.
[188] Chicago architect, partner in the firm of Elting & Bennett.
[189] A copy is in A.E.S., I.S.H.L.
[190] A copy is in A.E.S., I.S.H.L.

There is a prospect of a political journey to California in October. Evidently some of the candidates still think I am useful, although I suspect their good judgment.

All the best from the hottest place on earth — Chicago.

Sincerely yours,

The following letter was written in Denver, Colorado. Stevenson had just heard that Helen Kirkpatrick, a correspondent for the Chicago Daily News *whom he had known for years, had married Robbins Milbank.*

To Mrs. Robbins Milbank [191]

July 2, 1954

My dear Helen —

Even Colo. has heard the news of your changed status — and I don't want to be the last to report my elation at your "new happiness" — as the greeting cards would say.

Tonight, somewhere in the mountains in Bear Creek canyon, surrounded by howling Democrats I'll lift a silent toast to you and your fortunate gentleman — and also shed a tear for all the disappointed bachelors whose opportunities have sharply shrunk thanks to this bold step of the brave and beautiful Helen.

Cheers and all the best, and don't forget that Libertyville still yearns to be revisited — and my congratulations to you both. And now for the damned barbecue and more exhaustion.

Ever

P.S. And I was pleased to read that he's a Princetonian!

P.S.S. And Pres. Wright [192] is after me again — and all I want to do is shut up forever!

To Mr. and Mrs. Ernest L. Ives [193]

[no date]

Dear Buffy & Ernest:

We've spent a day with Nan McEvoy & her mother at her *exquisite* ranch and are on the way back to ours by way of this incredibly beautiful place.[194] The political situation in Colorado is good & in Oregon there

[191] This handwritten letter is in the possession of Mrs. Milbank.

[192] Benjamin F. Wright, president of Smith College.

[193] This handwritten postcard is in the Elizabeth Stevenson Ives collection, Illinois State Historical Library. It is postmarked Crater Bend, Oregon, July 8, 1954.

[194] Crater Lake.

is a good chance of electing a U.S. Senator for the first time in decades. All well happy and healthy —

ADLAI

To Mrs. Edison Dick [195]

July 23, 1954

. . . I'm so excited! Just had a wire from Adlai — from Louisville! — that he's back. And here I am in Alaska — and a remote part — and about as far away as one could be, just as I was when he left a year ago! . . .

It's rained almost incessantly since we touched Alaskan soil, or rather rock, at Ketchikan. At the moment Bill [Blair], Bob Bartlett (Alaska delegate in Congress) and I are in McKinley Nat Park where I'm supposed to be resting for 48 hrs & writing "a major speech," as the local press says, for Anchorage. The rest of the party has gone off to the Bering sea and the Esquimo country. I wish I had too; but I've gotten darn tired again & must do this wretched speech well after all the foul mistakes Sec'y McKay [196] has made. I guess there's just no such thing as quiet travel any more and in spite [of] all Bill's precautions and mother hen protection, it has been the same old thing from morning 'till night even in this strange, incredible land. But the "vacation" part is still ahead of us and I pray the weather will lift and all will yet be well.[197]

And what of the dear Dicks — ? Are you gently broiling in the heat wave — dehydrated, shrunk, dessicated? (As for me, I'm regaining my fine round proportions of the past very rapidly!) . . .

To Katie Louchheim [198]

[no date]

Dear Katie —

So many thanks for your letter of July 20. Dollars for Democrats sounds good & we're arranging something. After 6 weeks of incessant travel I'm weary and oh so eager to get home!

Cordially,

[195] This handwritten letter is in the possession of Mrs. Dick. It was mailed from Fairbanks, Alaska.

[196] Secretary of the Interior David McKay.

[197] Bill Blair wrote of the Stevenson trip to the Northwest and Alaska: "I can assure you that our trip was anything but a vacation! The Governor made fourteen speeches in all, and there must have been 114 receptions, breakfasts, etc. Shades of '52!" Letter to Robert Tufts, August 17, 1954.

[198] This handwritten postcard is in the possession of Mrs. Louchheim. It is postmarked Missoula, Montana, August 5, 1954.

To William Benton [199]

August 10, 1954

Dear Bill:

I am just back after seven weeks in the Pacific Northwest, Alaska and British Columbia. Curiously, at a party for me in Vancouver who should walk in but David Beatty,[200] with the alarming news just received that the Yacht had caught fire. He seemed to know little of the details and was much upset, but confident that the Bentons had escaped with their lives, if not their clothes. Some time I shall expect to hear more of the details, and I pray to heaven that all is well with you; but what an unfortunate conclusion for that glamorous journey.

Borden is in Maine at the moment, but reports to me he is apologetic about not letting you know that his plans were kept in suspense due to his draft situation; and finally, and recently, when no permission from the draft board to leave the country was forthcoming, he was obliged to give up his hope for a trip abroad and possibly a trip with you.

My schedule for the autumn is still uncertain, but frightening, what with the weariness I have already accumulated with incessant speeches and public appearances this summer. Perhaps the best thing to do is to call me when you get to Chicago, and meanwhile I am putting down October 11–15 on my schedule.

Love to the family.

Yours,
ADLAI

To Sidney Hyman [201]

August 10, 1954

Dear Sid:

I am back at last after a long and exhausting journey in the Northwest, Alaska and British Columbia immediately following the June academic barnstorming, politicking and a family wedding.

During the journey I had a chance to sort out my "thank you's" and also to read something in "The American President." [202] As to the latter, you are entitled to all my thanks. It is a superb and enlightening book and I

---

[199] The original is in the possession of the estate of William Benton (see note 143, p. 352).

[200] Commander in the Royal Navy, grandson of Marshall Field and half-brother of Ronald Tree.

[201] Scholar and author of numerous books on contemporary American politics.

[202] Sidney Hyman, *The American President* (New York: Harper, 1954).

shall hope to dip further and deeper as time permits. As to the former I am afraid I have not yet thanked you for the most useful manuscript you have sent me in preparation for my ordeal at Columbia. It was good of you and helpful beyond measurement of specific use. I trust you have seen what finally emerged.

I hope you have not forgotten our earlier talk and that we can resume the discussion later on in the fall as your horizons clear.

With gratitude and warmest wishes, I am

Cordially yours,

To David L. Lawrence [203]

August 10, 1954

Dear Dave:

Ever so many thanks for your card from Tel Aviv. Had I not just finished seven weeks of travel it might have made me restless!

I hope all goes well and that Pennsylvania is going to add a few more real Democrats to its public life this fall.

Yours,

To John Sparkman

August 10, 1954

Dear John:

Thanks for the report from Libya.[204] I was delighted. And, as you know, anywhere in the world, *except* the Middle East, we would have had *all* the votes.

My journey in the West and Northwest was interesting, rewarding and exhausting. Politically the discontent and disillusion is general with, of course, different emphasis. There is much more concern, for example, with natural resources, public power, etc. in the Northwest now than there was two years ago.

I think there is one danger, John: while there *is* discontent and dissatisfaction with the administration there is also, I felt, an underlying patience with the administration which we Democrats may not evaluate properly. What I am trying to say is that I feel there are a lot of people who still want to "give Ike a chance" and that they are not as audible as our partisan friends who seize on every expression of dissatisfaction as evidence of a ground swell to the Democrats.

Hastily yours,

[203] Mayor of Pittsburgh, Pennsylvania, 1945–1959; later governor of Pennsylvania. A copy is in A.E.S., I.S.H.L.
[204] Senator Sparkman had sent him an article about Stevenson supporters in Libya.

To T. S. Matthews

August 13, 1954

Dear Tom:

At last I have returned from the Northwest, Alaska and British Columbia, after a fascinating and fatiguing journey, and the shameful truth is that I have not yet looked at your article [205] nor, for that matter have I even cleaned up the thank you letters from this journey. It was all I could do to meet the travel schedules, personal appearances, speeches, etc., along the way, and now I am confronted with mountains of accumulated mail, a disordered household, departing servants, ghastly writing and political commitments lurking in the dark background.

But enough. I shall look at it as soon as I can and tell you candidly what I think, which is worth very little, as you must know.

But I have not been without concern, and the attached are the comments of my friend Bernard De Voto, who read it anonymously one night while we were together in Montana on a field trip with the Forest Service.

As your schedule progresses, let me know. I shall hope to be here when you come this way, but there is an appalling speaking schedule in the making, I understand.

Yours,

To Gerald Johnson

August 16, 1954

Dear Gerald:

I am just back after a long, fascinating and fatiguing journey in the Northwest, Alaska and British Columbia, and I find your notes, including the superb script of July 4, which will be precious grist in my mill.

. . . The document, "The Republican Pursuit of American Communists" [206] I have not seen. What is it? Have I overlooked something?

I shall have to be speaking this fall in the congressional elections and I am somewhat at a loss as to how to pitch my voice — attack or patient disappointment from a high level.

On my journey to the West it has been mostly the former. I think now perhaps I should view it all anxiously and soberly, which, after all, is the way I feel, and resist the temptation to attack with undiscriminating partisan fervor. Of course you have views, and when time permits they are always welcome.

Sincerely,

[205] Mr. Matthews was unable to identify the article.
[206] Unable to identify.

To Arthur M. Schlesinger, Jr.

August 16, 1954

Dear Arthur:

Thanks so much for your letter. I am afraid it would be impossible to persuade Mitchell to continue,[207] although there has been talk here and there of a draft movement. He has the genuine respect and support of most of the National Committeemen whom I have seen on this last journey, for example, and many others who have communicated with me as to replacements. The best bets seem to be DiSalle,[208] who is actively seeking the job, Paul Butler [209] of Indiana and Jim Finnegan [210] of Philadelphia. I think I have detected an increasing feeling that it should continue Catholic for the present. I have unqualified respect for Butler, whom I am coming to know well. He is definitely the "new look" type, gentler than Mitchell, but physically not strong, and there are some difficulties in the Indiana organization. As to Finnegan, you know him as well as I.

I hope to have a chance to talk with Jim Rowe [211] some time, but I just can't try to manage this succession to Steve, nor can I insist on his further continuance. He has stayed a year beyond his commitment already.

I am much interested in your journey to Costa Rica. I hope it comes off and that I can hear all about it promptly. Latin America is something I know little about, and a field of importance which we must not neglect.

Yours,

P.S. The Alaska journey was a delight and a fright. I am educated and exhausted! I am returning Rowe's letter herewith.

To Edith Gifford

August 19, 1954

Dear Miss Gifford:

The new scrapbooks have arrived and again I can find out more about myself than I knew — and in such comfort and elegance — thanks to you.

---

[207] Stephen A. Mitchell was resigning as Democratic National Chairman.
[208] Michael DiSalle, mayor of Toledo, Ohio, and later governor of Ohio.
[209] Mr. Butler later succeeded Mr. Mitchell as chairman.
[210] President of the Philadelphia City Council.
[211] A Washington lawyer who had held a number of positions in the Roosevelt Administration.

You are so good to me and I marvel at your continued dedication to this tiresome chore.

Best wishes.

Sincerely yours,

Bernard Baruch sent Stevenson a picture taken on his eighty-fourth birthday. In addition, he remarked that he was reading the Godkin Lectures — Call to Greatness *— and had told reporters they showed "a well read thoughtful man," but one reporter misquoted him as saying they were "glib."*

To Bernard M. Baruch

August 19, 1954

Dear Mr. Baruch:

I was delighted to have your letter, and I am profoundly touched by your thoughtfulness. If you were misquoted by the press I am sure it is not the first time!

I am flattered indeed that you have even seen the little book of lectures at Harvard. Some day I must read them myself and see what I said!

I am ever so grateful for the picture, and I am now prepared to impress all of my descendants as a statesman if not a ballplayer. I shall hope to see you when and if I get back to New York and can escape for a moment.

Cordially yours,

P.S. Congratulations on your birthday! I only wish I felt as energetic and young as you look.

To Bernard DeVoto

August 19, 1954

Dear Benny:

Carol Evans tells me you were through here yesterday when I was in Springfield. I am distressed that I was not here, as I should have liked sorting my thoughts out a little with you after those delightful days in Montana. Some time I wish you could give me just a few paragraphs reflecting your idea of what should be done to return that marginal wheat land from cultivation. Is this the answer to the wheat surplus problem?

Hastily,

P.S. I don't believe I have thanked you properly for all you did for me and for as agreeable and educational a field trip as has fallen to my lot.

Lady Spears wrote Stevenson that she had been asked by the London Daily Mail *to write a feature story about him. The interview was published on October 29, 1954.*

To Lady Mary Spears

August 30, 1954

Dear Mary:

Of course, I should be delighted to have you interview me for the Daily Mail — and no commission either! My schedule is hideous, but I shall probably be in New York around the middle of October. If you wish I shall let you know the time definitely when the schedule for October is worked out.

In the meanwhile, I shall be traveling between Harrisburg, Pennsylvania, and Minneapolis, Minnesota, from now until the end of the month with little time in Chicago. After the first of October I go to California, returning to New York, I think, about the middle of the month. Perhaps that would be about the best time if you are still there. Otherwise, let me know precisely when it would be best for you and I shall try to fit it in.

Hastily and affectionately,

September 2, 1954

MEMORANDUM TO: Miss Evans
FROM: Governor Stevenson

For the Files

On August 12, I think, I wrote Mendes-France,[212] longhand in Libertyville, substantially as follows:

My dear Mendes-France:
Permit me to express my admiration for the courage and vigorous attack on the formidable problems of France which you outlined for me with such clarity and logic in Paris last summer.[213]
Emboldened by my regard for you and our brief acquaintance, I am presuming to write you this very friendly (?) and personal note

---

[212] Pierre Mendès-France, Socialist premier of France, 1954–1955.
[213] See *The Papers of Adlai E. Stevenson,* Vol. V.

because of the recent developments with respect to E.D.C. and because of my great concern for French-American relations.[214]

It would serve no purpose to review much that has happened and much that has been said that we both deplore. Nor is there any point in discussing the genesis and merits of E.D.C., or American impatience and misconceptions about France's misgivings. I think I well understand them.

What I want to report very simply and accurately, I think, at the risk of repeating what you already well know, is that to the mass of American people, E.D.C. has become a sort of symbol of the continuity and vitality of the Western coalition of which France is an indispensable partner. Also to many of our more thoughtful people, E.D.C. is considered, perhaps unduly, as a step in the direction of greater European unity and integration.

While I do not wish to exaggerate the consequences, if France finally rejects E.D.C. or "amends it to death," I feel that the isolationists and the more intemperate among us here in America will be encouraged.

I am sure you know that American attitudes on E.D.C. have developed over several years and that it is in no sense a partisan matter, but a question on which my countrymen are in agreement.

Please understand, my dear friend, that this note represents *nothing whatsoever* but the personal anxiety and opinion of a private American citizen and an old and devoted friend of France.

Forgive me for imposing on you. I know how harrassed you are and I shall expect no acknowledgment of this hasty and spontaneous note which I am entrusting to our mutual friend, Jean Lambert,[215] of New York, who tells me that he is departing for France almost at once.

With warmest wishes and my profound respect

/s/ ADLAI E. STEVENSON

Prior to writing this letter, I talked with George Ball in Washington and Jean Lambert in New York and told them that I was loathe to write Mendes-France without being sure that it would not embarrass the State Department in any way. Thereafter Lambert got in touch with Arthur Dean [216] who telephoned Dulles in Lambert's presence. In due course the latter called me back to report that Dulles had said it would be a con-

---

214 Secretary of State Dulles pushed for rearming of the Federal Republic of Germany within a European Defense Community. There was strong opposition to EDC in the French National Assembly. Dulles warned on December 14, 1953, that unless France joined EDC the United States would make an "agonizing reappraisal" of its policy toward Europe.

215 Unable to identify.

216 Special ambassador to Korea, 1953–1954, and partner in the New York law firm of Sullivan & Cromwell.

structive and generous act but that he was fearful it was too late. No one saw the letter before nor after I sent it to Lambert by air mail, special delivery, to deliver to Mendes-France's office personally.

On August 25, 1954, Stevenson issued the following statement.[217]

I wrote a personal letter to my friend, Mendes-France, with whom I had had several long talks during my trip last year, because I, like most Americans, was alarmed by developments in France with respect to EDC. I thought he might be interested in my views as a member of the opposition party, although just a private citizen. I wanted to assure him that EDC was not a partisan matter in America and that Secretary Dulles spoke for all of us on the European Defense Community plan which was developed during the Democratic administration.

My letter was not instigated by the State Department nor did they see it. Before writing the Prime Minister, however, I checked with the Secretary of State through an intermediary to make sure that such a letter would cause no embarrassment.

I earnestly hope that the events of the next few days will give a new vitality to the EDC. As a step toward European unification I believe it can greatly assist in building a strong, free and peaceful world.

To Paul H. Douglas

September 2, 1954

Dear Paul:

I appreciate your letter and want to do everything I can to help this fall.

Bill Blair has been keeping in close touch with Mike Howlett and Doug Anderson,[218] and I understand that meetings at which I am to speak have already been set up in Bloomington on September 21, in Evanston on September 24, and in Rockford on October 1.

I was hoping to keep some time open in October, but the National Committee has already scheduled me for California, New Mexico, Wyoming, New York, New Jersey, Delaware, Michigan, and a few other states. However, as you know, I intend to give top priority to your campaign as best I can — and I'm flattered that you want me.

Cordially yours,

[217] The text is based on a carbon copy.

[218] Managers of Douglas's campaign. For Douglas's relations with Stevenson, see *The Memoirs of Paul H. Douglas* (New York: Harcourt Brace Jovanovich, 1972).

To George F. Kennan

September 11, 1954

Dear George:

Thanks so much for your letter, and I am glad you approved of my speech in Harrisburg. It has been difficult for me to combine responsibility, sobriety and exhortation to the faithful and I never feel quite satisfied with the composite results of these labored efforts.

I am glad that the Stafford Little Lectures are to be published.[219] I had a devil of a time following them in the Times — and I am grateful to you for sending a copy along — inscribed, I hope, by a profoundly esteemed friend!

Cordially,

P.S. I took the liberty of suggesting to [Chester] Bowles, in response to a proposal from him, that he might want to try to arrange a meeting with you and some of the others to talk about what we should be talking about in foreign affairs.

Dr. Karl Menninger relayed the views of Frank Laubach, a missionary, that "what we need is a Pentagon filled with men who believe that love is more important than hate, and that our enemies can be overcome by a 'war of amazing kindness.' At any rate, how to win our enemies instead of how to defeat them ought to be the objective of a group of thoughtful people."

To Dr. Karl Menninger [220]

September 11, 1954

Dear Karl:

I was so glad to have your letter about Frank Laubach. I think he has touched a profound and resonant chord, but we must be realistic in this ugly world and I rather doubt, whoever is President, that we will ever fill the Pentagon with positive love. Just how to translate into action and policy the great objective of learning to win our enemies instead of defeat them is a subject I should like to see explored, because there is nothing more important.

Some day I hope we can talk of this — or just talk!

Cordially yours,

[219] *Realities of American Foreign Policy* (Princeton: Princeton University Press, 1954).

[220] A copy is in A.E.S., I.S.H.L.

To Chester Bowles

September 11, 1954

Dear Chester:

I have read and reread your most interesting letter of September 3. Although most of my speeches since June have not been extensively reported, I have in each talked about foreign affairs with a two-fold purpose: to invite attention to the sloganeering, bluff and bluster of the administration, and to attempt to keep people interested and concerned.

I feel that we should continue to talk about foreign affairs in the campaign, and I intend to do so. Just how to do it and what to do is another question.

The schedule that the National Committee has imposed on me would not permit me to come East for a meeting at this time. However, I would earnestly hope that you and Tom Finletter, Paul Nitze, possibly Dean Rusk, or George Kennan, could meet, and soon, and let me have the benefit of your discussion.

I have taken the liberty of discussing your letter with Arthur Schlesinger, who was here yesterday. He likewise would be glad to join a meeting, and I would be delighted to send Bob Tufts from Oberlin [College], who helps me from time to time and whose views and judgment I respect. Of course, his availability will depend somewhat on his teaching schedule.

However, the foregoing personnel suggestions are perhaps less important than the meeting itself, and you will have your own ideas as to who would be helpful consultants.

Personally, I am not and have not been as concerned with the "preventive war" talk as others, and I think the administration has evidently backed away from the Radford-Alsop line.[221] But I am dreadfully concerned with a lot of other things in the West as well as in the East, and most of all how to be critically constructive and responsible.

How I wish I could have had some of that cruise along the Maine coast with you!

Cordially,

P.S. C. B. Marshall, 420 East 23rd St., N.Y., formerly of the Policy Planning Staff and a first rate man without illusions would also be available for consultation if needed. Nitze would know him well and perhaps you do too. I suppose you have seen his recent book of lectures.

[221] Admiral Arthur W. Radford and columnists Joseph and Stewart Alsop favored military intervention against Communism.

P.P.S. I should have told you, also, that the schedule seems to indicate that I will not be in New York until after the middle of October.

AES

The Secretary-General of the United Nations wrote Stevenson praising Call to Greatness *and saying: "I do want to express my very deep appreciation of your clear interpretation of those values and methods in national attitudes and foreign policy which would provide an effective blueprint for peace for any nation."*

To Dag Hammarskjöld

September 11, 1954

My dear Mr. Secretary:

I am flattered indeed by your gracious letter of September 7 about the lectures at Harvard.

I do hope so much that I can have an opportunity for a quiet talk with you one of these days, but I am fearful that with the General Assembly ahead of you there will be little time for itinerant politicians!

With my utmost esteem and gratitude, I am

Cordially yours,

On September 18, Stevenson delivered a speech to a Democratic party dinner in Indianapolis. It set the tone of Stevenson's campaign to bring the Democrats back to power.

Vice President Nixon led the campaign for the Republicans. President Eisenhower announced that he was opposed to making Communism a campaign issue. As a result, the Vice President relied on insinuation. On September 16, he declared: "'Trumanism' had been rejected two years ago because it showed hopeless inability to deal with the fourheaded monster that was Korea, Communism, corruption, and controls."

On September 17, he said: "The Eisenhower Administration happens to believe that when American boys fought and died fighting communism overseas we ought to deal with it effectively here."

On October 24, he charged: "Mr. Stevenson has not only testified for Alger Hiss, but he has never made a forthright statement deploring the damage that Hiss and others like him did to America because of the politics and comfort they received from the Truman Administration and its predecessors."

On October 28, he added: "Mr. Stevenson has been guilty, probably without being aware that he was doing so, of spreading pro-Communist propaganda as he has attacked with violent fury the economic system of the United States and has praised the Soviet economy." [222]

In other words, Nixon set the issue of Communism in a more usable text than McCarthy's "Twenty Years of Treason."

"Communism should not be a political issue," Nixon said. *"There is no difference between the loyalty of Democrats and Republicans. But"* — and here, Cabell Phillips reported, he lowered the boom gently into place — *"some misguided officials of the previous Administration were blind or indifferent to the danger. They ignored the repeated warnings that J. Edgar Hoover and others including myself brought to them. . . . But this Administration is cooperating with J. Edgar Hoover and the F.B.I. We have not only fired the Communists and fellow-travelers and security risks off the Federal payroll by the thousands; we don't hire them in the first place. I can assure you that no one in this Administration regards Communism as a red herring."* [223]

THE CONGRESSIONAL CAMPAIGN BEGINS [224]

We are on the eve of another momentous election. The time is approaching when we must pass judgment on the parties and their candidates again — which is not just our privilege as citizens; it is also our obligation, and on the quality of our government.

The Republicans have been in office for twenty months — or long enough to elect Maine's first Democratic governor in twenty years.[225] About the only danger our Republican friends don't face this fall is the danger of overconfidence.

But of course there is nothing new about the loss of public confidence in the G.O.P., and the political doctors have been proposing larger and larger doses of expediency to salvage what they once called the "Great Crusade." A couple of months ago in Milwaukee, the Vice-President of the United States set the tone of Republican political education and statesmanship by blaming the defeat of the French in Indo-China on the Democrats in Washington. A couple of weeks ago in Cincinnati at the Republican strategy conference Mr. Nixon's ennobling advice for his teammates was mostly to avoid discussing the issues at all and to stay out of debates. And a couple of days ago, over in Ohio, Mr. Nixon defined

[222] See Stuart Gerry Brown, *Conscience in Politics*, pp. 72–73, for the Nixon quotations of September 16, 17, October 24 and 28, 1954.

[223] "One-Man Task Force of the G.O.P.," *New York Times Magazine*, October 24, 1954.

[224] The text is from *What I Think*, pp. 72–75.

[225] Edmund Muskie.

the Republican task: it is to figure out what to do to win and then do it. Anything goes, apparently — and the farm program went quickly. Mr. [Ezra Taft] Benson, the Secretary of Agriculture, promptly took this advice and totally repealed his "total acreage allotment" plan to control farm surpluses. The farm belt, it seems, was chafing tender Republican skins. It will be interesting to observe how the nation's press, which recently applauded so vigorously the President's farm program and Mr. Benson's courage, will react to this hasty retreat and this application of the Nixonian doctrine of political expediency.

As in every election, state and local issues, the merits of the individual candidates, catchwords, and the weather will affect the results. Of the weather I have little to say and nothing to promise. As to the Republican slogans I've said quite a bit from time to time about government by merchandising. Nor can I say much about individual candidates, except, of course, that we are proud of ours. But I do want to say a word about the spirit of a Congressional campaign in this age of perpetual, troubled motion in human affairs. I want to say a word about the similarities of our great parties, which may seem a strange way to talk on the eve of a fateful political contest. And I hope this audience won't think it heresy for me to suggest that we Democrats could have anything in common with the Republicans.

An election tends, of course, to emphasize our political divisions. This is as it must be, for to vote is to divide and in selecting one candidate or party we necessarily reject the other. An election is both a selection and rejection; it is a choosing up of sides. It matters greatly whether reason or passion guides our choice. Reason will enlighten and elevate our understanding and it will discover in controversy the springs of a new unity. But passion will poison the political atmosphere in which the nation must meet the tests of the future.

The fact is that we are Americans, first, last, and always, and may the day never come when the things that divide us seem more important than the things that unite us. We have many differences with the Republicans on specific issues of national policy, and we want to discuss and debate them because we think they are important. But I hope we may never forget that we hold far more in common with our friends, the Republicans, especially Republicans like Wendell Willkie, than we hold in dispute. Were it not so, neither party could govern, for government rests less on majorities at the polls than on the abiding unity, good sense, and obedience of the people.

Even in these sobering times it would be too much to hope, I suppose, that there might be an end to extravagant claims that one party represents all that is good and the other all that is evil. And we know that shrill voices filled with bitterness and hate have already been raised in our land. A strange and, it seems to me, truly un-American violence has stained too many utterances in recent months. It was the Republican Governor of New York, twice his party's candidate for President, who damned all Democrats for all time with words too ugly to repeat and too grotesque to believe.[226] It was the Republican Attorney General of the United States [227] who impugned the very loyalty of a former President of the United States — a man who had done more to combat Communism at home and abroad than all the Republican politicians put together — Harry S. Truman. It was a Republican Senator [228] from this great state of Indiana who described Democrats as betrayers. And it was the Republican National Committee itself which sponsored, in memory of Abraham Lincoln, the slogan "Twenty Years of Treason" to describe the two great Democratic decades.

Now this, of course, is not the language of reasoned political debate. This is the language of clan warfare, of civil war, of flaming passions and unreason. And it is more dangerous than just the debasement of our political dialogue and our political morals, because as it exploits it also aggravates the unhealthy national mood of fear and suspicion of one another that has so hampered the unemotional discussion on which wise public policy must be based; a mood that has so dangerously diverted us from the main jobs of establishing sane foreign policies and evolving sound domestic programs.

We shall hear more and more of these unscrupulous, shrill voices before the people must judge in November. What will the response be? Will the people reject or applaud those who do not even hesitate to recklessly divide America into ugly, bitter factions?

I think the good sense of the American people will prevail and that America has already made its decision on those demagogues who rely on defamation, deceit, and double-talk. At any rate, whatever the provocation, we must not be guilty of contributing to irreconcilable divisions in our country and to political delinquency. And, whatever the provocation, I hope and pray that we Democrats will both recognize and respect the difference between cynical politics and principles, between ruthless partisanship and patriotism.

Now I have spoken seriously, indeed piously, about this because the preservation and strengthening of America requires above all the preservation and strengthening of our mutual trust and confidence. No election

[226] Governor Thomas E. Dewey, in December, 1953, had said: "Remember that the words Truman and Democrat mean diplomatic failure, military failure, death and tragedy."
[227] Herbert Brownell.
[228] William Jenner.

victory is worth the damage of these central elements of our strength. Weakness begins at home, in doubts, suspicions, and whispers, and if the spirit of America is enfeebled, it will be the result of self-inflicted wounds.

So I say let us dispute our honest differences honestly and let the people decide them on the merits, but let us Democrats at least not be guilty of sowing discord, mistrust, and hate in this lovely land. As bearers of an honorable and ancient political tradition let us so conduct this momentous campaign as not to weaken but to strengthen the nation in this troubled hour.

On September 12, Stevenson flew to Louisville, Kentucky, to be present at the announcement of the engagement of Adlai E. Stevenson III and Nancy L. Anderson, daughter of Mr. and Mrs. Warwick Anderson of Louisville.

To Warwick Anderson

September 19, 1954

Dear Warwick:

After beating my way from Cincinnati with the boys, thence to Oberlin and Indianapolis, I have paused briefly in Bloomington where I find your letter forwarded from Chicago.

I was delighted with the whole visit and enchanted by my new relatives. I hope the children were not in any confusion, and nothing troubles me whatever. All the same, I wish for my own enjoyment we had had more time to get together for quiet talk. I had, as you know, a great anxiety to be with the boys a little, especially Adlai, whom I have hardly seen for more than two years.

With affectionate regards to you and Mary San [229] and the delightful Emersons [230] —

Cordially,

P.S. I shall slow down abruptly after November 2 if I don't fall down before! Should circumstances permit a week end together it would be great fun for me thereafter.

---

[229] Mrs. Anderson.
[230] Mr. and Mrs. George Waldo Emerson. Mrs. Emerson was the Andersons' oldest daughter.

To Nancy L. Anderson

September 19, 1954

Nancy dear:

I came away from Cincinnati contrite with my deficiencies — among them my failure to thank you for something that touched me deeply — figs! The [Wilson] Wyatts shared my slight delirium at dinner Monday evening and we concluded to repeat the whole process at breakfast. If I was a little light-headed thereafter you are responsible! Now I have tried the same thing with seedless grapes and it works, but not as well.

The visit to Louisville was enchantment for me and I understand even better now why my son acts this way!

Some day if I ever come to slow down long enough you shall have an engagement present.

Affectionately,

Carl Sandburg wrote Stevenson on September 7: "I am amazed at how you meet great and difficult moments and make them your own. The perfection of your timing for the past two years borders on the marvelous."

To Carl Sandburg

September 19, 1954

Dear Carl:

Those little notes now and then do something to me — something very good. Bless you, and also for reminding me by the brigadier of 1864 that everything has happened before.

It is curious, but there comes to my attention your note and also the enclosed clipping from a friend with a scribbled note: "Wonder what office Carl is running for"! And I also find in the pile an invitation from Eugene Reynal [231] for the luncheon for you [232] on October 7, but the horrid schedule shows me in Wichita. To think of it — Wichita!, instead of the Havana Room, Blackstone, Sandburg!

Goodbye, and thanks.

Yours,

P.S. Allan Nevins writes me that the book is great.

[231] Vice president and director in charge of the trade department of Harcourt, Brace & Company.

[232] The luncheon celebrated the publication of a one-volume edition of Mr. Sandburg's *Abraham Lincoln: The Prairie Years and the War Years* (New York: Harcourt, Brace, 1954).

Mr. Truman wrote Stevenson on September 20, praising the Indianapolis speech and commenting that the Democrats had the Republicans on the run.

To Harry S. Truman

September 22, 1954

Dear Mr. President:

So many thanks for your gracious letter about the speech in Indianapolis. I am enormously pleased that you approve. And I hardly need tell you how difficult it is to write these things over and over.

All of the news is good, as you well know. Nor have I yet detected any serious danger of over optimism. At least it is a good sign when the Democrats are warning one another about it.

I hear good reports of your progress and I am personally relieved that the "Boss" [233] and the doctors have forbidden you to exert yourself this fall. There will always be time for that, and just now your health and strength are entitled to the first priority.

Cordially,

T. S. Matthews wrote Stevenson praising the Indianapolis speech and added: "Whether the Democrats have sense enough to nominate you in '56 and the country has sense enough to elect you — both of which I profoundly hope — it is your unavoidable destiny to be a voice for America: a voice that speaks truly for a nation we can all trust and admire and love. And that can crack jokes, by God! so we won't get too big for our britches."

To T. S. Matthews

September 22, 1954

Dear Tom:

Your letter I found in Chicago on my return from Bloomington and it pleases me no end. If you really believe what you say I am relieved. Making partisan speeches is not the most agreeable work!

I am more than a little disappointed about missing you and Martha.[234] I shall be in Libertyville from the 26th to the 30th in case there is any hope of an evening.

Yours,

[233] Mrs. Truman.
[234] Mrs. Matthews.

To Chester Bowles

September 22, 1954

Dear Chester:

Arthur Schlesinger writes that he has had a talk with you recently and that you may have some foreign affairs materials which I could use in speeches in the early future. Anything you could prepare for me would be most welcome. I am hard put to it to find either the time or the strength to do this job this autumn properly — so help! help!

I shall be speaking in Michigan on October 2, Wichita October 7, Los Angeles October 9, Albuquerque October 15, and San Francisco October 16. For your information I enclose copies of some recent speeches in which I adverted to the foreign situation. There are, of course, countless others but I shan't burden you.

Following the election I also have in mind that it would be a mighty wholesome thing in December, before Congress convenes, to make a thoughtful positive foreign policy speech pointing some directions for our congressional leadership. In the nature of things much of what we shall be saying and have said has been negative and critical and the time will come when we must talk more affirmatively. I think you will agree. The problem, from my point of view, is how to get the distillation or [of] our best positive thought.

Yours,

To Thomas K. Finletter

September 22, 1954

Dear Tom:

Ever so many thanks for sending me "Power And Policy." [235] How you got this done and so much more besides in the past year and a half baffles me.

Each day I think of something I want to talk to you about, and somehow our meetings are so infrequent and I am so rattled in those political gatherings that I never get important business attended to.

If we win the House and Senate, as well we may, the problem of congressional initiative and leadership in program is going to be perplexing and dangerous, as you well know. I suppose there is little that can be done, but I wish we were taping down some positive views on some specific problems which could be "packaged" — that horrid word — and passed along to our "guys" after the elections.

[235] *Power and Policy: U.S. Foreign Policy and Military Power in the Hydrogen Age* (New York: Harcourt, Brace, 1954).

But all this is very fuzzy and so am I after days of this weary traveling and yammering. As for me, all I want to do is to change my life after the elections, speak very infrequently and try to earn a little money on the fringes of the law. But I would like to make one thoughtful, positive, nonpartisan foreign policy speech some time in December, trying to suggest some alternatives and setting the tone for our people to the extent that I have any resonance with them. The problem is how to distill the best thinking of our best people — you, [Chester] Bowles, [Paul] Nitze, [George] Kennan, et al. Maybe we should plan a talk in New York when I am there about October 30, if not before.

Yours,

To Mrs. Averell Harriman [236]

September 22, 1954

BRAVISSIMA AND HOORAY TO AVE [237] AND COURAGE TO YOU DEAR MARIE. I AM VERY HAPPY.

ADLAI

Stevenson stayed with Mr. and Mrs. Barry Bingham in Louisville at the time of the engagement party of Adlai Stevenson III and Nancy Anderson. He had been concerned that this necessary meeting with his divorced wife might provoke a scene that would disturb the occasion.

To Mr. and Mrs. Barry Bingham

September 22, 1954

My beloved Binghams:

I seem to be always thanking you for something and this time it is for the best of all: your hospitality and help in a crisis. And how relieved I was to find it really wasn't a crisis! So many, many thanks for those wonderful hours at your place and all of your infinite kindnesses to the young people. I understand better all the time why Adlai lost his heart in Louisville.

Affectionately,

---

[236] A telegram.
[237] Mr. Harriman had just received the Democratic nomination for governor of New York.

To Mr. and Mrs. Wilson W. Wyatt

September 22, 1954

My dear Wyatts:

It is futile to try to thank you for those exquisite, happy days. You were sweet to us, thoughtful, sensitive, and the management was up to the Wyatt standard. But can you forgive me for such an imposition? I hope so, so I can come back.

Thanks, dear Ann, and affectionate regards to you both and to those wonderful children.

Yours,

To Malcolm MacDonald [238]

September 23, 1954

My dear Mr. MacDonald:

You will remember, I hope, an evening in your fine garden in Singapore when you were good enough both to feed and enlighten me. That you were so good to me and so helpful and courteous is perhaps all the more reason why I should not impose on you. However, I have taken the liberty of telling a friend here in Chicago that I met you on my journey in 1953 and would be bold enough to write this letter of introduction for — Kathryn Lewis of the Chicago Sun-Times.

Kathryn Lewis is the widow of my beloved and gifted friend, Lloyd Lewis, an American biographer and writer of great significance. She is traveling extensively in the next few months, doing an occasional piece for the Sun-Times of Chicago, and I could think of no one better equipped to tell her the facts of life in Asia than yourself. If you are in Singapore when she reaches there and could give her a few minutes I don't believe you will find it altogether tiresome for she is well informed about this country.

We watch your region of the world with anxious fixation.

Cordially yours,

To David L. Cohn [239]

September 23, 1954

Dear Dave:

Word comes to me via the New York Times that you have gone and

[238] Commander-General for the United Kingdom in Southeast Asia and son of former Prime Minister Ramsay MacDonald. For Stevenson's visit with him in 1953, see *The Papers of Adlai E. Stevenson*, Vol. V.

[239] The original is in the Mississippi collection, University of Mississippi Library.

done it. Well, while I hate to see my bachelor friends dropping off you have a better standing in that league than I and have earned your escape long since.[240] Blessings — congratulations — and all similar salutations in all languages to you and your victim — no doubt intelligent, charming, tolerant I pray, and a Democrat — I hope.

Yours,

ADLAI

Dore Schary prepared a documentary film of Stevenson's 1953 world trip from newsreel and television coverage. It was hoped that the film might be useful if Stevenson decided to run for the presidency again in 1956. William Blair took considerable footage on the trip, but his camera broke down at intervals.[241]

To Dore Schary [242]

September 25, 1954

Dear Dore:

I have seen the picture and thought it was fine; likewise the commentary seemed to me excellent. In view of the present pressures I doubt if there is very much we can do about it until after the congressional elections. Perhaps then Bill [Blair] can come out there and I could do a little work on the commentary here. Professor Walter Johnson, who was with us on the trip, is doing some work on it now.

I wish it were possible to put in some of Bill's footage for I think it would personalize the film a lot more. As it is there seems to me rather too much of abstract shots and arrivals and departures of airplanes. The film he took which survived disaster with the camera and film is more personal about our party, where we were, etc.

I hope so much we will have a chance to discuss this when I come to Los Angeles. At all events, I look forward to seeing you again and I am enormously grateful to you and Mr. Hoffman [243] for going to all this trouble.

Cordially yours,

ADLAI

---

[240] Mr. Cohn married Lillian Millner on September 14, 1954.
[241] The film is in the possession of Mr. Blair.
[242] The original is in the possession of the State Historical Society of Wisconsin.
[243] Herman Hoffman, who worked with Mr. Schary at MGM, helped to edit the documentary.

To Alicia Patterson [244]

September 26, 1954

. . . Thanks for the scrawl — and as for me — its a horror. I've hardly caught my breath since May; and it goes on & on until after the Congressional elections — Mich[igan], Kans[as]. Calif[ornia], N[ew] M[exico] next — coming last the last week about. Surveying the ghastly details it looks as tho my only time here — Libertyville — will be between Oct 3 and 6 when I suppose I'll be distracted with speech preparation.

In short things are lousy — but I'll pray for a glimpse in N.Y. & lots more after Nov 2 when I propose to sharply change my mode of life and speak very seldom and try to earn a little money at the law somehow.

Yes — its "I can't give you anything but love baby" — and I shall have to "help out." Its tough for me & will be tougher, but he's a wonderful guy, that oldest son of mine, and she's a charming, fine, bright gal.[245] And what am I living for anyway — I sometimes wonder —

Love from
THE GOV.

To Franklin D. Roosevelt, Jr.

September 27, 1954

Dear Frank:

I just want to say I think your behavior has been superb. I have an idea how disappointed you and Jim Lanigan and all of your devoted staff must have been. But to accept defeat so gallantly and then with such good grace a place on the ticket and a major part in the campaign has, I am sure, won you new respect and admiration.[246] Everyone realizes, including Averell Harriman, I am sure, how much he and the ticket will need your remarkable talents in an election which has the nation's attention.

Good luck, my profound admiration, and warm regards to you and your wife.

Cordially,

P.S. "Frank" has arrived! Indeed I have just been out to see him and he is as handsome and well bred as his namesake.[247] My farmer is ex-

---

[244] This handwritten letter is in the possession of Adlai E. Stevenson III.
[245] Nancy Anderson.
[246] Mr. Roosevelt lost the gubernatorial nomination to Averell Harriman but was nominated for New York attorney general.
[247] Mr. Roosevelt had sent Stevenson a purebred Suffolk ram.

cited and so am I — but as yet the ewes seem to be contented with green grass! I am sure a Roosevelt on my place is going to encourage the Democrats in Lake County — which hasn't gone Democratic since the Civil War. A thousand thanks — and the crate is on its way back.

To Mrs. Franklin D. Roosevelt

September 28, 1954

Dear Mrs. Roosevelt:

I regret so much that I cannot be in New York on October 11 for your Birthday Party. I must be in the Far West on political business — strange to say.

Personally I am not sure we should celebrate your birthday or that we should be reminded that time passes for you as for the rest of us. There are some people for whom time seems to stand still and who can bridge all the generations of their interval on earth, but they are very rare. You are one, and for me you will always be the same age, and no age.

With warmest good wishes, I am

Faithfully yours,

To Nancy L. Anderson

September 29, 1954

Dear Nancy:

I am sending you the first known newspaper photograph of that gent of yours. If you have any misgivings about his structure this photo should explain everything. I am happy to say that most of the deformities of his infancy seem to have vanished, however.

Affectionately,

Senator Kefauver wrote on September 25 that he had just heard a report that he had circulated rumors — or had been responsible for them — about Stevenson at the 1952 Convention. Kefauver explained that he had instructed his staff that he wanted no one connected with him to circulate derogatory words about Stevenson or any other candidate. The senator added that he had just campaigned in California and the situation was encouraging for the Democrats.

To Estes Kefauver

October 2, 1954

Dear Estes:

Thanks for your letter and the spirit which prompted it. I would expect nothing other from you.

But as to the "rumor" I must say that I had never heard of it until your letter arrived nor have I the remotest idea what it was. Had I heard of it I would have known at that time that you had nothing to do with it.

All good wishes, my gratitude — and gratification with the news you send from California.

Cordially yours,

To Warwick Anderson

October 4, 1954

Dear Warwick:

I have succeeded in engaging the Onwentsia Club here in Lake Forest for Sunday afternoon, December 26. If possible for you and Mary San [248] to be here that day, I should like very much to have a sort of reception for my friends hereabouts to meet Nancy. You know how thick things are at the holiday season in a place like Lake Forest, and after consultation with my sister and others hereabouts we concluded this was the best possible date. I have not had an opportunity to consult Nancy and Adlai but I am sending the latter a copy of this letter with the hope that it will meet with his approval and that I can discuss it with them at the next opportunity.

And this paragraph is of no interest to thee, but to thou, Mary San: I have some lovely Chinese brocade that I brought from Hong Kong and I should like awfully to have an evening wrap (Mandarin coat?) made up for Nancy for a Christmas present. Should I send the material down to you, and could you, would you, be able to instruct a dressmaker what to do and how to do it, and also instruct her to send me the bill!!! If not, my dear, I shall await measurements and try to arrange it myself — with God knows what consequences.

Please forgive a confused, harrassed itinerant politician who talks, eats, travels, writes and manages everything and everybody simultaneously.

Hastily,

[248] Mrs. Anderson.

[405]

To Nancy L. Anderson

October 7, 1954

My dear Nancy:

I am sending you a little engagement token, a shawl that I got in Srinagar — which a Smith College senior will at once identify as the "capital" of the province of Jammu-Kashmir, and the heart of the Vale of Kashmir.

Love from a harried politician,

During October, Stevenson embarked on a speaking tour through the West,[249] and published an article outlining the role of the Democratic party in the preceding two years.[250] The following letter was written from Taos, New Mexico.

To Porter McKeever

October 11, 1954

Dear Porter:

I was so glad to have your thoughtful letter — and to know there were some old friends who could still distinguish my personal happiness from my political success. This is something quite new and I'm the more grateful to you and Susan.[251]

But you are wrong about being "after the nomination." I'm afraid I'm not sure what I'm after except to pay in full my debt to the Democratic Party, and a congressional victory on the heels of the defeat of 1952 would, of course, be a most agreeable conclusion to that effort.

After the election, I'm by no means sure, except that I must give some attention to earning a living again and also conserving my health and enlarging my wisdom — which should not be hard!

Thanks for your charity about the speeches. It gets harder and harder and the way wearier and longer. I was delighted, of course, by the

---

[249] On October 7, he spoke at Wichita, Kansas. The text is in *What I Think*, pp. 76–81. Two days later he spoke at the Hollywood Bowl in California. A portion is in *What I Think*, pp. 82–83. The complete text, with an analysis of the last-minute changes inserted in the text released to the press, appeared in Ralph Richardson, "Adlai E. Stevenson, Hollywood Bowl, October 9, 1954," *Western Speech* (Journal of the Western Speech Association), May, 1955, pp. 137–174. October 15, Stevenson spoke at Albuquerque, New Mexico. The text is in *What I Think*, pp. 133–139.

[250] "Rapier versus Ax: A Constructive Opposition," New York *Herald-Tribune*, October 13; reprinted in *What I Think*, pp. 84–87.

[251] Mrs. McKeever.

McKeever sallies, especially Deutschland uber Dulles.[252] I wish I dared use it but my critics persist in saying I'm just a joker — and it is demons like you who keep reassuring me that "a merry heart doeth good like a medicine."

Yours,

Stevenson delivered the following speech at a Democratic rally in the Civic Auditorium of San Francisco on October 16.[253]

In two weeks we the people will have to elect a new Congress. So, in accordance with our ancient and honored custom, the air is full of voices these days telling you what to do, why you should have a Democratic Congress or why you should have a Republican Congress.

Well, I am here to add my voice to the controversy and to thank, from the bottom of a full heart, thousands of you for your encouragement and support of a native son of California in the campaign of 1952. If I don't recall the whole of that ordeal with undiluted joy, I can say that my visits here to San Francisco during that campaign — to the Veterans Auditorium and to the Cow Palace — and the warmth of your welcome on both occasions, are among the happiest and most enduring memories of a busy life.

My affection for this beautiful San Francisco and for California, which began when I began, is so strong that I've long since forgiven you for what you didn't do in 1952. Actually, it could hardly have been otherwise for about the only states I carried were the only ones I didn't visit at all and I visited California not once, but twice.

At all events I welcome this opportunity to pay my respects to all of those fine Democratic candidates who are here with me, and especially to Dick Graves [254] and Sam Yorty.[255]

I have been Governor of a great state — a responsibility, an opportunity and an honor in our public life with great potential for good or evil. I left that office convinced that the best equipment for an effective Governor (besides the courage to say "no" and say it often) was an

[252] Mr. McKeever had written that a current political quip about town was this alteration of the title of the German national anthem, in reference to Dulles's position with respect to rearming West Germany within the European Defense Community. See note 214, p. 388.

[253] The text is from the New York *Times*, October 17, 1954. The editors have corrected obvious errors.

[254] Richard Graves, a Democrat, ran unsuccessfully for governor against Goodwin J. Knight.

[255] Democratic Congressman Samuel Yorty ran unsuccessfully for the U.S. Senate against Thomas H. Kuchel.

intimate familiarity with the intricacies of government at all levels — local, county and state — and their interdependence in the service of the human needs for which government exists.

I believe such knowledge in a Governor is far more important to the people he serves than political charm, dexterity and know-how, and especially in California, which confronts the infinite problems of a population that has trebled and an industrial output that has increased eightfold in thirty years, with no end in sight. I firmly believe that the governing of this state is about as stern a task as there is in our public life. And I am pleased and proud that the Democratic party has offered the people of California for that task not a man whose credentials are just political but a man who has made a career of the theory and practice of government in California at the state and local level. It is seldom indeed that the people of any state have had the opportunity or have seized the opportunity to elect a man with such remarkable qualifications as Dick Graves.

And it seems to me that California has another conspicuous opportunity to better itself this fall — by sending Sam Yorty to the Senate. It may have come to your attention that the voice of California in the nation and the world has become the voices of Vice President [Richard M.] Nixon and Senator [William F.] Knowland — voices that are seldom still and always confusing.

Mr. Nixon expresses his views on foreign policy and everything else, freely and frequently, and changes them in the same manner. Senator Knowland tells off President Eisenhower and denounces Secretary Dulles also freely and frequently and loudly, which is the more remarkable considering that he is the President's leader in the Senate.

While the President talks about peaceful coexistence with the Communists, Senator Knowland talks of war with Red China. When he publicly demands that we sever diplomatic relations with Russia, the President has to issue a quick and angry "no."

In the current Republican parlance this is what is known as "team play."

In March Mr. Nixon, the Administration's chief spokesman these days, took to the television to tell us that massive atomic retaliation is the key to peace and we want no more small wars, no more Koreas; we are not going to be "nibbled to death."

Yet, in the following month he was in favor of sending American forces to fight in Indo-China. Then after the Communist triumph, he told political meetings that the Truman Administration was to blame for the French disaster in Indo-China. (I think that kind of political trip must be an ill-will tour.) But, meanwhile, the President was talking amiably about bipartisanship. This I understand is known as the smile and smear technique of campaigning: The President smiles while the Vice President smears. Finally to complete this story, now that the fighting is over and the free world has lost half of Vietnam to the Communists, our agile Vice President points to peace in the world as an achievement of the Eisenhower Administration.

Now all of this also suggests why, in my judgment, this great, majestic state of California, our western gate, badly needs some new voices in the United States Senate — some temperate, sensible voices — why, in short, California needs Sam Yorty.

Of course there are many explanations for the catastrophic loss of our moral and political prestige in the non-Communist world during recent months, losses which we and our world can ill afford at a time when the first objective of Soviet policy is to drive a wedge between us and our friends and enfeeble our Grand Alliance. The reasons for our sudden decline in world esteem stem mostly, it seems to me, from the unhappy divisions that have all but paralyzed the Republican party's initiative and effectiveness as an instrument of government. I warned you about the Old Guard, about the men who have had to be dragged, screaming and kicking, into the Twentieth Century. Just two years ago yesterday I said here in San Francisco (and I'm not embarrassed about repeating what I said during that campaign, for you see I wasn't a very promising candidate):

"These men opposed our policy of strength at home. They opposed labor's right to organize and bargain collectively. They opposed effective supports for farm income. They opposed the whole conception of security in economic life. They wanted labor to be weak, the farmers to be weak, Government to be weak — and only themselves to be strong. They never understood the central truth — that the strength of the nation resides in the strength of the whole, and not in the strength of one of its parts."

That was two years ago and meanwhile in the giveaway of our natural resources, in the economic retreat, in tax legislation for the benefit of corporations and the well-to-do, we have seen emerge the traditional Republican platform of government of the many by the few and for the few.

But two years ago here in San Francisco I also said that the Old Guard would not support even the foreign policy of their own Republican candidate. As an illustration I specifically mentioned foreign trade on which our allies, like Britain, Japan and Germany, are wholly dependent and on which we are becoming more dependent as our productive capacity exceeds our needs, especially in agriculture. And what happened was even worse than I foresaw. In the last session of Congress even President Eisenhower's modest proposals received not a single Republican vote and the best he could get was a one-year extension of the old Democratic Reciprocal Trade Law.

Our foreign affairs take, in effect, two-thirds of our Federal taxes, and the question of war or peace in the hydrogen age is the question of survival or extinction. So foreign affairs are [our] most important affairs, and, as in 1952, I want to talk soberly about foreign policy tonight — here on the rim of the Pacific where the destiny of the world for long years to come may well be decided.

What I want to say, briefly, is that in spite of all the domestic reasons for electing a Democratic Congress this fall there are even better and more insistent reasons in the foreign field where our loss of prestige and confidence and the spread of anti-Americanism is alarming.

Why is this? Why has the impression got around that we are heedless of the risks of war in the atomic age? Why are our friends fearful that a distant United States — that has never been occupied or bombed — may drag them into another war? How has the Administration continued to increase worldwide fears of America's belligerence while steadily reducing America's effective strength?

There are many contributing reasons for our present plight. Among them the Republicans have to bear the responsibility for nourishing our thinking since the war on myths — the myth, for example, that Truman and Acheson and a few sinister men in the State Department caused the Chinese revolution; the myth that Roosevelt gave Eastern Europe to the Communists at Yalta and Teheran; the myth that other peoples have to be for us or they are against us, and so on.

The Republicans created and cultivated these myths to discredit the Democrats. Now the Republicans are in power and the victims of their own mythology. With unsolved problems on all sides, they still mumble the old myths and waste our national reputation trying to give meaning to empty words and to prove that the Truman foreign policy which saved Europe, forged the Grand Alliance and held the walls of the free world for years was made in Moscow.

Also, the violence which has lately marked our domestic politics is not unrelated to the alarming deterioration of our world position. The Republicans have painted a picture of bitterly divided America for all the world to see. The image is not one to evoke confidence in our leadership but one of an uncertain and unreliable ally, powerful beyond compare and all the more disturbing for that reason.

While the rest of the free world drew courage and inspiration from our defense of freedom in Korea, Governor Dewey of New York, twice his party's candidate for the office of President, told the American people that the word Democrat was synonymous with murder and treachery; the Republican National Committee celebrated Lincoln's Birthday last winter with a series of speeches by Senator Joseph R. McCarthy entitled "Twenty Years of Treason," and the Attorney General of the United States impugned the very loyalty of a former President — a man who has done more to fight communism than all the Republican politicians put together — and I mean Harry S. Truman.

With mounting wonder and disbelief the world has seen and heard many other strange sights and sounds. McCarthyism, fear and mistrust have tarnished the bright vision of strong, confident, free America. Books were banned, respected people slandered, and frightening, arrogant slogans followed one another — into oblivion:

"Let Asians fight Asians," "liberation of the satellites" (which sounded like war in Europe), "unleashing Chiang Kai-shek" (which sounded like war in Asia), the "new look" in defense, "massive retaliation" (which sounded like total atomic war everywhere), "agonizing reappraisal," etc. At first our friends trembled lest the Government of the United States meant what it said, but then they gradually learned that the Administration did not mean what it said — a lesson, by the way, which the American people have had to learn about farm policy, public power, labor relations, balancing the budget, etc.

Is it any wonder that the leaders of other nations and their peoples have begun to doubt whether they can have confidence in America and the continuity of our policy? What's wrong? Why is this?

Basically, it is because the Administration is trapped in a dilemma of its own making — it is trying to conduct a responsible foreign policy and appease the extremist wing of the Republican party at the same time. It is trying to reconcile the irreconcilable. And it acts as though it was more important to unite the Republican party than to unite our country and the free world. They talk tough to satisfy the extremists and reduce the Army and the Air Force to satisfy the budget cutters. Driven by the extremists they announce goals exceeding their willingness or ability to act. Secretary Dulles demands united action on Indo-China and settles for united inaction, with nothing to show for our part in the Geneva Conference but the preposterous boast that we had refused to speak to our adversaries, because the right wing Republicans have successfully identified negotiation with appeasement. The President announces firm support of a liberal trade policy and not only accepts defeat without a struggle, but actually raises various tariffs.

Over and over we are wobbly when we should be firm and rigid when we need flexibility. We shake our fist and then our finger. Repeatedly we have bluffed friend and foe alike. Repeatedly Secretary Dulles has waved the diplomatic big stick and threatened our allies.

The Administration acts as if bluff and bluster were the essence of statesmanship. Its public utterances are designed more often to impress not our friends abroad, nor even our adversaries, but the right wing of the Republican party at home — the gentlemen who aid and abet the Communist policy of breaking up our alliances by abusing our allies. In order to achieve good relations with these gentlemen the Administration has impaired our relations with Britain, France, India. For harmony in the Republican party it has paid the price of harmony in the free world.

Some of you may wonder why the issue of foreign policy arises in a political campaign. Let me make it absolutely clear that it is in this campaign through no desire of the Democrats. The leaders of my party have expressed again and again their hope that the kind of bipartisanship in foreign policy which existed in the days of Truman and Roosevelt would be brought back to Washington.

Why is there no bipartisanship in the formulation of our foreign policy these days? Why are there no Democrats in high positions in President Eisenhower's Administration when there were so many Republicans in President Truman's Administration? Is it because the Republicans are imprisoned by their own irresponsible slander? Only this week the Administration is playing its cynical numbers game again about the subversives and security risks they have fired, but I haven't heard of a single Communist or traitor that they have exposed. Or has bipartisanship in the State Department been subordinated to job hunger and the Republican spoils system?

Why have they sharply cut our Air Force and Army while warning us about growing enemy strength — cuts, by the way, which account for most of the budget reduction to which they point with such pride? Has tax reduction, for the few, taken priority over national defense? Why have they cut economic and technical assistance programs, just as the Soviets venture into that field?

Why have they failed to keep their foreign trade promises, just as the Moscow-Peiping axis dangles seductive trade proposals before our hard-pressed friends?

Why has the State Department and Foreign Service been terrorized by a protege [256] of Senators [William] Knowland, [Styles] Bridges and [Joseph] McCarthy?

[256] R. W. Scott McLeod, chief security officer for the State Department. As a friend and follower of Senator McCarthy, who had earlier described the Department as infested with Communists, McLeod proved troublesome to the new Administration, which wished to avoid such extremism. See Emmet John Hughes, *The Ordeal of Power: A Political Memoir of the Eisenhower Years* (New York: Atheneum, 1963), pp. 84–85.

Why, indeed, are all the tools of our foreign policy in disarray? Why is our economic assistance program today a tool of little or no value? Why is our Point IV program limping aimlessly? Why is our foreign information program disorganized and voiceless? Why, indeed, do we even have to talk about the foreign policy and performance of this great nation in a Congressional political campaign when the goals, the objectives and ambitions of all of us, Democrats and Republicans alike, are identical?

The answer to all these questions is the same: political expediency, appeasement of the Republican extremists, party unity at the price of national unity and international influence. After all these months of babble and bewilderment is it any wonder that we have become unpredictable to our friends and predictable to our enemies? In Europe and Japan they fear we may heedlessly involve them in unnecessary war. Our enemies look at cutbacks in our defense expenditures, withdrawal of troops from the Pacific, the bluff that failed in Indo-China, delays in our continental defense program, tensions in our relations with our allies, our withering programs for building economic strength and unity, our reliance on military strategy and neglect of the underlying political and social problems. Our enemies look at these hard facts rather than Mr. Dulles' hot words — and believe they have little to fear.

Yet the President said the other night in Los Angeles: "Over the world we have brought strength where there was weakness. We have brought realism where there was wishful thinking. We have brought frankness, candor and force to foreign policy."

Well, if he really believed that it would be positively dangerous, because the success of our foreign policy far transcends in importance the political success of his party or mine. And until our leaders distinguish words from reality and foolish elocution from effective action, we will be in trouble, and our alliances, our security, in jeopardy.

I could add, too, that we will be in trouble as long as the Administration tries to placate the implacable, and yields to that little band of right wing Republicans. At the risk of mixing my metaphors, perhaps here in San Francisco I could remind our leaders of an old Chinese proverb: "He who rides a tiger may not dismount."

But with the great losses of the past months there have been some gains, too. I would even add that while Republicans, like Mr. Nixon, still blame the Democrats for the Communist conquest in China, I don't blame the Republicans for the Communist conquest in Indo-China. I don't even think there are any traitors among the responsible Republicans in Washington. In fact, I think they are just as patriotic and just as loyal, if not quite as wise and intelligent, as we Democrats.

But I must add about Indo-China that I hope I never again see the United States in such nervous disorder and confusion. Unable to fight, unable to negotiate, we ended up unable even to speak coherently, while the Communists drove a wedge into Southeast Asia, and the free world suffered its greatest disaster since the fall of China.

But, as I say, there have been gains. In Iran the long negotiations have come to a happy end, and our Government is, I believe, entitled to a large share of the credit.

In the Middle East the British and the Egyptians have settled the menacing dispute over Suez. But after seven years there is no peace between the Arabs and Israel, whose fears are now aggravated by our Government's plan to arm her Arab neighbors. Yet we can hope that the important and conciliatory proposals Israel has lately made may point the way at least toward direct negotiation with the Arabs.

At long last a settlement has been reached between Yugoslavia and Italy over Trieste, which is solid progress.

In Guatemala a Communist cell in the New World has been exposed and eliminated. While we lost the European Defense Community, on which we banked too heavily and threatened too much, the position and participation in European defense of Germany has been worked out through NATO. And if Mr. Dulles played a passive, secondary role I don't criticize, I applaud him. The time has come for us to calm down a bit, step aside and let our allies take some initiative — those allies, by the way, like Britain and France whom the Republican extremists constantly vilify.

And in the East the debacle of Indo-China ought to make it clear that military power alone will not carry the day, for the greatest power in Asia is nationalism and the greatest problems are political and social. But the Southeast Asian Defensive Alliance Secretary Dulles has negotiated has definite military value,[257] and it could and will, we hope, become far more than what the Asians call the "White Man's Protective Association."

So, I repeat, there have been some gains in the past two years and certainly our Government and Secretary Dulles are entitled to credit and gratitude for their contribution. But I pray let us understand the full significance of our situation and let us state our successes with modest realism and not boastful reassurance. For we confront a trembling alliance in Europe, less than confidence in Asia, the growing attraction of monstrous China, Russia's military and economic might, a restless Africa, and a South America we have too long taken for granted.

We exclude as solutions either world destruction or world tyranny; we exclude, in short, preventive war or surrender as offering any possible

[257] The Southeast Asia Treaty Organization, pioneered by Secretary Dulles after the Geneva Conference, agreed on French withdrawal from Indochina and a temporary division of Vietnam to be ended by elections in 1956.

solutions of the predicament of western civilization. The only course remaining is coexistence, and I confess I get a little impatient with the semantic debate for and against coexistence, for it is either coexistence or no-existence — until the evil of the dread design of imperial communism is clear for all to see.

But coexistence with our obnoxious, aggressive and perfidious neighbors can never be peaceful. Workable coexistence can only be based on a balance of effective strength, military, economic and moral, with evil neighbors who will relentlessly and tirelessly expand wherever they scent weakness or vulnerability. So military power is essential.

But imperialist communism is not just an armed threat and an underground conspiracy. It is also a social movement which grows and prospers especially in the great underdeveloped areas of discontent, while we concentrate on combating the conspiracy. Having checked their military efforts we would be foolish to let them win easy victories in the social and economic battle. So we must push steadily forward in developing the economic and moral strength of the non-communist world.

Can the United States meet this vast challenge? I doubt it so long as the Administration in Washington places the welfare of the right wing of the Republican party above the welfare of the country. The "agonizing reappraisal" and the "liberation" which Secretary Dulles has talked about must begin at home and now, before we lose any more precious, hard-won ground. And the way to liberate our Government from its present thralldom is to elect a Democratic Congress in November.

By electing a Democratic Congress, we can turn the Republican Old Guard out of control of the committees of Congress. We can demonstrate that this small group has no mandate from the American people. We can even encourage the Secretary of State to be himself and to sponsor a foreign policy which will represent the country as a whole and not just a reactionary minority; a policy which is not a hydra-headed compromise that frightens everyone, and pleases no one, and demeans our country.

But a Republican victory in November would confirm the Administration in its futility and error. It would encourage the spirit of "go it alone" in the world and "go it alone" in the nation. It would postpone indefinitely the restoration of genuine bipartisanship and mutual confidence in foreign affairs.

Only a Democratic Congress can free foreign and defense affairs from those suffocating influences which the Administration seems to regard with such fear and trembling.

With a Democratic Congress perhaps we can all join to rebuild our unity, our strength, the tools of our policy, respect for our word in the world, the faith and constancy of our allies, the confidence of mankind everywhere in the essential honor, decency and good will of America. Then we would merit the respect, and even the just fear, of those who choose to be our enemies.

A Democratic victory in November can lay the basis for national unity. For we Democrats do not believe that to be a Republican is to be a traitor, to be corrupt, or even always to be confused. We have, in fact, prided ourselves on the cooperation and service of able Republicans in matters affecting the welfare of our country, particularly in the great areas of foreign affairs and national security.

With a Democratic Congress we can review the problems of our defense budget, the level to which our economy can be expanded, and the nature of an equitable tax structure to give us financial stability while meeting our proper defense and foreign policy outlays.

With a Democratic Congress perhaps the President and Mr. Dulles will no longer feel compelled to tolerate insubordinate agents of right wing Republican Senators. The morale and efficiency of the State Department could be rebuilt; new and talented men could be trained for its work; honest reporting and careful analysis could once again become subject to reward, not reproach.

With a Democratic Congress we could adopt a liberalized trade policy and resume the never-ending task of building that better functioning world economic system so necessary not only to give others economic hope, but indispensable to our own continued growth and prosperity.

With a Democratic Congress we could address ourselves once more to the interrupted task of assisting the underdeveloped areas of the world in making the transition to the opportunities of the world of the future.

We could then speak to our allies again in accents which they can understand and believe. We could strengthen our alliances, and contribute leadership commensurate with our other contributions. We could move from disunity, mutual recrimination, and antagonism to that mutual respect and well-wishing which are the pre-conditions of political maturity and responsibility.

We could stand prepared to meet whatever thrusts our enemies might plot against us with unity at home, with growing military and economic strength, with efficient organs of Government, with our allies' understanding of our purposes and of the limits of those purposes.

And, finally, remembering that strength is not an end in itself but a means to an end, we could explore with greater confidence the possibilities of negotiation with our friends, yes, and with our enemies — negotiations for settlements here and there and for safe and sound disarmament, thus inching our way along the weary path to peace. Negotiation without strength, which some of our European friends seem to want, is madness. Strength without negotiation is futility. Negotiation on the basis of strength and solidarity is the only policy which can hold out hope to patient and suffering mankind.

The world at the moment is in a long and dark valley. Science offers us mass suicide. But it also offers the world a greater abundance than we have ever known. Our generation will have to make a fateful choice.

Just two years ago, here in San Francisco, I said that: "America has been called to greatness. The summons of the twentieth century is a summons to our vision, to our humanity, to our practicality. If these provide the common purpose of America and Asia (and I might have added, of the free world) we need have no fear for the future. Because it will belong to free men."

I am still content to leave it there, adding only that the Democratic party is faithful to this vision and ready to work with all like-minded men and women in answering this summons.

To Arthur M. Schlesinger, Jr.

October 19, 1954

Dear Arthur:

Last night after returning from San Francisco I read your Atlantic piece on the Oppenheimer case.[258] You have done it again! And how you do it so deftly, understandingly and often still eludes me. Anyway, thanks for that, and thanks also for the San Francisco draft. I don't know whether it was published in the East, but I am asking Miss Evans to enclose a copy of what finally emerged from my adobe retreat in New Mexico.[259]

The West Coast reception was exhilarating and exhausting — to the degree in both directions that only they can achieve.

Hastily,

P.S. I still have in mind doing something after the election, but I am not sure that Chester [Bowles]'s total emphasis on the economic is either what I want or wholly believe. Anyway, it will be an expression of views from several people which will help me to state my own — pray God!

---

[258] "The Oppenheimer Case," *Atlantic*, October, 1954.
[259] Stevenson had spent several days at the ranch of Stephen A. Mitchell, just outside Taos, New Mexico, while preparing his Albuquerque and San Francisco speeches.

To Paul H. Nitze

October 19, 1954

Dear Paul:

I am so grateful for all your time and help in connection with the foreign policy presentation. I retreated to an adobe room in New Mexico and wrote a couple of speeches, including the one for San Francisco. A copy of what finally emerged is enclosed, and you will recognize some portions — for which I am most grateful.

I hope it isn't unfair or overdrawn. I was trying to both please a tumultuous and monstrous audience on the eve of an election and also put this scene in proper political perspective. I probably failed on both counts, but the Californians liked it.

Hastily yours,

To Bernard DeVoto

October 20, 1954

Dear Benny:

I should have thanked you before this for helping me out with the speech in New Mexico. It has been a long and weary journey and the end of this campaign can come none too soon. I have found it so hard to do the writing, the traveling, and the everlasting "appearances." The ordeal makes useful contributions the more precious. For your information I enclose what finally emerged from my adobe retreat for Albuquerque and you will recognize a lot of it. Actually, when it came to delivery I had to cut it almost in two and then was over time — to which you will say "as usual." But I will have you know I have been doing better lately. The trouble is there was too much of you I wanted to keep.

Warm regards.

Cordially and hastily,

To William Benton [260]

October 20, 1954

Dear Bill:

I hope I can see the Benton gals, and even their Old Man during my campaign visit to New York. It would be a lark for me if not for them.

As to Thanksgiving, I find the situation still unclear. With my oldest

[260] The original is in the possession of the estate of William Benton. See note 143, above.

son engaged to a girl at Smith and evidently no Thanksgiving vacation from Harvard Law School, and also his mother's plans indefinite, I am literally unable to determine whether I shall have the boys for Thanksgiving, or, if so, whether we can leave Boston. Borden will probably be in the Army, and on the whole I think possibly you better write us off, although there is a possibility that John Fell and I might turn up, or even John Fell, Adlai and his fiancee if that were possible and Southport [Connecticut] not too distant from Cambridge.[261]

It's hell trying to manage a family and a campaign simultaneously!

Hastily,

ADLAI

To Mrs. Warwick Anderson

October 25, 1954

My dear Mary San:

I am so mortified that I have not answered your letter. My life lately I shall not attempt to describe, but it has been twice as bad as anything you can imagine. Yesterday, Sunday, I got off a letter to Adlai making in effect two points to sustain my opinion, which I assume he had requested, that the wedding should take place in June: (1) Nancy should finish college, getting her degree, do her job and not be diverted when so close to the end. This, I think, is largely his responsibility. (2) I can think of no worse way to start marriage than as a law student with a 12 or 14-hour work day, in contrast to a relaxed summer.

I gather both from what Adlai says and from what you say, and what

[261] Stevenson spent Thanksgiving with Mr. and Mrs. Benton. Mr. Benton later recalled:

"On the evening before Thanksgiving, with perhaps 12 or 15 guests of the ages of our children John and Louise who were then still at home, I showed ten or 15 Britannica films. After each film the Governor made a little speech. And a fascinating speech each one was. I remember one of the films dealt with policemen, and the Governor of course had a whale of a background on policemen. At the end of the evening I said to him, 'Adlai, where the hell did you learn so much about so many subjects?' In that sad way of his, he said 'Bill, I have spent my life collecting useless information.'

"This is indeed in part a clue to the Governor's life. His knowledge was encyclopaedia in countless fields — such as in the field of British history and the background of the British aristocracy. As a young man, when many of the rest of us were working day and night developing our careers, he could afford to indulge himself and did indulge himself. He was the most avid tourist I have ever seen. On our yacht in the Mediterranean, in his two or three sailings with us, he was frequently the first one off the boat in the morning and the last one back at night. His appetite as a tourist was insatiable, far exceeding that of anyone I've ever met or observed. This curiosity, this insatiable lust to extract the last bit of information about anything that interested him — this was one of his most pronounced characteristics. This was his way of 'collecting useless information.'" Letter to Walter Johnson, September 26, 1966.

I hear elsewhere, that the decision has already been made. I shall have no objection, of course, if that is the case, and I have the utmost confidence in their good judgment, although the tempo and intensity of it all, as you know, is a little fast for such a tiresome, orthodox old man as I seem to be. I am sure on the present basis it is impossible, and that they should not attempt to see each other so often at such a terrible price in time, travel and distraction.

I was distressed to hear that I missed Warwick. Evidently he has been here since I returned from the West Coast, but I did not hear from him.

In view of all the confusion, I think I shall call off, or at least put on ice, any idea of a party for Nancy at Christmas. If you could let me know at your convenience how many yards of material will be needed for the coat I shall be most grateful. I can send it along, and I am sure you will know best what to do about the seamstress, finishing, etc.

I hear the most wonderful things about her from others and what she means to the students as well as the staff at the college. I have always thought well of my son's judgment and each fragment of news from Nancy confirms it.

Yours,

P.S. As to the type of wedding, if a wedding, I think I shall leave that entirely to you and the children. Given some advance notice I can prepare lists of any size, and I think I can also well control how many might come from here, at least, so have no fear of special trains, of politicians, and plastered Republicans!

I emphatically agree that he *is* an unusually ardent young man!

To John F. Kennedy [262]

October 26, 1954

Dear Jack:

I was distressed to hear you were back in the hospital again, but relieved to learn that the operation was a success.[263] Needless to say, we are all counting on you to make a full and speedy recovery because I have a hunch you will be needed more than ever come January of next year!

I caught a glimpse of Peter and Pat [264] in Beverly Hills a couple of weeks ago and they seem to be most content — and I can't say I blame them!

Best of luck and warmest good wishes.

Sincerely,

[262] Democratic senator from Massachusetts, 1953–61. A copy is in A.E.S., I.S.H.L.
[263] Senator Kennedy had had a back operation.
[264] Mr. and Mrs. Peter Lawford, Senator Kennedy's sister and brother-in-law.

On October 30, Vice President Nixon sent Stevenson a lengthy telegram — which he released to the press — accusing him of "covering up"
the record of the Truman Administration and "failing to answer the
facts" by screaming "smear, slur, and slander." Among the Vice President's alleged facts were:

(1) "The Acheson Foreign policy, which in seven years, lost 600,000,000
people to the Communists . . .

(2) "Blindness and ignorance of the threat of Communism which resulted in clearing and hiring of over 6,000 security risks which this Administration has investigated and fired."

After listing four other "facts," the Vice President challenged Stevenson in his speech that evening to name one misstatement of fact that he,
Nixon, had made in the campaign.[265]

Stevenson spoke to a Democratic rally at Cooper Union in New York
City on October 30, 1954.

THE CONGRESSIONAL CAMPAIGN ENDS [266]

As this campaign approaches its end, I want to discuss as soberly as I
can what is at stake on Tuesday for us all — what is at stake so far as
government measures and policies are concerned; and then what is at
stake so far as the election affects the health and responsibility of our
democratic system.

Let me first discuss with you why I think a Democratic Congress
would be good for the country — indeed, why it might even be good for
the Republican party!

Now it is both customary and fitting that the President should desire
and ask for a Congress of his own political persuasion, for the President
is also the leader of his party. But it is an entirely different matter to say
that the President is somehow and in some way *entitled* to a Congress of
his own choosing. It is not the President but the people who choose the
Congress; and our biennial Congressional elections were specifically designed by the Founding Fathers to provide the people an opportunity
to periodically record their judgment of an administration.

I might add that I do not recall the Republicans ever advancing the
argument that a President was entitled to a Congress of his own party
when there was a Democratic administration in Washington. Nor do I
think it very likely that they will be making this argument in, say, 1958!

But President Eisenhower has been offering another argument as to
why the people should give him a Republican Congress. He has said a

[265] Stevenson apparently did not reply to the telegram. He felt Nixon was without
principles or conscience.
[266] The text is from *What I Think*, pp. 88–95.

Democratic Congress would usher in a cold war with the White House, but if we are to judge by the record of the last Republican Congress, there can be no war colder, or hotter, than the internal conflict in the Republican party. I need only remind you of the proposed Bricker Amendment which was perhaps the most serious Congressional attempt in recent times to strike at the authority and integrity of the presidential office. It was conceived and executed by Republican Senators. And the coldest political warfare waged within living memories between the executive branch of government and members of Congress was the attack on the Eisenhower administration by Senator McCarthy and his Republican followers — an attack which heartened our enemies and dismayed our friends. The contradictions of the President by his majority leader, Senator [William] Knowland, of the cabinet by one another, of the Vice-President by the Secretary of State and so on, have become a subject of sorry mirth not only here but abroad where it is no longer clear who speaks for America.

But on Thursday night General Eisenhower once again summarized his case for a Republican Congress by suggesting that "confusion can be avoided and steady progress assured only by electing a Republican majority." After two years of confusion and retreat under a Republican Congress, I could hardly believe my eyes when I read this. Indeed I would like to use these words of the President's as my own text. For I deeply believe that the only way to avoid the lamentable confusion which has characterized our policies at home and abroad in the last two years — the only way to achieve a resumption of social and economic progress — is to elect a Democratic Congress next Tuesday.

A Democratic Congress would not only be more likely to enact legislation for the benefit of all the people. The irony is that in addition a Democratic Congress would be more likely to enact more important parts of President Eisenhower's own program than a Republican Congress would.

I could even add that it is the only way to rehabilitate as an effective instrument of government the Republican party, now so hopelessly divided on policy, program, and philosophy.

Let us consider foreign affairs. Our foreign policy, the level of our military strength, and our system of alliances have been systematically imperiled by compromises, contradictions, and appeasement of the Republican Old Guard; except, that is, when the Democrats have rescued the President from his own party and his own leadership. Democrats, for example, tried to resist the policy of reducing our national strength. Democrats tried to save President Eisenhower's own foreign trade program from the Republican protectionists. Democrats effected the confirmation of his Ambassador to Moscow [267] against Republican opposition.

On twelve key administration bills on foreign policy the Democrats not only provided the margin of victory, but on each one the Democrats actually gave the President more votes in both Senate and House than he received from his own party.

But the Democratic minority could not always save us from the Republican Old Guard.

When the President insists, as he did on Thursday, that his administration has been more faithful to bipartisanship in foreign policy "than any previous administration," one must charitably assume that he has been misinformed again. Under the Roosevelt and Truman administrations, dozens of Republicans shared in the responsibility for the formulation and execution of foreign policy in exalted positions — including General Eisenhower and Mr. Dulles, themselves. Where, I respectfully ask, are the Democrats who play similar roles in this administration? Where, even, are the Republicans who served under Democratic administrations and have been dismissed to please the Old Guard?

Either to please the Old Guard, or to get votes, the administration embarked on a perilous course of foreign-policy-by-slogan and foreign-policy-by-bluff. The reckless words about "liberation," "atomic retaliation," "seizing the initiative," "unleashing Chiang Kai-shek," and the like may have warmed the hearts of the Old Guard. But abroad they frightened our friends if not our enemies — whose aggressions have steadily increased in the past two years.

Thanks to the Republican primitives, the administration put a muffler on the Voice of America [268] and our overseas psychological warfare at just the time that Soviet propaganda was scoring new triumphs.

To please the Old Guard, in short, our Army has been cut back, our foreign trade program scuttled, our foreign service harried and demoralized, our allies intimidated and alarmed, our unity of purpose exploded into a sorry mess of conflicting statements, conflicting policies, and conflicting hopes. And, on every one of these issues, it is the Democrats in Congress who have consistently stood for steadiness and strength.

The President asks us to believe that all will be different in the next two years — that he can do with a Republican Congress what he couldn't do — with a Republican Congress! He asks us to believe that a Republican victory will somehow cause the Old Guard to change its spots and re-

[267] Charles E. Bohlen.
[268] The radio broadcasting service of the U.S. Information Agency, intended in part to combat Soviet propaganda by broadcasts aimed at citizens of Iron Curtain countries.

appear in the next Congress purified and repentant. But I say that experience is the best teacher and that a Republican victory will only give them new confidence and deepen the divisions in the Republican party, and the peril to all of us. It will encourage their attacks on the great coalition of free peoples and on our own political and military strength. Indeed, is there any way to liberate our foreign policy from these baleful influences and destructive divisions — is there any way to end the compromise, babble, and confusion which this appeasement has produced — except to elect a Democratic Congress on Tuesday?

And all this holds equally true for democratic policy. At first the Republicans laid claim to a record of legislative achievement. Latterly we've heard less about this record and more about Communists in government, subversion, and sin. Probably this is because most of the positive accomplishments of the administration were made possible only by Democratic votes. But I shall only mention the other parts which were put through without Democratic votes — for only that represents the distinctive contributions of this administration and only that would be threatened by a Democratic Congress.

What has President Eisenhower sought in the domestic field against Democratic opposition?

Against Democratic opposition, he put through a tax program in which the main benefits went overwhelmingly to the corporations and to stockholders. Against Democratic opposition, he has sponsored a wide and various give-away program. Ranging from public power development to grazing lands, from Dixon-Yates [269] to oil, from atomic patents to water-power sites, the administration has not only reversed a bipartisan conservation policy of fifty years but has disclosed an alarming disposition to transfer our national possessions and resources from the many to the few.[270]

[269] Memphis needed more power, but the Eisenhower Administration refused to allow the TVA to build a steam plant. Instead, the Atomic Energy Commission signed a contract with the Dixon-Yates combine. In February, 1955, Senator Lister Hill revealed that the special consultant who helped prepare the contract was an official of the First Boston Corporation, the investment house that was to act as financial agent for the Dixon-Yates combine. On July 11, 1955, the President canceled the contract.

[270] President Eisenhower in his first State of the Union message said: "The best natural resources program for America will not result from exclusive dependence on Federal bureaucracy. It will involve a partnership of the states and local communities, private citizens and the Federal Government, all working together." The offshore submerged oil lands were granted to the coastal states, the budget of the Bonneville Power Administration was slashed, a number of dam projects already approved by Congress were abandoned or shelved, and the Democratic plans for a high federal dam in Hell's Canyon were blocked and the area turned over to the Idaho Power Company.

Against Democratic opposition, the administration has enacted a new farm program. As a matter of good faith in politics, it seems to me reprehensible that this program was erected on a foundation of false pledges and broken promises. But, what is more important is that it means lower farm prices, with no corresponding decrease in sight in the cost of what the farmer has to buy.

More disturbing still is that not just the Vice-President and the Republican campaigners, but now the President himself, has affirmed the proposition that prosperity under the Democrats was achieved only at the price of war and bloodshed. This, of course, has been standard Communist propaganda for years and is believed by many to prove that the United States is ready to precipitate war in order to save capitalism. I am sure that the President must have spoken thoughtlessly and carelessly; and let me say to our friends and our enemies beyond the seas that no one who sincerely believes in free capitalism can believe that war or preparation for war is the price of prosperity.

Moreover the facts contradict it. The President evidently forgets the successful transition from war to peace in 1945 and 1946, when in a single year eight million men were released from the armed services and defense spending fell ten times as much as in the past year. Yet, in 1946, we had far less unemployment than we have today. One must assume, too, that the President has not been informed about the prosperous peacetime years of 1947 and 1948 when defense spending was less than one-third as large as it is today, and yet unemployment was at least a million less.

Of course, a Democratic Congress will not solve all our problems. But the election of a Democratic Congress on Tuesday will check the tendency of the last two years to separate the United States from our allies in world affairs. It will stem the drive to cut back further on our own armed strength. It will diminish the passion to give away our natural resources. It will stop further Dixon-Yates deals. It will restore the dignity of the Congressional investigation and will strengthen the atmosphere of individual freedom. It will chasten the administration's complacent attitude toward the millions of Americans who cannot find jobs. It can do much to bring back intelligence, sobriety, and purpose, to the American government. And a Republican victory this fall can only confirm and intensify the tendencies which have brought us into such disrepute abroad and into such disunion at home.

And a Democratic victory will mean a gain for responsibility in another way — in a way perhaps more important than the substantive issues at stake in the campaign. For the success of our democracy depends on the extent to which politics can serve the end of education, of justice, and of truth. Those who would degrade our political processes threaten to destroy the very essence of a free system. If these methods succeed today, then they will be used again and again, until freedom, dignity, decency themselves sink from sight into quicksands of confusion, mistrust, and fear.

All thoughtful citizens have been concerned about the progressive degeneration of this present political campaign. We have observed with sorrow the effect that the pressures of partisanship and political ambition have had on the top leaders of the Republican party. When the campaign began, the President said that the only issue was the record of his administration. But the end is a reckless campaign of smear, misrepresentation, and mistrust. No reputation, no record, no name — no Democrat in short — has been immune from savage or sly attack on his integrity, his good sense, his very loyalty. A few days ago, when the President was asked what he thought of this kind of campaign, he said that he had not heard about it.[271] But within twenty-four hours — and despite his earlier protestation that Communism was not an issue in the campaign — he wrote the Vice-President expressing gratitude and admiration for his contribution to political enlightenment. And yesterday on his airport tour the President himself found it in his heart — or in his script — to take up these themes himself.

This is the end of the "Great Crusade." This Republican campaign has become a program of slander that began a year ago when Mr. [Herbert] Brownell, President Eisenhower's Attorney General, impugned the very loyalty of President Truman, when Governor Dewey identified all Democrats with death and tragedy in Korea, and when the Republican National Committee sent Senator McCarthy around the country to characterize the Democratic administration as "Twenty Years of Treason." Evidently the President couldn't control the campaign of slander, then, and evidently he has embraced it now.

I am sure that President Eisenhower could have accepted this strategy only because he has forgotten what I believe he really knows, and will once again remember — that *how* one wins in politics is as important as *what* one wins.

If ever our system should rise to the highest dignity of its tradition and its responsibilities, it is today. If ever we needed politics which would

[271] The President was asked at his October 27 press conference whether he had approved the change in Republican strategy from praising the Eisenhower program to charging the Democrats with being soft on Communism. The President looked puzzled and then replied that he had heard two or three speeches in Washington and had not heard the word Communist mentioned. James Reston commented that the President would never imply that the Democrats winked at treason, nor would he knowingly condone it, "but things are done in his name that he knows not of." New York *Times*, October 28, 1954.

leave our people informed and united, not confused and divided, it is now. If ever smears, slander, innuendo, misrepresentation were out of place in our national life, it is in this time, at this place, in this world.

Our nation faces grim years ahead — years which will test to the utmost our resolution, our will, and our faith. The realities of our existence — the severe and menacing problems which hang over us — will be as harsh on the day after the election as they were the day the campaign began. After a responsible campaign our country and our people would have been better equipped to cope with these realities than we were three months ago. Instead, the nation has been recklessly torn apart in the search for votes with careless disregard for our self-respect and our unity of national purpose.

The challenge is not just to win elections. The greater challenge is to live in pride and freedom in a future so precarious and so threatening that we can risk no missteps or miscalculations. We need to unite our country, not to divide it; to heal wounds, not to enlarge them. The times demand, not mistrust and suspicion and fear, but more mutual respect and confidence and understanding than ever before.

This does not mean a suspension of hard and healthy debate, for that is the essence of democracy. But hard and healthy debate has to do with real problems. It has to do with legitimate differences in policy and program. There is plenty in the realm of valid differences between our two parties to provide material for a dozen hard-fought political campaigns. No one needs to invent issues or to misrepresent them or to falsify them. No one needs to make confusion a policy and corruption a faith.

I say corruption, because this kind of campaign threatens to corrupt the very processes on which the functioning of democratic government depends. To say that one or another American or party lacks patriotism or favors Communism or wants to subvert our society — when his only crime is disagreement — is to shake our system to the foundations. If we lose our faith in each other, we have lost everything; and no party victory is worth this. Those who seek victory at this price can be rebuked in only one way — that is, at the polls. And this, I think, is the deepest meaning and the greatest opportunity for the American voters on Tuesday.

I would plead with all Americans to cleanse their minds of suspicion and hate; to recognize that men may differ about issues without differing about their faith in America or their belief in freedom; that politics must be a means, not of compounding our weakness, but of consolidating our strength.

If we do justice at the polls to our own conscience and sense of responsibility, then alone can we do justice to the nation we love; then alone can we make our beloved land a symbol and shrine of hope and faith for all free men.

As a result of the vote on November 2, the Democrats captured the Senate by a margin of one, and elected nineteen new members to the House, giving them a majority of twenty-nine. The Democrats also elected nine new governors. Candidates identified with McCarthyism did poorly.

On November 2, President Truman wrote Stevenson that he had made an outstanding contribution to the campaign and would deserve much of the credit if the Democrats won control of Congress. Congressman Michael J. Kirwan, of Ohio, chairman of the Democratic Congressional Campaign Committee, wired Stevenson on November 2: ". . . I want to sincerely congratulate you upon a job well done. You have been tireless in your efforts, unstinting in your time, and have had no concern for your health. . . . In behalf of our party you have been a tower of strength to all of us. . . ."

To Michael J. Kirwan [272]

November 2, 1954

Dear Mike:

I am writing this Tuesday evening, before the returns are in, to thank you for your thoughtful telegram. It gave me a big lift and has dissipated some of the accumulated fatigue of these weary endless weeks from Alaska to the Atlantic.

Friends like yourself have sustained this new aspect of my life for the last two years more than you realize. I am also sure you will now understand if I fade out for a bit and try to recover my strength, my equilibrium and my fortunes.

Cordially yours,

Jack Kroll, director of the C.I.O. Political Action Committee, wrote Stevenson on November 1: "The job you have done has been tremendous and the contribution you have made to elevating the standards of political debate in this country is without parallel in my memory."

---

[272] A copy is in A.E.S., I.S.H.L.

To Jack Kroll [273]

November 5, 1954

Dear Jack:

So many thanks for your thoughtful letter. I am personally quite content with the results and if I contributed to them I am the more so! I do hope we can have a talk.

Cordially yours,

To Ralph McGill [274]

November 5, 1954

Dear Ralph:

You were so good to call me on the phone, and I enjoyed and profited from our talk. I wish there were more frequent talks as I find it difficult to get detached, reflective points of view.

As to Steve [Mitchell], I am afraid he is adamant, and I really don't feel that I can bring any more pressure to bear. He has already stayed a year beyond his original commitment to me. I suspect, therefore, that a change will have to be made at the meeting in New Orleans in early December. This is not to say that he would not give a successor some weeks or even months to get ready to take over. I think he can clearly be persuaded to do this if he was sure a successor was going to replace him.

Yours,
ADLAI

To Nancy L. Anderson

November 5, 1954

My dear Nancy:

How nice you are to send me those two fine letters. I really wish you and Ad could have come down to New York for the ceremony [275] and some of the excitement. Perhaps there will be other opportunities.

I feel so detached somehow and remote, and also mournful that I have not been more useful in all of your difficult decisions — and negotiations! But now things are going to be different! Indeed, I shall start by trying to arrange a visit with your family at an early date.

Affectionately,

[273] A copy is in A.E.S., I.S.H.L.
[274] The original is in the possession of Mrs. Ralph McGill.
[275] Stevenson received an honorary degree from Columbia University on June 6, 1954.

Stanley Woodward, treasurer of the Democratic National Committee, wrote Stevenson on November 2 praising his leadership during the campaign as "inspiring, intelligent and ardent." He added that he planned to resign his post in order that the new national chairman could select his own treasurer.

To Stanley Woodward [276]

November 6, 1954

Dear Stanley:

So many thanks for your letter and your gracious words about my concluding "effort" — and what an effort it all became after all those weary weeks.

I suppose you are right to step aside with Steve [Mitchell] and make room for a new Chairman's choice if he has a choice. I shall always be grateful to you for helping us out, and I hope and pray that we can keep intact the quality and spirit of the Committee, to which you have contributed so much.

I shall look forward to seeing you soon.

Cordially and gratefully,

ADLAI

Arthur M. Schlesinger, Jr., wrote Stevenson on November 3, enclosing a speech by liberal Southerner Martha Ragland to the Democratic National Committee. The next day Schlesinger wrote that Dean Acheson was thinking of writing a series of essays outlining the historical philosophy of the Democratic party. Schlesinger enclosed a letter, praising Call to Greatness, *from José Figueres, president of Costa Rica, who wrote: "Being still under the emotions of his book, I wonder once more where a thinking man is more useful — as President of a Republic or behind a typewriter. With all their advantages, modern republics have made Plato's philosopher-king impossible."*

To Arthur M. Schlesinger, Jr.

November 11, 1954

Dear Arthur:

Thanks for your letters. I believe we discussed, or I discussed with someone, right after 1952, the possibility of restatement and reaffirmation of the Democratic party's philosophy. I think Dean's ideas excellent and

[276] The original is in the possession of Mr. Woodward.

I had rather fancied my role in the past two years as occasionally expressing such restatement and affirmation. Unhappily, that has not been the way it has turned out, at least lately.

Perhaps we can talk about this, as it would be a more congenial place for me, and I am sure there is room for others and for much work.

I think I have abandoned the idea of a separate speech on foreign policy by inertia and weariness if not for other reasons. However, I likewise feel that if I am obliged to make a long speech in New Orleans it should be on the election, our party's responsibility in these special circumstances and wind up on foreign affairs, where in 10 or 12 minutes it should be possible to strike the necessary themes.

I have talked with Tom [Finletter] about this and he indicates that maybe someone will draft something for me, and probably he has you in mind, which mortifies me a little!

I am off in a couple of days for my week's holiday in Carolina and will be in and around New York, I guess, from about November 23 until time to go to New Orleans. If you do have anything in mind I can't tell you how welcome it would be. The best place to reach me is care of Senator William Benton, Encyclopaedia Britannica, 342 Madison Avenue (phone Murray Hill 6-7020; secretary Miss Kay Hart).

I shall certainly hope to see Dean at the first opportunity.

And thanks for Miss Ragland's remarks. I get a little amused by the Northern liberals who damn us for making friends with the Southerners whom they seem to consider all conservatives and reactionaries and then Southerners like Miss Ragland, who seem to be fearful that the liberal movement is being neglected.

I also have for acknowledgement a copy of President Figueres' remarkable letter. How I can understand and sympathize with him. He must be a remarkable man. He even understands about contemplation and solitude and that "compelling yearning." I hope you will tell him how touched and pleased I was.

Sincerely,

To Henri Bonnet [277]

November 11, 1954

Dear Henri:

I have just heard of your impending retirement. Needless to say, it reminds me of many scenes, including our meetings here in Chicago, in North Africa, Paris, etc., and I shall view your departure as a milestone

[277] French ambassador to the United States.

and I shall hope it will not mean the last of our encounters, all of which I recall with such satisfaction and admiration.

Affectionate regards and the utmost good will to you and Madame Bonnet.

Sincerely yours,

Stevenson vacationed with Mr. and Mrs. Ernest L. Ives at Southern Pines, North Carolina, and then visited New York City and Washington, D.C. While there he dined with Mr. and Mrs. Dean Acheson. On November 24, Mr. Acheson sent Stevenson a draft of a speech.

To Dean Acheson

November 30, 1954

Dear Dean:

The rewards for my visit were richer than I expected! A thousand thanks for all your writings and I am sure I shall be even more thankful after I have had a chance to read them.

I hope there will be more talks like ours at your house the other evening — but I shall not impose upon you too often, I hope.

Faithfully,

At a meeting of the Democratic National Committee in New Orleans, Paul M. Butler of South Bend, Indiana, was elected chairman of the committee. Stevenson spoke at a dinner on December 4.

THE CHALLENGE TO POLITICAL MATURITY [278]

Now that the dust of the campaign has begun to settle, following the recent elections, we are in a better position to discern the permanent realities in our national life — above all, to recover that sense of unity as Americans which underlies the discord and conflict between us as Republicans and Democrats.

I have always insisted that far more unites us than divides us. And I have always regarded this, not just as a fortunate fact, but as a grim necessity for our survival. If we cannot achieve essential harmony, especially in the conduct of our foreign policy, then our divisions will expose us to ghastly possibilities of catastrophe in this troubled world.

The last campaign, it must be frankly said, seriously imperiled our

[278] The text is from *What I Think*, pp. 96–104.

sense of unity. Cruel, unjust, and foolish things were said, patriots were slandered, evil motives imputed, parties traduced and defamed. And by the most exalted of our adversaries too.

Frank and responsible debate is the essence of the democratic way; but recklessness and irresponsibility in our political discourse — frauds, hoaxes, and falsehoods — can strain our democratic fabrics to the breaking point. And the technique of "the big lie" must never become a standard weapon of democratic dialogue.

Let us never forget that self-government was designed for men who had first of all learned to govern themselves.

Perhaps it was too much to hope for an end in this campaign of the sort of guerrilla warfare that has been waged against us Democrats in the past few years; perhaps it was too much to hope that ambitious men would forswear low roads to high places; perhaps it was too much to hope that the awesome circumstances of these times would elevate our discourse, or at least halt the downward drift of our political controversy.

Indeed, there is probably much political realism for Democrats in Carl Sandburg's little poem about the soldier of fortune who entreated the Sphinx to reveal the wisdom of the ages in one sentence, and the Sphinx replied: "Don't expect too much."

But not expecting too much does not mean that we should reconcile ourselves to accepting this sort of campaign with resignation. It means something very different. It means that we should recognize these methods as a degradation of the democratic process that strikes at the very foundations of the republic. To remember this, to resist the provocation of retaliation in kind, to match evil with good, falsehood with honesty, is never easy and the results are not always reassuring. But this remains the greatest challenge to our political maturity, a challenge that our party met, I think, with honor in this last unlamented campaign.

In the end the people reaffirmed their confidence in the Democratic party in Congress and in many state governments. But, as Democrats, we must not merely rejoice in what victory has done for our party; rather we must look forward and ask what our victorious party now can do for the country.

There is a relation between legitimacy of power and responsibility. The insecurity of knowing that power must be gained by tricks and deception breeds dynamic words coupled with irresponsible action. But power which comes legitimately, as ours has, can be responsibly exercised with reason, patience, prudence, and wisdom. It is only from that sense of security that wisdom can be joined with innovation and that new paths can be explored with security.

From the past we all have a heritage of error. But we cannot dwell on the past, for the future is too challenging and too peremptory. I am sure that the great majority of Democrats and of independent voters agree in wanting this administration to succeed as it never has before in its task of defending the security and property of our own people and of expanding the hope for freedom and justice for all peoples. It is in this spirit that I speak tonight. It is in this spirit that the Democrats will act in the Eighty-fourth Congress.

We Democrats do not propose to usurp the powers and responsibilities of the Republican executive. As the loyal opposition we should not propose either to find the answers for executive problems or to impede the executive in the proper carrying out of its responsibilities. We wish to see the government do its job better; not to impede its operations.

I foresee as a consequence of the campaign the beginning of a restoration of responsibility to our discussion of public affairs. Nowhere is this responsibility more greatly needed than in the discussion of foreign policy. And nowhere is unity, manifested in intelligence and harmony of purpose, more important. I should add that unity — bipartisanship — can never be an end in itself. No man or party would be justified in surrendering principles deemed essential to national honor and safety simply for the sake of harmony. But where the independence and survival of the nation may hang in balance, we must all work together, lest we all perish together.

Bipartisanship, or whatever we choose to call it, in foreign policy cannot mean an artificial or coerced unity. It cannot mean a device for restricting legitimate discussion or suppressing honest criticism of the conduct of foreign affairs. Nor can it mean the development of new mechanical arrangements which might impair the constitutional and traditional authority of the Executive in the foreign field.

But what it must mean, first of all, is the elimination of domestic politics from the conduct of foreign affairs.

We all know that domestic politics have had too often a powerful influence in determining the tone and even, on occasion, the measures our government had adopted in the foreign field. We all know that decisions have been made in foreign affairs in the late years less to produce results abroad than to produce applause at home. We all know that great damage has been done to our national interest abroad for the sake of showing the domestic audience what big, tough boys we were. We all know that appeasing Republican leaders at home has sometimes had priority over recognizing realities abroad. If our foreign policy is to be manipulated in order to score political points in the domestic debate, then obviously unity in foreign affairs is not very likely.

Actually, the problem of co-operation between the two major parties in foreign policy has not arisen from the Democratic party in modern times. Since the first World War and Woodrow Wilson's heroic exertions, the Democratic party has been willing to co-operate at home and abroad in effective action. The problem has always been a Republican problem — the problem of how to get unity where one of the parties continues bitterly divided within itself, the problem of trying to ascertain the mind and will of the restless and contradictory combination of forces within the Republican party.

Currently, indeed, the matter can be put in more specific terms. How the government functions in domestic affairs as well as foreign affairs during the next two years will depend more upon the President's success in leading his own party than upon Democratic willingness to co-operate with him. If President Eisenhower can conclude a non-aggression pact with Senator [William] Knowland, and if he can find some means of peaceful coexistence with a large segment of his party, I think he will find us Democrats easy to get along with.

There will continue, of course, to be sharp divisions between the parties in the new Congress. I am sure that the Democrats will fight as manfully as they can for the public welfare, as they see it — against the giveaway of the people's property; for a better deal for the farmer, the wage earner, and the small businessman; for an expanding economy; for our traditional Democratic belief in equal rights for all — special privileges for none. I am sure that the Republicans will fight us back just as hard in terms of their beliefs.

But this conflict on domestic issues need not mean inaction in the foreign field. What should our main objectives in foreign affairs now be? To answer "peace" is to express an aspiration rather than to define a policy. All Americans — all human beings — want nothing more than to live at peace with their brothers. But wishing will not make it so.

To attain it we must have within ourselves an affirmative vision of hope which we can share with the rest of mankind. We cannot be any stronger in our foreign policy — for all the bombs and guns we may heap up in our arsenals — than we are in the spirit which rules inside the country. Foreign policy, like a river, cannot rise above its source. The image we project to the world will, in the end, reflect what we ourselves are and what we feel in our minds and hearts.

If we do not stand unequivocally at home for civil freedom, we cannot hope to stand as the champion of liberty before the world.

If we do not stand at home for equal rights for all our citizens, regardless of race or color, we cannot hope to stand as the champion of opportunity before the world.

If we do not stand at home for steady economic growth and widening social welfare, we cannot hope to stand as the champion of progress before the world.

We should stand for all these things because they are the least to which our people are entitled. We must stand for them because they are our great sources of strength in the world conflict. Unless we stand for them, our moral pretensions are hollow. Unless we stand for them, we have no hope of achieving the peace we long for.

This is the vision which must underlie our foreign policy. The main obstacle to realizing this vision, of course, is Communism, but it is not the only obstacle. If the Soviet problem could be solved tomorrow, our present-day world would remain ravaged, hungry, and explosive. Many of the people of Asia, Africa, South America would be in about the same state of aspiration, unrest, and upheaval as they are today.

Yet while the social revolution of these times must lie always in the background of our mind, the implacable power of the Soviet Union, the new turbulence and attraction of Communist China, and the intricate and sinister operations of the world-wide conspiracy clearly represent the immediate threat to peace.

Personally I am weary of the long semantic argument about coexistence. If we exclude the solution of atomic war, and if we exclude the solution of surrender, all we have left is some form of armed truce which we can call coexistence or anything else you like. Armed coexistence is certainly a bleak prospect. But it is better than no-existence.

The problem we face is how to restrain this new Communist imperialism, and at the same time maintain peace in the world and hold out hope to peoples presently striving for a new life. It is my belief that we are seeing today an important shift in Soviet tactics. The massive Western rearmament after 1950 has checkmated the armed power on which the Soviet relied for intimidation and aggression. Hence, they have begun to switch to the social and economic battlefield and to try, through diplomatic means, to split the Western coalition. Employing these new tactics, Communism has made significant gains in those parts of the world striving for a new power and a new dignity. And it may gravely disturb the unity of the alliance of the free peoples of the West.

Yet, while the Soviet policy has become more flexible, we have become more rigid. While Soviet leaders astutely utilize the weapons of social agitation and political subversion, we continue to act as if Communism is primarily a military threat. While we cannot for a moment relax our vigilance on either the military or the conspiratorial fronts, Communism is also a powerful social movement, making a profound appeal wherever people are aspiring or insecure or frustrated. The probability is that, so long as we maintain our own military strength at sufficiently high levels, the chief threat in the next period will be Communist exploitation of social and political unrest. This analysis implies two main obligations for the United States.

If it has been the growing strength and unity of the free world which has deterred new adventures on the Korea model, then obviously our first obligation is to maintain our own strength and the unity of our coalition.

And if the conspirators are concentrating today on social and political aggression, then our second obligation is to show peoples struggling for economic and national deliverance that they can fulfill their aspirations better in association with free peoples and by the methods of consent than they can by submitting to the iron yoke of Communism.

Let us look first at our strength — our strength in unity, in purpose, in dedication, in productivity; our strength in military equipment, trained manpower, and readiness; our strength in the skill and morale of our foreign representatives, in the clarity of our policies, and in the nobility of our ideas. Everything which contributes to our strength heartens and encourages our allies, our friends around the world, and particularly those who would like to be our friends. Everything which contributes to our strength increases the respect and the caution of those who are hostile to us.

But we have permitted our armed strength to decline, and we have abused that other bulwark of our national safety, our system of alliances. Some Americans, indeed, have made a career in recent years of attacking our allies.

I hope these tendencies will be sharply reduced in the new Congress; I hope it will ask the most searching questions concerning the adequacy of our air-atomic power, the adequacy of our Army, and of our system of defenses. I believe a Democratic majority in Congress can be relied upon to restore a serious and realistic concern for national defense and for the proper development of our military strength.

And along with this goes the necessity of assuring our allies that our determination to play our part with them in the common defense is fixed and permanent. This is essential to our joint strength, and it is essential to the restoration of confidence in the United States as a trustworthy, steady, and respected power in world affairs.

The act of the Senate this week (adoption of the McCarthy censure resolution) [279] in reaffirming its dignity and the simplest principles of

[279] The Democrats' victories in the 1954 elections gave them a majority in Congress, depriving Senator McCarthy of his committee chairmanship. The Senate on December 2, 1954, voted 67 to 22 to condemn him for abusing the 1951 Subcommittee on Elections and for attacking a special committee, headed by Senator Arthur Watkins, which was investigating a motion by Senator Ralph Flanders to censure McCarthy.

conduct will go a long way in restoring not alone our self-confidence and self-esteem, but also the respect of our friends. And I am glad that among the Democratic members at least there was no confusion about the standards of behavior of the Senate of the United States.

So, in brief, I feel that we have much to do in developing our own strength and alliances and helping the less fortunate in their struggles for life and freedom. If we employ serious and sensible analysis in place of slick phrases and the techniques of advertising, we will be able better to recognize our problems and make headway with their solution. I wish, for instance, we could in an atmosphere of open and reasoned discussion examine the dilemmas facing us from across the Pacific instead of pretending that they do not exist.

Although the two great parties have fought bitterly, sometimes recklessly, on almost every other issue, our policies in Europe have largely remained on neutral ground. There have been differences and criticisms, of course. I have voiced my own concern on many counts. But on the whole we have worked out common policies. And with a Democratic Congress the prospect for now moving forward toward more liberal foreign trade is brighter.

But in Asia our performance is in sharp and melancholy contrast. The fall of China, the war in Korea, the disaster in Indo-China, all have been accompanied by discord and disunity and some of the worst demagoguery in the history of the republic. While Communist influence has steadily increased in Asia, sentiment in many areas has steadily turned against us. And this situation presents both political parties with a challenge of profound importance. While the initiative is clearly in the hands of the Republican administration, the responsibility of the Democratic Congress is also clear.

The first step in the development of a sensible Asian policy, while there is still time, is to take Asia out of American party politics.

Next I believe we must recognize the limitations of American military power in any situation short of a world war. It is, for example, folly to assume that we can somehow painlessly bring about the collapse of world Communism through the good offices of our good friends Chiang Kaishek and Syngman Rhee.

And then we must face the fact that security and freedom in much of the world depends today more on economic progress than military defense. The number one problem in Asia today is not Communism but that millions of people want a better life and have discovered that poverty, hunger, and pestilence are not the immutable destiny of man. If they can't make progress by the voluntary democratic methods of consent, they will turn to the involuntary methods of coercion, as China already has.

There is some evidence, and it is welcome to me, that our government is beginning to perceive this and to change its major emphasis from military to economic considerations.

So our obligations are many and complex. Military strength, allied unity, economic growth — these I think are the solid foundations of the collective power of the free peoples.

Peace is not the work of a single day, nor will it be the consequence of a single act. Yet every constructive act contributes to its growth; every omission impedes it. Peace will come, in the end, if it comes at all, as a child grows to maturity — slowly, imperceptibly, until we realize one day in incredulous surprise that the child is almost grown.

So patience may reward itself. Let us cleanse our minds of the recriminations of the past. Let us abandon the illusion of quick and final solutions. And as we face — all of us together — a journey into an unknown future, let us recognize that there is no substitute for restraint, honesty, and work — yes, and most of all, for the loyalty of Americans to one another.

I am confident that I speak not only for you, the leaders of our great and triumphant Democratic party, but also for all my fellow Americans when I say to President Eisenhower, to his associates in the executive branch of our government, and to the new Congress — may God grant you the fortitude, the forbearance, and the wisdom to lead a united nation toward our goal of peace and security for all people.

When Stevenson had completed his prepared speech, he read a handwritten statement to the audience:

Now that we are off the air, let me add a final, personal word. . . . As in the past I have no political ambitions. . . . For more than two years I have sought as best I could to discharge my obligations to the Democratic party which had honored me, and to the millions of my fellow Americans who have given me their confidence. . . . But now I must devote more time to my own concerns. So if henceforth I cannot participate in public and party affairs as vigorously as in the past, I hope you will understand and forgive me, and I assure you that it reflects no lesser interest in our party's welfare and no ingratitude for the inspiration and encouragement you have given me in such abundance.

Kenneth S. Davis wrote: "In later years he would express surprise that this statement received virtually no attention in the press. He would speak

*of it as though it were an announcement of his intention to withdraw
from political life. Actually, of course, it was no such thing. What it did
do was give party leaders an opportunity to withdraw their support from
him, should they choose to do so, while encouraging his supporters to express their wishes. More than four months passed before he again made a
public speech."* [280]

To Mrs. Warwick Anderson

December 8, 1954

Dear Mary San:

I am back at work today and find your letters and wire. While I know
nothing about Borden's and John Fell's plans, I think John Fell and I
might plan to come down on Thursday on a noon plane, returning with
Nancy and Adlai on Sunday morning. I shall make plane reservations accordingly, but you will understand if I am obliged to cancel everything
on short notice when my masters — the young gentlemen — advise me of
their wishes!

I have asked John Fell what he wanted for Christmas. Modestly, he has
confided to me he would be content with a new automobile. How nice it
is to have such considerate, thoughtful and thrifty boys.

Yours,

To David L. Cohn [281]

December 8, 1954

Dear David:

Somehow my visit to New York this time was unsatisfactory. I have
just discovered why. I didn't see you except for that brief glimpse at the
banquet.[282] And that, in turn, reminds me to thank you once more for
providing me with a large part of what I did — which I hope was not too
unsuitable.

All best wishes.

Yours,

ADLAI

P.S. I spent a day in Memphis and visited with some old friends on a
huge plantation where there was much talk of Dave Cohn as the
authentic voice of Mississippi, past and present.

[280] *The Politics of Honor: A Biography of Adlai E. Stevenson* (New York: Putnam, 1967), p. 302.

[281] The original is in the Mississippi collection, University of Mississippi Library.

[282] Stevenson spoke on December 2 at a banquet of the American Committee for
the Weizmann Institute, held in New York City. The text is in *What I Think*, pp.
210–214.

To Thomas K. Finletter

December 11, 1954

Dear Tom:

Bill [Blair] tells me about the meeting you are having. I am not sure whether I can come, but it occurred to me that I might send for information and possible consideration the attached copy of letter from Jack Fischer. I have talked with him subsequently at some length and I believe there is much merit, as well as many difficulties, in his proposal.

While, as I said in New York, I would like to see the Finletter group go ahead, perhaps working advance ground, I think we also need a more formal program research project with an executive secretary who would stick at it full time in an effort to run down good people for as many subjects as possible. Of course Paul Nitze would be ideal were he available to help us whip in shape ideas on all manner of domestic as well as foreign problems, blocking out the areas of agreement and the areas of new and "controversial" ideas. For example, special attention must be given to the Rocky Mountains and the West. It is far more involved than public power. I could let my mind wander a bit and maybe suggest the old concept of railroad rate regulation needs reexamination in view of the present competition from trucks and the forthcoming new subsidies from federal construction of highways. Likewise, for example, is 160 acres any longer a proper limitation on water benefits in the West? How long can we ask the people to support enormous subsidies for a shipping industry and have our water friends paralyzed periodically by union jurisdictional quarrels and rackets? And what can one do about it?

But this isn't the place to discuss agenda. My point is that there is a vast amount of imaginative work to be done if we are going to have anything resembling a coherent, well thought out party "program" a year or a year and a half hence.

This is written in haste and confusion, which is not to say it wouldn't be confused if it wasn't in haste.

Yours,

P.S. I don't know what sort of a meeting it is that Bill mentioned, but it is not easy or economical to be travelling too much, as I am sure you realize. Also, maybe you will want to consider John Fischer to talk about his ideas, which are not dissimilar from our original ideas for the future of the "Finletter group."

P.P.S. I am told that a man named [Royden] Dangerfield, in political science at the University of Illinois (about 50 years of age) might be available and worth considering for some full time work. I also know where you could get some money on the West Coast to help underwrite the cost.

A.E.S.

p.p.p.s. Of course anything done through the National Committee must now be discussed with [Paul] Butler, but I think it would be well to have the project pretty well formulated before presentation to him in view of the myriad things he has to attend to.

A.E.S.

To Richard J. Daley [283]

December 15, 1954

Dear Dick:

This will introduce to you Douglas Flood, a classmate of mine at Northwestern Law School long ago. He has had an interesting and honorable career in the foreign service of the United States on most of the continents of the world, and now he is back in Chicago after retiring from the foreign service and eager to keep active in some useful work. With my approval he has hit upon the idea of helping out in the office of the Public Defender. I have never found that we had a surplus of useful and competent citizens who were eager to help with secondary concern for remuneration. Hence, I recommend him highly, while quite unaware of his professional qualifications or the needs of Mr. Getty's [284] office.

With warm wishes, I am

Sincerely yours,

To Arthur M. Schlesinger, Jr.

December 15, 1954

Dear Arthur:

I am suddenly the beneficiary of a modest amount of political philanthropy from an admirer and I want to share it with you because I can't tell how long I will be able to mislead such admirers! Now, please, please don't return the enclosed this time. It is the meagerest sort of acknowledgement of my infinite impositions. I hope there will be more such acknowledgements, and you must think of those little Schlesingers if you never think of yourself.

Yours,

p.s. I now have your note of December 6. The news about John Fell's infatuation suggests that there may be something to co-education as it

283 County clerk of Cook County, Illinois.
284 Gerald W. Getty, the Cook County public defender.

seems to have improved his marks. I shall see Carl [McGowan] presently, and I am pleased that the speech was not too bad. It was exceedingly difficult to prepare what with all that material and all those interruptions.

To Vincent Sheean

December 16, 1954

Dear Jimmy:

I am not surprised that the Library of Congress wants "the Sheean papers" and I have no objection whatever to the papers that relate to me. I have checked the file and the only one I find of any consequence seems to be a letter of July 14, 1952, in which I attempt to explain in simple language why I was avoiding the Democratic nomination for President. It may be that other letters are missing from my file, but even if they are I am not concerned. Looking at the file afforded me a chance to reread that exquisite letter of yours of October 24, 1952. I hope you have a copy for the Library because I would hate to part with mine.

I am glad you think well of my behavior of late. It has been a wearing, tearing and interminable travail, and I look forward now to some of the serenity and peace — and I hope profit — that I have wanted and missed these past fifteen years. I hope there are visits with you also in my future.

Cordially,

Stevenson was considering joining the Presbyterian church in Lake Forest, where so many of his friends worshipped. He also had attended this church for many years, the nearest Unitarian church to his home in Libertyville being in Highland Park. Stevenson wrote Jack Mendelsohn, minister of the All Souls Unitarian Church, Indianapolis, about it. Mendelsohn wrote the Governor on December 17: "The possibilities for misinterpretation are quite staggering, and not only by the Unitarians. The reaction of the religiously orthodox is almost certain to be that you made the change in order to strengthen your political position. I am reasonably sure that no one but the Presbyterians would be happy. Unless, of course, you were, and that would outweigh all other considerations."

To the Reverend Jack Mendelsohn

December 22, 1954

Dear Jack:

Thanks for your letter — helpful and understanding, as always. I am a little concerned about the church situation and rather wish I had never started the negotiations with my old, old friends in Lake Forest. We shall see.

To avoid the political implication you mention, the intention was, of course, to affiliate without any notice. But, after all, I can attend services as I did in Springfield without becoming a member. Highland Park is a little remote, but I shall look forward to meeting the new minister.

Sincerely,

To the Reverend Richard Paul Graebel

December 22, 1954

Dear Dick:

I have just finished a conversation with Ed Day,[285] who tells me how you stood by in his crisis. I am not surprised, but I am reminded how much all of us who lived there owe to you — myself most of all. With the passage of some time our perspectives sometimes get clearer, I suppose; at least the things that are important are distilled. And the experience of knowing you I count perhaps my most important church experience as well as a personal delight. How I wish I were to be in your congregation on Christmas Eve once more. Instead I will be in Louisville in a congregation of Adlai III's young and hilarious friends!

My affectionate regards to you and Dorothy [286] and the children, and all best wishes for the future.

Cordially,

P.S. I have been struggling with Bob Andrus [287] and the problem of joining the church in Lake Forest. I have discussed it with a discreet Unitarian minister in Indiana who is very much concerned. And now a Unitarian Church has been opened in nearby Highland Park. It is all very perplexing, and I suppose I will do nothing formal, but go to Presbyterian services more and more in Lake Forest. I am still hoping that I shall discover before it is all over the advantages of public prominence.

Harry Ashmore, of the Little Rock Arkansas Gazette, *wrote Stevenson on December 14: "I am, as you know, one who refuses to tolerate the notion that you will not be the nominee in 1956." He warned that many Southern political leaders did not know Stevenson well and the "myth*

---

[285] Administrative assistant to Governor Stevenson, 1949–1950, afterward director of the Department of Insurance during Stevenson's governorship.

[286] Mrs. Graebel.

[287] The Reverend Robert Andrus, pastor of the Presbyterian church in Lake Forest.

persists that you are cold, impersonal, and unapproachable." He urged Stevenson to meet in small groups with political leaders for informal conversation. Ashmore then noted that the Republican party was growing in the South and particularly in "Southern suburbia."

To Harry Ashmore

December 23, 1954

Dear Mr. Ashmore:

. . . I am flattered, of course, by your characteristic and gracious words about 1956. In my present state of mind, however, I rather feel as though I had done what I could and my interest in further "combat" politics is burning very low indeed. However, I am much interested in our party and I share your view about the imperative importance of preserving our position in the South. As you know, I have been at some pains to go to the South a number of times during the past year, and Steve Mitchell has devoted himself tirelessly to this problem. The New Orleans meeting was, of course, for the same purpose.

I am sure your analysis is correct, and I suffer no personal distress at the prospect of the evolution of a genuine two party system. But I hate to see it go in the direction already apparent, of separating the respectable and privileged from the Democrats! Surely we have an important problem in this connection and it was perceptible even in this last visit to New Orleans. I wish we could talk about this, and, more importantly, that you could talk to Paul Butler, and that some coherent plan of continuous action could be developed.

I think much of it will have to be done at the local level by our local leaders.

I too am conscious that I have by no means established a good relationship with masses of our leaders around the country and that some myths still persist about my aloofness. However, I have since the 1952 election spoken and visited in some 33 states, and Alaska and Hawaii and Puerto Rico. It has been about all I could do, together with the trip around the world and the writing, and now I must pay a little attention to my health, my finances and my family and personal affairs.

Bill Fulbright has written me in similar vein and I have told him that I hoped I could have some leisurely evenings in Washington this winter and spring and could have a better opportunity to meet some of our Congressional people. But as for traveling about, as you suggest, I am afraid I have done about all of that I can.

Most of all I wish I could resume my Southern education with a good quiet evening with you! Perhaps you will come to see me some time, or, if I come in that direction, you would permit me to stop off for an evening.

With best wishes for Christmas and the New Year, I am

Cordially yours,

Stevenson spent Christmas in Kentucky visiting with Mr. and Mrs. Warwick Anderson, soon to be the father- and mother-in-law of Adlai III. While there he wrote a number of handwritten letters. The following is a sample.

To Norman Cousins [288]

December 25, 1954

Dear Norman —

While trying to look forward I can't help looking back! And one of the most conspicuous hindsights is — Norman Cousins. Somehow I feel that not only have I not seen you in this crowded year but I haven't even thanked you for all you have done for me. Both failures I want to correct — and besides I want to talk! I hope there will be a leisurely evening either here or there and soon! —

ADLAI

Mrs. Bogart wrote that Darryl Zanuck had told her that on good authority he understood that Stevenson would not be a candidate in 1956. She then added that her five-and-a-half-year-old son, when asked on Art Linkletter's television program who was the smartest man in the world, replied, "Adlai Stevenson."

To Mrs. Humphrey Bogart [289]

December 28, 1954

Dear Betty:

I was amused by your note — both the content and your delectable style, at least with hot news from Zanuck! As for the future, who can tell? I think you know my continual state of reluctance about a job that staggers me, if not some others! But I shall try not to confirm his information. At least he could have gone to no worse source!

---

[288] The original is in the possession of Mr. Cousins.
[289] A copy is in A.E.S., I.S.H.L.

I had already heard of your boy's answer on the television show. Evidently it has reverberated far and wide and, of course, leaves me with a profound sense of respect for you and yours. But that is nothing new. Sometime you must bring him with you on one of your cross country journeys.

I am glad to hear that you are working hard, and profitably I assume. The former is true here if not the latter, but as to that we are going to take steps in 1955, or try to.

All good wishes and my very warm thanks for your always flattering and heartening words.

Sincerely,

Bernard DeVoto wrote Stevenson that he wanted to talk to him privately about issues for the 1956 campaign as well as about mechanisms to coordinate the campaign. He added he would join him any time at a place within the "fare-range of a not too opulent journalist."

To Bernard DeVoto

December 28, 1954

Dear Benny:

I have read that wonderful piece and I emphatically share your conclusion that "the eggheads are indispensable to the Democratic party." [290] I am not so sure, however, just how indispensable I am to either the party or the eggheads.

I am much interested in what you say about new mechanisms. Certainly one thing we must do is the issue study with a view to positive as well as negative program in 1956. I have had some talks with Paul Butler about this, and I am going to take the liberty of seeing that he reads your January piece.

As for our foregathering, I hardly know what to suggest. I should be delighted for you to come and stay a night with me anytime, or I can make a note and a very determined effort to arrange an evening on my next trip to New York. As for short or long range fares for not too opulent journalists let me say that a not too opulent politician has some funds, or soon will, for just such purposes. I marvel at your restless spirit when all I want is an end of controversy and contest. Intellectual lethargy is my heart's desire!

Best for the New Year.

Yours,

[290] *Harper's,* January, 1955, p. 17.

Adlai E. Stevenson III and Nancy Anderson were to be married on June 25, 1955. She had visited at Libertyville over the holidays.

To Nancy L. Anderson

January 4, 1954 [1955]

My dear Nancy:

Thank you for the charming letter. I think you have talents which arouse my professional admiration!

It was a wonderful holiday for me, and a new daughter is the best thing that has happened to me or any of us for a long while, especially one who is so understanding and patient with all the difficulties she has encountered. Ad is not the only one who loves you — we all do.

Affectionately,

P.S. I am hoping to have Mr. and Mrs. Warwick Anderson,[291] of Louisville, for dinner Saturday night.

To Edith Gifford [292]

January 4, 1955

Dear Miss Gifford:

I get a little confused by your many kindnesses and whether I have thanked you for them. If I have neglected to acknowledge the Christmas scrapbook, please forgive me, for I am most grateful indeed.

It has been on exhibit during the holidays, and has baited the trap for my boys and their young friends to look further into your great opuses! The result is a vast enhancement of my prestige where it does the most good, and my friends are full of wonder that anyone would bother to do for me such meticulous, painstaking and monumental work! And so am I.

Again my warmest thanks, my dear Miss Gifford, and may this be your very best year.

Cordially,

Mrs. Bethia Currie, who was working for Stevenson's nomination in 1956, wrote him, asking, among other things, "Are you an idealistic amateur or an expedient professional?" She noted that some people in Connecticut were charging that he was the latter.[293]

---

291 Nancy's parents.

292 The original is in the possession of Miss Gifford.

293 Mrs. Currie later wrote: "The question was not a reflection of my actual conviction, but an attempt to evoke a statement from him." Letter to Carol Evans, May 12, 1972.

To Bethia S. Currie [294]

January 4, 1955

Dear Mrs. Currie:

I always find your letters stimulating and your last one was no exception. I doubt, however, if I can shed any light on your dilemma.

Since it is impossible to please everyone, I try to do what I think is best — whatever that is depends on your point of view, I suppose. And now for the first time in years, I have returned to the practice of law and the business of earning a living.[295] I expect all factions can agree that I have been unemployed far too long!

With every good wish, I am

Sincerely yours,

James P. Warburg wrote Stevenson on December 30, 1954, saying that he had drafted some policy papers and that he would be happy to send copies of them.

To James P. Warburg

January 4, 1955

Dear Jim:

What a man! Since I saw you I have done nothing, and you've written another half dozen books. Of course I should like to see this material, but I wonder how and when I can read it. Moreover foreign affairs is more Bill Wirtz's field. Anyhow, if you have spare copies pray send them along.

The season's greetings, and may your New Year be as prolific as the past — I mean intellectually!

Cordially,

To Harry Golden [296]

January 10, 1955

Dear Mr. Golden:

Every now and then I look through the Carolina Israelite and invariably end up in a gala of mirth or with a knitted brow — or both! I am your

---

294 The original is in the possession of Mrs. Currie.

295 Stevenson had opened a law office at 231 South La Salle Street in Chicago, with William McCormick Blair, Jr., W. Willard Wirtz, and Newton N. Minow as his partners.

296 Editor and publisher of the *Carolina Israelite*, Charlotte, North Carolina.

debtor, either laughing or anxious. Thank you most recently for "Bigger And Better Invocations" — because you really haven't heard anything yet until you have run for public office in a great state and a great country.

Now don't print this or I will have to believe all I have heard — that it isn't safe for a politician to set pen to paper any longer. The results, of course, are obvious. We politicians can no longer write!

Cordially,

To Benjamin V. Cohen [297]

January 10, 1955

Dear Ben:

I have at last read your memorandum on the defense treaty with Formosa.[298] I agree with your anxiety and many of your conclusions. What, of course, we should be trying to do is to bring about a separate status for Formosa and a unanimity of view in the non-Communist world to that end. I am afraid this administration is a prisoner of much of its own propaganda of the past and has less flexibility in this region than almost any other.

In this connection you might be interested in the enclosure sent to me by an Englishman long resident in China and now in Hong Kong. Possibly Dean Acheson or Paul Nitze, or someone else, might find these gratuitous remarks which he sent me interesting. . . .

Sincerely yours,

On January 3, 1955, the Santa Monica Bay Area Democratic Club wired Stevenson: "We wish to express our hope that recent rumors of your retirement from public life are erroneous. We feel that you are the only person who can provide the leadership we need to win in 1956."

[297] New York lawyer and former member of the U.S. delegation to the United Nations. Stevenson had worked with him on the UN, and earlier had known him in Washington during World War II. See *The Papers of Adlai E. Stevenson,* Vol. II.

[298] In December, 1954, the United States signed a mutual defense treaty with the Nationalist government of Chiang Kai-shek which stated that an attack upon the territory of the Republic of China would be a threat to American security. While Formosa and the Pescadores Islands were included in this territory, the Eisenhower Administration retained the option of defending the offshore islands, including Quemoy and Matsu.

To the Santa Monica Bay Area Democratic Club

January 11, 1955

My dear Friends:

This is the first opportunity I have had to thank you for your very thoughtful telegram.

I have no intention of retiring from public life, but just feel that henceforth I will have to devote a little more time to my personal affairs which have been neglected for so long.

You were good to think of me and I am grateful indeed for all your past help and encouragement.

Sincerely yours,

To Carl Sandburg

January 19, 1955

Dear Carl:

I hear that in Louisville you said that Adlai Stevenson "could tell you what to do." Okay. You asked for it!

Now, I'll tell you: (1) Live forever, and (2) never pass this way without letting me know, in advance if possible.

Further instructions will come from time to time.

Affectionately,

To Lyndon B. Johnson

January 20, 1955

Dear Lyndon:

I "see by the papers" that you, too, are afflicted with kidney stones.[299] As a two-time veteran of that affliction I am praying for you; and perhaps on your return you will pass through Chicago and will give me a clinical report!

Cordially,

To Archibald MacLeish [300]

February 1, 1955

Dear Archie:

I am visiting Eastern positions in the forthcoming fortnight, with a hope, if not a certainty, of coming to Cambridge for the weekend of

[299] Senator Johnson was in the Mayo Clinic, Rochester, Minnesota.
[300] The original is in the MacLeish papers, Library of Congress.

February 12 to see my sons. Meanwhile, I shall be first in Washington and then in New York, arriving at the latter on February 5th, where I will be staying at the Savoy Plaza. Will you and Ada be in Cambridge, and, if so, could I beg a bed for Saturday night, February 12, and just possibly Sunday as well?

> Hastily,
> ADLAI

Stevenson delivered the following statement over the Columbia Broadcasting System, February 1, 1955.[301]

Carl Sandburg is one of the few living men whose work and whose life epitomize the American dream. He has the earthiness of the prairies, the majesty of mountains, the anger of deep inland seas. In him is the restlessness of the seeker, the questioner, the explorer of far horizons, the hunger that is never satisfied. In him also is the tough strength that has never been fully measured, never unleashed, the resiliency of youthfulness which wells from within, and which no aging can destroy.

Irv Kupcinet mentioned in his column in the Chicago Sun-Times *that Stevenson was celebrating his fifty-fifth birthday in New York City.*

To Irving Kupcinet [302]

> February 14, 1955

Dear Kup:

Thanks to you, I was kept busy in New York all week acknowledging birthday cards and telegrams — so I don't know whether to thank you or not for what you did!! However, I guess all is forgiven and I did appreciate hearing from you and Essie.[303]

I hope you will drop by my new office sometime when you are downtown and have a few minutes. In the meantime, many thanks for your thoughtfulness.

> Sincerely,

[301] The text is from a carbon copy.
[302] The original is in the possession of Mr. Kupcinet.
[303] Mrs. Kupcinet.

To Sam Rayburn [304]

February 14, 1955

Dear Sam:

I am back in Chicago today and find your note enclosing the telegram.

It was a most agreeable interlude for me and I wish they came more often, but I shall not disturb your busy routine soon again. Every time I go down there I am appalled by the pressures and chaos which you seem to survive and resist so gracefully.

Let me know if I can ever be of any possible help; and a thousand thanks for the delightful luncheon.

Cordially yours,

To Mr. and Mrs. Archibald MacLeish [305]

February 14, 1955

My Dearly Beloveds!

How can I thank you for that refuge — not to mention music, university presidents, and wise and beautiful aliens. Somehow there is always light and warmth and a little magic about your menages — and I shall be back!

"Once aboard the lugger" I discovered I had not seen the manuscript that Archie mentioned. I am disappointed, but I am sure you will know how to maintain cordial relations with your old friend [Walter] Lippmann in spite of a difference of view. And speaking of views, if I only had an occasional exposure to the society of the Master's Lodging at Eliot House,[306] I too might have some views about something.

With thanks and affection,

ADLAI

To Benjamin V. Cohen

February 15, 1955

Dear Ben:

I was disappointed that I didn't have a chance to confer with you while in Washington for a day or so recently. I did see some of the Senators and found them almost uniformly skeptical of the treaty [307] but loathe to vote against it for fear of misunderstanding. To the problem of foreign

---

[304] Speaker of the House of Representatives. A copy is in A.E.S., I.S.H.L.
[305] The original is in the MacLeish papers, Library of Congress.
[306] Mr. MacLeish was temporarily serving as master of Eliot House at Harvard.
[307] With the Republic of China. See note 298, p. 450.

policy, to serve domestic political purposes, we may have to add the hazard of foreign policy for the appeasement of our allies and beneficiaries. It is all very perplexing, and I am glad to have your supplemental memo. I shall not be surprised if we live to regret this treaty when the time comes for the ultimate disposition of the Formosa problem.

Cordially yours,

To Mr. and Mrs. Marshall Field [308]

February 17, 1955

Dear Fields:

At last I have extricated myself from my difficulties and I am off tomorrow for Jamaica and a fortnight's holiday. The utter joy in this prospect is only diluted by my disappointment that I cannot come to Chelsea [309] too and see you both. Moreover, my visit would not have diminished the quail population either!

I shall hope that you won't write me off your future book altogether.

Affectionately,

To Harry W. Rowe [310]

March 7, 1955

Dear Dean Rowe:

So many thanks for your letter and the clipping, which is a precious addition to my meager store of mementoes and material about my grandfather Stevenson.

Of course the election in Maine last fall was as heartening as anything that has happened to me.[311] While traveling around the country I hear much about the emergence of a genuine two-party system in the South. I should like to think that Maine is also leading the way towards the emergence of a genuine two-party system in the one-party section of New England. Evidently you think that Governor Muskie's election is indicative of enduring change. I pray that you are right and have heard much similar testimony, but one can't overlook that he is an exceedingly

[308] A copy is in A.E.S., I.S.H.L.
[309] Chelsea Plantation, the Fields's winter home in Ridgeland, South Carolina.
[310] Dean of Bates College, Lewiston, Maine.
[311] Democrat Edmund S. Muskie had shattered Republican supremacy in Maine when he was elected governor in 1954.

personable man and must have won a lot of votes on his own account regardless of party.

I hope some time we have an opportunity to meet and to discuss these and other things. Meanwhile, my thanks for your thoughtfulness.

Cordially yours,

To Nancy L. Anderson

March 7, 1955

Nancy dear:

Thanks for that charming letter which melted acres of snow hereabouts. I have also had one from Ad — far more illegible. The advice about commencement I shall remember when I get around to thinking about that speech, which will probably be a couple of days before.

I had a good holiday but with altogether too many interruptions — mail, visits, etc., and no productive work, aside from a good tan. But I did buy you a present in Jamaica — a skirt. You know my fondness for skirts! But I have no idea about sizes and I am timid about sending it lest you find yourself in a handwoven tent or scanty.

Love,

P.S. Any ideas that occur to you for suitable and important wedding presents, please pass along — shamelessly, after the manner of modern brides. It will be so helpful to a harrassed modern father-in-law.

To Everett Case [312]

March 8, 1955

Dear Ev:

Thanks for your letter. What I think we overlook is that the administration really has *no* policy with respect to Formosa and China. If we had a more discerning or independent press we would have perceived long since that the "policy" is a mixture of realism about Asia and domestic expediency, i.e., the reconciliation of the Republican right wing. The two, of course, are incompatible, as they have been for the past several years. And so it will continue to be at the expense of allies, prestige, and, I hope, nothing more, until time and circumstances force the issue as they are doing and at a price which we cannot readily evaluate.

In Puerto Rico the other day I had lunch with Mr. and Mrs. Laurance

[312] President of Colgate University and a Princeton classmate of Stevenson. The original is in the possession of Mr. Case.

[455]

Rockefeller, who informed me in detail of certain romantic entanglements, of which I heartily approve.[313]

Cordially,

ADLAI

Edith Stern was the daughter of Sears, Roebuck executive and philanthropist Julius Rosenwald, with whom Stevenson often stayed when he was in the New Orleans area. She wrote Stevenson on March 7 that an "Adlai Brooch," which had cost $1.00 in 1952, was now appraised at $10.00. She added: "I wanted you to be sure to know how much your value has been enhanced."

To Mrs. Edgar Stern [314]

March 8, 1955

My dear Mrs. Stern:

I was enchanted with your note. Evidently "Adlai" brooches have enhanced in value somewhat more than Adlai. I suppose this is just material inflation while the spirit struggles to hold its own!

Cordially,

To Mrs. Humphrey Bogart [315]

March 11, 1955

Dear Betty:

. . . You were thoughtful indeed to remember my birthday — the more so considering my antiquity. And now, my dear, you may forget them henceforth and consider that you have discharged all the amenities!

I too would like to come to the Coast again for a more leisurely visit than has been my lot in late years, but unhappily to all the other difficulties I must now contrive to earn a living. As to the latter, things have gone well, if not as well as in the movies. And to think that when I come I must be content with a Mercedes. Ho hum. What a lot you have to contend with.

I have just returned — brown and plump — from a fortnight in Jamaica. The color will last approximately four days and the plumpness forty years I fear.

---

[313] Mr. Case's son James had just become engaged to Laurance Rockefeller's daughter Laura. They were married in June, 1956.

[314] A copy is in A.E.S., I.S.H.L.

[315] A copy is in A.E.S., I.S.H.L.

With good wishes and gratitude, and the usual anxiety to see your next "production." [316]

Cordially,

Stevenson, on a trip to the East Coast, visited with Governor and Mrs. Averell Harriman in Albany, New York.

To Mrs. W. Averell Harriman [317]

March 23, 1955

My dear Marie:

It was a gala weekend, and I only hope it didn't exhaust the beloved Gov. His stamina and equilibrium astonish me and I can attribute it only to long and total immunization to crises! As for what his lady has done and how she has done it, to re-animate the Executive Mansion and the hearts of Albany — well, we all stand in awe and admiration.

All in all, the memorable visit reminded me that being a Governor really *has* its charms. You were an angel to take us in, and I'll be back!

My best to Averell, and so many thanks.

Affectionately,

To Dag Hammarskjöld [318]

March 23, 1955

My dear friend:

I enjoyed dinner so much, and you were good indeed to take me in. I thought afterward how many things there were I wanted to talk with you about and how little we had covered. As I have to go abroad in mid-April and have a myriad things to do, I think I shall not be able to testify at the Review Conference hearings in Washington, at least at this time.[319]

It was good to see you again and I left with renewed admiration — and gratitude!

Cordially yours,

[316] Mrs. Bogart does not recall what this refers to. Letter to Eric Sears, September, 1973.

[317] A copy is in A.E.S., I.S.H.L.

[318] A copy is in A.E.S., I.S.H.L.

[319] Senator Walter F. George, chairman of the Senate Foreign Relations Committee, invited Stevenson to testify before the committee in mid-April on proposed revisions to the United Nations charter. Stevenson was unable to testify, since he was leaving the country on April 18 for a one-month business trip through South Africa.

Jonathan Daniels wrote in the Raleigh News and Observer *on March 7, 1955, that North Carolina wanted no part of attempts by Senator Harry F. Byrd of Virginia and Governor Robert F. Kennon of Louisiana to nominate a "Jeffersonian-Democrat," and that had these men been living in Jefferson's time they never would have voted for "that radical." Daniels also criticized Senator Sam J. Ervin, Jr., of North Carolina for suggesting that the Democrats should nominate "someone between Stevenson and a more conservative candidate."*

To Jonathan Daniels [320]

March 23, 1955

Dear Jonathan:

So many thanks for that splendid editorial of March 7, which I have just seen on my return to Chicago. While I don't have any aggressive notions myself, as you know, I hate to see people like Ervin drifting off under foolish banners. Poor Jefferson; he would never recognize many of the Democrats now traveling in his train. But think of Lincoln!

I think the idea of pointing out repeatedly Jefferson's advanced ideas in the context of his time is excellent, and I propose to talk to Julian Boyd [321] about it when he comes here to see me soon.

Yours,

To Adlai E. Stevenson III

March 26, 1955

Dear Bear:

I enclose a check in the amount of $1,618.70, representing 1954 income from the Trust I established for you and the other boys of the manuscripts of my speeches in 1952. Mr. [R. Keith] Kane, the Trustee, indicates that there may be a little more forthcoming.

I have read with much interest your proposal about buying an income-producing building down there and I think it *does* make a lot of sense if you can get something at a fair price that does not require an awful lot of capital investment for repairs and rehabilitation. Everybody who bought houses in Washington during the war time expansion, at what looked like extremely inflated values, sold them at a profit, and meanwhile lived rent free. While I foresee nothing of that kind at Cambridge, where the student population is more or less stable, I am sure the demand will be continuous, as you suggest. There is, of course, the summer

[320] A copy is in A.E.S., I.S.H.L.
[321] Professor of history at Princeton and editor of the papers of Thomas Jefferson.

problem, when I guess living space is a drug on the market. The only other headache is looking after your tenants and real estate, especially old buildings which can be an awful headache. But I don't think it a bad idea at all, if you can find anything suitable for your own occupancy for the next two years. The interest deduction will not be too important in your bracket, especially when you are married. And please don't worry about getting off my back. You are not breaking it, at the moment at least. Moreover, I am counting heavily on that chinchilla ranch to lift us all to new living levels! Thank heavens, the hamster population is decreasing. But what's this about fish! My God! And all the time I thought you were down there to study law and not ichthyology and animal husbandry!

The plans for the honeymoon sound promising, but if I was a bride I might have some reservations about sleeping bags, tents, lanterns and gasoline stoves. But, of course, I am not a bride — just a tired old man I guess. Shall I start gently nudging the Kelloggs [322] in the right direction? You should also consider stopping in Desbarats on your way across Ontario. I am sure you would be welcome at Thorne Camp.[323]

I am sorry to hear about the loss of the pearls, but why not get some better ones this time, maybe spend $100 or $200? Would you like me to give them to Nancy as a personal wedding present? I should be delighted, and that raises again the problem of the major present for both of you, on which I am getting little help from Mary San.[324] If you have any ideas yet — silver, glass, etc., let me know. About all Mary San has suggested is money, evidently thinking it would be more useful than presents which might just be stored at the time. However, there may still be time to talk more about this in June, and meanwhile I have to get Marnie Dick [325] a present!

I was distressed to have a notice that John Fell had been put on probation for the naval science course. I can't see why it should cause him so much trouble. From the way everyone talks it sounds simple.

I am planning now to leave on Monday the 18th of April for Africa, to be gone until about the middle of May. I shall try to have the wedding lists worked up, although it will be a difficult chore at best. As I won't be here during your holiday, I wonder if you would like to come to Washington on the 16th, meeting me there in the afternoon. I might try to get Borden up from camp [326] in the evening and we could all stay at the Paul Magnusons. In the evening we could go to the [Sam] Rayburn testimonial

---

[322] Mr. and Mrs. John P. Kellogg, Libertyville neighbors and friends of Stevenson's. They had a summer home in Canada.

[323] The summer home of Mr. and Mrs. Herman D. Smith in Canada.

[324] Mrs. Warwick Anderson.

[325] The daughter of Mr. and Mrs. Edison Dick, now Mrs. James T. Last.

[326] Borden Stevenson was in the Army, stationed at Fort Bragg, North Carolina.

dinner and then have the following day, Sunday, together. Monday I would have to go back to New York to get my plane for overseas. You could stay in Washington, go on down to North Carolina to see Aunt Buffy, or up to New York or Cambridge — or home! At all events, I wish you would let me know promptly because I must make my plans and this will be my only chance to see you before I leave. Also, I would like to see Borden who writes me a depressing letter about the inaction in psychological warfare and the fatuity of his officers, etc. . . . .

Love,

While she was in New York City, Barbara Ward sent Stevenson a draft of a speech and mentioned that she would return to the United States in November to fill speaking engagements.

To Mrs. Robert Jackson

March 26, 1955

Dear Barbara:

The draft has come and I am about to read it. A thousand thanks. The advice is coming from all directions. As the Bastard in King John said: "I was never so bethump'd with words."

So you are making engagements for next November without consulting your American adviser?

Gratefully and affectionately,

To Mrs. Paul B. Magnuson

March 26, 1955

My dear Laura:

Once upon a time you were kind and foolish enough to suggest that there might be a refuge for Stevensons in your Washington establishment. I find now that I may be there on the 16th and 17th of April, prior to a business journey to Africa. It may be my one opportunity to get together with some or all of my boys, and rather than the exposure of a hotel, where I seldom find any peace, I was wondering if you could take one or more of us in at that time. I am obliged to come because of the testimonial dinner for Sam Rayburn on the night of Saturday, April 16. My thought was to perhaps get Borden up from his camp in North Carolina and to have Adlai down from Cambridge and take them with me to the dinner and then have a little time with them on Sunday before our departure to discuss all our family plans and problems. I am not so sure about John Fell or his availability.

If you were to write me a note and say that you were sorry but a Stevenson invasion would collide with some other invasion, or simply collide, I should not be surprised. If you were to say you could take one or two of us in I would be delighted, but I would have to still leave it uncertain until I could work out the details with the boys.

Please forgive a ghost from the past arising in your comfortable present.

Affectionately,

The Senate ratified the mutual defense treaty with Nationalist China in January, 1955. Shortly afterward, in order to avoid the kind of attacks that had been made on President Truman for his intervention in Korea without congressional support, President Eisenhower secured a resolution from Congress approving the use of armed force to protect Formosa and the Pescadores. The resolution left the People's Republic of China guessing as to American action toward the offshore islands. Eisenhower stated: "The authority that may be accorded by the Congress would be used only in situations which are recognizable as parts of, or definite preliminaries to, an attack against the main positions of Formosa and the Pescadores."

During the early months of 1955 tensions over the Formosa Straits mounted. James Warburg wrote Stevenson on March 20: "As you know, I was not among those who thought it terribly important for the Democrats to capture control of Congress last autumn — except to get rid of McCarthy as a committee chairman — because I feared precisely what is now happening; namely, that the Democratic leadership in Congress would compromise the position of the party to the point where its Presidential candidate in 1956 would have no issues upon which to stand. This is certainly happening in the field of foreign policy. How can the Democrats hope to beat Ike if the best claim they can make is that they gave him better support than his own party?" Mr. Warburg urged Stevenson to speak out and among other things recommend recognition of the People's Republic of China and propose negotiations.

To James P. Warburg

March 26, 1955

Dear Jim:

Thanks for your letter. I can't dispute what you say and have been disturbed by the lack of positive reaction in Washington, but I have felt that it was my turn to keep still and, moreover, practicing law leaves little choice, or rather sharply limits alternatives. I have been getting it in shock treatment form of late, both for and against speaking out on foreign policy, Asia, and war over the little islands.[327] Mostly "for" speaking out. Perhaps I will, although I suspect the administration is preparing another withdrawal after all the bluff and bluster.

Ever so many thanks for the working paper. I hope to get at it this week-end.

Cordially yours,

The Finletter Group had met irregularly since 1953. It did not work exclusively for any one Democratic leader. It was an unofficial policy-planning group, its purpose being to prepare material for the 1956 campaign and policy positions after the Democrats won the Presidency. Theodore H. White wrote: "The Finletter Group reflects a Democratic recognition that new issues, new programs are needed not only to meet the new perplexities of a prosperous citizenry, but to cajole it out of its current political placidity." [328]

To Paul Samuelson [329]

March 30, 1955

Dear Mr. Samuelson:

I just want to tell you once again how very grateful I am for your contribution to the seminar at Tom Finletter's. It was an important educational experience for me, and, I should like to think, for some of the other laymen. I marvel at the deftness with which you handled not only substance but colleagues!

With every good wish and the utmost gratitude, I am

Cordially yours,

To Barry Bingham

April 4, 1955

Dear Barry:

On March 9 I eagerly accepted your invitation to the [Kentucky] Derby, which I assume is on May 7th. Now I must report that I set sail, or rather wing, for Africa on April 18, returning about May 13, if all goes

---

[327] Quemoy and Matsu.

[328] "The Democrats: They're Off and Running for '56," *Collier's*, October 28, 1955.

[329] Professor of economics at Massachusetts Institute of Technology.

well. How I wish you were coming. Lloyd and Ellen Garrison and Cass and Jane Canfield have signed on but there is always room for the Binghams.

At all events, I must miss the Derby, and I am desolate. This is the third year in a row, and it was my time to earn some money, and see some beloved friends. But I'll be there in June!

Yours,

On March 8, Secretary of State Dulles spoke to the nation of his recent trip to Formosa and the meaning of the mutual defense treaty: "The political decision of what to defend has been taken. It is expressed in the treaty and also in the law whereby Congress has authorized the President to use the armed forces of the United States in the Formosa area. That decision is to defend Formosa and the Pescadores. However, the law permits a defense which will be flexible and not necessarily confined to a static defense of Formosa and the Pescadores. How to implement this flexible defense of Formosa the President, President Eisenhower, will decide in the light of his judgment as to the overall value of certain coastal positions to the defense of Formosa, and the cost of holding these positions."

In the days following the speech there were many reports of "off-the-record" meetings at which members of the Administration were said to have stated there was an American commitment to fight for Quemoy and Matsu. Senate Democrats had supported Eisenhower on the mutual defense treaty and they had backed Eisenhower's request in January, 1955, for a congressional resolution approving the use of armed force to protect Formosa and the Pescadores. By April some Democratic senators were disturbed over the situation but they did not speak out.

To Dean Acheson

April 5, 1955

Personal and Confidential

Dear Dean:

I am enclosing the first rough typescript of what I have written, somewhat in line with our telephone conversation. I would be so grateful if you could read it hastily and let me have your comments, if any, by collect telephone at Financial 6-5180.

I shall spend no time now explaining the "whys" of this text but I should certainly welcome your comments on the political aspects as well as the foreign policy. As I explained to you, I should be quite content to

[463]

make no speech but the pressure has not subsided, although the Democrats evidently have!

Hastily and gratefully,

P.S. Of course I need not tell you that I write in confidence in view of the uncertainty about making any speech. Also, I have more and more misgiving about consulting the Congressional leaders. Evidently the view there is to raise no questions, or not many! But that doesn't help me much.

To Adlai E. Stevenson III

April 6, 1955

Dear Bear:

Those week-end plans are okay and you can come back from Washington when you please. I had hoped you might spend part of your holiday there or with Aunt Buffy, or even around New York, rather than going back to New England so promptly. Meet me, then, sometime Saturday afternoon at the Magnusons.

As to the investments, if you don't want to invest it all why don't you just keep what you've got in the account and I will instruct Brown Bros. Harriman to invest the additional $3,000 I am now giving you. That means in effect that you are retaining $2,720.42 of principal in your "fund." I don't know what that "fund" is, by the way.

I can imagine the trouble you had with Mother. I had it too and the Andersons had it worse than ever before. I talked with Warwick yesterday and found him really shattered this time. I think they are worried about Nancy having to be exposed to this sort of thing but I did my best to try to reassure them. I hardly know what to do about the party and I so much wish the whole business had been handled quite differently. However, there is no point in crying over spilled milk. I just so hope that with your help we can all come to understand this situation a little better and handle it a little better. Warwick and I decided not to decide what to do yet and think things over a while until perhaps Mother's passion had cooled. I have no objection to a single party instead of two parties and if she is properly buttered up you know she will purr like a kitten. All it takes is a little management. I sort of felt it would have been well for you to come home during your vacation and be with her, but I guess you will have to be the judge of that. What would you think of my writing her a note saying that I felt very strongly that she should let the Andersons handle the wedding affairs the way they pleased but if she insisted, of course they could ask the two hosts [330] to cancel their parties and give a joint party for out of town friends themselves.

[330] Mr. and Mrs. Wilson W. Wyatt and Mr. and Mrs. Barry Bingham, among other of Stevenson's and the Andersons' Louisville friends, gave parties before and

I have been distracted with work and have written a speech on Quemoy and Matsu which I will have to give as soon as radio time can be cleared. That, together with all the usual work, plus the income tax, plus getting off to Africa, have delayed my work on the list. I hope to heaven I can get something done before I leave.

Love,

P.S. If you really need that fund, okay, but I don't like to see you using principal for current expenses.

John Anson Ford, of the Board of Supervisors of the County of Los Angeles, wrote Stevenson on March 24 that he had just been in Asia and "people spoke in highest terms of you and your visit." Mr. Ford expressed his concern over Senator William Knowland's bellicose position on the Formosa Straits.

To John Anson Ford [331]

April 6, 1955

Dear John:

Thanks for your letter and the *New Outlook* with your article. I shall read it with the utmost interest.

I am so glad that the recollections I left in Asia were not too bad. As to the future of democracy I think it is good and will get better and better if and when our paralysis breaks and the Democrats ever begin to open up on the administration.

With all good wishes, I am

Cordially yours,

To Mrs. Robert Jackson

April 6, 1955

My dear Barbara:

So many thanks for your departing note. I am afraid you will wish you had never seen the late Governor of Illinois, let alone the insatiable travelers Stevenson and Blair. Of course we would love to carry on with you in any manner in Rome. I think of only one thing I should do, which is to make a courtesy call on the Prime Minister if he can receive me, and

---

after Adlai III's wedding to Nancy Anderson. Mrs. Warwick Anderson does not know whether these might be the hosts referred to, but recalls that the situation was eventually resolved by having one large recepion, given by the Andersons, the night before the wedding.

[331] A copy is in A.E.S., I.S.H.L.

that I shall do on April 20 if it can be arranged. We arrive on April 19 at 6:00 P.M. and leave at 6:00 P.M. on April 21, so do with us as you will on the 20th and 21st. You may be sure that Mrs. Luce [332] will not have that opportunity! We will have the spaghetti cooking on the evening of the 20th when you arrive.

The African trip has now assumed incredible proportions and complexities. We seem to be going to Uganda, Kenya, the Rhodesias, the Congo and heaven only knows what else — including pygmies, giants, and the mountains of the moon. Indeed, I am now persuaded that the Jacksons should join up with us and wobble back to the Gold Coast along our wobbly route.

I can barely wait to set foot on the — road to Rome!

Affectionately,

P.S. Better than the foregoing is the enclosed late edition of the itinerary. Read it and weep.

P.P.S. I have written the speech — for better or worse, and a lot of the better you would recognize! I shall probably give it in the next few days. Easter is rather an interruption. There has been a great deal of consultation and the long distance expenditures are appalling.

Jonathan Daniels wrote Stevenson on April 5: "The simple fact at this point is that both you and I who want the party to provide an enlightened program for this country have to stay behind Adlai Stevenson." He added that he planned to attend a meeting of the Committee on Rules for the 1956 Democratic Convention "as a Southerner insistent that the party cannot go far in appeasing those arrogant 'Democrats' from the South who pretend that they are the South and the Democratic Party. Some kind of loyalty emphasis must be made, not so much to protect the national party from Southern bolters as to protect true and loyal Democrats in the South from devices which would serve future bolters in the domination of the party in Southern States."

To Jonathan Daniels [333]

April 8, 1955

Dear Jonathan:

How you can write! It was a grand letter and my blood is hot. But I worry about too much "loyalty emphasis" just now when we are in

[332] Clare Boothe Luce, wife of publisher Henry Luce and United States ambassador to Italy. Stevenson had avoided her on his 1953 trip to Italy. See *The Papers of Adlai E. Stevenson,* Vol. V.

[333] A copy is in A.E.S., I.S.H.L.

better and better shape in much of the South and some of the gentlemen you mention are losing ground I am told. I have not been exactly exhilarated by the Democratic performance in Washington. Haven't we been missing some opportunities to hit the administration and to contradict the "unbeatable Ike" mythology so vigorously cultivated by the Republican press?

I have been under considerable heat of late to speak out after my four months of silence on Formosa. I shall do so on Monday — for better or for worse.

Sincerely yours,

George B. Young and his wife, the former Mary Seymour Adams, were Chicago friends of Stevenson. Young worked with a small group of people, Louis Kohn and William Blair, particularly, who attempted to organize support for Stevenson to run for public office in 1948. In 1954 Young became an officer of Field Enterprises, Inc., and later its president. Because of Stevenson's friendly association with the Field family, he continued to see Young with some regularity until his death.

The Youngs were Libertyville guests of Stevenson at the time of the incident referred to in the letter. After returning from dining out in a borrowed car that had an automatic transmission, Young parked the car and failed to put it in neutral. As a result, the car crept slowly over one of the low yew trees flanking the front door. Young wrote on April 5 referring to this accident and stating that now, after he had visited Stevenson again and realized the extent of the damage, he wished to have a new tree planted.

To George B. Young [334]

April 8, 1955

Dear George:

What a thoughtful and punctilious man you are! I have had a lot of trouble with *ewes,* but this is the first *yew* I have had in some time, and you were good to think of remedying it.

Actually, I should imagine this was a very bad time to transplant, so why don't we just let it go for the present and I will see how the old one looks as the summer wears on. If it is too ragged perhaps I will take advantage of your kindness in the fall, when I assume transplanting is safer. How's that? And a thousand thanks for reminding me that 18th Century courtesy isn't extinct.

Cordially yours,

[334] A copy is in A.E.S., I.S.H.L.

To Mrs. Franklin D. Roosevelt [335]

April 11, 1955

ALL AMERICANS WHO LOVE FREEDOM AND JUSTICE JOIN WITH YOU IN
MOURNING THIS TENTH ANNIVERSARY OF THE DEATH OF FRANKLIN D.
ROOSEVELT. AS LONG AS MEN CARE DEEPLY ABOUT LIBERTY AND SO-
CIAL PROGRESS HIS MEMORY WILL BE FRESH IN THE MINDS AND
HEARTS OF THE PEOPLE OF THE WORLD.

On April 11, Stevenson spoke to the nation by radio.

THE FORMOSA CRISIS
A Peaceful Solution [336]

My Fellow Countrymen:

I have not spoken to you for more than four months. And I do so tonight only because I have been deeply disturbed by the recent course of
events in the Far East and because many of you have asked me for my
views. I have waited until the first excitement about the islands, Quemoy
and Matsu, has subsided and we can more calmly examine our situation
in the Straits of Formosa and in Asia. In matters of national security
emotion is no substitute for intelligence, nor rigidity for prudence. To act
coolly, intelligently, and prudently in perilous circumstances is the test of
a man — and also a nation.

Our common determination, Republicans and Democrats alike, is to
avoid atomic war and achieve a just and lasting peace. We all agree on
that, I think, but not on the ways and means to that end. And that's what
I want to talk about — war, and ways and means to a peaceful solution
in the present crisis in the Straits of Formosa.

On this April evening, I remember vividly that it was in April just ten
years ago that the largest conference in all diplomatic history met at
San Francisco to write the Charter of the United Nations — a charter of
liberation for the peoples of the earth from the scourge of war and want.

The spirit of San Francisco was one of optimism and boundless hope.
The long night was lifting; Hitler's armies were on the eve of collapse; the
war lords of Japan were tottering. Our hearts were high in that bright
blue dawn of a new day — just ten years ago.

But tonight, despite the uneasy truces in Korea and Indo-China, our

---

[335] This telegram is in the Franklin D. Roosevelt Library, Hyde Park, New York.
[336] The text is from *What I Think,* pp. 215–224.

country once again confronts the iron face of war — war that may be unlike anything that man has seen since the creation of the world, for the weapons man created can destroy not only his present but his future as well. With the invention of the hydrogen bomb and all the frightful spawn of fission and fusion, the human race has crossed one of the great watersheds of history, and mankind stands in new territory, in uncharted lands.

The tragedy is that the possibility of war just now seems to hinge upon Quemoy and Matsu, small islands that lie almost as close to the coast of China as Staten Island does to New York — islands which, presumably have been fortified by the Chinese Nationalists with our approval and assistance.

Having loudly hinted at American intervention in Indo-China just a year ago, and then backed away; having forced General Chiang Kai-shek to evacuate the Tachen islands when the Communists made menacing gestures just a couple of months ago, we now face the bitter consequences of our government's Far Eastern policy once again: either another damaging and humiliating retreat, or else the hazard of war, modern war, unleashed not by necessity, not by strategic judgment, not by the honor of allies or for the defense of frontiers, but by a policy based more on political difficulties here at home than the realities of our situation in Asia.

Given these unhappy choices it appears that President Eisenhower will decide what to do if and when the attack comes, depending on whether in his judgment it is just an attack on these islands or a prelude to an assault on Formosa. While our President has great military experience, perhaps it is not improper to ask whether any man can read the mind of an enemy within a few hours of such an attack and determine whether, at some later date, the enemy plans to go further and invade Formosa. Is it wise to allow the dread question of modern war to hinge upon such a guess?

Many of the President's most influential associates — including the Republican leader in the Senate [337] and the Chairman of the Republican Policy Committee [338] — have been insisting that he pledge us to the defense of these islands. They say that another bluff and backdown, another retreat in Asia, would add substance to what the Chinese Communists say about the U.S. being a "paper tiger."

Those who demand a pledge to go to war also say that having gone this far with Chiang Kai-shek to let him down now, when he is reinforcing these islands and preparing an all-out stand, would deal a heavy blow to the morale of his forces and endanger the defenses of Formosa itself.

Now there is undeniable merit to these and other arguments, but I

[337] Senator William Knowland of California.
[338] Senator Styles Bridges of New Hampshire.

must say in all candor that they seem to me overborne by the counter-arguments, and I have the greatest misgivings about risking a third World War in defense of these little islands in which we would have neither the same legal justification nor the same support as in the defense of Formosa. They are different from Formosa. They have always belonged to China. But Formosa belonged to Japan and was ceded by the Japanese peace treaty. We have as much right to be there as anybody, except perhaps the real Formosans.

But, of course, the President's judgment must be final. He asked for and got from Congress the sole responsibility for making this decision. His word is our law, and, as Senator Lyndon Johnson, the majority leader, has said: "We are not going to take the responsibility out of the hands of the constitutional leader and try to arrogate it to ourselves." So the ultimate decision must rest with the constitutional leader, the President, and he will have my prayers for his wisdom and fortitude in making this critical decision, if he must and when he must. I only hope that the inflammatory voices in his party and his administration do not unbalance his consideration of these critical questions:

Are the offshore islands essential to the security of the U.S.?

Are they, indeed, even essential to the defense of Formosa — which all Americans have been agreed upon since President Truman sent the Seventh Fleet there five years ago?

Or is it, as the Secretary of Defense says, that the loss of Quemoy and Matsu would make no significant military difference?

Can they be defended without resort to nuclear weapons?

If not, while I know we now have the means to incinerate, to burn up, much of living China, and quickly, are we prepared to use such weapons to defend islands so tenuously related to American security?

Finally, are we prepared to shock and alienate not alone our traditional allies but most of the major non-Communist powers of Asia by going to war over islands to which the United States has no color of claim and which are of questionable value to the defense of Formosa?

Are we, in short, prepared to face the prospect of war in the morass of China, possibly global war, standing almost alone in a sullen or hostile world?

These are the questions that must be answered, this time I hope with more concern for realities in Asia and for unity with our allies, than for fantasies in Formosa and for placating implacable extremists in America.

At this late date there may be no wholly satisfactory way of resolving the dilemma. But if we learn something from this experience, then perhaps we can turn our present difficulties to good account and devise an approach more in keeping with the realities of Asia and of the Hydrogen Age.

And that causes me to say that the division of our coalition over these offshore islands, the weakening of the Grand Alliance of free nations pledged to stand together to defend themselves, is in my judgment a greater peril to enduring peace than the islands themselves.

I know some politicians tell us that we don't need allies. Life would certainly be much simpler if that were so, for our friends can be highly irritating. But it is not so. We need allies because we have only 6 per cent of the world's population. We need them because the overseas air bases essential to our own security are on their territory. We need allies because they are the source of indispensable strategic materials. We need, above all, the moral strength that the solidarity of the world community alone can bring to our cause. Let us never underestimate the weight of moral opinion. It can be more penetrating than bullets, more durable than steel. It was a great general, Napoleon, who wrote that: "In war, moral considerations are three-quarters of the battle."

Should we be plunged into another great war, the maintenance of our alliances and the respect and good will of the uncommitted nations of Asia will be far more important to us than the possession of these offshore islands by General Chiang Kai-shek ever could be. Moreover, the maintenance of a united front is of vital importance to the defense of Formosa itself, since, in addition to the material and military support our friends might contribute, their moral support, and the knowledge by the Communist leaders that they would be facing a united free world, would be a much more effective deterrent to an assault on Formosa than is our present lonely and irresolute position.

How shall we mend the walls of our coalition? How shall we frustrate the supreme aim of the Moscow-Peiping axis — to drive a wedge between America and her allies? And is there any hope of a peaceful solution of the offshore island question?

I think so. Senator [Walter F.] George, the Chairman of the Foreign Relations Committee, has recently pointed the way: "We nations of the free world," he said, "must understand each other and reach a measure of unity before any hopeful approach can be made to a re-examination of . . . our Far Eastern problems."

And Governor [Averell] Harriman of New York, long familiar with the problems of maintaining a coalition, warned us the other day that in Asia "the whole world is a party at interest," and that it has been not only illogical but deadly dangerous, he said, "to arrogate to ourselves the sole responsibility for decisions which involve the future of many people."

So I would urge our government to promptly consult our friends, yes, and the uncommitted states too, and ask them all to join with us in an open declaration condemning the use of force in the Formosa Strait, and agreeing to stand with us in the defense of Formosa against any aggression, pending some final settlement of its status — by independence, neutralization, trusteeship, plebiscite, or whatever is wisest.

Nor do I see any reason why we should not invite Soviet Russia, which is united by treaty with Red China, to declare its position, to indicate whether it prefers the possibility of ultimate settlement by agreement to an unpredictable, perhaps limitless conflict, started by an arrogant, foolhardy Communist China, either by miscalculation or by design.

Fortified by such an international declaration denouncing the use of force; with the assurance of such collective support for the defense of Formosa; and with the addition, thereby, of moral solidarity to military strength, I should think Quemoy and Matsu would have little further importance to the Nationalists, let alone to us — and that they could then be relinquished, before we stumble any farther down the dismal road to war that nobody wants.

Diplomacy prescribes no rigid formula for accomplishing our objectives, and another major avenue in the quest for a peaceful solution in the Far East remains unexplored: the United Nations. I should think that the United States, together with friends and allies in Europe and Asia, could submit a resolution to the United Nations General Assembly, calling upon the Assembly likewise to condemn any effort to alter the present status of Formosa by force. And I think we could afford to go further and call upon the United Nations Assembly to seek a formula for the permanent future of Formosa, consistent with the wishes of its people, with international law, and with world security.

One of the weaknesses of our position is that we have been making Formosa policy as we thought best regardless of others. We have not made it clear that we are helping to hold Formosa not as an offensive but as a purely defensive measure. We have not made it clear because the administration has not been clear itself. But we can't expect other nations to support policies they disagree with, let alone ambiguous and dangerous policies.

Joint action along the lines I've indicated would put Formosa policy on a much broader and more comprehensible basis. In the eyes of the Asian nations we would thereby achieve a consistent and morally unquestionable position in providing for the protection of the Formosans according to the principles and ideals of international law. In the eyes of our European friends we would once more have asserted our full belief in the value, indeed in the indispensability, of maintaining the alliance of the free world against the slave world. And in the eyes of our Nationalist friends on Formosa, surely the understanding and support of the bulk of the non-Communist world is a much stronger defense of Formosa than these islands can possibly be.

But, if the Chinese Communists refuse; if they insist on force and reject any peaceful solution, then at least it would be clear to everyone who the aggressors were. And, clearly, if the Chinese are so bent on violence, so intoxicated by their success, so indifferent to the grisly realities of modern war, then we have no alternative but to meet force with force. But let us at least meet it with our allies beside us and the blame placed squarely where it belongs — not on America's fantasies and inflexibility, but on the unteachable and unquenchable ambition and the indifference to human life of China's Communist regime.

To profit from this unhappy experience we might ask ourselves how we ever got in this position, how the prestige and honor of the great United States, not to mention the peace of the world, could be staked on some little islands within the very shadow of the China coast in which we have no claim or interest.

The answer, of course, lies partly in the fact that domestic political considerations have influenced our Formosa policy lately. Domestic politics should not enter our foreign affairs, least of all factional conflict between the two wings of the President's party, but they have, and too often our hot and cold, vacillating behavior has reflected efforts to please both of the views that divide our government and the Republican party, especially on Far Eastern policy.

And, while I do not belittle some recent achievements in the foreign field, for the same reasons too much of our foreign policy of late has disclosed a yawning gap between what we say and what we do — between our words and deeds.

For example, you recall that just a year ago as the Communist pressure rose in Indo-China, so did our warlike, menacing words. The Vice-President of the United States even talked of sending American soldiers to fight on the mainland of Asia. But what happened? Nothing.

Likewise all the bold, brave talk about liberation that raised such vain hopes among the peoples behind the iron curtain has long since evaporated, with the loss of half of Vietnam and much of our prestige and influence.

So also we hear no more of last year's dire threats of instantaneous and massive atomic retaliation. Instead, the President has spoken lately of pinpoint retaliation with tactical weapons. I fear, however, that the psychological effect of the use of atomic weapons, large or small, will be most unfortunate.

But there has been plenty of massive verbal retaliation, and the administration's policy of extravagant words has alarmed our friends a good deal more than it has deterred the aggressors. For our allies assumed that the great United States meant what it said.

Now let me be clear. I am not criticizing the administration for abandoning these extravagant positions; I am criticizing it for taking such positions, for making threats which it is not prepared to back up, and thereby undermining faith in the United States. Theodore Roosevelt said: "Never draw unless you intend to shoot," and I fear this wordy warfare has made more friends in Asia for China than for us.

Another example of these winged words, as we have seen, was President Eisenhower's dramatic announcement two years ago that he was unleashing Chiang Kai-shek, taking the wraps off him, presumably for an attack on the mainland to reconquer China. However, it was apparent to everyone else, if not to us, that such an invasion across a hundred miles of water by a small, overage, underequipped army against perhaps the largest army and the largest nation on earth could not possibly succeed without all-out support from the United States.

Since it seemed incredible to sober, thoughtful people that the government of the United States could be bluffing on such a matter, the President's unleashing policy has caused widespread anxiety that we planned to support a major war with China which might involve the Soviet Union. Hence we find ourselves where we are today — on Quemoy and Matsu — alone.

What, then, are the lessons to be drawn from the past two years?

In the first place, I think we should abandon, once and for all, the policy of wishful thinking and wishful talking, the policy of big words and little deeds.

We must renounce go-it-aloneism.

We shall have to face the fact that General Chiang's army cannot invade the mainland unless we are prepared to accept enormous burdens and risks — alone.

The world will respect us for recognizing mistakes and correcting them. But if our present posture in the offshore islands, for example, is a wrong one, who will respect us for stubbornly persisting in it? If we cease to deceive ourselves over the hard realities of power in the Formosa situation, we shall have taken the first step toward our first essential — the restoration of unity of purpose and action between ourselves and our allies in the free world. But our friends have made it clear that so long as fantasy, rigidity, and domestic politics seem to stand in the way of peaceful Formosa settlement, they will not support us if, in spite of our endeavors, a conflict should break out.

So, finally, let us face the fact that keeping friends these days calls for more statesmanship than challenging enemies, and the cause of world peace transcends any domestic political considerations.

But, preoccupied as we all are these days with the immediate problem of these islands, we must try to keep things in perspective somehow, and not lose sight of our main objectives. For beyond Quemoy and Matsu, and even Formosa, lie the urgent and larger problems of Asia — the growing attraction of enormous, reawakened China, the struggle of the underdeveloped countries to improve their condition and keep their independence, and the grave misgivings about America.

If the best hope for today's world is a kind of atomic balance, the decisive battle in the struggle against aggression may be fought not on battlefields but in the minds of men, and the area of decision may well be out there among the uncommitted peoples of Asia and Africa who look and listen and who must, in the main, judge us by what we say and do.

It is not only over the offshore islands crisis that we need a new sense of direction and to mend our fences. Too often of late we have turned to the world a face of stern military power. Too often the sound they hear from Washington is the call to arms, the rattling of the saber. Too often our constructive, helpful economic programs have been obscured, our good done by stealth. Thus have we Americans, the most peaceful and generous people on earth, been made to appear hard, belligerent, and careless of those very qualities of humanity which, in fact, we value most. The picture of America — the kindly, generous, deeply pacific people who are really America — has been clouded in the world, to the comfort of the aggressors and the dismay of our friends.

As best we can, let us correct this distorted impression, for we will win no hearts and minds in the new Asia by uttering louder threats and brandishing bigger swords. The fact is that we have not created excess military strength. The fact is that compared to freedom's enemies we have created if anything too little; the trouble is that we have tried to cover our deficiencies with bold words and have thus obscured our peaceful purposes and our ultimate reliance on quiet firmness, rather than bluster and vacillation, on wisdom rather than warnings, on forbearance rather than dictation.

We will be welcome to the sensitive people of Asia, more as engineers and doctors and agricultural experts, coming to build, to help, to heal than as soldiers. Point Four was an idea far more stirring, far more powerful, than all the empty slogans about liberation and retaliation and unleashing rolled together. So I say, let us present once more the true face of America — warm and modest and friendly, dedicated to the welfare of all mankind, and demanding nothing except a chance for all to live and let live, to grow and govern as they wish, free from interference, free from intimidation, free from fear.

Let this be the American mission in the Hydrogen Age. Let us stop slandering ourselves and appear before the world once again — as we really are — as friends, not as masters; as apostles of principle, not of power; in humility, not arrogance; as champions of peace, not as harbingers of war. For our strength lies, not alone in our proving grounds and our stockpiles, but in our ideals, our goals, and their universal appeal to all men who are struggling to breathe free.

Stuart Gerry Brown wrote:

Thus Stevenson cast his influence against the risk of war over Quemoy and Matsu, and for a positive approach to the world crisis. There is no doubt that, partisan though he was, he spoke for the great majority of Americans. The next day, April 12, as though he had never suggested military intervention in the islands, Secretary Dulles said that Stevenson's proposals "copied" those of the administration. "Mr. Stevenson," he said, "has in fact endorsed the administration's program in relation to Formosa." Whether the Secretary's words meant what they seemed to say or were merely politic, there is no doubt that national unity on the Formosa question followed Stevenson's speech. No more was said of going to the military defense of Quemoy and Matsu, and in the discussions of the General Assembly overwhelming sentiment was expressed against the use of force in the Formosa Straits.

There is no reason to suppose that President Eisenhower ever personally wished to go to war over Quemoy and Matsu. And, of course, it was the Communists who preserved peace by refraining from further attack. But Eisenhower was under severe pressure from leaders of his own party and from Nationalist China. Stevenson's intervention on behalf of a peaceful solution provided Eisenhower with the unity of American opinion he required to resist these pressures. In the moment of crisis the image of Eisenhower as peacemaker seemed to waver, but it was fortified and secured by Stevenson's leadership.[339]

Stevenson received many telegrams and letters commending his speech.

To Herbert H. Lehman [340]

April 14, 1955

My dear Senator:

I could not be more pleased or touched than by your wire and also by

---

[339] *Conscience in Politics*, pp. 144–145.
[340] A copy is in A.E.S., I.S.H.L.

your gracious and eloquent statement about my "effort" the other night. That you approve is a reward in itself; that you approved so heartily delights me.

I have grown progressively anxious as the administration continues to use foreign policy for domestic political purposes. It is worse than shameful; it is dangerous.

I look forward to seeing you.

Cordially yours,

To Harry S. Truman

April 14, 1955

Dear Mr. President:

I am profoundly grateful for your thoughtful telegram. I have grown more and more alarmed as the administration continues to persist in its practice of using foreign policy for domestic political purposes.

With affectionate regards to you and Mrs. Truman, and my utmost thanks, I am

Cordially yours,

P.S. I am taking the liberty of enclosing a copy of the speech herewith.

To Lyndon B. Johnson

April 14, 1955

Dear Lyndon:

So many thanks for your thoughtful and kind wire. I believe the President will have to choose sides within his party before much longer.

I look forward to seeing you this week-end.

Cordially yours,

To Carroll Binder [341]

April 15, 1955

Dear Carroll:

Thanks for your letter and the enclosures. That Binder approves fortifies my conviction! I am so glad that you have challenged the absurdities about the loss of China and I hope you never lay off.

I have become increasingly alarmed of late, which has been confirmed by advices from literally ever[y] corner of the earth, about the administration's continued use of foreign policy to serve domestic political pur-

[341] The original is in the possession of the Newberry Library, Chicago.

poses. Perhaps even more alarming is the apparent indefiniteness or actual approbation of the press. Evidently unity in the Republican party is a much more positive concern than unity in the free world or among our allies. I am told by some formidable historians that probably we have no similar counterpart, in recent history at least.

If you were surprised by [John S.] Knight's editorial on [Robert R.?] McCormick you should have seen the one on the Yalta papers.[342] He said they were proof that Roosevelt gave away everything but the kitchen stove. I have seldom seen anything as incredible or intemperate over the signature of a responsible man.

It was good to hear from you, as always.

Cordially yours,
ADLAI

On April 14 the Finletter Group met at the Chicago Club. Harvard economist Seymour Harris was among those who presented papers.

To Seymour Harris

April 15, 1955

Dear Seymour:

Before the memory wears off, I must thank you again for all the enlightenment you brought to me yesterday. I am literally amazed by your versatility and I am grateful indeed for all of your pains and efforts to educate me.

Cordially yours,

On April 16, Stevenson flew to Washington, D.C. At the airport he told reporters that he had not made up his mind as to whether he would run for President again in 1956. He lunched with Speaker of the House of Representatives Sam Rayburn, Senate Majority Leader Lyndon B. Johnson, and Paul Butler, chairman of the Democratic National Committee.

This was Stevenson's first stop on his trip to Africa, a trip of self-education, and he wrote in the diary he kept of that journey:

Saturday April 16

. . . Johnson rationalizing why they don't attack Eisenhower's management more, but seemed to approve my criticism re foreign policy this

[342] Chicago *Daily News*, April 3, 10, 1955.

week. Rayburn very critical, but uncertain about political tactics — aging and a little indifferent . . .

That evening Stevenson introduced Sam Rayburn at a huge $100-a-plate testimonial banquet to Mr. Rayburn. Stevenson wrote in his diary:

. . . Made good intro. of Sam Rayburn on Radio-TV. Rayburn's eloquent and philosophical speech not in character but very good — written by David Cohen [Cohn]. Pres. Truman looking himself again — also spoke in old attack vein, and as usual caught hell from Rep[ublican]. press which never even mentioned his criticisms. Very friendly to me.

On April 18, Stevenson and Bill Blair flew from New York City to Rome. Stevenson wrote in his diary:

Tues — Ap. 19
Arrived Rome in evening in rain. Hassler Hotel.

Wed — Ap. 20
Shopping — prices seemed high. Rome beautiful, cool, fresh and still to me the world's most wonderful and exciting city.

To Villa Madonna on hill on outskirts overlooking Mussolini's great sports park — for lunch with Prime Minister [Mario] Scelba. Long talk thru interpreter in the *magnificent* Villa Madonna. Wants $300 million more annually for 5 years to "save the south" from communism. Same story — almost — I heard 2 years ago. But Italy from Rome north is an incredible picture of recovery and well being.

Scelba firm, pleasant, unpretentious, simple little man — more interested in Italy than the "world." His wife plump and pleasant & unaffected.

Delicious lunch with foreign minister etc etc — and Mrs. [Clare Boothe] Luce — who tries hard to be pleasant and considerate.

Returned to Embassy with her and talked a bit about the new oil discoveries and the proposed oil law etc. Shook a few hands — and then to Hotel to finish & polish my poor and long neglected article for Sat Eve Post [343] on party cooperation.

Barbara (Ward) & Robt. Jackson arrived in time for late gay dinner at

[343] Probably a reference to *Look* magazine, in the September 20, 1955, issue of which Stevenson's article "Memo to the President: Let's Make the Two-Party System Work" appeared.

Palassis fine restaurant — Mussolini's modern villa for his mistress. Then a night club!

Recognized everywhere — autographs, photos!

Thurs — Ap 21

Scelba sent a fine car for day. To Catacombs of St. Calistus — to see again the imperishable sights of 1912! [344] The professor in charge showed us thru; learned a lot I didn't know, also a reminder there among the hundreds of thousands of dead stacked on shelves — that we're not very important.

Lunch at Villa d'Este & a walk thru the fabulous gardens in bright soft sunshine — with the charming, witty, totally cultivated Barbara.

Thence to St. Peters for a "conducted tour" by the "authorities" of the new excavations beneath the alter where they think they have found St Peter's bones at last — at the legendary place beneath the alter of Constantine's basilica.

Airport and off at 7 by Scandinavian Airlines to Athens. . . .

Stevenson and Blair arrived in Nairobi, Kenya, on April 22. Mr. and Mrs. Lloyd Garrison [345] and Mr. and Mrs. Cass Canfield [346] joined them there for the African journey. As had happened before, Stevenson's attempt to keep a diary proved abortive. For two days he wrote rather fully of his experiences, but after that it became brief notes and lists of names to serve as reminders. Instead of publishing this material, the editors decided to use the following memo. It was probably written on May 15 or 16 since Stevenson reached New York City on May 17 and returned to Chicago on May 18.

MEMO TO MY SONS ON A MONTH IN AFRICA
by Adlai E. Stevenson
Dakar, French West Africa, May 1955 [347]

My homeward bound airplane has broken down and I have an unscheduled and welcome day here in Dakar. After inspecting the city and environs with the French officials and American consul, I am going to

[344] Stevenson had traveled to Europe with his parents and sister in December, 1911. See *The Papers of Adlai E. Stevenson*, Vol. I, pp. 10–11.

[345] Mr. Garrison wrote six "reports" or "notes" to his family while he traveled with Stevenson. He made this material available to the editors.

[346] See Cass Canfield, *Up and Down and Around* (New York: Harper's Magazine Press, 1971), pp. 214–219, for an account of this trip.

[347] The text is based on a carbon copy.

improve "the shining hours" with a brief report to you on my journey through sub-Sahara Africa during this past month. (And the hours really "shine" here high above the sun-tamed sea at the Westernmost tip of the "great bulge of Africa.")

Perhaps the place to start is where I am — on the edge of the vast area of French Africa which covers a fourth of the continent. Behind me to the East stretch almost empty deserts and semi-deserts for thousands of miles, but to the South from whence I've just come lie the steaming, equatorial rain forests of the Guinea coast — the slave coast of old — and the rich Congo basin. Beyond the tropical forests and the head waters of the Congo, 4,000 miles to the South and West, the country changes to high "savanna," sometimes well watered, green, rolling and lovely, as in the highlands of East Africa, and sometimes impoverished scrub and arid, treeless grasslands that stretch endlessly over so much of the Rhodesias, Angola and Bechuanaland.[348] Still further south, at the tip of this huge, little known continent, lies the healthy, rolling, beautiful "velts" of South Africa, the best known part of all. It seems a little curious that the extremities of this continent, 5,000 miles apart, are both restless. Along the northern fringes, in Morocco, Algeria and Tunisia the dominance of a European minority has been violently challenged by an Arab-Berber majority. In the far South a dominant European minority is afraid it will be challenged by an African majority.

However, my journey has not been in the troubled zone of French North Africa but below the Sahara, the Sudan and Ethiopia. It is customary and dramatic nowadays to write of Africa as if it were all "seething" and "in ferment," but I cannot in honesty dramatize the racial unrest in the country through which I have just travelled. Except for the Mau Mau terrorism in Kenya (and those bloody devils ambushed, mutilated and murdered two small English boys near Nairobi during my stay) there are no riots or anti-white or anti-foreign demonstrations as in North Africa.

But it would be a bold optimist indeed who did not detect trouble ahead if the awaking Africans' demands for greater freedom and better economic opportunities are not satisfied. It is what is being done in response to these urges that interested me most. And everywhere something *is* being done, except in South Africa, which has taken a quite different approach, although the leaders there would assure you that what they are doing is not only right before God and man, but also in the long run best for the Africans.

I want to tell you something of *what* is being done and *how*, to meet the emergence of a whole new race on the world's stage. But first a few

348 Since 1966 the independent nation of Botswana.

generalities, hazardous though they be, about this strange new land which has such variety of climate, scenery, population, and civilization, from the oldest, in Egypt, to the youngest — in some of the places I've just been! I say "new" land because our knowledge of much of Africa is very recent, less than 100 years, and there is still much to learn. Even now scores of geological teams are probing unknown fabulous resources. In the Congo we heard that they had teams at work discovering areas where there *weren't* minerals where they could build towns!

But physical exploration is the least of it; understanding the people and what is happening to them under the impact of western civilization is harder. One obvious thing that is happening is the transition to a western money economy. People who have known nothing but shifting cultivation by the most primitive methods; people who have always tended cattle or goats; people who have produced for subsistence and barter only, are learning about money and how to get pots and pans, bicycles and beer, and those brightly colored cloths that make any public place or roadside in Central Africa the most colorful in the world.

European civilization, the missionaries, traders, settlers, planters and industrialists have also brought with them new faiths, new moral values, sanitation, disease control, tribal peace, better tools, new skills, a little education — and that inevitable partner of law and order — taxes! But don't think the African is getting rich. Money incomes probably range from $30 a year in the more primitive areas to $250 in the most developed, the Union of South Africa.

The consequences of all these things that have been gathering momentum for a century are many, some good, some bad. Population, both human and animal, is increasing as the death rate goes down. Cattle are still the measure of wealth in some places, and you will be interested to hear that the price of wives is rising alarmingly. Speaking of wives, women are still doing most of the work among the Africans and, as is often said, "they call these people uncivilized!" A common sight is an African on a bicycle, donkey, or afoot, carrying a light spear or nothing at all, followed by his women folk with huge jars of water, loads of wood or stems of bananas on their heads and the inevitable babies lashed to their backs. Babies in Africa, by the way, seldom cry — a curious fact for which I heard no satisfactory explanation.

But let me wander back to the consequences of European impact. The pressure of population increase has been aggravated in the areas of white settlement, like Kenya, Southern Rhodesia and South Africa, by the reservation of the better lands for Europeans. And the use and ownership of land is now certainly about the hottest subject south of the Sahara. You hear more than once, as I did from a missionary, the plaintive remark of the African who said: "When the European came he had the Bible and we had the land; now he has the land and we have the Bible."

Again, the migration of labor into money earning not only reduces the food supply by reducing the productive males available to keep the subsistence economies going, but it also separates families. The demand has been largely for male labor and families are left behind in the villages. Indeed I can't recall ever seeing even a female African house servant anywhere. Such separations result in high turn-over rates in industry and have retarded the growth of a skilled African labor force. But that pattern is changing now and at the great Roan Antelope mine on the Copperbelt of Northern Rhodesia,[349] for example, workmen are now encouraged to bring their families and hundreds of new small houses are being built for them. But to an African, "family" has a much broader meaning than it does to us and includes relatives as well as wife and children. Indeed the mine manager told us that an average of three people in addition to his family lived off each of his African miners.

Why is it, you will wonder, that there is no demand for female labor? Well, for one reason, the women are not yet as advanced as the menfolk and often have a status little above a chattel. Indeed one of the major handicaps to education is the superstition and backwardness of the children's mothers.

Even more serious and profound than the transition to a money economy have been the non-economic, the psychological and political stresses, especially in areas of large European settlement. For here the African collides head on with economic and political discrimination, as well as social segregation. He quickly learns that he can climb the economic ladder only so far, that ability and initiative will not earn for him the same advancement in status and income as the white man. The discovery of his inferior status, economically, politically and socially, provokes resentment and bitterness.

This points, I think, to one of the most acute problems for harmonious, peaceful development requires not only enlightened European but also cooperative and rational African leadership. Its development is not easy in such circumstances. I often asked Africans what priority of importance they attached to economic opportunity, political participation, education, or respect. Almost always the educated ones said respect and recognition, and almost always the illiterate said they didn't know or didn't understand. I was reminded of G. K. Chesterton's words about the British working people of an earlier day: "We do not know them because they have not spoken yet."

You may also wonder why I always say "European" and "African" in-

[349] Since 1964 the independent nation of Zambia.

stead of "white" and "Negro" as we do. Well, I don't believe I ever heard the word "Negro" in Africa — "African," "native," "Bantu," yes, but never "Negro," which seems to be an American word. And "European" is used in distinction to "Asian" or "Indian," for there are almost a million Asians, mostly Indians, along with five million Europeans in Africa. How many Africans are there? No one knows. But the "guesstimate" is upwards of 170 million. There are also the "coloreds" of South Africa, a million descendants of the early Boer settlers and native stock or women imported from the Dutch East Indies. It is these unfortunates, the most race conscious of all, whom the South African government is striking from the voting rolls by the extreme device of "packing" the Senate.

We have seen the collision of the indigenous population with the Europeans in the North — the Arabs with the French; the Egyptians with the British. And in the rest of the continent it is the relations of these minorities — European, Asian, Colored — with one another and with the awakening and overwhelming majority, the African, that now occupies so much of the attention of thoughtful people of all races.

Travelling rapidly through these countries you are constantly reminded that a handful of white men have brought to this continent and to these friendly, simple people most everything they have, save what nature gave them. And you also realize that without African labor little could have been done or can be done to develop the country, exploit its wealth and better the lot of its peoples. While you marvel at the majesty of the scenery, from the stately forest mansions of the tropics, across the green rolling savannas to the Mountains of the Moon, you marvel too at the mighty gulfs between white and black, and between the East African tribesmen who eat blood and milk and the West African eggheads educated at the London School of Economics. But everywhere the question is not *if* the African is advancing, but *how* and how *fast*. And that varies from country to country.

Whether what is happening is for the best; whether it would have been kinder as some say to leave the African in a state of nature with his tribal chiefs and fetish priests doesn't concern us. For the die has been cast long since — not, I like to think, by the "Christian" West's first relationship with Black Africa — the slave trade — but a hundred years ago by Livingston[e] and Stanley and their followers — the early Christian missionaries who brought to Africa medicine, science, education and Christ's teachings, and who bravely died untimely deaths of yellow fever, cholera, malaria and the lethal bite of the tsetse fly. I've seen their forgotten graves by the roadsides. And I have wondered too about the bewildering effect on the African of the variety of his successors, the Catholic and the Protestant missionaries from many denominations, but all of whom preach to him from the same Book and teach him the same lessons of the Fatherhood of God and brotherhood of man. I shall long remember a visit to Swaziland,[350] a mountainous, beautiful and primitive British Protectorate on the Portuguese East African frontier, and its King, Sobhuza. Plaintively he told me that there were some six Protestant missions in his little domain ministering unto his bewildered pagan subjects. The separatism of Western Christianity has fallen on fertile ground in Africa and I was told that there are more than 700 African Christian sects in the Union!

But I can't proceed to what is important without another word about King Sobhuza. You must approach him, unless you are a white man, on all fours. To my consternation one of his fully grown daughters crawled to his feet while I was there. But he was a charming, hospitable man, Oxford educated, and looked very imperious on his red plush sofa. I sat on it too and kept slipping off because the front springs had collapsed. I can't tell you how he was dressed, because he didn't have much "dressing." But his handsome queen did — a bright green silk dress. He is said to have 56 wives and, of course, numerous children. Last winter, we were told, he asked who a particularly accomplished dancer was and the reply was: "Sir, that is your son!"

But to return to what the colonial powers are doing about the one sure thing in Africa — advancement of the native. Here in the French territories the policy is political integration with metropolitan France. The African territories send African delegates to the National Assembly and the Council of the Republic in Paris. (I could not confirm the story of the African delegate who returned from Paris and was promptly eaten by his constituents, and whether it was from joy or indignation!) Territorial assemblies with real powers have been created and Africans have a majority of the seats. Literally millions of Africans are voting. Public investment is on a large scale. While I was in Dakar during the war I would hardly have recognized the place due to the expansion and building. France is spending a lot more than it is earning in these vast territories on health, housing, education and commercial development, and the political reforms have given to the Africans the power to enforce to some extent their claims to a better life.

While the British aim is generally the creation of new self governing

[350] Stevenson, Blair, Mr. and Mrs. Lloyd Garrison, and Mr. and Mrs. Cass Canfield were accompanied on their two-day motor trip to Swaziland by Clara Urquhart, Albert Schweitzer's translator, and her brother, Fritz Rosenberg, of Johannesburg.

units, the French objective is political incorporation in the French Union.[351] And certainly they have stepped up the pace of assistance to the Africans to take their place as French citizens alongside other French citizens. Although aloof and often rough and arbitrary with the natives, the French system seems to work, and they seem to succeed in convincing the African that their distinctions are not *racial*.

The French territories surround Nigeria and the Gold Coast,[352] British colonies that are now on the threshold of self-government and independence within the British Commonwealth. What happens there may well affect the future elsewhere in Africa where it has been standard thinking that the African is incapable of self rule.

If anywhere, the experiment with African self rule should succeed in the Gold Coast where Europeans of all nationalities have been building fortresses and trading for gold, ivory and slaves since the 15th Century. Some of those great European castles still rise above the white sands, black rocks and green palms along the coast, incongruous reminders of an irretrievable past.

The Gold Coast is rich, the richest of all British dependencies — and supplies much of the world's cocoa and manganese. Its gold mines in the Ashanti province still yield the world's richest ore, and its bauxite and water power potential are enormous. Like Nigeria, the Gold Coast has an educated urban class better prepared to deal with the modern world than elsewhere in Africa. And it has very able leadership, headed by Dr. Kwame Nkrumah, leader of the revolution, national hero, Prime Minister — and educated at Lincoln College in Pennsylvania.

But perhaps even more important than money, leadership and the beginnings at least of a middle class, the Gold Coast has no European problem. I mean Europeans never came to settle in West Africa, "the white man's grave," as they did in the East, Central and South Africa. So there is no dominant white minority with a large stake in the community to reconcile with a rising, restless, disenfranchised African majority. In that respect the Gold Coast and Nigeria are like the surrounding French territories, the Belgian Congo,[353] the Portuguese colonies, British Uganda, but quite unlike Kenya, the Central African Federation of Rhodesias and Nyasaland [354] and, most of all, South Africa. Indeed the only Europeans that Dr. Nkrumah and company have to worry about

[351] In the years following Stevenson's visit the French government abandoned its plan and country after country became independent.

[352] Since 1960 the republic of Ghana. While visiting the Gold Coast, Stevenson stayed at the Accra home of Robert Jackson and Mrs. Jackson (Barbara Ward).

[353] From 1960 to 1971 the Democratic Republic of Congo, now the Republic of Zaire.

[354] Since 1964 the independent nation of Malawi.

are British experts and civil servants working their hearts out to help. And the African leaders have to worry about persuading them to stay.

There are other formidable obstacles on the road to independence and dominion status. "Palaver," talk, is one. Probably because the African literary tradition is oral rather than written, endless talk, eloquence, chatter and just plain recreation are an African affliction. Corruption is another. Political morality does not come easily to a people who have always associated authority with wealth.

But the big hazard is separation, fragmentation. Nigeria is divided into four or five regions and tribes that have little in common except that they have been part of a British administration unit. How and whether they can subordinate their jealousies and unite or federate effectively remains to be seen. Certainly they cannot afford the luxury of separate states.

It is simpler in the Gold Coast, but there the Asantehene of Ashanti, the hereditary ruler of the warrior tribe in the rich center of the country, is already finding the rule of Dr. Nkrumah and his "young men" very irksome and is insisting stoutly and violently on some sort of "federation" which leaves his region considerable autonomy, and himself, I daresay, considerable authority. I went up into the interior and had a long talk with this interesting and agreeable ruler who must have no physical imperfection or he will be promptly dethroned, or rather destooled. His hereditary throne is the "Golden Stool" and I'm glad I didn't see that sacred article of furniture, for the story is that the penalty for an unauthorized glimpse is to be blinded!

I can't move on from the Gold Coast without telling you about the small boy in Accra to whom my host handed a letter to mail. He promptly popped it on top of his wooly little head, leaned down and carefully picked up a stone to put on top of it, and trotted off on his errand, hands empty. They really use their heads in the Gold Coast! And if you have never seen fetish priests madly pouring libations of gin and shouting incantations when their team was near the goal line in a soccer match, well, you "ain't seen nothin'" in cheerleading. (My British hosts suggested that it was not unlikely that the gin had not gone to waste and the bottles were filled with water.)

And, speaking of the British, I left the Gold Coast marvelling again, as I did in Asia, how those "hated imperialists" have somehow managed to liquidate their empire and withdraw respected and liked, even loved, by the most extreme nationalists who, more than likely, spent some time in a British jail reading [Edmund] Burke on Freedom for the Colonies!

The great Belgian Congo, eighty times as big as Belgium, is the heart of Africa and from its untold riches pours a mounting flood of copper, uranium, diamonds, tin, gold, cobalt, zinc, manganese, vegetable oils, cotton and coffee. And the Congo offers something entirely different from African self government a la the British, or the French policy of integration and common citizenship. For the Congo is frankly a colony and operated with a beneficient paternalism that commands everyone's respect, if not everyone's confidence that it is the best solution to "Africa." In the Congo they do everything to keep the African happy and economically progressive — "give him everything — except a vote." But the 90,000 Europeans among the 14 million Congolese can't vote either.

It takes a brave man to speculate on the Congo's economic future. Aside from the mineral wealth, agricultural development has only started and the hydroelectric potential is among the greatest in the world. But everyone speculates on the Belgian approach to accommodation with the African population and compares it with the British, French and Portuguese. In the Congo, control is firmly in white hands and there they mean it to stay — for the present. How? By, as I say, keeping the Congo for the Congolese and setting no limit on their economic advancement. No European can buy land. Permanent residence is discouraged. Even tourists are not wanted, and Indians, so conspicuous in British Africa, are not admitted. Officials of the government and the industries come to work not to stay.

So the African can have no quarrel with a dominating white settler class in the Congo. Nor can he claim discrimination in employment — a Belgian goes home when an African can take his job, and nowhere, I daresay, are Africans performing so many and such advanced tasks and for such good wages as in booming Leopoldville and Elizabethville. In the latter we found that 20% of the Africans in the houses built by the Belgian copper company now *owned* them. But the most important news of all may be the beginning of a university in Leopoldville.

All this and much more is consistent with the Belgian theory of a lot of economic advancement and a little education first giving the Africans a "stake in the community," before exposing them to dangerous ideas or political power. Sandwiched between freedom in the Gold Coast and suppression in South Africa, the hard-headed Belgians who run the Congo are confident that their way is best, and they can point with pride to the fact that there is practically no racial tension in the Congo. A Belgian said to me "We will be here at least 25 years more. Can you say that about any other colony?" [355]

[355] Five years after Stevenson's visit, the Belgian government suddenly granted independence and withdrew. Immediately after the effective date of independence, June 30, 1960, internal strife broke out, and the United Nations intervened to restore order.

It may be that they are right and certainly the performance is impressive. But usually economic development and education bring with them demands for a share in one's political destiny. There are dangers in delaying some political participation too long. Perhaps that is why even in the Congo they are now establishing municipal councils with African participation.

Ruanda-Urundi, adjoining the Congo on the East, was part of German East Africa and is now a United Nations trusteeship administered by Belgium.[356] We motored into it from British Uganda — and that is the finest scenic motor trip in mid-Africa. In contrast to so much of this empty land, this breathlessly beautiful and mountainous country is grossly over-populated. The Belgians have taught the very poor people about contour plowing and hill terracing, and the countryside in many places looks much like green, over-populated Java.

Ruanda-Urundi is also over-populated with cattle, and a cow's value to the Watutsis seems to depend not on milk or beef production but the length of its horns and tail. The Watutsis are the "giants" you have seen in the movies. They are tall and straight and look very dignified in their white togas. At Kisenyi, between the great green volcanoes and lovely Lake Kivu, we saw the famous Watutsi dances. I can still hear the drums and the thunder of their footbeats in that incredible rhythm. I sat beside the huge chief, resplendent in a saffron toga, and the dancers even in their wildest moments never seemed to divert their eyes from his. But they weren't giants! — except for the "dance master," a seven-footer, with the traditional half-moon headdress, who pranced around in front, evidently urging the dancers to greater exertion. Frequently he flung his spear flat on the ground with a mighty gesture of total anger and indignation. But it was approval!

North of Ruanda-Urundi lies more beautiful highland country — the prosperous British colony of Uganda, flanked on the West by the soaring Ruwenzori, the Mountains of the Moon, and on the East by Lake Victoria, beautiful, placid and full of crocodiles. We drove across the high divide between the Congo and the Nile watersheds, wary of wandering elephants. And we crossed the equator. It was cool. In fact, in a fortnight along the equator in East Africa we were never uncomfortable. I mean hot, because I was hardly "comfortable" one afternoon in a small boat amid a herd of hippos with elephants and buffalo along the shore and the water infested with "crocs." Actually, that preposterous animal, the hippo, with only his eyes and nostrils showing above the surface, is both amusing and harmless unless he surfaces too close to your boat with a mighty whoosh and snort for he's awfully clumsy.

[356] It became the independent nation of Rwanda in 1962.

As in the other colonies, the British are following the policy of pre-paring Uganda for self-government.[357] At Kampala there is a fine little college, Makerere. Uganda is prosperous and many Africans have gotten rich off of cotton and coffee. Indeed, we heard Englishmen complain that not only are they forbidden to own land in Uganda but they have to pay income taxes while the rich African farmers don't. Evidently there are all kinds of discriminations in Africa.

Uganda is tranquil but the authorities are watchful, for next door, the other side of Lake Victoria, is Kenya and Mau Mau land.[358] I have neither time nor competence to tell you much about the magnificent, highly civilized "White highlands" which British settlers have pioneered and where scores of them have recently died violently and suddenly, along with thousands of terrified Africans. Mau Mau springs from deep, deep wells — land hunger, nationalism, bewilderment, resentment, pa-ganism, witchcraft and, some say, just plain boredom. (Like all Africans, the Kikuyu tribe of Kenya used to let a little blood now and then, what with ritual killings and sanguinary ceremonies. But law, order and Chris-tianity have stopped all that and there hasn't been much excitement for quite a while.)

Be that as it may, Mau Mau with its unspeakable horrors is on the wane now, but the British face the monumental task of de-brainwashing, rehabilitating and protecting from reprisal some 40 or 50 thousand "in-fected" Kikuyus still in concentration camps.

In contrast to the countries I've talked about so far, where the white man is only a transient governor and business man, Kenya has a large settled European population — about 40,000 — among five million Af-ricans. Add another 120,000 Indians and you have the root of the trouble. The Europeans monopolize the land, the Indians monopolize the trade, and the emerging African is taking another look at things.

Mau Mau has served a purpose. It has brutally directed the attention not only of Africa but the world to the problems of permanent multi-racial society in this revolutionary era. How to accommodate small domi-nant minorities to huge subordinate majorities is the big question, and beautiful Kenya has been the scene of its most explosive manifestations.

There are as many ideas as to what to do about it as there are about colonial management in the all-black countries. But Michael Blundell,[359] a strong man in the Kenya government who seems to personify the new enlightenment among the white settlers, is confident that they can work out a "multi-racial" government and society which would recognize the

[357] It became independent in 1962.
[358] Kenya became independent in 1963.
[359] Minister without portfolio in charge of defense against the Mau Mau.

dignity and rights of all. He and other Europeans, if by no means all, see the solution as more education, more job opportunities for Africans, and voting rights based on some minimum qualifications.

We were to hear much more about "partnership" and "interracial" society in the Rhodesias. But how the land distribution problem can be settled, how jobs can be created, how education can be financed, how voting qualifications can be fixed to give Africans any real participation without being swamped, are mighty stubborn problems.

But one thing is sure in Kenya — responsible people realize that the old strong-arm methods are not good enough and that development depends on inter-racial cooperation rather than mutual isolation. Cooperation in turn implies the elimination of discrimination, restriction and special privileges, which is just what they are *not* doing in South Africa.

I must tell you about an engaging Englishman [360] who took us into the big game reserve near Nairobi where we saw more animals than I knew existed, and practically joined a family group of lions for tea. This delightful character in a matter-of-fact way assured us that the great attack on the tsetse fly had been Africa's undoing for human beings and their cattle were now "swarming all over the place and the wild game is disappearing."

In the Rhodesias we witnessed at sundown and sunup the storied grandeur of the Victoria Falls on the Zambezi, and we crossed the "gray, green, greasy Limpopo" of Kipling's story. We heard much about the birth pains of a new nation — the Central African Federation of the Rhodesias and Nyasaland.[361] But we heard a lot more about the emerging concept of social and political "partnership" and about job discrimination in the great copper mines of Northern Rhodesia.

Here in a much larger country we have another case like Kenya of a considerable settled white population, some 200,000, among six million Africans, with all the same problems — and more! More, because on the great copper belt of Northern Rhodesia the European miners' union, in order to keep the better jobs, has, until very lately, prevented the upgrading of African workers regardless of competence and also preserved wide disparities in pay scales. The result has been strikes, trouble and many investigations. We visited for several days in the remarkably modern communities that have been created in the wilderness of central Africa around the mines. And we were glad to hear that the company in which there is a large American ownership has pressed insistently for

[360] Colonel Mervyn Cowie, in charge of the royal game preserve.
[361] This federation ended in 1963. In 1964, Northern Rhodesia and Nyasaland became independent states. On November 11, 1965, Southern Rhodesia unilaterally declared its independence from Great Britain.

African advancement. Progress is being made now and more jobs are being made available for Africans.

But land distribution is even a tougher problem in the Federation. With constantly growing population more Africans must find employment in industry. And the government is counting heavily on a project for large hydroelectric development on the Zambezi River.

In Salisbury, the capital of the Federation, one of the ministers of the government said to me: "You must first put your fundamentals right, then later your politics won't develop along nationalistic racial lines. Good race relations result from a human process of development. The major problems are settled by populations mixing in their day to day lives. Legislatures can't blueprint this development."

This is exactly the opposite of the Afrikans policy of apartheid in South Africa. And, although segregation is still sharp in Rhodesia, the direction appears sound and the principle of African participation and racial partnership is accepted. If success *cannot* be certainly predicted in Kenya and the Federation, it seems to me that failure *can* be in South Africa where the official policy of government is total separation.

Here the proportion of permanent European settlers is the greatest in all of Africa; almost a third, and the problem is therefore the greatest. Likewise, to the outsider and casual visitor at least, it appears to be the area that is furthest from a solution of one of the great problems of our century — racial coexistence.[362]

Moreover, South Africa influences the rest of Africa. What happens there increases African suspicions of sincere attempts to deal with the question elsewhere, and at the same time encourages the more uncompromising and reactionary Europeans not to yield to the "soft new ideas."

It is always easy to criticize and often hard to understand another's views — especially if they conflict with your own prejudices! But my impression of much of what I saw and heard of apartheid in practice in South Africa is summarized by a remark about the new Bantu Education Act: "Like many other acts of this Government, it gives much that is better and withholds all that is best." [363]

[362] Lloyd Garrison wrote of a meeting Stevenson had with African intellectuals on the outskirts of Johannesburg: "They gave us the impression of being leaderless, without a program, baffled, discouraged, frustrated and deeply hurt." Notes for the Family, #5, p. 20. The original is in the possession of Mr. Garrison.

[363] Lloyd Garrison described a conversation with three Afrikaners who insisted that black people were inherently inferior and that because of their superior numbers apartheid was essential. "Adlai asked them whether any dire results had occurred in the West Indies, where the natives greatly outnumber the whites but there is no segregation save such as occurs voluntarily and naturally. . . . It was answered merely by the assertion that in the West Indies the Christians had made greater efforts to teach the natives true religion, and had penetrated deeper into their characters." Ibid., p. 22.

But I am not going to attempt to tell you about that great country, South Africa, which we read so much about in our newspapers and magazines. Instead I will conclude this hasty survey of a memorable month with what I said to the reporters' questions when I left the big, bustling city of Johannesburg, where I received so much hospitality and kindness:

"History is moving very fast in Asia and in Africa. South Africa — the land where Asia, Africa and Europe have met — has, I think, a grave responsibility to itself and to the world in this interval of rapid change and turmoil.

"The *present* generation of South Africans did not make the problem that they confront — they inherited it. But it is for *this* generation to find the solution. This problem is of such gravity and complexity that you have to come here to appreciate it. I feel for every South African old enough to share the responsibility.

"If anyone not involved in these conflicts and with such a superficial understanding as mine, is entitled to an opinion, then I would express the hope that the people of this lovely land take care lest fear lead them along the wrong path. Perhaps it is always best in human affairs to do what is right and ethical and just to all of God's creatures, and leave the consequences confidently to God.

"Speaking with the utmost diffidence, I cannot foresee the success of apartheid as applied to industry and economic development with any confidence. And let me add I have great misgivings about efforts to arrest the progress of a whole race when the rest of the world is moving so rapidly in the other direction. It is seldom wise to close safety valves, and a nation's greatest resources are, of course, the willing hands and the loyal hearts of its people."

P.S. I had one disappointment on this journey to Africa. I wanted to see and talk again with Dr. Albert Schweitzer, whom many call "the greatest living man." He had invited me to visit him — "I hope you will find the road to Lambarene," he wrote. But my close schedule forbade me to go up into the jungle in French Equatorial Africa where this remarkable man works among the natives. I wanted also to confirm the epitaph he has written in case he is eaten by cannibals: "He was good to the last."

If I write any more you boys will be sorry I wrote at all!

Stevenson's mail throughout the years brought him letters from unknown women admirers who fancied themselves to be in love with him. These were watched carefully by his staff and Stevenson rarely saw them. They were kept with other "crackpot" mail in a large file entitled "Eccentric Letters."

On May 18, when Stevenson returned to Chicago he faced a heavy accumulation of mail, one handwritten letter being from one of his unknown lady admirers who said she was leaving the country because he did not really need her. It was put on his desk with a note from Carol Evans saying: "You complain that you don't get enough of this kind of mail!" Stevenson scribbled: "Thanks, I liked it! But why do I never see the dames?" [364]

Also among the letters was an editorial from the May 8 Little Rock Arkansas Gazette, *entitled "Mr. Stevenson Must Put It on the Line." The editorial stated: "Mr. Stevenson . . . has slipped back into his Hamlet role and there are many who believe his indecision is based on his private belief that Ike will be the nominee and that Ike can't be beat." Editor Harry Ashmore, who sent the editorial, wrote: "Please give us the word."*

To Harry Ashmore

May 18, 1955

Dear Harry:

Your editorial almost makes me wish I were back where the elephants know what they're doing and the donkeys have stripes around them.

Does it strike you that "coyness" is what the other fellow does while you yourself are engaged in the honorable pastime of "playing them close to the chest"? Or that some who use this particular form of criticism — to which I admit a special sensitivity — would be among the first to comment condescendingly right now on any alternative action as premature?

But why don't you tell me, just for fun, when and where and what kind of "clear-cut statement of interest" you would think appropriate.

As for your question about whether I count the President "unbeatable" — I do not, either as a candidate or as a President.

I'd love to have a personal version of what you cover in the editorial.

Cordially yours,

P.S. There's a difference between primary and election campaigns. I would find it awfully hard to confidently assure my fellow Democrats that I am the best among them for President!

---

[364] The original is in the possession of Miss Evans.

Coming Out Swinging

Stevenson confers with Senator Estes Kefauver during the campaign

Stevenson writes a speech on the porch of
Wilson Wyatt's home in Kentucky, 1954

*With Adlai III, Nancy Anderson, Borden, and John Fell at the
Louisville, Kentucky, airport, September 13, 1954. The engagement
of Miss Anderson and Adlai III was announced that weekend*

At the home of Mr. and Mrs. Ernest L. Ives,
Southern Pines, North Carolina, 1955

With Mr. and Mrs. Ernest L. Ives and Borden
in Southern Pines, 1955

On vacation in Jamaica, September, 1955

*With Adlai E. Stevenson III and his bride Nancy Anderson in
Louisville, Kentucky, on their wedding day June 25, 1955*

To Dr. Robert McMillan [365]

May 21, 1955

My dear Doctor:

My sister, Mrs. Ives, once told me that you were collecting stamps. I have just returned from a trip to Africa. While in Swaziland — a strange and distant little British protectorate — I acquired the enclosed — for you.

Sincerely yours,

On May 24, Stevenson addressed the General Federation of Women's Clubs at Philadelphia on the topic "Faith, Knowledge and Peace." [366] *On June 2, he spoke on "Medicine and Public Policy" at the dedicatory exercises at the New York University–Bellevue Medical Center.* [367] *While in the East he visited with friends in Philadelphia, Princeton and New York. On June 6, he delivered the following address at the Smith College commencement, where his future daughter-in-law was graduating.*

WOMEN, HUSBANDS, AND HISTORY [368]

Countless commencement speakers are rising these days on countless platforms all over the world to tell thousands of helpless young captives how important they are — as citizens in a free society, as educated, rational, privileged participants in a great historic crisis. But for my part I want merely to tell you young ladies that I think there is much you can do about that crisis in the humble role of housewife — which, statistically, is what most of you are going to be whether you like the idea or not just now — and you'll like it!

To explain what I mean I must ask you to step a long way back and recall with me that over vast periods of history and over most of the globe the view has prevailed that man is no more than a unit in the social calculus. Tribal life — the way of life pursued by man for by far the longest period in his history, of which there are many remnants today in Africa — knows no individuals, only groups with disciplines and group sanctions. But then at a certain point in time and place there took place the most momentous revolution yet achieved by mankind — a revolution

[365] A resident of Southern Pines, North Carolina, where Stevenson's sister and her husband had their winter home. A copy is in A.E.S., I.S.H.L.

[366] The text is in *What I Think*, pp. 157–163.

[367] The text is in *What I Think*, pp. 124–132.

[368] The text is from *What I Think*, pp. 182–189.

compared with which such achievements as the discovery of fire or the invention of the wheel seem modest. In the origins of our Western civilization, among two small peoples of the eastern Mediterranean, the Greeks and the Jews, the great Copernican revolution of politics began: the discovery that the state exists for man, not man for the state, and that the individual human personality, spirit, soul — call it what you will — contains within itself the meaning and measure of existence and carries as a result the full range of responsibility and choice.

Once the Greek vision of reason and the Jewish concept of moral choice had sent man forth onto the stage of history in this new guise of self-determination and responsibility, clearly only one form of society would provide a framework for the new energies and capacities that could now be released. That form of society is the free society upon which the peoples of the West have been engaged for the last two thousand years, with disasters and setbacks, with triumphs and tragedies, with long sweeps of history's pendulum between the extreme of freedom and tyranny, of individualism and collectivism, of rationalism and spiritualism.

The peoples of the West are still struggling with the problems of a free society and, just now, are in dire trouble. For to create a free society is at all times a precarious and audacious experiment. Its bedrock is the concept of man as an end in himself, as the ultimate reason for the whole apparatus of government, and the institutions of free society fulfill their task only in so far as this primary position of the free citizen — the *homo liber et legalis* — is not lost to sight. But violent pressures are constantly battering away at this concept, reducing man once again to subordinate status, limiting his range of choice, abrogating his responsibility, and returning him to his primitive status of anonymity in the social group. And it is to these pressures in their contemporary forms that I want to call your attention because I think you can be more helpful in identifying, isolating, and combating these pressures, this virus, than you girls perhaps today realize.

As you have learned here at Smith, science, among other things, arose out of the disintegration of feudal society and the rebirth of individualism in the Reformation and the Renaissance. As the individual mind was released from medieval bondage, as reason again became the test of faiths, the processes of free inquiry opened vast new fields of knowledge and human endeavor. There followed an almost explosive expansion of mental horizons. Science, born of freedom, and technology, born of science, grew by leaps and bounds into a giant of power and complexity. Certainly the material well-being of Western man was advanced with a speed and to an extent never before seen on earth. And there were great spiritual advances.

But, as always, history's pendulum swung too far, this time toward the extreme of social fragmentation, of individualism, of abstract intellectualism. And it seems to me that the very process which, in the name of individual liberty, disintegrated the old order — this very process has developed into a powerful drive toward the precise opposite of individualism, namely totalitarian collectivism.

Let me put it this way! Individualism promoted technological advances, technology promoted increased specialization, and promoted an ever-closer economic interdependence between the specialties. The more intense the specialization, the more complete the interdependence of the specialties — and this necessity of interdependence constitutes a powerful economic drive toward that extreme of a machine state in which individual freedom is wholly submerged.

As the old order disintegrated into this confederation of narrow specialties, each pulling in the direction of *its particular* interest, the individual person tended to become absorbed — literally — by *his particular* function in society. Having sacrificed wholeness of mind and breadth of outlook to the demands of their specialities, individuals no longer responded to social stimuli as total human beings: rather they reacted in partial ways as members of an economic class, or industry, or profession whose concern was with some limited self-interest.

Thus this typical Western man — or typical Western husband! — operates well in the realm of means, as the Romans did before him. But outside his specialty, in the realm of ends, he is apt to operate poorly or not at all. And this neglect of the cultivation of more mature values can only mean that his life, and the life of the society he determines, will lack valid purpose, however busy and even profitable it may be.

And here's where you come in: to restore valid, meaningful purpose to life in your home; to beware of instinctive group reaction to the forces which play upon you and yours; to watch for and arrest the constant gravitational pulls to which we are all exposed, your workaday husband especially, in our specialized, fragmented society that tends to widen the breach between reason and emotion, between means and ends.

And let me also remind you that you will live, most of you, in an environment in which "facts," the data of the senses, are glorified, and value judgments are assigned inferior status as mere "matters of opinion." It is an environment in which art is often regarded as an adornment of civilization rather than a vital element of it, while philosophy is not only neglected but deemed faintly disreputable, because "it never gets you anywhere." Even religion, you will find, commands a lot of earnest allegiance that is more verbal than real, more formal than felt.

You may be hitched to one of these creatures we call "Western man," and I think part of your job is to keep him Western, to keep him truly purposeful, to keep him whole. In short — while I have had very little experience as a wife or mother — I think one of the biggest jobs for many of you will be to frustrate the crushing and corrupting effects of specialization, to integrate means and ends, to develop that balanced tension of mind and spirit which can be properly called "integrity."

This assignment for you, as wives and mothers, has great advantages. In the first place, it is home work — you can do it in the living room with a baby in your lap, or in the kitchen with a can opener in your hands. If you're really clever, maybe you can even practice your saving arts on that unsuspecting man while he's watching television. And, secondly, it is important work worthy of you, whoever you are, or your education, whatever it is — even Smith College — because we will defeat totalitarian, authoritarian ideas only by better ideas; we will frustrate the evils of vocational specialization only by the virtues of intellectual generalities. Since Western rationalism and Eastern spiritualism met in Athens and that mighty creative fire broke out, collectivism in various forms has collided with individualism time and again. This twentieth-century collision, this "crisis" we are forever talking about, will be won at last not on the battlefield but in the head and heart.

If the Colosseum at Rome is, as some say, the symbol of Roman failure to integrate mind and spirit, or means and ends, the hydrogen bomb, we might say, is the symbol of our own very similar self-betrayal. And one may hope that Hiroshima, like Rome's bloody arena, may be remembered at some distant day as a scene symbolizing a new beginning for mankind.

So you see, I have some rather large notions about you young ladies and what you have to do to rescue us wretched slaves of specialization and group thinking from further shrinkage and contraction of mind and spirit. But you will have to be alert or you may get caught yourself — even in the kitchen or the nursery — by the steady pressures with which you will be surrounded.

And now that I have dared to suggest what you should do about your husbands and friends, I am, recklessly, going to even make some suggestions about your children as well.

In the last fifty years, so much of our thinking has been in terms of institutional reform — reform of the economic system, social security, the use and misuse of government, international co-operation, etc. All this thinking has been necessary and salutary, but somewhere along the line the men and women whose personalities and potentialities will largely determine the spirit of such institutions have been lost to sight. Worse than that, we have even evolved theories that the paramount aim of education and character formation is to produce citizens who are "well adjusted" to their institutional environment, citizens who can fit painlessly into the social pattern.

While I am not in favor of maladjustment, I view this cultivation of neutrality, this breeding of mental neuters, this hostility to eccentricity and controversy, with grave misgiving. One looks back with dismay at the possibility of a Shakespeare perfectly adjusted to bourgeois life in Stratford, a Wesley contentedly administering a county parish, George Washington going to London to receive a barony from George III, or Abraham Lincoln prospering in Springfield with nary a concern for the preservation of the crumbling Union.

But in this decisive century it seems to me that we need not just "well-adjusted," "well-balanced" personalities, not just better groupers and conformers (to casually coin a couple of fine words) but more idiosyncratic, unpredictable characters (that rugged frontier word "ornery" occurs to me); people who take open eyes and open minds out with them into the society which they will share and help to transform.

But before any of you gallant girls swear any mighty oaths about fighting the shriveling corruptions and conformations of mind and spirit, before you adopt any rebellious resolutions for the future, make no mistake about it — it is much easier to get yourself and yours adjusted and to accept the conditioning which so many social pressures will bring to bear upon you. After all tribal conformity and archaic dictatorship could not have lasted so long if they did not accord comfortably with basic human needs and desires. The modern dictators are reviving a very ancient and encrusted way of life. Hitler discovered this. The Fascists knew it. The Communists are busy brainwashing all over Asia. And what they are washing out is precisely independence of judgment and the moral courage with which to back such judgments. And there are, alas!, some leaders in our country who certainly have a brainwashing glint in their eye when they meet with an unfamiliar idea.

Now, as I have said, women, especially educated women such as you, have a unique opportunity to influence us, man and boy, and to play a direct part in the unfolding drama of our free society. But I am told that nowadays the young wife or mother is short of time for the subtle arts, that things are not what they used to be; that once immersed in the very pressing and particular problems of domesticity many women feel frustrated and far apart from the great issues and stirring debates for which their education has given them understanding and relish. Once they read Baudelaire. Now it is the *Consumer's Guide*. Once they wrote poetry. Now it's the laundry list. Once they discussed art and philosophy until late in the night. Now they are so tired they fall asleep as soon as the dishes are finished. There is, often, a sense of contraction, of closing horizons and lost opportunities. They had hoped to play their part in the crisis of the age. But what they do is wash the diapers.

Now, I hope I have not painted a too depressing a view of your future, for the fact is that Western marriage and motherhood are yet another instance of the emergence of individual freedom in our Western society. Their basis is the recognition in women as well as men of the primacy of personality and individuality. I have just returned from Africa where the illiteracy of the mothers is an obstacle to child education and advancement and where polygamy and female labor is still the dominant system. The common sight on the road is an African striding along swinging his stick or his spear, while a few feet behind comes the wife with a load of firewood on her head, a baby on her back and dragging a couple more children by the hand.

The point is that whether we talk of Africa, Islam, or Asia, women "never had it so good" as you do. And in spite of the difficulties of domesticity you have a way to participate actively in the crisis in addition to keeping yourself and those about you straight on the difference between means and ends, mind and spirit, reason and emotion — not to mention keeping your man straight on the differences between Botticelli and Chianti.

In brief if one of the chief needs in these restless times is for a new quality of mind and heart, who is nearer to the care of this need, the cultivation of this quality, than parents, especially mothers, who educate and form the new generation?

So, add to all of your concerns for Western man, your very special responsibility for Western children. In a family based upon mutual respect, tolerance, and understanding affection, the new generation of children — the citizens of tomorrow — stand their best chance of growing up to recognize the fundamental principle of free society — the uniqueness and value and wholeness of each individual human being. For this recognition requires discipline and training. The first instinct of all our untutored egos is to smash and grab, to treat the boy next door as a means not an end when you pinch his air rifle, or deny the uniqueness of your small sister's personality when you punch her in the stomach and snatch her lollipop.

Perhaps this is merely to say that the basis of any tolerable society — from the small society of the family up to the great society of the State — depends upon its members learning to love. By that I do not mean sentimentality or possessive emotion. I mean the steady recognition of others' uniqueness and a sustained intention to seek their good. In this, freedom and charity go hand in hand and they both have to be learned. Where better than in the home? And by whom better than the parents, especially the mother?

In short, far from the vocation of marriage and motherhood leading you away from the great issues of our day, it brings you back to their very center and places upon you an infinitely deeper and more intimate responsibility than that borne by the majority of those who hit the headlines and make the news and live in such a turmoil of great issues that they end by being totally unable to distinguish which issues are really great.

Yet you may say that these functions of the home could have been as well fulfilled without your years of study, performed perhaps better by instinct and untroubled by those hints of broader horizons and more immortal longings which it is the purpose of a college education to instill.

Well, there are two things to say to that. The first, of course, is that in modern America the home is not the boundary of a woman's life. There are outside activities aplenty. But even more important is the fact, surely, that what you have learned here can fit you as nothing else can for the primary task of making homes and whole human beings in whom the rational values of freedom, tolerance, charity, and free inquiry can take root. You have learned discrimination. You have the tolerance which comes from the realization of man's infinite variety. Because you have learned from history the pathos and mutability of human affairs, you have a sense of pity. From literature you have learned the abiding values of the human heart and the discipline and sacrifice from which those values will flower in your own hearts and in the life of your families.

There can be no waste of any education that gives you these things. But you can waste them, or you can use them. I hope you'll use them. I hope you'll not be content to wring your hands, feed your family, and just echo all the group, the tribal ritual refrain. I hope you'll keep everlastingly at the job of seeing life steady and seeing it whole. And you can help others — husbands, children, friends — to do so too. You may, indeed you must, help to integrate a world that has been falling into bloody pieces. History's pendulum has swung dangerously far away from the individual, and you may, indeed you must, help to restore it to the vital center of its arc.

Long ago at the origins of our way of life it was written of a valiant woman in the Book of Proverbs:

> Strength and beauty are her clothing; and she shall laugh in the latter day. She hath opened her mouth to wisdom and the law of clemency is on her tongue; she hath looked well to the paths of her

house and hath not eaten her bread idle. Her children rose up and called her blessed; her husband and he praised her.

I could wish you no better vocation than that. I could wish a free society no better hope for the future. And I could wish you no greater riches and rewards.

To Mr. and Mrs. Ronald Tree [369]

June 7, 1955

My beloved Trees!

This is both a bread and butter and a farewell note. It was a refuge, as it always is in your hospitable vicinity. Thanks; and my prayers for a happy journey. I shall be eager for a full report exchange. I shall be glad to tell you about the state of sheep culture on St. Mary's Road with incidental references to the care and feeding of Democrats.

Affectionately,

To Mrs. Harold Hochschild [370]

June 7, 1955

My dear Mary:

In spite of cumulative fatigue I enjoyed our evening more than I can tell you. It was sweet of you to go to all that trouble and I am touched and grateful. Moreover, I am determined to invade your Princeton precincts and see more of an old and dear friend and more of a new and remarkable one — her husband.

With affection and warmest thanks, I am

Cordially yours,

P.S. As for your Aunt, Mrs. Cross, I lost my heart. Oh, to be 75!

Sargent Shriver sent Stevenson a picture of his brother-in-law Senator John F. Kennedy receiving an honorary degree. The accompanying news story quoted the senator as stating that Stevenson was the strongest Democratic candidate for 1956.

---

[369] A copy is in A.E.S., I.S.H.L.
[370] The former Mary Marquand, of Princeton, New Jersey, whom Stevenson had known when he was an undergraduate.

To R. Sargent Shriver, Jr.[371]

June 9, 1955

Dear Sarge:

Thanks for the clippings from the Worcester paper. I am delighted to hear that Jack is getting about again and appears to be so well and sound — although I might have some reservations as to his judgment about Presidential candidates!

Cordially yours,

p.s. I hope some time soon we may have a quiet talk together — preferably with Eunice! [372]

p.p.s. I even read the newspaper account of Jack's speech and bow deferentially to a philosopher.

Stevenson sent the Wyatts the following telegram on the occasion of their twenty-fifth wedding anniversary.

To Mr. and Mrs. Wilson Wyatt

June 14, 1955

I HEAR IT'S THE 25TH. IT MUST HAVE BEEN AN ILLEGAL MARRIAGE. AFFECTIONATE CONGRATULATIONS.

THE GOV

Mrs. Wright Morrow, of Houston, Texas, wrote Stevenson on June 6 asking him to explain why, if in 1952 he expressed doubts as to his qualifications for the presidency, he now was a candidate for the 1956 nomination.

To Mrs. Wright Morrow [373]

June 14, 1955

Dear Mrs. Morrow:

I am sure you are familiar with Lincoln's expressed misgivings about his qualifications for the Presidency and others in our history.

As to your other questions, what I said in the convention hall in 1952

[371] A copy is in A.E.S., I.S.H.L.
[372] Mrs. Shriver.
[373] A copy is in A.E.S., I.S.H.L.

has, of course, been frequently published and I am sure you will find a copy readily at hand to check your recollection.

As to my position in 1952, I thought I had made it clear that I was a candidate for re-election as Governor of Illinois, that I had been nominated without opposition at the primary in April and I felt, and still do, that it is entirely improper for anyone to run for two offices at the same time.

As to the balance of your letter, I have not yet announced what my position will be with respect to the nomination by the Democratic party in 1956.

Cordially yours,

Mrs. Eugene Meyer, the journalist wife of newspaper executive Eugene Meyer, wired Stevenson that his speech on "Medicine and Public Policy," June 2, at New York University–Bellevue Medical Center was "admirable." She invited him to visit at her home at Mt. Kisco, New York.

To Mrs. Eugene Meyer [374]

June 14, 1955

Dear Mrs. Meyer:

Careful, please; I'm falling in love!

Would Wednesday, June 29, be convenient for a visit to your farm? I should like very much to talk with Mr. Meyer, but I hope you won't be wholly excluded! I shall be in New York at that time and could let you know by telephone at what hour in the afternoon I would be free. I should like to take advantage of your offer of a ride out, which would give me more flexibility with my appointments.

And now, your speeches, even a book! I wish you would prescribe the vitamins, diet, exercises or the alchemy of your extraordinary energy and productivity.

Cordially yours,

To Lady Mary Spears [375]

June 15, 1955

Dear Mary:

I have written Louis at long last at the end of two months of almost incessant travel and I am profoundly distressed that I neglected

[374] The original is in the Agnes Meyer files, Princeton University Library.
[375] The original is in the possession of General Sir Louis Spears.

his gracious and flattering invitation so long. I just don't dare come, much as I should like to — if not to make a speech!

It looks as though that old devil "destiny" was creeping up on me again and that I shall be doing the Democratic honors, although I still live in some light-hearted — or headed — hope that it may all blow away.

The situation with Ellen [Stevenson] as I have told you, is, I fear, an illness well known as persecutory paranoia and it is not very likely that much can be done or that it will improve. The boys understand it all better and better, and I think the extreme difficulties this spring have advanced their enlightenment and understanding. This, however, is not to say that you could not be extremely useful, were it necessary to impose upon you, and I shall certainly bear that gracious and gallant offer in mind, although I rather doubt if you fully appreciate what you are bargaining for.

In any event, I shall try not to let her and her difficulties control decisions. They have, as you know, influenced me continuously in the past, largely in my anxiety not to aggravate things and thereby perhaps make it harder for the boys. We face a critical test at Adlai's forthcoming wedding in Louisville on the 25th, but everyone is alerted and it is to be a small and informal affair with a minimum of pressure and, I hope, opportunity for a blow-up.

I talked with Betty [376] in New York on the phone not long ago and she sounded better and more self-confident and cheerful than I have heard her in a long while. I think she is mending rapidly. My youngest son, John Fell, is leaving today for a trip through Asia with a Moral Re-Armament group. Horrors! It's an expense his grandmother is underwriting and an opportunity I could hardly deny him. I have reasonable confidence that such a calm and self-reliant lad will survive the religious emotion. If he gets to London I am sure he will be in touch with you.

Affectionately,

ADLAI

Professor Galbraith wrote Stevenson that he was planning to spend a year in Switzerland writing a book on economics.

---

[376] Mrs. Ralph Hines, Lady Spears's niece.

To John Kenneth Galbraith [377]

June 15, 1955

Dear Ken:

Assuming that you have no trouble identifying "the interest of the Republic" with the interest of the Democratic party or the interest of Stevenson and will respond to that interest on call, then you have my grudging consent for your year abroad, and even for the book. God knows, it's about time somebody wrote something on economics that I can understand. I am only resentful that you haven't done it before!

I hope while you are in Alpine valleys you will not forget the wheat fields. I still bite my nails with anxiety about an agriculture program that doesn't just repeat the old line about 90% [of parity].[378]

Have a good time, and if you run into anything you don't understand how about sending for *me!* I am sure intellectual misery must love company and I sometimes suspect that is why there are so many folks all around me these days.

Yours — with everlasting gratitude and affection,

AES

P.S. Have just had a stimulating visit with a Mr. Roswell Garst,[379] your great admirer, & heard something of his ideas. What do you think of him? Shall I encourage him? And now I'll bother you no more — today!

AES

Professor Henry Steele Commager, of Columbia University, wrote Stevenson on June 4 that four great issues clamored for discussion: the conservation of natural resources; the conservation of human resources; a vastly enlarged federal aid to education at all levels; and a real housing program. He added that a long campaign of public education was necessary to bring about massive government intervention in all these fields.

---

[377] The original is in the possession of the National Archives and Records Service, Washington, D.C. The postscript is handwritten.

[378] The purpose of parity is to maintain, by a system of price supports and subsidies, the buying power of farm products based on the levels of 1910–1914, when prices received and paid by farmers were theoretically in good balance. Until 1952, neither party had opposed high parity prices and subsidies after they were introduced. But in 1954, the Eisenhower Administration backed a new law reducing supports to 75 to 90 per cent of parity, hoping thereby to discourage production and diminish agricultural surpluses.

[379] An Iowa farmer noted for his innovations. Stevenson and Nikita Khrushchev visited the Garst farm in 1959.

To Henry Steele Commager

June 15, 1955

My dear friend:

I was distressed to miss you and I hope you got the message. Your letter did not come to my attention until the very day of your arrival and I was obliged to leave for Oberlin [College] and another commencement — the last for 1955, thank heavens.

I agree as to the issues and I am pleased that we have made something of record by opposition at least and something positive on housing. Some time I would like to wrap all of this up in a speech about human beings, which are human resources as you say, and their conservation and development in philosophical terms rather than precise programs. The function of government is to advance the welfare of the governed, of which peace in the world is only one aspect. It would seem to me that it could be restated from time to time in the ever changing contexts.

But I suppose I am saying precisely what you have said — a speech in a long campaign of public education. The problem, of course, is money and the everlasting conflict with the budget, taxes and rigid attitudes. What you call "bold and imaginative programs" are, I agree, what we need but when they translate into terms of large additional federal expense I am afraid the opposition is indiscriminate and not without reason.

I was interested in your statement that our delinquency problem is more urgent than in any other western nation. I wish I knew more about that.

Perhaps some time in a spare moment — if any! — you might want to draft something along this line touching both the foreground and the distant background of the whole panorama. But keep it within bounds of reason — I mean reason in 1955!

Your letters are always good and stimulating and I wish there were to be conversations too.

Cordially yours,

To Ralph McGill [380]

June 14, 1955

Dear Ralph:

I have recently read some pieces by you which both flatter and pro-

380 The original is in the possession of Mrs. Ralph McGill. The second postscript is handwritten.

voke my anxiety to see you. Are you by any chance going to be in this vicinity during the summer? I am told that even Georgians occasionally venture as far as Canada's lakes. There is much I should like to talk about, of which politics is not more than ninety-five per cent!

Cordially yours,

P.S. As for Attorney Stevenson coming South this summer, he is going to have to pay some attention to his law business and his sanity, which would probably suggest the extreme desirability of a little sedation in Chicago and the green pastures of Lake County, Illinois!

P.P.S. How to offset the church and peace propaganda is something I should like to hear more of!

After seeing Stevenson at the Smith College commencement, Mrs. John Currie wrote that they were moving to Connecticut because many people in the town where they lived in the Berkshires objected to their politics and their children were being harassed. Mrs. Currie added that she and her husband wanted to write articles or a book to make Stevenson's views better known.

To Mr. and Mrs. John Currie

June 15, 1955

My dear friends:

Another letter! And as good as ever. I enjoyed my little glimpse of you and I am mortified that I didn't identify you more readily as my conscience in the Berkshires!

Having been raised in McLean County, Illinois I am not unfamiliar with the brutality to which those charming children must be exposed. In my case it did no lasting harm aside from a broken nose, a deformity which was added to by subsequent fractures, and not always for political offenses either! But I can hardly blame you for moving. There is such a thing as fruitless heroism.

And now as to what you could do for me. Of course, that presents the question as to whether I want anything done, and of course I really don't, yet I may very well need it desperately. All this is so confused that it must be clear to you! Various books are cooking, I hear, although I am not clear about it, except a frightening thing my sister has been surreptitiously writing — I hope for an ample price! [381] As to articles, of course they all help, especially to put across the very point that you

[381] Elizabeth Stevenson Ives and Hildegarde Dolson, *My Brother Adlai* (New York: William Morrow, 1956).

mentioned, that I am not a dangerous radical. This sort of balance has been hard to establish, especially when the press has developed such blanket, meaningless and sinister sounding terms as "Trumanism" to characterize Democratic party positions. But all this you know too well.

As to materials, they are plentiful, but I hardly know what to send you or what you want. In short, this letter isn't very helpful; and maybe someone like Arthur Schlesinger, 95 Widener, Harvard University, Cambridge, Massachusetts, who is a historian and was with me in 1952 could make a suggestion as to what you could do. Certainly such talents and such precious friendship should not be permitted to escape unscathed.

With all good wishes, I am

Sincerely yours,

Dr. Albert Schweitzer wrote expressing disappointment that Stevenson had not been able to visit Lambaréné while he was in French Equatorial Africa. Schweitzer added that he liked Stevenson's Unitarian mentality and Unitarians since "religious thought free of dogmatism" was of great importance for the "creation of a spiritual civilization."

To Dr. Albert Schweitzer

June 15, 1955

My dear Doctor Schweitzer:

I was profoundly touched by your gracious letter which Clara Urquhart has sent along. I am sure now that I should have plunged into Lambarene and your busy life there if only for a day. It seemed to me at the time an imposition on you and so brief and hurried that it would appear more perfunctory than sincere.

Perhaps the future has another journey to Africa for me. I hope it does, as I eagerly look forward to paying my homage to you, Sir, and to seeing in that strange setting one whom I am honored to call friend — one who even respects Unitarians!

With warmest good wishes and my enduring gratitude for your thoughtful and revealing letter which I shall always cherish, I am

Respectfully yours,

To Walter W. Heller [382]

June 21, 1955

Dear Dr. Heller:

So many thanks for sending me your appraisal of the administration's

[382] Professor of economics at the University of Minnesota.

tax policy. I shall most certainly read the pages to which you refer — and maybe some more.

I too missed you at the [Finletter Group] meeting in New York some time ago, which was most informative to me. I earnestly hope that your illness is yielding and that I shall see something of you in the near future. Perhaps you would be good enough to let me know when you are in Chicago. I am profoundly grateful for the help you have given our little research work.

Cordially,

To Robert Jackson

June 21, 1955

Dear Robert:

While gasping for air on the Gold Coast one day I saw a mirage — sparkling blue water in a Northland forest. I communicated my lovely vision to Barbara,[383] who looked at me a little apprehensively, I thought, and soothed my fever with "a squash."

But I have recovered, and the fact is that I am now prepared to translate my mirage into reality — if you should stop off on your way West for a visit with me in the summer lodge of some friends[384] in southern Ontario near Sault Ste. Marie.

Alternatively, if you flew from Montreal to Chicago, a brief visit to the Illinois corn country in July would give me great pleasure — and would probably give you a reminder of the Gold Coast climate!

All of which is by way of saying I would welcome a visit in mid-America on your journey across the continent, and I can offer either the North woods or my little farm. I am eager to talk with Barbara about some of the issues, ideas and speeches that are tumbling around in my weary head — which gets more addled and battered daily. I think I shall probably ask her to take charge of my Department of Political Philosophy (at least its higher altitudes!), and I suspect it is not unlikely there is also work for her to do in the Political "Conscience" Department too.

It would be nice if both projects could be combined and that I could expose some of my "team" (that awful word!) here to her for a couple of evenings of talk and also have a little holiday with you in Ontario. Possibly she could fly ahead to Chicago for some skull practice and then we could all meet at the Sault and drive out to the "Dutch" Smith's camp

---

383 Mrs. Jackson.

384 Mr. and Mrs. Hermon Dunlap Smith. See Mr. Smith's "Politics and R & R," in *As We Knew Adlai: The Stevenson Story by Twenty-two Friends,* edited with preface by Edward P. Doyle, foreword by Adlai E. Stevenson III (New York: Harper & Row, 1966), pp. 28–41.

in Desbarats, and you could even go on to Vancouver from Sault Ste. Marie without returning to Chicago. Smith's credentials, by the way, are enclosed, clipped from this morning's *New York Times*. Such service! I am not sure they will be back from Europe or could join us even if they are, but it would make no difference as the summer place is available and tenanted only by their young people at that time.

Of course, as I dictate, I begin to realize that Canadian woods are probably old stuff to you old "Alcans" [385] and that your Montreal business may have a lot of that in it. In any event, do try to visit me one place or the other if you can. And lest I be charged with misrepresentation of material facts, I warn Barbara herewith that I shall shamelessly impose on her good will and gracious proffers of counsel and help. Some of which, I remind her, were uttered without benefit of brandy. Give her, if you will please, the attached note, and do try to work out something if possible. I long to hear of progress with your project and even to talk about some other aluminum affairs.[386]

Cordially yours,

To Mrs. Robert Jackson

June 21, 1955

My dear Barbara:

Yesterday morning I had a letter from Archie MacLeish, excerpt as follows:

> Nate is determined to have Barbara here for a spell. Entirely lost his heart to her. Mac Bundy [387] is working on the details — if you can call anything which involves money at Harvard a detail. But there are great hopes of pulling it off for several weeks or a month or so next spring. And how does she look against the wet air of Accra?

You will identify Nate as Nathan Pusey, the juvenile President of Harvard. Also you may be sure I have reported that your appearance in the wet air of Accra is starched and brilliant.

Don't you think you had better appoint me your agent to negotiate with competing universities?

Yesterday I sat next to your great admirer, Cecil King,[388] at luncheon

---

[385] Alcan was the name of a large Canadian aluminum company. The Jacksons were members of the company at this time, but they later withdrew.

[386] Mr. Jackson was chairman of the Preparatory Commission for the Volta River Project in the Gold Coast.

[387] Dean of the Faculty of Arts and Sciences of Harvard University.

[388] A Chicago artist.

and we talked of you — which is becoming my almost daily and not distasteful routine.

Enclosed find the last of my academic efforts — Oberlin College, prepared in confusion, haste and disorder, all of which are transparent. Attached is the heartening reaction of that distinguished pundit David Lawrence.

I hope we can contrive a visit while you are here, as per my letter to Robert. I am so eager to get you for a little leisurely talk with me and some of my advisers, which would be, of course, more convenient in Chicago, and it would also be fun if we could all have a few days in the Canadian woods if that does not bore you. At all events, I have suggested alternatives and I hope something can be worked out. You can always reach me by phone from Montreal where, if my recollection serves me well, you will arrive around the first of August. I believe I could make reservations for transportation to Vancouver for you either from Chicago or the Sault.

I am glad you have had a chance to see the 20th Century Fund report.[389] I have not read it, but there are a dozen others hereabouts that are also neglected. How I wish I could put you in charge of a research and drafting staff!

It looks more and more as though I would have to run, willy nilly (which is one of our language's most foolish expressions). Some careful planning of what I say might influence in advance the platform which could be very helpful. We shall have to meet the usual "socialism," extravagance, waste and traditional anti Democratic nonsense, as well as peace and prosperity, but I am sure there are strong currents of subtle anxiety and that I must find some new ways of expressing bold and sound views. If I could get you here for a few days for conferring it would be a blessing, but I am loathe to press the point if it is inconvenient for Robert or you to come ahead of him from Montreal.

John Fell has gone to Asia, Borden leaves presently for Hawaii,[390] and Adlai with bride [391] to the forests of Canada — and I to the forests of New York.

Affectionately,

---

[389] Lady Jackson cannot identify the report specifically but does remember it concerned a study on American resources. The report was probably Murray R. Benedict, *Can We Solve the Farm Problem? An Analysis of Federal Aid to Agriculture* (New York: The Twentieth Century Fund, 1955).

[390] Borden Stevenson was stationed in Hawaii with the Army.

[391] Adlai Stevenson III was to be married on June 25.

To Hermon D. Smith

June 21, 1955

Dear Dutch:

I am informed — not by Hermon D. Smith or Mrs. Hermon D. Smith, or even by Miss Adele Smith, but by the *New York Times* — words and pictures — that you have been elected President.[392] I have always wanted to know a President, and I am delighted but a little jealous that you got there first.

Congratulations and affectionate regards to you and your lady folks.

Yours,

P.S. I am now conspiring with my remarkable friends, the Robert Jacksons, of the Gold Coast, to visit your establishment in August for a couple of days on their way across Canada. You and Ellen would enjoy them if it works out. Please note, however, that I shamelessly proceed with the use of your property.

To Mr. and Mrs. Joseph Bohrer [393]

July 4, 1955

Thank you, my dear old friends, for coming to L'ville [Louisville] for Adlai's wedding. It was an exertion I know and I am very grateful. I only hope *you* know what a comfort it was to me in those difficult circumstances —

Affectionately —
ADLAI

To Mrs. Lyndon B. Johnson

July 5, 1955

My dear Mrs. Johnson:

I need not tell you how distressed and anxious I am about Lyndon and his condition.[394] I wish I were nearer at hand and I also wish I felt that I could be of some help to you in this emergency.

We pray that all will be well and that he will shortly recover his vigor. Somehow the full perspective of people and their importance, per-

[392] Mr. Smith was with Marsh and McLennan, insurance brokers, in Chicago.

[393] This handwritten postcard is in the possession of Mr. Bohrer.

[394] Senator Johnson had just had a heart attack and was in Bethesda Naval Hospital.

sonally and nationally, emerges especially in a crisis like this. My heart is very much with you in these anxious days.

Sincerely yours,

To Harry S. Truman

July 5, 1955

Dear Mr. President:

I read your fine speech at San Francisco and it brought back a flood of memories of those exciting, hopeful days ten years ago.[395] Then I saw Pinay [396] in New York before his return to France and he told me with emotion of the reception you had there, using with undisguised emphasis "the *incomparable* respect of the delegates for President Truman." It must have made you feel good — even if it did not hasten the proof-reading of your book! [397]

I also saw, too briefly, your charming daughter in New York last week. She was well, gay, and full of anticipation of her trip abroad. That little visit with Margaret also reminded me that I hope I can see you somewhere before long for a leisurely talk. Will you be in Independence all summer? Or are you coming this way and could you stop off with me in the country?

I feel an acute need — growing acuter! — for communion with you. I had not thought I would be facing this decision again, and before I say or do anything more about it I should like to talk with you. There is ample time and I hope we can work out something to suit your convenience.

Faithfully yours,

To Mrs. Robert Jackson

July 6, 1955

My dear Barbara:

(1) Thanks so, so much for the might[y] mss. It has survived the Fourth of July — untouched. But I shall digest it carefully before a week-end meeting out in Libertyville with a "bunch of pols" — and I expect to surprise them, as well as myself, with my penetrating thoughtfulness and perception. I can already hear the "how does he find time to do it all," etc. etc., and you may be sure you will get no credit line!

[395] At the tenth anniversary session of the United Nations on June 24, 1955, Mr. Truman praised the UN's peacekeeping role.

[396] French Foreign Minister Antoine Pinay.

[397] Volume II of Mr. Truman's memoirs, *Years of Trial and Hope* (New York: Doubleday, 1956).

(2) Herewith $450 U.S. — representing one-half of $1,000 sale proceeds of Smith commencement [speech] to *Woman's Home Companion*, less $100 agent's commission. I send you this as ghostly compensation on the fine, fine West African principle of female labor. You do the work, I collect the profits, and return an insufficient portion. However, to return anything at all is obviously a sign of Western weakness.

(3) Oberlin [speech] enclosed. Pardon oversight; but don't bother to read. Important only that the feeble little effort to be of help provoked the indignation of David Lawrence and many writers for the provincial Republican press.

(4) And, finally, I am elated at the prospect of your visit and will be waiting with eyes bright, pencil sharp and mind blank; but I am sorry about Robert [398] and I hope my presumption has not made planting harder for the planter.

At the moment I am acutely ill — or think I am — with a cruel cold, or something. If, however, I don't recover from my present horrible malaise I shall not be here and you will also be too late for the funeral. Lucky you.

> Hastily, gratefully and affectionately,

To Chester Bowles

July 6, 1955

Dear Chet:

Your letter prompts me to say at once that I should like to come for the cruise up the Maine Coast, but, unhappily, I am told that I should be here during the Governors' Conference August 9–12 to do something about the Democratic Governors. Is there any possibility of joining up with you somewhere about the 14th for a week? Or is it too complicated, taking into account my continuing uncertainties of obligations and health. The latter at the moment is lousy and uppermost in my mind or that part of my head that is not occupied by a hideous cold!

If I could contrive both to cruise with you a bit and also drop off for a day or so with the [Thomas] Finletters it would be fine; and I hope we can work it out. Let me know the details and any deadlines on yes or no.

As for the future, your letter and penetrating understanding of my predicament and problems also prompts me to say that I would feel better about things if you were available for a lot of thought and work commencing this autumn. The image I create now and this fall, if and when I make some announcement, becomes important, obviously. There

[398] Mr. Jackson had written that he would have to remain in Montreal.

are, I gather several alternatives, and I have none of you smart Madison Avenue folk, even graduates!, hereabouts. But this in turn gets us to your own indecision (?) — about the Senate.

As for those travels to key sections of the country that Mrs. Roosevelt, and Paul Butler also, talk about, I am afraid I have more to do than even a vigorous, determined hungry man could do, and even if I wasn't afflicted with an awful weariness after some fifteen years of uninterrupted motion.

Yours,

P.S. The index of your book excites me, but how the hell have you the energy, time and wisdom to absorb and write so much. You depress me! All the same, I await it eagerly.

On July 6, Stevenson addressed the national convention of the National Education Association in Chicago.

EDUCATION, A NATIONAL CAUSE [399]

No single issue of domestic policy is more in need of clarification, public understanding, and bold action than education. It is unfortunately true that educational inadequacy is less obvious to the naked eye than is the sight of a man out of work, of a factory shut down, or of a hungry family. Yet to look squarely at the issue of education is to face nothing less than the central question of whether civilization is to prove a fulfillment of divine and rational purpose — or a bitter mockery.

In a very real sense the central issue of education is the central issue of today: how a civilization which has reached, at least in America, unprecedented heights of material well-being and unlocked awesome secrets of the physical world is also to master the ways for preserving its spiritual and moral and intellectual values — for preserving, if you please, those very things that are the essence of civilization.

In a narrower, more political sense the issue of education is how democracy can be made an instrument by which a people work together to mobilize the strength of the community to fight ignorance as effectively as we have fought every other enemy which has threatened us.

Yet crucial as these issues are, I would nevertheless emphasize first that any discussion of education cannot be cast just in terms of national needs, or a national policy, or a national program. For education can

[399] The text is from *What I Think*, pp. 140–148.

serve the ends of democratic society only as it meets those of the individual human being. The essential condition of the system of free choice between conflicting ideas and leaders, which we call democracy, is that it be made up of all different kinds of people — which means that what we demand most of education is the development of informed people who are at the same time unique, different, unpatterned individuals. I think this means, in turn, that any national educational policy must encourage difference, experimentation, and flexibility in educational practice.

May I add a word about the things that have happened these past two or three years which undoubtedly make some teachers think that we want our children taught only certain things in a certain way. This just isn't so!

It was an unprecedented historical coincidence that brought together the flames of war across the world, the atom's unlocking, and the emergence of aggressive Communism that created dangers — at first not fully realized — of insidiously organized disloyalty. This coincidence of crises induced the fever of fear, and there were unfortunately those among us who insisted on treating this fever in medieval manner by applying leeches to the bloodstream of freedom itself. Public servants, particularly teachers, were regrettably the victims of these frightened attacks of scared people.

But the fever is now subsiding. We know about the precautions which are necessary against organized disloyalty, and we have also experienced the excesses of overcaution which are both unnecessary and dangerous. The Supreme Court has forthrightly rebuked the government's abuse of education's Dr. Peters.[400] And the Senate has voted, despite administration opposition, to review the whole security program.

This battle for freedom, of course, is not over — as freedom's battles are never over. But it is very important, I think, that teachers realize that America's confidence in itself is coming back after our unpleasant nightmare — and that we insist no less strongly than before that the teacher's job is to teach the way of inquiry, to prepare each generation to meet its new problems, to improve its new opportunities, to explore civilization's always new horizons, to open minds and not to close them.

---

[400] Dr. John B. Peters, a part-time consultant to the U.S. Public Health Service, had passed an investigation conducted in 1949 by the loyalty board of the Federal Security Agency. In 1953, the Loyalty Review Board conducted a post-audit which concluded that Peters's loyalty could not be proved to be beyond a "reasonable doubt." Upon being released from his job, Peters appealed, and ultimately, on June 6, 1955, the U.S. Supreme Court ruled that the government had "wrongfully dismissed" him because the Loyalty Review Board was legally without jurisdiction in the case. See the New York *Times,* June 7, 1955.

A second principle underlying our national educational policy is that whatever control of public education is required should be exercised by local authorities. Our public schools take much of their strength from the millions of private citizens who are involved directly in their affairs — the boards of trustees, the parent-teachers associations, the room mothers, and all the others. Local control keeps alive continuous debate and the freedom to experiment. It insures a wholesome diversity in educational plans and practices. It helps to keep public education from becoming an instrument of stifling conformity and uniformity. Not sentimental attachment to tradition, but hardheaded good sense demands that by keeping control of education in the local community we keep the spreading branches of an ever-enlarging democracy always close to its roots.

Yet we have reached the point where the financing of education, as distinguished from its control, can no longer everywhere be taken care of entirely from local or even from state and local revenues. This is not a matter of more, or more expensive, education. Nor is it a matter of opinion or of politics. It is a matter of plain arithmetic, and it is a matter of necessity.

The key fact is that by law most schools must rely very largely for their support on property taxes. But property tax revenues do not go up as the population and the community income and production go up. And the tax revenues which do rise in proportion — the income and excise taxes — have been largely taken over by the state and federal governments.

Our thinking about adequate financing of public education must still start from an insistence that it is first of all a responsibility of local and state governments; that they must make available the largest possible revenues to sustain our public education system. State and local governments have no higher duties and there are too many instances today of failure to do that duty courageously and imaginatively.

Yet it is obvious, over all, that some measure of assistance to public education from the federal purse has now become necessary, and that this necessity will become increasingly acute in the next few years.

Two centuries of American history and experience testify that this need for federal financial assistance can be met without the slightest degree of domination by the central government.

No such domination followed Congress's grant in 1785 of a section of every township in the federal domain for the maintenance of public schools.

Nor has President Lincoln's approval of the Land Grant College System resulted in federal control.

The GI Bill of Rights has done great good. So has the Fulbright Fel-

lowship Program.[401] And there has been no accompanying federal domination.

It seemed a fair conclusion some years ago when Senators and Representatives from both parties, notably Senators Lister Hill and Robert Taft,
sponsored government aid-to-education proposals, that there was at least
to be no political division on party lines about federal action in this field.

And in February, 1953, just after he assumed office, President Eisenhower said: "Our school system demands some prompt, effective help."

Yet when this need has become acutely critical, nothing has been done.
Instead of "prompt, effective help," we await a conference on education
to be held at the White House next fall. Now a conference is fine and it
will dramatize the great significance of our educational system and its
critical deficiencies. But it seems to me a pitifully inadequate excuse for
years of doing absolutely nothing about America's number one domestic
need — schools and teachers.

I do not mean to ignore the President's recommendation to Congress
last February. We need, he said, seven billion dollars' worth of new
schools. But to help get them, he recommended that Congress pass not
a law but a miracle. For meeting this seven-billion-dollar need the
President proposed grants of $66 million a year for three years. This is
33¢ a year to meet every $35 of admitted present, crying need.

The President's recommendations also included federal loans for school
construction to be repaid with interest. But the proposed amount was
sufficient to cover only one-seventh of the needs the President listed, and
when the fine print was read it developed that even these loan provisions
were so drawn that they could never be used.

It is, I think, interesting if disheartening to reflect that while proposing
an effective grant of only $66 million a year for three years for school
construction aid, the President at the same time proposed a federal grant
for highway construction aid — mostly on a matching basis — of three
billion dollars every year for the next ten years! This is $45 of federal
funds for highways to every $1 for schools.

I will resist the temptation to draw inferences from the unequal competition between automobiles and education in our government these
days, but I deny that this 45-to-1 ratio between highways and schools
represents the standards or the priority of values of the people of
America.

There is, however, no point in belaboring the inadequacy and decep-
tiveness of this administration's school program. The chief education
officers of forty states have said that it would be of no help whatsoever

[401] See Walter Johnson and Francis J. Colligan, *The Fulbright Program: A History*
(Chicago: University of Chicago Press, 1965).

in their states. And Congress has long since buried the President's bill.

What then should our federal school financing policy and program be?

It should be to face, honestly and forthrightly, our educational shortages, to hold the states and local communities responsible for meeting all of these shortages they can, and then to allocate from the taxes we collect from ourselves whatever is necessary to do the rest of the job.

The figures on the shortages are well known despite the efforts in Washington to conceal them by confused and conflicting pronouncements. Enrollment in primary and secondary schools increased as much in the school year just ended as it did in the entire twenty years between 1930 and 1950. Six million children went to school this year in firetraps. Seven hundred thousand children are on a split session basis and get only half-day schooling.

We are currently short at least 250,000 classrooms — which is rooms for 7½ million children. Extraordinary efforts by local communities throughout the country are improving the situation a little bit. But with a million and a half more school-age children every year now drastic measures obviously have to be taken — and there can be no excuse for further delay.

The shortage of teachers is in some ways even more ominous than the shortage of schoolrooms. It is generally agreed that we need 180,000 more teachers than are presently available. Yet only 70,000 qualified teachers enter the profession each year. Somehow we must double the number. We note the urging today in Washington for a strong military reserve. It seems to me high time that we also pay attention to the schools' crying need not just for a teacher reserve, but for filling the large gaps in education's front-line trenches.

To meet this appalling situation we must start, it seems to me, with immediate support of the proposals now before Congress for $400 million of federal funds each year for the next four years for school construction to be matched by state funds.

While this program, together with the provisions for extending credit to certain school districts, will by no means meet the whole construction need, it would be a long American step in the right direction. And I hope that what is good for all will not be lost to all by any linking together of the school aid and desegregation issues which would delay realization of our hopes and expectations on either or both of these vital fronts. In the long run segregation and discrimination, like other obsolete heritages, will yield quickly to the general advance of education.

The need for more teachers — 145,000 new teachers a year to man the teaching ranks and meet the deficit — also means more money, higher salaries to make teaching a more attractive profession, and more funds for educating teachers. Careful calculations indicate that a federal grant to the states of approximately $50 million a year, if matched by an equal amount of new state funds, will at least break the back of the problem — instead of breaking the teachers' backs.

So much for the present. Over the longer run it may be best not to tie federal assistance to specific purposes, such as school construction, but rather to make unrestricted cash grants to the states on a per pupil basis. State governments would then have much greater flexibility to distribute these funds among local school districts for whatever purpose would most effectively advance education.

In view of the financial difficulties of the states, I also have misgivings about making federal grants to education permanently on a matching basis. But in any event, to insure that federal assistance is given only to those states which already make a proper effort to support public education, and to avoid the further risk that federal aid might result in relaxed state and local effort, some stated minimum local effort should be required as a condition of federal assistance.

Moreover, in the interest of narrowing somewhat the present wide gap in educational opportunity among the children of the various states, it seems to me that there are cogent reasons of fairness and good sense for higher per pupil assistance to states with the least ability to finance education as proposed by that great champion of our schools, Senator Lister Hill.

Finally I would suggest a modest program of national scholarships to promising candidates who upon graduation would undertake to give some years to teaching. To encourage outstandingly competent teachers, scholarships might also be awarded for special teacher training to graduate students, or for advanced work for already experienced teachers.

Just as we recruit promising young people for West Point and Annapolis, and for such professional fields as the Merchant Marine, science and engineering, we should now consider the same methods of attraction to our great public school system. Moreover, the cost of such scholarships would be small; the return on our investment would be immeasurable.

Yet there should be no evading the fact that the composite program I am suggesting here will be expensive, and it is just a beginning. Beardsley Ruml [402] has proposed federal expenditures to salvage our public school system of about $700 million next year, and possibly as much as $3 or $3½ billion a year ten years hence.

These are sobering figures and demand the closest scrutiny. Yet they are no excuse for either economic alarm or political timidity.

[402] Former dean of the Social Sciences Division of the University of Chicago and originator of the payroll deduction system for collection of personal income taxes.

It is said that our national income should be rising at the rate of $15 billion a year during the next decade. This will mean increased federal tax revenues, at present rates, of $4 billion a year. So what I suggest, in effect, is that we agree with ourselves, to spend on education — until we have caught up with our children's needs — say 20 per cent of our federal tax collections from our new national wealth.

Bad education isn't cheap either. Its high costs are paid from other budgets — for poverty and sickness and unemployment and juvenile delinquency. The question is not only "What will an adequate education program cost?" The question is even more "What is the cost of not having such a program?" I cannot imagine the American people responding with anything but eagerness and enthusiasm to a proposal to give our children better education, which means a better chance, and fuller education, which means fuller lives.

I have suggested here what seems to me the outlines, the elemental necessities, of our public educational system. Yet we all recognize that there is infinitely more to the problem than simply providing a classroom and a person with a teaching certificate for every thirty children between the ages of five and seventeen.

The larger challenge that we must meet together — as teachers and parents and public and private citizens — is to prove that mass education can also be a good education.

Good school buildings are an asset — but they are not the essence of good education. The real heart of good education remains, as always, good teaching. We must, if we want to improve the quality of education, attract into teaching and hold there a far larger number of our ablest young people. Compensation must be geared to ability and performance, and opportunity afforded for advancement to a high level based on merit, as in other professions.

And, above all, teachers must be freed of the shackles of bigotry and anti-intellectualism, and the indignities of loyalty oaths and unwritten blue laws which no longer apply to other citizens.

It is another accepted requirement for improving educational quality, I think, that we be clearer as to the tasks and priorities of our schools. Today they are being asked to perform not only their traditional jobs but, more and more, functions traditionally recognized as the obligation of the family, the church, the employer, and other social institutions. Under pressure of this group or that, courses of study are becoming laden with activities whose educational value is at least subject to serious question.

In a growing and changing society, the primary tasks of the school must also grow and change. But we must be clear that if we expect the schools to do too much, if we expect the teacher to play too many roles, we are bound to be disappointed with the results. If our educational purposes are unclear, if the curriculum is chaotic and cluttered with distractions, if the teaching staffs are overburdened with an indiscriminate array of responsibilities well beyond their reasonable capacity to carry, we must expect that our children will be educated for mediocrity instead of for something better.

I do not mean to trespass upon areas of what I know to be strong — and healthy — controversy among you who are so much more experienced in this field than I. But it is our common concern that we recognize and that we resist the pressures to let mass education become education for mediocrity. The dangers of mass education seem to me as much our problem as are its necessities.

We are well advised, I think, to take very seriously the admonition that education for all may come to mean real education for none. The struggle is very real today between massiveness, standardization, conformity on the one hand, and on the other the spirit of individualism which has given freedom and democracy and life itself their meaning.

We must, then, work together to forge better tools for the ever-enlarging job of educating fast growing numbers of our children for an always more complex life. Equally must we struggle everlastingly to keep education a process of enrichment — of the mind and spirit of the young American whose destiny is measured only by his wisdom.

Roswell Garst, who had traveled in the Soviet Union, visited Stevenson in Chicago and then wrote him.

To Roswell Garst [403]

July 7, 1955

Dear Mr. Garst:

Thanks for your interesting letter to Adams [404] about export of surplus food to the Iron Curtain countries. I should like to know about the restriction on CCC [Commodity Credit Corporation]. Has the administration proposed any amendments this year? Also, I should like to see Adams' reply.

Of course you know why this administration has been so timid and reluctant about trade and barter with the communist states. After all the bragging for years about [what] they were going to do — "roll back" communism, "liberate" the satellites — and all the denunciation, indeed manu-

---

[403] The original is in the possession of Mr. Garst.
[404] Sherman Adams, assistant to President Eisenhower.

factured suspicion, of Truman, Acheson and Democrats generally, and the right wing, [William] Knowland, [Joseph] McCarthy et al, frenzy about the way our allies were trading with the enemy, for the Eisenhower administration to reverse itself and send food and extend credits to Russia, China, etc. might even be hard for the Republican press to laugh off.

This "split personality" is why I think and have repeatedly said that the Republican party is incapable of governing.

Cordially yours,

Mrs. Eugene Meyer, after an operation, wrote Stevenson several letters from the hospital. She strongly advocated his running for President again in 1956.

To Mrs. Eugene Meyer [405]

July 10, 1955

Dear Mrs. Meyer:

Bless you for all those gallant and tonic messages from your "grave." And now I write you from mine. Following a relentless week in New York I returned home quite ill and with barely time to write the education speech. The doctors propped me up with sprays and drugs long enough to utter it and then I was hauled off gasping to a hospital with bronchial pneumonia. Here I now languish, but I am recovering rapidly and I, too, will go home for a brief period of recuperation presently. I was so relieved to hear that you have been released and that you are now at your lovely country place. I hope that you can master all of your obvious congenital urges and submit utterly to the doctor's orders. I promptly overdid after a kidney stone operation a year and a half ago and it was a long time before I recovered my strength and confidence. That "well again" feeling is deceptive and dangerous and I am sure you will have it, like all the rest, and probably gaily embrace it in spite of all these solemn warnings.

. . . As to my plans: a number of my "friends" had planned to meet here this week-end from around the country to discuss futures but my illness made it impossible. They will probably do so later. At that time I shall hope for some "guidance" on several counts, including timing. The impression I have is that in the circumstances there is a growing feeling that nothing should be said before late in the fall, but that much should be planned. I really need more expert advice than relying on my intuition in so many things. But you must not think badly of me for "not wanting

[405] The original is in the Agnes Meyer files, Princeton University Library.

it." To say so is something else and there I concede you are right. To know the proper measure of this task precludes anybody but the light-headed or ruthless from "wanting it," it seems to me. I think we do what we must do, and the job is to do it as well as it lies within us. To summon more savage fervor is, I fear, beyond me. Your advice is always eagerly welcome and so will a talk be which I am sure will come one of these days. I think the basic problem is to find a formula on which a campaign can be pitched and which goes to the heart of what you call "the whole political, economic and cultural philosophy of our nation is at stake." Actually, superficially, there seems to be little at stake, but I think we realize that mediocrity, materialism, social indifference and repulsive showmanship cannot be forever disguised by wholesome smiles, golf clubs and a Bible firmly clutched beneath the right arm if seldom read; and somehow I feel that ways and means must be found to get at these imperfectly perceived realities and incomprehensible language by means that touch masses. It will be hard, if not impossible, I am sure, with prosperity, peace and a contented press.

Speaking of press, I think what I need most in the world is a "press man." What I mean is something much more important than a technician to handle public relations henceforth. My political staff now consists of one man and some devoted girls in my law office. I think the first addition should be someone who could reflect thoughtfully over the news and the image I present henceforth and help me not just with cheese cake and handouts, but with backgrounding friendly writers, and generally envisioning the picture that emerges six months hence. Mostly the people who are really good and sensitive and perceptive are, of course, unavailable. I think of Al Friendly [406] in your husband's organization,[407] and several others. If you have any ideas don't hesitate to pass them on to me.

And now, my dear friend, farewell. I must lie down and cough my head off for a while.

Blessings on you, and my enduring gratitude.

Faithfully yours,
ADLAI

P.S. . . .

To John Kenneth Galbraith

July 15, 1955

Dear Ken:

Thanks for your jolly little note which made life brighter for me in the

[406] Assistant managing editor of the Washington *Post* from 1952 to 1955, when he became managing editor.

[407] Mr. Meyer was chairman of the board of directors of the Washington *Post*.

local pest house where I have been experiencing the agonies of bronchial pneumonia.

I shall await the "compulsory reading" and assume confidently that you have found the answer to all our agricultural problems. It will make things so much easier with Mr. Garst, Senator [Clinton] Anderson, Charlie Brannan [408] and several characters who are closing in from all sides. If you find any hidden valleys over there [409] mark them well, for I may need one.

Here all is well, except for my health, and the tractor is broken, also the hay wagon, and my farmer has lacerated his arm with a hay hook; and now the truck is broken down and the bailer hasn't turned up. Ho hum!

Yours,

To Lyndon B. Johnson

July 15, 1955

Dear Lyndon:

I am sitting on my little farm recuperating from bronchial pneumonia. They are making hay out here. But now the tractor has broken down; the hay truck has broken down; the hay wagon has collapsed dumping fifty bales in the middle of the driveway; and my farmer has lacerated his arm on a hay hook. Besides it is hot.

I think I will just go back to bed, cough for a while, and take it easy. And that would be the best thing you can do too.[410]

Cordially,

To Mrs. Warwick Anderson

July 15, 1955

Dear Mary San:

I am convinced that you Anderson women have remarkable literary talents. I shall read and reread many times what you have sent me and each time bless you and my lucky starts [stars] to have such perception, depth and gentleness, not only in my son's life but in mine too.

I had an ugly time for a few days with bronchial pneumonia but I am at home now and recuperating very rapidly. Next week I shall be going to the office again. The temptation to come down and join you and relax in that happy, loving atmosphere was formidable — but so was the dour

---

[408] Charles F. Brannan, Secretary of Agriculture, 1948–1953.
[409] Mr. Galbraith was in Switzerland.
[410] Mr. Johnson was still in Bethesda Naval Hospital recuperating from the heart attack he had suffered early in July.

doctor! And my instructions are not to move off this place for at least a week.

I am sure you have had many bulletins from our romantics, but I wonder if you have had anything so good as this one from Nancy. Please return it for my "imperishable" file.

And again a thousand thanks for your sweet letter and that extraordinary essay.

Affectionately,

To William Benton [411]

July 15, 1955

Dear Bill:

I seem to have you to thank for both wine and speeches! You were good to send me the wine, and I am going to try it as soon as I feel like anything stronger than water and gargle. The speeches, however, will be consumed promptly; and so many thanks for sending both.

I am recuperating from my foolishness and confidently look forward to a visit with you before you take off for Russia.

My affectionate regards to Helen [412] and the children.

Yours,
ADLAI

To Harold Hochschild [413]

July 15, 1955

Dear Harold:

I have Baron von Kimmelmann's letter to you, forwarded by your Secretary. I would be delighted to see Sir Roy Welensky [414] during his visit, and I am sure once his available time is known to me we can work out a convenient meeting, either here or in New York.

As I believe I told you, I was much impressed with this bold and forthright man, and I hope political circumstances permit him to continue to play an enlightened role in the resolution of the Federation's infinite difficulties.

Do tell him that I am at his service and look forward to seeing him.

I am home on my little farm near Chicago at the moment. We are in the midst of making hay. The tractor has broken down; the hay wagon

[411] The original is in the possession of the estate of William Benton. See note 143, p. 352.
[412] Mrs. Benton.
[413] Chairman of the American Metal Company in New York City.
[414] Deputy prime minister of Rhodesia and Nyasaland.

has collapsed dumping fifty bales in the middle of the driveway; my farmer has lacerated his arm on a hay hook. It is hot; I am recovering from bronchial pneumonia. All in all, I wish to hell I was in Switzerland with the Hochschilds!

My affectionate regards to Mary [415] if she is with you.

Cordially yours,

Senator Hubert Humphrey wrote Stevenson on July 8 praising his speech to the National Education Association. He advised him, however, that regardless of how inadequate President Eisenhower's proposals for education were, Congress was controlled by the Democrats and no bill could come out of committees until there was agreement on the segregation issue. The National Association for the Advancement of Colored People, he added, was urging an antisegregation amendment. But, if such an amendment was added, the bill would be defeated on the floor of the Senate by Southern Democratic votes. Humphrey suggested that Stevenson consider calling together leaders from education, labor, and Negro groups to discuss the problem. Humphrey also urged Stevenson to call a meeting of his supporters to plan the 1956 campaign.

To Hubert H. Humphrey

July 15, 1955

Dear Hubert:

Thanks for your letter about the School Bill. I think I know the awkward position that the NAACP stubbornness has created and the possible, even probable, Democratic embarrassment that may ensue. I am loathe, however, for reasons that I am sure are obvious to you, to take any personal initiative from where I sit along the lines you suggest of attempting to reconcile the conflicting interests. Actually, this is one case in which I don't in the least sympathize with the attitude of the Negro leaders. I am convinced, as I said in the speech (copy enclosed), that desegregation and improved relations are going to gain more from advancing education than from stubbornness and perhaps even reaction.

Having to make a speech on the school subject I saw no alternative but to express my views as best I could regardless of the current situation in Congress. I am most fearful that we may have much to answer for if Southern Democratic votes kill all we agree upon for extraneous reasons. But it won't be the last time that we have scratched our own backs with our own daggers.

[415] Mrs. Hochschild.

I look forward eagerly to a visit with you about the matters you mentioned. I need your counsel and I hope, as I suggested earlier, that you can stop off for a little visit with me on your way home after the session or on your next trip West.

Hastily yours,

P.S. I seem to constantly read remarks of yours, and most recently those at Colgate [University], with which I emphatically agree. And, as ever, I marvel at your vitality and versatility.

To Richard J. Daley

July 16, 1955

Dear Dick:

That you were present at the Stevenson School [416] dedication last week surprised and flattered me; that you spoke so beautifully touched my sister and me very much. I wish your secretary could send me a copy of your remarks. Buffy Ives and I would like to have them among our papers relating to Grandfather Stevenson. Thanks!

Like other friends of yours I have been disturbed of late by Democratic inertia with respect to judicial reform in Springfield. I hope we don't have to look back a year hence to public charges of Democratic failure of neglect of duty by democracy's leader — Mayor Daley.[417] I think you know what I mean, and it occurs to me that regardless of what you are doing quietly the public record ought to be clear. A statement such as the enclosed that Fred Hoehler [418] has suggested would seem to me appropriate, although the details are not as clear to me.

Cordially yours,

To Harry S. Truman

July 18, 1955

Dear Mr. President:

It was good to see you in Chicago and to see you looking so well — and feeling so optimistic! I hope that there can be another and more leisurely visit soon.

Meanwhile, I trust you will pass along to me any advice you have from time to time. As I explained, I am more interested in the Democrats winning than *who* wins. The important thing, it seems to me, is to

[416] A public school in Chicago named for Stevenson's grandfather.
[417] Mr. Daley was beginning his first term as mayor of Chicago.
[418] Executive director of the Citizens of Greater Chicago and formerly director of the Department of Public Welfare during Stevenson's governorship.

restore public interest in government as quickly as possible, and I seem to want that more than anything for myself. In short, I want our strongest candidate in 1956, which makes it a little hard for me to do what you suggest — "make up *my* mind that *I* want the job and say so." I hope you will understand.

With affectionate regards to Mrs. Truman, I am

Faithfully yours,

Beardsley Ruml sent Stevenson a report entitled "Essentiality of the American Horological Industry" and expressed concern that there was confusion as to the value of the watch and clock industry to national defense.

To Beardsley Ruml

July 18, 1955

Dear B:

I am sorry to be so slow in acknowledging your thoughtfulness in sending the Horological — what an egghead word! — Report on to me. But I've been outnumbered by a swarm of microbes which have me still, as a matter of fact, somewhat in their grip. (No pun!)

All right, I'm persuaded that what I have always thought of in plainer terms as the watch makers are essential to the national defense. But does this constitute the complete case for the 50% tariff increase? And was this the reason it was granted — or doesn't that matter? These aren't rhetorical questions. I'm frankly unclear about all this.

Many thanks for the Report — and best regards.

Sincerely,

To David L. Cohn [419]

July 19, 1955

Thank you dear friend for reminding me so vividly of my horrid fate. It was just the remedy that I needed for bronchial pneumonia! But I've weathered the relapse and all and sundry are now pointing out the extraordinary resemblance of the shuffling figure — "Out of Office" — and his lean and hungry dog to me and Artie.[420] Thank you, suh!, but it won't be the gallows; I'm oiling my revolver!

ADLAI

[419] This handwritten postcard is in the Mississippi collection, University of Mississippi Library.
[420] Stevenson's Dalmatian, King Arthur.

To Carol J. Hardin [421]

July 20, 1955

My dear Carol:

Thank you for your sweet letter. I do need another daughter and consider yourself mine henceforth. I was disappointed that you couldn't come to the wedding, but I suspect there will be more!

I was delighted to hear that you were going to have your junior year at Geneva. I have known so many girls who have done that and they all seem to profit by it, and I am sure you will too. What a wonderful opportunity; and I know that you fully appreciate it.

Do give my love to your mother, father and Adlai,[422] and much much love to you, dear girl.

Your affectionate Uncle,

To John Paulding Brown [423]

July 20, 1955

Dear John:

I have been ill with pneumonia and hence have neglected my affairs, including your letter. How I envy you your trip to London! I should like to escape myself — even just to Prout's Neck [Maine].

It was good to hear about Fanny McPherson.[424] I love her dearly.

The daughter I have acquired is an enchantress and I hope you get to meet her before long. She and Adlai will be living in Cambridge this year when he will be in his second year at Harvard Law School. Perhaps you could look in on them some time if you pass that way.

I can think of one thing you *can* do for me some time at your convenience, and in confidence. If I should run again and should by any chance be elected, what is the law and what are the proprieties with respect to a President's investments? May I hold stocks? What about the Pantagraph, a closely held family corporation? I presume there would be no question about that; but what about industrials? No hurry, and nothing elaborate, please.

Yours,
ADLAI

---

[421] The daughter of Adlai S. Hardin, the sculptor. Although Stevenson signed this letter "Uncle," he was in fact her first cousin once removed. A copy is in A.E.S., I.S.H.L.

[422] Miss Hardin's brother.

[423] The original was in the possession of the late Mr. Brown.

[424] A mutual friend in Chicago.

To Eugenie Anderson [425]

July 20, 1955

My dear Mrs. Anderson:

Thank you so much for your very good letter. I agree with you about the necessity for pointing out the administration's deficiencies — and the Democratic deficiency in doing so! Actually, with the exception of Dixon-Yates, it seems to me our party has not been too audible, and what with the protective Republican press and the difficulty of getting through to people it is bad enough if we were talking incessantly.

I hope so much that we *can* have the talk you suggest, and trust you will let me know if you come my way.

Cordially,

Benjamin V. Cohen wrote Stevenson on July 20 that President Eisenhower's chief aide, Sherman Adams, had told him that the Administration had decided not to appoint him to the United States delegation to the United Nations. Secretary of State Dulles hinted to Mr. Cohen that the decision not to appoint him was because right-wing Republicans objected to his views on Formosa.

To Benjamin V. Cohen

July 25, 1955

Dear Ben:

Your letter shocks me a little, but it doesn't surprise me. Such timidity seems to me neither necessary nor good political judgment, regardless of the value of your services to the UN Delegation.

If you are not going to do anything about it, would you have any objection to my hinting at the story — or even more! — to the [St. Louis] Post-Dispatch or the [Louisville] Courier-Journal or some other interested and friendly paper? It is an example of the sort of Executive timidity which should not pass unnoticed.

Hastily yours,

[425] The original is in the possession of Mrs. Anderson.

To Mrs. Eugene Meyer [426]

July 28, 1955

My dear Agnes:

"Why hasn't anybody told *me* this before"? — I mean about Herblock's book.[427] I have just read the chapter you sent me, and this is doubtless the most effective campaign document of 1955 plus 1956. I was enchanted, and I think the very restraint and accuracy with which he has done it will magnify its usefulness and earn him a larger public respect than his extraordinary talents as a cartoonist have already done.

The press exploitation of the President's melodramatics of the Geneva Conference [428] is, I suppose, a preview of the shape of things to come. I wonder if you are right about any hesitancy on the part of Ives [429] in the '56 campaign. It could be important in view of the importance of New York. My own guess is that if this popularity holds they will all be for him whether they like it or not, and all out.

I agree with you, however, on the danger of trying to magnify small issues into big ones. This sounds good for a while during the shouting but the people's sober second thought restores the perspective. Can't we, however, put together a great multitude of small ones somehow and emerge with a large one — general disillusion? I think it undoubtedly the most important preparation problem that the Democratic party will confront. Now that McCarthy, the security terror, etc. have receded, most of what we will be able to count on for issues will be relatively small but of those there seems to be a multitude. I hope you will be thinking of how best to handle this by consolidation, or shall I say merger?

I still haven't read your book or even the marked passages. I have a curious habit of trying to keep the good things until the end. I used to do it with food when I was a child, and it still operates on my desk.

I wish I had a stronger heart for the work ahead and did not wish it was ahead quite so much.

I hope you are making some proper progress and your concern for me fills my heart with gratitude. But spare your anxiety. I am restored and have even played golf. My big problem now is to repair, in a few

[426] The original is in the Agnes Meyer files, Princeton University Library.

[427] Herbert Block, *Herblock's Here and Now* (New York: Simon & Schuster, 1955). Mr. Block was a syndicated cartoonist with the Washington *Post*.

[428] President Eisenhower had just met with the leaders of the Soviet Union, France, and the United Kingdom at Geneva, Switzerland.

[429] Senator Irving M. Ives, a New York Republican.

weeks, the physical ravages of fifteen years of unremitting tension and pressure.

Faithfully yours,

Adlai

P.S. I wonder if I should call Philip Graham [430] about the "press man." I want to keep this situation as confidential as I can for the present for obvious reasons. I am still uncertain as to my own future, but I am sure that a man of stature, stability and statesmanship is indispensable to me or to anyone who may move into what appear to be my shoes.

P.P.S. I suppose you wanted the Herblock text returned and I am enclosing it herewith.

Professor Arthur M. Schlesinger, Jr., wrote Stevenson that he was leaving for Europe to speak at a conference in Milan and asked if there was anything he could do for him while there.

To Arthur M. Schlesinger, Jr.

August 1, 1955

Dear Arthur:

Yes, there *is* something I would "like you to look into." I would like you to look into your suitcase — the large one — and find me all curled up but unwrinkled and eager to travel, especially to Venice! Beyond that I can't think of a thing, beyond what you will pick up anyway.

I would hope to talk to you after your return, and will probably be in New York on my return from the West Indies about that time. Try to check with me if your circumstances permit, through Miss [Kay] Hart at Bill Benton's office.

The speaking program for the autumn begins to look something as follows:

Thursday, September 15 — Jamaica.

Friday, October 7 — State Democratic Convention, Wisconsin (probably agriculture).

Thursday, October 13 (?) — University of Texas (probably something about the purposes of government, with some solid blows at economic mythology).

Saturday, October 15 — Queens University, Kingston, Ontario (very brief speech about what?) Any ideas of A.S., Jr. gratefully received.

[430] Publisher of the Washington *Post* and Mrs. Meyer's son-in-law.

Saturday, October 22 (?) — Duluth political rally for [Hubert] Humphrey, Freeman,[431] Blatnik.[432] Ten-minute speech about what?

Monday, October 31 — Democratic National Committee dinner, New York. This I will probably decline.

Friday, November 11 — University of Virginia, Woodrow Wilson Centennial. (I have asked [Arthur] Link [433] of Northwestern and Barbara Ward for suggestions).

Saturday, November 19 — Democratic National Committee dinner, Chicago. This is too distant to think about.

Have a good time and don't worry about the foregoing too much.

Yours,

P.S. Thanks for the letter from Morris Cooke.[434] I shall take it home and read it in due course.

P.P.S. Are you sure you don't need some help from me about what you say in Milan? I hope not!

Trygve Lie congratulated Stevenson on his new daughter-in-law and mentioned that he was about to become governor of Oslo and Akirshus.

To Trygve Lie [435]

August 1, 1955

Dear Trygve:

You were more than good to write me about Adlai's wedding and my illness.

I was much interested to hear that you were doing your memoirs, and as a veteran may I congratulate a new Governor! I am sure you will enjoy it, but it seems as though your visits to America will diminish rather than increase. I had hoped that the latter might be the case.

With all good wishes and my enduring admiration.

Cordially,

---

[431] Orville Freeman, candidate for governor of Minnesota.
[432] John A. Blatnik, a candidate for congressman.
[433] Arthur Link, professor of history at Northwestern University and biographer of Woodrow Wilson.
[434] Unable to identify.
[435] A copy is in A.E.S., I.S.H.L.

To Bernard Baruch [436]

August 1, 1955

Dear Mr. Baruch:

I have only now come across your speech of May 25 at Woodrow Wilson House.

It is splendid, and I hope you will forgive me if I shamelessly appropriate large segments when I must speak of Wilson on November 11. I shall try to remember to give you a byline — but occasionally politicians forget such amenities, I understand.

With my congratulations — and thanks — from another Wilsonian.

Cordially yours,

Robert Woetzel visited Stevenson in January in Chicago, and later wrote to him from Fort Belvoir, Virginia.

To Robert Woetzel

August 1, 1955

Dear Robert:

I am mortified that I have not long since acknowledged your letter of April 7. As you know, it came just as I was preparing to leave on a long journey abroad — this time to Africa — followed by six weeks of almost incessant travel, and, I fear, almost incessant speech-making!

I have only now had an opportunity to read it, on the heels of pneumonia and other diversions, pleasant and painful.

It is a remarkable letter, and you write with a perception and depth that surprises me. I must say that I emphatically agree that "a growing uniformity of thought is favored rather than competition between different conceptions"; and this malaise has been the theme of endless words of mine from public platforms, as I am sure you know.

I am sure, gifted with insights beyond your years, that you can profit mightily from your experience in the Army, despite its "dehumanizing process." After all, there you are dealing with the raw material of the world — mankind as it comes off a production line, still unstandardized, thank God! And it is these people you must know and understand if you are to know, understand — and influence! — your generation *now*. There are the realms of thought, and there are the realms of action, and there is the realm of a little of both. You must take your choice of that in which you are to live and work — if not wholly live.

[436] A copy is in A.E.S., I.S.H.L.

Your visit was not an imposition and I hope there will be more. With all good wishes, I am

Cordially yours,

Norman Thomas, Socialist party candidate for President, wrote Stevenson about the need to develop the case for universal and controlled disarmament.

To Norman Thomas [437]

August 1, 1955

Dear Mr. Thomas:

Thank you for your letter of July 20. I regret that I have not yet surmounted my mountainous mail and incessant visitors, hence Mr. Klein's memorandum [438] is still in the waiting heap. I do hope that in questions of disarmament the liberals and thoughtful people can this time concert their reasoning and eschew all the doctrinaire ideas of the past. Like you, I expect, I have heard more flat assertions of half truths as whole truths, from our friends as from our enemies. I wish a liberal conference of some kind on disarmament were possible, but I dread to think of the conflicting views that might emerge. I hope I am wrong, and I hope likewise that there is concurrent thinking about economic substitutes for full employment and expanding economy after fifteen years of armament transfusions.

Thank you for writing me, and I hope to read what you have sent soberly.

Cordially yours,

To Archibald MacLeish

August 2, 1955

Dear Archie:

I'm so, so grateful for your delightful and stimulating letter. I'm bubbling with ends not means — or is it the boiling heat! If more people could put so much so well in four pages my mail would be more profitable — and take up a good deal less of my time!

Now may I selfishly take up some more of your time! As you know, we are in substantial agreement about our present dilemma in the fields of both foreign and domestic policy. (And, incidentally, I liked your

[437] A copy is in A.E.S., I.S.H.L.
[438] The editors were unable to locate this memorandum.

thought that "they are not so much pursuing as being pursued by" *our* domestic policy!)

But, granted that it is ends rather than means that we should be talking about today — and that the great common end is peace — how does one build a campaign on this? In other words, what "positive policy to achieve peace" do I propose? (And *since* your letter was written the press universally seems to report that Eisenhower has seized the peace "initiative" with "strong, firm, sincere hands"! [439] But the reaction will come — or will it with a press that never denounces the situations he creates but always applauds his last minute efforts to save them?

I don't mean to sound naive or skeptical. I am impressed by your reasoning. I would simply ask you — if and when you have the time — to push it a little further in the direction of what one says: how it might be embodied in a program and expressed through a campaign. Perhaps this is asking too much, but it is just this sort of problem that I am up against. If I *must* do it again, I shall need all of the thinking and help and advice I can get from my friends. I am extraordinarily fortunate in my friends, I know, but few of them can be truly helpful in the way you have always been. So I'd be deeply grateful for any further thinking that you can give me on ends in lieu of means; restating the American position; restating, even, the meaning and purpose of government in America.

It was good of you to stop off to see the invalid and I proceeded to mend rapidly, thanks to your therapy. But my recovery would have been even more rapid if Ada [440] had been along. Give her my love, and don't let my problem spoil too much of your summer's fun.

Yours,

P.S. Jane [Dick] has told me a little about your conversation with her en route to the train. I know that it is difficult to put views of this sort on paper, but it would be helpful to me to know more specifically what you feel are the main shortcomings, from my point of view, of the people you mentioned to her. Needless to say, I value your judgment and would keep anything you had to say completely confidential.

Archibald Alexander, who had been executive director of the 1952 Stevenson for President Committee, wrote that he was going to Paris to be at the birth of his second grandchild. He stated that peace and pros-

[439] After the Geneva summit conference, President Eisenhower spoke of the "evidence of a new friendliness in the world."
[440] Mrs. MacLeish.

perity were contributing to the popularity of the Eisenhower Administration. Nevertheless, Mr. Alexander concluded it was Stevenson's duty to run in 1956.

To Archibald Alexander

August 2, 1955

Dear Archie:

I have read and reread your excellent letter of July 27. In the first place, let me say that I hope we can have a little time together after you return from abroad. I may be in New York around the 20th of September, and if circumstances permit maybe we could get together then. I pray that all goes well in Paris and I am sure Grandpa will be most helpful!

I suspect your analysis is not far off the mark. Certainly on any reasonable calculation the prospects for victory could hardly be an inducement for running. But, curiously, perhaps I attach less importance to that than other factors, personal as well as political, as to why I am not eager to undertake the assignment again.

While I am not sure about the state of the economy a year hence, I am sure there is bound to be a reaction to the maudlin embrace at Geneva. The Russians are, of course, following their classic program of retreating when the West is strong and pressing forward when the West is weak. This is a period of retreat, but they will yield little in reality, all of which will be perceptible, I presume, in time and make the jerky inconsistency of the administration's foreign policy the more apparent.

I had rather thought someone else was entitled to the honor and labor this time, but that is not to say that I have any less doubt about the importance of restoring public interest [in] government, and quickly. My mistrust of the superficial in Washington is only slightly aggravated by the President's enthusiastic approval of Mr. Talbott's contribution to our government while kicking him out.[441] This constant coating of piety and approval of Dixon-Yates, [Herbert] Brownell, [Richard M.] Nixon, etc. must break through even the wall of the press sooner or later. But I am wandering — and I wish it were in the direction of Paris!

Yours,

P.S. I will probably be at my farm near Chicago the first week in September, before I have to go to the West Indies.

[441] Secretary of the Air Force Harold E. Talbott was discovered by a Senate subcommittee investigation to have used his official stationery and telephone to conduct business activities on behalf of a New York management engineering company. He resigned on August 2, 1955. See the New York *Times*, August 3, 1955.

Democratic National Chairman Paul M. Butler wrote Stevenson that he felt Clayton Fritchey should remain as editor of the Democratic Digest *rather than join Stevenson's campaign staff. Mr. Butler praised the work of his predecessor, Stephen A. Mitchell, for bringing a "new look" to his office and refusing to be a "smoke-filled room" type of political leader. Mr. Butler also mentioned that he had designated Hyman B. (Hy) Raskin to be Chicago manager for the 1956 Democratic National Convention.*

To Paul M. Butler [442]

August 4, 1955

Personal and Confidential

Dear Paul:

I was delighted to have your letter and I am most grateful for all the thoughtfulness that lies behind it.

I think you are right about Clayton [Fritchey] and that he ought not to be disturbed. I only hope you can get on a more personal and compatible basis with him with manifest advantage to your common objectives.

You may be right about the organization situation. I know that we have no time to waste and that dissipating the current mythology and disclosing the moral duplicity of this administration is going to take a legion of speakers and much effort. Hence I feel that we should be looking toward the *election* rather than just the intermediate step of the *convention*. It becomes, in a sense, hardly a personal problem but a party problem. That I should be delighted to campaign for someone else this time I think you well understand, but if it is to be otherwise, then I believe we should know it as early as possible and start planning and organizing in that direction. It is for this reason that I have felt we needed more than a single person assuming some active responsibility for the whole effort, but I am not sure that I see the situation clearly. Yet I do see what you say clearly, and I think it is both exceedingly well said and very cogent.

I have spoken to [Hyman B.] Raskin as you suggested, and he does not think that anything he is doing, at least thus far (and I'm not clear what he has been doing) is inconsistent or could be embarrassing. Perhaps that situation should be re-examined from time to time.

I wish I could be of more help to you and that our opportunities to talk were more frequent.

Cordially,

---

[442] A carbon copy is in the possession of the editors.

To Mr. and Mrs. Charles Fahy [443]

August 4, 1955

My dear old friends:

Word comes to me from Louisville that you have sent Adlai and his bride a wedding present. I am not only grateful, I am also touched by such thoughtfulness, and it reminds me again of many other kindnesses from the same source. I only wish there were some more meetings with the source!

Cordially,
ADLAI

To Hector McNeill [444]

August 5, 1955

Dear Hector:

Please note the enclosed letter from the President of the Glasgow University Liberal Club.[445] You will recall in London a couple of years ago I told you I had been flattered by the persistence of some of your fellow Glasgow students to accept nomination for Rector of the University. This I declined because it involved a commitment there, once, to come and make a speech, which I did not feel I could guarantee.

This request, however, seems to entail no obligations, and while I have done nothing of the kind I would not decline if there were no commitments and you saw no objection. Of course I have no way of knowing whether the club is good, bad or indifferent. If enlightening me about this very unimportant matter involves any difficulty on your part, or any extensive research, please return the enclosed and spend no time on it. I can decline, consistent with my practice of declining virtually everything of this kind. If on the other hand it would be harmless and at all helpful, well, I am quite willing to be thus honored!

I hope you find the late Senator from Connecticut [446] in good form. He reports on you periodically and always with Bentonian enthusiasm. Perhaps he has also told you that I am now a director of the Company and can greet you as a "business associate."

Cordially yours,

443 Old friends from Washington, D.C. Mr. Fahy was judge of the U.S. Court of Appeals for the District of Columbia. The original is in the possession of Mr. Fahy.
444 Director of the London office of the *Encyclopaedia Britannica.*

445 Students at Glasgow University had voted to invite Stevenson to be honorary president of the Liberal Club for 1955–1956.
446 William Benton, chairman of the board of the *Encyclopaedia Britannica.*

Mr. Bowles wrote Stevenson on August 3 recommending that he visit the Soviet Union to meet the Russian leaders and thus be in a better position to make his own independent judgment of the situation.

To Chester Bowles

August 8, 1955

Dear Chet:

Your letter interests me very much. I think you have made a suggestion that must be considered very very carefully. Certainly it fascinates me at this stage. I presume you would exclude the possibility of my going with Bill Benton the end of September as premature.

Hastily,

Mrs. Eugene Meyer wrote Stevenson that whether he was elected President or not, he was bound to become the outstanding leader of the nation provided he overcame his "fear" of his own greatness and destiny.

To Mrs. Eugene Meyer [447]

August 8, 1955

My dear Agnes:

No, you are wrong, I insist, It isn't just self distrust; it is prior experience and also a genuine anxiety to be sure the Democratic party is doing the best thing for it and its cause, which is the restoration of public interest government. However, let us not argue about my frailties, of which I have a great many; nor will I argue about my virtues of which I am afraid you see more than there are. I am, in fact, quite ready for the task, if equally ready to see someone else, and I would hope a better man, undertake it. That you feel about me as you do I must add fills me with confidence measured only by my gratitude, and I think perhaps I did need some of that kind of faith you talk about.

This week-end we had a meeting that lasted the better part of two days at my home in the country. It was very gratifying, and I think now some realistic preliminary organization work is going to proceed. A real estate man named Roger Stevens, in New York, an old friend, has undertaken to raise $100,000 promptly to enable us to get some staff. This, together with your help, gives me a feeling that I can now expand my entourage and relieve myself somewhat of other things. . . . I am thinking now about an idea and editorial assistant rather than just the press

[447] The original is in the Agnes Meyer files, Princeton University Library.

man. For the latter I have a lead that is promising: John Steele, now of the Time Bureau in Washington, who has for years corresponded with us and is a dedicated supporter.

I most emphatically agree that a campaign must have much more imaginative and grand content than the mere bread and butter issues and the minor irritations that can be exploited at a lower level. You have stated it superbly: "the hope that great things will be hatched by this miscegenation." But I should very much doubt if a ringing declaration for world government was the answer. Of that perhaps we can talk again.

I am distressed that you are still shaky. But what did you expect with major operations and pneumonia? I am still shaky too, with a fraction of what you must have had and the advantage of a few years. You *must not* — and now it is my turn to be a little tough — exert yourself mentally over my affairs at the expense of your recuperation. This would not be serving me, let alone yourself and your family.

Affectionately,

ADLAI

Mrs. Meyer wrote to Stevenson about Eisenhower's attending the summit conference in Geneva, Switzerland. She added that international law had to be strengthened and mentioned the contribution Grotius made to international law in the seventeenth century. She said that she would talk to Senator Herbert Lehman about making sure New York was for Stevenson's nomination. She added, however, that Stevenson should not closely identify himself with her since she was going to speak at a White House Conference on Education in November and object to parochial schools receiving any federal funds. She also wrote that she was to make a speech favoring birth control. "After that you will have to pretend that you do not know me," she remarked.

To Mrs. Eugene Meyer [448]

August 12, 1955

My dear Agnes:

I have so much to report and so little time to report it in.

. . . I do not altogether agree that Eisenhower had nothing to do with the relaxation of tensions. Of course the firm policies of Truman and Acheson, Stalin's death, and [Anthony] Eden's initiative, paved the way but had Eisenhower not seen fit to reverse most of what they had said and done for two and a half years I doubt if much of value could have

[448] The original is in the Agnes Meyer files, Princeton University Library.

come from Geneva. Whether anything of value comes, of course, remains to be seen. I find from this illustration an example of the extraordinary naivete and disarming innocence of our President. But it is not every man who can let things get into a frightful mess and then get universal applause for correcting his own errors in part. I think even you would have to acknowledge this as an amazing talent! But, of course, the meeting proves, as you say, only one thing: people want peace. And I agree, further, that threats from without and anxiety from within create a noxious climate for democratic plants. But I think we are learning to live in an age of perpetual peril, albeit slowly, with convulsions of pessimism and optimism. While I know that international organization on a broader scale must lie at the end of this long corridor I can hardly believe that the time is ripe for much progress yet. What do you think of Streit's [449] proposal for a conference on the Atlantic Community? Even that seems to me *avant garde* thinking as of now. It seems to me, first, we ought to unify segments of Europe and then move onto larger spheres. Actually, the progress since the last war is phenomenal if you step back and shut your eyes.

I hope I *can* do something with this, and I wish you could be thinking in something short of final terms, which would be of help and hope to many earthy mortals.

All week the Democratic Governors have been coming out to call.[450] Their attitude is unanimous, confidentially, with the possible exception of [Abraham] Ribicoff of Connecticut, whose state chairman listens to him and then whispers confidentially that they really want to know what I want and when I want it. The others have been forthright to the last man, and I have talked to some 22 of the 27, including Averell [Harriman], whom I really like and respect and have for a long while. He has the inclination and has seen some lush green valleys from Tammany's heights. I am a little at a loss as to what to do other than be quite candid with him: if I am wanted and if the party thinks I am the strongest. This is what I have done. Meanwhile, he is canvassing the situation to get a more accurate measure of his own strength. He will get a lot of encouragement in a lot of places, which, knowing politics as you do, will be contradicted by the same people in talks to me.

I most eagerly want to see Herbert [Lehman] when he comes back. I think he will be most effective in avoiding any misunderstanding be-

[449] Clarence Streit, president of Federal Union, Inc., and a member of the board of the Atlantic Union Committee.

[450] The Governors' Conference was meeting in Chicago. The encouragements of the governors who visited Stevenson in Libertyville, and the statements issued by many of them afterward, were a major factor in Stevenson's decision to prepare for the 1956 campaign. See Davis, *The Politics of Honor*, p. 305.

tween Averell and myself, which is terribly important to me. I expect to be in New York for a couple of days around the 7th and 8th of September. I hope he is back by then; and I also hope you will be on exhibition for visits from admirers!

I see better what you mean about secrecy and an "inside job." What a wonderful phrase! We can talk more of this another time, but is all that religious and birth control activity necessary? At that point I suppose any "honest" politician has to say goodbye, and that I cannot do.

. . . Grotius' teachings didn't take root at once and at the moment what we are talking about is political material.

. . . I was literally enchanted by your remark: "If the administration boys keep on with their sudden love of the Russians, they will soon be using their security program to persecute civil servants for being *anti*-communist." It reminded me of what I had felt while the reports of that romance on the shores of Lac Léman were oozing in. In consequence I said at a press conference here the other night that I had never expected to see an American President pleading with a third-string Communist to please believe that he wanted peace. I suspect it did me no good — as usual! I shall read your Commonweal clip at the first opportunity, which will be in Canada since I am retreating for a fortnight of rest and writing.[451] I am 'way behind on some assignments and must catch up before the autumn catches up with me. How wonderful it would be to sit down and do nothing for quite a while — or would it!

. . . Mr. Meyer's intuition about coming financial trouble confirms rumblings that I have heard elsewhere. Surely a major item in a useful campaign will have to be thoughtful talk about the implications of peace to the economy. Isn't conversion to production for undeveloped countries on bold, imaginative financing plans an area worth much more exploration? And what would Mr. Meyer think of that?

But enough for now; and bless you my dear, dear friend.

Yours,
Adlai

Barbara Ward, during a visit with Stevenson, had lost a trinket in the form of an elephant. She had returned to Melbourne, Australia, when the following letter was written.

[451] In fact, while staying with Mr. and Mrs. Hermon Dunlap Smith in Desbarats, Ontario, he hired one campaign staff member and prepared to hire others. Ibid., p. 305.

To Mrs. Robert Jackson

August 12, 1955

My dear Barbara:

This morning I have your acknowledgement of the telegram. A few days ago I received the piece on Criticism and the day before that your exquisite "Collins." I am revelling in this flourishing and charming correspondence, but you are altogether too good to me. There was no trouble in sending out the little posse in search of a strayed or stolen golden elephant. That it came home empty handed distressed me so I was the more relieved to hear it was at least insured. I can't understand its disappearance and I suspect humbug and African magic of some kind. You may find it back in Accra nibbling in the garden. At all events, we have searched high and low and they have done likewise at and around the airport.

How Borden (not John Fell, who is resisting the blandishments of MRA [Moral Re-Armament] in distant parts) would have enjoyed lunch with you on board that fine ship. But I doubt if he could have made it on short notice in view of the rigors of his discipline and training, which seem to consist mostly of policing the camp and writing leaflets to fling at an imaginary enemy. Please tell me no more about voyages with nothing to do but sleep and eat and doze in the sun. That is what I was going to do this summer, as you well know. Instead, the place has been chaos, and some twenty-odd governors have been eating my food, drinking my liquor and chewing my ear for the past week, and some yet to come. But come Sunday or Monday I hope to drive away to Canada with my friends for a week or ten days of rest and fun. The latter is a conventional phrase meaning writing an introduction for the speech book on Criticism [452] (by and with some help from a charming, charitable and gifted ghost), doing a speech for Jamaica,[453] and the article for Coronet,[454] and an article on Africa.[455] It is equally certain I shall accomplish none of the foregoing and come back more agitated than ever (a) by the failure to have any rest, and (b) by the failure to accomplish any work. Anyway, it's always nice to know what is going to happen.

I am really so very, very grateful for all your contributions to my empty storehouse. Things have marched apace at increasing speed and I suspect I am for it "either willy or nilly," as the little boy said. I have

[452] The introduction to *What I Think.*

[453] Stevenson wrote his speech for the Jamaica Tercentenary Industrial Exhibition at Kingston on September 15, 1955, by hand.

[454] "If I Were Twenty-one," *Coronet*, December, 1955.

[455] "Africa: The Giant Awakens," *Look*, November 15, 1955.

resisted manfully and made fine speeches of genuine disinterestedness, so long I am afraid they have lost their sincerity as well as their eloquence. Averell [Harriman] has been here, panting with anxiety, but gallant, good and gracious as always. I am afraid he has seen some valleys from Tammany's highest peaks and will see more; or perhaps it is I who have seen the valleys and they don't look as green and inviting.

But I go on and on to no end or purpose. So enough — and my affectionate regards, to you dear Barbara, and to "himself" himself!

Love always, and much gratitude —

To W. Averell Harriman [456]

August 15, 1955

Personal and Confidential

Dear Averell:

I am anxious above all to avoid misunderstanding that might affect our personal relations. The friendship of Marie [457] and you and your constant counsel, encouragement and kindness have meant a great deal to me. I think you agree that in our circumstances we must take care not to be divided ourselves or let others divide us — which is S.O.P. in politics as you well know.

So I felt, after reflecting on the past week here in Chicago, that I should attempt to leave no doubt about my position, with you at least.

While avoiding any commitment to be a candidate for the past two years, I have lately told many party leaders that I would gladly attempt it again if there was extensive feeling in the party that I would be the strongest candidate against the Republicans. I have also said that because I have done it before I did not feel I should selfishly seek the nomination aggressively at this time or make any immediate announcement.

As you know, I have expressions of preference from many areas and more this past week from the Governors. And I strongly suspect because of the difficulty of precise communication many of our Democratic friends now consider me committed to run, and to say so at some opportunity in the not too distant future.

I gather from our talk that you are also importuned, and I am sure that many feel that you would be a stronger candidate than I. In these circumstances, I gather that sentiment on your behalf will be measured

---

[456] A carbon copy is in the possession of the editors.
[457] Mrs. Harriman.

around the country promptly. If you then feel our party's best interests will be served by your candidacy I hope you will promptly let me know so that we can talk it over to avoid misunderstanding and embarrassment. (As the delicatessen clerk said: "Lady, let's not get the wrong misunderstanding.")

Meanwhile, I will not make any public statement, although my friends will doubtless proceed with some preliminary planning.

It was good to see you — and I am ever so grateful to you for making the effort to come out to the country.

My tenderest sentiments to Marie.

Yours,

To Frank Lausche [458]

August 15, 1955

Dear Frank:

I was sorry I did not see you and Mrs. Lausche during the Governors' Conference. I had not wanted to talk "politics" (of which I've had altogether too much of late and doubtless you too) — but to have a reunion with friends whom I've seen all too little of late.

Knowing how busy you were I suppose I should have come into town to see you, but I didn't want to get caught up in that mass of press and people. Perhaps there will be another opportunity and if there is, please let me know. If you are by any chance coming this way again I should be delighted if you could stop off with me in the country.

My warm sentiments to your lady — who once introduced me to Ohio Liederkranz!

Yours,

The following letter was written from Desbarats, Ontario, Canada, where Stevenson was vacationing.

To Carol Evans [459]

August 19, 1955

Dear Miss E —

Borden & some of his pals want to buy a second hand auto in Honolulu. As usual I've capitulated. So please check his Spfd. [Springfield]

---

[458] Governor of Ohio. A copy is in A.E.S., I.S.H.L.
[459] This handwritten letter is in the possession of Miss Evans.

balance as of Aug. 1 and if it is not up to $1000 send a check for deposit to make up the difference.

All is well here — hot but it doesn't hurt. Lots of noise, children and commotion, but I doubt if I could have accomplished much anyway. I have a reservation returning on the 24th on Capitol airlines leaving the Soo at 2:50 and arriving Chicago via Detroit at 6:32. At least I think I have, but I can't now find my memorandum. I must have left it at home. The reservation is in the name of A. E. Stevenson. Please check with Capitol to see if it is correct. I'll assume it is unless I hear from you. Also please ask Midwest Airlines, Reliance 5-2813, to reserve a place for me on their #46 to Northbrook leaving Midway at 6:55 (Hope my plane isn't late) and tell Barney [460] to meet me at 7:15 at Sky Harbor that night.

I'll be in the office, early if not bright, on the 25th. And now to work — mid the wail of the outboards and the screams of children!

Yrs
AES

To Marc Connelly [461]

August 25, 1955

Dear Marc:

I was distressed to miss you and insist hereafter that all visits to my precinct be attended with proper advance notice.

I am the more disappointed because I have wanted to ask you for a long while if your wonderful "O! Caesar" story has ever been printed. That is, if there is lying about anywhere a copy of it which I could read again and again when my spirits are low — and the Romans too plentiful!

Yours,

Secretary of State Dulles, on August 24, sent Stevenson a copy of a statement he planned to make on the Israeli-Arab situation. The President would recommend that the United States make the following contributions to a settlement of existing problems:

1. Subscription to an international loan to enable Israel to discharge its obligation to the refugees which in turn will help them to get resettled;

[460] Stevenson's chauffeur.
[461] American playwright, author of *The Green Pastures* and numerous other works.

2. United States contribution to water projects which will develop more arable land which will aid in resettlement;

3. Good offices, if desired, to assist in making the frontier adjustments needed to convert the present armistice lines into permanent boundary lines;

4. United States participation in an international treaty guarantee, preferably sponsored by the United Nations, of the resultant boundary lines.

To Harry M. Fisher [462]

August 25, 1955

Personal and Confidential

Dear Harry:

Seeing you the other day reminded me that I have not had your counsel for a long time — even on Israel!

I enclose a copy of letter and speech received from Dulles today, and copy of my reply. While the proposals contain little that is new, they have the novelty of official sanction, and I thought they would interest you. You will recall that I have, on several occasions, suggested allied guarantee of the boundaries and American assistance toward refugee compensation. Water development projects have, of course, been American as well as United Nations policy for a long time, with the implication of assistance when agreement could be found. I personally rather doubt if our good offices in the border adjustment could be as effective or helpful as those of an outsider not previously implicated.

As the Secretary has written me in confidence, I must ask you to treat his comunication in the same way and to return the speech for my files.

With warm wishes, I am

Cordially yours,

To John Foster Dulles

August 25, 1955

Personal and Confidential

Dear Foster:

Thank you for your letter and copy of your speech on the Israel-Arab problem. I earnestly hope that these proposals, coming from an official source, will improve the situation, which, I agree, is both menacing and stubborn.

[462] Chicago judge and prominent Zionist.

I note that you make no reference to the Arab blockade of Israel, but I assume from the speech that you have reason to expect some reassurance on this score will be forthcoming if progress can now be made on refugees, border rectification and the fears of aggression.

In connection with the proffer of good offices for border rectification, it occurred to me, both during my visit and subsequently, that conditions being as they are, some other less involved nation might be more welcome in that regard.[463]

Good luck.

Sincerely yours,

To J. Scott Birnie [464]

August 26, 1955

My dear Mr. Birnie:

I am mortified that I have not acknowledged your letter of July 22 long before this. Actually, I have not only been away but I have also been wrestling with my decision — and I am not sure whether I have won or lost the match! At all events, you *are* "presenting an honor" to me, your letter to the contrary notwithstanding, and because I know what a good and lively lot the Liberals of Glasgow are, I have wanted all the more to accept the Honorary Presidency of the Club.

But I have reluctantly come to the decision that I must not. My reasons are manifold, but they largely relate to a consistency of behavior, both here and elsewhere, which, once broken, would cause me no end of difficulty and embarrassment. In short, if I do this at Glasgow University, why won't I do something similar at an American University; and if I do it at an American University, why not at many others, etc. etc.

I hope you will understand, and I hope you and the other members can also appreciate the depth of my gratitude.

With so many thanks, and warmest good wishes, I am

Cordially yours,

Gerald Johnson wrote Stevenson on August 11 that in 1952 Eisenhower was elected by eight million "sentimentalists" who never had voted before

---

[463] Dulles replied on August 30 that the question of the Arab blockade was sufficiently indicated by his statement that the Israelis "suffer from the economic measures now taken against them." The blockade question, he added, was "very much in my mind." He also wrote that the United States would welcome the good offices of another nation.

[464] President of the Liberal Club of Glasgow University.

and probably never would vote again. Johnson added that he never had encountered a person who voted for Stevenson who regretted it, but he had encountered a number who regretted voting for Eisenhower. Johnson also wrote that Eisenhower's "cold political war" against Democrats and his refusal to invite President Truman to lunch at the White House were "snide" and "petty." Johnson concluded by saying there was a whispering campaign in New York that Stevenson had one foot in the "grave and the other slipping."

To Gerald Johnson

August 26, 1955

Dear Gerald:

Nothing has lifted me — I was about to say uplifted me — more than your letter of August 11 for a long while. I would have acknowledged it before but have only now seen it on my return to [from] a brief escape to the dark woods of Canada.

I am fascinated and interested by your estimate of the situation and I hope it is published somewhere. It is the sort of thing that our rank and file desperately needs to hear. I have heard the same reasoning, but not as well expressed, from several sources. But it seldom breaks through the shrill drumbeat of the Republican press.

I emphatically agree that there has been an insensitivity and artlessness about this operation — sometimes called "administration" in Washington — which I could not altogether foresee. The pious way that good things are proclaimed and the way in which they are sabotaged and forgotten or repeatedly warmed over for fresh exhibition has, I hope, not gone unperceived. The treatment of Truman which I know about in detail is little short of an historical discourtesy.

I think you know my position and have expressed it to me better than I can to you. I have been a candidate once. There is no novelty or honor in a repeat performance which I have not already enjoyed. I can campaign only one way, I fear — my way. The important thing is to defeat this administration at the first opportunity, which is 1956. Therefore, the important thing is to select the strongest candidate. I have been loathe to assume by my own conduct that I was that person. Hence, I have tried to keep moderately quiet yet alive and listen to the voices. Of one thing I am positively sure, I want to beat the Republicans more than to advance Stevenson.

As to that rumor you heard about "one foot in the grave and the other slipping," let me say I never felt better, which may be a mistake from the party's point of view as well as mine!

Bless you.

Yours,

To Mrs. John S. Currie

August 30, 1955

Dear Mrs. Currie:

Your letter amused and stimulated me as always! I don't know about Norman Thomas and the New Republic, as my reading seems to have lapsed a little of late. (I have been vacationing in the wilds of Canada.)

I should like to do all of the thing you suggest, speaking incessantly, moving around, shaking hands, seeing things and people, etc. etc. The fact of the matter is I can hardly look after my home and family, my law practice, the Democratic party here and there — and I am bound to disappoint you and my dearest friends. Besides, if it falls to my lot to go into combat again I don't want to exhaust myself in the hot summer when the temperature is high. It is best illustrated by a remark I just read in the letter preceding yours in the pile:

Man on the street in Springfield, Illinois meets a friend and says: "I would like to see Stevenson the next President." Friend: "Oh no, he thinks too much. Ike is the greatest President since Washington, he is so friendly."

Yes, thinking is a lonely business and perhaps we should all give it up and join the Republicans.

But as to you, carry on, my charming battle axe!

Cordially yours,

p.s. Nor did I overlook that wonderful remark about "the Cheshire Cat has taken off for the golf course leaving the Grin to run things."

To Harry S. Truman

September 6, 1955

Dear Mr. President:

I seem to have the worst possible luck with your trips to Chicago. I am obliged to leave today for a political meeting in New York and then, on the 8th, down to the West Indies on a law job — and only one speech! — so I shall miss you at the Executives' Club. Moreover, I shall miss you in your hotel room, or at my house for the night which is what I have hoped for so often. I am more than a little disappointed.

[553]

I had thought to warn you about the Executives' Club but H.S.T. will take care of himself in such Republican surroundings and by the best possible method — candor.

With affectionate wishes to the "boss," [465] I am

Faithfully yours,

To Mrs. Eugene Meyer [466]

September 9, 1955

My dear Agnes —

After another frenzied day, including an interesting visit from Mayor [Robert] Wagner, I flew away from New York in this bright blue morning and have now arrived with my friends and clients in rain swept Miami for the night. We go on to Haiti in the early morning, and *before* I go I *must* get off this note to you, because my visit to your chateau is still very much with me.

First, my thanks for the bread and butter — and what B & B! Such a chef must be a constant moral duel. As for me, I should capitulate with hardly a struggle, and die with a very large trace. But, oh so happily! The fruit that Mr. Meyer thoughtfully gave me has accompanied us down here and enlarged the number of your debtors. What plums!

And, *secondly,* my visit has reminded me, or rather worked a miracle I somehow find it hard to explain. Never before have I dissolved so utterly with another human being. I don't understand your alchemy. But it has worked some magic with my spirit, my confidence and my perceptions of my role. I suppose I needed someone to whom I could unburden without self consciousness or affectation, someone who was both wise without being superior, and devoted without being maudlin. I could go on — if they were not clamoring so loudly for me "to join them in the bar" — but I think you detect what I mean in spite of these opaque and futile words. My visit, in short, was an important interlude for me. I can't, and have ceased to try to understand how an older woman, a total stranger, could suddenly, without at least the normal preliminaries of acquaintance give me both feminine understanding and masculine fortification, and mental provocation and moral confidence. Its a comfort. It is quite a lot of comfort! And I hope the tonic "takes" in this frail vessel.

Thanks, my dear Agnes, and I know better what people mean by a much abused phrase — "a remarkable woman."

And "remarkable" reminds me to add that Mr. Meyer's interest, friend-

---

[465] Mrs. Truman.

[466] This handwritten letter is in the Agnes Meyer files, Princeton University Library.

liness and helpfulness touched me deeply. The glimpses I had of the wide horizons of his life and experiences, the grace and humor that bubble up incessantly and the sober perspectives of a very wise and sophisticated man fascinated me. I hope I shall have more opportunities to drink at that fountain — and I don't mean just ancient scotch! I hope you will also thank him for his hospitality and, even more, for all the time he gave me. I'm afraid I may have kept him up much too late!

And now to Hispaniola!

> Affec.
>
> ADLAI

P.S. Mr. Meyer indicated that the Washington Post normally endorsed no candidates and that that would be its position, I gathered, next year. I guess that confirms what you suggested.

> AES

Robert Sherwood wrote on September 14, thanking Stevenson for writing him while he was in the hospital. Sherwood added that an editor of Fortune *told him that Stevenson's article "My Faith in Democratic Capitalism" (*Fortune, *October, 1955) was "superb."*

To Robert E. Sherwood [467]

September 23, 1955

Dear Bob:

Today I returned to Chicago after an interlude in the Caribbean — on business! Imbedded in my horrid pile is a pleasant surprise — your letter. Thanks. And thank God you are emerging with spirits and grip unimpaired. And what do you think was lying right next to your letter? Your article from Fortune,[468] sent to me by some egghead no doubt. And now I can read — and regret that I didn't write it.

> Love to you both,

To Estes Kefauver

September 23, 1955

My dear Estes:

So many thanks for your note from Russia. I envy you that journey, and hope to do it myself again after thirty years.

---

[467] A copy is in A.E.S., I.S.H.L.
[468] "There Is No Alternative to Peace," *Fortune,* July, 1955.

I have just returned from a visit to the West Indies — on business! — and also for a speech in Jamaica on the 300th anniversary of the British colony. On my way back I stopped in Washington briefly and tried to reach you by phone, thinking you might have returned during my absence. I am disappointed that I missed you and I hope I can hear something of your journey, somehow, after you return.

Cordially,

J. N. Heiskell, president of the Little Rock Arkansas Gazette, *announced on September 27 that Harry Ashmore, executive editor, had been granted a leave of absence to serve as personal assistant to Stevenson.*

To J. N. Heiskell

September 27, 1955

Dear Mr. Heiskell:

I feel as though I owed you a profound apology, or that you owed me an indictment for grand larceny, daylight robbery — call it what you please. At all events, I am grateful to you, sir, for the sportsmanship and charity with which you have permitted me to raid your staff and purloin Ashmore. I was tempted to say "my need is greater than thine," but I didn't have to say it.

I hope I shall have a chance to thank you in person for not obstructing my use of this delightful and gifted man. I hope some time also to counsel with you about the perils of public life.

With great respect and my warmest wishes, I am

Cordially yours,

James Warburg wrote Stevenson that enough people would vote for him if they were convinced that he rather than President Eisenhower offered the best hope of a lasting peace. Warburg added that he would send galley proofs of a new book that he had written.

To James P. Warburg

September 27, 1955

Dear Jim:

I have just returned from a trip to the Caribbean and find your letter of September 8. I am grateful. However, I wish it were possible for you to abstract (I hate that word) your ideas of the *essence* of the policy issues, as you say, and your ideas as to the overall approach to each. But, please, not another book! (My God, I am getting as bad as Ike!) But my desk is groaning and my staff — well, he's out to lunch!

Yours,

Dore Schary sent Stevenson a copy of a statement he made at a Democratic National Committee meeting in Los Angeles. Schary added: "Come on, coach — when do we start the schedule?"

To Dore Schary [469]

September 30, 1955

Dear Dore:

Well, it was certainly entitled to more than "proper" applause. What a remarkably versatile man you are: business, politics, money raising, speaking — and writing! — which warms my heart most.

Thanks for your kind reference to me. I have been listening attentively to the voices for a couple of years, and if what I think I hear is sincere, then I shall not evade the ordeal.

Just back from a University lecture in Texas; the lecture was good enough, the welcome far beyond that deserved, and Democratic politics improving briskly.

Regards to you, my dear friend.

Cordially,
ADLAI

To Mrs. Eugene Meyer [470]

October 3, 1955

Dear Agnes:

I find that the picture has not gone forward but it will presently. Evidently it was so large they could not find proper wrapping!

. . . I am so glad you thought well of my sister's piece.[471] I agree with you about that coy photo — and, indeed, photos, I suspect, will be my undoing — in sailor suits, Bermuda shorts, and heaven knows what is to come. I hope you can meet my sister some time. . . .

---

[469] The original is in the possession of the State Historical Society of Wisconsin.
[470] The original is in the Agnes Meyer files, Princeton University Library.
[471] Excerpts from Elizabeth Stevenson Ives and Hildegarde Dolson, *My Brother Adlai*, appeared in the *Ladies' Home Journal*, October, 1955.

I am distressed about the visit to Libertyville. I had looked forward to this on several counts — and I still will.

What you say about your writing I am sure is correct, and you are likewise accurate about my painstaking and profitless habits in that field. I have always felt that I was more self-conscious about utterances than anything else and still feel an incessant restlessness about their quality. I think you are right, that I shall have to learn something more about relaxation.

Further evidence comes from various directions that Averell [Harriman] *is* intent and determined and that your estimate of his intentions was more accurate than mine. I am a little disappointed, and I hope we can avoid any conflict. Your "intelligence" on this score is as helpful as anything that has happened to me thus far.

Affectionately,
ADLAI

Philip Graham wrote Stevenson suggesting that he and Mrs. Graham have lunch or dinner with him when they were in Chicago. Graham concluded his letter: "I view the possibility of my wife's meeting you with some trepidation, knowing the influence of her maternal inheritance" (she was the daughter of Mrs. Eugene Meyer).

To Philip L. Graham [472]

October 5, 1955

Dear Phil:

I have your letter and will be glad to lunch with you either day or dine with you on the evening of the third. Perhaps you and your wife would like to come out to my house at Libertyville and have dinner with me quietly and stay the night. If you prefer staying in town and dining at the [Marshall] Fields it is quite all right with me so far as I can foretell at this time.

Having "fallen" for her mother, I shall doubtless fall for your wife too, but it seems to me I am the one to worry, not you! After all, how much can a man stand in such anxious times!

Cordially,

Gerald Johnson wrote Stevenson that his speech at Green Bay, Wisconsin, on October 7 [473] was a splendid exposition of why the existing farm

[472] A copy is in A.E.S., I.S.H.L.
[473] See *What I Think*, pp. 30–37.

policy did the farmer no good, but that Stevenson failed to emphasize that the policy "doesn't do anybody else any good." Johnson concluded his letter: "Washington is going to be a nauseating mess for the next 12 months, for Ike isn't half as sick as the government.[474] It is the GOP elephant that has had the fatal heart attack."

To Gerald Johnson

October 11, 1955

Dear Gerald:

Either I'm handcuffed by circumstance and you aren't, or you have a combination of intestines and words I'm supposed to have but don't. It would be consoling to hang on to the first theory. I suspect the second has more to it.

Every word you say in your letter and notes about this farm business seems to me complete good sense. Except that I'm not sure the farm problem is not to some extent one of overproduction. I may have to leave out your ultimate description of the horny-handed gentry, and Lord only knows when and where I'll be able to use some of the rest of this double barreled language, but I'll be unhappy until that time comes. (It seemed to me that last week, when I dabbled with the problem at Green Bay, was not the time for it.)

Many thanks — and please keep on insulting what — in your only compromise with facts — you call my intelligence.

Cordially,

To Alicia Patterson [475]

October 11, 1955

Thanks & blessings for that wonderful edit.[476] It heartened me when I needed it! I'm a little irked by the goings on in N.Y. after all that has been said and done by and between us. I've done my best for the party & tried to play it straight and impersonally for 3 yrs. I've made no campaign on my own behalf feeling that the leaders about the country should indicate if they want me *again*. And then when they have — almost unanimously — along comes this crafty business.

I don't care, frankly, too much and it will force a lot of characters to come clean, but with the press, the money and the government all stacked against us plus peace and prosperity, it will not be easy for a

[474] President Eisenhower had suffered a coronary thrombosis on September 24, 1955.

[475] This handwritten letter is in the possession of Adlai E. Stevenson III.

[476] An editorial in *Newsday* supporting Stevenson for the 1956 presidential nomination.

Democrat, *any* Democrat, to win, with or without Ike. And now, to exploit an outside chance, A[verell] H[arriman] has or is kicking away the first chance in modern times for a major party out of office to agree on its candidate 10 months in advance and concert its effort and resources against the enemy instead of against each other, with all the lost momentum, injured feelings, wasted money and precious time.

Ho! Hum! But this was not to complain, but to thank you. . . .

Ever
AES

To Mrs. Eugene Meyer [477]

October 14, 1955

My dear Agnes:

I am way behind you and have many comments on your letters, but for now let me just say that I have had a call about Dean [Acheson] and have written him hoping that we might meet, if possible, in New York while I am there on Tuesday or Wednesday of next week. I should be glad to hear anything that Senator K[efauver]. has to say, but I would rather doubt the wisdom of putting any suggestions about "deals" into his head so far as I am concerned. The rumor is widespread, as you know, that Harriman will finance him in order to try to damage me on the off chance that Harriman would benefit ultimately. Personally I would doubt it, but one can hear anything you please from politicians about Senator K., who, as a matter of fact, I have always liked.

I haven't been troubled particularly by what has transpired, but I have been a little injured in my spirit by Averell's performance and, of course, Mr. Truman's intervention will have the effect of slowing up some of the professionals. In consequence the agreement in all directions seems to be that Stevenson clubs etc. should begin emerging rapidly and endorsements from leaders as quickly as possible to both get people committed and also to head off the head-off! I yearn for a talk with you, but New York looks pretty hopeless what with the encircling crowd, etc.

As to Mr. Gallup, I don't know him but should be glad to if a convenient occasion arose. I have never been a believer in polls, however, and have seen so many examples of rapid change of public opinion and the sheeplike qualities of my fellow men that while I think they have indicative value I feel that the attention politicians pay to them is disproportionate.

And would you, could you, ghost an article entitled "A Program For Children" for Parents' Magazine for me — about 2500 to 3000 words?

[477] The original is in the Agnes Meyer files, Princeton University Library.

The letter from the publisher, which I have disregarded for some two months or more says: "We would like your ideas about school construction and federal aid to schools, juvenile delinquency, aid to dependent children, child welfare, school health services, the school lunch program, etc. Our preference for the article would be to present a constructive program with very few political comments, but we still want the article, whatever you wish to say." I hate to impose on you and I usually reject these countless requests out of hand, but I am told this one has value because of the circulation in so many homes and with so many women who *should* be sympathetic to my views. Also, the editor, George Hecht, is a fan.

Affectionately and all too hurriedly,
ADLAI

P.S. I look forward so much to meeting your daughter and son-in-law [478] when they are here early in November, and I hope circumstances will permit me to hear his speech.

On October 9, 1955, the New York Times *reported that former President Truman at a press conference called by Governor W. Averell Harriman, of New York, gave Harriman high praise, saying: "If I were a resident of New York I know who I'd be for." Truman declined to say who he would be for if he lived in Stevenson's home state, saying, "They have three or four good men in the state of Illinois," and added that he would wait until the state convention had nominated a candidate.*

To Harry S. Truman [479]

October 15, 1955

Dear Mr. President:

I want you to know that all the feeling which seems to have been generated by what happened in New York last week-end has in no way affected my regard for you or my respect for your opinion. I am sure your motives are, as always, the best interests of the country and the party. I hear you are to be in Chicago October 29. I guess I am destined to miss you again, as I have a long standing engagement to speak in Duluth that night. If you are coming the day before, however, I hope I can call on you for a visit. I think it can be arranged quietly and

---

[478] Mr. and Mrs. Philip Graham.
[479] Stevenson made a copy of this letter, which he wrote by hand while in Syracuse, New York.

without publicity. Also, I should be back by Sunday noon in case you are staying over the week-end.

With warm regards to Mrs. Truman, I am

Cordially,

*Stevenson spoke at Queen's University, Kingston, Ontario, on October 15 on the subject "Partnership and Independence." *[480]* Afterward he visited New York City. The following letter was written in New York.*

To Arthur Krock [481]

October 18, 1955

Dear Arthur:

I've just read yrs of the 18th. Thanks! — this is the first time I've known what was going on or the utility of polls and samples.[482] Now I know — and I feel better — about politics, polls, pundits — and post toasties.

Bravo! Carry on and don't be discouraged if commoner clay is slow in catching up with such avant garde perception. Know, at least, that *I* am not far behind, and *ever* grateful —

Yrs

A. E. STEVENSON

To John Fischer [483]

October 21, 1955

Dear Jack:

Two things occur to me that I had wanted to talk to you about by telephone before I left New York, but circumstances did not permit.

(1) Can I *really* count on you for a draft of a letter thanking the State Central Committee of Minnesota for its endorsement, agreeing to enter their primary, and explaining why I am glad to offer myself for the battle against the Republicans?

(2) Cass Canfield's reminder of the report to the boys which I wrote about Africa causes me to wonder if it should be included in the book [484] as a little variant on the politics, statecraft, etc. If so, I suspect it will take a little editing. *Look,* I believe, is using only a couple of thousand

---

[480] See *What I Think,* pp. 225–231.
[481] This handwritten letter is in the possession of Mr. Krock.
[482] The October 18, 1955, column by Mr. Krock in the New York *Times* was a satire on "quickie poll samplings" on potential candidates.
[483] The original is in the possession of the State Historical Society of Wisconsin.
[484] *What I Think.*

words,[485] and there would be no objection to publication in January of the whole thing.

Hastily,

ADLAI

To Dean Acheson

October 21, 1955

Dear Dean:

I have your letter, which I find a little perplexing. I was referring to a conversation with Mr. Kopper.[486] However, be that as it may, I did not feel I could ask you to come up to New York to enlighten me on the Harriman and Secretary of State and H.S.T. situation, but another time I may.

Ever so many thanks for your interest and helpfulness.

With much affection to you both, I am

Cordially,

To Mrs. Eugene Meyer [487]

October 27, 1955

My dear Agnes —

. . . Thanks, thanks, thanks for all the news. There is so much to report and no time now to report it — except that I called Estes K[efauver]., as you suggested, by telephone, and we've arranged to meet without fanfare and trumpet about Nov. 10. (I'm still getting postcards from him from Asia! One today)

And now may I ask something more? Could you sometime sit down, close your eyes, think a little and put on paper the 3 or 4 things you object to most in this administration, and then the 3 or 4 things that should govern the thinking & direction of a new administration. I said somewhere that I was against Erratic foreign policy, single interest govt. and moral duplicity — and the reaction was that I was attacking the President's morals! Ho Hum!

Its wonderful to have a friend — with a brain!!!

Affec —

ADLAI

P.S. So glad to hear of Eugene's improvement.

---

[485] "Africa: The Giant Awakens," *Look*, November 15, 1955.
[486] Samuel Kopper, deputy director of the Office of Near Eastern Affairs of the Department of State, 1950–1952.
[487] This handwritten letter is in the Agnes Meyer files, Princeton University Library.

Gerald Johnson wrote Stevenson on October 15: "Well, nothing will induce me to admit that my ideas are unsound, but if you ever were reduced to expressing them in my words you wouldn't be nominated, you would be committed as having lost your mind."

To Gerald Johnson

October 28, 1955

Dear Gerald:

All right, if you won't let me use your words I will continue to use your ideas — and send along any new ones that occur to you from time to time.

I am seeing H.S.T. tomorrow to pay my courtesy call. I can hardly wait to hear what we both have to say!

Yours,

Senator John F. Kennedy wrote on October 23 that he was ready to issue a statement calling on the Democratic party to nominate Stevenson. Sam Rayburn, who had intended to issue a statement of support for Stevenson, withheld it because Lyndon B. Johnson was at work trying to win the Democratic nomination.

To John F. Kennedy

October 29, 1955

Dear Jack:

Thanks for your letter. I have talked with Sam Rayburn. He is withholding his statement pending the resolution of some Texas problems which I think you can surmise. He has little doubt that they will work out satisfactorily. Meanwhile, he suggested instead of talking to the [House] majority leader [488] by telephone he will write him a note of the same import.

In these confused circumstances I cannot be sure what effect it will have. He was quite candid in saying that the gentleman did not "like me" and I gathered that it was because of the fact that I was divorced.

I trust that you and Paul Dever [489] will proceed as you think best. As to the time of any announcement you care to make, for my part I don't have any strong feeling but the "advisers" seem to think the sooner the better for all concerned.

[488] Democratic Representative John W. McCormack of Massachusetts.
[489] Democratic governor of Massachusetts, 1949–1953.

I shall communicate with you from time to time as circumstances indicate. Meanwhile my warm wishes to you and your wife.

Cordially yours,

To Dean Acheson

October 31, 1955

My dear Dean:

Thanks for your letter. The mystery is resolved. Will you be in Washington the 9th and 10th of November? I have in mind that I might come there en route to Charlottesville where I must speak on the night of the 11th. I would like to take refuge in the seclusion of P Street [490] for a "spell." What would suit you best from the evening of the 9th to the 10th? The latter evening is promised to certain dark conspiracies. . . .

Yours,

P.S. Buffie may have made a swimmer out of Alice, but look what she did to me! [491]

To Gore Vidal [492]

October 31, 1955

Dear Mr. Vidal:

A brief trip to Canada and New York made it impossible for me to tell you before now how very pleased I am to have your good wishes. As you probably know, I plan to make an announcement soon and am greatly encouraged by your kind message.

Cordially,

MY FAITH IN DEMOCRATIC CAPITALISM [493]

I am invited by the editors of *Fortune* to look forward with them toward 1980 and to join in the suggestion of goals for American achievement during the next quarter-century. The ultimate goals are, of course, very clear: peace, freedom for ourselves as individuals, and a realization of man's place in a meaningful scheme of things. But it is to a narrower

[490] The Achesons' home in Washington.

[491] Mrs. Acheson, the former Alice Stanley, had spent summers in Charlevoix, Michigan, as a child and had been a playmate of Stevenson and his sister. See Ives and Dolson, *My Brother Adlai*, pp. 45–46, excerpts from which appeared in the *Ladies' Home Journal*, October, 1955.

[492] The original is in the possession of the State Historical Society of Wisconsin.

[493] The text is from *What I Think*, pp. 3–17. The article appeared in *Fortune* magazine, October, 1955.

focus that I am asked to address myself; namely, the future of the relationship between two great forces in America's structure — the force of business and industry on the one hand, and on the other, the force of government, particularly the federal government.

If it is expected that comment on this subject by one sometimes close to government — particularly a Democrat! — must inevitably be antagonistic and critical, and slanted against "Big Business," I promise disappointment. I think of this relationship between business and government as essentially one of co-operation between two institutional forces wholly dependent upon each other. If there were but one twenty-five-year goal to fix upon in this area it would be, for me, to stop the talk about a basic antagonism between American business and government, and replace such nonsense with a recognition of the common purposes and obligations of these two cornerstones of democratic capitalism.

We all make the mistake of thinking about institutions, such as business and government, as ends in themselves. Most of the friction between businessmen and bureaucrats in this country has arisen from their constantly having to remind each other that neither government nor business is an end in itself, that they both are only institutional means to the ends of individual purpose; and that whether the relationship between them is "good" or "bad" is measureable solely in terms of how the relationship pays off in the lives and satisfactions of 165 million people, or, more broadly, of all humanity.

I find the measure of the strength of this relationship in the fact that the past quarter-century has seen in America the most extraordinary growth any nation or civilization has ever experienced. Our rise in population has been largely a function of our increased prosperity and productivity; our millions of new mouths to feed are better fed than fewer mouths were only twenty-five years ago. The possessions of a modest family today exceed those of a "prosperous" one in 1930. While the population of some unhappy countries rises against the most dreadful counterpressures and in spite of wishes that it could be restrained, our numbers increase out of a sense that we can well afford such an increase. An important part of the example we show the world is the fact that we are the nation of the most powerful consumers on earth.

It was not always so. It was not so twenty-five years ago. It is a curious thing that the two institutional forces in the democratic capitalistic society that contributed most directly to this emergence of the powerful consumer during this quarter-century seemed to snarl at each other every step of their common way. The bounding prosperity of postwar America has been due in large measure to processes in which government and business have in effect played complementary and co-operative roles.

The New Deal legislation of the thirties helped to provide a "built-in" consumer demand that business could then work to satisfy, and the increase of 70 per cent in the scale of the American economy between 1939 and 1944 was achieved by the closest co-operation between government and industry in America's war effort.

Yet, in spite of this practical realization of common interests and common goals, it became part of the ritual of New Deal politics to castigate a business system that has always been recognized by Americans as the only permanent source of the jobs and consumer purchasing power which "the government" was trying to restore. And in the meantime the businessmen, who rose from prostration to record-breaking prosperity through satisfying a multibillion consumer demand that was stimulated and buttressed by New Deal legislation, became the bitterest critics of this New Deal legislation.

I know the arguments that business *might* have recovered even faster in the later thirties if it hadn't been for government "regimentation" (also referred to as "drift") and "exercise of arbitrary power" (also referred to as "indecisiveness"). If those arguments ever needed answer they have it in the decision of the present "businessman's government" in Washington not to curtail the federal programs that underwrite consumer purchasing power but to enlarge them. Nor in current talk of "getting government out of business" does there appear to be much recognition that government is in business to the tune of about $15 billion worth of military orders each year and is therefore playing, whatever the theory of the matter, a decisive part in keeping demand steady through the whole economy.

One of the future goals for American government and American business must surely be a fuller recognition that the maintenance of demand in the interests of the consumer — which is one of the few things everybody in this country is — is basic to both.

A broader aspect of the common purpose of business and government in America emerges from recognition of the new and tremendous sense of commonality that has come over this nation in the past twenty-five years. The individual no longer stands alone. His smallest community is larger, and more diverse in its services. His light and power come no longer from his own windmill or from some small local utility company, but usually from a vast network. His bank is strongly interconnected with its fellows, and his deposits are insured. The same news reaches him and his neighbors, and faster than it ever did before. An incredible linkage of wires and roads and co-operative enterprises, public and private, has taken isolation (and now isolationism) from all but the remotest homes in America.

In ways we hardly realize, this commonality brings inevitable interweavings of the functions of business and government. When the services of even two people are joined there are decisions of "governing" to be made; and when thousands and then millions invest or work together in a common business enterprise, their dealings together become more and more like the relationships we call government. What we used to think of as the "decentralized decision-making of the market place" has given way to various processes of large-scale private institutional decision-making remarkably like that of government in both its methods and its results. We constantly see in such things as labor unions, corporations, and trade associations, and in the "bargaining" that goes on between them, a reflection of the private institutional needs for "government."

As a people we are doing world-shaking and history-making things today — partly as the result of individual genius, but perhaps even more because we have learned of the powers of individuals working together. A brilliant professor turned businessman, Beardsley Ruml (who reformed the nation's thinking on how to collect the income tax and has more recently been trying to perform an equal miracle on our notion of the federal budget),[494] has declared that the greatest economic discovery of the twentieth century so far is the realization that the wisely directed actions of all of us, *as a whole*, can compensate for the aberrations or misfortunes of a few. A. J. Toynbee suggests that three hundred years from now the twentieth century will be remembered, not for its wars, not for its conquests of distance and disease, not even for the splitting of the atom — but for "having been the first age, since the dawn of civilization, some five or six thousand years back, in which people dared to think it practicable to make the benefits of civilization available for the whole human race." I hope the judgment of this great historian comes true. My instincts tell me it will.

It was in America that the first practical stirrings of this great idea began. We must bring the idea to such perfection that it will save the very civilization it has awakened. Another goal, then, for 1980 America — so that we may disprove George Orwell's terrifying prediction for 1984 — is that this process of our growing commonality must and will be everywhere recognized and acknowledged, *not so that it can be senselessly accelerated, but so that it can be wisely guided and controlled.* I hold no belief in economic determinism; I bow to Shakespeare, not Marx, when I declare that there is a tide in the affairs of men, and that we had better acknowledge it.

This new sense of commonality is not without its dangers. Security,

[494] See "The New Old Plan," *Newsweek*, August 8, 1953, and "What Is the Ruml Budget Program?" *Newsweek*, October 5, 1953.

whether economic, political, or social, has become an individual and national obsession. I wonder if we fully realize the relationship between this yearning for security and the problem of maintaining our civil liberties. Security doesn't come free. Sometimes its price — or the price some would charge for it — is conformity and groupthink, and so it becomes part of the future joint obligation of the forces of business and government to respect, yes and protect, those elements of individuality that commonality threatens.

It is not true that the individual rolls around today like a kernel of grain between the upper and nether millstones of Big Government and Big Business — but there is a danger here that is great enough to warrant our keeping such a picture always in mind. Even as we become increasingly vigilant in our battle against the debilitating force of Communism we must be aware of another enemy that creeps upon us even more quietly and insidiously: the army of mass mediocrity, with banners flying.

Democracy's literature is full of warnings against the overpowering of the individual by the agencies of government and business. A hundred years ago John Stuart Mill deplored society's encroachments on the individual. John Ruskin prophesied the destruction of aesthetics by the industrial revolution. Lord Acton used some of his careful, rationed counsel to warn that democracy's flaw might prove to be — despite its protestations of the state's sublimation to the individual — a lack of moral criteria. Learned, sensitive, eloquent, these eminent Victorians voiced their concern that progress in the arts of statecraft and industry might make its intended beneficiaries its victims. Perhaps our survival in the face of these unhappy prophecies shows how wrong they were. Surely the individual is still today not *wholly* fenced in, except by the Kremlin, which Mill did not happen to be thinking of. As for the destruction of aesthetics, it turns out that in some ways — in modern design, in support of artistic efforts — industry is one of the best friends aesthetics has in the modern world.

Yet we know, from warnings that are more sensed than seen or heard, that all is not well with our status as individuals. Consciously or unconsciously, we are erecting battlements against our own accomplishments. Man in the individual sense today is not man's only adversary. We are concerned, too, about a strange, not wholly definable force in which there are at least the identifiable elements of "government" and "technology" and "massiveness" in this age of mass population, mass education, mass communications — yes, and mass manipulation. Indeed it seems that at mid-twentieth century mass manipulation is a greater danger to the individual than was the economic exploitation in the nineteenth century; that we are in greater danger of becoming robots than slaves. Surely it is part of the challenge of this next quarter-century that industry and government and the society they both support must find new and better ways of restoring scope to that strange eccentric, the individual.

Nostalgia won't help. We shall never dis-invent the airplane, which sets down the evil of Communism in our back yard instead of leaving it to fester outside our notice five thousand miles away. We shall never recover the quiet privacy the individual had before the telephone, the hand camera, and the microphone. We shall not relock the atom. A small fraction of our citizens have already come out flatly for government by lie detector. Some businesses maintain, in the name of security, "black lists" that in effect can deprive a man of the right to work without inquiry, due process, or even hope of ultimate redress. I can't help suspecting that some social scientists and even psychiatrists would love to find a combination of electronic devices by which every citizen could be measured for the slightest personal or social aberrations from some assigned "norm," and I suspect they will get it from our onrushing technologists. On this kind of assault on the individual I stand precisely where Calvin Coolidge stood on sin: I am agin it. I propose to keep on being agin it.

But we shall have to learn the art of coexistence with many strange things in the future, some of them perhaps even stranger than Communism. Technology, while adding daily to our physical ease, throws daily another loop of fine wire around our souls. It contributes hugely to our mobility, which we must not confuse with freedom. The extensions of our senses, which we find so fascinating, are not adding to the discrimination of our minds, since we need increasingly to take the reading of a needle on a dial to discover whether we think something is good or bad, or right or wrong.

Deepest pride in the accomplishments of America's inventive genius is no warrant for congratulating ourselves on any best-of-all-possible-worlds. Materially we can — and will — do better still. But spiritually, morally, and politically, I don't think we are doing so well. Both industry and government are contributing enormously to the almost unbelievable advance of technology in America — but both must become increasingly aware of their moral and spiritual responsibilities. The representative of a great manufacturing concern, speaking about the phenomenon we call automation, concluded: "I don't think it is the part, nor can it be the part, of industry to try to plan the social aspects of this thing." It seems to me, to the contrary, that industry is eventually, with government, going to have to do its full share of thinking about the sociology as well as the economics of such things as automation and the split atom.

The more realistic and broad-gauge view is suggested by David Sarnoff's comment, in an earlier article in this *Fortune* series, that "if freedom is lost, if the dignity of man is destroyed, advances on the material plane will not be 'progress' but a foundation for a new savagery." [495]

There is increasing realization that one of the biggest problems of these next twenty-five years will be what we are going to do with "the new leisure" which it appears will develop as one of the fruits of the new technology. As people learn how to live longer after their service in the regular work force is done, as machines and "feedbacks" and push buttons take on more and more of the job of production, as the inevitably shortened work week materializes — with these things there comes a whole host of new adjustments to be made. No one need fear the long-range effects of machines replacing men, but the adjustment is going to require responsible and thoughtful administration, and the new leisure will mean new happiness only if care is taken not to confuse leisure with just plain having nothing to do.

It is inevitable that government in America will be called upon during this next quarter-century to meet the social implications of these ever more rapid technological advances, and I see no reason why American industry should not participate fully and freely in this enterprise. There seems to me no escape from this obligation. It just will not do to leave all worrying about our souls to the educators, the clergy, and the philosophers. The men to whom mass America tunes its ear today are businessmen — indeed, they seem to have more influence on youth than the schools, more influence on the devout than the clergy, more influence on the wicked than the thought of perdition. With this prestige goes a responsibility that can be given no artificial boundaries.

I shall not attempt to suggest a particular role for industry in the transforming of technology's dark threats into bright promises. Part of this role will undoubtedly lie in an increased laying aside of great funds to foster education in all fields, not confining such funds to the sciences or to what is of immediate or "practical" significance. The day of the great individual philanthropist is nearly over, and industry must step into this breach. Even as I write this there comes to my desk a list of fifty research memoranda being prepared as part of a joint project of a large private corporation and a branch of the federal government. Would that just one of the fifty memoranda related to the heart of industrial progress — instead of all of them to its hands and feet and muscle! Adolf A. Berle, Jr., suggests in his recent book [496] a broader emergent

[495] David Sarnoff, "Fabulous Future," *Fortune*, January, 1955.
[496] *20th Century Capitalist Revolution* (New York: Harcourt, Brace & World, 1954).

concept of the corporation as an instrument of social leadership and responsibility, chargeable with a stewardship as broad as all the implications of its economic effects. This, it seems to me, must be the direction of our progress.

It could be hoped that one of the dividends of a "businessman's government" might be a merging of the thinking *both* in business and in government about economic and human affairs. And yet there has been quite a lot of talk from high government spokesmen about being "conservative" in economic affairs and "liberal" in human affairs. I don't know how this works where something like unemployment or social security is involved. Are those "economic" or "human" affairs?

If there is value in a definition of "conservatism" that would cross economic-human and business-government lines (and even Republican-Democratic lines), may I reiterate what Thomas Carlyle said a hundred years ago: the conservatism that *really* conserves is that which lops off the dead branch to save the living tree. Our American economy has fewer dead branches than that of any other nation, I am sure; but that we shall need pruning and spraying and the application of new fertilizers and growth regulators in the future as in the past, I have no doubt. Should it perhaps be part of our purpose in these years ahead to recognize that the process of conservation must be a joint government and business responsibility, and that division of function between "human" and "economic" is unrealistic in today's complex society?

I hope this quarter-century will see a frank recognition that every new frontier in American progress has been, and will always be, opened up by the *joint* enterprise of business and government. Great respect for the concept of the "rugged individualist" (usually incorporated) is no warrant for the illusion that modern America was *created* by businessmen — any more than it was by Senators or the Founding Fathers. Before colonial America could emerge from its colonialism, and a few cities could become interconnected with a subsistence agriculture and the tinkering sheds of a few ingenious Yankees, the federal government had to assert its power. Before America could become a great industrial nation the federal government had to assert its power over territory in terms of a U.S. Army that would explore and protect; in terms of a federal treasury that would regulate and expand the national credit; and in many other terms of a state that would hold title to the whole public domain until private entrepreneurs could slowly, on terms adjudged to be for the public benefit, take over vital business and industrial procedures. There were very few businessmen (and no government officials) in the Conestoga wagons that toiled across the West only a little more than a century ago; their time and place and function came later.

No; business did not create America or the American way. The American way was created in a complex collaboration whereby the federal government offered to individuals the best soil and nurture for enlightened capitalism ever devised — and the individuals took it on the generous terms offered.

Nor is this interdependence of government and business reflected only in historical vignettes. We accept today as one of our great principles that operation of industry is a properly private function. Yet so long as technology burgeons, the interrelationships between government and industry will continue to grow more complex, not less. Where technology disemploys workers, government will be asked to help. It must help. Where it creates surpluses, government will be asked to help. It must help.

There is no reason to be afraid of growing complexity; indeed our option is to deal cheerfully and courageously with growing complexity — or to go over the authoritarian abyss. I see no reason why the need to confront complexity is more ominous merely because it may require new formulas of private-public co-operation.

A fascinating future relationship between government and business, for example, will occur when Alaska is truly "opened." Before business and industry can begin to pour Alaska's resources into the mainstream of the world's commercial life, millions of dollars' worth of trunk and access roads will have to be built, and someone will have to complete the geological mapping of 586,400 square miles of territory so that private mining companies will have some notion of what, where, and how great the mineral treasure of Alaska really is — facts unknown today. Shall we organize a purely private Alaskan Corporation of America to take all these risks? Or may it be necessary to accept some subvention from the federal government to get things going? Regardless of our preachments we may be sure it will be the latter, as in large part it already has been.

In spite of resounding keynote speeches and business-convention oratory, it is an obvious fact that this pattern of co-operation between government and private enterprise runs through our economy from end to end. One of the most pervasive of all influences is without doubt the tariff — that massive governmental intervention that is generally left off the standard anathema list of many businessmen. Much of the work of the Atomic Energy Commission is undertaken through the agency of private corporations. Business in the Northwest has certainly not been retarded by cheap public power. And just how much of the newspaper and magazine industry is carried by the taxpayer through the government's massive subsidy of second-class mail?

There will be a testing of a good deal of unthinking talk when it comes time to consider translating into action the Hoover Commission's recommendations for liquidating the structure of government lending agencies. It seems a conservative prognosis that these recommendations will be loudly honored for their expression of the sacrosanct and sound principle of the least-government-possible and that it will then be more quietly decided that most of these agencies (with perhaps a little exterior redecoration) come within the least-possible limits.

I am not suggesting that American business and industry owe either an unpaid debt or any attitude of servile gratitude to the federal government. The creative record of American capitalism is altogether too strong and dignified in its own right to call for subservience to any other force. What I am suggesting, however, is that there could be a good deal more realism and quite a lot less nonsense in the recognition by the business community of the interdependence, if you will, of the two essential democratic capitalistic institutions of business and government. We are past the point of adolescence in a relationship where it once was perhaps understandable that those who profited in largest sum from the operation of our system of things might still clamor about the federal government as a childishly operated nuisance, which hampers business, which intrudes, which confiscates or expropriates profits, and in a thousand ways spoils all the fun and is constantly threatening to "socialize" all America by creeping. It seems to me an essential element of our present maturity to recognize that the relationships between the two institutions do not consist exclusively of government's recourseless taxation or browbeating of business.

We too rarely realize how very great and needless a strain is placed on this relationship just by the verbal violence that is indulged in in describing its elements. "Economic royalists" was an unfair and unfortunate epithet. To call the TVA "Communism," or rural electrification "Socialism" — the list of such cliches is long — is a kind of nonsense that insults the facts and serves only evil. It is an important goal for America-1980 that what is publicly said or reported regarding such things be better adjusted to what is generally true. This will require, among other things, an enormous improvement in the standards and practices of American journalism.

Before leaving the subject of the interaction of government and industry, I should speak of a vital area in which failure to formulate joint and consistent policies can have the effect not simply of weakening the domestic economy but of imperiling America's position of leadership in the free world. I refer, of course, to those tariff, trade, and custom practices that hamper and addle world commerce to the disadvantage of the whole Western world, ourselves included. As a goal for the future, to be achieved many years sooner than distant 1980, I would certainly hope for relaxed restrictions on world commerce — a relaxation not just on tariffs — to the end of freer and freer trade among the nations. Policies that were appropriate only in the day when it was accurate to speak of "our infant industries" can lead to social, political, and economic misfortune in our industrial manhood. And insofar as the need for capital and technical assistance in the less developed areas has become perhaps the greatest limiting factor on expanding world trade, I would hope, too, for new and courageous action by public and private agencies in this field as well. On tariff reductions the government (under Democratic administrations, at least) has led the way since 1934 and earlier. In providing capital and technical "know-how" for world development, it is the government that has made the start. Business must educate its members to follow.

But perhaps the most urgent problem that will be set before government and business alike by pressures generated beyond America's frontier will prove to be the issue of disarmament. We cannot deny that the overwhelming desire of our own people and of all the world's peoples is to be rid of the nightmare of atomic war. There are some signs that the Communists are feeling this enormous pressure of popular longing for peace. It is not inconceivable that in the next decade we shall be required to take the lead in dismantling a part of our vast military structure of preparedness. The impact upon the national economy of falling expenditures for arms will be profound and it will take the best efforts and the concerted efforts of government and business to see that the transition from a large measure of military spending to an overwhelmingly civilian economy is accomplished without a downward spiral and grave dislocation in the whole economic system. Neither government nor business can manage that alone. It would be well if its implications were examined jointly — and soon.

Perhaps most of what I have mentioned here comes together in a suggestion that we might profitably think in terms of a doctrine of "separation of powers" in this area of business and government relations — a separation resembling the constitutional differentiation between the executive, the legislative, and the judicial in government itself. This is a formula for "checks and balances," and yet essentially for co-ordination and co-operative functioning toward common goals. The future of government and business does not consist in *either one* having ambitions to take over the functions of the other. It is an essential goal for the future to keep their separation jealously guarded.

Government in America has *always* regarded the operation of industry as a purely private function. To return to an earlier example, even the newest-biggest of all governmental agencies, born in the early days of the Atomic Age and the Fair Deal — the AEC [Atomic Energy Commission] — operates its vast, complex, "monopolistic," and largely secret domain through private industrial contractors. But business has yet to show a comparably broad and tolerant understanding of the legitimate domain of government. In fact, some sections of the business community could not do better than follow, in this regard, Dr. Johnson's advice, and clear their minds of cant and prejudiced misinformation, not to say the downright nonsense about "governmental dictatorship," and, of course, "creeping Socialism" that all too often, as a species of businessmen's groupthink, takes the place of responsible consideration of the proper functions of government in free society.

This idea of a different kind of "separation of powers" does not require being against "businessmen in government." Not at all. But it does suggest that when businessmen, like anyone else, are being selected for government posts, it should be because of their talents for the job of government and for no other reason. To the extent that "businessmen in government" means the introduction into government of the ideals and practices of efficiency for which American business is justly famous — and to the degree that it also means adding to government councils an intimate understanding of industry and commerce — to that extent and degree this is all to the good and none should object. The case is very different, though, wherever a businessman brings with him to government any ideas other than a completely objective and independent concept of the public good.

An intelligent businessman,[497] now a member of the current administration, said before he reached his present public eminence: "Commercial interests are not the same as national interests." How right he was, and is. Although commercial interests and national interests can and usually do walk a certain distance hand in hand, no full identity between them can ever be forced, and any attempt to force it would be apt to end in misery, or disaster, or both — and for both.

Over the years, the federal government, in Republican and Democratic administrations, enacted the Sherman and the Clayton [antitrust] acts to prevent concentrations of power in plutocratic hands, and no wiser or more beneficial legislation has ever been enacted in America — for business. In Europe, where these laws are incomprehensible, and a cozy hand-in-glove-ism between governments and industries has its expression in the cartel system, we see many brilliant accomplishments. But we do *not* see any properly significant diffusion downward of the profits and benefits of the industrial system, which, in this country, con-

[497] Unable to identify.

stitutes our most effective safeguard against radical infection in any large masses of our public.

It was governmental intervention, beginning about fifty years ago, that broke up the trusts. If American business had remained in the image of the "oil trust," the "steel trust," the "sugar trust," the "whiskey trust," America as we know it today would never have come into existence, and the leadership of the modern world would almost certainly reside elsewhere — doubtless in a totally Prussianized or Communized Europe, with the British Isles reduced to the status of a tourist resort, and America still a giant agricultural bumpkin among the nations.

Events took a very different turn. We are not yet fully grown up to our responsibilities of world leadership, and we groan understandably under the burdens placed upon us. But despite two hideous wars, the history of the twentieth century is by no means so tragic — yet — as it might be, and the vast area of hope still alive in the world lies squarely here, with us. The past interactions between American government and American business, brawling and ill-natured though they were, have been a major determinant of the shape and course of the modern Western world. Given an improved respect and understanding between these properly separated forces in America, I can look forward to the next twenty-five years with confidence, and think of all the Western world, potentially, as a land of hope and glory, Mother of the Free.

"What is past," says the inscription in front of the National Archives Building in Washington, "is prologue." To this I say amen.

Stevenson spoke at a Democratic party rally at Duluth, Minnesota, on October 29.[498] Governor Orville Freeman and Senator Hubert H. Humphrey endorsed him for the nomination for President.

In the week following his return from Minnesota, Stevenson spent two days in Passavant Hospital in Chicago for a complete physical examination.[499]

To Orville Freeman [500]

November 2, 1955

Dear Orville:

We arrived alive! It was a wonderful visit and Bill [Blair] and [I] exchanged weary remarks on the way back about the vitality of the

---

[498] See *What I Think*, pp. 38–42.
[499] See Davis, *The Politics of Honor*, p. 318.
[500] A copy is in A.E.S., I.S.H.L.

Minnesota leadership. Even more remarkable than you and [Hubert] Humphrey, however, are Jane [501] and Muriel.[502] To the former please give my love and sympathy, although I suspect she needs none of the latter.

You are more than good to me and it is less than adequate to say that I was more than delighted by my visit. I learned a lot, not the least being what a miracle you and Hubert have wrought in Minnesota. In time your biographies will be standard reading for young and politically conscious Americans — but I am afraid it will discourage more than encourage!

And now I will detain you no further except to say thanks — and my affectionate regards to you both.

Yours,

To Mr. and Mrs. Hubert H. Humphrey [503]

November 2, 1955

My dear friends:

The doctors have discharged me — with a satisfactory report of condition. Indeed, I seem to be better off than a man has any right to be [at] my advanced age. So that avenue of escape is closed. I reflected long and happily, between the tortures, about my visit to Minnesota and your infinite kindness. But I also felt a little weary, I confess, when I thought again of the energy of Messrs. Humphrey and Freeman and their remarkable wives. However, it is infectious, and with a little more of you two around I might feel somewhat vigorous and combative myself. Perhaps I will have to ask for a blood transfusion one of these days.

At all events, it was a happy experience and I was profoundly touched by all that befell me there, and most of all by your loyalty and good will. Blessings!

Yours,

To Eugenie Anderson [504]

November 2, 1955

My dear Eugenie:

I enjoyed my little visit with you in Duluth but it was altogether too little! As I am sure you realize, I was profoundly flattered by what tran-

---

501 Mrs. Freeman.
502 Mrs. Hubert Humphrey.
503 A copy is in A.E.S., I.S.H.L.
504 The original is in the possession of Mrs. Anderson.

spired there and the apparent confidence in me by the Minnesota organization. And I should feel even better about it all if as this situation develops I could be sure of your active participation and leadership.

With warm regards and my thanks for your kindness, I am

Cordially yours,

ADLAI

Edward J. Miller, Jr., Stevenson's friend from his State Department days (1945–1948), wrote on November 1 that he had joined the Stevenson for President movement.

To Edward J. Miller, Jr.

November 2, 1955

Dear Eddie:

Bless your heart. And welcome aboard. But I am not quite sure when the boat is going to sail, although I have a vague idea of the destination. I hope to heaven it won't be long before we can have a proper talk, and if you come this way reserve an evening for me.

Yours,

To Mrs. Eugene Meyer [505]

November 2, 1955

My dear Agnes:

I am just back after two days in the hospital and all the horrid tests and Chinese tortures they could contrive. I felt I dare go no further until I had my "cardiac certificate" and other medical passports. So I advanced my annual medical checkup a bit. The results were satisfactory. Indeed, I seem to be healthier than a working man of my age has a right to be. And on top of my desk your letters and the Post and Times editorials about Eugene Meyer's 80th birthday. It makes me feel a little humble and weary. How can anyone stay in such spirits, such health and such usefulness so long?

It must have been a memorable party, and how I wish I could have been there to see you amiably slaying your bewildered adversaries. I wish so much that you would send me Earl Warren's speech [506] if you can conveniently lay hands on a copy. Or, rather, I will ask Philip [Graham] for it when I see him tomorrow. . . .

[505] The original is in the Agnes Meyer files, Princeton University Library.
[506] Unable to identify.

From what I have heard about him, a proper reply to that gentleman from Arizona, Mr. Goldwater,[507] might be if he is alive in this century so is Pharaoh. As to Reuther,[508] I have had some calls from him lately, but we have so far failed to make a mutually convenient appointment because of my week-end in Minnesota and the two days in the hospital. I suspect we will meet before long, but just when I don't know, possibly in Washington en route to Charlottesville. But if I don't see him first I think the thing for you to do would be to find out precisely how he feels before he knows too much about how you feel. Other top CIO people have been here pledging me the usual undying fealty.

I am afraid you have been misinformed about my position on labor in 1952. I took the position that we had to improve the Taft-Hartley Act and that we should repeal it. The question of method is where the word "repeal" came in. I believe I often used the phrase "repeal and replacement." Actually, as you know, my position was identical with [Robert] Taft's, whose draft bill was in the form of the repeal of the Taft-Hartley Act and an enactment of a new bill. That was my idea and it was constantly misrepresented by Arthur Krock and others. But if that was the only misrepresentation I suffered I might be less suspicious of the press. Any friend of labor would be a fool to propose repeal without replacement of the Taft-Hartley Act, because with it would go the collective bargaining procedures.

My trip to Washington I want to keep as closely guarded as possible to avoid embarrassment and pursuit. I shall certainly talk with you on the phone, and come out for that lunch if I can. But meanwhile I look forward to an animated evening with your daughter and son-in-law tomorrow at my little house in the country. Indeed, I shall drive them out, which will be the most perilous experience they have had for quite a while.

And among the most famous of last lines will be Agnes Meyer's: "Nothing amuses me more than when people take me seriously."

Affectionately,

ADLAI

Modie J. Spiegel, chairman of the board of Spiegel, Inc., wrote praising Stevenson's Fortune *article, "My Faith in Democratic Capitalism." Mr. Spiegel expressed his opinion that sustained consumer purchasing power was vital to American business and added that he felt the humor in Stevenson's 1952 campaign speeches "went over the heads of the average voter."*

[507] Republican Senator Barry Goldwater.
[508] Walter Reuther, head of the United Auto Workers.

To Modie J. Spiegel [509]

November 4, 1955

Dear Modie:

It was good to have your letter, and it reminds me of our "collaboration" a long time ago in a worthy cause.[510]

I am glad we agree again on the importance of consumer purchasing power as the precedent to investor prosperity, not to mention the economic balance that is impossible when agriculture is depressed. I am sure you will appreciate full well that the real reason for the stable level of prices to which the Republicans have pointed with such pride in recent years has been due to the fact that falling agricultural prices have offset the rising industrial price level.

I suspect you are right about my speeches last time, and I shall probably be less "humorous" anyway — because I am older and wearier! I am glad to hear that Elmo Roper [511] and Lou Cowan [512] are on your Board. There are few people whom I like and admire more than that pair.

Cordially,

P.S. I neglected to thank you for liking my *Fortune* piece. The hostility of businessmen to the Democrats and the New Deal is one of the absurdities of our time. Also, it is an acute danger, because the more business rejects liberalism and even what's good for it the more it drives Democrats in other directions for support. To me there is nothing wrong with business, labor, farmers or any of the other smaller special interest groups, except *dominance*. That's the trouble now.

Mrs. Hubert Humphrey wrote Stevenson apologizing for having allowed a photographer friend of hers to take a picture of him with the Humphreys at church in Duluth, Minnesota, and saying that she had no idea he was about to take the picture. She went on: "I just want you to know and understand that have the sincerest and highest affection and regard for you." She promised that she and her husband would support him for President in 1956 regardless of who his running mate might be. She closed: "I sincerely hope I have not gone too far in expressing my feelings. I think I will wait about two years from now to tell Hubert what I have done."

[509] A copy is in A.E.S., I.S.H.L.
[510] The Committee to Defend America by Aiding the Allies.
[511] Marketing consultant and public opinion researcher.
[512] Radio and television producer Louis G. Cowan.

To Mrs. Hubert H. Humphrey [513]

November 7, 1955

My dear Muriel:

Yes, let's have a little conspiracy and we will admit Hubert when we get good and ready, or even not at all!

I am glad you wrote me as you did. I think you know how I feel about him and I have little doubt that he will be accorded among the most conspicuous places in our generation. As to his immediate political future I can say and do little or nothing now, nor can I foresee developments with any certainty. I do, however, know what I should like!

I hope that we shall have many more days together, although for the benefit of the older members let's cut the pace just a little!

Cordially,

P.S. Please don't be concerned about the photos in the church. It was as nothing compared with the indignities I have already suffered. It reminds me of the rancher who complained when a neighbor moved in a mile away: "It's getting so there ain't no privacy even in the privy."

To Mrs. Franklin D. Roosevelt [514]

November 7, 1955

Dear Mrs. Roosevelt:

Barry Bingham and Mrs. [Edison] Dick asked me the other day if I had heard from you about the possibility of Mr. Baruch's being an honorary co-chairman with you of the new volunteer organization they are planning. I told them I had not heard and would drop you a note. Hence this. If you have an opportunity to ask him you can let me know, or inform Mrs. Dick, in Lake Forest.

Our plot thickens, and satisfactorily on the whole. I expect now to make a "statement" on the 14th, although as you will understand the date is confidential for the present. I have held off at the insistence of the National Chairman in order not to affect the "box office" for the fund-raising dinner on the 19th. I had not realized there was any commercial value or surprise left in my plans.

Cordially yours,
ADLAI

---

[513] A copy is in A.E.S., I.S.H.L.
[514] The original is in the Franklin D. Roosevelt Library, Hyde Park, New York.

To Adlai E. Stevenson III

November 9, 1955

Dear Bear:

I have your letter about Christmas, and I heartily agree that you must go to your mother's for Christmas dinner. I enclose, by the way, the report of a message from her which came after a message indicating that she was planning to join you all for Thanksgiving at Aunt Lucy's.[515] However, as I have to be in Miami on November 30 I don't believe I can come to Boston on the 24th and I trust you will let Aunt Lucy know I must forego her kind invitation. If the situation should change I will telephone you.

I am glad John Fell is not upset by the club business, and I hope he gets what he wants and suffers no scars.[516]

Please give him my love and tell him that damned sow has arrived with ten pigs and dear Barney[517] is preoccupied with its care and nurture while everything else is neglected. I can't imagine what he was up to but I will pay for it — as usual![518]

And now for the important business! Would you, could you, and Nancy, come out on Saturday the 19th to join me at the Democratic affair[519] that night? You could go back Sunday night and, of course, I will underwrite the cost. It isn't that I feel I need support at this late date, but I do get terribly tired of being alone in all of these ordeals and I am repeatedly advised that a little family around once in a while would be mighty helpful. If I am going to do this thing again I want to do it right this time, and to have you two hang around and help out, exposing your fine features to the cameras with me, would be both a comfort and a desirable improvement in my usual background.

I don't want to embarrass you as I am sure you realize, and I doubt

[515] Mrs. A. Kingsley Porter, Ellen Stevenson's aunt, who lived in Cambridge, Massachusetts.

[516] Harvard's "final clubs," more or less exclusive undergraduate social organizations, elect their new members in the late fall after screening candidates in a lengthy series of parties and dinners known as "punches." See Cleveland Amory, *The Proper Bostonians* (New York, 1947). John Fell joined the Delphic Club.

[517] Stevenson's farmer and chauffeur in Libertyville.

[518] John Fell had a brief fling in pig raising, contemplating no cost but the original cost of the sow, which was pregnant. The farmer at Libertyville was to take care of the pigs while John Fell went off to school. John Fell hoped ultimately to sell the fattened brood, but expenses were so great that the venture was abandoned.

[519] A $100-a-plate Democratic dinner at the Chicago International Amphitheater, at which Stevenson was to deliver a speech giving a preview of issues he planned to emphasize in the 1956 campaign.

if I will need to impose on you again for a long time, but if you could do it this time without too much inconvenience I will be most grateful.

I will be staying in town most of that week at the Hilton Hotel and you can stay with me that night, or with Grannie or Mother, or even go out to the country if you wished.

Love,

P.S. I am off to the University of Virginia to pontificate on Woodrow Wilson on the occasion of his 100th anniversary, Friday morning. I trust you will be listening in animated suspense for my imperishable words. Miss [Carol] Evans says the broadcast begins at 9:30 and is coast-to-coast on ABC.

On November 11, 1955, Stevenson spoke at the Woodrow Wilson Centennial at the University of Virginia.

THE ROAD AWAY FROM REVOLUTION [520]

We can see now a painful but just irony in the designation "Armistice Day." For November 11, 1918, brought only an armistice; it did not bring peace. Instead, the years since 1918 have been a parody of peace, a series of intervals between wars; and war itself has grown more ghastly and more appalling. The crisis in human history which Wilson perceived with such clarity thirty-five years ago is now upon us with redoubled urgency. In an age when total war threatens not just a setback to civilization, but its total destruction, it will profit us Americans to revisit Woodrow Wilson and reconsider his contributions to the struggle for peace.

When one thinks of Wilson and the peace, one thinks of the League of Nations — and rightly so. Yet, I doubt if the concept of the League, noble as it was, exhausted Wilson's search for peace. If I have any thesis here tonight, it is that Wilson's war against war depended only in part on the creation of new international mechanisms. It depended even more, in my judgment, on the creation of a new international spirit. And he deeply believed that the new international spirit could emerge only from new values in our own social and economic life. Wilson knew that his crusade for peace could never succeed unless the world was committed equally to a crusade for justice.

One must not forget that President Wilson first came upon the national scene, not as a student of world affairs, but as the eloquent exponent of

[520] The text is from *What I Think*, pp. 232–240.

the gospel of the New Freedom in our domestic affairs. The rise of industry and business, he felt, had transformed the economic order. There was need for a new liberation — "for the emancipation of the generous energies of a people." His mission was to work for liberation; to work for social justice; to establish public policy on the basis of the welfare of all, not on the welfare of a narrow group.

Let us remember the context of the times. The last years of the nineteenth century had seen an ominous concentration of wealth, and with it of political power, in a few hands. And the economic system, left to itself, would not reverse a process which it had, in fact, set in motion. *Laissez faire* could not cure what *laissez faire* had helped to start. Only one agency commanded enough authority to redress this dangerous unbalance, and this was the national government. It should use its great powers, derived from the popular vote — from "the just consent of the governed" — to restore equilibrium in the community and ensure that all interests shared in the expansion and enrichment of American life.

This was Wilson's greatest undertaking. And his central effort was to establish, as the standard of public policy, at the very core of his party's faith, the concept of the common good. As he once said: "In a self-governed country, there is one rule for everybody and that is the common interest." Wilson was by no means the first or only American politician to devote his political career to the advancement of the general welfare. But what Wilson achieved was to translate this dedication into the terms of the new industrial society.

Of course, lamentations and predictions of catastrophe ushered in such Wilsonian reforms as the Federal Reserve System, the income tax, the Federal Trade Commission, the Clayton Antitrust Act, and the rest. Reforms are always frightening to some, and his enduring achievement lay in introducing, lastingly and indelibly, the principle of the common good into the welter of confusion and conflict of the modern economy. Wilson's concept was based on the rights and interests of *all* sections of the community. He knew, as Lincoln did, that government *for* the people had to be government *by* and *of* the people.

What Wilson sought was a new birth of freedom, based on equality of rights and social justice. What he feared was government by a single interest. Wilson saw the public good in the co-operation and balance of the various sectors of the community; farmers, workers, businessmen — all must be considered. "We shall not act either justly or wisely if we attack established interests as public enemies," he wrote. And all had a right to be represented in the processes of governmental decision. Nor — may I add, in this university town which knew Wilson as well as Jefferson — nor did he propose to banish experts and even professors from the operation of government! Once, indeed, in his retirement he wrote to another great Southern statesman, Cordell Hull: "I am not afraid of making ours a 'highbrow' party, for highbrows at least think and comprehend the standards of high conduct."

In the years since Wilson, we have enlarged much of his original program. Public control of credit policy has become more effective, a more progressive income tax has helped widen the distribution of wealth, the first steps toward federal protection for the worker have been expanded into a general system of social security, the farmers have been helped not only by soil conservation and credit but by the underpinning of prices. These measures have extended the spirit of the New Freedom. Far from acting as shackles upon the independence of the economy, they have helped create a stability of purchasing power, a width of consumption and a scale of market of which business could hardly have dreamed in Wilson's day.

Nor has the business community suffered from the rising political and economic power of the other sectors. On the contrary, the intervening years have vindicated triumphantly his concept of the common good, of the government's role in securing it, and of the realizable harmony of diverse economic interests within an expanding democratic community. If you require a monument to his achievement, I would ask you to look round at the American economy of which he laid so many secure foundations.

The Wilsonian reforms thus helped produce the vast material abundance we have today. But, more important still, they contributed to a renewal of the American moral purpose. They gave meaning in a world of affairs to the fact that we are, in the words of Paul, members, one of another; they reminded us that the vital community depends on integrity, upon generosity and decency in human relationships, and on equality in human opportunities.

What Wilson saw in the nation he came to see even more urgently in the world. In the international anarchy of his day — an anarchy which plunged Europe into war within eighteen months of his election — he had the vision, all over again, of the strife, the bitterness, the disaster which must follow if uncontrolled forces are allowed to struggle with each other with no restraints imposed by the community as a whole. The philosophy behind the League of Nations, indeed, was Wilson's guiding idea of the common good applied to international society.

As we all know, he failed to convey this vision to his people, or at least to a sufficient number of their leaders. Our nation took no part in the world's first experiment in international order. But, looking back today with the hindsight of over thirty years, we also know that his vision of a community of nations under law was — and is — the only road to lasting peace. The dream of 1919 has become the reality of the United Nations.

And so, once again, if we look for monuments to the work of Wilson, we can find them built into the very foundations of our postwar world.

This does not mean that, for Wilson, the League then — or the United Nations today — would constitute the whole of a strategy of peace. The grounds of the universal unrest and perturbation lie deeper; they lie, Wilson himself suggested, "at the sources of the spiritual life of our time." Underneath the recriminations of diplomats and the conflicts of nation-states, there boiled up then — as there boils up today — the hopes, resentments, and aspirations not just of leaders but of great masses of people seeking for themselves and their children the rights and privileges which, Wilson said, "all normal men desire and must have if they are to be contented and within reach of happiness."

This, it seems to me, is the heart of the matter — and the heart not only of democracy and of freedom but of peace itself. Violence is, after all, the confession that mutual relations of respect and good will have broken down and the web of common life has been torn apart. The most urgent task before any society, domestic or world-wide, is to check grievances, clashes, blind oppositions of interest, long before they reach the flashpoint of war.

These subterranean pressures rising round the world — of dire need, of hunger and disease, of awakened hope, of nationalism, of envy, of impatience to make up for lost centuries — these are the explosive stuff of international life. And this Woodrow Wilson knew, just as he knew that poverty and underprivilege and the gulfs between rich and poor were fire hazards in America's basement. In one of his last public utterances, he discussed the phenomenon which so threatens and alarms us today — the rise of Communism.

"The sum of the whole matter is this," Wilson said, "that our civilization cannot survive materially unless it is redeemed spiritually." What we require, he said, must include "sympathy and helpfulness and a willingness to forego self-interest in order to promote the welfare, happiness, and contentment of others and of the community as a whole." This, he said, thinking of the terror of the Communist alternative — this "was the road away from revolution."

I would suggest that Wilson still has much to say to us today. And that what he has to say is that we must wage more fiercely than ever the same twofold struggle of a generation ago: the war against want and oppression, and the war against war itself.

We have made a start in the war against poverty and oppression. But our world is not moving by the action of some inscrutable "hidden hand" toward spreading prosperity, rising standards, and the extension of freedom. On the contrary, the drift is the other way, to population outstripping resources in backward lands, to wealth accumulating in the already wealthy West, and to the Communists' propaganda and infiltration. If they succeed in capturing the revolution of the underdeveloped areas — the uncommitted third of the world — as they have already captured the revolutions of Russia and China, the circle of freedom on earth will dangerously shrink.

Yet anti-Communism and self-interest should not be our only motive in offering a helping hand to people struggling for dignity and independence. Unselfishness and magnanimity are also part of the American record. And there is much we can do to help reverse the fatality in less fortunate lands whereby poverty breeds ever more poverty and hatred breeds ever more hatred. We can set our overwhelming resources of wealth and skill to work to improve the productivity and standards of life. We can furnish more of our brain power for activity abroad and widen the opportunities for giving education and training to our foreign friends here in the United States. And we can convince the peoples of the world that we do this not just to check Communism or to impose Americanism or to perpetuate colonialism, but because we believe that the dream of a fearless, free, and equal society, first cherished within these shores, is more potent than ever and can be spread around the world.

But perhaps the most urgent struggle of all is the war against war itself. Our past failures to control war caused great wreckage in the world and took many lives, but they did not destroy the world itself. Total war in the nuclear epoch will not let civilization off so lightly.

What humanity now demands is a great leap ahead in our thinking and in our action. We talk of "limiting" war. But that is not enough. War in the Hydrogen Age resists limitation: one cannot keep a chain reaction on a leash. So the ultimate goal is not limitation, it is not an uneasy balance of weapons, or of terror, but the abolition of war by the abolition of the means of war.

The difficulties in the way of achieving an enforceable system of disarmament are immense. Maybe the problem is insoluble now as it has been in the past. But it seems to me that the urgency is such that we can settle for nothing less than a sustained and dogged search for effective disarmament with the best brains we can muster, and that we have no greater foreign policy objective.

That we must move ahead creatively and decisively along all the world's fronts in the struggle for the common good of freedom becomes more imperative every day. Each day's news is another plea for sober realism. For now that the rosy mists around last summer's meeting at the summit are rising we see all about us signs of the disintegration of our whole security system. The fabric is unraveling. Most recently Arab-Israel hostility has risen to a new pitch of intensity along the Egyptian frontier, just as the Soviet design to split the Arab world from the West becomes more apparent.

It is interesting and relevant to recall that Wilson believed in encouraging Jewish settlement in Palestine and took an active part in making the Balfour Declaration a vital part of the Palestine mandate under the League of Nations. Since then the state of Israel has become a fact, and, unhappily, so also has the bitter hostility of its Arab neighbors. For five years violence along the armistice lines has been mounting. Unless these clashes cease there is danger of all-out war developing while we debate which side was the aggressor.

A major effort of statesmanship is required if we are to avert a political disaster in this troubled area. We have shown little initiative within or outside the United Nations in devising measures to prevent these border clashes. After years of experience it would seem evident that the only way to avoid bloodshed and violence along the border is to keep the troops of these antagonists apart. And I wonder if United Nations guards could not undertake patrol duties in the areas of tension and collision. Certainly both sides would respect United Nations patrols where they do not trust each other.

In this country we have been dismayed by the arms deal between Egypt and Russia. Of course there should be an equitable balance of armed strength so that neither side feels that it lives by the grace of its none-too-kindly neighbor. We must help, if need be, to counteract any Soviet attempt to upset such a balance, and we must make it emphatically clear that the status quo shall not be changed by force.[521] But we do not want to see an arms race in this area where the principles of Woodrow Wilson's fourteen points once shone like a lighthouse after centuries of dark oppression.

The Middle East has long been an area of Russian ambition. And we trust our friends there have neither overlooked the fate of nations which have listened to the siren songs of Moscow, nor forgotten that the Soviet Foreign Minister told the Nazi Foreign Minister in 1940 that one of the conditions of a Nazi-Soviet agreement was that the Persian Gulf was to be a sphere of Soviet influence.

---

[521] In September, 1955, Czechoslovakia sold Egypt jet aircraft, tanks, and other equipment, thereby threatening the delicate military balance between Israel and the Arab nations.

The contagious flames of undeclared war between Israel and her neighbors have smoldered too long. We applaud the peaceful efforts of the Secretary General of the United Nations and we must bestir ourselves to help create conditions which will work toward peace, not conflict, in this troubled area. The United States does not choose sides when it chooses peace.

Let us, I say, not deceive ourselves. The Soviets have sharply altered their tactics and stepped boldly forth from the shadows of conspiracy and secrecy. To our dismay they are now competing openly and directly with the West. We must take care lest the illusions of the new charm policy further weaken our defenses, moral and physical. And we must take care, too lest a rigid military-security diplomacy hobble our foreign policy. We cannot meet each new problem in the war against war and the war against want just in terms of air bases, military alliances, and nuclear stockpiles. If we do, our influence will steadily ebb away in those crucial areas of the world where progress and peace are the major concerns.

So, let us keep our powder dry, our minds supple, our hearts warm, and our spirits high as the great contest of our times moves forward into a new, even more perilous phase.

As Woodrow Wilson devised new methods to promote the common good among men and among nations, so must we devise new methods to meet the challenges of our times. Surely this is what the spirit of Wilson has to say to us today. And it commits us to the institutions for world understanding and for peace which Wilson tried so nobly to establish.

It commits us to labor relentlessly against the causes of war and against the means of war — a labor which must go on and on until men everywhere can live in the sunlight without oppression and fear.

This image from the greatness of America's bright past commits us most of all to enliven the new international spirit without which Wilson knew that neither institutions nor material programs could succeed. It is the spirit that recognizes that justice transcends victory, that "humanity is above all nations," that "every man beareth the stamp of the human condition," that in the words of our Illinois poet:

> There is only one man in the world and his name
> is All Men.
> There is only one woman in the world and her name
> is All Women.
> There is only one child in the world and the child's
> name is All Children.[522]

[522] From *Names*, by Carl Sandburg. Copyright 1953 by Carl Sandburg.

Let us take this occasion to consecrate ourselves to these purposes, until at last Wilson's words will no longer mock us — until at last the world will be truly safe for democracy.

By November 15, 1955, when Stevenson announced that he was a candidate for the 1956 Democratic nomination, he had assembled his immediate campaign staff. James A. Finnegan, of Philadelphia, the Pennsylvania secretary of state, was the campaign manager. Hyman B. Raskin, of Chicago and former deputy to Stephen A. Mitchell when Mitchell was Democratic National Chairman, was deputy campaign director. Stephen A. Mitchell and Wilson Wyatt were to be advisers. Harry S. Ashmore was personal assistant to Stevenson. Roger Tubby, who had recently resigned as director of publicity for the New York State Department of Commerce, was in charge of press relations. Mrs. Edison Dick and Barry Bingham were named cochairmen of the National Stevenson for President Committee and Archibald Alexander was director of the organizing committee.

STATEMENT BY ADLAI E. STEVENSON
Chicago, Illinois, Tuesday, November 15, 1955 [523]

I shall be a candidate for the Democratic nomination for President next year, which I suspect is hardly a surprise.

I shall do all I can to persuade my party to entrust that immense responsibility to me again because:

In the first place, I believe it important for the Democratic party to resume the executive direction of our national affairs.

Second, I am assured that my candidacy would be welcomed by representative people in and out of my party throughout the country.

Third, I believe any citizen should make whatever contribution he can to search for a safer, saner world.

It is of the first importance to return the executive branch of our government to the Democratic party because it is apparent that wisdom and responsibility began to reappear in the conduct of our affairs only with the return of Congress to Democratic leadership in the 1954 election.

Seldom before has the United States faced a period of greater opportunity — and of greater danger.

Our great opportunity lies in the fact that our prosperity and wealth can now be used to give all of our people the higher standards and wider opportunities which are mankind's universal dream. These are now

[523] The text is from a mimeograph copy of the press release.

within our reach, not simply for the favored few, but for every family in America.

Our danger lies, of course, in the ambition of a new tyranny for mastery of the world, and in Communist exploitation of the hopes and discontents of the two-thirds of mankind who now demand a larger share in the good things of life.

In partnership with our friends and allies, with confidence born of magnanimity, we must work to uproot the causes of conflict and tension and to outlaw the very means of war in this atomic age.

The task of the Democratic party is to make "prosperity and peace" not just a political slogan but an active search for a better America and a better world.

I am ready to do what I can to that end either as a worker in the ranks or at the top of the ticket if my party sees fit to so honor me.

The day after his announcement, Stevenson held a press conference in Chicago. It was transcribed by the New York Times. *In publishing the transcript on November 17, 1955, the* Times *explained: "Because many of the reporters did not identify themselves, all questions following a reporter's name were not necessarily asked by him." Because of the many typographical errors in the text as printed in the* Times *the editors have taken the liberty of correcting them for easier reading. Also, in one or two instances where the text was hopelessly garbled a few words have been deleted, with the deletions indicated by three dots.*

MR. STEVENSON: Gentlemen, good morning and welcome.

I would like to, at the outset, perhaps express my sympathy for you that you shall have to see and listen to me not just for three months, but for an indefinite time. I have a few things that I thought I should say at the outset before you ask me questions.

In the first place, I wanted to take this occasion to tell you that I have asked Jim Finnegan of Philadelphia to assume the job of campaign pre-convention manager in my pre-convention campaign. Mr. Finnegan was active in the convention of 1952, where I was nominated before, and has been a friend for a long time. His credentials as an expert, I think, are well known to all of you. Not only did Philadelphia show exceptionally good judgment in 1952,[524] but all over Pennsylvania went Democratic in 1954, as you know, and only within the last week or ten days the Democrats have swept the municipal elections in Philadelphia by even larger margins.

[524] Stevenson had carried Philadelphia by a larger margin than any other large city.

Serving with him as deputy or executive director will be Hy [Hyman B.] Raskin, with whom I have been associated for a long time in Illinois politics, who worked both in 1952 and subsequently as Steve Mitchell's deputy when he was chairman of the Democratic National Committee.

I shall continue to look to Steve Mitchell, who was chairman of the committee, and whom I believe is entitled to much of the credit for the rehabilitation of the Democratic party since the election of 1952, for continuous advice and counsel.

I shall also take full advantage of the experience and the wisdom and the friendship and loyalty of Wilson Wyatt of Louisville, who was my personal manager at Springfield during the 1952 campaign. These two gentlemen have proffered their assistance on a continuous basis and I count it both invaluable and indispensable.

I have one other matter that I would like to dispose of. Some time ago the State Central Committee of the Democratic Farmer-Labor party of Minnesota adopted a resolution expressing its eagerness for me to be a candidate for the nomination and inviting me to enter the Minnesota primaries.

Yesterday, following our meeting here and my announcement, I sent a letter to the state chairman, Ray Hemingway of Minnesota, advising him that I would accept that invitation and that I had announced my candidacy.

Should you care for copies of that letter, I am sure that we can make them available to you through Roger Tubby.

That is the only firm decision that I have made with respect to primaries. The others we will consider as we come to them.

I think that is all I have to tell you, and now I will be glad to submit to your questions and answer them as best I can.

JACK ANGELL of the National Broadcasting Company: Mr. Stevenson, I am Jack Angell, N.B.C., Chicago. Yesterday you announced your decision to run again. I would like to know if you made your decision before the President's illness.

MR. STEVENSON: The circumstances are these: he asked me when I had made my decision to be a candidate for the nomination, and whether it was before President Eisenhower's illness.

During my very extensive travels around the country in 1954 raising money for the Democratic National Committee and in the Congressional campaign from coast to coast, I discovered that there was a surprising degree of interest in my being a candidate again. I did nothing for it. I had been inactive most of this year politically. I continued to receive, however, evidence of this support both in breadth and depth, and during the Governors' Conference here in Chicago in the month of August, further extensive evidence of support, indeed, enthusiasms for a future candidacy.

When I could see my two sons who were in this country, which was not until the end of August and early September — one of them when I returned from Europe at the end of August and one of them went with me to the Caribbean the last of September — after having an opportunity to consult with them and the other one who is stationed in Hawaii in the Army, by mail, I reached my decision that I would be a candidate again subject to further evidence confirmatory of what I thought I had already detected.

That evidence has been forthcoming in the intervening month of October. I have not made this statement before for a variety of reasons, mostly to do with my convenience, with the forthcoming Democratic dinner which the party's leaders, and the treasurer particularly, attached some importance to keeping some element of this uncertainty alive, and also because I wanted to make quite sure about certain regions of the country and certain individuals in my candidacy. I do not know whether that answers your question, but I could —

Q: Well, in a word, sir, you would say that it was not contingent on what happened to the President?

A: Well, not at all. It was based, as I say, largely in the course of the summer and confirmed by my children around the first of September.

Q: Thank you.

Q: You say it was made in the early part of summer, Governor? We couldn't quite hear that.

A: I said it was largely made as a result of the evidence of support I had received. It was culminated at the Governors' Conference early in August, then I felt I should discuss it with my children.

W. H. LAWRENCE of the New York *Times:* Governor, could you tell us with regard to some of these other primaries what your line of thinking is as to which ones you might go into, New Hampshire, for example, California?

A: I am afraid I can't. I am afraid I can't, because I just haven't gone into them nor have I done very much thinking about them. This is something that I will have to consult with Mr. Finnegan about, and I don't know that he has been able to give it much attention thus far.

I should say in this connection that Mr. Finnegan will not be able to come here to Chicago on full time for a little while yet, but we will take up these as we come to them.

The reason for the importance of deciding with respect to Minnesota now is not one with respect to the invitation, but under the Minnesota law — I have forgotten what the requirements are, but there have to be district conventions, and they take about six weeks to hold them, and then they have to file a list of delegates early in January, or something, and they have pressed me for an early decision.

EDWARD J. MILNE of The Providence (R.I.) *Journal:* Governor, do you agree in principle with Estes Kefauver that a candidate ought to go into primaries as broadly as possible?

A: I don't have any well-defined views as to what a candidate should do with respect to primaries. I think it depends on the primary; it depends on the circumstances, the region, the presence of a favorite son and what not.

CHARLES FINSTON of The Chicago *Herald-American:* What role will Mr. Mitchell and Mr. Wyatt play in your convention campaign, sir?

A: Advisory to Mr. Finnegan and to me.

JACK BELL of The Associated Press: Governor, will Mr. Finnegan resign his state office to become campaign manager?

A: Yes, he will. I just interrogated him [laughter] and if you have, then you are wasting our time.

WALTER KERR of The New York *Herald Tribune:* Are you confident that as head of the Democratic ticket you could defeat any Republican candidate for the election?

A: Well, let me say to you that while I believe, as I said yesterday, everyone should do what he can consistent with our political traditions to serve his country and his party, therefore, I think one runs regardless when he feels it is consistent to do so, consistent with that principle whether he feels he can win or not. I might say I am not entering this campaign for the exercise [laughter].

Q: Can you tell us what Mr. William Blair is going to do in your campaign?

A: He will be my personal assistant as he has for a long time.

Q: As appointment secretary and so forth?

A: Yes, sir.

Q: And Mr. Ashmore, is he going to be head of the publicity?

A: Well, he will be in my immediate entourage. Mr. Tubby — I don't know that we have any formal distribution of responsibilities. But Mr. Tubby, generally speaking, is going to look after public relations, and

Mr. Ashmore is going to advise me on substance, issues and problems.

CHARLES A. DAVIS of the Chicago *Defender:* The support that was indicated at the Governors' conference, does it include such promises from the Governors of the Southern states that were not with the Democratic party in 1952?

A: No, I didn't have any reports from them, sir. [Laughter]. In fact, what I had from them was mostly through the newspapers.

ALLEN DUCKWORTH of the Dallas *News:* Governor Stevenson, will you comment on Governor Shivers' qualifications to sit in the next national convention? [525]

A: No, sir, I won't, because I don't know what they are [laughter].

EDWARD P. MORGAN of The American Broadcasting Company: Governor, it has been said that the Democrats are going to have to campaign in 1956 more or less on negative issues, that is, more peace and prosperity rather than conversion. What is your comment on that, and what do you think are the main positive issues that the Democrats must campaign on?

A: Well, if you will permit me, I will say something about that at length on Saturday night.

ROBERT E. LEE of The St. Paul *Pioneer Press:* Governor, you have received a strong invitation from Democratic leaders in California to enter their primary.

A: Yes.

Q: Do you have any idea now when you will give them an answer? Isn't that in a slightly different category than other states?

A: Yes, I think that is perhaps in a slightly different category. As to when I will make that decision, in view of the invitation from some of the leaders out there, just when I will be able to answer that question with respect to California I don't know. I suspect it would be within, say, a month, wouldn't it? Possibly before the end of the year.

JOHN DREISKE of the Chicago *Sun-Times:* Governor, in view of the fact that the New Hampshire primary is the first on the schedule, I presume that you will make your decision concerning primaries on that first?

A: I don't think I can answer the question because I just don't know.

Q: Do you have any estimate, Governor, as to the convention strength you have?

[525] Governor Allan Shivers of Texas had bolted the Democratic party and supported Eisenhower in 1952.

A: You know, I don't have any idea about the schedules for filing and so forth.

Q: Would you consider that one first?

A: No, I wouldn't think necessarily. I should think the ones that have legal requirements within the states.

Q: When will you start giving out with decisions on entry in the primaries?

A: I don't know. I don't know. Certainly by the end of the year.

Q: Governor, do you have any estimate now of the strength of delegates you now have in view of the fact you talked to many leaders?

A: No, sir, I have not. I have made no such calculations.

RICHARD J. H. JOHNSTON of the New York *Times:* Governor, there has been a great deal of discussion of Senator Lyndon Johnson's heart attack, his recovery, and its possible effect on the candidacy for President or Vice President. Do you have any comments on this business of heart attacks and the aftermaths?

A: Well, I would hope, indeed I pray, that Senator Johnson's misfortune will in no way limit his future activities or his usefulness. And the same goes for anyone else who has suffered a similar misfortune, and most specifically it goes for the President of the United States.

Q: Governor, would you accept Senator Kefauver as your running mate for Vice President?

A: Well, I would say this about Senator Kefauver or anyone else: that after all the national convention has to make that decision. As far as I am concerned, I think he is eminently qualified for exalted public office, indeed he already holds one, and that isn't to say that there are no others likewise qualified, equally qualified, and also there is a question of whether he would be available for such an office, and I gather from what I have heard that he would not.

JOHN C. O'BRIEN of The Philadelphia *Inquirer:* How will you finance your pre-convention campaign?

A: With money, I hope. [Laughter]

Q: Will you have a finance committee to raise the funds?

A: You say, have we?

Q: Yes.

A: Yes, I have one. I have an individual, I don't know that it is a committee, and I am not at the moment prepared to tell you about it. I will later. I hope he is busy. [Laughter]

GRIFFING BANCROFT of The Columbia Broadcasting System: Governor —

A: Who is paying for this room, by the way? [Laughter]

Q: Governor, do you expect your opponent to be President Eisenhower?

A: I can't speculate on that. I hadn't thought so, but I read in the paper that his recovery is rapid and encouraging, and that there are those who believe that he may be fit to be a candidate again. That I just don't know. I can't speculate.

ROBERT G. SPIVAK of The New York *Post:* In this morning's newspapers there was a story that the Administration has decided to hold back as much as 20 per cent of economic aid to distressed areas, and this was supposed to be a holdback or cutback of about one hundred million dollars in that aid, India to be cut from fifty million to forty million dollars. Could you give us your views on this whole subject?

A: Well, I don't know that. I know what the reasons are. Do you know what the reasons were?

Q: Well, I am not sure from the story.

A: I couldn't very well comment on it unless I knew the reasons.

Q: They said to establish a reserve fund, but I don't know any more than that. I mean, I presume it is to give them more flexibility.

A: I don't believe I can comment on it intelligently now.

Q: Well, in general could you [comment on?] economic aid to distressed areas?

A: Do you mean underdeveloped areas?

Q: Yes.

A: You mean foreign assistance, not domestic.

Q: Right.

A: Well, I shall talk about that somewhat on Saturday. I have before, and I will for the next ten months, probably, from time to time.

Q: Governor, on this question of the Vice Presidency but not as to personalities, Mr. Eisenhower has given some of his philosophy as to how they should be picked and the importance of the office. What is your philosophy on those points?

A: I think the Vice President should be chosen with virtually the same care and consideration that a major party selects its Presidential candidate.

Q: Governor, does that mean that you might accept the Vice Presidential nomination if the party said so?

A: I haven't reached that bridge. Until I do I don't think I will attempt to cross it.

Q: Governor, on the list of those qualified to run with you as a Vice Presidential candidate do you include John Sparkman of Alabama?

A: Sir?

Q: I say, do you include John Sparkman of Alabama?

A: Oh, yes, indeed so, yes. I think he is a highly qualified citizen and senator.

A: Governor, did you tell Governor [W. Averell] Harriman in August or later that you were going to run?

A: Did I tell him in August or later that I was going to run?

Q: He was here at the Governors' Conference, he came out and said there was an understanding between you as I recall. Did you tell him at that time —

Q: Well, I am not at liberty to discuss with you what the understanding was, but in answer to your specific question, did I tell him at that time that I was going to run, the answer is no, because I hadn't made up my mind, as I just told you.

ARNOLD E. MARTIN of the Newark *News:* Governor, a story was published within recent days that Governor [Robert] Meyner assured you at Charlottesville that New Jersey's thirty-two votes had been pledged to you. Is that true?

A: No such assurances were asked for and no such assurances were given. In fact, they were never mentioned.

NED BROOKS of The National Broadcasting Company: Do you expect to have the support of Mr. Truman in your campaign?

A: Do you mean for the nomination?

Q: For the nomination.

A: Mr. Truman has already made it, I think, emphatically clear that he is going to be neutral in the selection of a Presidential candidate, and then will accept the nominee of the convention. I believe what he states.

Q: What about some of these stories that you and he disagree on rather fundamental issues?

A: I don't know what substance they have. So far as I know there is none.

CHARLES T. LUCEY of The Scripps-Howard Newspaper Alliance: What did you think Harriman said [meant?] when he said he was for you?

A: I don't think I choose to comment on that.

Q: Governor, what is your attitude toward Senator Anderson [526] as a Vice Presidential prospect?

A: I think he is a splendid man and he just happens to be one of my oldest friends in the Senate.

Q: How about Governor Meyner?

A: I feel the same about Governor Meyner. I haven't known him as long as I have Clint Anderson, but for the years I have known him, which is the last three, I have come to like him immensely.

MR. ANGELL: Governor, Senator Anderson believes in the flexible price support. He stood behind Secretary Benson, and you would support him, yet you have come out for a 90 per cent parity program. Wouldn't there be a difference there?

A: No, I don't think he and I have any great differences. If we do on the farm issue, I haven't heard them. The point is that I have said regardless of what some of you may have written, what I felt about the farm issue and I have said the same thing consistently since 1952, and I might say that that is more than certain Republicans have done, and among other things I have said that neither flexible nor fixed price supports were an adequate solution of the farm problem, and this is precisely the position of Clinton Anderson.

By the way, if any of you, in view of what I read in the press from time to time, would like to see what I have said since 1952 on the farm subject Mr. Tubby can give it to you. You will find I have said the same thing.

Q: Governor, would you express any opinion whether or not any delegation from Texas would come up favorable to you next year?

A: I have no opinion on that.

ZYGMUNT BRONIARER of *Trybuna Ludu* of Warsaw: I represent a Communist newspaper in Warsaw, Poland — if you are the United States President what will be your policy towards the Communist world?

A: Well, I hope that we can preserve peace between one another, and that we find accommodation of our differences in the interest of all mankind, but there will be no disposition on my part to submit to the demands of international communism here or elsewhere.

Q: Governor, Senator Russell [527] recently said that maybe you are a little bit too far to the left for his liking. I notice one of the editorials this

---

[526] Senator Clinton Anderson of New Mexico.
[527] Senator Richard Russell of Georgia.

morning, after your announcement, spoke of you as a middle-of-the-road Democrat. I wonder if you would give us your thinking on where you stand, in the middle of the road or —

A: I don't know that I can be very helpful to you. I have tried to make my views clear from time to time on a number of things for a number of years. I am not one of those who believes that you can characterize a philosophy on public issues by slogans. I have never been sure what progressive conservatism means, or was it conservative progressivism? [Laughter] I have forgotten, and I am not sure what dynamic moderation or moderate dynamism means. I am not even sure what it means when one says that he is a conservative in fiscal affairs and a liberal in human affairs.[528] I assume what it means is that you will strongly recommend the building of a great many school [buildings for?] children to accommodate our needs, but not provide the money. [Laughter]

MR. JOHNSTON: Governor, I have a question, please. I don't think it is improper in the circumstances now. Can you give us a brief comment on your state of health and your physical condition? [Laughter]

A: But I am so modest. [Laughter] Well, perhaps, using the doctors' phrase, I had my semi-annual ordeal a week or ten days ago and they checked me out of the Passavant hospital with a formidable sheaf of papers, the net of which was for one of my age I was in better than normal condition. I have no excuse from now on.

Q: Governor, are you going to make a special effort in the April primary in Illinois to secure the election of delegates who are known to favor your nomination?

A: Well, I hadn't given any thought to that. I had no such plan, no.

Q: Do you contemplate a unanimous delegation in back of you?

A: No sir, I haven't any view on that subject. I haven't inquired. I think a unanimous delegation would be very agreeable, I would certainly like to have it. It would be flattering, but whether it is possible or not I don't know. Did I have one last time?

Q: You were for Governor Harriman last time.

A: That's right, I voted for Governor Harriman last time so that I guess there was not a unanimous delegation.[529]

---

528 President Eisenhower had used these phrases to describe his program.

529 This is misleading. Stevenson apparently meant that he favored Harriman for the 1952 nomination. One Illinois vote was cast for Harriman on the first ballot, perhaps by Stevenson's alternate, but it could not have been cast by Stevenson himself, since he did not appear on the floor of the convention after his speech of welcome until he returned to accept the nomination.

WILLIAM THEIS of *The Interview:* . . . what you said about a heart attack not limiting the activities of anyone in public life should we interpret that as meaning that you would not make health an issue in your campaign?

A: I said I hoped it would not limit the activities of Lyndon Johnson. I believe that was the question. And then I said —

Q: Or anyone else.

A: And I said I felt exactly the same with respect to anyone else who had suffered a similar misfortune.

Q: Can we take it from that, sir, that you mean that health should not be an issue in the campaign for the Presidency?

A: Well, obviously it would be foolish to say that people don't take into account the survival of a candidate in office or his fitness to perform the office. I should certainly never make health an issue myself. I should certainly think — I should hope earnestly, as I have said — that such limitations as health may have imposed could be remedied by total cure.

Q: Governor, how do you plan to campaign for the nomination? Do you have a number of special dates across the country? Do you plan to go into Minnesota extensively? Can you give us a general idea of it?

A: I have made no such plans, I haven't made extensive speaking engagements across the country beyond the immediate future, I think up to early December. Beyond that I don't think I have made any at all.

Q: Will you go into Minnesota extensively to campaign?

A: I just don't know I just don't know. I probably won't know until just that time, depending on what the circumstances are there and what my circumstances are.

MR. MORGAN: Governor, it has been speculated in principle that among the non-southern possibilities you would be most acceptable to the South as a nominee, and it has also been speculated that this has been caused by certain sacrifices, if that is the word, or compromises, on your part on the issue of civil rights. What is your comment on that?

A: Well, I never heard it before. That is my first comment and if there are sacrifices, I don't know what they are, because I made none.

Q: I meant to say compromises, not sacrifices.

A: Or compromises. I made none. I think what I said has been audible, I hope.

Q: Governor, do you think that when President Eisenhower went to

Geneva the first time, this last time, that he made a real achievement, a substantial achievement, or was it just a way station in the cold war?

A: I think there was a substantial achievement in that he assured the world that the United States was not a menace to peace. That it was necessary to do for a President of the United States is something else.

Q: Governor, do you plan conferences here this week with Governor Harriman and Senator Kefauver?

A: I haven't made any such plan but I hope to see them both. They are both going to be here on Saturday, I am told, but I have arranged no conferences. I hope very much to see them both. They are both old friends, particularly Averell Harriman.

G. GOULD LINCOLN of The Washington *Star:* . . . Senator Lehman of New York has declared himself for you; [also] some of the others in New York. Do you expect to get some New York delegates?

A: I have been very much gratified and flattered by Senator Lehman's continued support, and well, I would not, if Governor Harriman is to be a favorite son, would not want in any way to cause any difficulty or be the occasion for any embarrassment in New York to him or to the New York leadership. I would, of course, hope to have some support in New York.

Q: Do you see any possibility in the future for the reunification of Germany?

A: I do.

Q: May we hear the question?

A: Do I see any possibilities in the future for the reunification of Germany. I think that, while I am not going to go into the details at this time on the alternatives of neutralization of Germany and free elections under the Soviet interpretation, the Soviet interpretation of free elections or under the western interpretation of free elections, I think that it is inevitable that a great country with people of identical tradition and language and race must sooner or later reunite, and that ultimately Germany will be reunited. The sooner the better, I hope, and under circumstances which will leave Germany where it belongs, which is with the West.

Q: Mr. Stevenson, in London they are quite interested in your policy towards Red China. Do you envisage any recognition of the Peking government in the future?

A: By the United States?

Q: Yes.

A: I don't, not in the immediate future.

Q: Governor, it is obvious that you are changing your strategy in this pre-convention campaign, and using major league political pros, according to all reports, instead of so-called bush league advisers. [Laughter]

A: Will you bush men all stand up, please? [Laughter]

Q: The final part of the question is: Have you made any deals for patronage or anything else to assure yourself the nomination and election if you are nominated?

A: Well, in response to the first part of your question, have I changed my methods or something or other, I remind you that I was not a candidate for the nomination in 1952, that I had no organization whatever, that I said repeatedly then and repeat now that as a candidate for Governor of Illinois at that time I could not, even if I had wanted to, have been a candidate for President. One does not run for two offices at the same time in good conscience.

As to any changes that have taken place, I was not conscious of any unless you are referring to Jim Finnegan, whom I have valued always, whom I respect enormously as a political leader and who did invaluable service during the campaign of 1952.

I will welcome the help of big leaguers and bush leaguers.

Q: What about the last half of the question, Governor?

A: I thought I just answered it.

Q: You were asked about deals.

A: Oh, deals, I have made no deals. Not only — I don't want to be too pious about that. I was going to say in the first place that I am rather surprised that anyone would suspect me of making a deal and in the second place, let me say that nobody has proffered me a deal, and I don't anticipate any. [Laughter]

I don't anticipate any deals from people who want to be Vice President. I think they have about the same disrespect for deals or attempts to commit a convention as I would have.

Q: Is Colonel [Jacob M.] Arvey in the pros, Governor, who are going to help you.

A: Well, I certainly hope so.

Q. Because he has no specific assignment?

A: Well, he is Democratic National Committeeman of Illinois, which, according to most people, is a pretty big assignment. I think he probably thinks so, too.

Q: Governor —

A: I don't expect his perspiration will ever dry this year. [Laughter]

Q: Colonel Arvey said a couple of days ago he thought Senator [Hubert] Humphrey would be, I think his word was, an outstanding running mate for you. Do you agree with that assessment?

A: I think he is an admirable Democrat and a most competent and gifted man. I have said, I think, the same thing about some half dozen by this time. I will have to get some new adjectives. I have great respect for Senator Humphrey. He happens to be another old friend.

Q: Governor, Senator Lyndon Johnson of Texas was reported to have said that the recent decisions of the Supreme Court about civil rights would tend to remove it from the political arena. Would you like to comment on that?

A: Well, I think that is inevitable, that certainly from the decisions of the Supreme Court on the law of the land, and the matter of the desegregation of the schools, it has been removed from the political arena and disposed of by the judiciary.

Q: Well, would you like to comment upon the refusal or failure of some states in the Union to abide by the law of the land in relation to school desegregation and other such matters?

A: I don't know that I can comment about it in the abstract. I think the Supreme Court's decision speaks for itself, and I believe that the law should be supported by all of the citizens of the country.

Q: Governor, if there is a budget surplus next year, would you use the money to reduce taxes or deduct [reduce?] the national debt.

A: If there is a budget surplus?

Q: Yes.

A: I would certainly have to assess on the one hand the threat of inflation which would be an occasion for maintaining taxes; on the other hand, the needs, be it for schools, be it highways, be it hospitals, be it soil conservation or what-not, against the desirability of giving business a stimulant and the taxpayer a break. I don't see how I can foretell any of those things now if I don't have a much more accurate estimate of what the needs are and also what the revenue situation is to be.

Q: Governor, on the Emmett Till case,[530] could you tell us how you —

A: Excuse me. I would like to say with respect to the tax situation that I

[530] Emmett Till, a Negro youth from Harlem, visited a relative in Mississippi in September, 1955, and allegedly whistled at a white woman. Several days later his battered body was found, and the woman's husband and brother-in-law were tried and found not guilty of the murder, a verdict that was bitterly criticized as racially inspired.

expressed some view up in Wisconsin the other day — I have them here — and I read in the paper that I opposed tax reductions. What I said was that I would oppose tax reduction in the abstract without consideration for the country's needs; that you can never determine what the national requirements are merely for [from] the last budget.

You have to also assess the current needs as they increase or change or alter from year to year, and it is only against that that you can determine whether or not you have a surplus, because a surplus merely represents an arithmetic figure against a given total expenditure which is a projection for another year of the same expenditure.

You continue to determine whether your needs for expenditures are greater than your needs for tax potential, for a tax reduction. I don't see how you can determine.

I also think that the question of tax reduction and tax adjustment are two separate things and ought not be overlooked. While I might be against tax reduction, which would mean revenue reduction, I might be in favor of tax adjustment.

MR. DREISKE: Thank you, Governor Stevenson.

Acknowledgments

W e are most grateful to Adlai E. Stevenson's sister, Mrs. Ernest L. Ives, for her infinite patience and considerate help at all stages in the preparation of this volume.

Professor Stuart Gerry Brown, Edward D. McDougal, Jr., Newton N. Minow, William McCormick Blair, Jr., W. Willard Wirtz, Wilson W. Wyatt and Stephen A. Mitchell have read all or portions of the manuscript. The entire manuscript was submitted to members of the Advisory Committee to *The Papers of Adlai E. Stevenson,* and their suggestions have been most helpful.

The following generously provided funds to defray the editorial expenses of this volume: Little, Brown and Company, Mrs. Eugene Meyer, Mrs. Marshall Field and the Field Foundation, Mr. and Mrs. Harold Hochschild, Arnold M. Picker, Robert Benjamin, Newton N. Minow, James F. Oates, Jr., Francis T. P. Plimpton, Benjamin Swig, Philip M. Klutznick, Mrs. John Paul Welling, William McCormick Blair, R. Keith Kane, Simon H. Rifkind, Wilson W. Wyatt, the late William Benton, Daggett Harvey, Mr. and Mrs. Edison Dick, William McCormick Blair, Jr., Lloyd K. Garrison, J. M. Kaplan, Jerrold Loebl, Hermon D. Smith, Edward D. McDougal, Jr., Glen A. Lloyd, Mr. and Mrs. Gilbert Harrison, Irving B. Harris, Edwin G. Austin, Archibald Alexander, Jacob M. Arvey, Paul Ziffren, Frank E. Karelsen, Jr., George W. Ball, C. K. McClatchy, Maurice Tempelsman, Barnet Hodes and Scott Hodes, and the J. M. Kaplan Fund, Inc.

Roger Shugg, of the University of New Mexico Press, and Ned Bradford, of Little, Brown and Company, have been constant in their encouragement.

William E. Dix, Alexander P. Clark and Mrs. Nancy Bressler, of the Princeton University Library; Phyllis Gustafson; John Bartlow Martin; Roxane Eberlein; Carla Ley Fishman; Albert Dalia; and Paul Edlund, of the Library of Congress, have been most helpful. Linda Inlay proofread the manuscript. Louis B. Cella, of Elmhurst, Illinois, kindly sent us his collection of newspaper clippings.

WALTER JOHNSON
CAROL EVANS
C. ERIC SEARS

Index

Acheson, Dean, 349, 430, 431, 450, 543, 560; quoted, 117; Republican accusations of, 410, 421, 524; letters to, 432, 463–464, 563, 565

Acheson, Mrs. Dean (Alice Stanley), 432, 565

Adams, Franklin P., letter to, 89

Adams, Mary Seymour (Mrs. George B. Young), 467

Adams, Sherman, 523, 532

Adenauer, Konrad, 276

"Adlai Brooch," 456

Africa: AES trip to, 457n, 459, 460, 463–464, 465, 466, 478–493, 495; AES "Memo to My Sons" from, 480–493; and Central African Federation, 491, 527; AES article on, in *Look* magazine, 546n, 563n

Agar, Herbert, 28, 149, 242; letter to, 242–243

Agar, Mrs. Herbert, telegram to, 149

Agricultural Adjustment Administration, 143, 166

Agronsky, Martin, 365

Aiken, George D., 165n

Air Force, U.S., 309, 317, 411, 412

Alaska, 573; AES trip to, 367, 378, 381–384

Albright, Mrs. Ivan (Josephine), 149

Alexander, Archibald, 538, 591; letter to, 539

Alsop, Joseph, 5, 227, 326, 391n

Alsop, Stewart, 5, 326, 391n

Altgeld, John Peter, 12, 355

Altschul, Frank, 326; letter to, 326

American Bar Association, 71

American Committee for the Weizmann Institute, 440n

American Legion: AES speech before, 22, 34, 39, 49–54, 69; Eisenhower speech before, 69n

American Medical Association, 8n

American Newspaper Publishers Association (ANPA), 227

American Scholar (Phi Beta Kappa publication), 235

Americans for Democratic Action (ADA), 37, 312, 346, 350

Anderson, Clinton, 526, 600

Anderson, Douglas, 389

Anderson, Mrs. Eugenie, 114; letters to, 114, 532, 578–579

Anderson, Harrison Ray, 11

Anderson, Nancy L. (Mrs. Adlai E. Stevenson III), 403n, 405, 419, 440, 448, 464, 512, 527, 531, 583; engagement and wedding of, 396, 400, 420, 459, 465n; letters to, 397, 404, 406, 429, 448, 455

Anderson, Warwick, 396, 420, 446, 448, 464, 465n; letters to, 396, 405

Anderson, Mrs. Warwick ("Mary San"), 396, 405, 446, 448, 459, 465n; letters to, 419–420, 440, 526–527

Andrus, Robert, 444

Angell, Jack, 593, 600

Antioch College, 272, 273

Appleby, Paul, 205

Arab states, 414, 549–551, 589–590

"Area of Freedom, The" (AES speech, October, 1952), 140–147

"Armistice Day," AES on, 584

Army, U.S., 411, 412, 423, 437

Army-McCarthy hearings, 328n–329n, 357n

Arvey, Jacob M., 6, 313, 604–605; letter to, 313

Ascoli, Max, 240; letter to, 240

Ashanti, Asantehene of, 487

Ashmore, Harry S., 444, 494, 556, 591, 595–596; letters to, 445–446, 494

Association of American Law Schools, AES speech before, 305–310

Atkinson, Brooks, 222, 272; letters to, 222, 273

Atlanta *Constitution,* 292n

Atlanta *Journal,* 292n

Atlantic Community, 544

Atomic Energy Commission, 424n, 573, 576

"Atomic Future, The" (AES speech, September, 1952), 93–98

Auriol, Vincent, 362

Bacall, Lauren (Mrs. Humphrey Bogart, "Betty"), 446; aricle in *Look* magazine, 285–286; letters to, 286, 356, 379–380, 446–447, 456–457

Baggarly, H. M., 316; letter to, 316

Balfour Declaration, 589

Ball, George, 27, 388; quoted, on defeat of AES, 188

Bancroft, Griffing, 597

Bankhead, Tallulah, 271–272; letter to, 272

Barbados, AES trip to, 192, 232, 238–239, 241–242, 244, 245, 260

Barkley, Alben, 5, 21, 33; AES on, 17, 115; letter to, 311

Barney (AES's chauffeur), 549, 583

Bartlett, Robert, 381

Baruch, Bernard M., 44, 95, 201, 386, 582; letters to, 201, 386, 536

Battle, John S., 47; letters to, 47–48, 65, 130

Baumgarten, Judy Hardin (Mrs. Walter Baumgarten, Jr.), letter to, 362

Beatty, David, 382

Belgian Congo, 487–489

Bell, David, 28, 267, 279

Bell, Jack, 595

Bell, Laird, 265

Benét, Stephen Vincent, 222

Benson, Ezra Taft, 394, 600

Bentley, Elizabeth, 136

Bentley, Richard, letters to, 38, 131, 233

Benton, John, 419n

Benton, Louise, 419n

Benton, William, 377, 419n, 431, 534, 541n, 542; letters to, 352–353, 382, 418–419, 527

Benton, Mrs. William, 352n, 419n

Berendt, Mrs. Carol, 286; letter to, 286

Berle, Adolf A., Jr., 571

Bevan, Aneurin, 279

Bill of Rights, 53, 57, 139, 252, 299

Binder, Carroll, letters to, 30, 267, 296, 477–478

Bingham, Barry, 9, 243, 400, 465n, 582, 591; letters to, 9–10, 400, 462–463

Bingham, Mrs. Barry, 400, 465n; letter to, 400

bipartisanship (in foreign policy), 184, 219, 313, 329–330, 333, 366; and HST; 46, 56, 65n, 331, 368, 412, 423; AES speech on, 65–68; and Eisenhower, 321, 408–409, 412, 423

Birnie, J. Scott, letter to, 551

Bishop, L. F., 310; letter to, 310

Blackburn, Catherine ("Casey"), 220

Blair, William McCormick, Jr. ("Bill"), 449n, 467; AES at home of, 13, 41n; as aide to AES, 27, 243, 337, 367, 389, 441, 577, 595; accompanies AES on trips, 345, 348, 377n, 381, 402, 465, 479, 480, 485n; quoted, on Alaska trip, 381n

Blatnik, John A., 535

Block, Herbert, 533n

Blundell, Michael, 490–491

Bogart, Mrs. Humphrey, *see* Bacall, Lauren

Bohlen, Charles E., 423n

Bohrer, Joseph F., 354–355; letters to, 205, 355, 513

Bohrer, Mrs. Joseph (Margaret), 205; letter to, 513

Bokum, Mrs. Richard (Fanny Butcher), 8, 283n; letters to, 9, 215

Bonnet, Henri, letter to, 431–432

Bonneville Power Administration, 424n

Bowers, Claude G., 230, 299; letters to, 231, 299–300

Bowles, Chester, 274, 295–296, 315, 349, 390, 400, 417

LETTERS TO: 274, 296, 302, 515–516, 542; on foreign affairs, 368–369, 391–392, 399

Bowles, Mrs. Chester, 274; letter to, 274

Bowra, Sir Maurice, 236

Boyd, James, 287; letter to, 287

Boyd, Julian, 191, 458

Bramblett, Ernest K., 331n

Brandt, Raymond P., 186

Brannan, Charles F., 526

Brehm, Walter E., 167n, 331n

Brevard, John, 289n

Brice, Don, 325; letter to, 325

Bricker, John W., 143, 167

Bricker Amendment, 302n–303n, 315, 316–317, 422; AES statement on, 317–319

Bridges, Styles, 412, 469n

Brightman, Sam, 357, 358

Broniarer, Zygmunt, 600

Brooks, Ned, 599

Brown, John Paulding, letters to, 357, 531

Brown, Stuart Gerry: quoted, on AES, 27, 204, 333, 476; letter to, 204–205

Brownell, Herbert, 292n, 395n, 411, 426, 539

Broyles Bill, 39n

Buck, Paul H., 87; letter to, 88

Bundy, McGeorge, 511

Bunting, Joseph M., 284

Burgess, Kenneth F., telegram to, 235

Burke, Edmund, 487; quoted, 373

Burke, Thomas A., 277

Busch, Noel F., 9; *Adlai Stevenson of Illinois*, 9n, 283

Butcher, Fanny, *see* Bokum, Mrs. Richard

Butler, Paul, 217, 385; letters to, 268, 540; as Democratic National Chairman, 432, 442, 445, 447, 478, 516, 540

Byrd, Harry F., 458

Cain, Harry, 92

Call to Greatness (Stevenson), *see* Godkin Lectures

Cameron, George, 87n

"Campaign Is Over, The" (AES speech, November, 1952), 181–186

"Campaign Mythology and the Public Weal" (AES speech, February, 1953), 255–259

Canfield, Cass, 218, 349, 463, 480, 485n, 562

Canfield, Mrs. Cass (Jane), 463, 480, 485n

Canham, Erwin D. ("Spike"), 87

Carlyle, Thomas, 572

Carnegie Endowment for International Peace, Alger Hiss at, 65, 167–168

Carolina Israelite, 449

Carr, Francis, 329n

Case, Everett, letter to, 455–456

Case, James, 456n

Case, Mrs. James, *see* Rockefeller, Laura

"Case for Stevenson, The" (Cooley), 43

Cash, Mrs. Albert D. (Betty Cassatt), letter to, 36

Central African Federation, 491, 527

Central Intelligence Agency, 137, 138

Cerf, Bennett, 216

"Challenge to Political Maturity, The" (AES speech, December, 1954), 432–439

Chandler, Kent, 121

Chapin, Mr., 230

Chapman, Oscar, 31n, 217

Chelf, Frank, 125

Chesapeake and Ohio Railway, 319–320

Chiang Kai-shek, 137, 411, 423, 438, 450n, 469, 471, 474

Chicago Sun, 147n

Chicago Sun-Times, 147, 401

Chicago Tribune, 37, 180

Childs, Marquis ("Mark"), 247; letter to, 31

China, People's Republic of (Communist), 96, 256, 360, 408, 455; Communist conquest in, 52n, 62, 115, 116, 323, 360, 410, 413, 414, 436, 438, 477, 588; and recognition of, 461, 603–604; and offshore islands, 470–475, 476

China, Republic of (Nationalist), 84–85, 115, 116–117, 137, 314, 323, 472, 476; U.S. treaty with, 450n, 453–454, 461, 463, 469

Choate School, AES at, 93n

Christian Century magazine, article on AES in, 214

Churchill, Winston S., 9, 86, 118, 192, 203, 276, 375

Citizens for Eisenhower and Nixon, 99n

civil rights, 47–48, 57–58, 63, 157, 205, 435, 602, 605; AES speech on, 54–60; in 1952 Democratic platform, 110n–111n, 151

Civil Service Commission, 137, 326

Clapper, Mrs. Raymond, 147; letter to, 148

Clark, Kitty, letter to, 312

Clayton Antitrust Act, 576, 585

Clements, Earle C., 256

Cleveland, Grover, 38, 79, 106, 156, 172n

coexistence: AES on, 82, 415, 436–437; Eisenhower on, 115, 169, 408

Cohen, Benjamin V., 532; letters to, 450, 453–454, 532

Cohn, David L., 28, 239, 298, 300, 358, 479; letters to, 239, 298–299, 352, 401–402, 440, 530

Cohn, Mrs. David L. (Lillian Millner), 402n

Cohn, Roy, 329n

Columbia University, 237, 300, 316, 367n, 429n; AES speech before Bicentennial Conference (June, 1954), 369–376

Commager, Henry Steele, 506; letters to, 234, 507

Commission on the Health Needs of the Nation, 8n

Committee to Defend America by Aiding the Allies, 581n

Commodity Credit Corporation (CCC), 523

Commonwealth Club (Chicago), 204

Communism, 111, 119, 128, 145, 212, 250–251, 342, 350, 369–370, 372, 373, 415, 437, 517, 569, 570, 587–588, 600; as campaign issue, 52–53, 255n, 294, 392–393, 410, 426, 427; and China, 62, 85, 116–117, 120, 256n, 414, 436, 471; and Asia, 83–86, 127, 245–246, 359–360, 408–409, 414, 438, 469, 499; in government, 126, 169–170, 231, 292–294, 303, 307–308, 325–326, 328–330, 334, 412, 421, 424, 425; AES speeches on, 134–140, 327–333; under FDR and HST, 143, 258, 292–293, 303, 325; and American Negro, 290. *See also* Union of Soviet Socialist Republics

Communist party, in U.S., 137

"Congressional Campaign Begins, The" (AES speech, September, 1954), 392, 393–396

"Congressional Campaign Ends, The" (AES speech, October, 1954), 421–428

Congressional Record, AES speech inserted in, 337

Congress of Industrial Organizations (CIO), 206, 214, 296, 580; AES speech before, 209–212

Connelly, Marc, letter to, 549

Connelly, Matthew, 36, 199

Constitution: Confederate, 109–110; U.S., 111n; and Bricker Amendment, 317–319

Continental Divide, 71

Cooke, Alistair, 324; on AES's nomination, 15–16; letter to, 324–325

Cooke, Morris, 535

Cooley, Harold D. ("The Case for Stevenson"), 43

Coolidge, Calvin, 135, 307, 570

Coombs, Philip, 280

Coronet magazine, AES article in, 546

Council of Economic Advisers, 100

Council on Foreign Relations, 317, 320; AES speech before, 302

Country Gentleman magazine, 43

Counts, George S., 60

Cousins, Norman, 234; letters to, 92–93, 221–222, 446; "Whither A.E.S.?," 221

Cowan, Louis G., 581

Cowie, Colonel Mervyn, 491n

Cromwell, Oliver, 99

Cross, Mrs., 502

"Crusades, Communism, and Corruption" (AES speech, March, 1954), 327–333

Cummings, Milton, 298; letter to, 300

Curie, Eve, 200; letter to, 200

Currie, Mrs. Bethia S., 448; letter to, 449

Currie, Mr. and Mrs. John, 322, 508; letters to, 508–509, 553

Currie, Lauchlin, 136n

Cuyler, Mrs. Lewis B. (Margery), 379n

Czechoslovakia, 589n

Daily Pantagraph, 39, 40n, 277, 283–284, 531

Daley, Richard J., 261; letters to, 261–262, 351, 442, 529

Dangerfield, Royden, 441

Daniels, Jonathan, 458, 466; letters to, 458, 466–467

Davis, Charles A., 596

Davis, John W., 163; letter to, 163

Davis, Kenneth S., quoted, on AES, 439–440

Day, J. Edward, 444

Dean, Arthur, 388

Dean, Vera Micheles, 304; letter to, 304

Declaration of Conscience, 165

Declaration of Independence, 57, 111n

Defense, U.S. Department of, 325, 360, 390

"defense perimeter," 117

Democratic Congressional Campaign Committee, 218, 428

Democratic Digest, 356, 357, 540

Democratic National Committee, 27, 36, 254–255, 275, 283, 367, 385, 430, 432, 442, 557; HST charges against, 90; revitalization of, 198, 202, 204, 205, 215–216, 217, 220, 221, 231, 232, 253, 265, 302; AES speeches for, 265, 268, 269, 302, 315, 322, 327, 389, 535, 583n, 593

Democratic National Convention, 54; AES arrives at, 10–11; AES speech of welcome to, 11–14, 282; conduct of, 17; AES speech of acceptance at, 17; Official Report of Proceedings (1952), 110n–111n; for 1956, 466, 540

Democratic Organizing Committee of Wisconsin, telegram to, 218–219

Democratic party, 19, 108, 120, 132, 143, 182, 247–249, 251–253, 283, 383; and AES draft, 3, 4–6, 11; AES on twenty years of, 13, 18, 100, 125–127, 135–137, 139, 156, 158, 183, 184, 282, 328; platform of, 17, 54–60, 61, 63–64, 71–74, 78, 177–179; defections from, 32, 204, 596n; and ADA, 37, 312; foreign policy, 56, 68, 85–86, 96–97, 120, 140, 154, 313–314, 409–417 (*see also* bipartisanship); and civil rights, 57–58, 63, 110n–111n, 151, 157, 205; farm program, 71, 73–74, 257, 290; AES on contributions to, 123, 148; AES as leader of, 195, 198, 201, 204–205 (*see also* Stevenson, Adlai E.: AND LEADERSHIP OF DEMOCRATIC PARTY); future of, 219, 230, 231, 254, 261–262, 265, 278–279, 287, 291, 292; as labor party, 221; in South, 230, 231, 290, 445, 466, 467, 528; in 1954 Congress, 266, 292, 347, 428, 437n, 461, 463, 528; and Finletter Group (policy planning), 267, 315, 441, 462, 478, 510; and "how to be a Democrat," 281–283; HST on, 365; "new look," 385, 540; and AES in 1954 campaigns, 392, 393–399, 403, 406, 407, 417, 418, 421, 428; and business hostility, 566–567, 581. *See also* Democratic National Committee; Democratic National Convention

Democratic State Central Committees: Virginia, 65; Illinois, 261–262, 351–352, 354, 604; Minnesota, 562, 577, 578–579, 593

Democratic State Convention, AES speeches at: New York, 47, 54–60; Wisconsin, 534

Depression, Great, 135–136, 142–143

Desbarats, Ontario, 44, 459; AES vacations in, 545n, 548

Dever, Paul, 564

DeVoto, Bernard, 28, 199, 384, 447; letters to, 30, 199–200, 367–368, 386–387, 418, 447

DeVoto, Mrs. Bernard, 199, 200

Dewey, Thomas E., 93, 116, 224n, 324; denounces Democrats and HST administration, 323, 330, 395n, 410–411, 426

Dick, Jane Warner (Mrs. Edison Dick), 27, 37, 92, 207, 538, 582, 591; letters to, 38, 212–213, 376, 381; quoted, on ghostwriting, 376n

Dick, Marnie (Mrs. James T. Last), 459

DiSalle, Michael, 217, 385

Dixon, Sherwood, 262

Dixon-Yates combine, 424, 425, 532, 539

Dodds, Harold W., 113; letter to, 113

"dollar diplomacy," 246, 251

Dollars for Democrats, 381

Douglas, Mrs. Helen Gahagan, 231; letter to, 232

Douglas, Paul H., 125, 351; letters to, 354, 357, 389

Doyle, James E., 217; telegram to, 218–219

Dreiske, John, 596, 606

Dubinsky, David, 60

Duckworth, Allen, 596

Duff, Alverta, letter to, 304

Dulles, Allen, 138

Dulles, John Foster, 246, 276, 317, 388–389, 407n, 413–416 *passim*, 422, 423, 532; and Alger Hiss, 65, 167–168; consults AES, 266, 549–550, 551; letters to, 266, 278, 550–551; AES visits, 274, 297; quoted, 251n, 317n, 331, 463, 476; criticisms of, 56, 320, 359–360, 408, 411–412

Dunne, Edward F., 12

Durkin, Martin, 256n

Eaton, Cyrus, 378; letters to, 319–320, 378

"Eccentric Letters," AES file, 493–494

Eden, Anthony, 543

"Educated Citizen, The" (AES speech, March, 1954), 337–345

"Education, a National Cause" (AES speech, July, 1955), 516–523

Edwards, Mrs. India, letter to, 275

"eggheads," AES on, 140–141, 223, 225, 227, 305, 447, 530

Egypt, 414, 589

Einstein, Albert: quoted, on AES, 174; letter to, 200

Eisenhower, Dwight D., 208, 224, 319, 363; AES and, 10, 37, 49, 56, 62, 78, 176, 225–226, 247, 249, 252, 270, 476; and foreign policy, 10, 66–68, 69n, 74, 80–81, 85, 86, 158, 160, 184–185, 313, 317, 364, 391, 408–415, 422–423, 477, 523–524, 539; quoted, 10n, 42n, 256n, 424n; supporters of, 32n, 37, 44n, 147n, 180, 191, 197n, 227, 596n; campaign strategy, 34–35, 40, 138–139, 169, 178, 181, 184–185, 421–422, 425, 426, 601n; and HST, 62, 292n, 552; and General Marshall, 62, 93n, 165; and domestic policies, 71, 73, 107, 124,

Eisenhower, Dwight D. (*continued*)
394, 424–425, 506n; and the press, 76,
538; reconciliation with Taft, 90, 99,
163, 177, 183; and Republican candidates, 93–94, 164–166, 183; on Oliver
Cromwell, 99; and Old Guard, 99, 125,
165, 174, 423; and Korea and Far
East, 115–119, 184, 185n, 231, 408–
409, 450n, 461, 463, 469, 474, 476;
on coexistence, 115, 169, 408; appeal
and image of, 133–134, 204, 222, 476,
551–552, 553; and Communist menace
and security program, 138–139, 177,
265, 276, 292n, 294, 309n, 325–326,
329–330, 392, 545; and Hiss case, 164–
169; AES concession telegram to, 186;
AES "message" to, from White House,
212; AES meets with, 254, 273, 274,
278; on Yalta agreement, 255; administration, 256n, 266, 274, 292–294, 299n,
347, 383, 416, 435, 539; as "unbeatable" in 1956, 467, 494; and aid to
education, 519–520, 528; at Geneva
Conference, 533, 539, 543–544, 545,
602–603; illness and 1956 candidacy
of, 559n, 593–594, 597, 598
Eliot House, Harvard, 453
Elks Club Group, 28n, 194, 239
Elting, Winston, 379
Emancipation Proclamation, 57, 213
Emerson, Mr. and Mrs. George Waldo,
396
England, *see* Great Britain
equal rights, *see* civil rights
"Equal Rights" (AES speech, August,
1952), 47, 54–60
Ervin, Senator Sam J., Jr., 458
Europe: AES's popularity in, 114, 242,
274–275; U.S. foreign policy in, 251n,
258, 413
European Defense Community (EDC),
251, 276, 407n, 414; AES letter to
Mendès-France on, 387–389
European Economic Co-operation, 251
Evans, B. Ifor, letter to, 280
Evans, Carol, 213, 243, 281, 337, 386,
417, 494, 584; letters and memoranda
to, 244–245, 288, 345, 387–389, 494,
548–549

Fahy, Mr. and Mrs. Charles, letter to,
541
Fair Deal, 576
Fair Employment Practices Commission
(FEPC), 47, 48

"Faith in Liberalism" (AES speech, Au-
gust, 1952), 60–64
"Faith, Knowledge and Peace" (AES
speech, May, 1955), 495
Farley, James A., 230, 231
farm program: as campaign issue, 34, 71,
107, 124, 257, 290, 394, 506, 581; AES
on, 44, 73–74, 425, 559, 600
Farrar, Straus & Company, 238, 283
Farrell, James T., 379; letter to, 379
Faulkner, William, 109
Federal Bureau of Investigation (FBI),
126, 137, 138, 139, 303, 393
Federal Reserve System, 585
Federal Security Agency, 517n
Federal Trade Commission, 585
Fell, Jesse W. (great-grandfather), 325
Field, Marshall, III, letters to, 147, 301,
454
Field, Marshall, IV, 147n, 223n, 311n,
558
Field Enterprises, Inc., 467
Fifer, Joseph W., 354
Figueres, José, 431; quoted, on AES, 430
Finletter, Thomas K., 267, 279, 280, 295,
391, 431, 515; letters to, 268, 302–303,
315, 399–400, 441–442
Finletter, Mrs. Thomas K. ("Gay"), 302,
515
Finletter Group, 267, 315, 441, 462, 478,
510
Finnegan, James A., 5, 217, 385; as 1956
campaign manager, 591, 592, 594, 595,
604
Finston, Charles, 595
First Boston Corporation, 424n
"First Fireside Speech" (AES speech,
September, 1952), 121–130
Fischer, John, 28, 218, 441; letter to,
562–563
Fisher, Eddie, 275, 276
Fisher, Harry M., letter to, 550
Fisher, Walter T., letter to, 214
Fitzgerald, F. Scott, 142
Flanagan, W. H., 303; letter to, 303
Flanagan, William I., 3, 103n
Flanders, Ralph E., 334, 437n
Fleeson, Doris, letter to, 35
Flood, Douglas, 442
Floyd, M. A., letter to, 327
Force Bill, 156
Ford, John Anson, 465; letter to, 465
foreign affairs and policy: of Eisenhower
administration, 10, 66–68, 69n, 74, 80–
81, 85, 86, 158, 160, 313, 317, 364,
391, 408–415, 422–423, 477, 523–

524, 539; as partisan issue, 34, 56–57, 90, 119–120, 313–314, 320–321, 368–369, 421, 461, 473, 477; AES on, in letters, 46, 68–69, 267, 349, 391, 399, 400; AES on, in speeches, 56–57, 62, 69n, 74, 140, 251–252, 258, 294, 318, 368–369, 372–373, 409–417, 422–423; AES speeches on (1952), 65–68, 79–86; (1956), 432–439. *See also* Bricker Amendment

Foreign Policy Bulletin, 304

Foreign Service, U.S., 271, 278, 412

Formosa, 117, 120, 256, 455, 465, 467, 532; mutual defense treaty and, 450, 454, 461, 463, 468–476

"Formosa Crisis, The" (AES radio speech, April, 1955), 468–476

Forsyth, Donald, 262

Fort Bragg, North Carolina, 459n

Fortune magazine, AES article in, 555, 565–567, 580

Fourth Presbyterian Church, Chicago, 11

France and the French, 259, 260, 359, 379, 393, 533n; Eisenhower and, 10n, 158; and EDC, 251n, 387–388, 389; AES in, 362; in Indochina, 408, 414n; and African colonies, 485–486, 488

Franklin, Benjamin, 60

"Franklin Delano Roosevelt" (AES speech, October, 1952), 172–174

Freeman, Orville, 535, 577, 578; letter to, 577–578

Freeman, Mrs. Orville (Jane), 578

Friendly, Alfred, 525

Fritchey, Clayton, 356, 540; letters to, 316–317, 357

Fry, Joshua, 130n

Fulbright, J. W., 27, 125, 186, 445

Fulbright Fellowship Program, 519–520

Galbraith, John Kenneth ("Ken"), 28, 88, 267, 278, 296, 505; letters to, 278–279, 336, 506, 525–526

Galbraith, Mrs. John Kenneth, letter to, 88

Gallagher, William F., 226n

Gallup, George H., 560

Garrison, Lloyd K., 463, 480, 485n; letters to, 29–30, 218, 238–239, 349; and AES in Africa, 492n

Garrison, Mrs. Lloyd (Ellen), 463, 480, 485n

Garst, Roswell, 506, 523, 526; letter to, 523–524

Gellhorn, Martha, *see* Matthews, Mrs. T. S.

General Federation of Women's Clubs, 495

General Motors Corporation, 250

Geneva Conference, 359, 411, 414n, 533, 539, 543–544, 603

George, Walter F., 289, 457n, 471

Georgia: 1952 election returns in, 197n, 289n; AES speech before legislature of, 288–294, 298–299

Germany, 260, 271, 308, 414; Nazi government in, 137, 589; Stalin on, 155; and EDC, 251n, 276, 388n, 407n; AES on re-unification of, 603

Getty, Gerald W., 442

ghostwriting, 89n, 149n; discussed by AES with writers: Archibald Mac-Leish, 22, 39, 49n, 199, 242; Gerald Johnson, 34, 195, 236–237; T. S. Matthews, 41, 316; Arthur M. Schlesinger, Jr., 43, 114, 131, 149–150, 194, 366; Samuel Rosenman, 46; Norman Cousins, 92–93; Nicolo Tucci, 208–209; Henry S. Commager, 234; Paul Nitze and Bernard DeVoto, 418; Barbara Ward, 510–512, 514–515, 546; Agnes Meyer, 560–561, 563; research and writing staff for, 28, 47, 196, 198, 280–281; Elks Club Group, 28n, 194, 239; AES on, 226, 295; Jane Warner Dick on AES's use of, 376n. *See also* Finletter Group

Gibbons, Mrs. Kitty Clark, *see* Clark, Kitty

GI Bill of Rights, 518

Gifford, Edith, 297; letters to, 297, 385–386, 448

Gill, Joseph, 262

Glasgow, Ellen, 109

Glasgow University Liberal Club, 541, 551

Glassford, Mrs. D. L., 10; letter to, 10

Glassford, Admiral William A., 10

Godkin Lectures (Harvard), 322, 327, 336, 346, 347; published as *Call to Greatness,* 304n, 335, 349; praise of, 386, 392, 430

Golden, Harry, letter to, 449–450

Goldwater, Barry, 92n, 580

Good Neighbor Policy, 154

Goodwin, Richard N., 29

G.O.P., *see* Republican party

"Government and Private Reputation," *see* "Reputation of the Government, The"

Governors' Conference (August, 1955), 515, 544n, 546, 547, 548, 594, 596, 599

Graebel, Rev. Richard Paul, 217, 285; letters to, 285, 444
Graham, Philip L., 534, 558, 561n, 579, 580; letter to, 558
Graham, Mrs. Philip L., 558, 561n, 580
Grand Alliance, 409, 410, 471
Graves, Anna Melissa, letter to, 362–363
Graves, Richard, 407, 408
Great Britain, 359, 414, 533n; and EDC, 251n; Labour party in, 279; and support of AES, 280; McCarthyism and, 297; and African colonies, 485–488, 489, 490
"Great Crusade," 99, 165, 169, 180, 293, 330, 393, 426
Green, Lewis Warner (great-grandfather), 217
Gridiron Club, AES speech before, 9n, 192, 207, 223–229
Griffith, Clark, 228
Grotius, Hugo, 543, 545
Guatemala, 414
Guggenheim, Mrs. Harry, *see* Patterson, Alicia
Gunn, Emmet V., 284
Gustafson, Phyllis, 243–244

Hall, Leonard, 294
Hamilton, Alexander, 252
Hammarskjöld, Dag, 392; letters to, 392, 457
Hardin, Adlai S., 531n
Hardin, Carol J., letter to, 531
Hardin, Mrs. Martin D. (Aunt Julia), 35, 362
Harding, Warren G., 307
Harper & Brothers, 218, 233, 283, 349
Harriman, Averell, 21, 37, 54, 279, 320, 336, 337, 346, 457; in 1952 campaign, 5, 6, 15, 601; letters to, 320–321, 547–548; nominated for governor of New York, 400n, 403n; and 1956 campaign, 544–545, 547, 558, 560, 561, 563, 599, 603; quoted, on Asia, 471
Harriman, Mrs. Averell (Marie), 346, 457, 547; letters to, 336–337, 400, 457
Harris, Seymour E., 478; letter to, 478
Harrisburg, Pennsylvania, AES speech at, 366, 376, 390
Hart, Kay, 431, 534
Harvard Law School, Adlai III at, 419, 531
Harvard University, 304; Corporation, 88; John Fell at, 583. *See also* Godkin Lectures

Havens, Gordon, 243; letter to, 243
Haydn, Hiram, letter to, 235
Hayes, John, 33
Hecht, George, 561
Heiskell, J. N., 556; letter to, 556
Heller, Walter W., letter to, 509–510
Hemingway, Ray, 593
Hendrickson, Robert C., 165n
Hersey, John, 95
Hill, Lister, 424, 519, 521
Hillbilly Festival, Meridian, Mississippi, AES speech at, 352, 368
Hines, Mrs. Ralph (Betty Borden, formerly Mrs. Robert S. Pirie), 242, 347, 505
Hiroshima, 95
Hiss, Alger, 34, 64, 65, 136, 392; AES speech on, 164–170
Hitler, Adolf, 64, 134, 136, 372, 499
Hochschild, Harold, letter to, 527–528
Hochschild, Mrs. Harold (Mary Marquand), letter to, 502
Hodes, Barnet, letter to, 147
Hoehler, Fred, 36, 529
Hoffman, Herman, 402
Holt, Mr. and Mrs. McPherson, 45
Hoover, Herbert, and Hoover Commission, 108, 574
Hoover, J. Edgar, 138, 139, 393
Horner, Henry, 12
House Military Affairs Committee, 115, 169
House Un-American Activities Committee, 136n
Howlett, Mike, 389
Hughes, Charles Evans, 18
Hull, Cordell, 154, 586
Humphrey, Hubert H., 63, 195, 346, 528, 578, 581, 582, 605; letters to, 195, 202–203, 528–529, 578; AES schedules speech in behalf of, 535; endorses AES, 577
Humphrey, Mrs. Hubert H. (Muriel), 578, 581; letters to, 578, 582
Hutchins, Robert M., 353
Hyman, Sidney, 28; letters to, 193–194, 382–383

Idaho Power Company, 424n
"If I Were Twenty-one (AES article in *Coronet*), 546n
Illinois: AES as governor of, 3, 16, 39, 43, 44, 57, 110, 122–123, 192, 194–195, 206, 224–225, 240, 241, 243 (*see also* Stevenson, Adlai E.: GOVERNORSHIP AND PUBLIC LIFE); University

of, 93, 140; Democratic party in, 261–262, 351–352, 354, 601

Illinois State Fair, 43

India, 62, 85, 157, 348, 598

Indianapolis, AES speech in, 392, 393–396

Indochina, 84, 120, 359, 364, 368n, 393, 411, 469; Nixon on, 408, 473; AES on, 413–414, 438

Iran, 414

Irvin, Lawrence, 261, 262

Israel, 414, 549–551, 589–590

Italy, 414

Ives, Ernest L., 32n, 345, 432; letter to, 380–381

Ives, Mrs. Ernest L. (Elizabeth Stevenson, "Buffie"), 32n, 35, 206, 345, 405, 432, 460, 464, 529; letters to, 274, 380–381; *My Brother Adlai*, 508, 557n, 565n

Ives, Irving M., 59n, 63, 165n, 533

Ives, Timothy Reed (nephew), 362

Jackson, Andrew, 141, 252

Jackson, Henry, 92

Jackson, Robert, 479, 486n, 512, 513, 515; letter to, 510–511

Jackson, Mrs. Robert, *see* Ward, Barbara

Jamaica: AES vacations in, 454, 455, 456; AES speech in, 534, 546, 556

Japan, 120, 127, 137, 155, 413, 470

Jebb, Sir Gladwyn, 37; letter to, 38

Jefferson, Thomas, 112, 144, 191, 222, 252, 299, 373, 585; quoted, 51, 79, 333; AES compared to, 208; as "radical," 458

Jefferson-Jackson Day Dinner(s), AES speech at: New York (1953), 242, 245, 247–253, 259; Los Angeles (1953), 255–259, 260–261, 262

Jenkins, Dick, 351; telegram to, 351

Jenner, William E., 34, 183, 303, 395n; attacks General Marshall, 52n, 93n, 165

Johannesburg, AES in, 492n

Johnson, Gerald W., 33, 236, 363, 364, 551, 559–560, 564; letters to, 34, 195, 236–237, 368, 384, 552–553, 559, 564

Johnson, Lyndon B., 249, 266, 313, 364, 470, 478, 605; letters to, 364, 451, 477, 526; heart attack, 513, 602; and 1956 nomination, 564, 597

Johnson, Mrs. Lyndon B., letter to, 513–514

Johnson, Walter, 402; telegram to, 4n

Johnston, Richard J. H., 597, 601

Justice, U.S. Department of, 111n, 135, 137, 138

Kane, R. Keith, 458

Karelsen, Frank E., Jr., letters to, 214, 312

Kefauver, Estes, 15, 92, 110, 125, 313, 404, 595, 603; letters to, 196, 202, 313–314, 337, 404, 555–556; consultations with AES, 560, 563; as vice presidential candidate, 597

Keller, Helen, 232; letter to, 233

Kellogg, Mr. and Mrs. John P., 459

Kem, James P., 34

Kennan, George F., 319, 349, 391, 400; letters to, 319, 390

Kennedy, John F., 352, 502, 503, 564; letters to, 420, 564–565

Kennon, Robert F., 458

Kentucky, AES's ancestors in, 114–115

Kentucky Derby, 351, 462–463

Kerr, Chester, letter to, 207

Kerr, Walter, 595

Khan, Muhammad Zafrullah, 296

Khrushchev, Nikita, 506n

Kilgore, Harley M., 347; letter to, 347–348

Kimmelmann, Baron von, 527

King, Cecil, 125, 511–512

Kintner, Robert E., 220; letter to, 220

Kirkpatrick, Helen, *see* Milbank, Mrs. Robbins

Kirwan, Michael J., 428; letter to, 428

Knight, Goodwin J., 407n

Knight, John S., 478

Knopf, Alfred A., Jr., letter to, 7

Knopf, Alfred A., Inc., 238

Knowland, William F., 408, 412, 422, 435, 465, 469n, 524

Knox, Frank, 10, 148, 289

Kohn, Louis A., 467; letter to, 213

Kopper, Samuel, 563

Korea, 160, 410, 437, 468; AES on war in, 56, 67, 84, 96, 100, 105, 115–121, 127, 230, 306–307, 328, 332, 372, 438; Truman and, 56, 118, 461; Republican party on, 67, 84, 96, 126, 323, 392, 408, 426; AES speech on (1952), 114–121; Eisenhower and, 115–119, 185n, 231; AES and journey to, 184n–185n

Krock, Arthur, 4n, 259, 322, 580; letters to, 260, 322, 562

Kroll, Jack, 428; letter to, 429

Kuchel, Thomas H., 407n

Kupcinet, Irving, 452; letter to, 452

labor relations, 73–74, 101, 211–212
Labour party (Great Britain), 279
La Follette, Robert, 144, 371
Lahey, Edwin A., letter to, 214
Lambert, Jean, 388
Laniel, Joseph, 276
Lanigan, James, 403
Last, Mrs. James T., *see* Dick, Marnie
Latin America, 154, 385
Laubach, Frank, 390
Lausche, Frank, letters to, 277–278, 548
Lawford, Peter, 420
Lawford, Mrs. Peter (Patricia Kennedy), 420
Lawrence, David, 261, 276, 277, 512, 515
Lawrence, David L., letter to, 383
Lawrence, W. H., 594
Leach, Paul R., 223; letter to, 9
League of Nations, 86, 338, 584, 586–587, 589
Lee, Robert E., 596
Lee, General Robert E., 112
"Legacy of Philip Murray, The" (AES speech, December, 1952), 209–212
Legge, Harry A., 274; letter to, 274
Lehman, Herbert H., 55, 58, 59n, 63, 543, 544–545, 603; letter to, 476–477
Lehrer, Tom, 323; letter to, 323
Lend-lease, 372
Lewis, John L., 186
Lewis, Kathryn (Mrs. Lloyd Lewis), 401
Lewis, Lloyd, 401
Lewis, Mrs. Raymond S., 282; letter to, 282–283
Liberal party (New York), 48; AES speech before, 60–64
Libertyville, Illinois, AES's house in, 223n, 467
Library of Congress, 443
Libya, AES supporters in, 383
Lie, Trygve, 201, 234, 535; letters to, 201–202, 234, 535
Life magazine, 254
Lilienthal, David E., quoted, on AES, 79, 269
Lincoln, Abraham, 106, 187, 222, 355–356, 499, 518, 585; uncertainty of, 7, 503; Republican party "descendants" of, 57, 328, 395, 458; quoted, 99, 160, 161, 188, 342, 358; AES sleeps in Lincoln Room, 212–213; AES on (interview), 323–324, 325
Lincoln, G. Gould, 603
Lindsay, Vachel, 12
Link, Arthur, 535

Linkletter, Art, 446
Lippmann, Walter, 5–6, 197, 227, 453; letter to, 197
Livingston, Edward, 299
Lloyd, David D., 253, 353; letter to, 353
Locke, Walter, 272, 273
London *Daily Mail*, 387
Look magazine: AES articles in, 244, 246, 271n, 479n, 546n, 562–563; Lauren Bacall's article on AES in, 285–286
Louchheim, Mrs. Katie, letter to, 381
Louisiana, 151–153, 156–158
Louisville *Courier-Journal*, 532
Lovejoy, Elijah, 192
Loyalty Review Board, 517n
Luce, Clare Boothe (Mrs. Henry Luce), 466, 479
Luce publications, 226
Lucey, Charles T., 599
Lynch, Robert J., 64; letter to, 64

McAdoo, Eleanor Wilson (Mrs. William Gibbs McAdoo), 132; letter to, 132
MacArthur, General Douglas, 117, 118
McCarran, Patrick, 303
McCarran Act, 252
McCarthy, Senator Joseph R., 62, 131, 166, 183–184, 208, 266, 303, 335, 346, 412, 422, 461, 524, 533; attacks General Marshall, 52n, 93n; accuses State Department, 135, 138, 270, 297, 298, 328n, 329; on AES, 164–165; and "Twenty Years of Treason," 323, 393, 411, 426; and Army-McCarthy hearings, 328–329, 357; repudiated and censured, 334, 437n
McCarthyism, 270, 293, 329, 362, 363, 366, 374, 411, 428
McCloy, John J., 335; letter to, 335–336
McCormack, John W., 564n
McCormick, Robert R., 164, 180, 478
MacDonald, Malcolm, letter to, 401
MacDonald, Ramsay, 401n
McDougal, Edward D., Jr., 322; letter to, 204
McEvoy, Mrs. Dennis (Nan Tucker), 87n, 288, 380
McFarland, Ernest, 92
McGill, Ralph, 292n, 363; letters to, 197, 295, 363–364, 429, 507–508
McGowan, Carl, 28, 133, 186, 443
McGrory, Mary, 29
McKay, David, 381
Mackay, John A., 298n
McKeever, Porter, letter to, 406–407

McKinley, William, 100

McKinney, Frank, 36, 90, 91

MacLeish, Ada (Mrs. Archibald Mac-
Leish), 452, 538; letters to, 199, 453

MacLeish, Archibald, 22, 28, 511; on
AES's speeches, 49n
LETTERS TO: 451–452, 453, 537–538;
re ghostwriting, 22–23, 39, 43, 90, 199,
241–242

McLeod, R. W. Scott, 412n

McMahon, Brien: AES on, 94, 95, 97–
98; quoted, 97–98

McMillan, Dr. Robert, letter to, 495

McNeill, Hector, letter to, 541

McPherson, Fanny, 531

Madison Square Garden, AES speech at
(October, 1952), 175–180

Magnuson, Laura (Mrs. Paul Magnuson),
8, 459, 464; letters to, 8, 460–461

Magnuson, Dr. Paul, 8, 459, 464

*Major Campaign Speeches of Adlai E.
Stevenson, 1952,* 192, 216n, 218, 242,
244

Malaya, 84

Malone, Dumas, 377; letter to, 377

Manchester *Guardian,* 15

Marines, U.S., AES speech before, 103–
105

Marquand, Mary, *see* Hochschild, Mrs.
Harold

Marshall, C. B., 367n, 391

Marshall, General George C., 203, 285n;
letters to, 32, 203, 285; attacks on, 52,
62, 165; Eisenhower on, 93n, 165

Marshall Plan, 74, 82, 159, 251, 285,
372

Martin, Arnold E., 599

Martin, John Bartlow, 28; *Adlai Stevenson,* 283

Martin, Joseph W., Jr., 167

Marx, Karl, 372, 568

Matsu Island, 450n, 462n, 463, 465; AES
speech concerning, 468–476

Matthews, T. S. ("Tom"), 40, 398; letters to, 41, 315–316, 378–379, 384,
398

Matthews, Mrs. T. S. (Martha Gellhorn),
315, 316, 379, 398

Matthews, William Alexander Procter
("Sandy"), 379

Mau Mau, 490

"Medicine and Public Policy" (AES
speech, June, 1955), 495, 504

Mellon, Andrew, 108

"Memo to My Sons on a Month in Africa" (AES, May, 1955), 480–493

Mendelsohn, Rev. Jack, 443; letter to,
443–444

Mendès-France, Pierre, letter to, 387–
388

Menninger, Dr. Karl, 390; letter to, 390

Merwin, Davis, 276, 277, 284

Merwin, Loring C. ("Bud"), 39–40, 276,
283; letters to, 40, 276–277, 284, 365

Meyer, Eugene, 504, 525n, 554–555, 563,
579

Meyer, Mrs. Eugene (Agnes), 504, 542,
543, 558
LETTERS TO: 504, 554–555; on 1956
plans, 524–525, 533–534, 542–545,
557–558, 560–561, 563, 579–580

Meyner, Robert, 297, 599, 600

Miami, AES speech in (March, 1954),
315, 322, 326, 327–333, 335, 337, 346

Middle East, 383, 414, 549–551, 589

Milbank, Mrs. Robbins (Helen Kirkpatrick), 380; letter to, 380

Milder, John B., Jr., 237; letter to, 237–
238

Miller, Edward J., Jr., 579; letter to, 579

Miller, John S., letter to, 7

Millner, Lillian, *see* Cohn, Mrs. David L.

Milne, Edward J., 595

Milwaukee *Journal,* 180

Minnesota: Democratic primaries in
(1956), 562, 593, 595, 602; Democratic party leadership in, 577–578,
579

Minow, Newton N., 449n

Mitchell, George, 123n

Mitchell, Stephen A., 232, 311, 417n; as
Democratic National chairman, 27, 40,
42, 215, 220, 253, 268, 445, 540; and
HST charges, 90–91; letter to, 216–
217; quoted, on ADA, 312n–313n; resignation, 385, 429, 430; in 1956 campaign, 591, 593, 595

Monroney, A. S. Mike, 36

Montagu, Lady Judith, 203; letter to, 203

Moody, Blair, 37

Morgan, Edward P., 596; interviews AES
(February, 1953), 245–247

Morrow, Mrs. Wright, 503; letter to, 503–
504

Morse, Wayne, 164, 165n, 184

Mumford, Lewis, 360; letter to, 360–361

Munn, Mrs. Margaret, 187n, 311; letter
to, 311

Munoz-Marin, Luis, 254

Murphy, Charles, 279

Murray, Philip, AES speech honoring,
192, 206, 209–212, 214

Murrow, Edward R., 323, 325; interviews AES (February, 1954), 323–324
Muskie, Edmund, 393n, 454–455
Myers, Francis J., 5
Myers, Maude, letter to, 194–195
"My Faith in Democratic Capitalism" (AES article in *Fortune* magazine, October, 1955), 565–577

Nagel, Brenda, 281; letter to, 281
Nassau Herald (Princeton), 338
National Association for the Advancement of Colored People (NAACP), 528
National Committee Stevenson for President (1952), 3–5, 538; (1956), 579, 591
National Education Association, AES speech before, 516–523, 528
National Labor Relations Board (NLRB), 211
National Press Club, 364
"Nature of Patriotism, The" (AES speech, August, 1952), 49–54
Navy Department, U.S., 43n; AES with, 10, 49–50
Negroes, AES on: in America, 47–48, 110, 290, 528; in Africa, 483–485
Neuberger, Maurine (Mrs. Richard L. Neuberger), 271, 301
Neuberger, Richard L., 301, 367; letters to, 271, 301–302
Nevins, Allan, 240, 397; letter to, 241
New Deal, 143, 173, 250, 567, 581
"New England Tradition, The" (AES speech, September, 1952), 98–102
"New Force in America, The" (AES speech, October, 1952), 175–180
New Freedom, 156, 585–586
Newsday, 20, 180n, 559n
"New South, The" (AES speech, September, 1952), 106–113
Newsweek magazine, 3
"New West, The" (AES speech, September, 1952), 70–75
New York *Herald Tribune*, 103
New York *Post*, 86, 103
New York *Times*, 11, 103, 121, 184–185, 360; and support of Eisenhower, 34n, 103, 133; anonymous contribution from employees of, 148; on AES Miami speech, 333–334; report of 1956 press conference, 592
New York University (Bellevue Medical Center), AES speech at, 495, 504

Niebuhr, Reinhold, letters to, 42, 229–230, 305
Nitze, Paul H., 320, 349, 391, 400, 441, 450; letters to, 327, 418
Nixon, Richard M., 59, 413, 422, 539; in 1952 campaign, 34, 67, 164–167, 364; and Nixon fund, 103, 121; repudiates McCarthy, 334, 336; and 1954 campaigns, 392–393, 425, 426; and accusations against AES, 392–393, 421; and foreign policy, 408–409, 473
Nkrumah, Kwame, 486, 487
Nobel Prize: for literature, 109; for peace, 285n
Noel-Baker, Philip, 68; letter to, 68–69
Norris, George, 55
North Atlantic Treaty Organization (NATO), 82, 119, 251, 414

Oates, Mr. and Mrs. James F., letter to, 350–351
O'Bannion, Dion, 350
Oberlin College, AES speech at, 507, 512, 515
O'Brien, John C., 597
O'Mahoney, Joseph, 217
O'Meara, Joseph, 318
"One-Party Press, The" (AES speech, September, 1952), 75–79
"On Liberty of Conscience" (AES speech, October, 1952), 158–163
Oppenheimer, J. Robert, 376, 417

Pakistan, 85; AES trip to, 348
Palestine, *see* Israel
Palmer, Dwight R. G., 215, 253; letter to, 215–216
Pantagraph, see Daily Pantagraph
Parents' Magazine, 560–561
parity, 506n, 600
"Partnership and Independence" (AES speech, Ontario, October, 1955), 534, 562
Pasley, Virginia, 180
Patel, Dahyabhai, letter to, 230
Patterson, Alicia (Mrs. Harry Guggenheim), 20, 86
    LETTERS TO: 86–87, 131, 149, 223, 273, 322, 346, 351, 403; on candidacy and campaigns, 20–21, 180, 193, 559–560
Patterson, Richard, letter to, 358–359
Pentagon, *see* Defense, U.S. Department of
Perry, Arthur, letter to, 300–301
Persian Gulf, 589

Pescadores Islands, 450n, 461, 463
Peters, John B., 517
Phi Beta Kappa, 235
Philadelphia, support of AES in, 592
Philadelphia Phillies (baseball team), 272
Phillips, Cabell, 393
Pierson, Juli, 217
Pierson, Lynn, 217; letter to, 217–218
Pinay, Antoine, 514
Point Four program, 66, 74, 372, 413
Pontrelli, John, 314; letter to, 315
Porter, Mrs. A. Kingsley ("Aunt Lucy"), 583
Portland, Oregon, *Journal,* 75
Potsdam Agreement, 255
Poullada, Leon B., 348; letter to, 348
Powell, Paul, 261
Pravda, 155
Presbyterian Church, 11, 298n, 443–444
President's Commission on Civil Rights (1947), 57
press, the, 230, 455, 525, 538, 539, 559, 574; Republican, and AES, 40, 76, 479, 524, 532, 552; AES speeches on, 75–79, 223–229; and AES need for "press man," 525, 534, 542–543
Priest, Madison, 305
Princeton University, 113, 344–345; AES speech at, 300, 336, 337–345; AES receives degree from, 376
Pulitzer Prize for photography, 226n
Pusey, Nathan M., 511
Pyle, Jack, 272

Queens University (Kingston, Ontario), AES speech at, 534, 562
Quemoy Island, 450n, 462n, 463, 465; AES speech concerning, 468–476
Quigg, Philip W., 204

Radford, Admiral Arthur W., 391n
Ragland, Martha, 430, 431
Random House, 218, 233, 242
Raskin, Hyman B. (Hy), 540, 591, 593
Rauh, Joseph L., 346; letter to, 346
Rawlings, Calvin, 217
Rayburn, Sam, 249, 266, 459, 460, 478, 564; letter to, 453; AES introduces at testimonial banquet, 479
Reader's Digest, 226
Reciprocal Trade Agreements program, 66, 81, 154–155, 410
Reddig, William, 28
Reinig, C. W., 275

Reporter magazine, 240
Republican National Committee, 328, 334, 366, 395, 411, 426
Republican National Convention, 3, 6, 10, 30n–31n, 143, 293
Republican party, 10, 57, 65, 136, 156, 157, 257, 289; AES on division within, 18, 66–68, 73, 78, 81, 176, 181–182, 183–185, 228, 292–294, 314, 328–330, 348, 409, 410–413, 422–424, 434–435, 455, 473, 524; policies and platforms of, 30n–31n, 32n, 61–62 (AES on), 72, 93, 154, 177–178, 249–252, 255, 366, 409; and campaign strategy, 34–35, 40, 46, 56–57, 183–185, 231, 392–395; and foreign policy, 34, 46, 56–57, 62, 66–68, 74, 80–81, 85, 86, 90, 96, 119, 140, 154, 313, 314, 409–417, 422, 455; and farm program, 34, 71, 73–74, 107, 257, 290, 581; and the press, 76–78, 479, 524, 532, 538, 552; and Korea, 67, 84, 96, 126; AES on tariffs and trade under, 80–81, 106, 107–108, 153–154, 270, 574–575; Old Guard, 81, 86, 135, 136, 139, 154, 174, 177–178, 409–410, 415, 422; AES on humor and, 98–99, 100, 225, 323, 324, 357; as G.O.P., 99, 292; and Eisenhower, 99, 125, 165, 174, 423; and campaign funds, 103; and the South, 106–107, 445; and Wendell Willkie, 185, 394; "new look," 317, 319, 320–321, 326, 331, 335, 336, 411
Republican Policy Committee, 469
"Reputation of the Government, The" (AES speech, December, 1953), 305–310
Reston, James ("Scotty"), 186, 251n, 260; quoted, 11, 359–360, 426n; letter to, 360
Reuther, Walter, 580
Reynal, Eugene, 397
Rhee, Syngman, 438
Riba, Dr. Leander W., 353
Ribicoff, Abraham, 544
Roach, Susan, 281; letter to, 282
"Road Away from Revolution, The" (AES speech, November, 1955), 584–591
Rockefeller, Laura (Mrs. James Case), 456n
Rockefeller, Mr. and Mrs. Laurance, 455–456
Romanes Lecture, 236
Rome, AES in, 479–480
Ronan, James, 261, 262

Roosevelt, Eleanor (Mrs. Franklin D.), 23, 45, 172, 299, 356, 516; on AES's speeches, 23n
   LETTERS TO: 23, 198, 220, 268–269, 299, 356, 365; on Bernard Baruch, 44, 582; birthday messages, 150, 404; on public speaking, 287–288; on ADA, 350; on tenth anniversary of FDR's death, 468
Roosevelt, Franklin D., 56, 58, 62, 76, 99, 106, 116, 299; AES on leadership of, 12, 100, 136, 143, 156, 175–176, 252, 257; administration, 46, 137, 154, 303, 368, 371, 423; as "Great Humanitarian," 99; AES speech on, 172–174; and dog, Fala, 364; and Yalta agreement, 410, 478
Roosevelt, Franklin D., Jr., 172, 403n; letter to, 403–404
Roosevelt, Theodore, 119, 256, 366, 371; quoted, 96, 146, 474
Roper, Elmo, 581
Rosenberg, Fritz, 485n
Rosenman, Samuel I., 28; letters to, 31, 45–46
Rosenwald, Julius, 456
Rowe, Harry W., letter to, 454–455
Rowe, James, 385
Ruml, Beardsley, 521, 530, 568; letter to, 530
Rusk, Dean, 303, 349, 391
Russell, Richard, 15, 37, 41, 48, 110, 289, 600; letters to, 41–42, 89
Russia, *see* Union of Soviet Socialist Republics

Sackville-West, Lionel, 38
"Safeguards Against Communism" (AES speech, October, 1952), 134–140
St. Louis *Post-Dispatch*, 149, 532
Salamon, Sidney, 213
Samuelson, Paul, letter to, 462
Sandburg, Carl, 397, 433; quoted, on AES, 174–175; writes AES after defeat, 192; birthday celebrations for, 215, 241; AES statements on, 241, 452; letters to, 397, 451; *Names*, quoted by AES, 590
Sandburg, Margaret, 175n
San Francisco, AES speech at, 407–417
Santa Barbara, California, *News-Press*, 216
Santa Cruz, Hernan, 299
Santa Monica Bay Area Democratic Club, 450; letter to, 451
Sarnoff, David, 571

Scelba, Mario, 479, 480
Schaefer, Walter V., 123n
Schary, Dore, 402, 557; letters to, 92, 334, 402, 557
Schine, G. David, 329n
Schlesinger, Arthur M., Jr., 37, 232, 279, 355, 509; as head of research and writing staff, 28, 87–88, 267, 391; on AES, 188
   LETTERS TO: 6, 385, 430–431, 534–535; on speeches, 43, 114, 131, 149–150, 194, 267, 334, 366, 417, 442–443
Schmidt, Mrs. Mott B., 321
Schricker, Henry F., 5, 114
Schuman Plan, 251
Schweitzer, Dr. Albert, 485n, 493, 509; letter to, 509
Senate Foreign Relations Committee, 359, 457n, 471
Senate Labor Committee, 59, 63
Sevareid, Eric: letters to, 33, 206; on appeal of Stevenson and Eisenhower, 133–134; on conduct of campaign, 205
Sevareid, Peter, 33n
Seventh Fleet, 255, 256n, 314, 470
Sharon, John, 280, 281
Shaw, Mrs. Jacqueline, 7; letter to, 7–8
Sheean, Vincent ("Jimmy"), letters to, 33–34, 443
Shepard, Lieutenant Thomas, 309n
Sherman Antitrust Act, 576
Sherwood, Robert E., 21–22, 28, 46, 555; letters to, 22, 555
Shivers, Allan, 32n, 151, 152, 596; letter to, 32–33
Shriver, R. Sargent, Jr., 502; letter to, 503
Shriver, Mrs. R. Sargent, Jr. (Eunice Kennedy), 503
Sidley, Austin, Burgess and Smith, 204n, 235, 243
Silver, James, 239
Simon, Paul, 48; letters to, 48–49, 314
Sloan, Alfred P., 48
Smith, Adele, 236
Smith, Alfred E., 58, 99, 166, 175–176, 247
Smith, Ellen (Mrs. Hermon Dunlap Smith), 44, 236, 321, 459n, 513, 545n; letter to, 45
Smith, Farwell, 321; letter to, 321
Smith, Mrs. Farwell (Nora Stone), 321
Smith, Hermon Dunlap, 27, 321, 459n, 545n; letters to, 130, 132, 236, 513
Smith, Margaret Chase, 165
Smith, Paul C., letter to, 87

Smith, General Walter Bedell, 137, 138, 139

Smith Act, 137

Smith College, 419; AES speech at, 495–502

Smoot-Hawley Tariff Act, 107–108

Sobhuza, King, 485

socialism and socialization, 90, 143, 157, 162, 370, 574, 576

Southeast Asia Treaty Organization (SEATO), 414n

Southern Pines, North Carolina, 32, 345, 432

Soviet Union, *see* Union of Soviet Socialist Republics

Sparkman, John, 36, 42, 48; AES on, 55; as 1952 vice presidential candidate, 110, 123, 187, 207, 289, 599; letters to, 207–208, 296–297, 383

Spears, General Sir Louis, 504; letter to, 235–236

Spears, Lady (Mary Borden), 261, 297, 387; letters to, 235–236, 298, 347, 387, 504–505

speechwriting, *see* ghostwriting

Spence, Linda, 45

Spiegel, Modie J., 580; letter to, 581

Spivak, Robert G., 598

Springfield, Illinois, 98, 106

Stafford Little Lectures, 390

Stalin, Joseph, 100, 119, 127, 308, 543; AES on, 155, 372

State Department, U.S., 196, 260, 266, 325, 360, 389, 390, 410, 416; AES with, 64, 116, 579; McCarthyism and, 135, 138n, 270, 297, 298, 328n, 329, 412

Steele, John, 543

Steinbeck, John, 191

Stern, Alfred W., 355

Stern, Mrs. Edgar (Edith Rosenwald), 456; letter to, 456

Stettinius, Edward R., Jr., 64

Stevens, Robert, 329n, 357

Stevens, Roger, 240, 542

Stevenson, Adlai Ewing (grandfather), 79, 106, 114–115, 155–156, 454, 529

Stevenson, Adlai E.

CAMPAIGN FOR PRESIDENCY, 1952: refuses candidacy, 3, 6, 21, 504, 604; and "draft Stevenson" movement, 3–6, 7, 9–10; arrival and opening speech at convention, 4–5, 10–11, 11–14 (quoted); goes into seclusion, 14–15; HST introduces at convention, 15–16; voting and nomination, 15–16, 247; acceptance speech, 16–19, 27–28; dis-

cusses in letters to HST, 20, 36, 42, 46, 91–92; as "Truman's candidate," 21, 37; organizes campaign, 27–28, 35, 36; "I don't *have* to win," 32n; on Republican and partisan strategy, 34–35, 40, 46, 56–57, 183–185, 231, 292–295; and "conservatism," 46; and foreign policy, 46 (*see also* foreign affairs and policy); and Western campaign, 69–70, 91–92; later criticism of, by HST, 90–91; reports on campaign funds and income taxes, 121–124; speaks at Madison Square Garden rally, 175–180; concludes campaign with Chicago speech, 181–186; concedes election, 186–188; receives many letters concerning, 191–192

CAMPAIGN FOR PRESIDENCY, 1956: 402, 406, 448, 502–503; announces candidacy, 266, 582, 591–592; discusses candidacy, 283, 447, 478, 503–504, 514, 524–525, 528, 529–530, 539, 540, 542–545, 561–562, 564; and need for "press man," 525; inquires re propriety of investments, 531; and Averell Harriman, 544–545, 547–548, 559, 560, 561, 563; and campaign staff, 545n, 591; visits HST to discuss, 564; endorsed by Freeman and Humphrey, 577, 581; and need for family support, 583–584; and vice presidential nomination, 598–599

CHARACTERISTICS, PERSONAL: eloquence and wit, 4n, 23n, 29, 79, 163, 191, 192–193, 201, 208, 222, 240, 269, 310; objectivity, 6; integrity, 16, 32n, 133–134, 174–175, 199, 205, 285–286; courage and intelligence, 19, 21–22, 188, 205, 208, 230, 325; complexity, 27; literary style, 28–29, 222; influence on American politics, 29, 353; conservatism, 46; and humor, 98–99, 179, 225, 286, 323, 357, 364, 398, 407; humility, 188, 285; statesmanship, 203; denies reading books about himself, 283; dread of speech-making, 287–288, 406; curiosity and lust for information, 419n; "unapproachability," 444–445

GOVERNORSHIP AND PUBLIC LIFE: as candidate for governor, 3, 6, 9, 15, 16, 504, 604; as governor, 39, 43, 44, 57, 110, 122–123, 206, 224, 225, 240, 241; with Navy Department, 10, 49–50, 289; and Alger Hiss, 34, 64, 65, 166–169; with State Department, 64, 166, 579; reports on campaign and

Stevenson, Adlai E. (*continued*)
supplementary funds during governorship, 122–124, 262; with AAA, 143, 166; turns over Illinois state affairs and makes Farewell Report, 192, 194–195, 215, 243; interviewed (1953) by Edward P. Morgan, 245–247; meets with Eisenhower, 254, 273, 274, 278; reports on world trip, 265, 269, 269n; interviewed (1954) by Edward R. Murrow, 323–324; announces "withdrawal" from political life, 439–440, 450, 451. *See also* LEADERSHIP OF DEMOCRATIC PARTY *below*

AND LEADERSHIP OF DEMOCRATIC PARTY, 201, 206; Walter Lippmann on, 5–6; and independence, 27; urged by Humphrey, 195, 202; and discussions with HST, 198–199, 206–207, 253; as "Loyal Opposition," 204–205, 207–209, 219, 221, 223, 246–247, 248–249, 254, 256–259, 273, 274, 278, 353; and Cousins's article, "Whither A.E.S.?," 221; and plans and "program" for 1956, 246, 441–442; and Illinois State Central Committee, 262; and speeches for National Committee, 265, 268, 269, 302, 315, 322, 327, 389; campaigns (1954) for Democratic candidates, 266, 392, 393, 399, 403, 406, 407, 417, 418, 421, 428; and avoidance of "brain trust," 279; HST on, 365; and "withdrawal" from political life, 439–440, 450, 451; and effect on Eisenhower's image, 476

PERSONAL LIFE: undergoes surgery, 8, 9, 345, 349–350, 351–358 *passim,* 360; trip to Russia, 20, 169, 362; vacations in Wyoming, 70–71; vacations in Barbados, 192, 232, 238–239, 241–242, 244, 245, 260; and world trip, 192, 223, 235–236, 238, 242–243, 244, 245–246, 253, 260–261, 265, 296n, 304, 349, 362, 363, 401, 402; sleeps in Lincoln Room at White House, 212–213; declines invitation to join editorial board of *American Scholar,* 235; reports on return from world trip, 265, 269, 296n; returns to law practice, 266; and management of *Daily Pantagraph,* 284; Thanksgiving, 1953, with sons and Tydings family, 295; receives honorary degree from Yeshiva University, 302; hospitalized in North Carolina, 345, 346; in India, 348; trip to Northwest and Alaska, 367, 378, 381–384 *passim;*

receives honorary degrees: Princeton, 376; and Columbia, 376, 383, 429n; Thanksgiving, 1954, with Benton family, 418–419; Adlai III's wedding, 419–420, 459, 464–465, 513; vacations in Southern Pines, 432; and church affiliation, 443–444; vacations in Jamaica, 454, 455, 456; and business trip through South Africa, 457n, 459, 460, 463–464, 465, 466, 478–493, 495; stopover in Rome, 479–480; "Memo to My Sons," 480–493; and "Eccentric Letters," 493–494; accompanies Khrushchev to Iowa farm (1959), 506n; suffers bronchial pneumonia, 524, 525–527, 530, 531; and difficulties on farm, 526, 527–528; inquires re investments proper to presidential candidate, 531; and business trip to West Indies, 539, 553, 554, 555, 556; vacations at Desbarats, 545n, 548; undergoes physical examination, 577, 578, 579; on being photographed in church, 582; 1955 Christmas plans, 583

QUOTED: on 1952 presidential nomination, 3, 4, 10–11; limerick of, re governorship, 15; on independence in 1952 campaign, 27–28; on party issues and independent thought, 27–28; on talking over people's heads, 28–29; 134, 179; "I don't *have* to win," 32n; on Eisenhower-Taft agreement, 90; on Nixon fund, 103; on Soviet Union, 116, 169n; on government salaries, 122; on free system, 132; on mail and messages after defeat, 192; on Democratic party leadership, 265; on conformity, 265; on materialism, 265–266; on fear, 312n; on his "useless information," 419n

SPEECHES, INTERVIEWS AND ORATORY, 4n, 23n, 79; welcoming address, Democratic National Convention (July, 1952), 11–14, 282; acceptance speech, 16–19, 27–28; and personal pride in style, 28–29; "The Nature of Patriotism" (American Legion Convention, August, 1952), 49–54; "Equal Rights" (New York State Convention, 1952), 54–60; "Faith in Liberalism" (August, 1952), 60–64; "Bi-Partisan Foreign Policy" (September, 1952), 65–68; "The New West" (Cheyenne, September, 1952), 70–75; "The One-Party Press," 75–79; "World Policy" (San Francisco), 79–86; at Albuquerque, 90; "The Atomic Future," 93–98; "The

New England Tradition," 98–102; on Nixon campaign funds, 103; "To the Young Marines" (Quantico), 103–105; "The New South," 106–113; "Korea," 114–121; "First Fireside Speech" (radio and TV speech), 121–130; "Safeguards Against Communism" (October, 1952), 134–140; "The Area of Freedom," 140–147; makes statement re contribution from employees of New York *Times*, 148; "Tidelands Oil — Foreign Trade" (New Orleans), 150–158; ends New Orleans speech in French, 158; "On Liberty of Conscience," 158–163; "The Hiss Case," 164–170; "The United Nations: Our Hope and Our Commitment" (radio speech), 170–172; "Franklin Delano Roosevelt," 172–174; "The New Force in America" (Madison Square Garden), 175–180; "The Campaign Is Over!" (Chicago, November 1, 1952), 181–186; "The Verdict — We Pray as One" (conceding election, November 4, 1952), 186–188; "The Legacy of Philip Murray" (December, 1952), 209–212; "An Address . . . before the Gridiron Club Dinner," 223–229; makes Farewell Report to citizens of Illinois (January, 1953), 192, 215, 243; compiles *Major Campaign Speeches*, 192; speaks at Los Angeles (February, 1953), 192; "Statement . . . 75th Birthday of Carl Sandburg," 241; at Jefferson-Jackson Day Dinner: New York (February, 1953), 247–253; Los Angeles (February, 1953), "Campaign Mythology and the Public Weal," 255–259; interviewed by Edward P. Morgan, 245–247; makes fund-raising speeches for Democratic National Committee, 265, 268, 269, 302, 315, 322, 327, 389; and dread of speech-making, 287–288, 406; before Georgia legislature, 288–294; at Council on Foreign Relations, 302; in Philadelphia, 302; Godkin Lectures at Harvard, 304n, 322, 327; "The Reputation of the Government," 305–310; "Statement on the Bricker Amendment" (January, 1954), 317–319; "Crusades, Communism and Corruption" (Miami speech), 327–333; interviewed by Edward R. Murrow, 323–324, 325; "The Educated Citizen," 337–345; at Charlotte, North Carolina, 345; at Hillbilly Festival, 352, 368; at Columbia Bicentennial, 369–376; at Vassar commencement, 376; at Harrisburg, Pennsylvania, 376; on Alaskan tour, 381n; interviewed by London *Daily Mail*, 387; on difficulty in composing, 390, 406; "The Congressional Campaign Begins" (Indianapolis speech), 393–396; on Western tour, 399, 403, 406, 407, 418; at Democratic rally, San Francisco (October, 1954), 407–417; "The Congressional Campaign Ends," 421–428; "The Challenge to Political Maturity," 432–439; statement (December, 1954) announcing "withdrawal" from politics, 439–440; speaks at banquet of Weizmann Institute, 440n; radio statement on Carl Sandburg (February, 1955), 452; "The Formosa Crisis" (radio speech), 468–476; introduces Sam Rayburn at testimonial dinner, 479; makes statement to reporters in Johannesburg, 493; "Faith, Knowledge and Peace," 495; "Medicine and Public Policy," 495, 504; "Women, Husbands, and History," 495–502; delivers commencement speech at Oberlin, 507; "Education, a National Cause," 516–523; speaks in Jamaica, 556; "dabbles with" farm problem in speech at Green Bay, Wisconsin, 559; "Partnership and Independence" (speech at Ontario), 534, 562; "The Road Away from Revolution" (radio speech), 584–591; announces 1956 candidacy (Chicago, November, 1955), 591–592; holds press conference, 592–606. *See also* ghostwriting

AND UNITED NATIONS: during formation, 22, 37, 65n, 66, 68, 80, 174, 450n; as delegate (1946), 20, 166, 169; at General Assembly (1947), 166; delivers speech on (October, 1952), 170–172

VIEWS, SOCIOPOLITICAL: on people and campaign issues, 27–29, 74; on quoting words of Christ, 41; on the press, 40, 75–79, 224–229, 230; on civil rights, 47–48, 57–58, 63, 110–112, 151, 157, 435, 602, 605; on patriotism, 49–54; on American leadership and greatness, 50–51, 86, 132, 144, 145–146, 159–163, 185–186, 372–374, 375, 410–417, 475–476; on liberalism, 55, 63–64, 222; on relationship between government and industry, 72–73, 94,

Stevenson, Adlai E. (*continued*)
100–102, 107, 132, 424, 565–577, 585–586; on labor relations, 73–74, 101, 211–212; on freedom, 81, 82–83, 140–147, 169–170, 228–229, 310, 375–376; on coexistence, 82, 415, 436–437; on nationalism, 82–83; on materialism, 85, 265–266, 374–375; on humor, 98–99, 179, 225, 286, 323, 357, 407; on corruption, 124–125, 306; on responsibility of democracy, 129–130, 310, 371–375, 433, 434–436; on Communism, 134–140, 327–333 (*see also* Communism); on "eggheads," 140–141, 223, 225, 227, 305, 447, 530; on socialization, 157, 162, 370, 574, 576; on future of Democratic party, 219, 231, 254, 261–262, 265, 278–279, 287, 291, 292; on "dollar diplomacy," 246, 251; on conformity, 265, 343, 365, 498–499, 536, 569; on decay of English language, 297; on retaliation, 317, 331–332, 473; on disarmament, 360–361, 537, 588, 589; on conservation, 367–368; on apartheid, 492–493

WRITINGS: in *Look* magazine, 244, 246, 271n, 479n, 546n, 563n; *Call to Greatness* (Godkin Lectures, Harvard), 304n; "Statement on the Bricker Amendment," 317–319; begins diary of African trip, 478–480; "Memo to the President: Let's Make the Two-Party System Work" (*Look*), 479n; "Memo to My Sons on a Month in Africa," 480–493; introduction to *What I Think*, 546n; "If I Were Twenty-one" (*Coronet*), 546n; "Africa: The Giant Awakens" (*Look*), 546n, 563n; "My Faith in Democratic Capitalism" (*Fortune*), 555, 565–577, 580; *Major Campaign Speeches of, 1952,* 192, 216n, 218, 242, 244

Stevenson, Adlai E., III ("Bear"), 345, 381, 403, 404, 405, 429, 440, 444, 446, 455, 460; in Marine Corps, 103, 301; engagement and wedding, 396, 397, 400, 418, 419–420, 448, 465n, 505, 512, 513; at Harvard Law School, 419, 531; letters to, 458–460, 464–465, 583–584; and father's 1956 candidacy, 583, 594

Stevenson, Mrs. Adlai E., III (Nancy L. Anderson), 531, 583. *See also* Anderson, Nancy L.

Stevenson, Borden, 92, 236, 274, 323, 419, 440, 548; and Army service, 382, 459, 460, 512, 546; and father's 1956 candidacy, 594

Stevenson, Ellen Borden (Mrs. Adlai E. Stevenson), 89, 352, 400, 419, 464–465, 505, 583, 584

Stevenson, John Fell, 274, 345, 346, 352, 419, 440, 442–443, 459, 461; at Milton Academy, 300–301; and trip to Asia, 505, 512, 546; at Harvard, 583; and father's 1956 candidacy, 594

Stevenson, Letitia (aunt), 362; letter to, 35

Stevenson, William E., 278; letter to, 196–197

Stevenson for Governor Committee (1948), 213n

Stevenson for President Committee (1952), 3–5, 538; (1956), 579, 591

Stevenson Press Corps, 15

Stevenson School (Chicago), 529

Stone, Melville E., 321

Stone, Nora, *see* Smith, Mrs. Farwell

Storke, Thomas M., letter to, 216

Streit, Clarence, 544

Stritch, Samuel Cardinal, 21; letter to, 21

Students for Stevenson, 93

Suez, 414

Sullivan, John Lawrence, 43

Sun Yat-sen, 85

Supreme Court, 151, 152, 517, 605

Tachen Islands, 469

Taft, Robert A., 34, 154, 167, 225, 228, 519, 580; and Republican nomination, 7, 10, 293; reconciliation with Eisenhower, 90, 99, 119, 163, 177, 183

Taft-Hartley Act, 62, 252, 580

Taiwan, 256n

Talbott, Harold E., 539

Talmadge, Herman, 289

tariff and trade, AES on, 66, 80–81, 106, 107–108, 153–154, 269–270, 574–575

Taylor, Chalmer C., 205

Taylor, Mrs. Lucille, 272; letter to, 272

Teheran Agreement, 255, 410

Tennessee Valley Authority (TVA), 424n, 574

Tenney, Henry, 233

Texas, University of, AES speech at, 534, 557

Theis, William, 602

Thomas, Benjamin P., 7, 187, 358; letters to, 7n, 355–356, 358

Thomas, J. Parnell, 331n

Thomas, Norman, 191, 537, 553; letter to, 537

Thye, Edward J., 165n

Tidelands Oil Bill, 424; AES on, 32n, 151–153, 256

"Tidelands Oil — Foreign Trade" (AES speech, October, 1952), 150–158, 256n

Till, Emmett, 605

"Time for a Change" (speech), 34, 131. *See also* "The Campaign Is Over," 181–186

Time magazine, 271–272

Toby, Charles W., 165n

Tonks, Lewi, 356

Tornincasa, Mary Anne, 275; letter to, 276

Tree, Marietta (Mrs. Ronald Tree), 192, 232, 241, 377; letters to, 232, 254, 260–261, 377, 502

Tree, Ronald, 192, 232, 241, 377, 382n; letters to, 254, 260–261, 377, 502

Trieste, 414

Truman, Harry S., 123, 213, 248–249, 377–378; and AES as candidate (1952), 3, 5, 21, 27, 37, 48, 90, 91; (1956), 560, 561, 564, 599; AES on leadership and tradition of, 13, 19, 56, 252, 257, 358–359, 395, 543; introduces AES at 1952 convention, 15, 16; writes to AES, 19, 46, 90; comments on AES's speeches, 69, 259, 269, 335, 398, 477; no party leadership, 198, 206, 365, 428; vetoes of, 32n, 252; administration denounced, 40n, 292, 293, 323, 411, 421, 426; and participation in 1952 campaign, 42, 46, 69, 90, 91; and bipartisan foreign policy, 46, 56, 65n, 331, 368, 412, 423; and Korea, 56, 118, 461; Eisenhower and, 62, 292n, 552; and the press, 76, 479; and Communism, 127, 137–138, 256, 303, 325, 326, 392, 395, 408, 410, 470, 523–524; speaks at tenth anniversary of UN, 514n

LETTERS TO: 20, 36, 42, 91–92, 335, 364, 377, 553; on foreign policy, 46, 269, 477; on Democratic party, 199, 206–207, 253, 365–366, 398; on departure from White House, 244, 259; on 1956 plans, 514, 529–530, 561–562

Truman, Mrs. Harry S., 213, 244, 253, 398

Truman, Margaret, 244, 253, 259, 514; telegram to, 378

"Trumanism," 392, 509

Truman Library Fund, 358

Tubby, Roger, 591, 593, 595, 600

Tucci, Nicolo: quoted, on AES, 208; letter to, 208–209

Tucker, Nan, *see* McEvoy, Mrs. Dennis

Tufts, J. E., 47; letter to, 47

Tufts, Robert, 28, 47, 196–197, 267, 391; letters to, 198, 320

Turner, Frederick Jackson, 144

"Twenty Years of Treason," 323, 328, 393, 395, 411, 426

Tydings, Joseph, 295

Tydings, Millard, 288, 295; letter to, 295

Tydings, Mrs. Millard, 288; letter to, 295

Union of Soviet Socialist Republics, 111, 145, 360, 423, 588, 603; AES on: dominion and imperialism, 13, 66, 83, 116, 119–120, 137, 169, 250–251, 332, 363; cold war, 50–51, 81, 160, 161; aggression, 96–97, 105, 127, 360–361, 588–590; foreign policy, 154–155, 409, 436–437; negotiation with, 270, 276–277, 472; AES and trip to (1926), 20, 169, 362; (1955), 542; Eisenhower and, 115, 408, 474, 533n; and Yalta agreement, 255

Unitarian Church, 443–444

United Kingdom, *see* Great Britain

United Nations, 12, 116, 117, 468, 488n, 489, 587, 590; AES with, 20, 22, 37, 65n, 66, 68, 80, 166, 169, 174, 450n; and arms race, 95–96, 97; AES speech on (1952), 170–172; FDR on, 174; and U.S., 372, 472, 589; charter revisions discussed, 457n

university, AES on function of, 343–344, 375

University College, London, 279

Urquhart, Clara, 485n, 509

Valentine, Mrs. Doris Dooley, 283; letter to, 283

Vandenberg, Arthur H., 37n, 65n; AES on, 65–66, 67, 68, 100; quoted, 117

Vassar College, AES speech at, 300, 316, 376

"Verdict, The — We Pray as One" (AES concession speech, November, 1952), 187–188

Vidal, Gore, letter to, 565

Vietnam, 409, 414n, 473

Vinson, Carl, 289

Virginia, University of, AES speech at, 535, 536, 584–591

Virginia Central Committee, 65

Virginia Statute of Religious Freedom, 57

Voice of America, 74, 423

Volunteers for Stevenson, 37, 122, 131, 132, 147; officers of, 27, 44, 95, 240, 278

Wagner, Robert, 554

Walker, Charles Morehead, Jr., 88n

Walsh, Donald J., letter to, 233

Warburg, James P., 133, 270, 449, 461, 556; letters to, 133, 271, 449, 461–462, 556–557

Warburg, Jennifer Joan, 229, 271; letter to, 229

Ward, Barbara (Mrs. Robert Jackson), 347, 376, 479, 480, 486n, 510–511, 513, 535, 545; letters to, 460, 466–467, 511–512, 514–515, 546–547

Warren, Earl, 328n, 579

Washington, George, 112, 499; quoted, 160

Washington and Lee University, 112

Washington *Post*, 133, 555

Washington Senators (baseball team), 228

Washington *Star*, 29, 35

Watkins, Arthur V., 34, 437n

Watson, James Eli, 224

Watts, Lyle, 367

Wechsler, James, 86–87

Weinstein, Jacob J., letter to, 353–354

Weizmann Institute, American Committee for, 440n

Welensky, Sir Roy, 527

Welling, Mrs. John Paul (Harriet), 192; letters to, 88–89, 193

What I Think (Stevenson), 562n

White, Edward Douglas, 152

White, Harry Dexter, 136n, 292n, 293, 308

White, Hugh L., 239, 352, 368

White, Theodore H., 29, 462

Whitehead, Donald, 265

White House Conference on Education, 543

"Whither A.E.S.?" (Cousins), 221

Wickenden, Elizabeth, 267

Williams, John Sharp, 111

Willkie, Wendell, 394; AES on, 181

Wilson, Charles E., 248n, 250n

Wilson, Woodrow, 13, 59, 86, 106, 108, 113, 156, 252, 303, 371, 435; AES's oratory compared to, 4n; as hero of AES, 132; quoted, 161, 257, 366, 586, 587; centennial, AES speech at, 535, 536, 584–591; on "highbrow" party, 586

wire-tapping legislation, 302

Wirtz, W. Willard, 28, 267, 449, 449n

Wisconsin, University of, 140, 144

Wisconsin tradition, 144–145

WJBC (Bloomington, Illinois, radio station), 365

Woetzel, Robert, 536; letter to, 536–537

Woman's Home Companion, AES speech published in, 515

Woman's Suffrage Amendment, 57

"Women, Husbands, and History" (AES speech, June, 1955), 495–502

Woodward, Stanley, 191, 269, 430; letters to, 270, 430

"World Policy" (AES speech, September, 1952), 79–86

World War II, 173

Wright, Benjamin F., 380

Wyatt, Wilson W., 33, 397, 465n, 503; in 1952 campaign, 27, 36–37, 40, 115, 188; quoted, on AES, 32n; letters and memoranda to, 34–35, 280–281, 354, 401, 503; in 1956 campaign, 591, 593, 595

Wyatt, Mrs. Wilson (Ann), 379, 465n, 503; letters to, 354, 401, 503

Yalta Conference and Papers, 255, 410, 478

Yeshiva University, AES receives honorary degree from, 302

Yorty, Samuel, 407, 408, 409

Young, George B., 467; letter to, 467

Young, Mrs. George B. (Mary Seymour Adams), 467

Young, Robert R., 320n

Young Communist League, 86

"Young Marines, To the" (AES speech, September, 1952), 103–105

Yugoslavia, 414

Zanuck, Darryl F., 446

Zwicker, General Ralph, 328–329